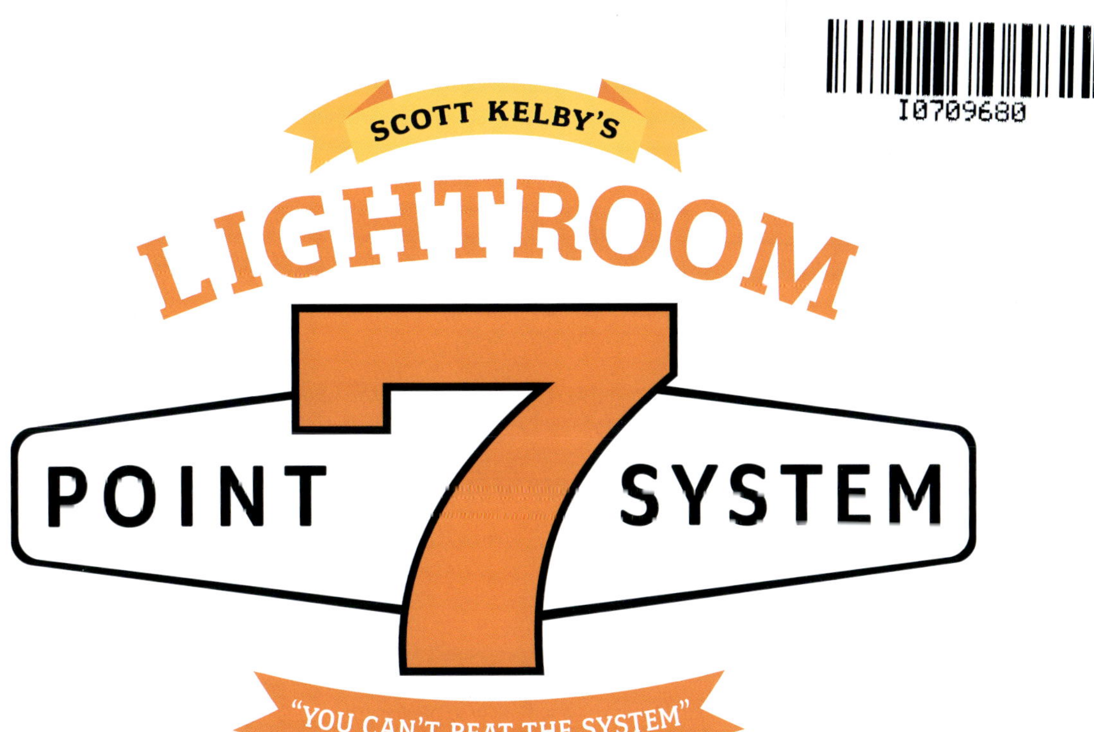

SCOTT KELBY'S
LIGHTROOM
POINT 7 SYSTEM
"YOU CAN'T BEAT THE SYSTEM"

MANAGING EDITOR
Kim Doty

COPY EDITOR
Cindy Snyder

ART DIRECTOR
Jessica Maldonado

PHOTOGRAPHY BY
Scott Kelby

Published by
Rocky Nook
1010 B Street, Suite 350
San Rafael, CA 94901

Composed in Myriad Pro, Program, and Ronnia by Kelby Media Group, Inc.

Trademarks
All terms mentioned in this book that are known to be trademarks or service marks have been appropriately capitalized. Rocky Nook cannot attest to the accuracy of this information. Use of a term in this book should not be regarded as affecting the validity of any trademark or service mark.

Lightroom, Lightroom Classic, and Photoshop are registered trademarks of Adobe Systems, Inc.

Warning and Disclaimer
This book is designed to provide information about Lightroom for digital photographers. Every effort has been made to make this book as complete and as accurate as possible, but no warranty of fitness is implied.

The information is provided on an as-is basis. The author and Rocky Nook shall have neither the liability nor responsibility to any person or entity with respect to any loss or damages arising from the information contained in this book or from the use of the discs, electronic files, or programs that may accompany it.

THIS PRODUCT IS NOT ENDORSED OR SPONSORED BY ADOBE SYSTEMS INCORPORATED, PUBLISHER OF ADOBE PHOTOSHOP LIGHTROOM 2021.

ISBN 13:   978-1-68198-727-9

9 8 7 6 5 4 3 2 1

Distributed in the UK and Europe by Publishers Group UK
Distributed in the U.S. and all other territories by Ingram Publisher Services

Library of Congress Control Number: 2021935015

Printed and bound in the United States of America

https://kelbyone.com
www.rockynook.com

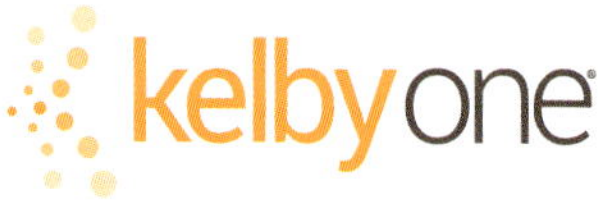

This book is dedicated to my niece, Sarah Crist.
Thank you for being such an important
part of our family. We love you and are
so proud of the young woman you are becoming.
We can't wait to see the amazing future
you have ahead of you!

ACKNOWLEDGMENTS

Although only one name appears on the spine of this book, it takes a team of dedicated and talented people to pull a project like this together. I'm not only delighted to be working with them, but I also get the honor and privilege of thanking them here.

To my amazing wife Kalebra: This year we'll be celebrating our 32nd anniversary and you continue to reinforce what everybody always tells me—I'm the luckiest guy in the world.

To my son Jordan: I just can't believe my "little boy" has already graduated from college and is now building a life of his own. It all happened so fast, but I'm so thrilled for you and for the many adventures, and for the fun, love, and laughter your future holds. If there's a dad more proud of his son than I am, I've yet to meet him. #rolltide!

To my beautiful daughter Kira: You are a little clone of your mom, and that's the best compliment I could ever give you. I love your sense of humor, your constant dancing, the hilarious faces you make, and your heart. I love the young woman you are becoming, and I particularly love when you and I go grab lunch or dinner together. Those times are so precious to me. I love you!

To my big brother Jeff: Your boundless generosity, kindness, positive attitude, and humility have been an inspiration to me my entire life, and I'm just so honored to be your brother.

To my editor Kim Doty: If there's a Book Editor Hall of Fame, you should truly be in it. You are so talented, organized, and awesome, and your amazing attitude, support, and ideas are what keep me going when I'm deep in the weeds. I'll be forever grateful to have you on my team. You rock!

To my book designer Jessica Maldonado: I love the way you design, and all the clever little things you add to everything you do. Our book team struck gold when we found you!

To my dear friend and business partner Jean A. Kendra: Thanks for putting up with me all these years, and for your support for all my crazy ideas. It really means a lot.

To Erik Kuna: Your suggestions, ideas, and good counsel have made this book, and the ones before it, that much better. I value your friendship so much, and feel very blessed to have you in my life.

To Cindy Snyder: Thank you so much for working on my books and catching tons of little things others would have missed.

To Ted Waitt, my fantastic "Editor for life" at Rocky Nook: Thanks for being such a great friend, a world-class sounding board, and for helping these ideas become a reality.

To my publisher Scott Cowlin: I'm so delighted I still get to work with you, and for your open mind and vision.

To all the gifted photographers and instructors who've taught me so much over the years: Moose Peterson, Joe McNally, Bill Fortney, Anne Cahill, David Ziser, Tim Wallace, Lindsay Adler, Peter Hurley, Cliff Mautner, Jeremy Cowart, Dave Black, Jay Maisel, Joel Grimes, and Helene Glassman.

To these wonderful photographers whom I, and the industry, already miss dearly: Jim DiVitale, Winston Hendrickson, Mike McCaskey, and Monte Zucker.

To my friends for just being my friends: Terry White, Dave Clayton, Jeff Revell, Peter Treadway, Ted Waitt, Paul Kober, Scott Stahley, Victoria Pavlov, Serge Ramelli, Kim Doty, Marvin Derezin, Dave Williams, Manny Steigman, Fernando Santos, Glyn Dewis, Robby Pisco, Larry Grace, Matt Kloskowski, Ed Biuce, Tony Llanes, Larry Becker, Rob Foldy, Frank Doorhof, Jeff Leimbach, Deb Uscilka, Karen Hutton, John Swarce, Bryan Hughes, Kathy Porupski, Mike Kubiesy, Vanelli, Rick Sammon, Greg Rostami, Bob DeChiara, Mike Larson, Kleber Stephenson, Kelly Jones, Brad Moore, Mimo Meidany, Juan Alfonso, Cathy Baitson, Eric Eggly, Ramtin Kazemi, Skip Cohen, and John Couch.

To my mentors John Graden, Jack Lee, Dave Gales, Judy Farmer, and Douglas Poole: Your wisdom and whip-cracking have helped me immeasurably throughout my life, and I will always be in your debt, and grateful for your friendship and guidance.

Most importantly, I want to thank God, and His Son Jesus Christ, for leading me to the woman of my dreams, for blessing us with such amazing children, for allowing me to make a living doing something I truly love, for always being there when I need Him, for blessing me with a wonderful, fulfilling, and happy life, and such a warm, loving family to share it with.

OTHER BOOKS BY SCOTT KELBY

The Natural Light Portrait Book

Photoshop for Lightroom Users

The Adobe Photoshop Lightroom Book for Digital Photographers

The Flash Book

The Landscape Photography Book

How Do I Do That In Lightroom?

How Do I Do That In Photoshop?

Professional Portrait Retouching Techniques for Photographers

The Digital Photography Book, parts 1, 2, 3, 4 & 5

Light It, Shoot It, Retouch It

The Adobe Photoshop Book for Digital Photographers

The Photoshop Elements Book for Digital Photographers

It's a Jesus Thing: The Book for Wanna Be-lievers

Professional Sports Photography Workflow

ABOUT THE AUTHOR

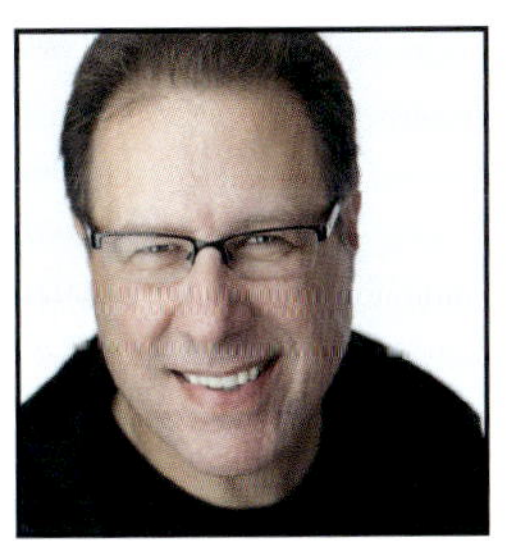

Scott Kelby

Scott is President and CEO of KelbyOne, an online educational community for photographers. He is Editor, Publisher, and co-founder of *Photoshop User* magazine; host of *The Grid*, the influential, live, weekly talk show for photographers; and is founder of the annual Scott Kelby's Worldwide Photo Walk.™

Scott is an award-winning photographer, designer, and bestselling author of more than 100 books, including *Photoshop for Lightroom Users*; *The Landscape Photography Book*; *Light It, Shoot It, Retouch It*; *The Adobe Photoshop Book for Digital Photographers*; *The Flash Book*; *The Natural Light Portrait Book*; and his landmark, *The Digital Photography Book*, which is the #1 top-selling book ever on digital photography.

His books have been translated into dozens of different languages, including Chinese, Russian, Spanish, Korean, Polish, Taiwanese, French, German, Italian, Japanese, Hebrew, Dutch, Swedish, Turkish, and Portuguese, among many others. He is a recipient of the prestigious ASP International Award, presented annually by the American Society of Photographers for "…contributions in a special or significant way to the ideals of Professional Photography as an art and a science," and the HIPA award, presented for his contributions to photography education worldwide.

Scott is Conference Technical Chair for the annual Photoshop World Conference and a frequent speaker at conferences and trade shows around the world. He is featured in a series of online learning courses at KelbyOne.com and has been training photographers and Photoshop users since 1993.

For more information on Scott, visit him at:

His daily Lightroom blog: **lightroomkillertips.com**

His personal blog: **scottkelby.com**

Twitter: **@scottkelby**

Facebook: **facebook.com/skelby**

Instagram: **@scottkelby**

CONTENTS

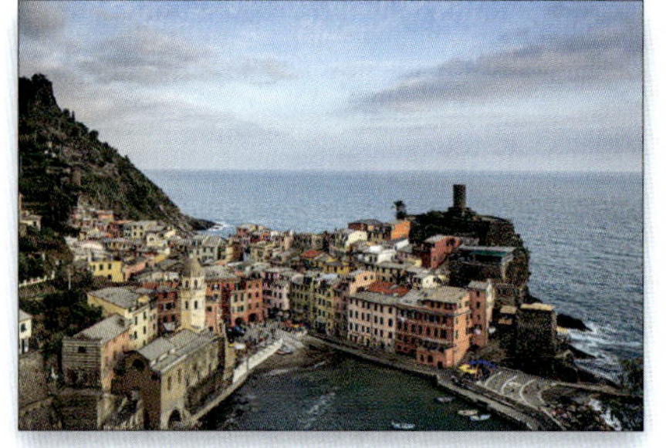

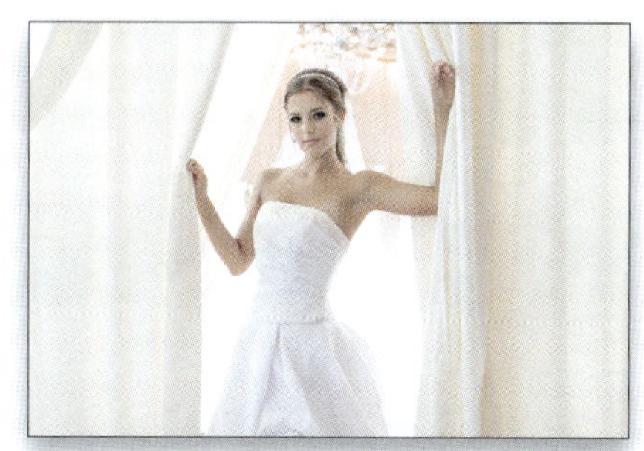
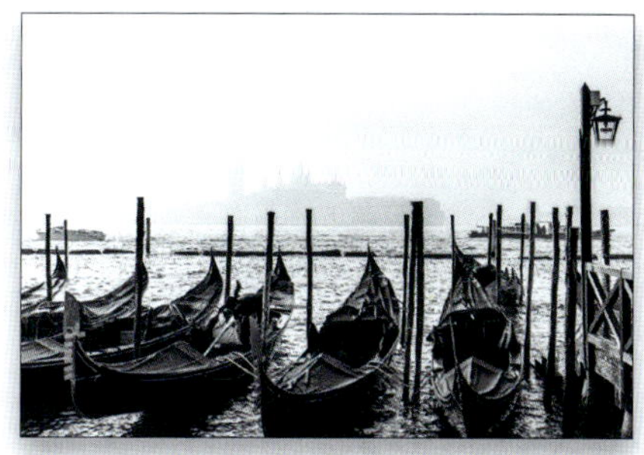
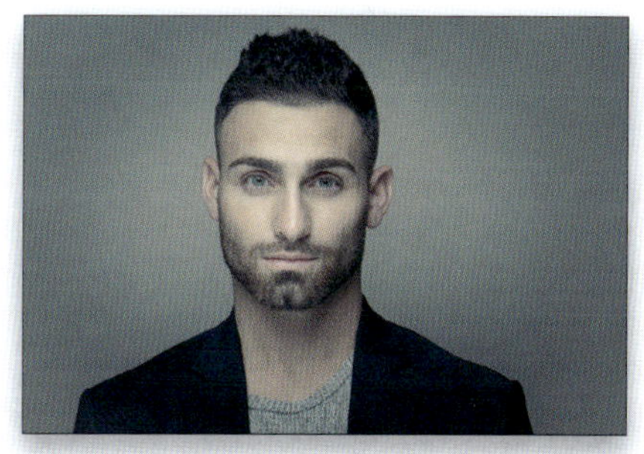
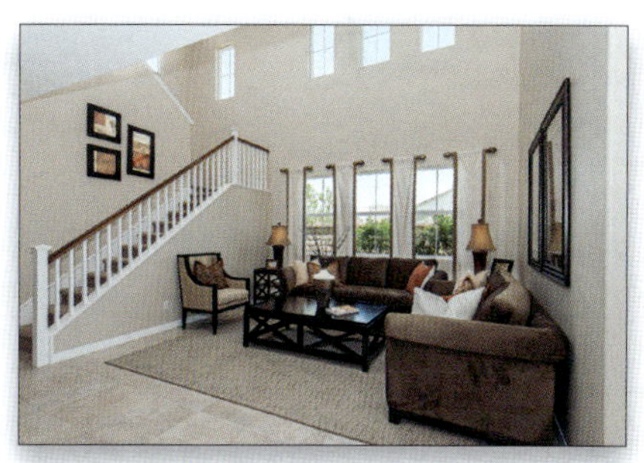
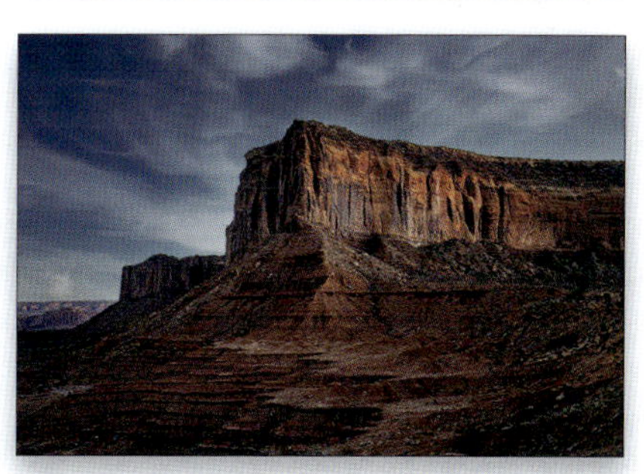

THE SEVEN POINTS ARE REVEALED RIGHT HERE!

How the 7-Point System Works:

Sorry for that *National Enquirer*-style headline up there, and I know you probably want to jump right over to Lesson 01 and start fixing photos, but if you do that (and skip this quick section where I reveal the seven points), you're going to wish you had read this (not now, but about halfway into Lesson 02, you're going to start saying things like, "Hey…" and "What the heck… ?" and other stuff with three dots after it). But, if you spend two minutes with me now, and let me explain the system so it makes sense, I promise you, you'll get much more out of the book, and from your Lightroom-editing experience. You'll totally "get" what we're trying to accomplish (and why I wrote it the way I did), and then the system will be a success for you.

I'll do this in a quick Q&A-style format, which is ideal for people with the attention span of a hamster. (Not you, mind you. Other people.) Here we go:

Q. So, how is this 7-Point System going to help me?

A. Hey, first can we lose the attitude?

Q. Oh, sorry. It's been a really hectic day.

A. That's okay. Well, this book addresses what I've learned are the three biggest problems people have with editing their photos in Lightroom:

(1) They open a photo, and they know it looks bad, but they have no idea where to begin to fix it. They don't know what to fix first, what to fix next, or even how.

(2) If they already have a book on Lightroom (perhaps even one of mine), and they read about using something like the Tone Curve or camera profiles, they can somewhat fix their photos while the book is open in front of them. But, when they come back to Lightroom after their next shoot (which might be three days—or three weeks—later), they've pretty much forgotten what they learned three weeks ago, and now they're back to reading the book again, so things are moving really slowly, and that's very frustrating for them. What they learned doesn't "stick."

(3) They know Lightroom can fix their problem—they know it can not only make their photos look at least as good as they looked when they originally took the shot, it can make them look even better—they're just not sure which buttons and sliders will get them there.

Q. So, this book is going to fix all three of those problems?

A. You betcha! We'll start with the first problem (we know it looks bad, but have no idea where to begin to fix it). You're going to do 21 lessons (they're like chapters, but they don't have chapter titles because they share a common theme, as you'll learn in a minute). Each lesson starts off with the original boring, flat, lifeless image as it came out of my camera (and a lot of them look like #@$, but don't judge). You download the exact same lousy RAW photos I used here in the book, so you can follow right along with me every step of the way as I take you through the entire process—leaving nothing out—of going from flat to fantastic in just minutes.

Q. *How is this different?*

A. Well, think about it. Most Lightroom books show you how to do one thing per section, or one thing per chapter. For example, they might have a chapter on sharpening, or a chapter on white balance, and so on. That's great, but here's the thing: as you've learned—that's not real life. You don't just open a photo, apply a quick single adjustment, and then save the photo because it now looks amazing. In real life, that white balance adjustment only fixes one thing in a photo that needs 10 things fixed. Once again—you're stuck.

Hey, I'm not casting aspersions on other authors—my own books are guilty of this same thing, too. My best-selling book, *The Adobe Photoshop Lightroom Classic Book for Digital Photographers*, has a chapter on local adjustments, and it shows you step-by-step how to edit just part of your image using the Adjustment Brush, Gradient Filter, and other local adjustment tools. But, which one will fix the problem you have right now? Which do you use first? Second? Last? Which one is most effective? Which ones should you avoid? What's the proper order? See, there's something missing in the way we teach Lightroom—something that makes it stick. That's why I really wanted to write this book for Lightroom, and change the way we learn Lightroom. This is actually the second book I've written like this—the first was a Photoshop version of this 7-Point System back when Photoshop was our main tool for editing images. Today, it's Lightroom, and my system has changed and evolved over the years, so I'm super-psyched to share this upgraded version of the system with you.

Q. *So, where did the seven points come in?*

A. Well, when I started collecting "crappy" photos for my first version of this book, and I would do what it took to take them from boring to beautiful, it wasn't long before I realized that I was using the same adjustments, the same tools, and the same techniques over and over again. In fact, once I really broke it down, I realized I was using the same basic seven techniques again and again, no matter which image I was trying to fix. Just seven things. Not 70. Just seven! Plus, for the most part, I was using them in a particular order (with some small variance).

That's when I realized two things: (1) if I can distill this down to just these seven techniques, these "7 Points," then anybody can learn this stuff (after all, learning everything about Lightroom is really daunting, but learning just seven things? Heck, that's a piece of cake!), and (2) if it's just seven things, I can have my readers repeat them again and again, so it finally, actually, really sticks. It's the repetition part that's missing. That's why, when you come back two or three weeks later, you can't remember what to do first. ("Am I supposed to do the white balance first? No, wait, should I expand the tonal range first?") Does any of this sound familiar? If it does, this is the book for you, my friend. (By the way, even if it doesn't sound familiar, this is still the book for you. Just ask my publisher.) ;-)

Q. *So, I'm going to be doing the same thing over and over again?*

A. Well, yeah. But, that's the beauty of this book—you'll get really, really good at this stuff because you'll do it over and over and over again. Luckily, each lesson is different—each image is different—but you still use the same seven points in pretty much the same way, in pretty much the same order. At some point, later in the book, you're going to go to do one of those seven points, and you're going to say to yourself, "Aw, this again? I already know this. I've done it 10 times now." Bingo!

That's it—that's the book at work. That's what it's all about. The whole idea is that you do this stuff again and again until it becomes second nature. You do it until my workflow becomes your workflow, and these seven points become just "stuff you already know how to do," so when you hear yourself say, "I already know this," you need to smile that "I-already-know-this" smile. You're getting "the system." The cool thing is the system works. I've heard from people—literally all over the world— whom I've taught this system to, and they've told me time and time again that it has changed their editing lives.

Q. Is it always the same steps in the same order?

A. Well, no. It usually is, but as you'll see in the book, sometimes we vary the order just a bit. For example, if we open an image where my white balance was set wrong in-camera, and the photo looks way too blue, it's so distracting that we jump ahead and fix that first. That way, once that issue is fixed, at least then we can make more reasonable decisions about things like exposure. So, occasionally, we'll go out of order, but I explain when and why as we go. So, just know if we do go out of order, it's no big deal. It doesn't mess anything up, so don't let it freak you out.

Q. Does this system work for the cloud version of Lightroom?

A. Absolutely! However, a few features have different names in Lightroom "cloud" (as I call it here in the book). For example, in Lightroom Classic, there is a feature for fixing problems caused by your lens, and that feature can be found in a panel called the "Lens Corrections" panel. However, that same feature is found in a panel called the "Optics" panel in Lightroom cloud. They do the same thing, and all the sliders have the same (or similar) names, but the panels simply have different names (thanks, Adobe. Arrrgggh!). Don't worry—it's only a few things that are different, and I point them all out in the book as we go, but I'm giving you a heads-up on it now, just so you know. There are also some features in Lightroom Classic that aren't available yet in Lightroom cloud. For example, Lightroom Classic has a side-by-side before/after view (that I use at the end of each lesson) that isn't currently in Lightroom cloud. Again, I let you know when a feature isn't available in Lightroom cloud, and it's not a whole bunch of them, but it's just enough to be annoying (again, thank you, Adobe).

Q. Should I do all the lessons even if I don't shoot people or landscapes or travel?

A. Yes, you absolutely should. This is about repetition, so it doesn't matter what the subject of the photo is—we still apply the same system. The nice thing is that you'll learn some techniques and features that may be used for things outside what you normally work on in Lightroom, but that's a good thing. So, in short, don't skip any lessons, even if the subject isn't something you normally shoot.

Q. I just leafed through the book, and some of these changes seem really subtle. Is that right?

A. Part of that is because we're limited in how big we can make the screen captures here in the book, and the changes don't look as obvious in print as they will when you try these yourself on your computer. Also, some of the changes you do will be really subtle, but a lot of little changes can add up to a big overall change in your image. So, yeah, sometimes the changes will be subtle, but they really do matter, and they do add up. The good news is they will usually be much more obvious when you see them on your own computer screen as you're working through the system.

Q. Okay, I get it. But, can you please tell me the seven points before I burst an artery?

A. Okay, you've waited long enough. But, before I tell you, just know this: you're not going to be blown away when I list them here. After all, they're all features already in Lightroom—probably ones you've used before. I'm not going to name some hidden feature that Adobe buried deep in the program that you have to unlock with a secret code. The secret to this system isn't the name of the techniques, it's how you use them, and that's what you'll learn through each lesson—putting this to work, in order, for you, and only using what you need to use. So, here are the seven points, starting with the first one:

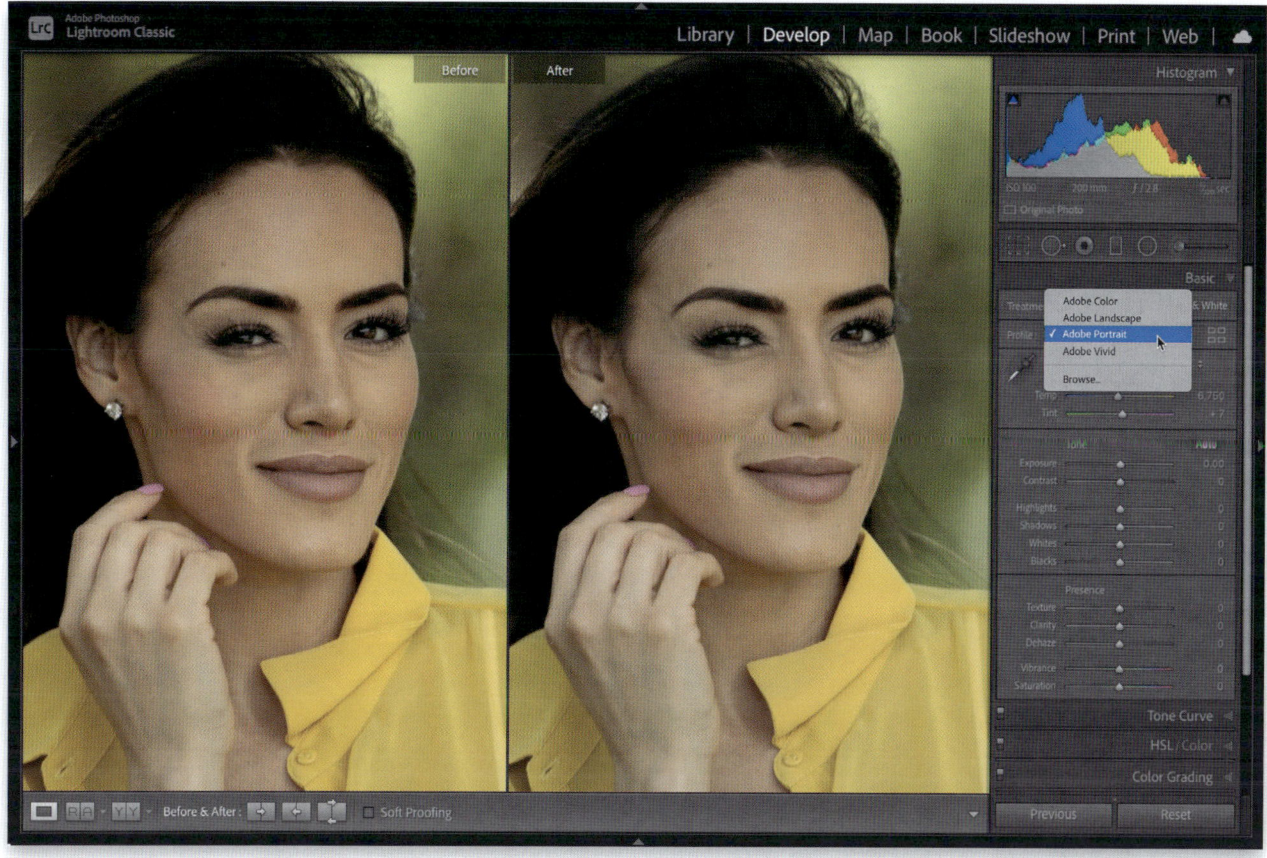

① Assigning a RAW Profile

If you shoot in RAW, you have a distinct advantage in that you get to decide your image's "starting place." You get to choose which of Adobe's built-in RAW profiles you should use to give your image an advantage, an edge, over the original unprocessed image and how it looks before you even begin to tweak it. If you shoot in JPEG or TIFF, you don't get the option to apply a RAW profile because...well...you're not shooting in RAW, and any profile you chose to apply in-camera (yes, you can apply built-in camera profile "looks" to your image right inside most cameras) will already be applied when you open your image in Lightroom. So, for you, it's going to be the Lightroom "6-Point System."

Note: This system absolutely rocks for JPEG or TIFF images, so don't let it throw you if you don't shoot in RAW. However, if you and I were at a bar, and you asked me, "Scott, should I be shooting in RAW?" I'd be like, "Absolutely!" Okay, why? Because (without getting technical and nerdy) when you shoot in RAW, your camera captures a wider tonal range, and later, when you're processing your images in Lightroom, you get better results, especially in a few key areas (as you'll learn as we go), and you get features (like assigning profiles or choosing white balance presets after the fact) that you can only apply to RAW images. You can push RAW images farther without damaging the images, and because a RAW photo is kind of like the old negatives we used to get when we shot film (back when dinosaurs ruled the Earth), your original is always protected. There are all sorts of advantages to shooting in RAW, especially in this post-processing stage, but again—you do *not* have to shoot in RAW to take advantage of "the system."

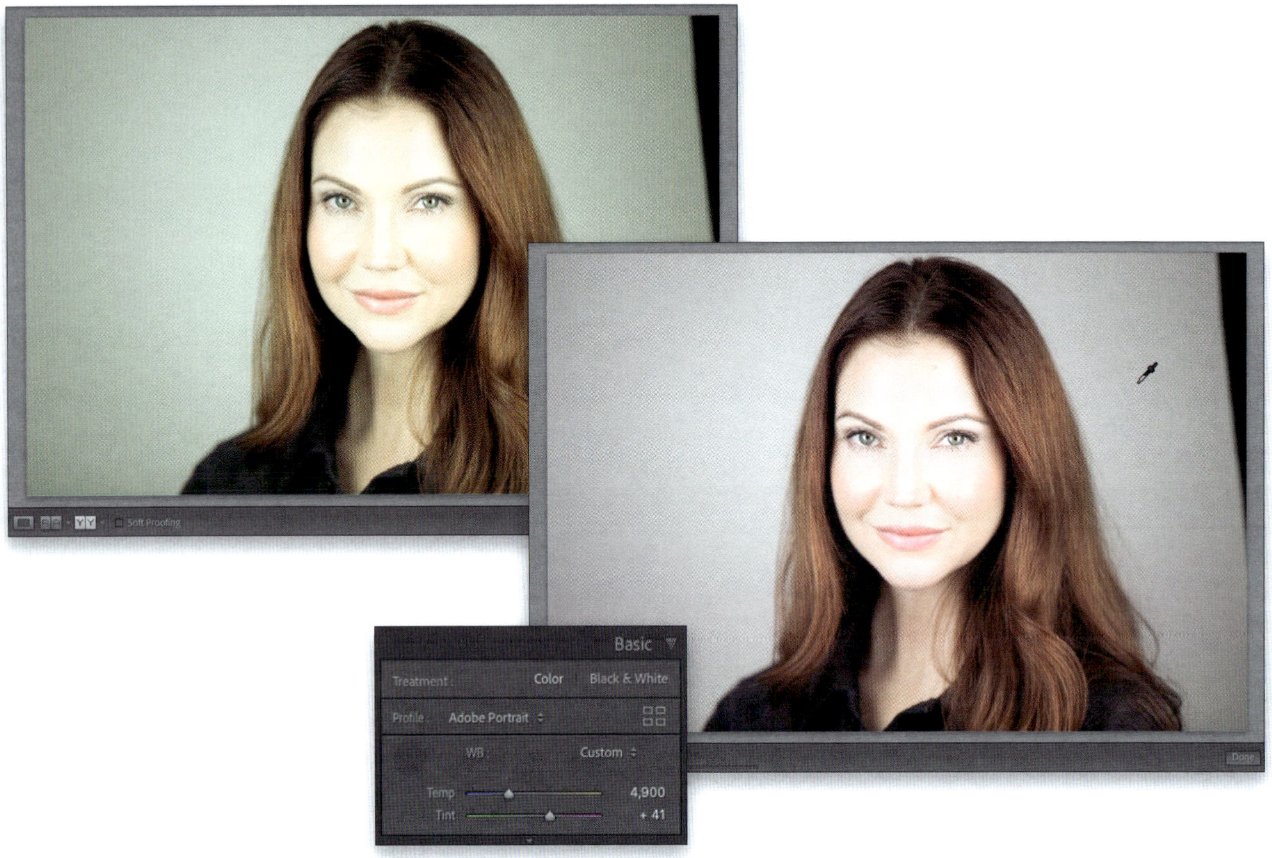

② Getting Your Color Right

If your color's not right…it's wrong, so the next thing we do is get our white balance right on the money. You'll learn a few different ways to do this (including my favorite), and you'll also learn when getting the proper white balance is not the goal, but for the most part, being able to get a proper white balance in "post" is really important. By the way, "post" is what we call everything that we do on our computers (or mobile devices) to tweak an image after we take it—it's short for the "post-production" stage. We just call it "post" because (a) it sounds way cooler, and (b) we can't be bothered to actually say two words. Anyway, that's the second point, and it's more important than you might think (and there's a reason we do it early in the process, as you'll learn in just a few minutes).

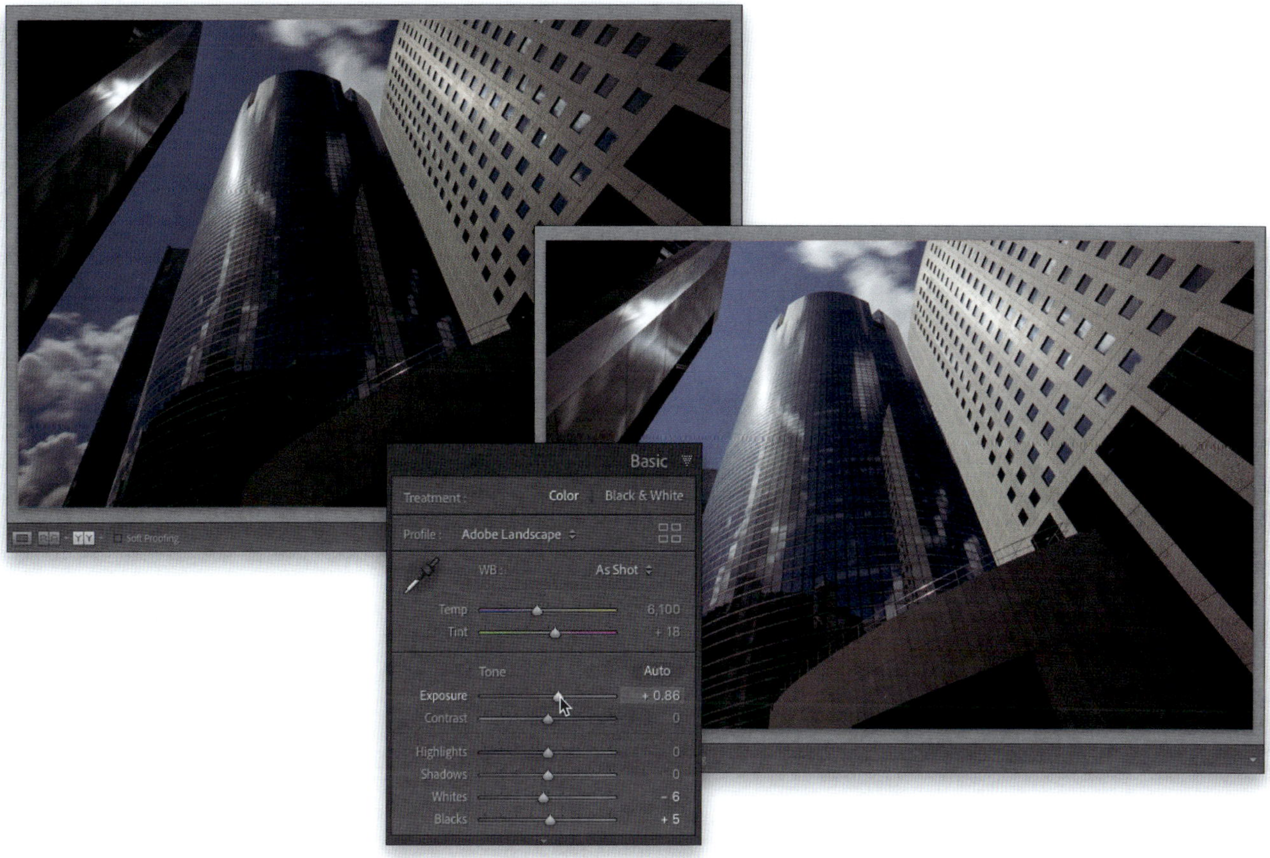

③ Expanding Your Image's Tonal Range

This is another one of those key things we do up front—we push the brightest parts of a photo as far as we can without actually "clipping" our highlights (letting parts of our image get so bright that the pixels in our highlight areas are destroyed), and then we expand the darkest parts of our image as far as we can. But, if we get a little clipping in the shadow areas (and they turn solid black), we can often look the other way and let that go. Back in the traditional film days (when we shot from the top of Conestoga wagons), we were careful to expose for the shadow areas of our images, and we'd let the highlights take care of themselves. Since digital photography came along, we now expose for the highlights (to make sure they're perfectly intact), and we let the shadows take care of themselves (if that sounds confusing, it won't a little later, and you'll casually toss that phrase out at your next camera club meeting and people will break into that slow clap at first, but then it will grow to a roar, until you're in a full standing ovation. At least, that's the way I always pictured it, but then again, my character was played by George Clooney, so there's that). Anyway, this process of expanding your tonal range is kind of hidden, but once you learn it (it's super-easy), you'll use it on every photo. I do, anyway, and it has worked so well for me that I'm portrayed by George Clooney in my dreams.

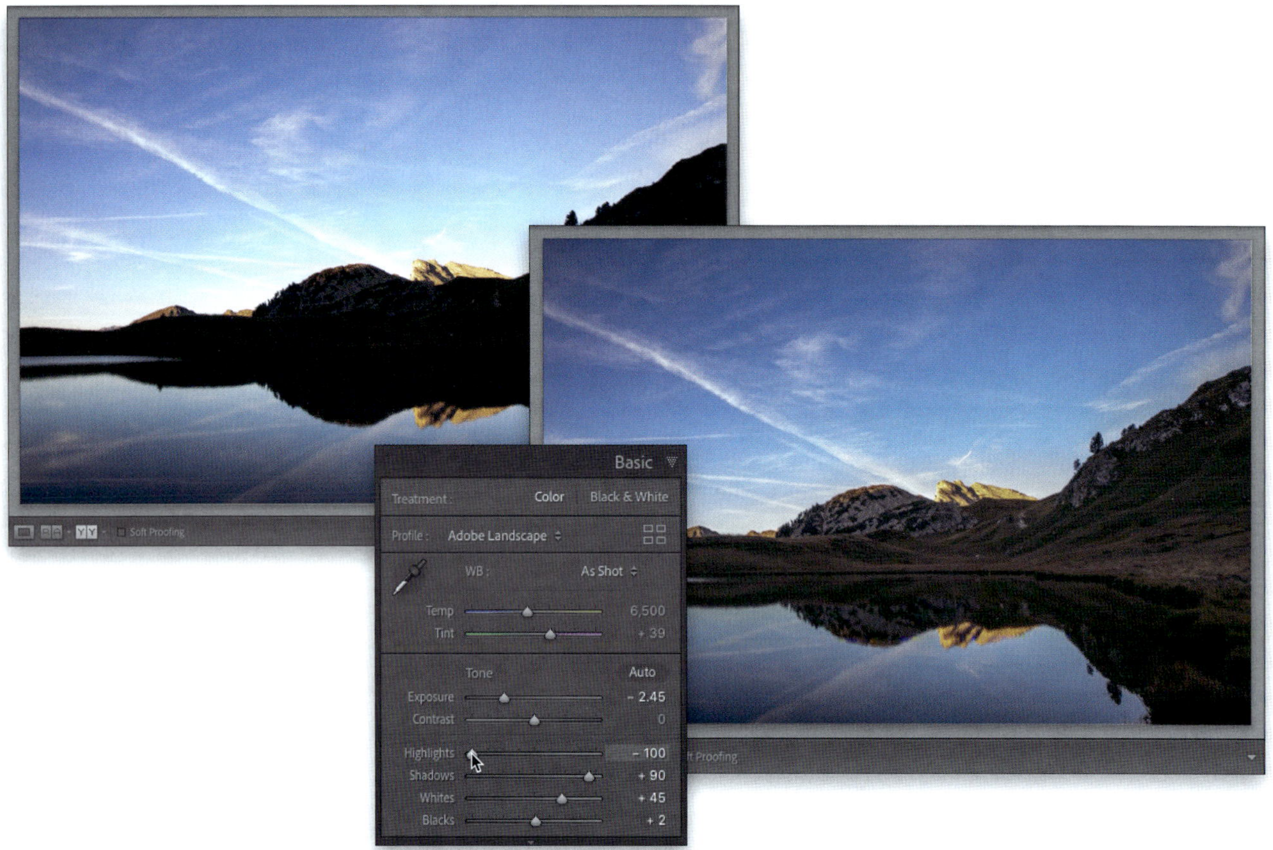

④ Dealing with Limitations Caused by the Sensor

Our eyes can see an absolutely amazing range of tones, but our camera sensors, as good as they are today, have not nearly caught up with our eyes, which is why we often shoot backlit images (as one example). We're standing there looking at the backlit scene in front of us, but it doesn't look backlit—with our subject being a dark silhouette—because our eyes automatically adjust for the scene and everything looks fine to us. Then, we take a picture and since our sensors don't have that amazing range, the image that looked fine to our naked eye has our subject looking like a dark silhouette. Sometimes we can adjust for this in-camera, but if we didn't catch it, we fix it here in post (see how I just threw "post" out there and it sounds pretty cool? This is the stuff I'm talking about. Take note). Anyway, another typical situation is: when we took the shot, we let the brightest areas of our photo blow out to where there's no detail—there are no pixels visible; we've clipped the highlights. This is stuff we can usually (not always, so we still need to keep our highlight warning on in our camera) deal with in post and recover those lost highlights. So, the fourth point of the system only kicks in if we have problems caused by our sensor, or by not catching the problem in-camera, or whatever. It's not about blame, it's about getting the problems fixed if we need to.

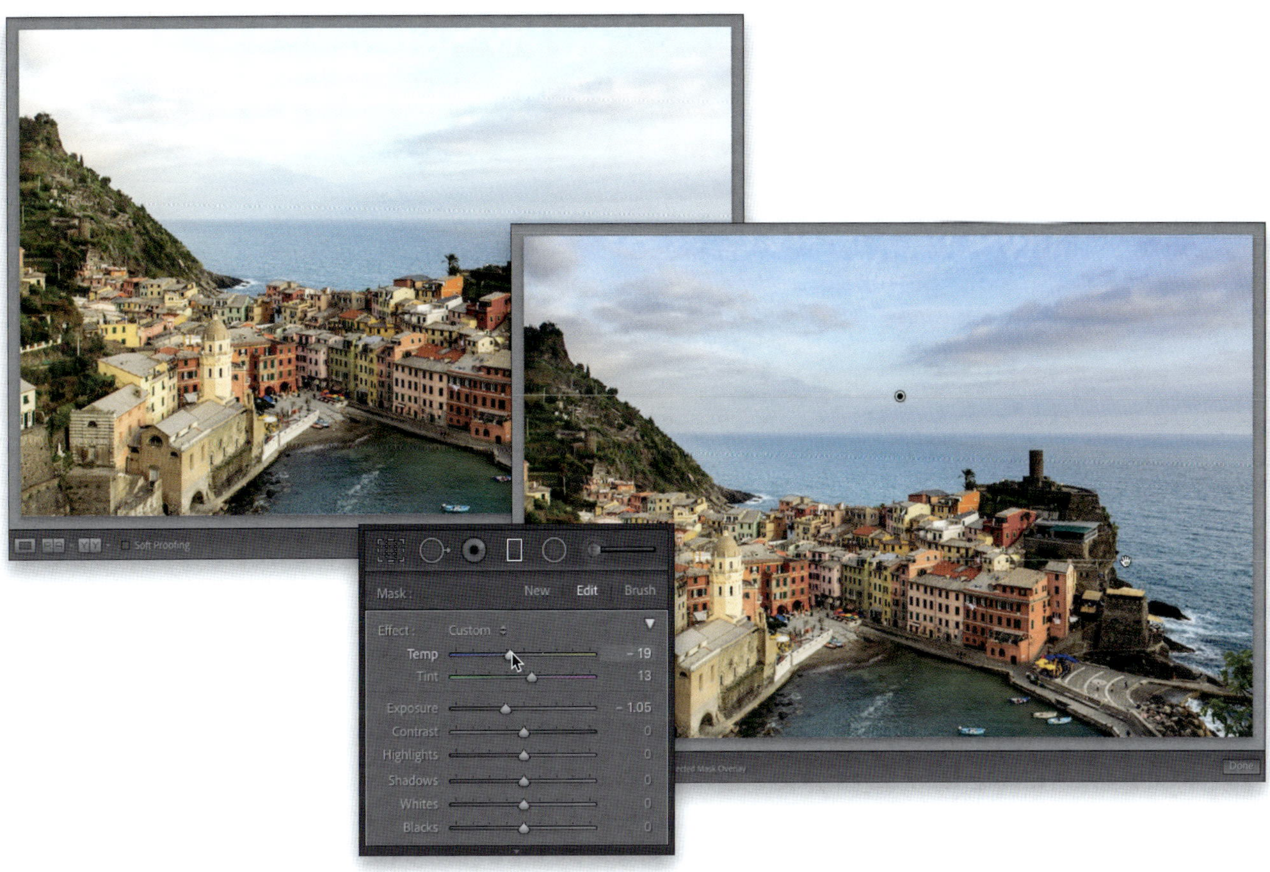

⟨5⟩ Painting with Light and Retouching

Back in the traditional darkroom days (when we used to listen to 8-track tapes and think, "Man, this is high-tech!"), this was called "dodging and burning," which is simply making certain areas of your image lighter or darker, but what we can do now in Lightroom goes way beyond that. We can literally "paint with light," and we can paint with color, and we can paint sharpness on parts of our image, and bring out details in certain parts while we leave other parts untouched. The power here is pretty incredible, and there are a number of different tools you're going to learn in this fifth point that let you do everything from fixing problems, to retouching portraits, to creating special effects.

This is one of the easiest, yet most powerful, ways to get your photos looking like you wish they did, and once you do it a few times (applying light right where you want it, but in a much better way than simply dodging and burning), the light bulb is going to come on for you in a big way. This alone will change the way you edit your images from here on out.

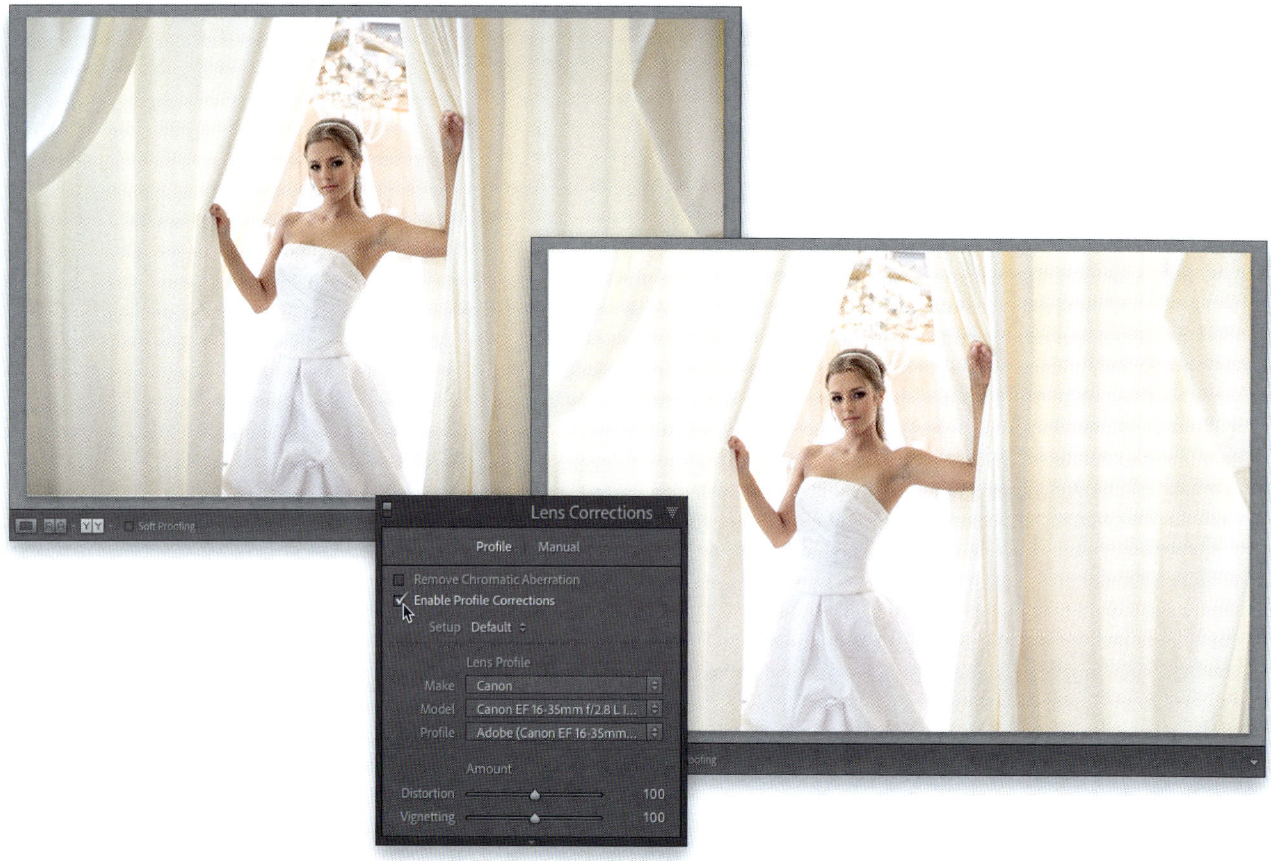

⑥ Fixing Lens Issues

Just like we have image issues that are caused by our camera's sensors, we also have some often pretty severe issues that are caused by lenses, and fixing these issues is not only super-easy, but it has a bigger impact on your final image than you probably would have ever imagined. It's one of those things where once you start fixing these common lens issues, and you realize what a difference it makes in your images, you'll not only start doing it from here on out, you'll go back to images you edited years ago and fix their lens issues, too. This is, in most cases, literally just the act of turning this feature on, and maybe moving a slider or two, but man what a difference that makes. By the way, using the term "man" is a surefire way to know that I'm a child of the '70s, which doesn't mean I'm in my 70s, because I certainly am not. I'm very young and youthful in a young, youthful way. Besides, if I'm a child of the '70s, does that mean I was (a) born in 1979, like a glorious Pontiac Firebird rising up from the factory floor, or (b) born in 1971, making me more of a Chrysler New Yorker (the best-selling car of '71), in which case I actually am old, because everyone who bought a Chrysler New Yorker back then was probably already in their 70s because that car was for "old fogies," and cool kids like me wanted a Dodge Challenger, or a Plymouth Barracuda, or (that's right) a Conestoga wagon? I'm not sure where I was going with all this, but suffice it to say, for now, lens issues are something we're going to be dealing with because it makes that big a difference.

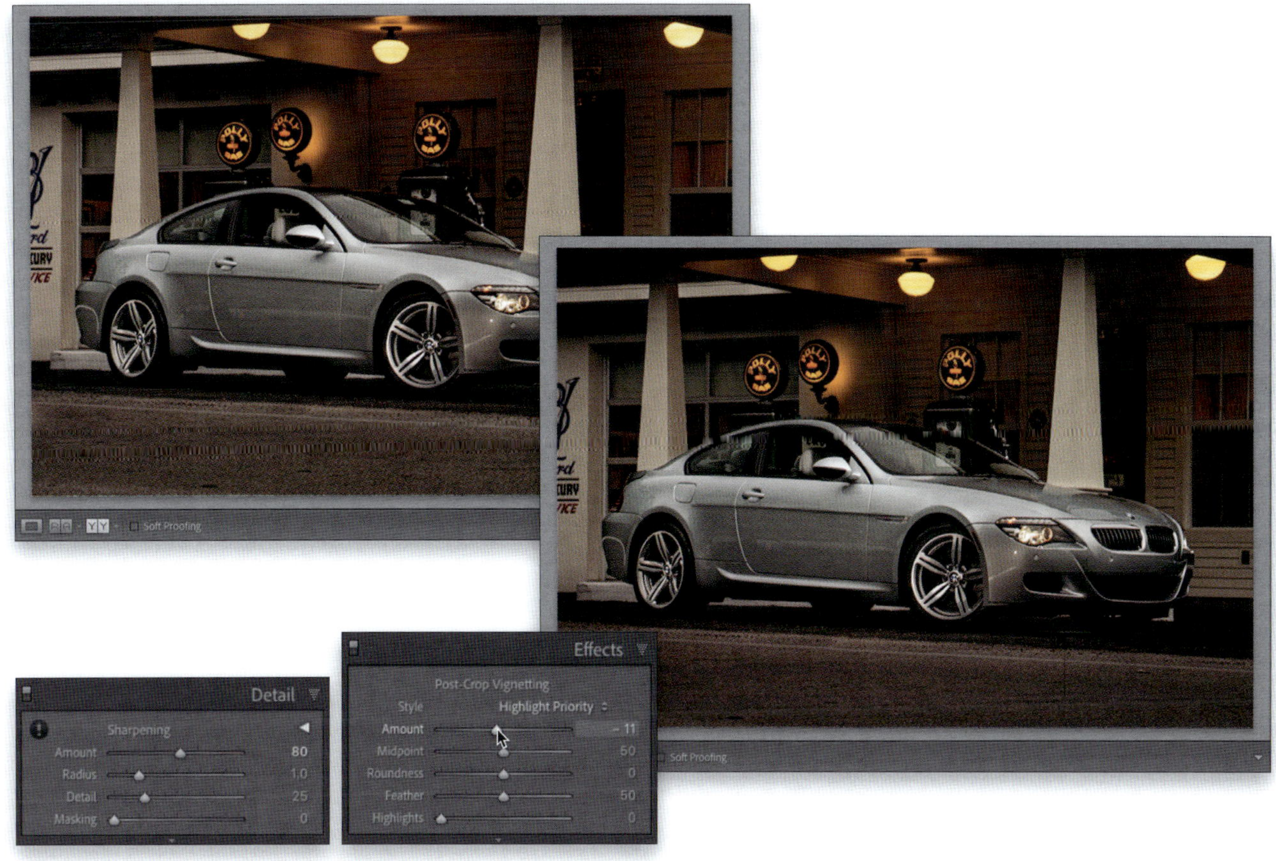

7 Finishing Moves

The final point of the 7-Point System involves some finishing moves we apply at the very end of the editing process to finish off our image. Some of it is production-type stuff (like sharpening, for example, which is something we do to every single image) and some things are special effect–type stuff that give our image a specific look, or feel, or address some other piece of our puzzle that makes our image look finished and ready to deliver to the client, or add to our portfolios, or just post on Instagram. Believe it or not, we didn't have Instagram when I grew up (back in the 1840s). Everything was all about the telegram, and the California Gold Rush, and stuff like that, so we hardly had time to get on the Internet back then. We spent a lot of time churning butter (I have no idea why). Perhaps I've gotten a bit off track here. Anyway, those are your seven points, and when you turn the page, we'll pick back up with some last-minute Q&As that we need to cover before you launch into the 21 lessons ahead, so…well…now is probably a good time to turn the page. But, feel free to stay here and linger a moment, staring at the white space that appears directly below this paragraph, and then turn the page only when you're ready. No pressure or judgment here.

So, those are the techniques that make up my 7-Point System, but don't let just the names of these fool you—this is very powerful stuff. When they're applied the way I'm going to show you, in the order I'm going to show you, they come together to give you a real plan—a real course of action that lets you know where to start, what to do next, and how to finish your photos, so they look the way you want them to.

Q. Will I use all seven points on every photo?

A. Nope. Thankfully, not every photo looks so bad that you'll need to apply all seven points every time. Most need at least four or five of the points, but don't worry, you'll get plenty of practice with all of them. Now, if you find that you need to apply all seven points to each and every photo you take, then perhaps post-processing shouldn't be your biggest concern right now. Just sayin'. Anyway, it's important to note that different photos will require different points, so again, you'll get plenty of practice determining which photos need which points. Also, at the beginning of each lesson, on the intro page, you'll see a list of which of the seven points are going to be used in that particular lesson, but even if you're already getting very comfortable with the seven points, you need to do every single lesson anyway.

Q. How come?

A. Along the way, I tossed in all kinds of other little tricks of the trade that aren't necessarily one of the seven points, but they made that particular photo look better. So, if you do every lesson, you'll pick up more than just the 7-Point System—you'll learn some slick bonus tricks, as well.

Q. I love slick bonus tricks!

A. We all do. It's what separates us from the animals. That and Netflix.

Q. So, do I have to start at Lesson 01?

A. Yeah, I'm afraid so. You need to start with Lesson 01 because in that lesson we cover some really essential stuff that you'll use in most of the lessons going forward, so you kinda need to start there.

Q. So, is the book the same all the way through?

A. Actually, toward the end, it starts to change as you start to change. By the time you get to the last four or five lessons, you're going to know this stuff pretty darn well, so I stop spelling every little thing out, like I did in the earlier lessons. For example, in Lesson 04, when I need you to paint with light, I might write an instruction like, "Click on the Adjustment Brush icon, up in the toolbar that appears directly below the Histogram panel, at the top of the right side Panels area." But, after you've done that a bunch, I figure you've been around the block a bit, so I talk like I would to a colleague. At that point, when I need you to use the Adjustment Brush, I just write, "Grab the Adjustment Brush," and that's it. I figure if you don't know where the Adjustment Brush is by Lesson 06 or 07, you're probably playing on your phone a bunch and texting and looking at TikTok while you're doing these lessons instead of paying the rapt attention required to become a Lightroom shark. So, put down your dang phone and just focus on the book. Well, that is unless somebody texts you a really funny meme. Then, all bets are off.

Q. Is there anything the 7-Point System can't fix?

A. Absolutely. It can't fix bad photography. Here's what I mean: if you've got a good photo (it's reasonably in focus and well-composed), you can use the system to take this good photo and make it a great photo. But, I can tell you this: it won't take a bad photo and make it a good photo. Believe me, I know. I've tried. The system just won't make a bad photo good. It'll make a decent photo better, a good photo great, and a great photo outrageous, but it can't fix bad composition, an out-of-focus image, or a bad concept. You're always better off getting it right in the camera. That way, you can spend less time fixing it in Lightroom and spend more time finishing it in Lightroom, which is infinitely more fun (and I've included many of my favorite finishing techniques right here in the book, so you'll pick those up, too).

Q. What's the deal with the "Refresher" at the end?

A. A friend of mine came up with the idea because sometimes he goes long periods of time between shoots (sometimes weeks, sometimes a month or more), and when he gets back, he said, since he's read the book once, he doesn't want to have to re-read the entire book again. He asked if I would include a quick refresher that will quickly bring it all back. So, at the end of the book, you'll find just that—a quick refresher you can come back to if you take a long break from Lightroom (I call it "Mike's Refresher," but feel free to insert your own name). This refresher keeps you from having to relearn things you already learned when you first read the book. There's just enough info there to really jog your memory and get you back on track fast.

Q. Do we get to use any Photoshop at all in the book?

A. Only in the final two lessons. Lightroom was designed, from the start, to work with Photoshop and Photoshop truly is "where the magic is," so I wanted to include at least a lesson or two to get you over there to see how easy working with the two together can be, but that's pretty much it. Remember, it's called "The Lightroom 7-Point System," so of course, it's going to focus on Lightroom. That being said, there is a version of Lightroom's Develop module built into Photoshop that you can pull up anytime you're in Photoshop when you need to do something you'd normally do in Lightroom (like adjusting the white balance, or painting with light, etc.). It's called the Camera Raw filter and it's found under Photoshop's Filter menu, right near the top of the menu. It's the same sliders, in the same order, using the same math, that do the exact same things. It's really handy.

Q. So where are the photos we can download?

A. You can download the same photos I used in the book from the book's companion website: **www.kelbyone .com/books/7pointphotoslr**. Of course, the whole idea is that once you're done with this book, you'll be applying my 7-Point System to your own photos, but for now, you should practice along with mine. See, I care.

Q. Some of the original photos in the lessons look pretty, well...crappy.

A. Yeah, I know. Once I started putting the book together, I soon realized why other photographers hadn't done this original-photo-to-finished-product thing. It's because normally you only see a photographer's very best finished work—you don't see their "before" photos that would otherwise never see the light of day. But, to do a book like this, you have to let people see some of your crappy photos, too, and I can tell you from doing that here myself, it stinks (and that's not the word I wanted to use). But, without these crappy originals, the book just wouldn't work, so I had to do it. (Of course, in retrospect, I could have just made up fake names for photo credits beside each image, rather than identifying them as my own. I guess I should have thought of that before I sent this to my publisher. Did I just say all that out loud?)

Q. Any final tidbits or advice?

A. Just remember that repetition is a key part of this system. It's designed to teach you just the most important parts of just seven points, and have you apply them again and again and again, until they become second nature. Until they become your workflow. Until you become a Lightroom shark, which only happens when you're no longer scared of any photo. When you open a photo in Lightroom and right away know which adjustment to use, when to use it, which settings to use, and how to take your photos from flat to fabulous in no time, you know it's feeding time (I'm not certain what that means, but I think I heard it once in the movie *Jaws*). I genuinely hope this book will give you a plan— a road map to follow—and help you finally get the results you've always wanted from your photography and Lightroom. My hope is that this learning methodology, with its simplicity and repetition, will ultimately help you spend less time in front of your computer, and more time doing what you probably love best: taking photos and enjoying your final images or prints. Okay, now you can turn to Lesson 01 and dig right in.

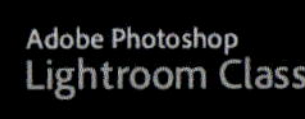

Adobe Photoshop
Lightroom Classic

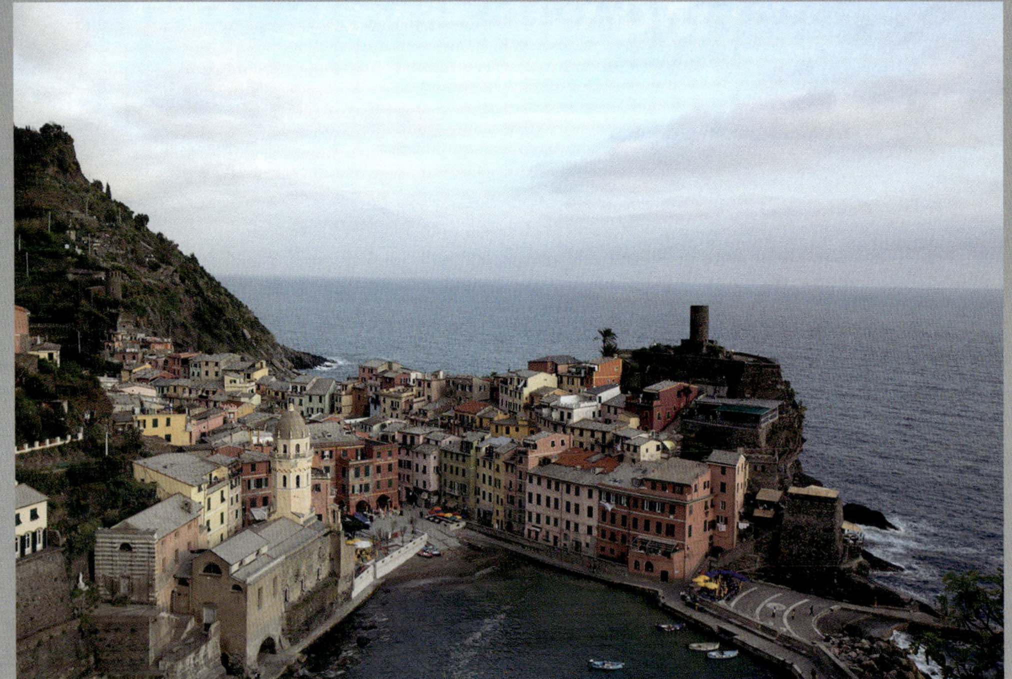

Before

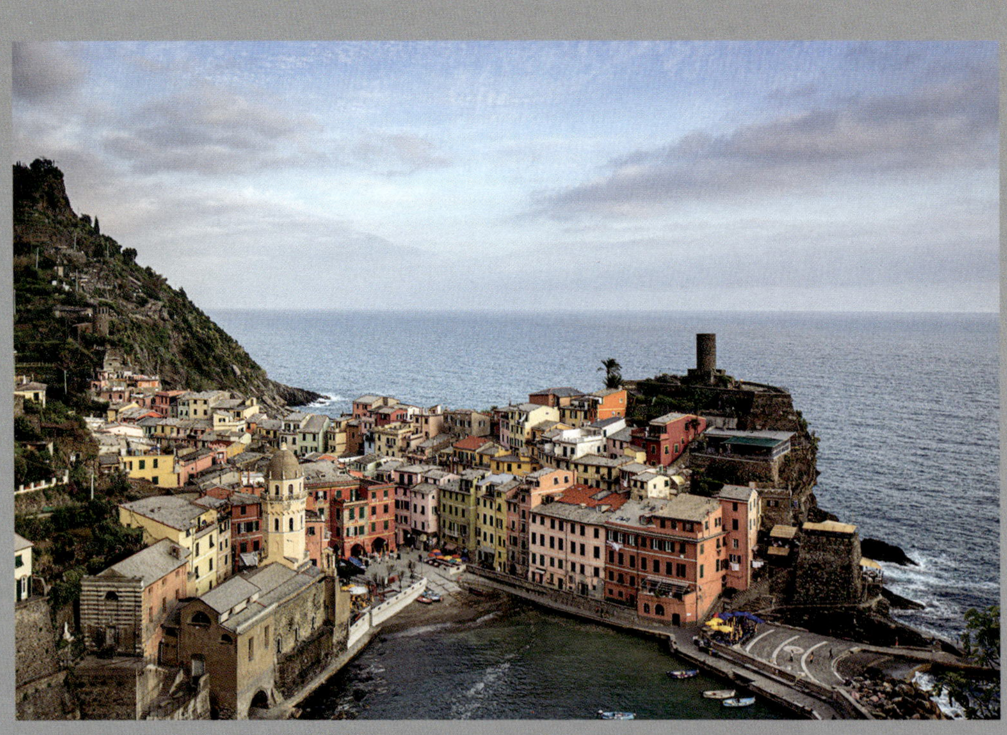

After

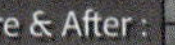

Before & After :

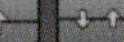
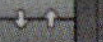

Soft Proofing

LESSON 01

SEASIDE VISTA

1. Assigning a RAW Profile
2. Getting the Color Right
3. Expanding the Tonal Range
4. Dealing with Sensor Limitations
5. Painting with Light and Retouching
6. Fixing Lens Issues
7. Finishing Moves

Before messing with any sliders, take a moment to analyze the photo. Look at it and ask (it helps to say this out loud), "What do I wish were different in this image?" Don't just say, "I wish it looked better." That doesn't help (it's also implied, right?), so be very specific. Let's evaluate this shot: Overall, it's a very flat-looking, low-contrast image, with one of my pet peeves—a crooked horizon line (an easy fix, but I should've paid more attention taking the shot). The colors are muted, including the sky, and the whole image really lacks snap.

THE STORY BEHIND THE SHOT:

This is the Italian village of Vernazza, which is one of the five seaside towns that make up a very charming and tourist-famous area of Italy known as Cinque Terra, which roughly translates to "be prepared to hike up a ridiculous amount of stairs." My wife and I had taken a trip to the South of France, staying right near Monaco. One night in our hotel, I was looking at Google Maps to see what else was around that we could go see, when I realized that we were just a 3-hour drive from one of my favorite places—beautiful Portofino, Italy—and Cinque Terra was just a short 30-minute drive from there. The next morning, we got up early and made the beautiful drive along the coast, and once we got to Vernazza (and after some incredibly yummy Italian food), we hiked up to a spot over-looking the town that's super-popular on Instagram. It was a bit of a hike up there, but totally worth it. We stayed until after sunset (and, yes, I took my lightweight travel tripod up there with me).

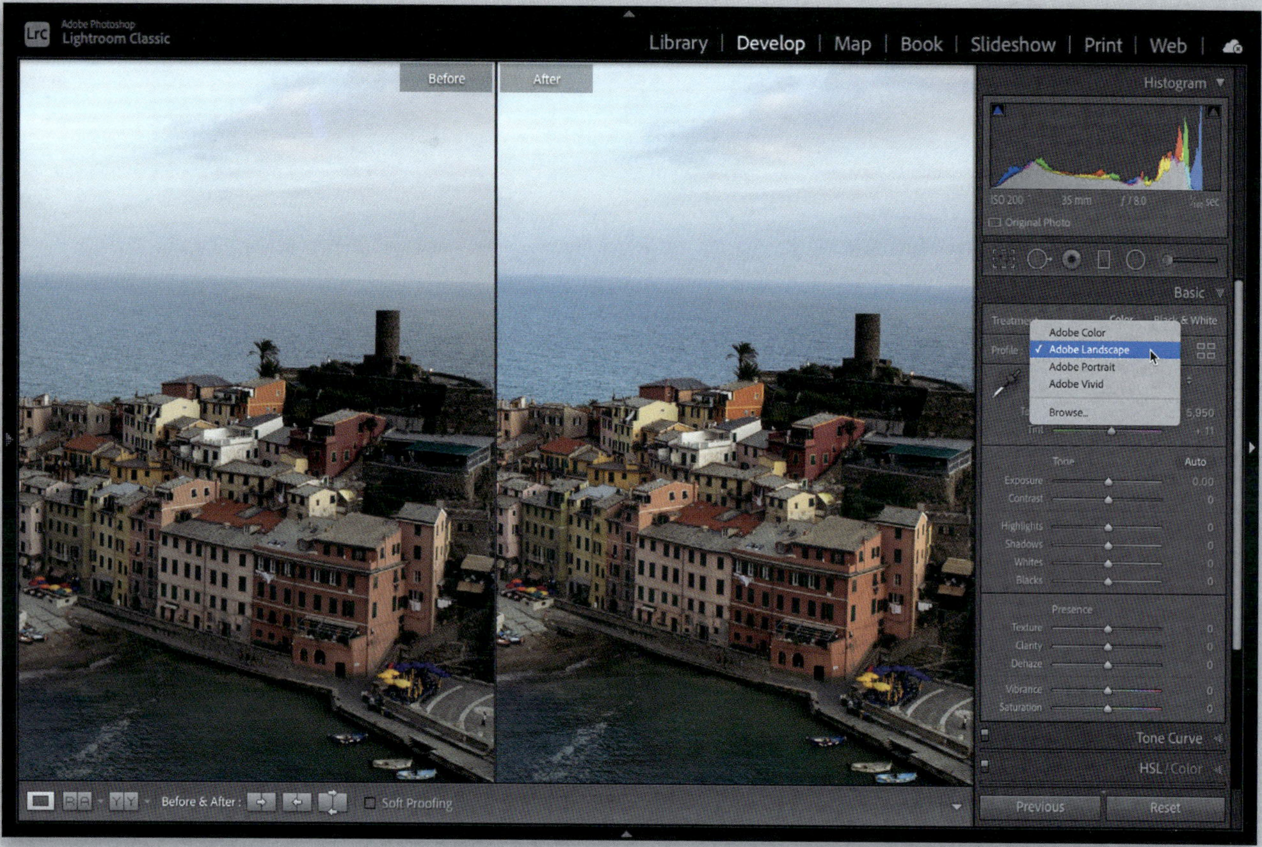

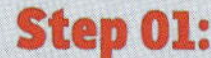

Camera: Canon EOS 5D Mark III

Aperture Value: $f/8.0$

Shutter Speed: 1/160 sec

ISO: 200

Focal Length: 35mm

Step 01:

Here's the original RAW image as it came out of my camera, in Lightroom Classic's Develop module (don't forget to download my RAW image, so you can follow along. The link to the book's companion webpage, where you can download all of the images, is on page xxi). Now, the first thing I do (as you already know if you read Point 1 on page xiii) is if I shot the image in RAW, I assign a better RAW profile than the default one that Adobe applies automatically, and this gives the image a better starting place. So, before I start tweaking sliders, the image will already look either a little bit better or a lot—it just depends on the image. You assign a RAW profile **(Point 1)** from the Profile pop-up in the Develop module's Basic panel (in Lightroom Classic; the Edit panel in Lightroom cloud). While the default Adobe Color profile looks okay, changing it to Adobe Landscape makes an immediate difference (you can see that in the before/after above), so go ahead and choose **Adobe Landscape** (as shown above. By the way, the Profile menu has profiles marked as favorites in the Profile Browser [we'll look at that later], so your menu may have a couple more). While it doesn't do a ton to the photo, it makes the tones a little bit flatter and opens the shadows a tiny bit. While you're at it, try Adobe Vivid, and you'll see why I didn't choose that one (and why I don't choose it more often). It's a very contrasty RAW profile, and it makes the already backlit buildings look even darker. Adobe Landscape boosts the color and it opens up those shadows a bit, so it gives us a better starting place to build from. *Note:* You can get this before/after view by pressing the **Y key** on your keyboard (this view is not available in Lightroom cloud, but you can press the **\ [backslash] key** to see your original image).

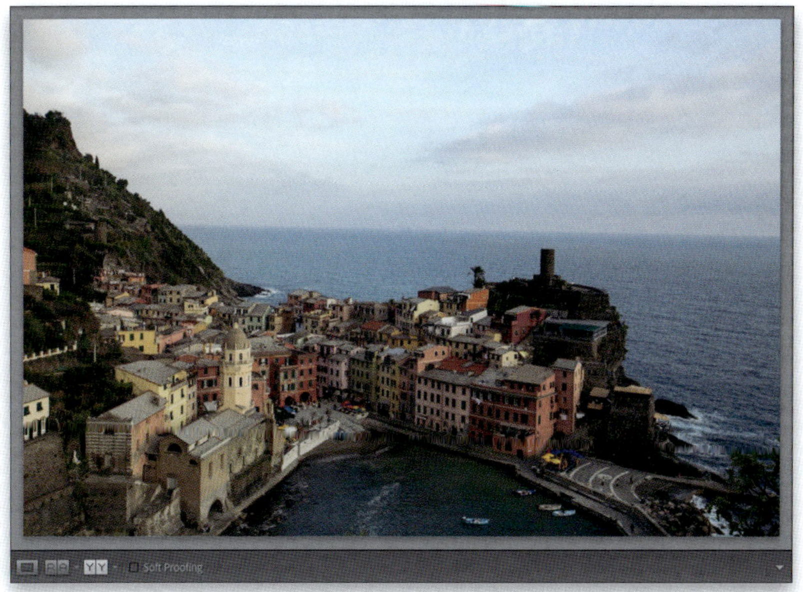

Step 02:

Okay, take a look at that crooked horizon line. We gotta fix that (well, I need to, actually, because it's really distracting, so help me out here). We should be able to get Lightroom to straighten that horizon for us if we fix the lens distortion issues in the image, including a perspective issue (the buildings are smaller at the base and look larger at the top), and there's darkening in all the corners. Lightroom's Upright feature can usually fix all of this, but (and here's a handy tip) the Upright feature actually works better if you apply a lens profile fix first, so let's start there (in the next step. Yes, we're jumping to **Point 6** here, which we looked at back on page xviii, because, like I mentioned on page xii, occasionally, we need to jump around in the system if something is really distracting and needs to be fixed right away).

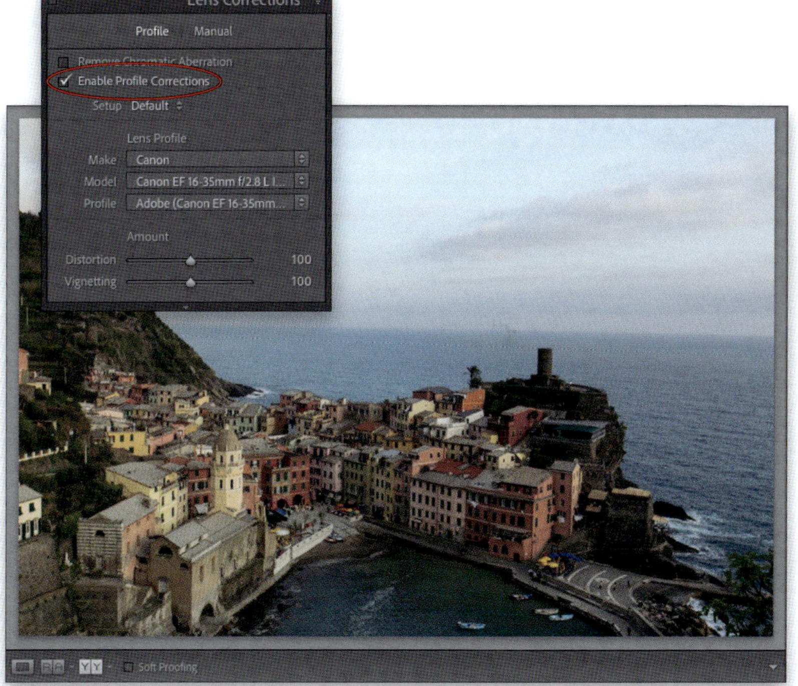

Step 03:

Go to the Lens Corrections panel (the Optics panel in Lightroom cloud), and turn on the Enable Profile (Lens) Corrections checkbox (as seen here). Look at that—it fixed some of the barrel distortion (because lenses are rounded, the middle of your image winds up bowing out a bit, and doing this flattens out and straightens the sides of the image. The wider the lens you use, the more pronounced this distortion is, but luckily, it's super-easy to fix for the most part—just turn on this checkbox). These built-in lens profiles in Lightroom not only address the distortion, but they also fix the darkening in the corners big time by simply brightening them. Look at the top corners here, versus those in the previous step, and you'll see the difference. So, two birds (lens distortion and corner vignetting), one stone (the Enable Profile Corrections checkbox).

Step 04:

Now that the lens profile has been applied, go to the Transform panel (the Geometry panel in Lightroom cloud) because that's where the Upright feature lives. You'll see six buttons at the top of the panel (in Lightroom cloud, there are no buttons—you choose these from a pop-up menu), and the one I wind up using 99% of the time is Auto. It gives what Adobe calls "a balanced correction" that fixes the level (straightening), perspective, and aspect ratio issues, and the results look the most natural of any of the options. If you were an architectural photographer where straight verticals are a must, you might wind up using some of the other options, but for most images, Auto does the trick. So, click on Auto (as shown here), and it applies an Upright correction. It did a really nice job here, fixing all those issues. Toggle on/off the visibility button in the left side of the panel header (click-and-hold on the eye icon in the right side of the panel header in Lightroom cloud), keeping your eye on the buildings, and you'll see what a big difference this one click makes.

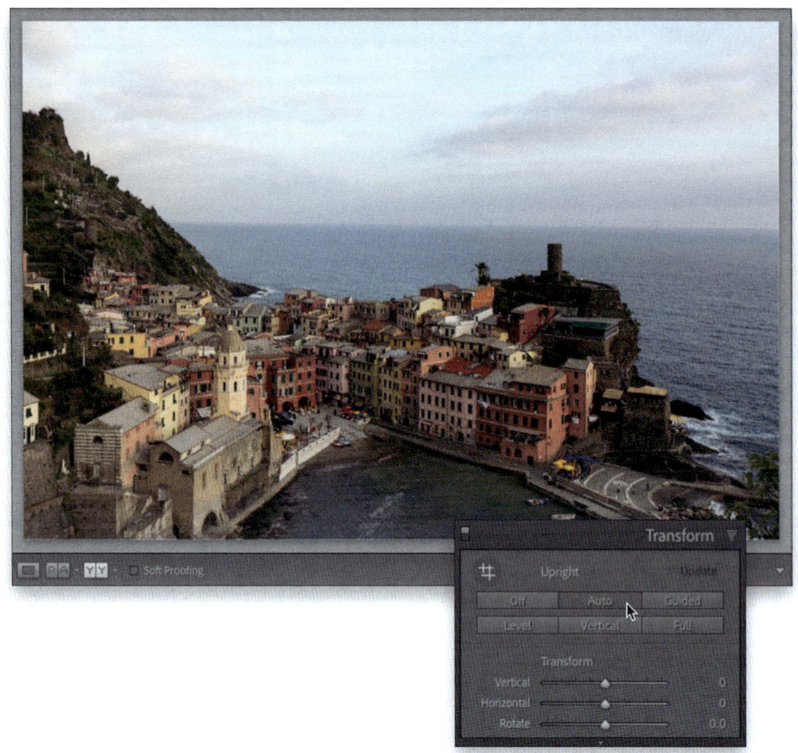

Step 05:

I'm tellin' ya—as good a job as Upright did, I think the horizon line is still off by a tiny bit. Maybe it's an optical illusion and, technically, it's straight, but if it doesn't look straight to our eye, it's not straight. Easy fix. In the same panel, drag the Rotate slider to the left to –0.3 (as shown here). I know that's just a smidgen of straightening, but I think that fixed it, and now it looks straight to my eye. Give it a try to see what you think (you might go with –0.4, as you could make a case for that being perfectly straight). Another way to do this is to get the Crop Overlay tool (**R**; the Crop & Rotate tool in Lightroom cloud **[C]**) from the toolbox, and use its straightening feature (drag it along the horizon line, from left to right, and it straightens the image based on that. In Lightroom cloud, use the slider). I tried it, and yup, it rotated the image straighter, so I guess it needed it.

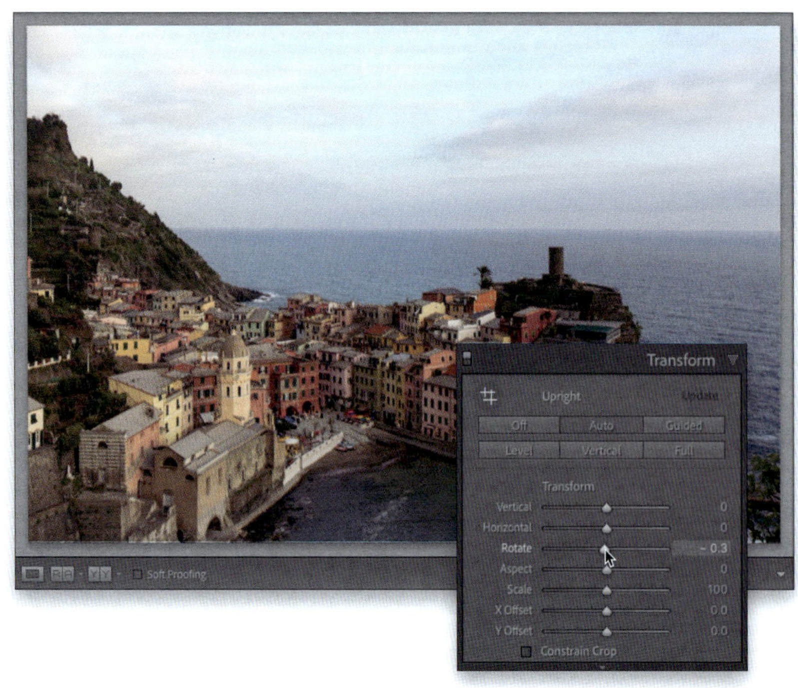

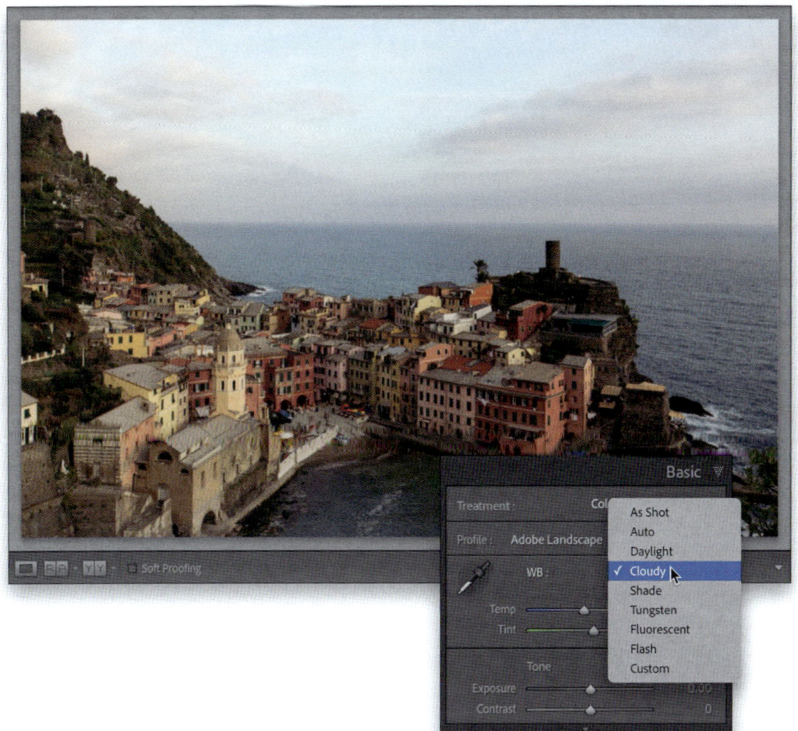

Step 06:

Now, let's check our color (**Point 2**, which you learned about back on page xiv). The overall white balance actually looks pretty good, but if you want, you can try out some of the WB (White Balance) presets at the top of the Basic panel (the Color panel in Lightroom cloud. These choices are only available if you shot in RAW). I tried them all (well, if you didn't shoot indoors, under artificial light, you can skip trying Tungsten and Fluorescent), and in this instance, **Cloudy** looks nice. It gives a little warmer look without losing the blue in the sea and sky, so choose that from the WB preset pop-up menu (as shown here).

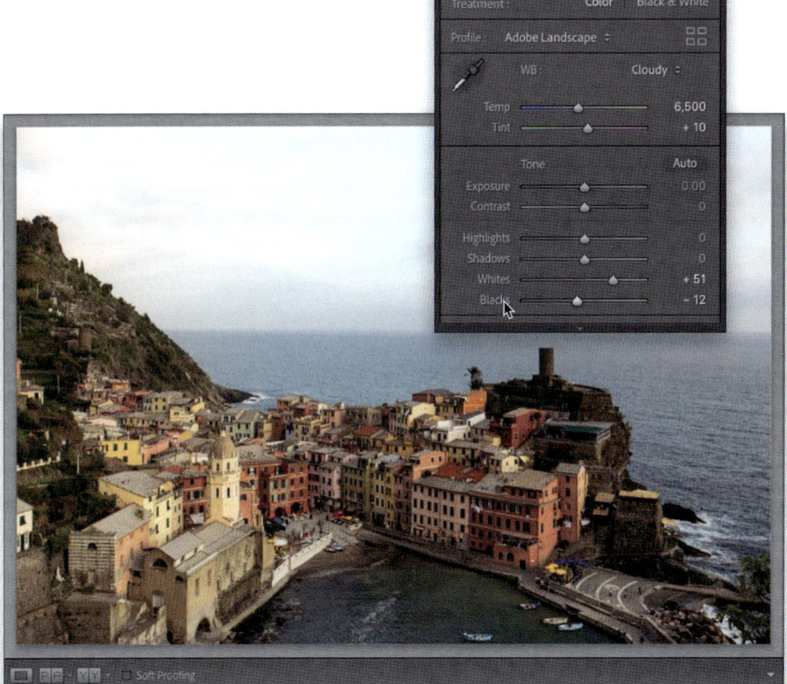

Step 07:

Next, let's work on expanding our tonal range (**Point 3**, which you learned about back on page xv), making the whites as white as we can and the blacks as dark as we can make them, without everything going totally solid black. Lightroom can easily do this for us (well, as long as you know the secret handshake, which you will in about 4 seconds). Just press-and-hold the Shift key, then double-click directly on the word "Whites," and then do the same thing and double-click directly on the word "Blacks" (as shown here. These sliders are in the Light panel in Lightroom cloud). Wow! Just doing this was like cleaning a dirty window—it was like a level of grime was just lifted off our image. The contrast looks better and the colors are more vibrant and it just looks better all the way around. Setting the white and black points (to +51 and –12) definitely expanded the tonal range in this image, and it's not nearly as flat looking as before. Compare it to Step 04 and you'll see what I mean.

Step 08:

Now that our white and black points are set, let's brighten the image just a bit to bring out some brightness in those backlit buildings. Drag the Exposure slider just a little over to the right (here, I dragged over to +0.35) and that helps brighten the overall image just a tad, but it makes a difference.

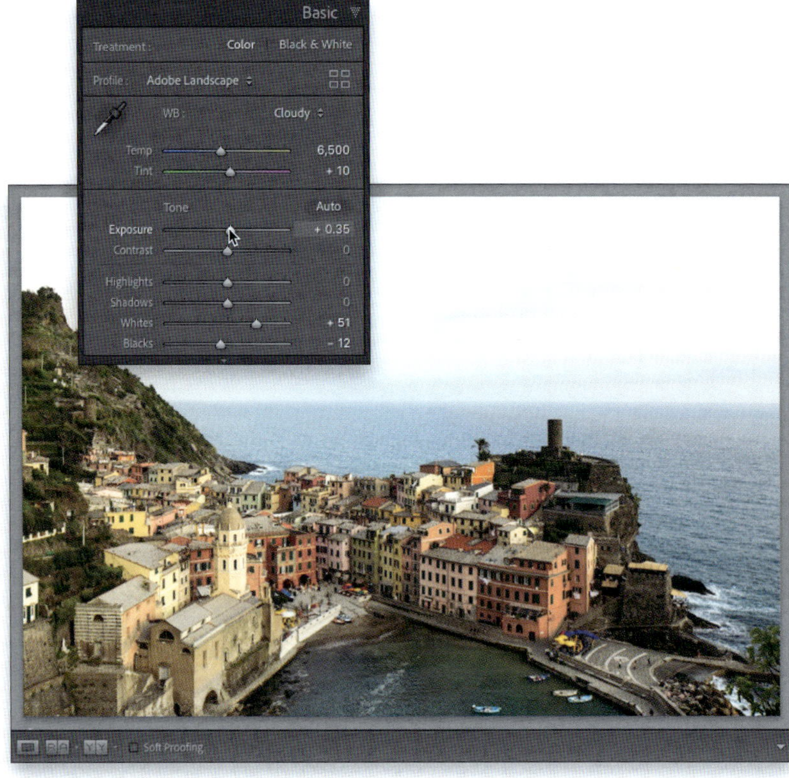

Step 09:

We can now fix two areas that need addressing (**Point 4**, which we learned about back on page xvi): (1) We can make our sky look better and help those clouds stand out a bit more by reducing the amount of highlights big time. This is a sky trick I've been using for many years: just drag the Highlights slider all the way to the left, to –100, and it makes a big difference in the definition of the clouds, and darkens the sky a bit, as well, but usually doesn't harm any other parts of the image. And, (2) we can help those backlit buildings on the right of center by dragging the Shadows slider to the right a bit to open up the shadows in that area (here, I dragged over to +28).

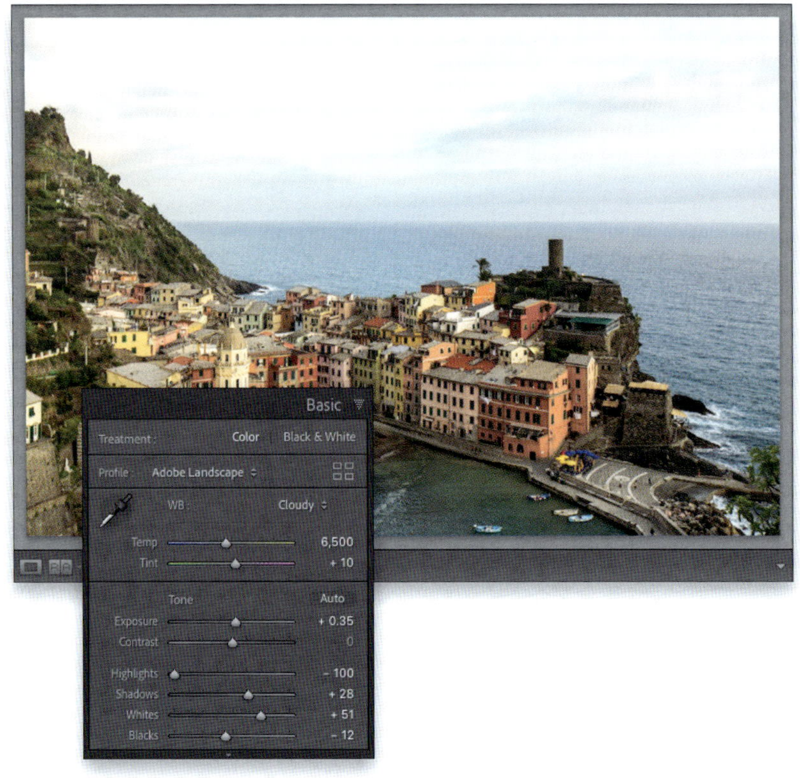

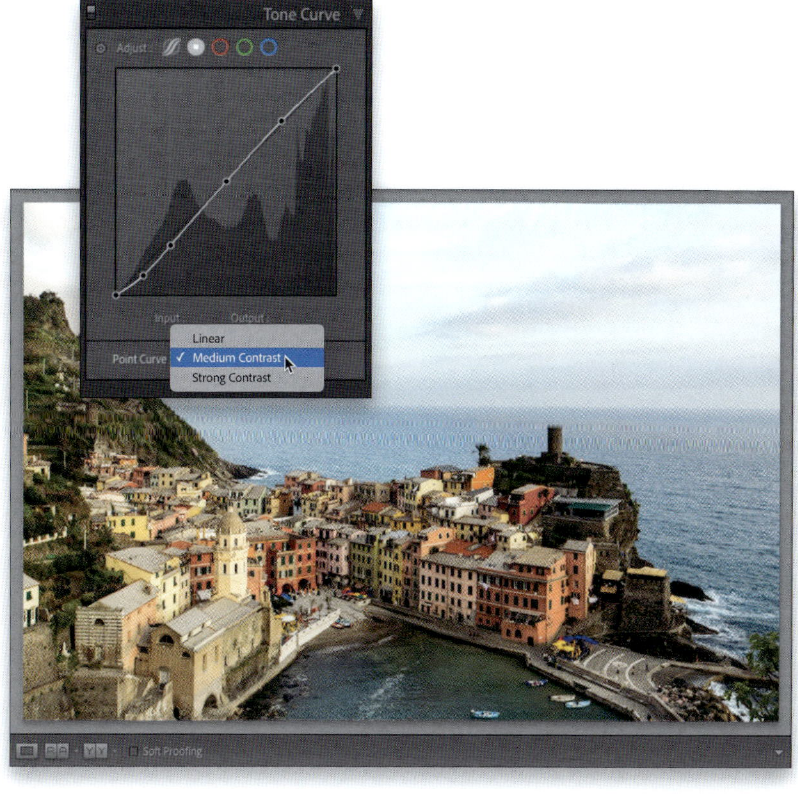

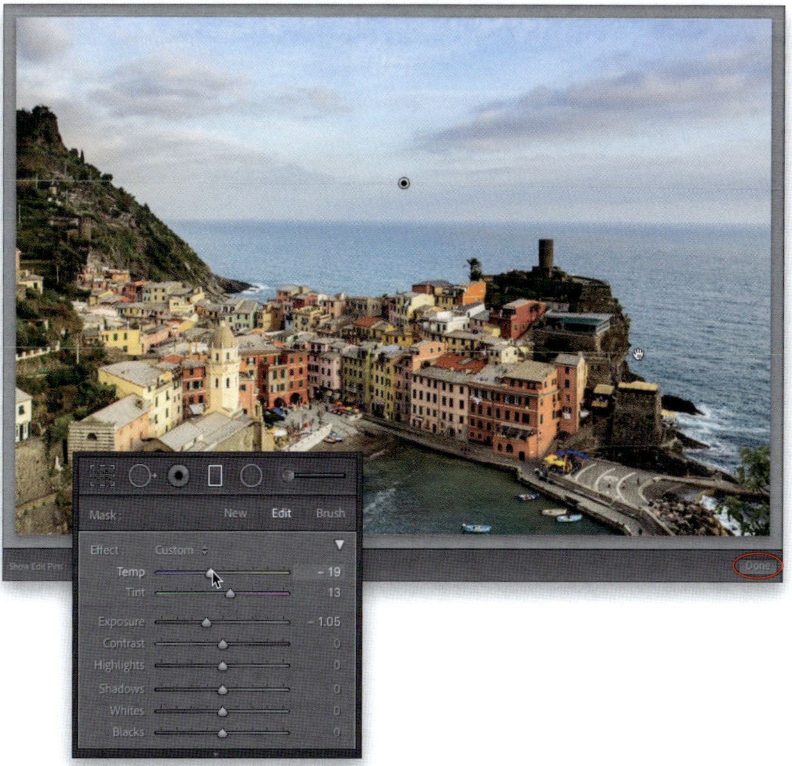

Step 10:

When opening up those shadows, and crushing the highlights like this, sometimes (well, often), we lose some contrast, but that's an easy fix. You could drag the Contrast slider to the right, or you could go to the Tone Curve panel and apply some contrast there, using its built-in contrast presets. From the Point Curve pop-up menu, choose **Medium Contrast**. If you want even more contrast, choose Strong Contrast, or adjust the curve yourself manually. The steeper you make that curve (click-and-drag the dots on the diagonal line), the more contrast it creates. The middle point controls the midtones, the point between the middle and top-right controls the highlights, and the point to the left of the center point controls the shadows. *Note:* There isn't a Point Curve pop-up menu in Lightroom cloud, so you'll need to adjust the curve manually.

Step 11:

Now, with an easy move, we can get that sky looking a lot better (**Point 5**, which you learned about on page xvii). Get the Graduated Filter tool **(M)** from the toolbox beneath the histogram (the Linear Gradient tool **[L]** from the toolbox on the right in Lightroom cloud), then double-click on the word "Effect" near the top left of the panel to reset all the sliders to zero (this happens by default in Lightroom cloud), and then drag the Exposure slider about 1 stop over to the left (I dragged it to –1.05). This will darken the top of the gradient, and then it will gradually go to transparent at the bottom. Click once at the top center of the image and drag down until your cursor is about at those center buildings' rooftops (that bottom line indicates where the gradient is transparent, so you're not darkening those rooftops). Now that it's in place, we can make the sky prettier (not just darker) by dragging the Temp slider a little toward blue (to –19), and the Tint slider a little toward Magenta (to 13). That makes a big difference in the sky. Click the Done button when you're finished.

Step 12:

Okay, let's bring out some detail in those buildings (and well…everything else) by dragging the Texture slider to the right (here, I dragged it over to +40. This slider is in the Effects panel in Lightroom cloud). That did a nice job (though, it might be a bit hard to see the awesomeness it added at the size we're seeing here in the book—you'll see the difference big-time onscreen when you apply it yourself).

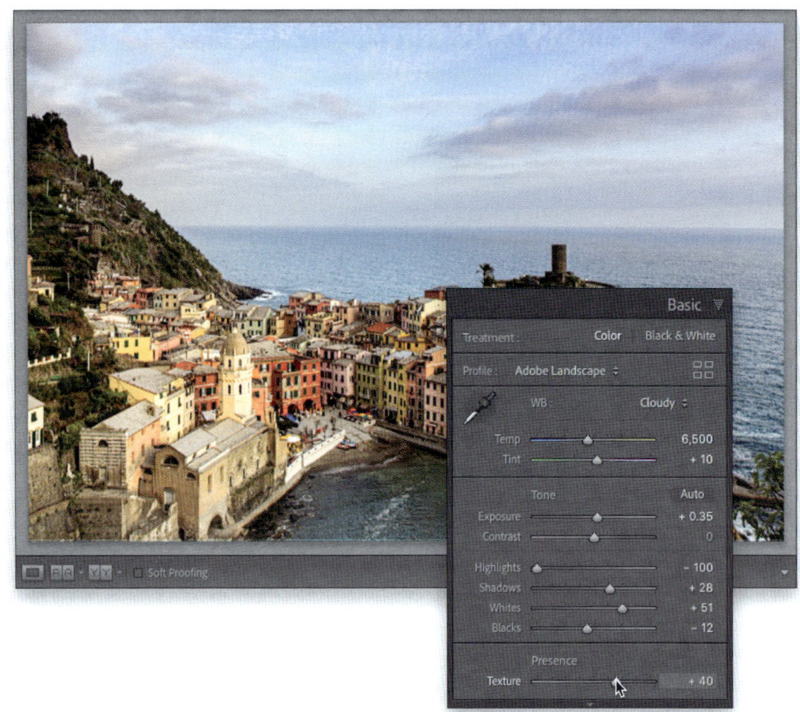

Step 13:

This might make it seem like I'm being really picky (so you can skip this step if you feel that way), but I'm trying to balance the overall tone in the image. I don't want something that's too bright drawing our eye, and to me, that yellow church and bell tower in the center left is pulling my eyes over there. It's not the focus of the image (the colorful buildings in the center and right are the focus), so I would darken them up just enough to where they don't pull the viewer's eye. Get the Adjustment Brush **(K)** from the toolbox beneath the histogram (the Brush tool **[B]** from the toolbox on the right in Lightroom cloud), double-click on the word "Effect" to reset all the sliders to zero, then drag the Exposure slider a little to the left (here, I dragged to –0.49, so about 1/2 a stop). Now, paint over that bell tower and the church (as shown here) and anything kind of bright in that general area. Ahhh, that's better! Click the Done button when you're finished (it's at the bottom right of the preview area. By the way, there isn't a Done button in Lightroom cloud. When you're done, just go to the next panel or tool).

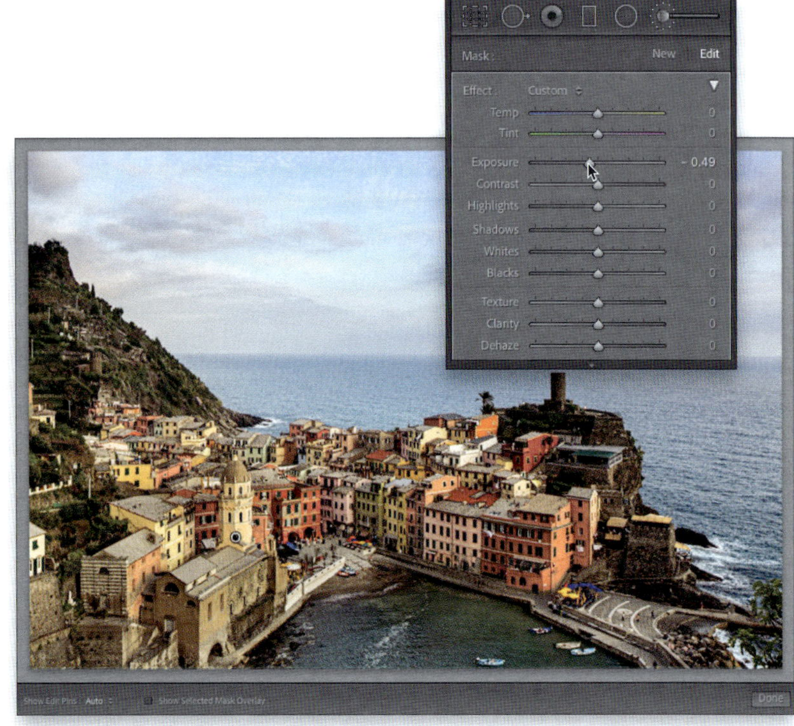

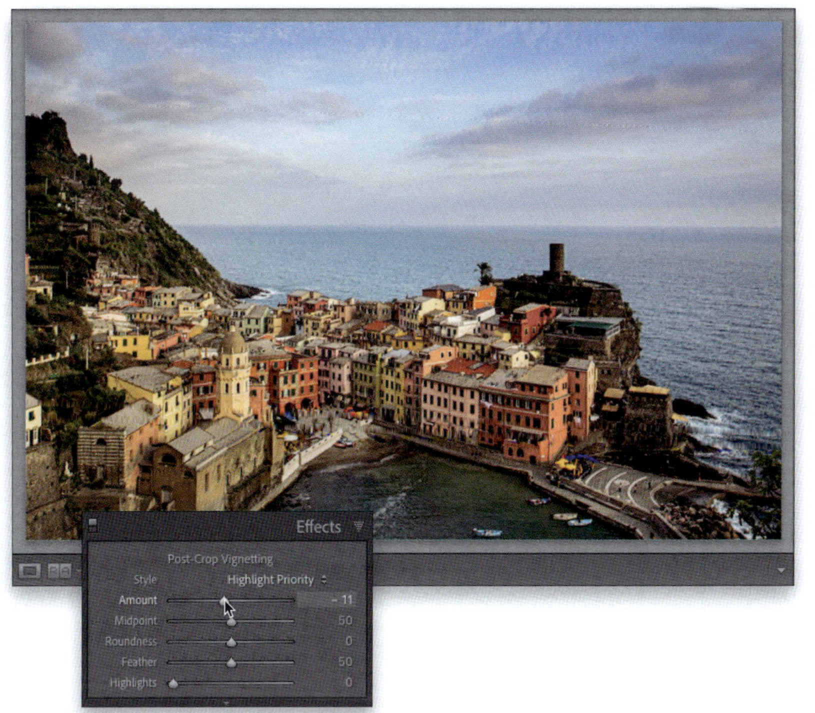

Step 14:

For the final point of the 7-Point System, (**Point 7**, which you learned about back on page xix), we're going to do some finishing moves. Let's subtly darken those outside edges of the image all the way around (drawing your attention to the center) by such a small amount that nobody will realize we did it—but it makes a nice difference. Go to the Effects panel, and under Post-Crop Vignetting, drag the Amount slider (the Vignette slider in Lightroom cloud) over to –11 (as shown here). That's the magic number I use to darken the edges without it looking like I added a vignette. If you don't think it does that much, toggle it on/off by clicking on the little visibility button in the left side of the panel header (click-and-hold on the eye icon in the right side of the panel header in Lightroom cloud), and you'll see why I usually add this as a finishing move. Easy and quick.

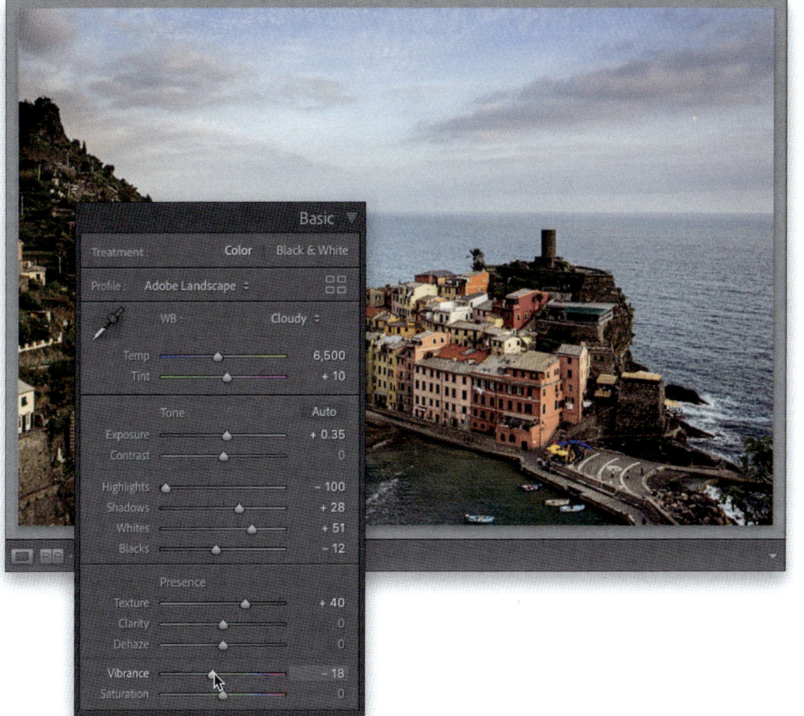

Step 15:

Now, I love really colorful images (almost as much as the public likes them, which is much more than photographers do), but throughout the system (and often at this point), when I pause, step back, and look at the image, I think it's a little too colorful. A lot of the things we did added contrast, which pumps up the color, and we could trim a little of that saturated color off. This is an optional step because if you like the color as it is, there's no sense in messing with it. But, if you think it's just a little too colorful (as I do), then go back to the Basic panel (the Color panel in Lightroom cloud) and drag the Vibrance slider to the left just a bit. Here, I dragged it to –18 to pull back that color just a little.

Step 16:

All that's really left is to add some sharpening (every image I process gets sharpened). So, go to the Detail panel and drag the Amount slider (the Sharpening slider in Lightroom cloud) to 60 (I tried dragging it higher and it started to look kind of crunchy, so I came back to 60). How your sharpening will look is often based on the things you did before you get to the sharpening stage, and in this case, 60 looks like it got the job done (and I didn't have to touch any of the other sliders. Though, if you were concerned about sharpening the clouds, you could avoid sharpening them altogether. Just press-and-hold the Option [PC: Alt] key and drag the Masking slider to the right until the sky turns solid black, and now that sky wouldn't get any of the sharpening— just the village and sea would be sharpened. We'll look at the Masking slider more later). Okay, you made it through Lesson 01, so we are off and running. Time for a different image, and to learn some other cool Lightroom stuff along the way.

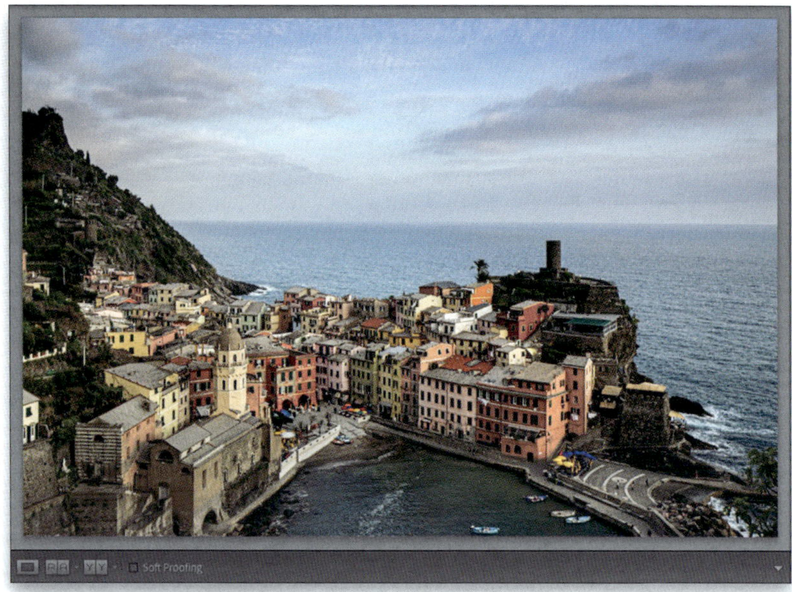

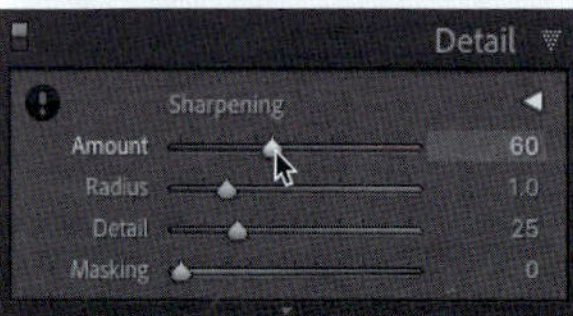

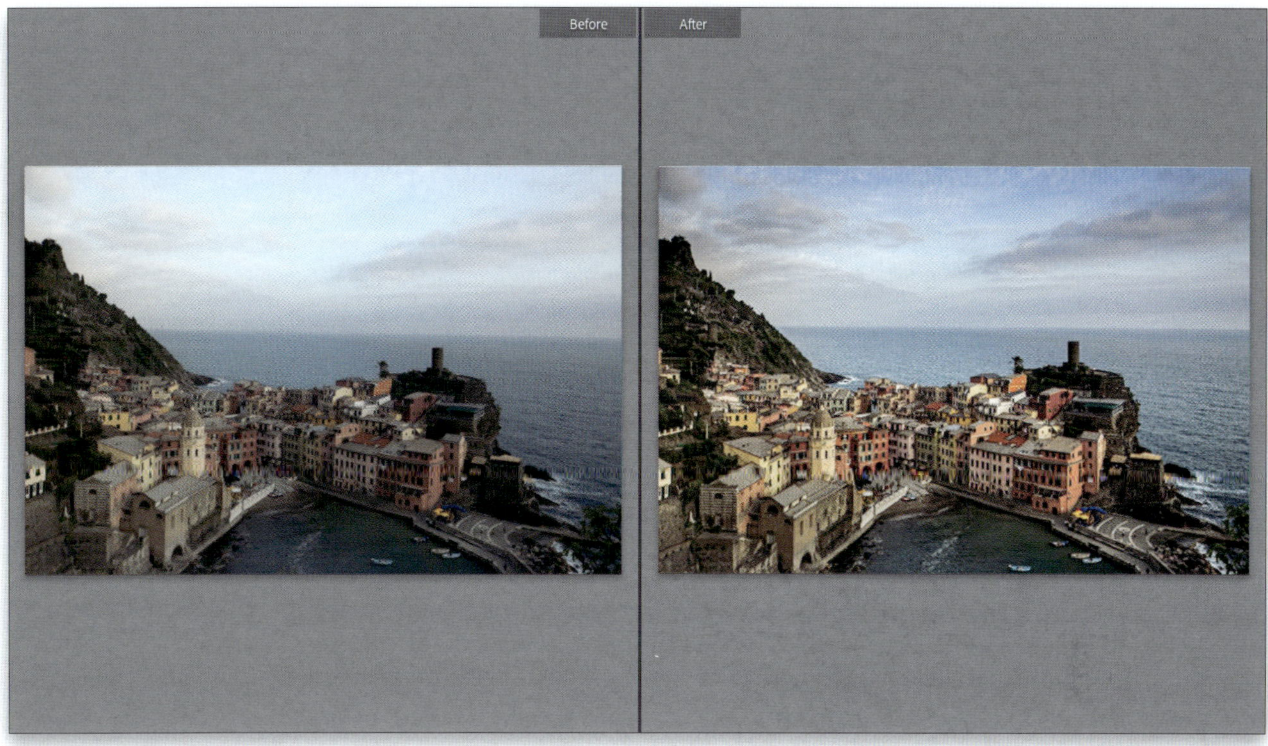

Here's our before/after.

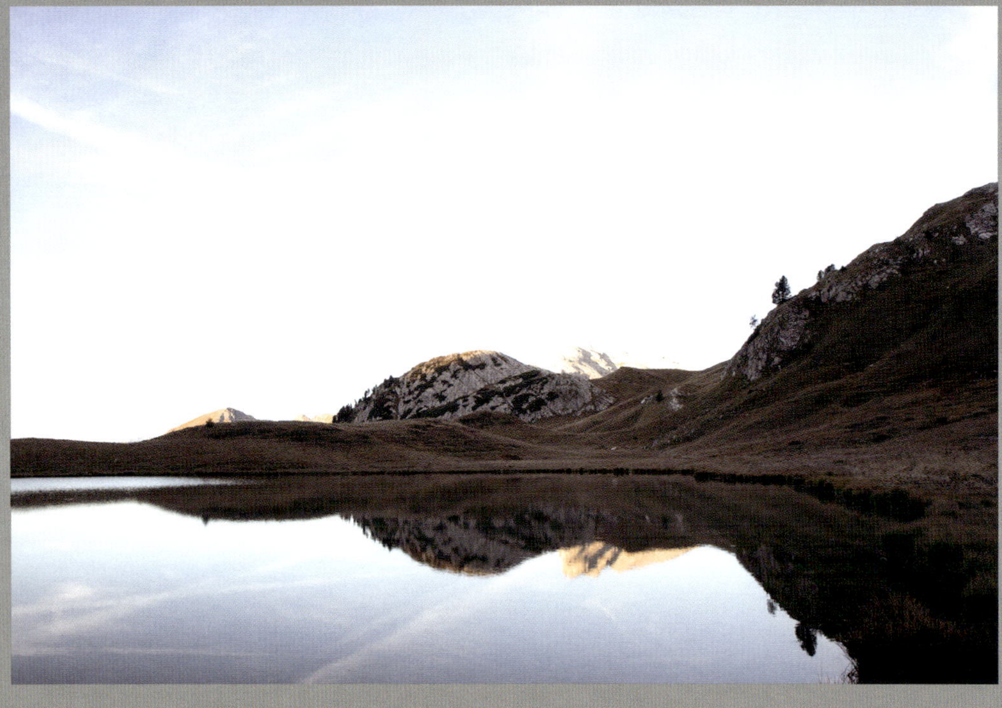
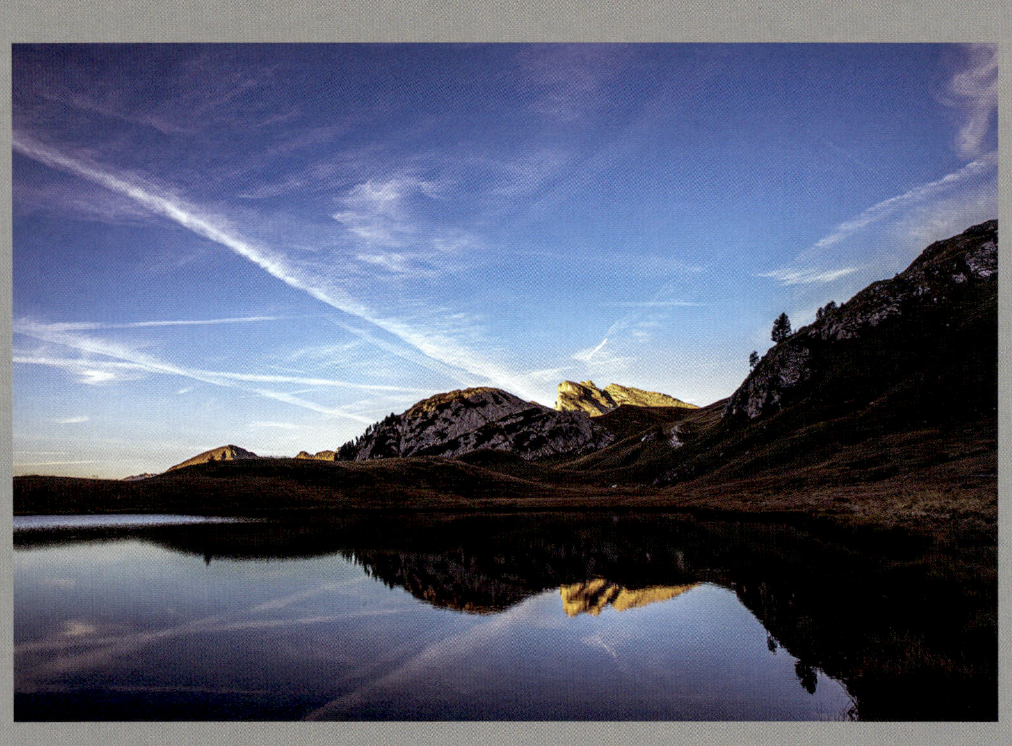

Adobe Photoshop
Lightroom Classic
Before
After
Before & After :
Soft Proofing

LESSON 02

LAKESIDE REFLECTION

1. Assigning a RAW Profile
2. Getting the Color Right
3. Expanding the Tonal Range
4. Dealing with Sensor Limitations
5. Painting with Light and Retouching
6. Fixing Lens Issues
7. Finishing Moves

Let's evaluate the shot: I wish the sky wasn't so washed out, that it was bluer and richer, and the clouds stood out more. I wish the hills in the foreground weren't backlit, that they were brighter. The image looks a little flat, so I wish it had more contrast and the colors "popped" more. I'd love to see more detail in the hills, and of course, like almost every similar photo, I want it to be really sharp and crisp looking.

THE STORY BEHIND THE SHOT:

This was taken on vacation with my brother Jeffrey, in the Dolomites of Northern Italy. I convinced him to get up really early one morning and drive to a location about 40 minutes from our hotel to shoot the sunrise (he's actually a really good photographer, with a great eye, but he's not so into photography that he wants to get up at 4:45 a.m., while on vacation, but he did it anyway 'cause he's an awesome brother). On the way to our dawn shoot, just off the road and right next to a small gift shop, was the scene you see here, and what drew me to it was the reflection from the absolutely still water. So, on the way back from our shoot, just a little after sunrise, we stopped at the gift shop (it wouldn't be open for hours). I grabbed my camera and tripod and headed down the little pathway to the lake where we spent about 30 minutes shooting, until the sun was above the little mountain (more a "big rock thing"), and then we headed back to our hotel for a great Italian breakfast. Perfect way to start the day.

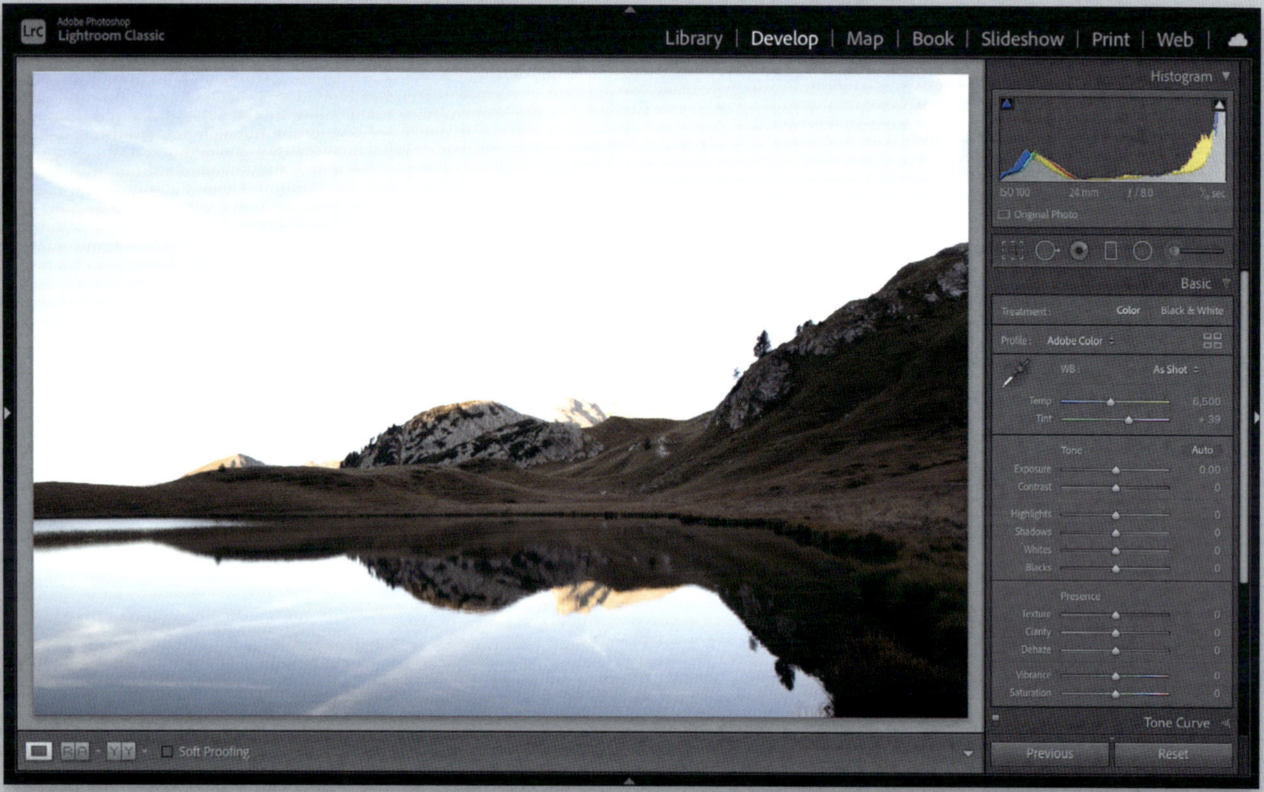

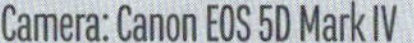
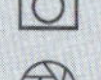
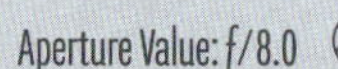
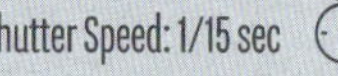
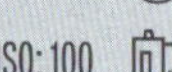
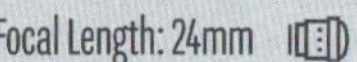

Camera: Canon EOS 5D Mark IV

Aperture Value: ƒ/8.0

Shutter Speed: 1/15 sec

ISO: 100

Focal Length: 24mm

Step 01:

Here's our original RAW image. It has a very common issue caused by the fact that our camera sensors, great as they are, still cannot capture the range of tones and light that our eyes can, so it's either going to make the sky look properly exposed or the foreground (the lake and that big rock). Our go-to choice is to make the foreground look good, and then darken the sky by putting a neutral density gradient filter over the front of our lens, or we can fix it later in post-production (also known as Lightroom). The nice thing about this one is, while we are applying the system, we're also getting to learn two of my all-time favorite editing tips for making our skies look great along the way. Okay, let's get to work.

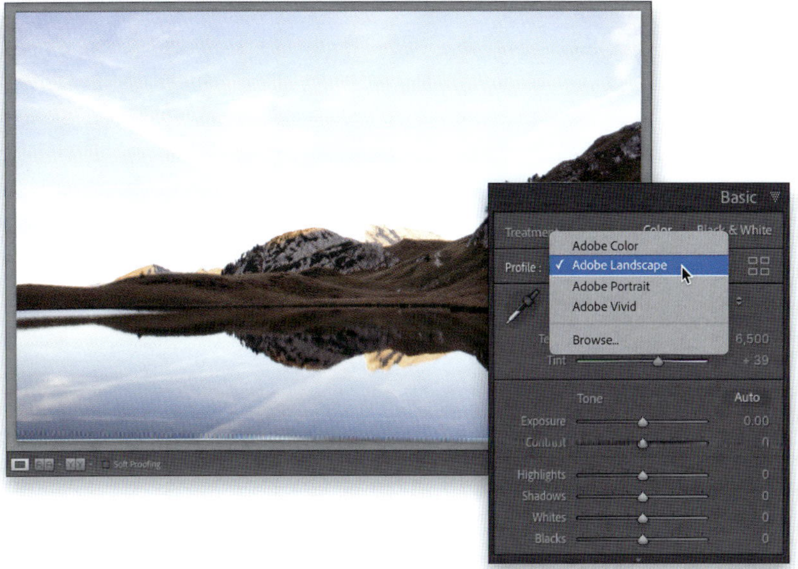

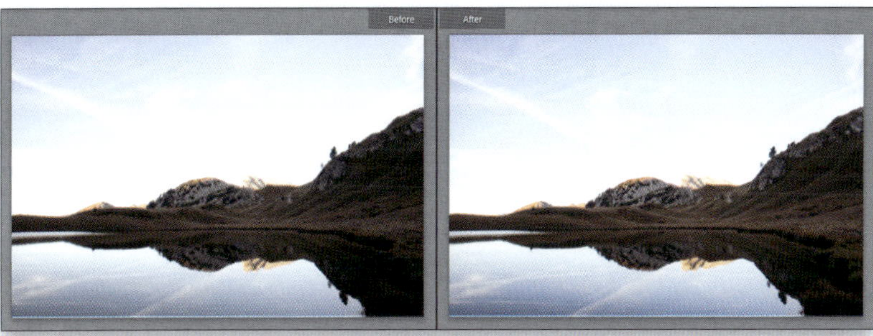

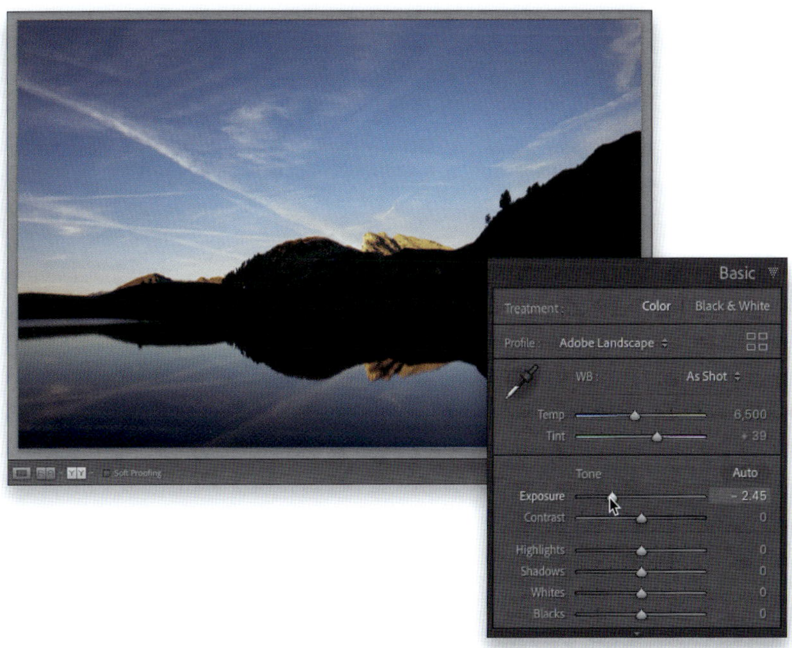

Step 02:

The first thing we do is choose a RAW profile to give our image a better starting place **(Point 1)**. We do this in the Develop module's Basic panel (the Edit panel in Lightroom cloud) from the Profile pop-up menu (as shown here). The one I choose in most cases (except if the image is a portrait) is **Adobe Landscape**. It generally makes your image a little more contrasty (which also makes it a bit more colorful), and for most photos, it just looks better. So, that's our starting point—applying the Adobe Landscape RAW profile—and while it's not a night-and-day difference on this particular photo, it is certainly better (see the before/after shown below. You can get this view by pressing the letter **Y** on your keyboard. This view is not available in Lightroom cloud, but you can press the \ **[backslash] key** to see your original image). Remember, if you shot in JPEG, you will skip this point in the system as you can't assign RAW profiles to JPEG or TIFF images.

Step 03:

Next, I normally fix the white balance, but this shot—taken on a bright day with my camera set to Auto White Balance—actually looks pretty good, so we can breeze right past that point in the system (Point 2). Instead, let's work on this problem: since I exposed for the foreground, the sky got washed out (a pretty typical problem). So, to get the sky looking great, I'm going to pull one of my favorite editing tricks: I'm simply going to darken the entire image until the sky looks richer and bluer by lowering the Exposure (it's the slider that controls the midtones, so it has a big effect on the overall brightness of the photo). In the Basic panel (the Light panel in Lightroom cloud), drag the Exposure slider to the left to –2.45, making the image about 2-1/2 stops darker.

Step 04:

Now, before we go any further, let's go ahead and expand the tonal range of our image **(Point 3)**, making the whites as white as we can and the blacks as dark as we can make them, without everything going totally solid black. Just press-and-hold the Shift key, then double-click directly on the word "Whites," and then do the same thing and double-click directly on the word "Blacks" (as shown here). Sometimes this will have a massive effect (which lets you know how badly you needed to expand that range), and sometimes it doesn't have a big effect at all, which is not a bad thing—it just means your tonal range is already pretty wide, so a big adjustment wasn't necessary. Here, it really made a difference in the Whites, where it bumped them up by +45. In the Blacks, not so much, only bumping them up by +2. Either way, it's totally worth doing—just two double-clicks. Now, this is normally what I do first in Point 3, but this photo needed that sky fixed so badly, I chose to fix the exposure first. I also increased it a bit, here, to –2.05.

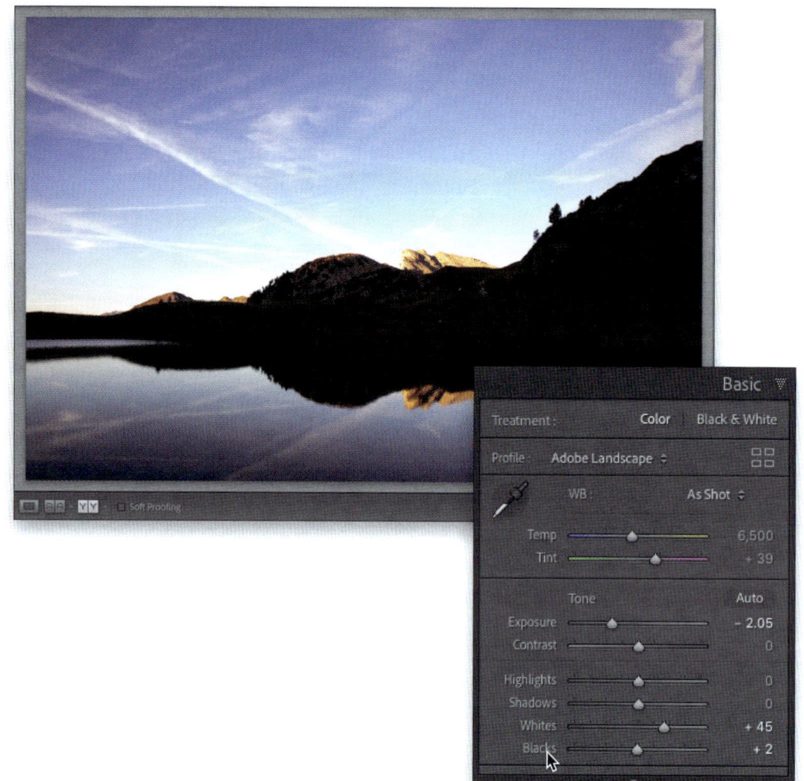

Step 05:

Once we darkened the sky, the backlit hills in the foreground looked even darker, so to fix that, we crank up the Shadows amount by a bunch **(Point 4)**. Here, I cranked it up to +90. You can usually get away with cranking it up that much in images like this (landscapes, cityscapes), but if you did that to a portrait, your subject's skin would start to look kind of weird and over-affected, so we don't generally open the shadows as much on portraits. Also, if you shoot bracketed on your camera (taking multiple photos with different exposures to combine into a single HDR image), you can crank that Shadows slider up to +100 easily without seeing a lot of noise. It's part of the magic of Lightroom's HDR feature (as you'll learn later in this book).

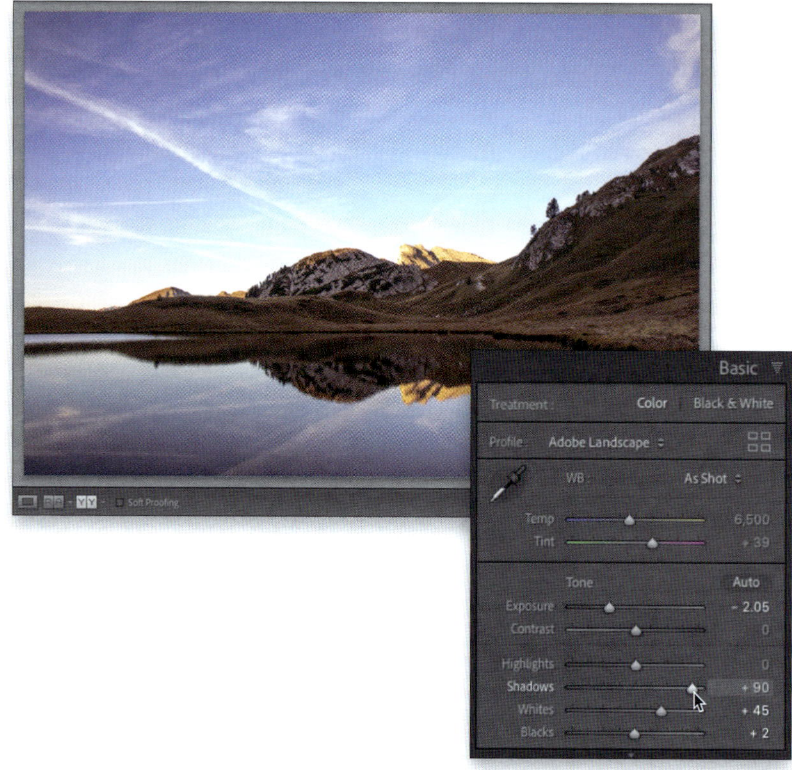

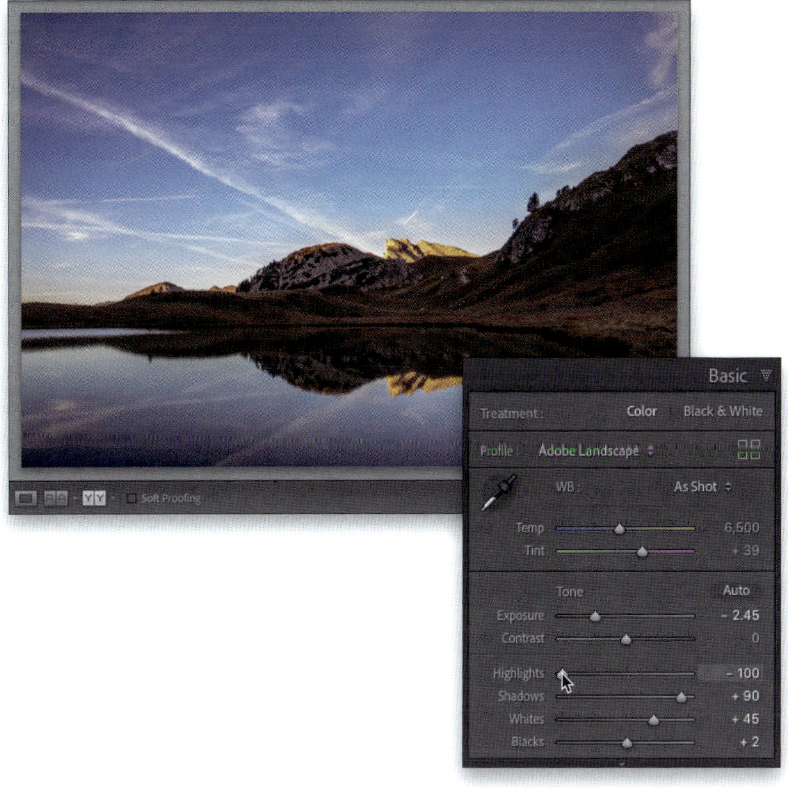

Step 06:

Now we're going to pull another trick I use for landscape and travel photos that sounds like it might mess up the photo, but it doesn't—it adds awesomeness to the sky without really messing anything up. To get more detail in the clouds (which are usually bright white), drag the Highlights slider all the way to the left to –100. Yes, I know that sounds crazy (well, I dunno, maybe it doesn't?), but it works like a charm in most photos (and I've used this trick on thousands of photos). Take a look at the sky now. Again, great on travel and landscape photos, but if you happen to try it on a photo and you don't like how it looks on that particular one, just drag the Highlights slider back to the right until it looks good again. No harm done, so it's definitely at least worth trying. Compare the sky here with the one in the previous step. The clouds look better and have more definition and the sky even looks better. This trick works way better (and way more often) than you'd think. I thought things looked a little too bright, so I also ended up decreasing the Exposure again to –2.45 here.

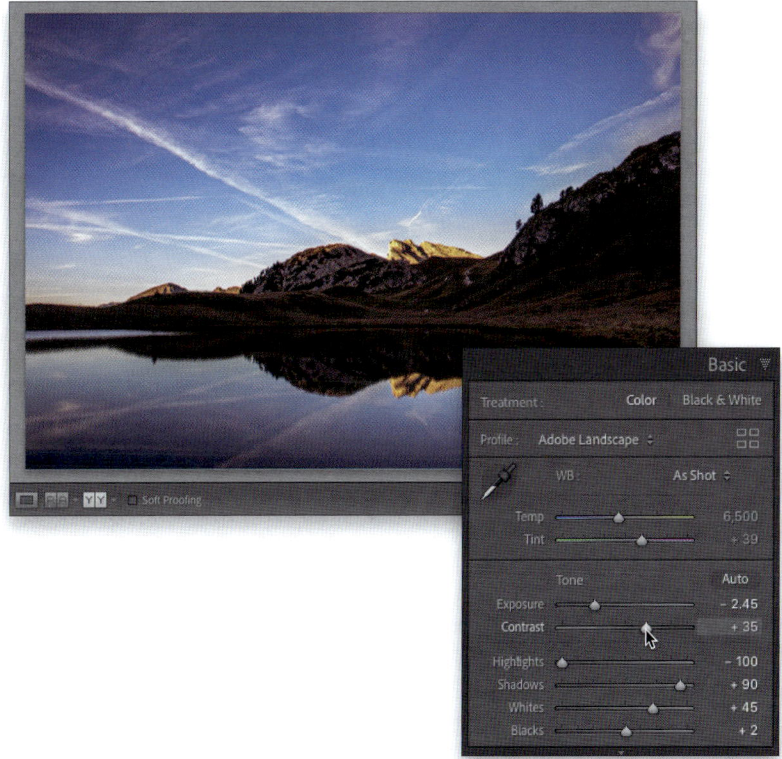

Step 07:

It's time to increase the Contrast now (I do this to almost every image), and just doing this (increasing the Contrast) makes your colors more vibrant and saturated. So much so that you probably won't have to apply any Vibrance to your photos here in Lightroom (not that you won't ever have to, but adding contrast usually does at least most of the job for you). Go ahead and increase the Contrast slider quite a bit (dragging it over to around +35), which gives you the snappy, colorful image you see here.

Step 08:

At this point in the system, this is where I look to bring out detail. I only wait until this point because I want to get pretty close to what the final exposure will look like before I start messing with the two sliders that enhance detail. I start with the Texture slider, which does a great job of bringing out detail and giving the image a crisp look without messing with the tone or brightness of the image. In this case, where I've got an image with lots of detail in the rocks, I know I can crank up the Texture amount quite a bit without things looking funky. So, drag the Texture slider to the right to around +30 and watch how the detail comes out and how it tightens up your photo, making it look sharper overall (and we haven't even added sharpening yet). *Note:* If you're using Lightroom cloud, you'll find the Texture slider in the Effects panel.

Step 09:

In a photo like this (one with lots of detail and sharp corners, so anything like a landscape, cityscape, an automobile, a motorcycle, etc.), after adding Texture to bring out detail, I'll add some Clarity. The Clarity slider (nerd alert) controls the amount of midtone contrast, and it does mess a bit with the tone of your image (for example, on portraits, it makes people look like they've been in a fight—literally), but for these types of images it does something wonderful: it makes water and metal very shiny (no metal here, but just for future reference, Clarity looks great on the chrome parts of cars, motorcycles, and buildings). So, drag the Clarity slider over to the right to around +23 (I don't apply the same amount of Clarity that I do Texture—usually about half—but in this case, it looked okay to push it a bit more), keeping an eye on that water and the rocks as you go. Makes a big difference, right? *Note:* You'll find the Clarity slider in the Effects panel, as well, in Lightroom cloud.

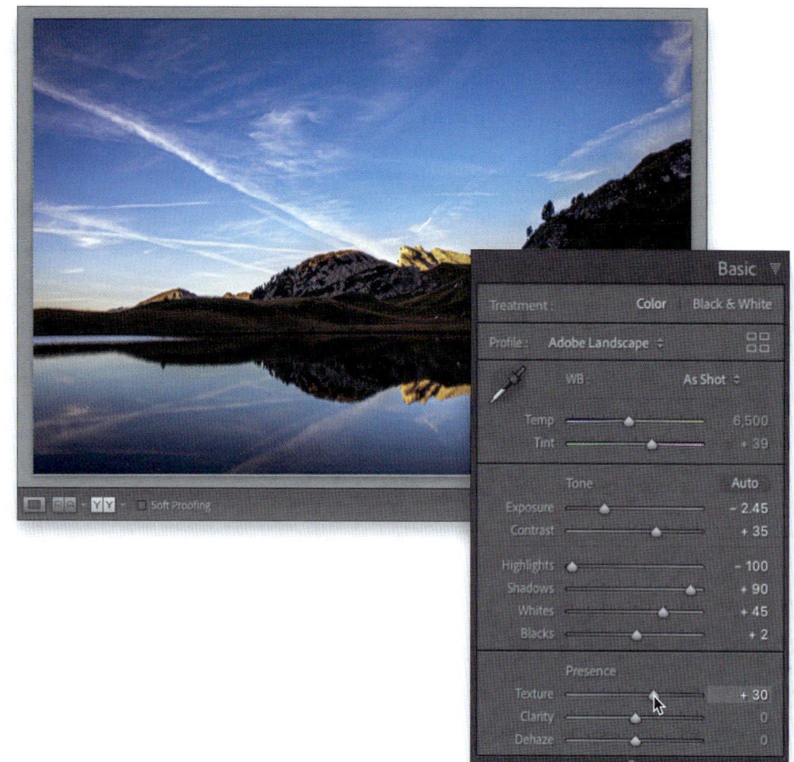

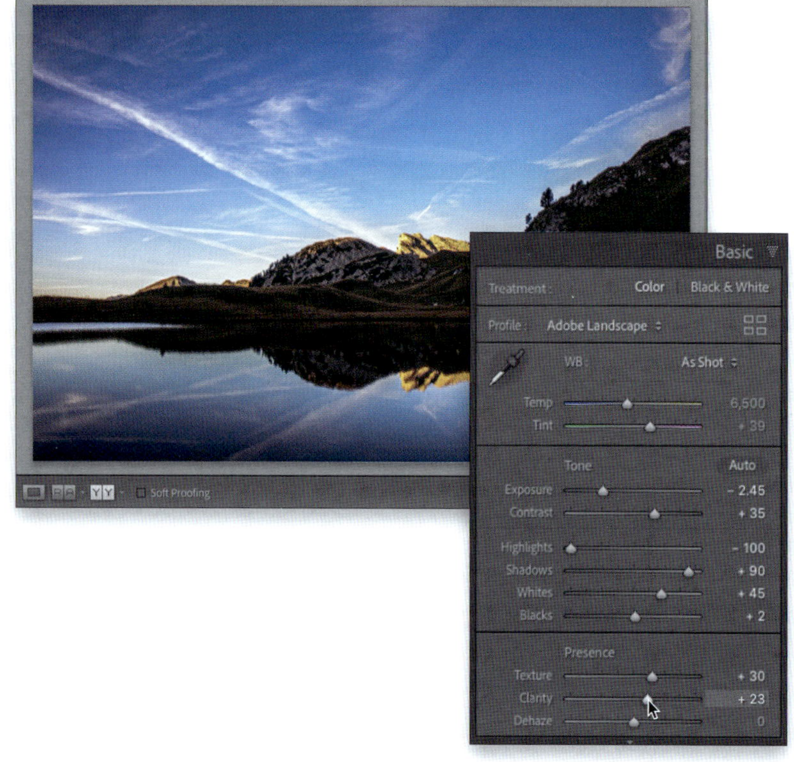

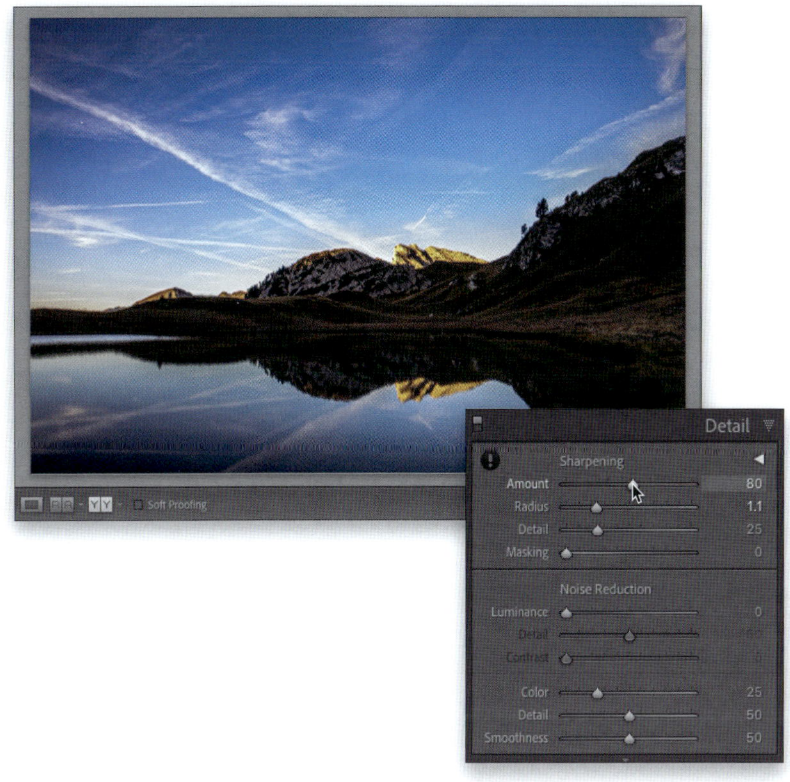

Step 10:

Lastly, and falling under our "Finishing Moves" of the system **(Point 7)**, is sharpening. Now, I sharpen every single photo. Period. Every photo gets sharpened, but just like we can add higher Texture and Clarity amounts to images with lots of detail like this, we can also add a lot of sharpening, as well. Sharpening in Lightroom happens in the Detail panel, so go to that panel and increase the Amount from its default setting (for RAW images) of 40, taking it up to around 80. That's quite a bit of sharpening, and depending on your image, it might be too much, but for a detailed image like this, you can probably get away with it. Also, if you have a higher megapixel camera (like 30 megapixels or higher), you can usually increase the Radius amount to 1.1, or even 1.2 if you have a 50-megapixel body, but leave the Detail slider at 25 (I don't ever increase it because it has the opposite effect than you'd imagine).

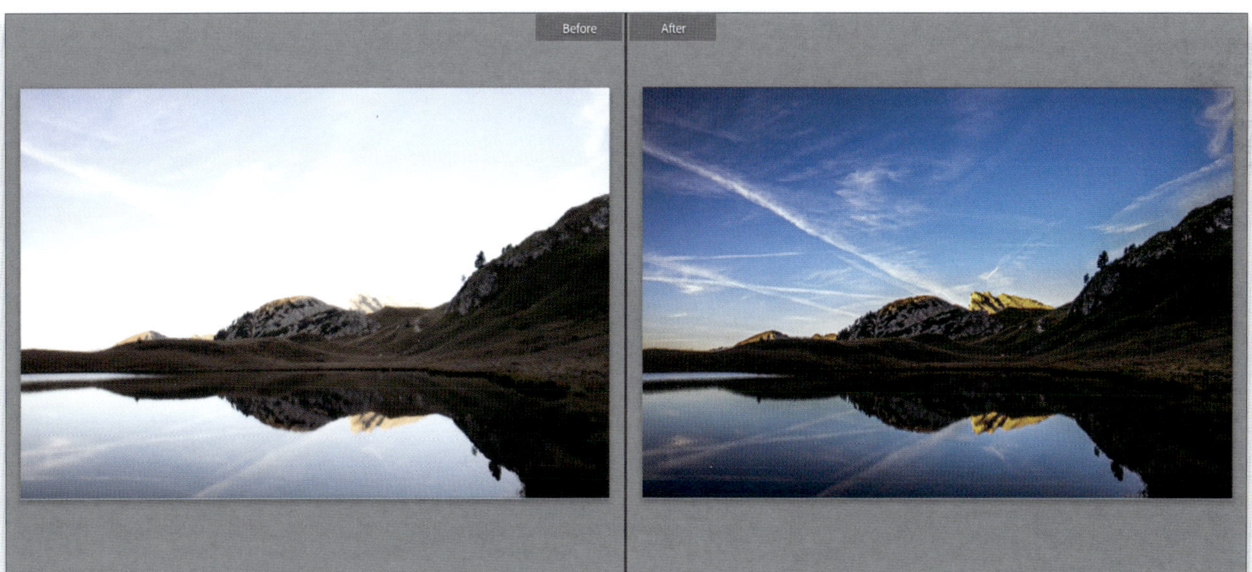

Here's our before/after of the image using just those adjustments. The things that I feel made the biggest difference were lowering the Exposure to get a great sky, and then enhancing the clouds by pulling those Highlights back to −100 (keep that trick in your back pocket—you'll use it often). Also, the Clarity made the water glassy, which is nice, and the Contrast gave us the nice rich colors without jumping through any hoops. In addition to Point 2, we skipped over Points 5 and 6 for this image because we didn't need to paint with light or retouch here, or fix any lens problems.

Adobe Photoshop
Lightroom Classic

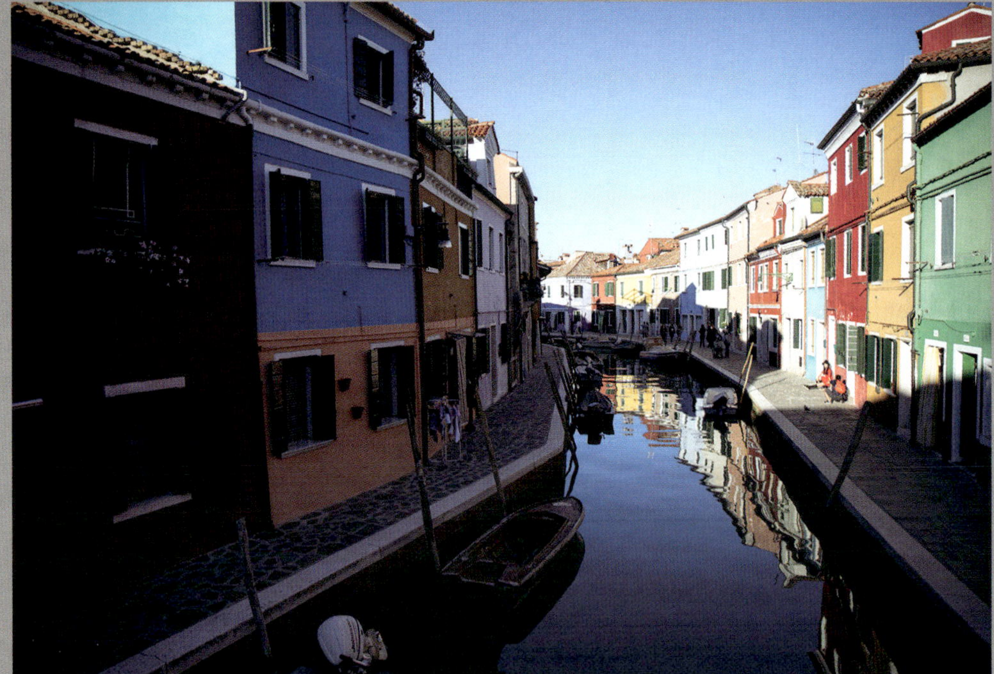

Before

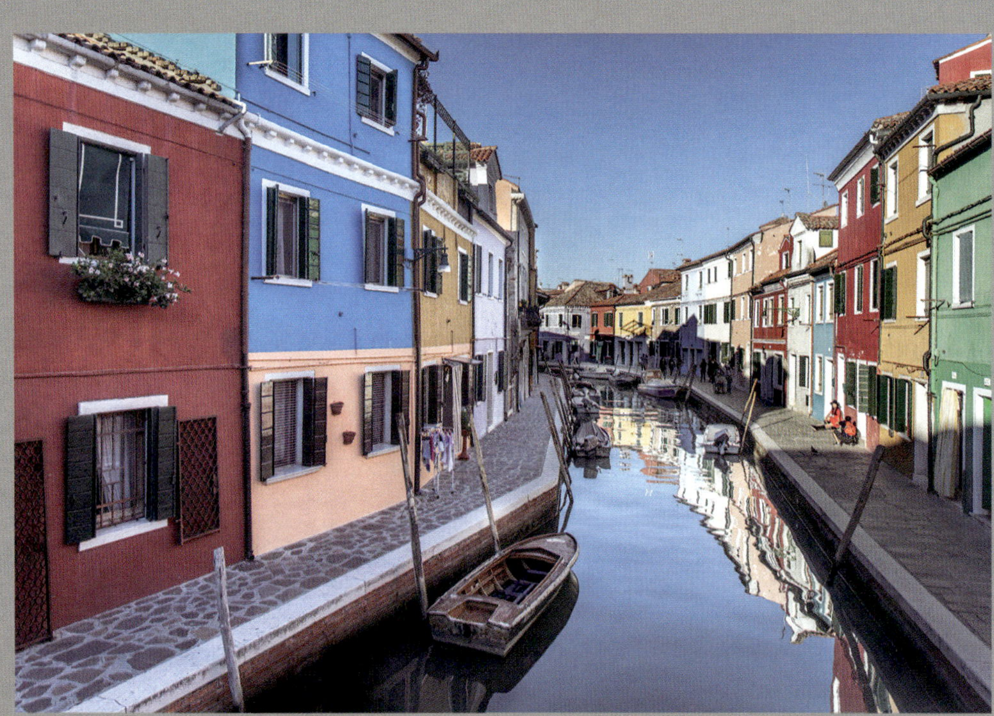

After

Before & After :
Soft Proofing

THE VIVID ISLAND

1. Assigning a RAW Profile
2. Getting the Color Right
3. Expanding the Tonal Range
4. Dealing with Sensor Limitations
5. Painting with Light and Retouching
6. Fixing Lens Issues
7. Finishing Moves

Okay, let's take a moment to evaluate the image: What do I wish were different? Well, one side of the canal is too dark and one side is too bright, the buildings are leaning backward (a lens problem we'll have to fix), and the buildings on the right, in direct sun, have their colors a bit washed out (this would have been ideal to shoot on a cloudy day where the lighting would've been much more even, and that would've helped make the colors look more saturated).

THE STORY BEHIND THE SHOT:

This shot was taken on the tiny island of Burano, Italy (just a short vaporetto ferry ride from Venice, and like Venice, it is made up of a series of small islands connected by bridges with winding canals and charming walking bridges. There are no cars, but the island is so small that you can easily walk the entire thing in just a few hours). I was there with my buddy Mimo, who lives in Venice, and as we learned, the main attraction of the island (and the reason to hop that vaporetto in the first place) is, unlike Venice, all the buildings are painted bright vivid colors, and that can make for some fun images (though, you certainly can't tell that from the Before picture on the opposite page). If I got the chance to shoot there again, I would (a) wait to go on an overcast day, and (b) I would only dedicate an hour or so to shooting there because the whole island pretty much looks the same—when you return from your trip, how many shots of similar brightly colored buildings are you really going to show?

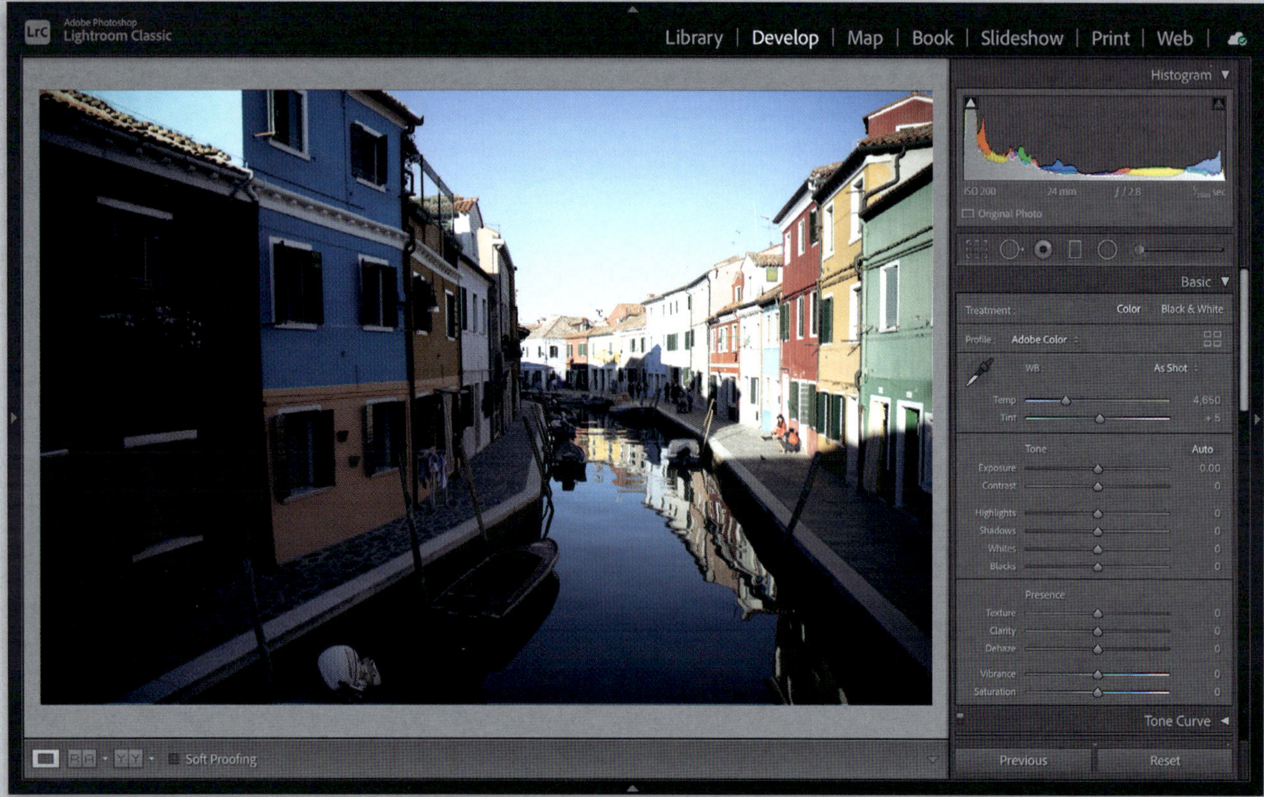

Camera: Canon EOS 5D Mark IV
Aperture Value: $f/2.8$
Shutter Speed: 1/2500 sec
ISO: 200
Focal Length: 24mm

Step 01:

Here's the original RAW image. It's hard to enjoy the vivid colors of Burano when they don't look very vivid, and that's mostly because of the bright, cloudless sky and the position of the sun, which left one side of the canal dark and in the shade, and other side brightly lit but washed out. The buildings on the left, in the shade, are much more saturated and vivid color-wise, but they're also underexposed. A scene like this, where part of the image is brightly lit (and washed out) and another part is dark is a challenge for your camera's sensor, but we can get this balanced out and looking much better using the 7-Point System.

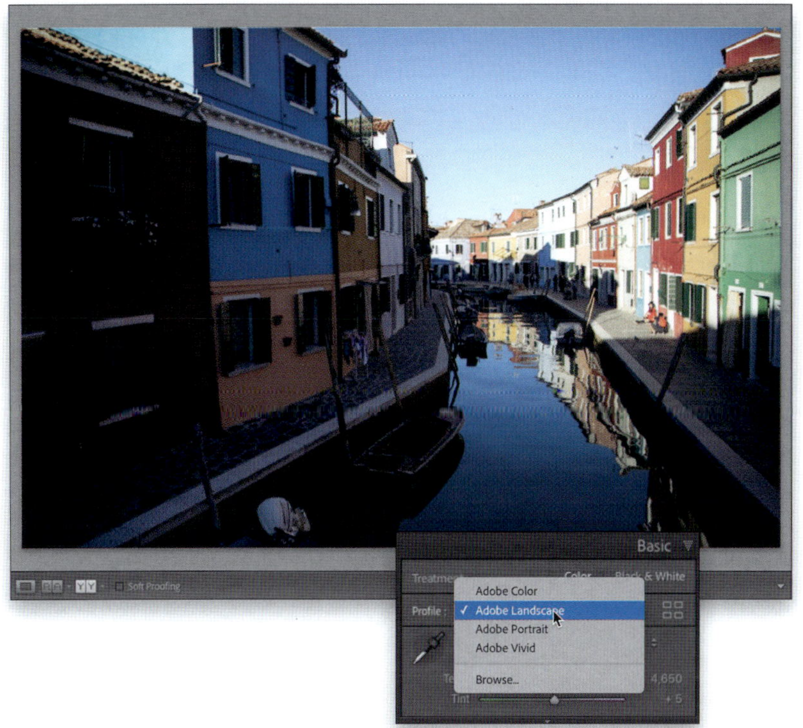
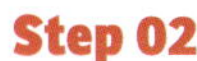

Step 02:

We'll start by applying a RAW profile, which gives us a better starting place (this is **Point 1**, and again, if you shot in JPEG, just skip this step). The profile I use the most by far is **Adobe Landscape**, as it usually gives a little better color and contrast, so let's go ahead and choose that one (since more color and contrast is what we want for this photo anyway) from the Profile pop-up menu at the top of the Develop module's Basic panel (the Edit panel in Lightroom cloud). It doesn't look a whole lot better (the colors on the buildings on the right do look a bit better), so it's not a home run, but still worth doing.

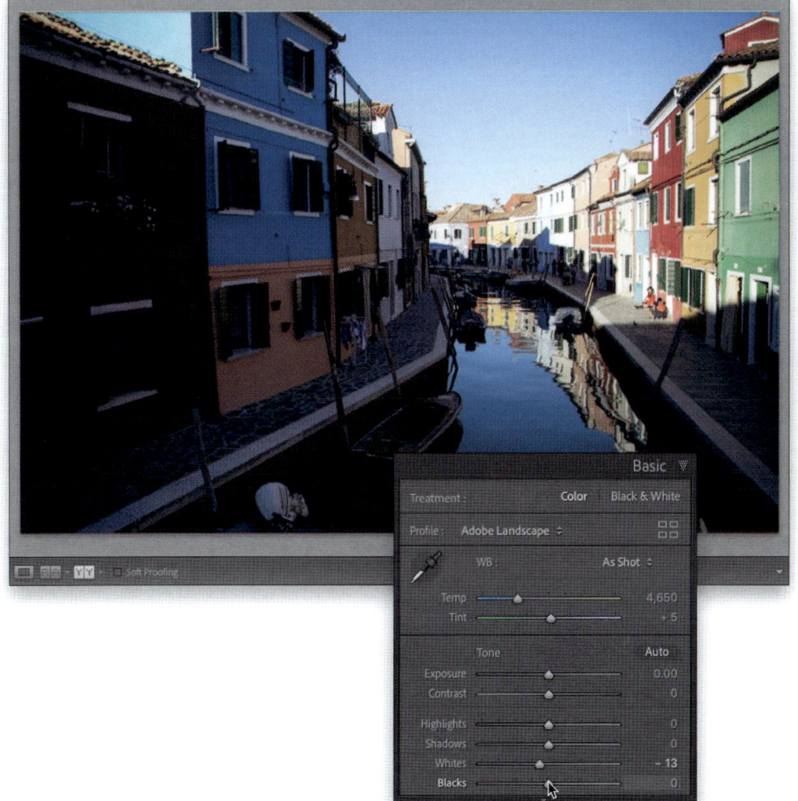

Step 03:

The white balance, overall, looks okay. It's a bright, sunny day, which is when your camera's Auto White Balance feature looks best, and while the buildings on the left are a bit blue (that blue tint is pretty standard for anything in the shade while you're shooting in Auto White Balance), if we adjust for it at this point, the other side of the image in the bright light will look too warm and yellow. So, we're going to skip Point 2 of the system (getting our color right) because, for the most part, our color looks good. Instead, let's go ahead and get our overall exposure **(Point 3)** right (though, as a whole, it doesn't look too bad either). Let's start in the Basic panel (the Light panel in Lightroom cloud) by pressing-and-holding the Shift key and double-clicking directly on the word "Whites," and then Shift-double-clicking on the word "Blacks" to expand our tonal range. Well, that didn't do a whole lot now, did it? It only moved the Whites down to –13, so we're off to a slow start, but I expect that will change shortly.

Step 04:

Next, let's work on fixing the problems caused by the fact that our camera sensor isn't as sensitive as the human eye **(Point 4)**. We'll start by working on making that right side not so bright (it's so bright that the white in the buildings is nearly blown out over there). Go to the Highlights slider and drag it way over to the left to pull back those really bright areas, which goes a long way in helping those buildings look more balanced overall. Of course, you're seeing the "after" image here (after I dropped the Highlights to –79). Go back and look at the image in the previous step and you'll see what a huge difference this one move made in balancing the overall tone of the image.

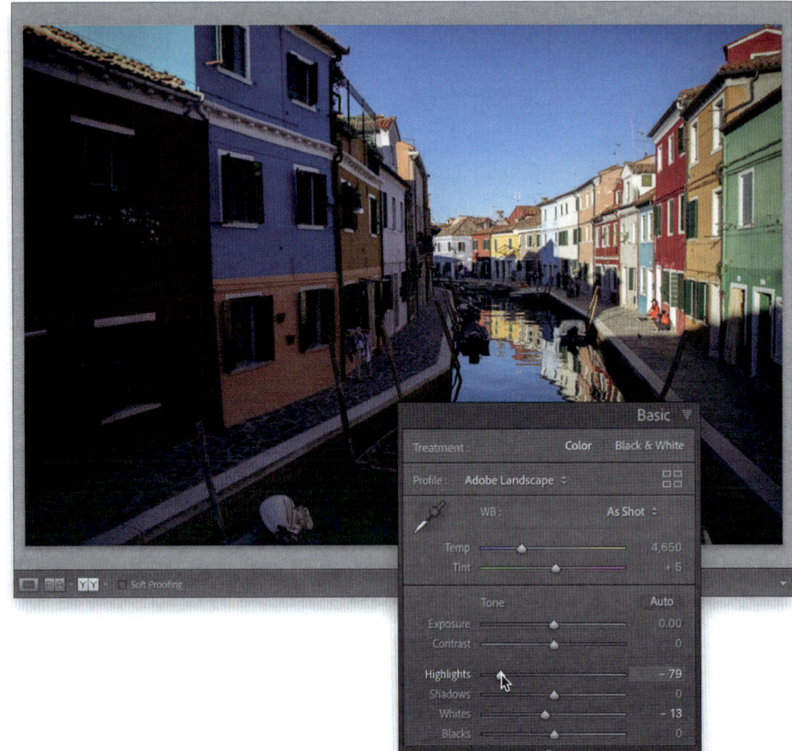

Step 05:

Let's work on the left side of the image next to try to bring it out of the shadows. Go to the Shadows slider and drag it to the right (here, I dragged it over to +82). This helped quite a bit, but it's not nearly as bright as I'd like it to be, so we'll have to go a step further to get that side looking good. For now, this is a good couple of first steps: backing off the bright highlights on the right side and opening up some of the dark shadows on the left side.

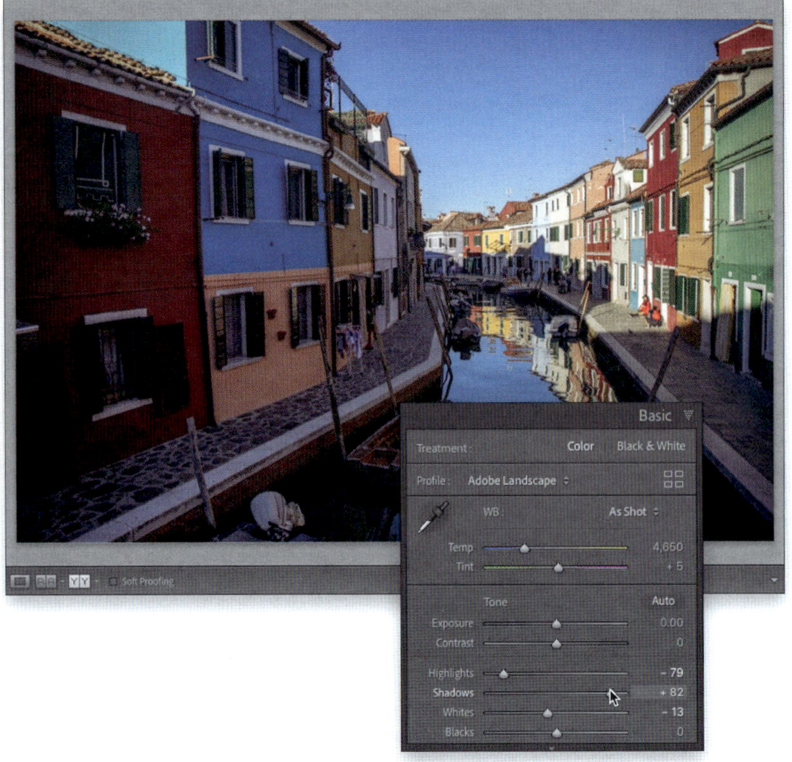

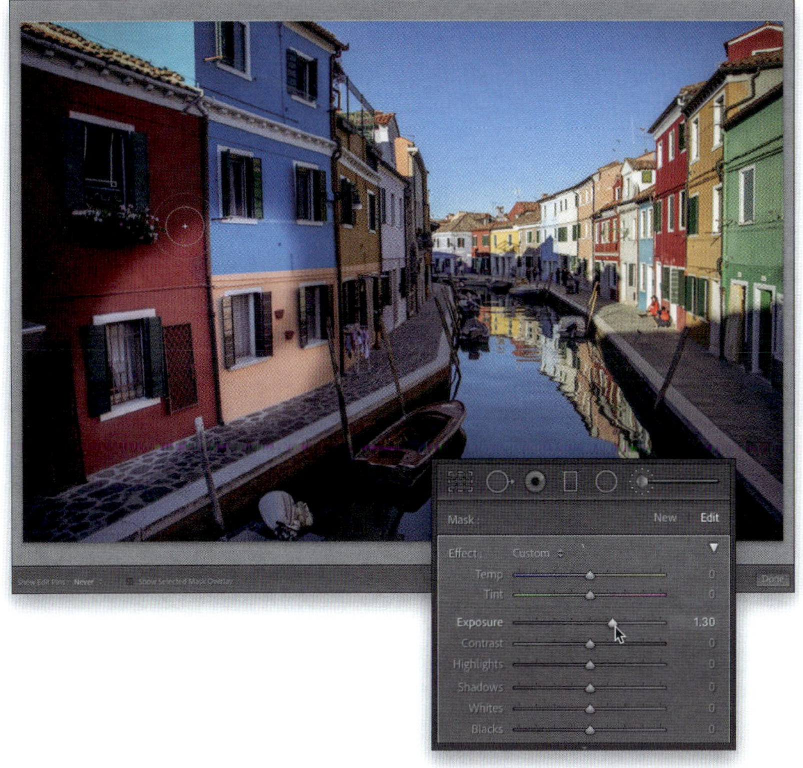

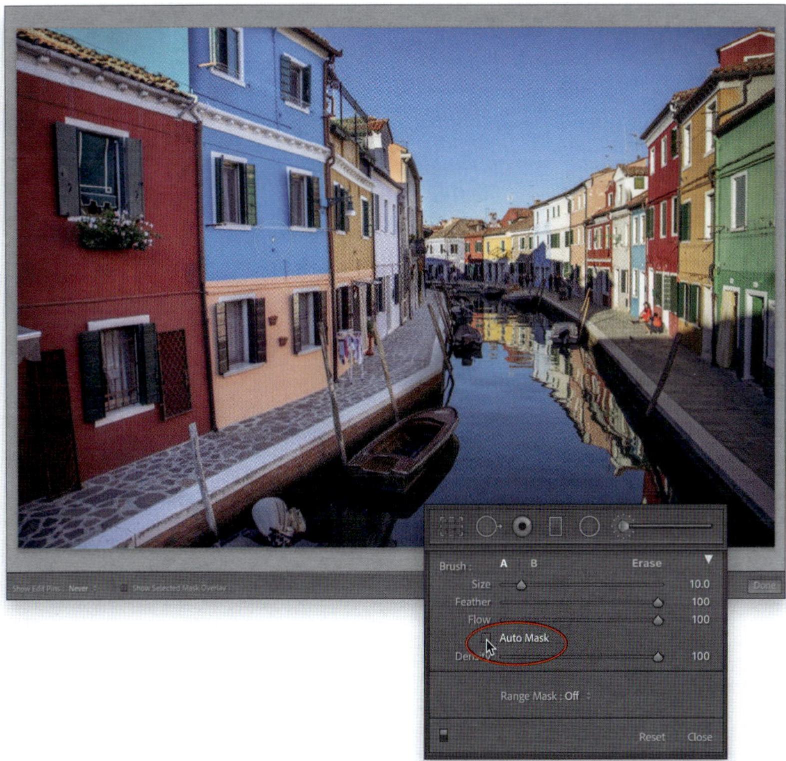

Step 06:

In this case, we're going to need to "paint with light" **(Point 5)** to get that left side as bright as we're going to want it to match better with the other side. Click on the Adjustment Brush (the keyboard shortcut to get it in Lightroom Classic is the letter **K**; in Lightroom cloud, it's the letter **B**). When it comes to making parts of my photo brighter or darker using the Adjustment Brush, I generally do this using just the Exposure slider. So, let's drag the Exposure slider a good way over to the right (here, I dragged it over to 1.30), then start painting over the buildings on the left (as shown here), as well as the sidewalk and the canal edge, and you'll see what a difference that makes.

Step 07:

Near the bottom of the Adjustment Brush panel, make sure the Auto Mask checkbox is turned off while you're painting (so your painting goes smoothly and quickly. If you don't see it, click on the left-facing arrow to the right of Erase). But, when you get near the edges of the roofline, press-and-hold the **Command (PC: Ctrl) key** to temporarily turn Auto Mask on, which helps keep you from painting "outside the lines" (and onto the sky). It's okay if the edge of your brush extends onto the bright areas when you have the Command key held down—it won't spill onto them, as long as you make sure the little + (plus sign) in the center of the brush doesn't touch them. Keep that + on the roofline and you'll be fine. Also, to change your brush size, press the **[(left bracket) key** to make it smaller, or the **] (right bracket) key** to make it larger. Okay, we're getting closer. Remember, you can change the brightness of the Exposure after you've painted (one of the great benefits of the Adjustment Brush), and you can even come back later, choose the Adjustment Brush, click on that adjustment's black Edit Pin (on the wall where you started painting, as seen in the next step), and it becomes active again.

Step 08:

By the way, if you make a mistake while you're painting with the brush (or Auto Mask messes up, which it sometimes will), you can erase any spillover by pressing-and-holding the **Option (PC: Alt) key** and then painting over that spill area to erase it. Okay, back to our lesson. So, now our buildings on the left are brighter, but the colors could be a bit more vibrant, and we can do that easily by increasing the amount of Contrast. It works wonders—just drag the Contrast slider to the right until those colors look nice and saturated (here, I dragged it over to around 65). Because adding contrast makes the brightest parts of your photo brighter and the darkest parts darker, if you add a lot of it (like we did here), it tends to make your image a bit darker, so you might have to increase the Exposure amount just a little to get your image back to the brightness you had it before you bumped up the Contrast (here, I increased it to 1.59).

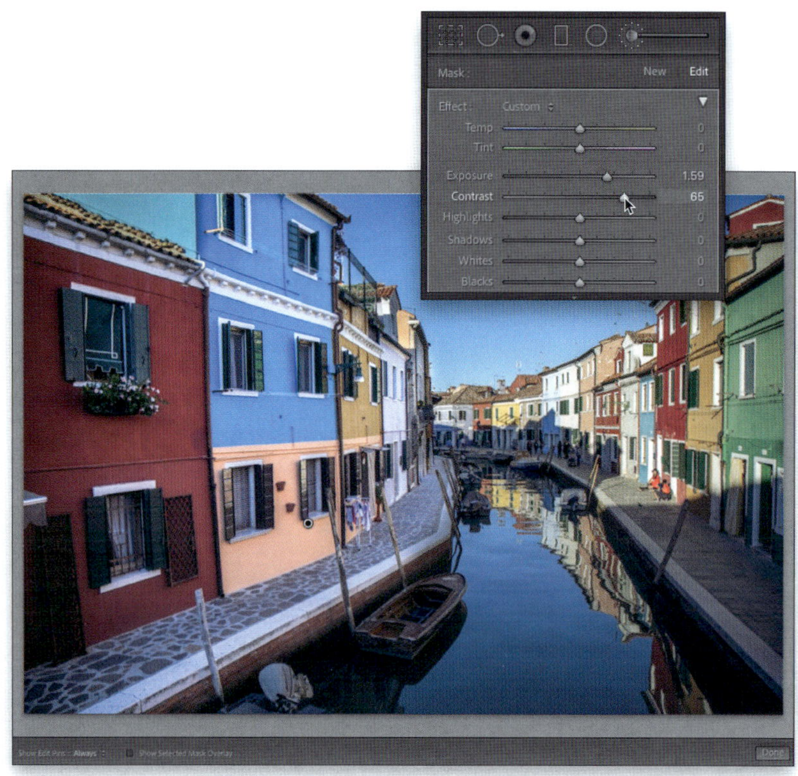

Step 09:

Now I've got a little kick-butt trick for you to get vibrant color from the other side of the canal—the right side. You'd think just lowering the Exposure would make the color more vibrant (since they were washed out by the sun), but that just makes everything darker, not more colorful. The trick is this: Go to the top of the Adjustment Brush panel and click New (in Lightroom cloud, click the + [plus sign] icon). This tells Lightroom to "leave what I've already done with the brush as-is, and let me start painting somewhere new." Next, double-click directly on the word "Effect" near the top left of the panel to reset the sliders to zero (this happens by default in Lightroom cloud). Now, let's drag the Blacks slider way over to the left, increasing the amount of blacks (I dragged to –43), paint over those buildings that are in the direct sun, and—bam—they get that color saturation. Be sure to put that one in your new bag of tricks for adding color to washed-out areas.

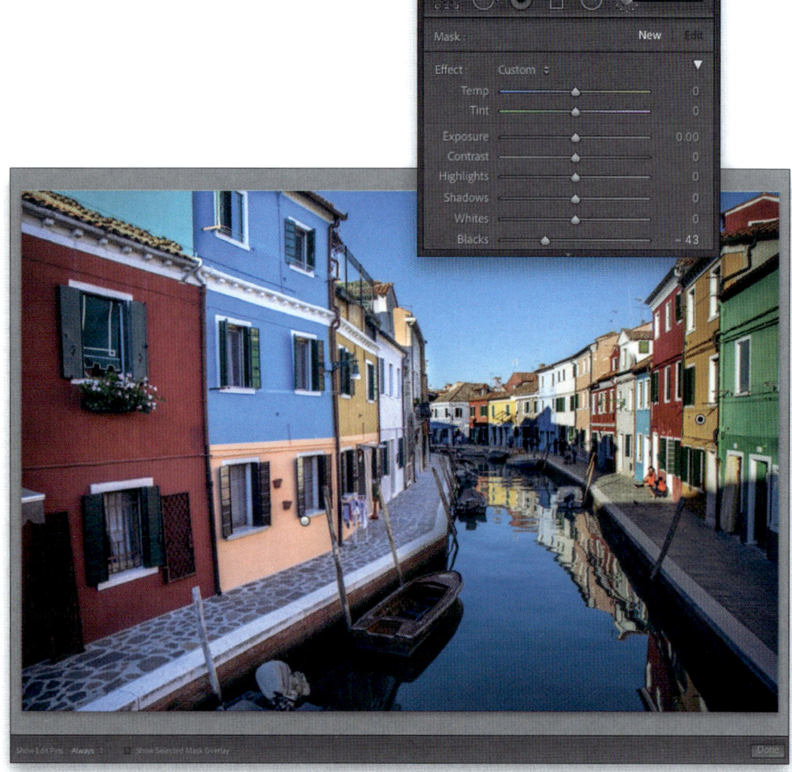

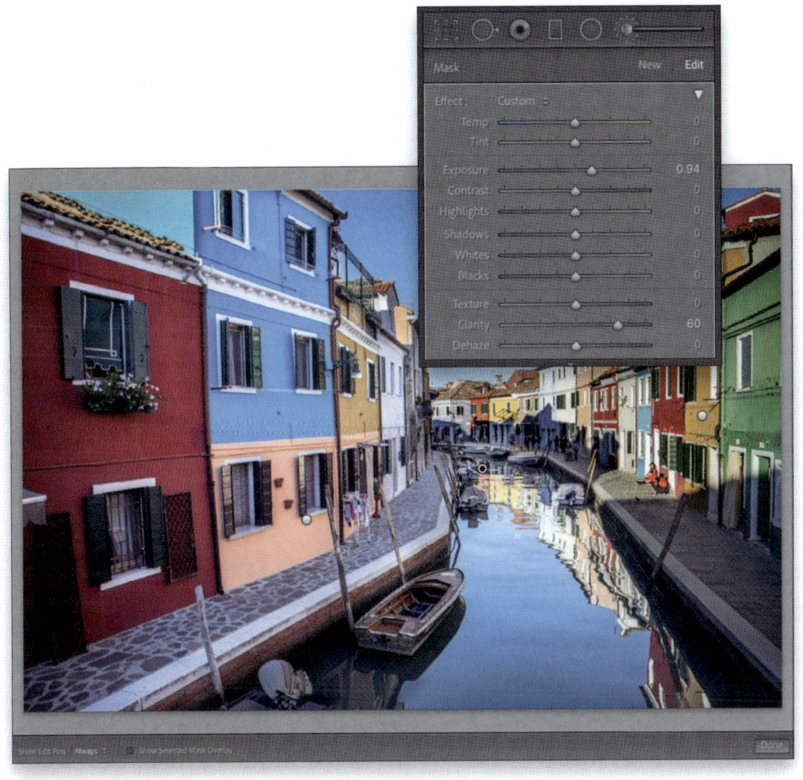

Step 10:

Next, let's make the water brighter using a trick that will also make it look shiny. Hit New (or the + [plus sign] icon) up at the top of the panel again. Then, double-click on Effect to reset the sliders to zero, and increase the Exposure amount to around +1 stop (in this case, I dragged to 0.94, which is almost a stop, right?). Now, paint right over the water to make it brighter. Once you've done that, we're going to do that trick that makes water look shiny—we're going to crank up the Clarity amount (I cranked it up to 60), and that's it. Works like a charm! Okay, this is starting to come together.

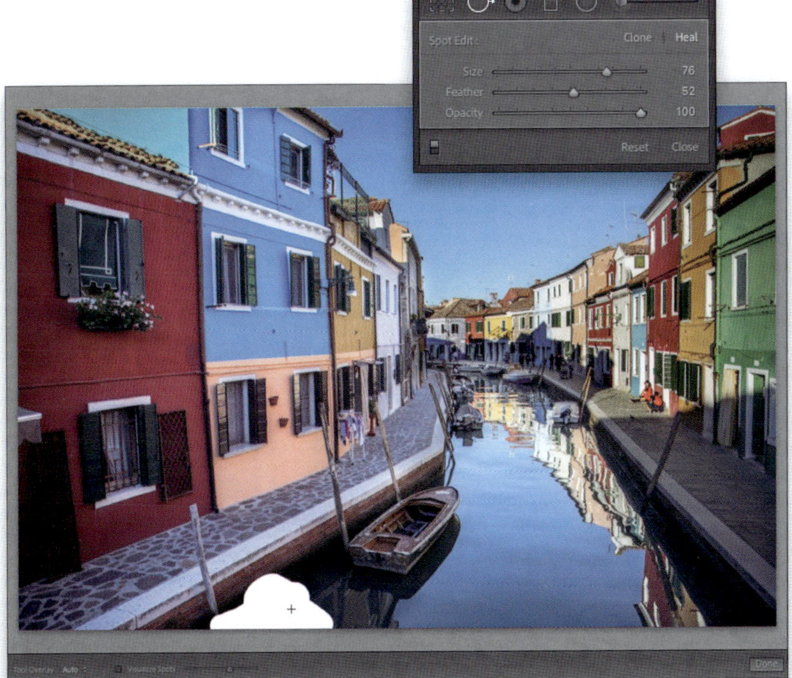

Step 11:

We're going to divert for a second because there's an ugly boat with a motor hanging off the back, near the bottom-left corner of our image that is totally killing the quaintness of the shot, so let's literally get rid of it. There's a tool for this—it's called the Spot Removal tool (its keyboard shortcut is **Q**. It's called the Healing Brush in Lightroom cloud and its keyboard shortcut is **H**). Get the tool (brush) and paint over the boat. As you paint, the area you're painting over turns white (as seen here, bottom left). You can change the brush Size using the same shortcuts as always (I mentioned them in Step 07). Once you paint over it, just release your mouse button and it will try to find another part of the photo to use as a source to remove that boat. Spoiler alert: it's not great at it. Well, let me clarify: it's great at removing spots (that's why it's called the Spot Removal tool), but for bigger stuff like this, it's pretty touch and go.

Step 12:

Here's kinda what I'm talking about. So, the first outlined area (where the boat used to be) shows the "spot" you're trying to remove. The white line points to a second outlined area, which shows the area in your image Lightroom chose to sample from to make its repair. Seriously? It chose the red wall with the green shutters, instead of choosing the canal? Yeah, that's what I'm talking about when I mentioned "it ain't great." Luckily, you can override what Lightroom chose and pick a better spot for it to sample from (like maybe something in the water, for example).

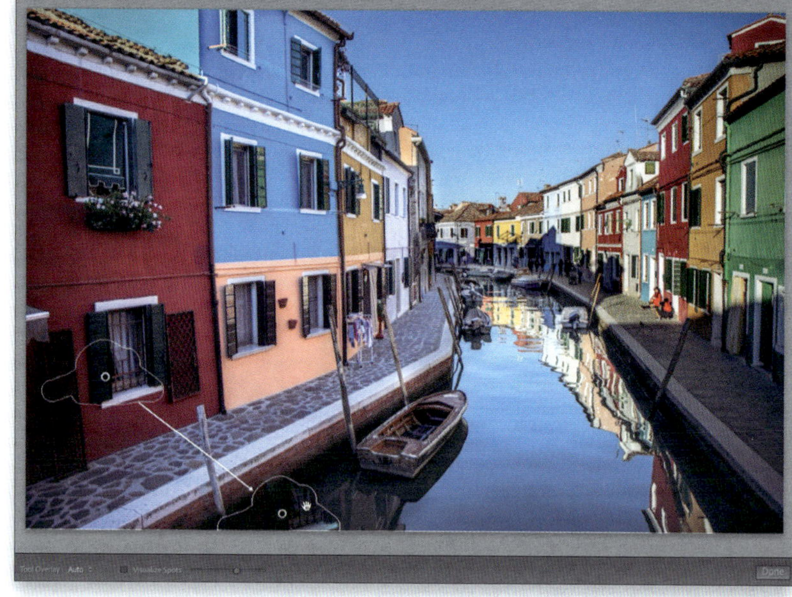

Step 13:

You get the best "healing" results if you click-and-drag that second outline (the one it's sampled from) over to something close to the area you're trying to cover. So, click inside that second outline (the one up on the red wall) and drag it down right behind the boat in front of the boat we're removing (as shown here), and as you drag it around, the area we're removing updates using the new info. While this didn't do a perfect job, it's a whole lot better (and it's just a start). We've got some leftovers right at the bottom left along the water, so we'll try again in the next step and see if we can get rid of that leftover area.

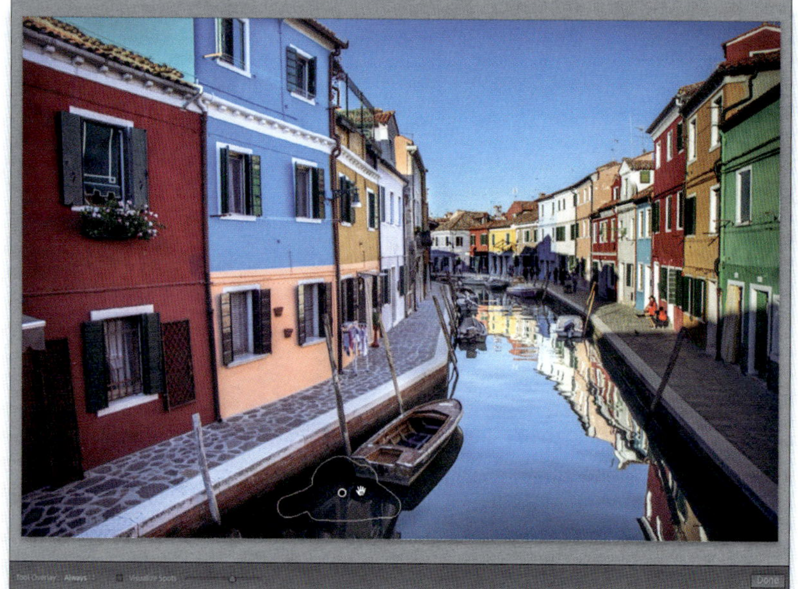

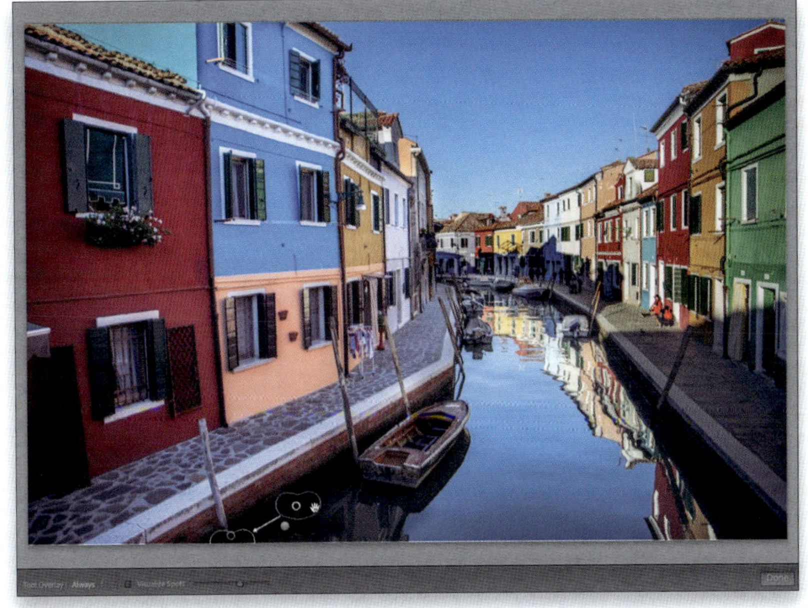

Step 14:

Make your brush size a lot smaller, paint over that little leftover area, and, again, don't be surprised if it puts the second outline (the area it samples from) in a completely ridiculous place. So, just be prepared to drag that second outline to someplace that makes more sense (like I did here, where I dragged it along the brick wall at the edge of the water), and then click Done (down in the toolbar) when you're finished. Okay, we dealt with that—let's move on 'cause now we're gettin' close.

Step 15:

Let's deal with the lens issues next (**Point 6**); the buildings are leaning backward, and the image isn't straight, and there's a little distortion with the buildings bowing outward a bit). We can fix this with two or three clicks. Go to the Profile tab in the Lens Corrections panel (the Optics panel in Lightroom cloud), and turn on the Enable Profile (Lens) Corrections checkbox. This fixes a bunch of lens issues (like barrel distortion and corner darkening) by quickly searching through Lightroom's built-in database of lens profile corrections and applying the proper fix. It knows which camera and lens you used (it reads the EXIF data embedded into your image by your camera), so it matches up that info to the proper profile and applies it. If for some reason it doesn't find your profile, you can choose your make and model of lens from the pop-up menus under Lens Profile (it has a *ton* of built-in profiles, so chances are the lens you used is already there—you just have to help Lightroom out a bit. In Lightroom cloud, click on the little camera icon to see the menus). Usually, just choosing the make will be enough for it to find your exact lens in its database.

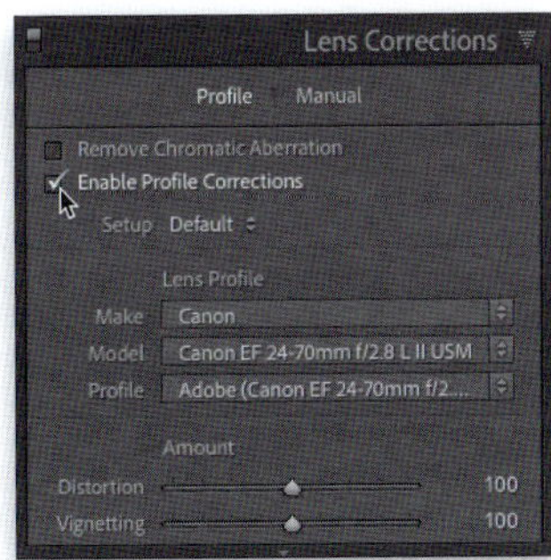

Step 16:

Now that the buildings are no longer bulging and the corners aren't darkened, let's get the buildings to stop leaning backward. Go to the Transform panel (the Geometry panel in Lightroom cloud), and at the top of the panel, under Upright, click on Auto (choose it from the Upright pop-up menu in Lightroom cloud). This attempts to make your buildings upright, and it usually does a pretty good job. In this case, it made the buildings on the left perfectly straight, but the ones on the right still looked a little funky, so you might have to use the Vertical slider (the slider that controls building tilt), moving it just a little to find that sweet spot where both sides of the canal look straighter (here, I ended up dragging it to the right to +5. A grid will appear over your image when you move your cursor over a slider to help you out). Lastly, to keep from having any little white gaps in the corners of your image (that happens sometimes when the Upright correction has to transform your image to make it look right), turn on the Constrain Crop checkbox (as shown here) and it trims those areas away.

Step 17:

For the final step of the 7-Point System **(Point 7)**, we're going to do some finishing moves. First, let's subtly darken the edges all the way around the outside of the image by such a small amount that nobody will realize we did it—but it makes a nice difference. Go to the Effects panel and drag the Post-Crop Vignetting Amount slider (the Vignette slider in Lightroom cloud) to the left to −11. That's the magic number I use to darken the edges without it looking like I added a vignette. If you don't think it does that much, toggle it on/off, using the little visibility button in the left side of the panel header (click-and-hold on the eye icon in the right side of the panel header in Lightroom cloud), and you'll see why I usually add this as a finishing move.

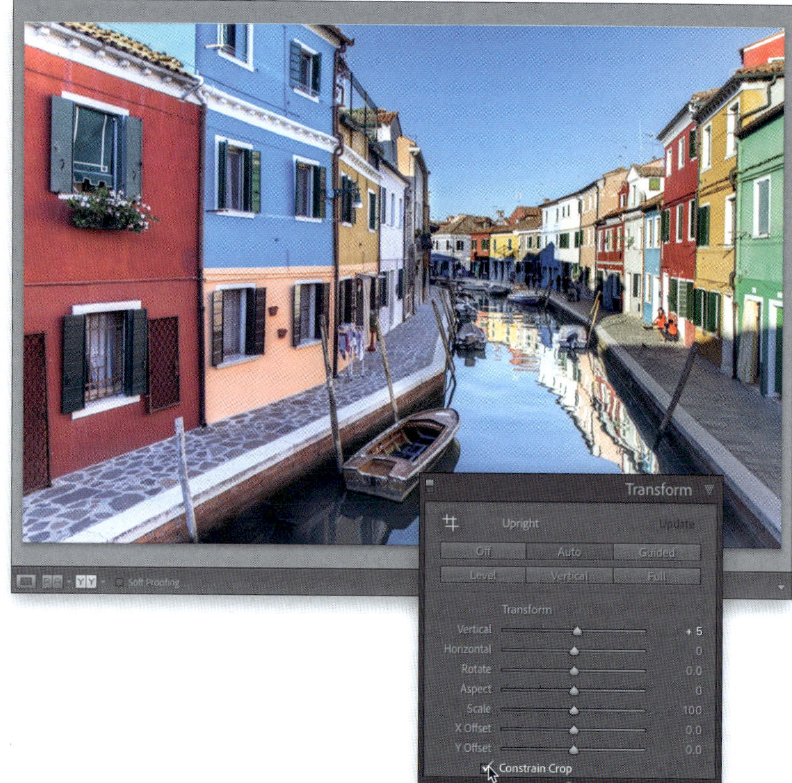

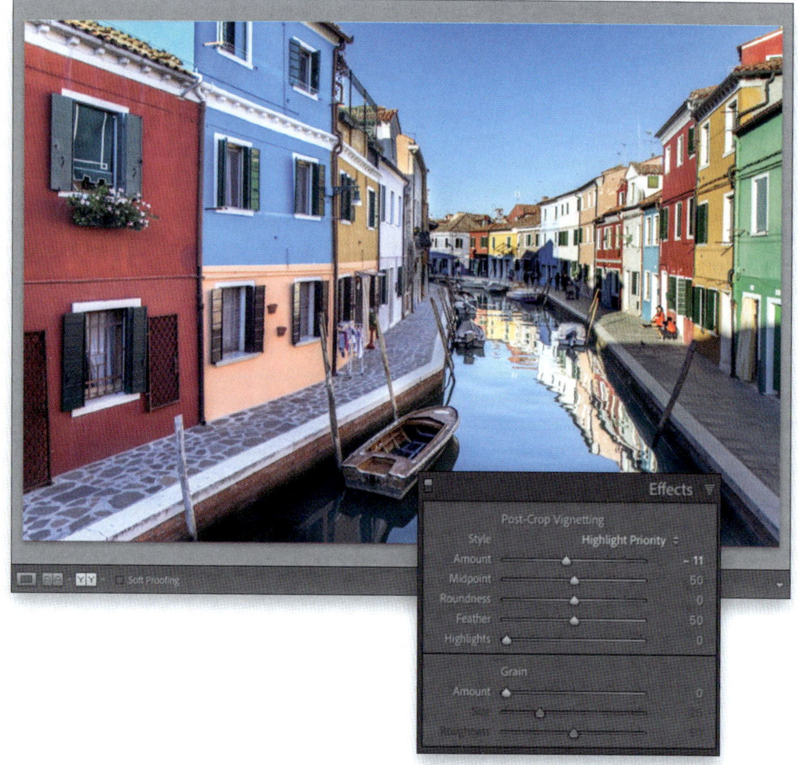

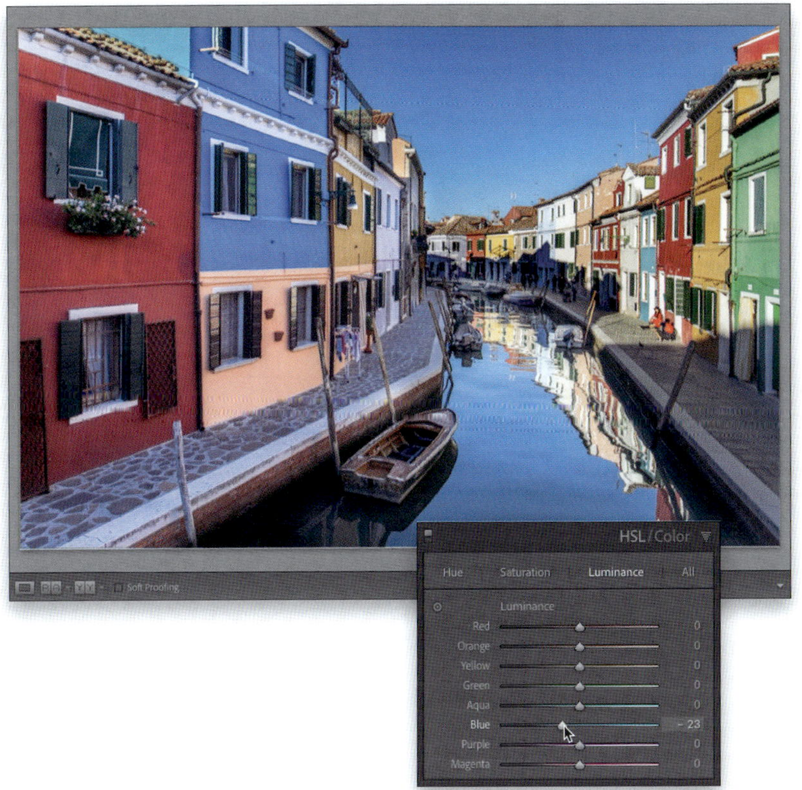

Step 18:

Now that I'm looking at the image, we've brightened it so much that I think I'd like the sky a little bluer and richer. I have three really handy tips for doing this (you're going to learn them all in this book), and the first one is to go to the HSL/Color panel, click on the word Luminance (in Lightroom cloud, go to the Color panel, then click on Color Mixer, and then from the Adjust pop-up menu, choose Luminance), and then drag the Blue slider to the left (here, I dragged it to –23). This makes all the blues in your image deeper and richer. This works great here because the sky is also reflected in the canal, and this move makes them both look better. It also makes the blue building on the left a bit bluer, and I'm perfectly fine with that.

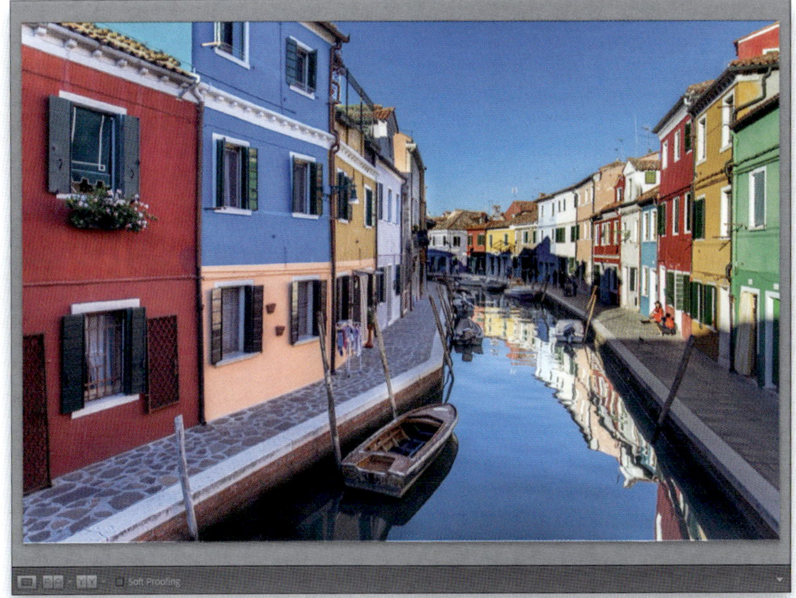

Step 19:

Next, we'll add some sharpening (like I've mentioned, every image I process gets sharpened). Go to the Detail panel and drag the Amount slider (the Sharpening slider in Lightroom cloud) over to the right to 80 to add a nice amount of sharpening (for more on why I chose this amount for an image like this, see Step 10 on page 19). If you have a higher megapixel camera (this shot was taken with one that was 30 megapixels), you might want to crank up the Radius to at least 1.1. If you have an even higher megapixel camera, go to 1.2 for some nice snappy sharpening.

Step 20:

I know the island of Burano's "thing" is the bright and vibrant buildings, but if you think the colors in the image are too bright and vibrant, you can do this optional step that backs off the overall vibrance. Here's what to do: go to the bottom of the Basic panel (the Color panel in Lightroom cloud) and drag the Vibrance slider to the left to desaturate the colors a bit (as seen here). Again, totally optional.

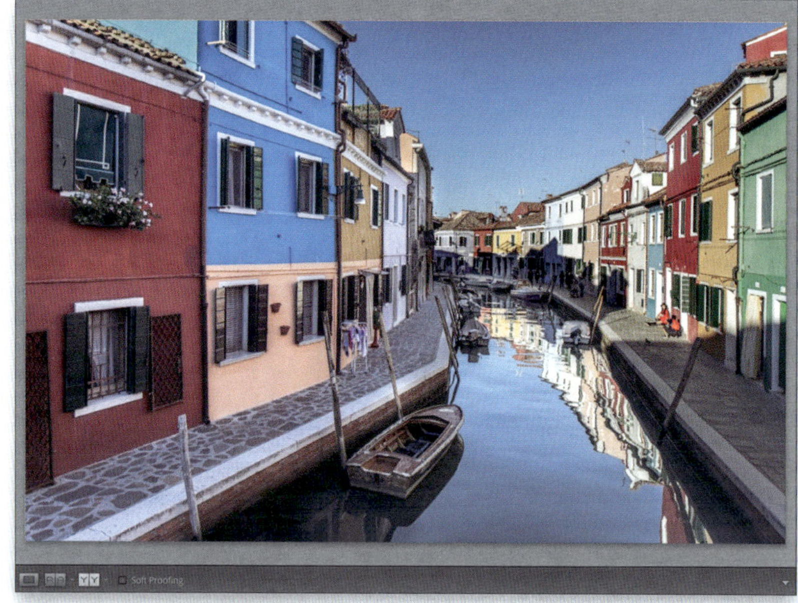

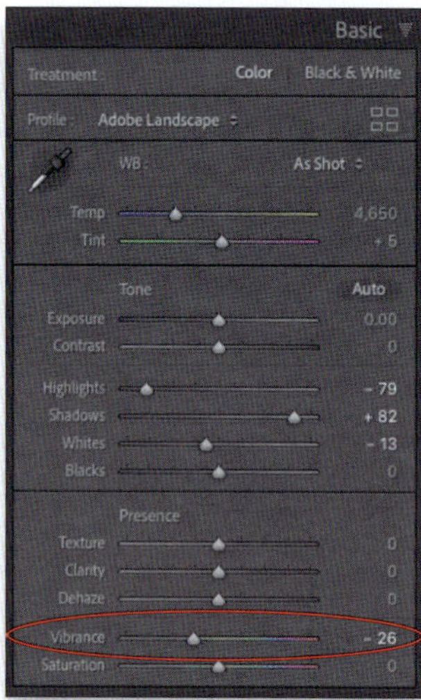

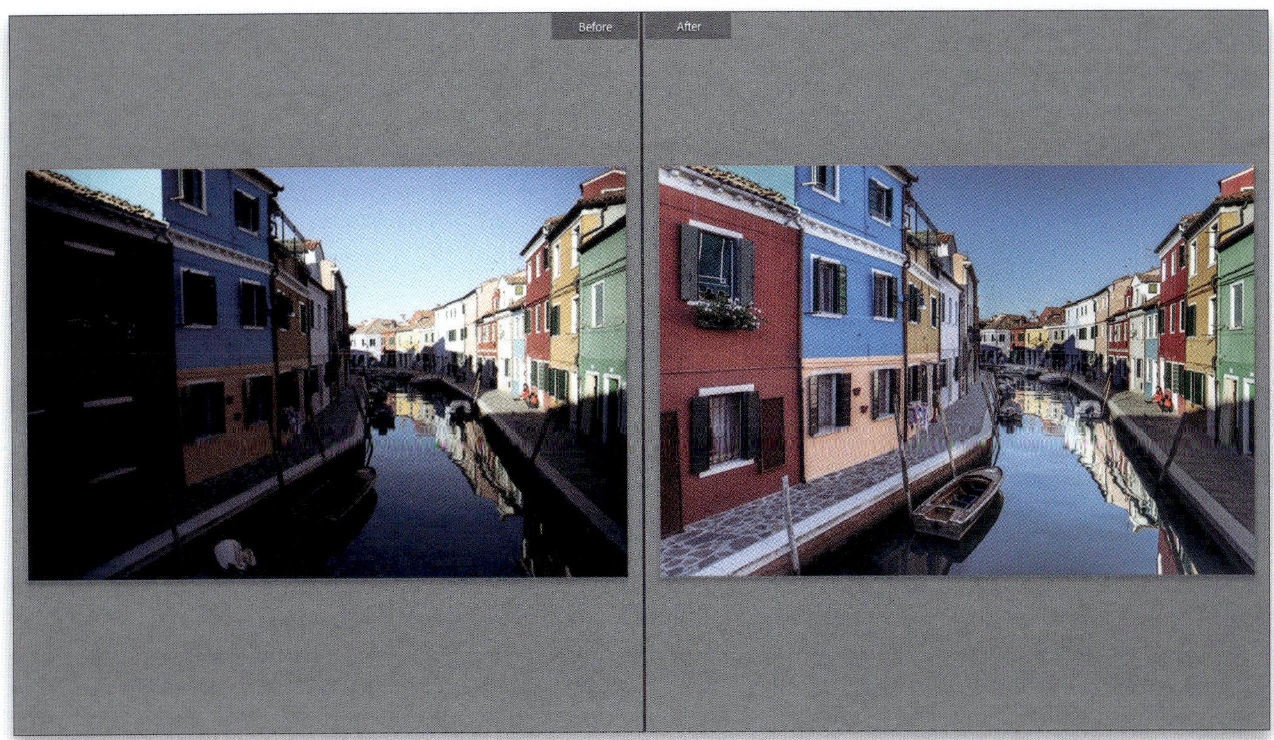

Here's our before/after.

Adobe Photoshop
Lightroom Classic

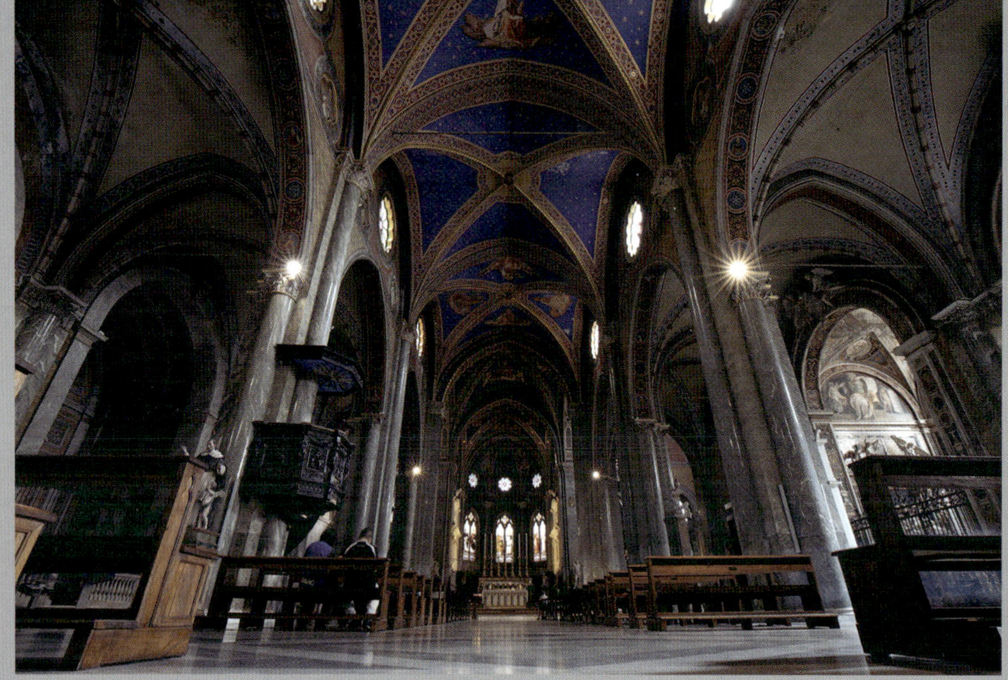

Before

After

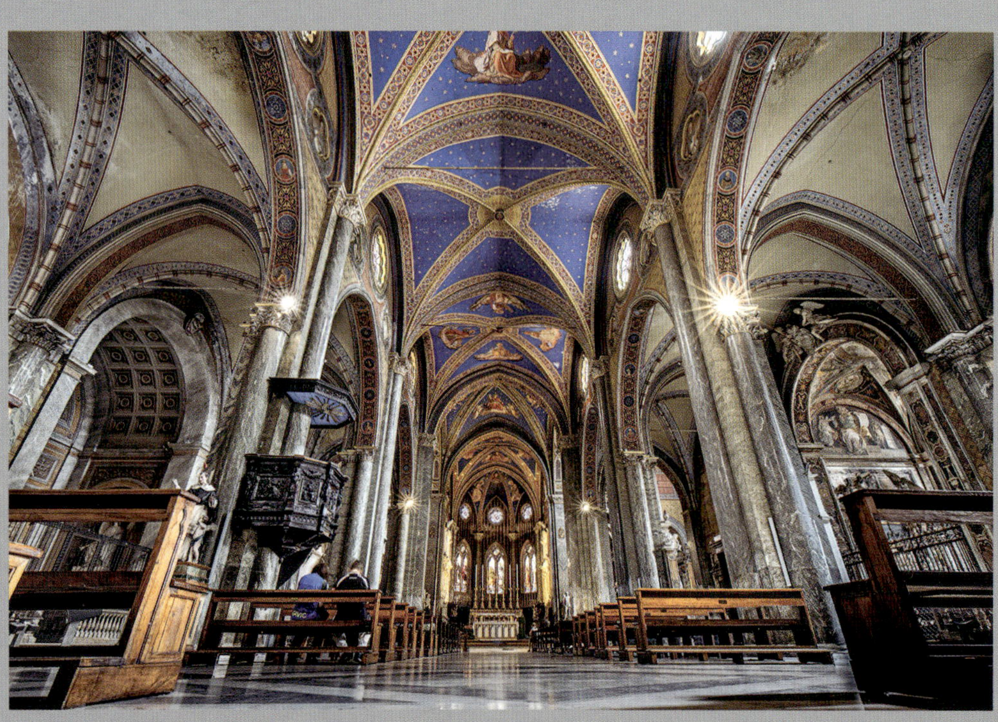

Before & After :
Soft Proofing

CLASSIC INTERIOR

1. Assigning a RAW Profile
2. Getting the Color Right
3. Expanding the Tonal Range
4. Dealing with Sensor Limitations
5. Painting with Light and Retouching
6. Fixing Lens Issues
7. Finishing Moves

In this lesson, we're going to overcome the limitation of our camera's sensor by shooting three bracketed shots. Lightroom will then combine those three images into a single image that captures a range of light that is beyond what our camera, just shooting a normal exposure, could ever capture. We'll then apply the system to the combined photo (and there's a hidden benefit to this whole process that we'll talk about).

THE STORY BEHIND THE SHOT:

I was teaching a travel photography workshop in Rome, and when I do a workshop like this, I go a couple of days early to check out potential shooting locations for my students and to get a few shots for myself (because during the workshop, I'm there to help the students and don't get a lot of chances to shoot). This shot was taken inside the beautiful Basilica di Santa Maria sopra Minerva, which you might walk right past, as it's diagonally right behind the super-popular Pantheon (a tourist hot spot). The shot was taken with a wide-angle lens, with my camera positioned down low—just a few inches from the tile floor—mounted on a Platypod Ultra (a small metal plate designed to mount a ballhead on top of that your camera attaches to). It's so small and inconspicuous that you can shoot in places where tripods are forbidden. I sat in a pew, centered the camera rig in the aisle beside me, tilted it up a bit, and fired it wirelessly from my camera's iPhone app.

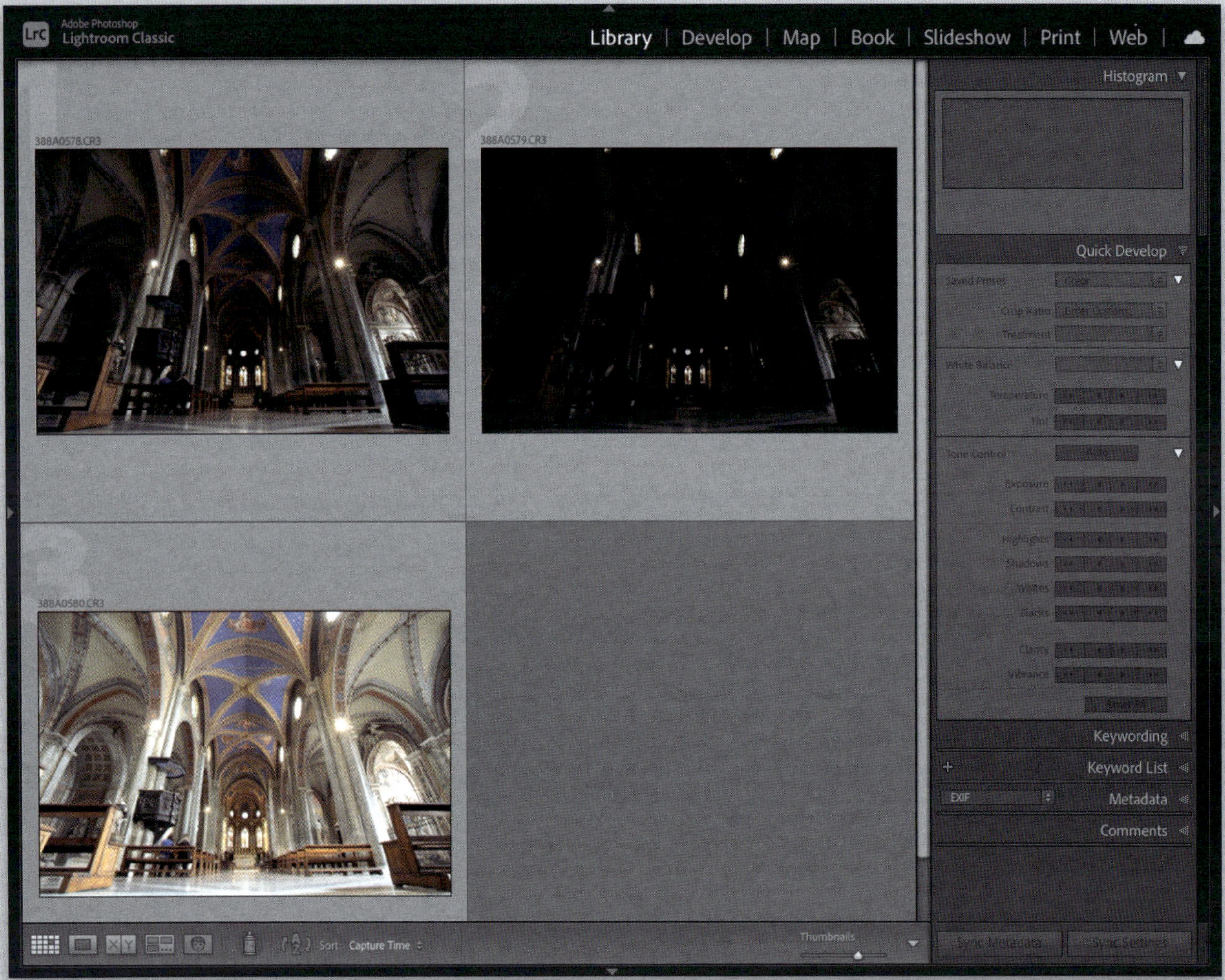

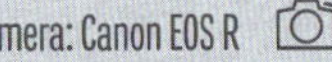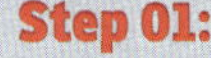

Camera: Canon EOS R
Aperture Value: ƒ/11
Shutter Speed: 8.0 sec, 2.0 sec, 30.0 sec
ISO: 100
Focal Length: 17mm

Step 01:

Here are the three original RAW images in Lightroom Classic's Library module. You'll want to set your camera to shoot in bracketed exposure mode, so it creates multiple shots at different exposures (normal, dark, and very bright) that Lightroom can combine into a single RAW image that has a much greater range of light than our cameras can capture with just a single frame. In this case, I set my camera to shoot three bracketed frames: one normal shot (top-left thumbnail), one shot that's two stops underexposed (top-right thumbnail), and one shot that's two stops overexposed (bottom-left thumbnail). What the dark shot allows us to do is keep detail in the stained glass windows and lighting, and the bright shot brings out glorious detail in all the beautiful architectural work inside the cathedral—it's just all too bright. That's why, when you combine these, you get the best parts of them all in one shot. I shoot bracketed like this in situations where I can see there is a large disparity in tones (really bright areas, and really dark areas, all in the same scene).

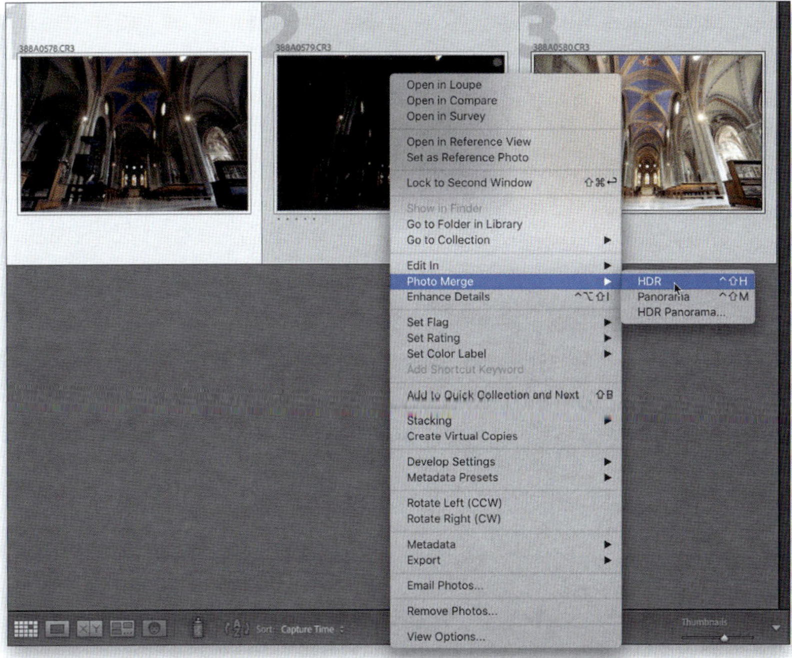

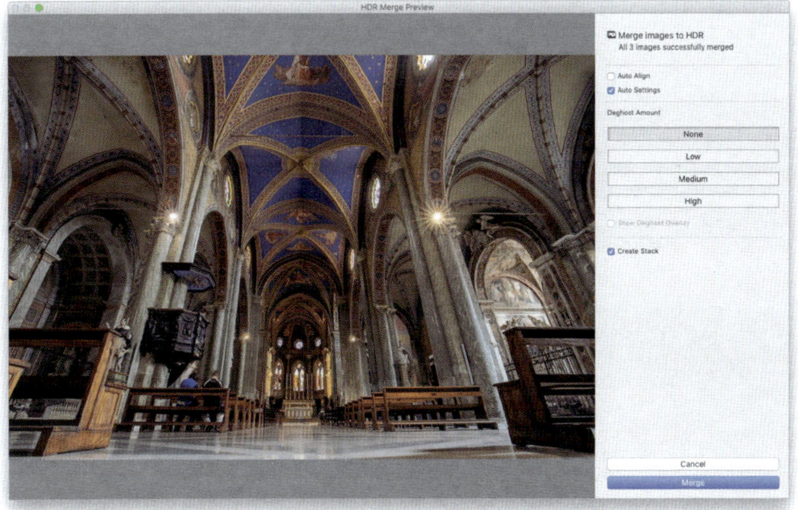

Step 02:

Select the three images (click on one, then press-and-hold the Command [PC: Ctrl] key and click on the other two to select them). Once they're all selected, Right-click on any one of them and, from the pop-up menu that appears, under Photo Merge, choose **HDR** (as shown here). HDR stands for "High Dynamic Range," and it's what combines the three images into a single image. It doesn't make things look crazy or "HDRed," like in the early days of HDR where everybody used this one third-party plug-in and their shots came out looking like something out of Harry Potter. So, don't worry—your image will still look normal throughout this process. One more thing: You don't actually need to select all three photos to do this. It works the same (and goes a little faster) with just two—the two stops underexposed image, and the two stops overexposed image. So, you don't really need to select that normal image at all.

Step 03:

This brings up the HDR Merge Preview dialog, with the images combined into a single image. The Auto Align checkbox should only be turned on if you hand-held your bracketed shots because it will try to align them for you (it does a surprisingly good job), but I shot this using a Platypod, so there was no movement between shots so it's not necessary. The Auto Settings checkbox (on by default) applies an auto-matic correction to your photo, and I usu-ally leave this turned on so I have a good starting point once the image is merged. The Deghost Amount stuff helps if some-thing was moving in your image—it helps alleviate the movement (if it can)—but nothing was moving in this image, so leave it set to None. Lastly, turn on the Create Stack checkbox for these images (three brackets and one HDR image) to be tucked behind a single thumbnail. (Light-room cloud doesn't have this checkbox. The images will be stacked automatically.) Now, click the Merge button.

Step 04:

Here's the combined HDR image, and behind that thumbnail are the three images we used to make that HDR (the number "4" up in the top-left corner lets you know that this thumbnail is a stack comprised of four images. If you want to see all four images, just click once directly on the number 4 to expand the stack). Okay, we have our HDR image and now we can begin to apply the system. Press the **D key** on your keyboard to take this image over to the Develop module in Lightroom Classic (or press the **E key** in Lightroom cloud to bring it into Edit mode).

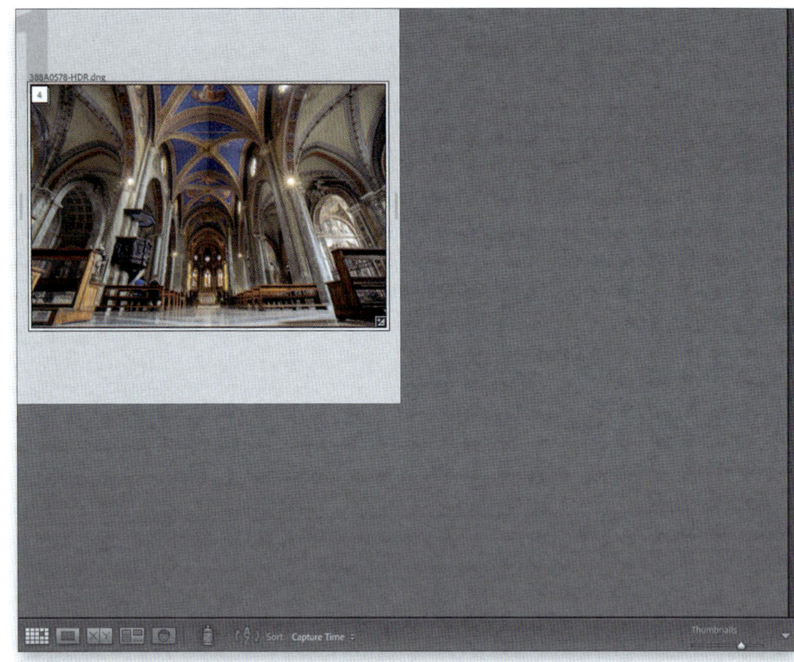

Step 05:

Point 1 of the 7-Point System is to see if we can get a better starting place for our editing by looking at the different RAW profiles built into Lightroom. The default RAW profile, Adobe Color, is "okay." It's not great, it's not bad, it's a good middle-of-the-road RAW conversion, but changing the conversion to Adobe Landscape (my most frequent choice) or even Adobe Vivid usually makes the image more contrasty and colorful, so why not try both? Just go to the Profile pop-up menu at the top of the Basic panel (shown here; or at the top of the Edit panel in Lightroom cloud) and try Adobe Landscape to see how that looks (I always choose it first since it's my go-to profile). In this case, it looks a little too warm, so I tried **Adobe Vivid** and—boom—that's the one (well, *I* thought it was. Try both to see what you think). Now, that was easy—we're starting in a better place already.

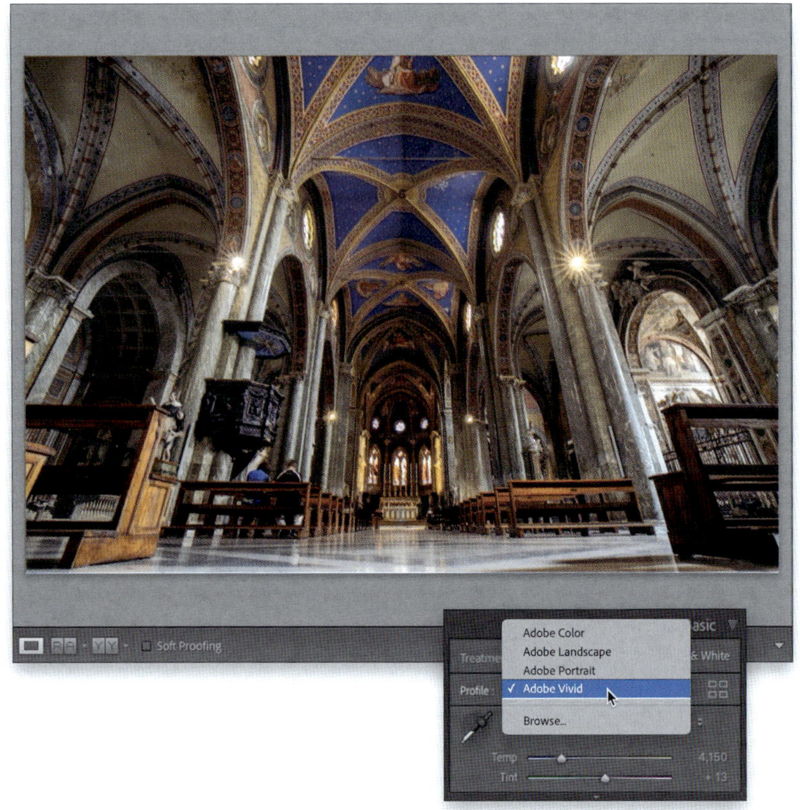

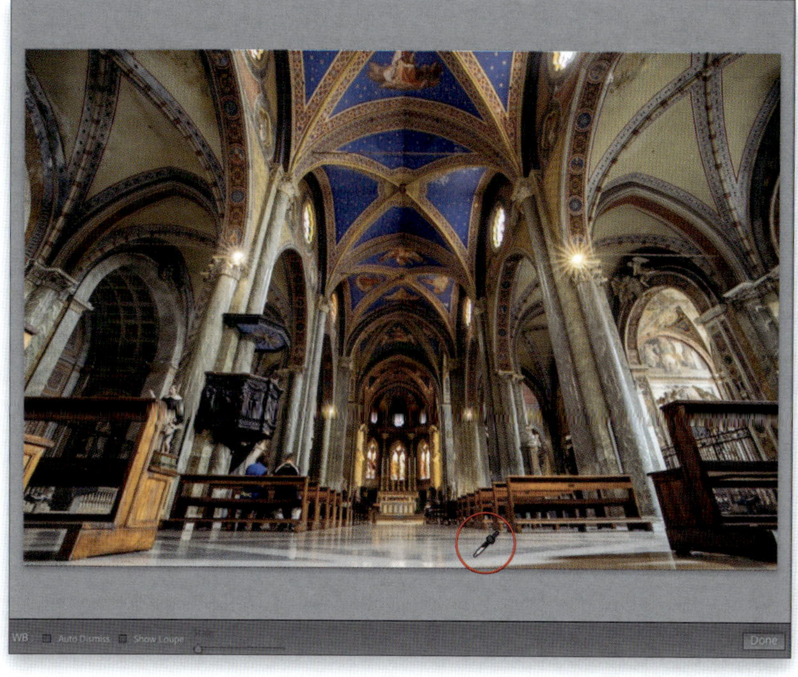

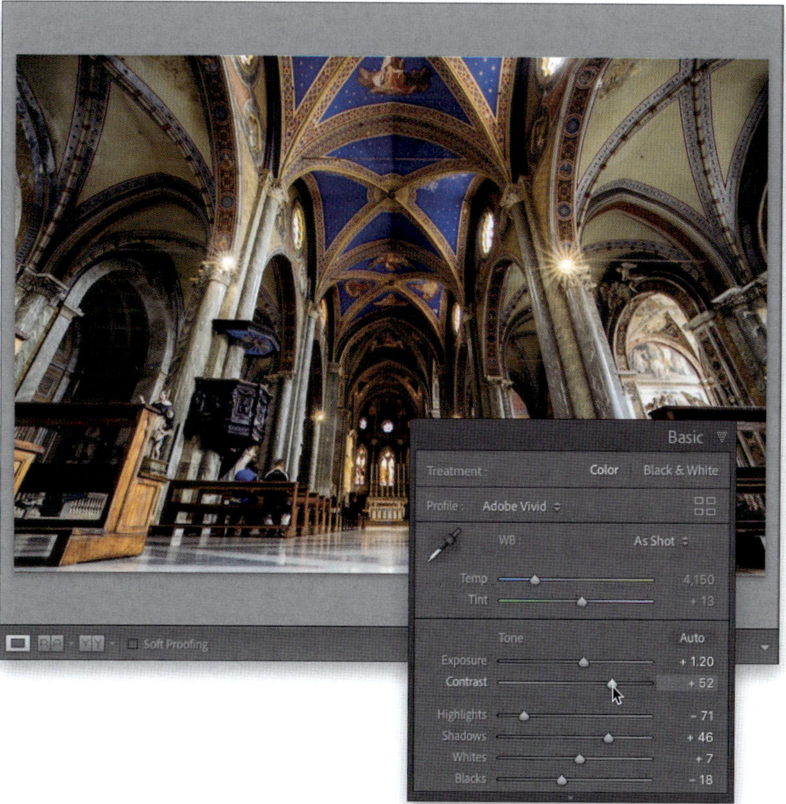

Step 06:

Next, we get our color right, but I have to say, the white balance looks pretty decent in this shot, so I'm not seeing a lot to do here for **Point 2**. If you want to make sure it's right on the money, get the White Balance Selector tool **(W)** near the top of the Basic panel (the Color panel in Lightroom cloud) and click it once on something in the photo that you know is supposed to be a neutral color (ideally, a light gray, but of course, not every photo has light gray in it). You can click around a number of times in different areas and each time you do, you'll get a different white balance look. This photo has a gray tile pattern on the floor, so I clicked it once on a gray floor tile (as shown here). It made the white balance a little warmer, and that looks pretty nice to me, but you're in charge of the white balance. If you like the look you get doing this, stick with that. If not, no harm done, just go to the WB (White Balance) pop-up menu and choose **As Shot** to return to the original white balance (that's what I ended up doing here).

Step 07:

For **Points 3 and 4**, let's look at our exposure. Overall, it seems okay, but there are some balance issues where parts are bright and parts are dark, and the ceiling is pretty dark, along with the altar area. The biggest issue is the whole image looks kinda flat. If your photo looks flat, it's probably because you haven't added enough contrast. Adding contrast has a bigger positive effect than you might think. So, let's drag the Contrast slider to the right (as shown here) until the image looks nice and punchy. Look at how much better the lights at the top of the columns look now, and the overall color is punchier and more vivid. It didn't help our dark ceiling problem (it made it a bit worse, but we'll fix that), but it's looking better. *Note:* You'll see other sliders have been moved already because we turned on Auto Settings in Step 03—it applied an auto edit when it made the HDR (so, your settings may be slightly different).

Step 08:

To help with that dark ceiling and altar area, we're going to open up the shadows big time. How much? Crank the Shadows slider up to +100. Wait!!! Won't that make any noise in the image really stand out? Not really, because the hidden, awesome, secret weapon of creating an HDR image is that you can crank up the shadows a ton (even to +100), and then crank up the exposure, all without having a bunch of noise. It's pretty amazing what you can do with the extra tonal range in an HDR image. It's crazy (and I love it!). So, crank away and don't worry about the noise. That helped our ceiling and altar issues quite a bit, but we're not done working on those areas.

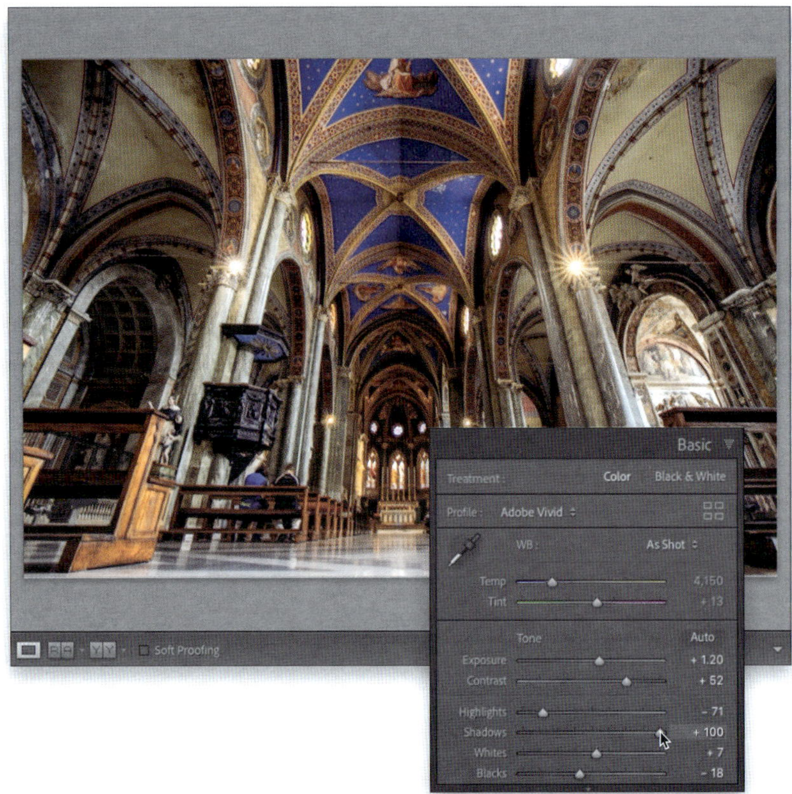

Step 09:

We're going to jump over to **Point 6** in the system to fix any lens distortion (or other) problems, and with wide-angle images it's pretty common to have some issues. So, start by going to the Lens Corrections panel (the Optics panel in Lightroom cloud) and turning on the Enable Profile (Lens) Corrections check-box. Lightroom will look at the make and model of your lens (it finds that info from the data embedded into your photo by your camera), and then it finds a matching lens profile to fix the issues from its huge internal database of lens profiles. In this case, just turning on this checkbox fixed the distortion on both sides of the image (toggle the visibility button in the left side of the panel header on/off [click-and-hold on the eye icon in the right side of the panel header in Lightroom cloud] to see what a big difference this actually made), and got rid of any corner darkening prob-lems. Look at that—one click and it looks a whole lot better (and even brighter now that the corners aren't darkened).

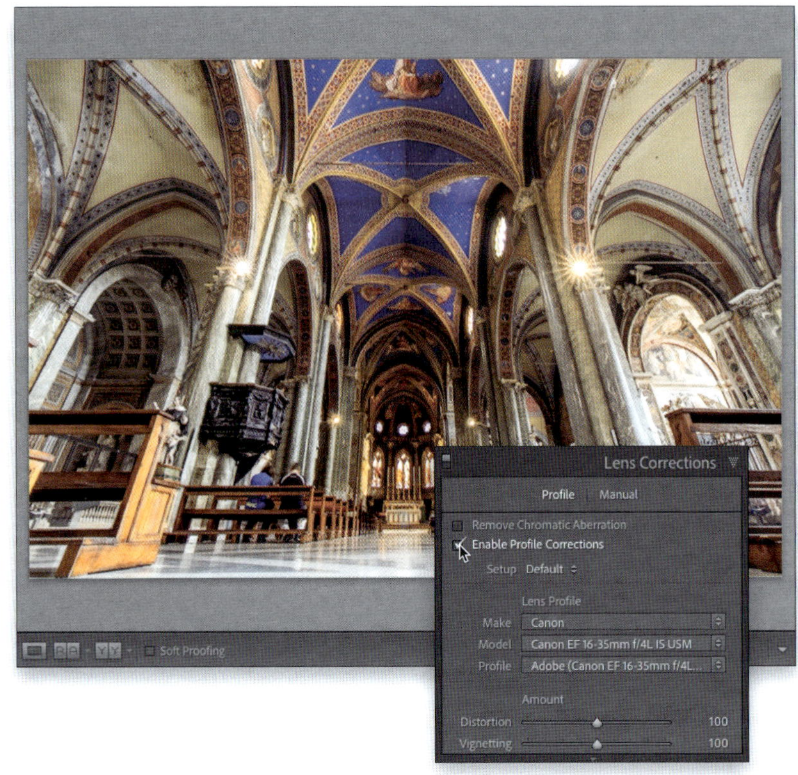

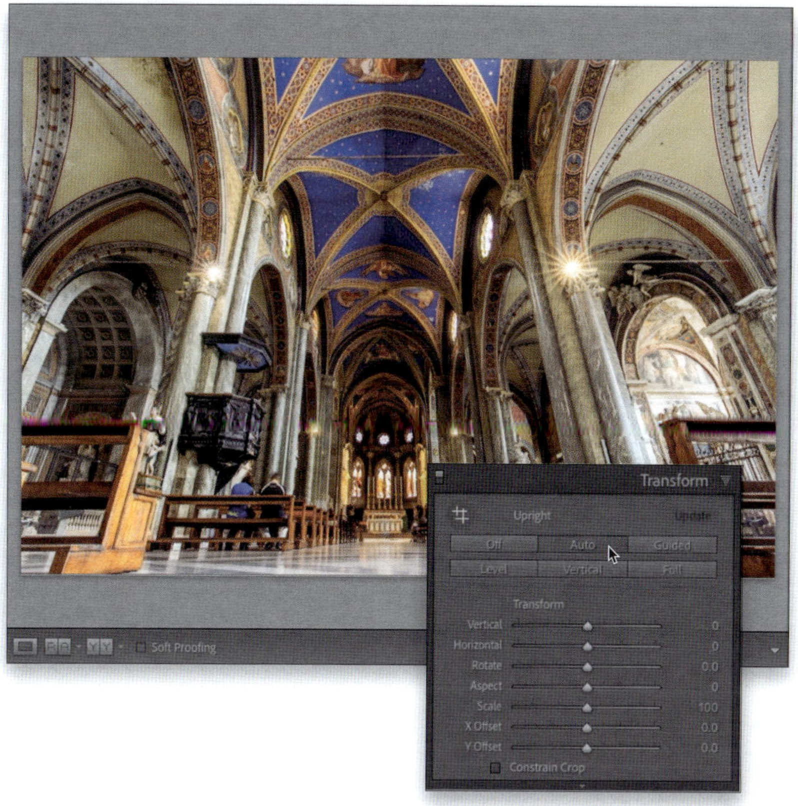

Step 10:

There's still another lens issue you may or may not want to fix, and that is how the columns and walls are not perfectly upright. Personally, I love this look and I rarely fix it, but some folks feel very strongly that those columns should be straight (or at least straighter). If that's you, go to the Transform panel (the Geometry panel in Lightroom cloud), and under Upright, click on Auto (choose it from the Upright pop-up menu in Lightroom cloud) for it to apply a nicely balanced automatic correction. It mostly straightened out the right side a bit, but those columns still aren't perfectly straight. If you feel like they should be, click on Vertical and be prepared to see something radical, because forcing those columns to be straight will take a lot of image manipulation on Lightroom's part and I don't think you'll like the results (and how much of the photo you'll have to crop away), but it's at least worth clicking once just so you know. In this case, we'll stick with Auto (for now).

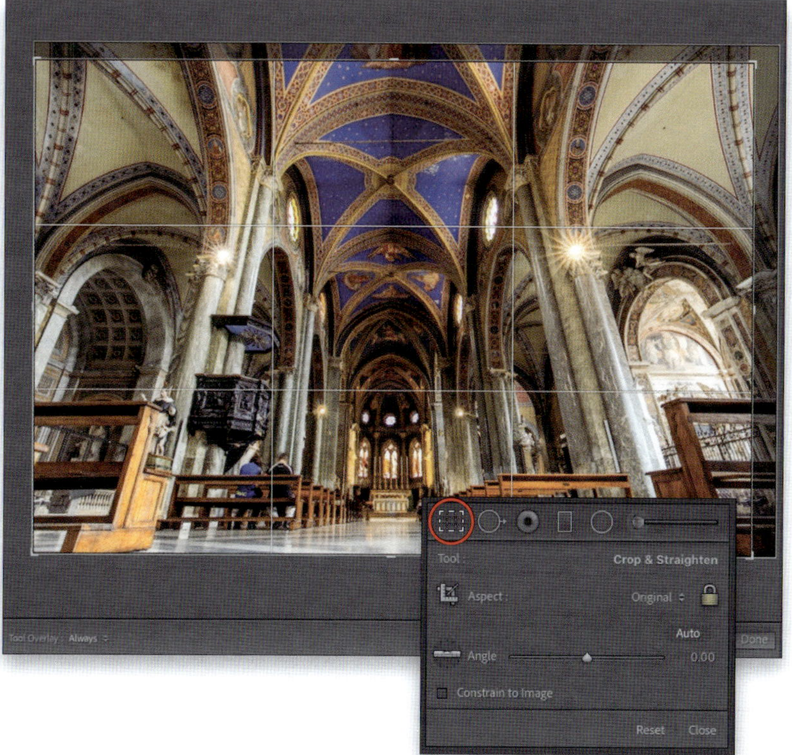

Step 11:

If you do decide to go with the Auto Upright correction, then you will need to crop the photo so it looks properly centered again, so get the Crop Overlay tool **(R)** from the toolbox below the histogram (the Crop & Rotate tool **[C]** from the toolbox on the right in Lightroom cloud) and click-and-drag the top-right corner in a bit until the image looks more centered. I'm not going to do this with the image we're working on, though, because I'm cool with how the columns and walls look—I think it adds to the epic feel, but that's just me. I just wanted to include what to do next if you went with the Auto Upright correction—it's gonna need this crop. Okay, so when we pick up with the next step, just know that I clicked on Off under Upright.

Step 12:

I mentioned earlier that there were a lot of areas that, lighting-wise, were out of balance (parts that are too bright, and draw your eyes to areas where you don't necessarily want them to start), like both sides of the image, and in particular, the bright floor area in the foreground. To deal with large areas with lighting issues like these smoothly and quickly, I use the Graduated Filter tool (the Linear Gradient tool in Lightroom cloud. This is **Point 5** of the system). It creates a gradient that is darker (or brighter—your choice) wherever you start dragging it, and then it fades off smoothly to transparent wherever you stop dragging. So, in this case, get that tool from the toolbox below the histogram (**M**; or from the toolbox on the right in Lightroom cloud, or press the **L key**), then lower the Exposure amount by –1.00 (1 stop), so we can darken that floor. Click at the very bottom of the image and drag your gradient upward (as shown here. The plus sign [+] is the top of the gradient and the dot [Edit Pin] is the center of it. So, it's darkest where you started dragging up from, and it's transparent where the plus sign appears).

Step 13:

Both sides of the image are also kind of a bit bright and while we could just paint over those areas with the Adjustment Brush, because it's so quick and easy to cover a large area with the Graduated Filter tool, it has become my go-to tool for this type of stuff. So, click-and-drag another gradient from the top-left corner down at an angle (to kind of match the direction of the light), like you see here. The –1.00 Exposure setting we used on the floor is too dark for the sides, so back off the amount to around –0.54. Remember, most of the darkening happens at the top-left corner and smoothly gets (graduates) lighter until it reaches the plus sign (or, in this case, the Hand tool, which lets you reposition the gradient when you move your cursor over a line), where it's transparent.

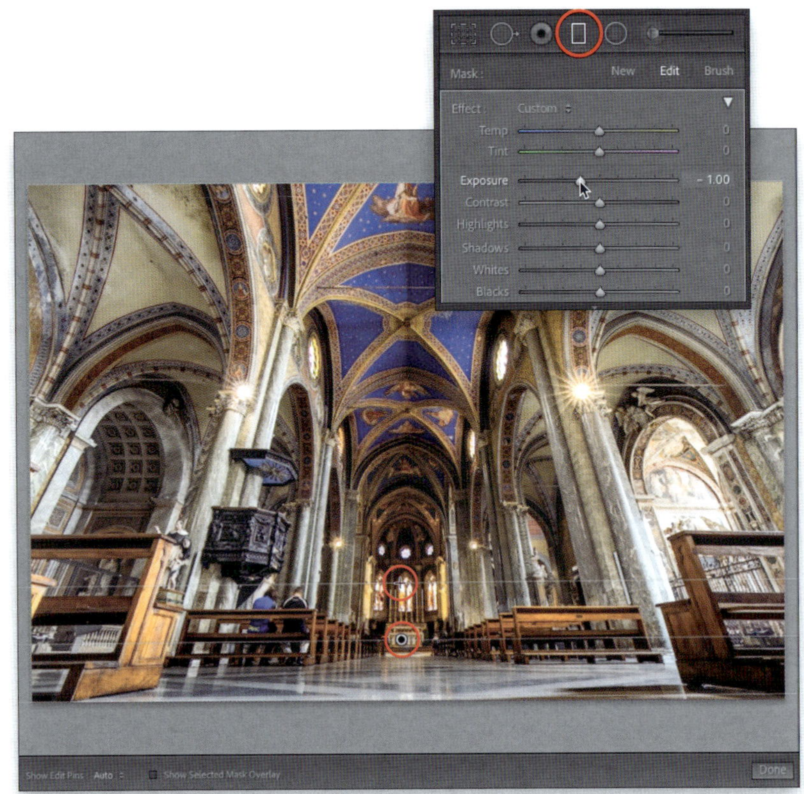

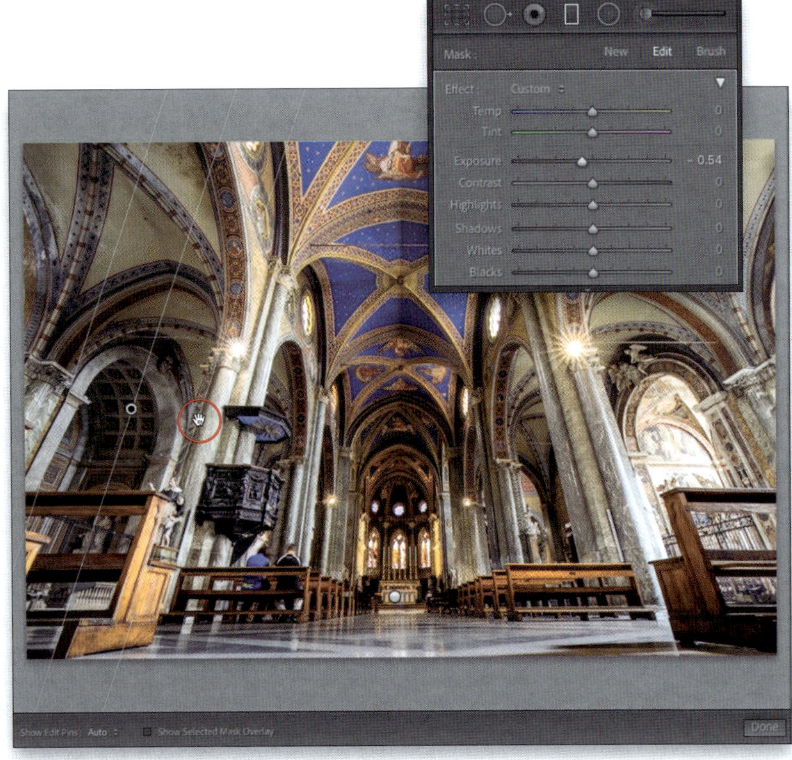

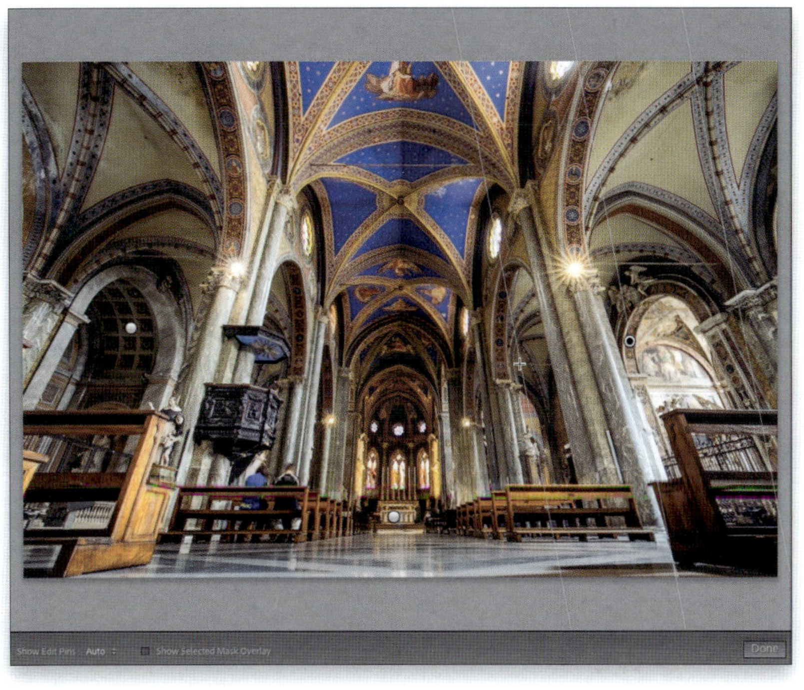

Step 14:

Let's do something similar to the right side of the image. Just click-and-drag another gradient from the top-right corner, and then see if the Exposure amount needs to be moved up or down after you've dragged it. Look at how much more balanced our light is getting. There are still three other areas we'll need to work on using a finer adjustment: (1) The bright area in the cove on the right side, (2) the column on the left that's too bright, and (3) we still need to brighten the ceiling right above the altar. These areas need a finer adjustment than a gradient will do, so we'll switch to the Adjustment Brush to get these smaller areas.

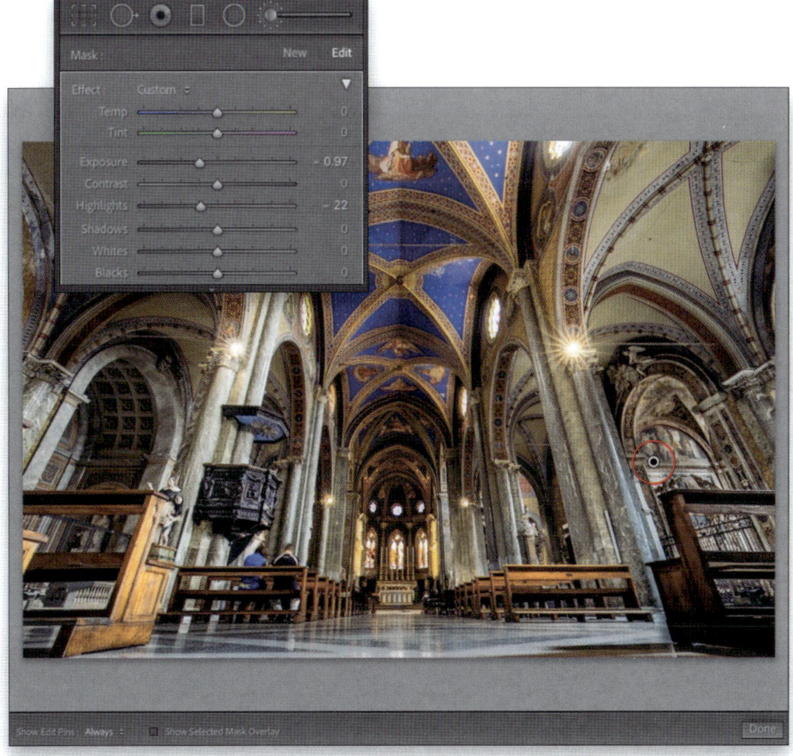

Step 15:

Get the Adjustment Brush (**K**; it's just called the Brush **[B]** in Lightroom cloud), darken the Exposure by around 1 stop (here, I have it set to –0.97), and the Highlights by a bit, too (I dragged the Highlights slider to the left to –22), and then paint over the area on the far right, inside that cove, and maybe even paint a little on the edge of that column on its left (my Edit Pin for this adjustment is circled here). We're trying to make this bright area balance with the rest of image—so it's not drawing our eye over there—and darkening it will help a lot. Remember, after you've painted over that area, if it looks too dark, drag the Exposure slider over to the right a bit. If it's not dark enough, drag it more to the left. Also remember that if you make a mistake and paint over an area you didn't mean to paint over, just press-and-hold the **Option (PC: Alt) key** and it switches to Erase, so you can paint away any areas you spilled over onto.

Step 16:

Next, let's slightly darken the left side of that archway on the left that looks a bit too bright (look back at the previous step to see this before I fixed it). First, click on New (the + [plus sign] in Lightroom cloud) at the top of the panel to leave the changes we've already made as is and start painting somewhere new. With a small-sized brush, paint over the left side of that archway. The −1.00 Exposure amount will be too much, so you'll need to back it off to at least −0.50 if not less (here, I increased it to −0.40 and the Highlights to −21). Okay, we're making some good progress.

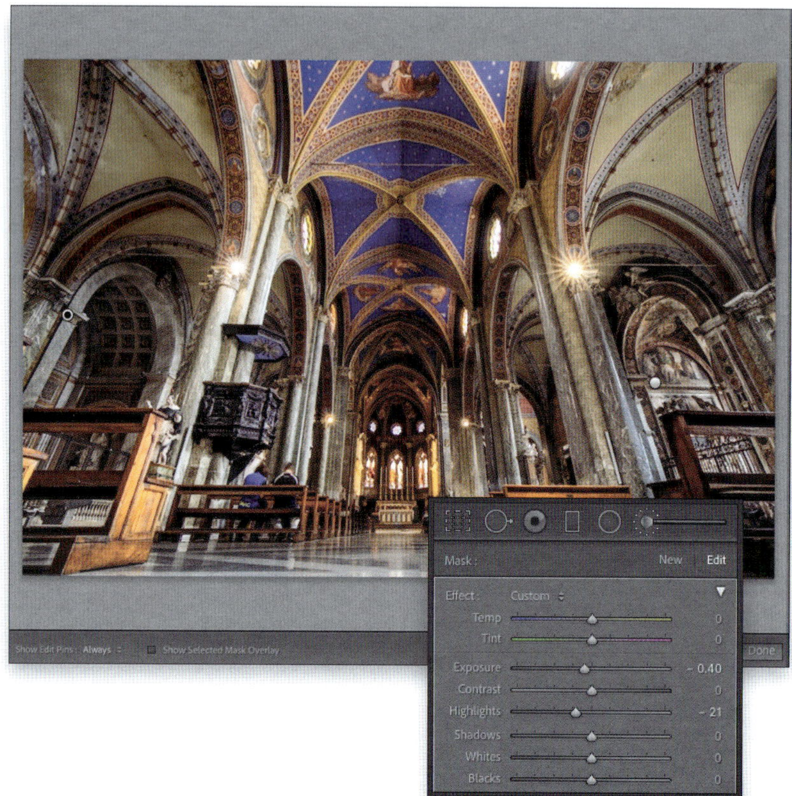

Step 17:

Now for that ceiling area above the altar. Click on New (the + in Lightroom cloud) again to start painting somewhere new. Increase the Exposure amount to around 0.59, set the Highlights back to 0, and with a small-sized brush, paint over the ceiling area above the altar (as shown here) to brighten that area. I even went and painted some of the blue ceiling areas to bring them out, as well, to help balance the overall lighting. That really made a big difference. Click Done in the toolbar beneath the Preview area when you're finished. There's one more thing we'll do (a finishing move) that will also help balance things out).

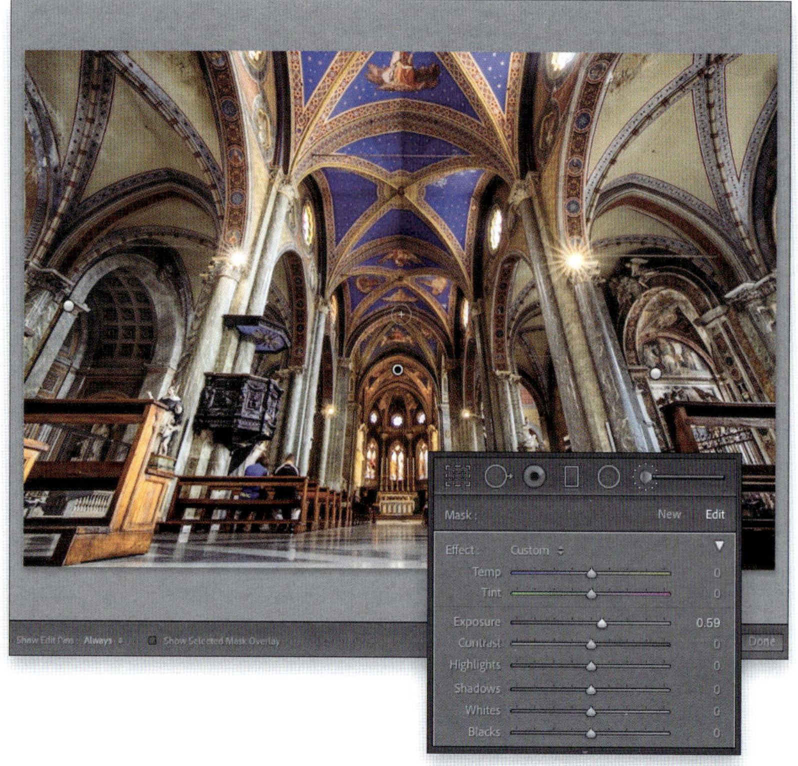

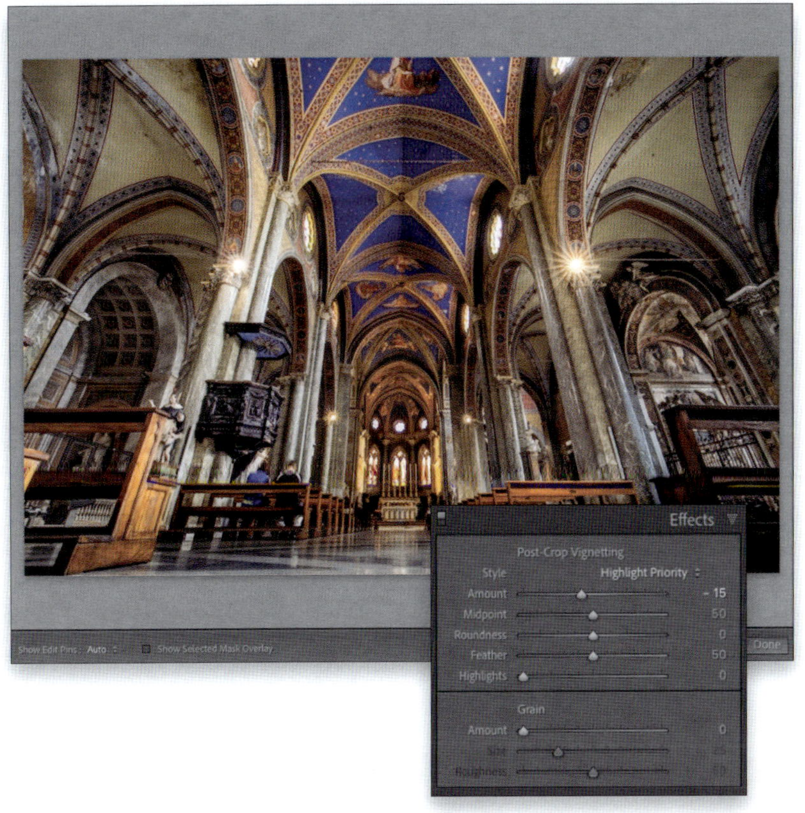

Step 18:

It's time for the final steps in the system, and **Point 7** is a series of finishing moves we do that make a big difference. The first is to apply a subtle darkening all the way around the image—so subtle you wouldn't really know it's there, until you undo/redo it, and then you realize how subtly powerful it is. Go to the Effects panel and under Post-Crop Vignetting, drag the Amount slider (the Vignette slider in Lightroom cloud) to –15 to darken the edges all the way around the image, which focuses your attention on the center of it. An Amount of –15 is more than I usually use (my go-to number is –11), but in this case, it seemed like the edges needed to be a little darker, perhaps because the image is of a darker feel anyway. Once I did this, the gradient we added earlier from the top-left corner now looks too dark, so click back on the Graduated Filter tool, click on the black dot (the Edit Pin) in that top corner, and then hit the Delete key on your keyboard to just remove that gradient altogether. There, that looks better.

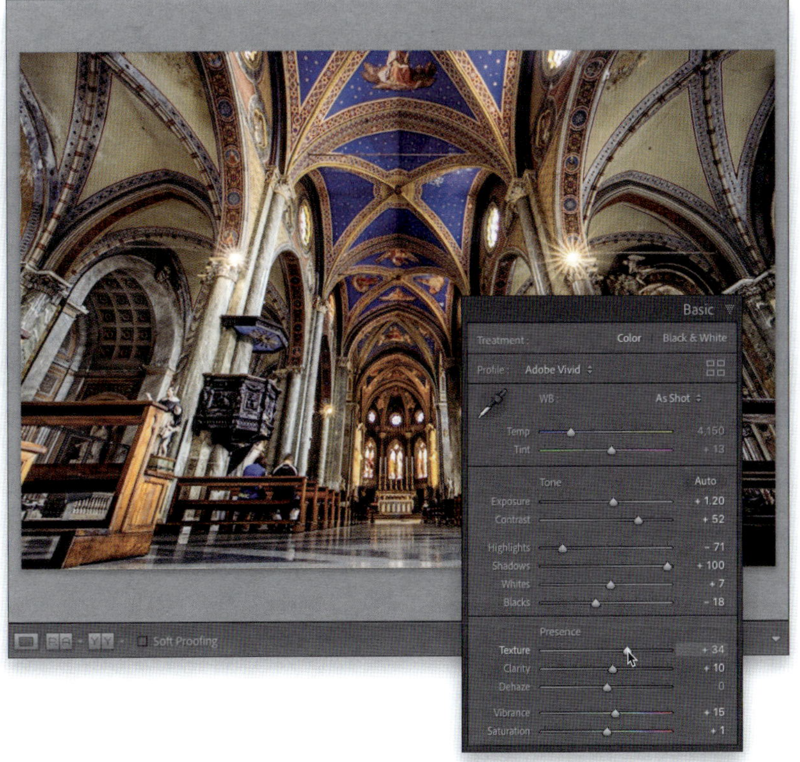

Step 19:

Now, let's enhance the detail and shininess by going back to the Basic panel (stay in the Effects panel in Lightroom cloud) and increasing the Texture slider by a lot (here, I dragged it to +34), and the Clarity slider a bit (+10), which helps add shininess. I don't drag the Clarity slider too far because it starts to change the tone of the image and it can make it start to look kind of grungy. That works great in some images, but for this type of image, you have to use it gingerly.

Step 20:

Every photo gets sharpened, and photos like this, with lots of edges and interesting detail, get lots of it. So, go to the Detail panel and increase the Amount to 80 (as shown here), and bump up the Radius to 1.1 (since this was taken with a 30-megapixel camera, you have to goose that Radius a bit to make the effect stronger. If you're shooting with a 50- or more megapixel camera, you'll need to bump that Radius amount to 1.2).

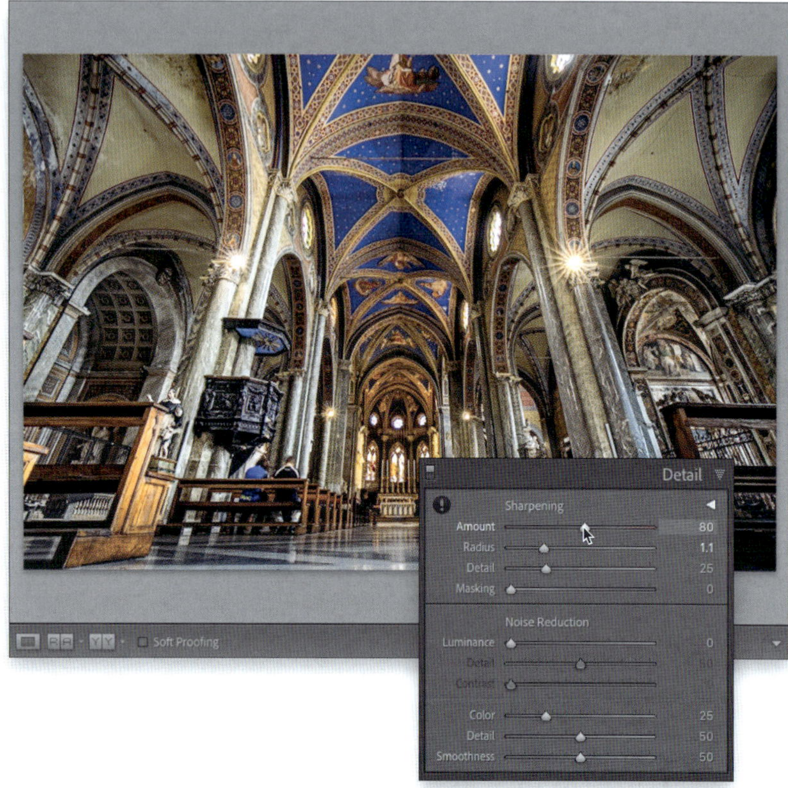

Step 21:

Normally, we'd be done at this point, but when I pause to take a look at the image, two things jump out to me (balance-wise) that I think we need to fix. The tall columns on the left center (to the right of the arch we adjusted earlier) look too bright (see the image in Step 20 to see what I mean), so those need to be darkened. Get the Adjustment Brush (the Brush tool in Lightroom cloud) again, lower the Exposure amount to –1.00, and then paint over those columns to help them closer match the ones on the right side. After I painted over them (and the red and gold areas of the arches right above them), I thought it was a bit too dark, so I backed off the Exposure amount to –0.88.

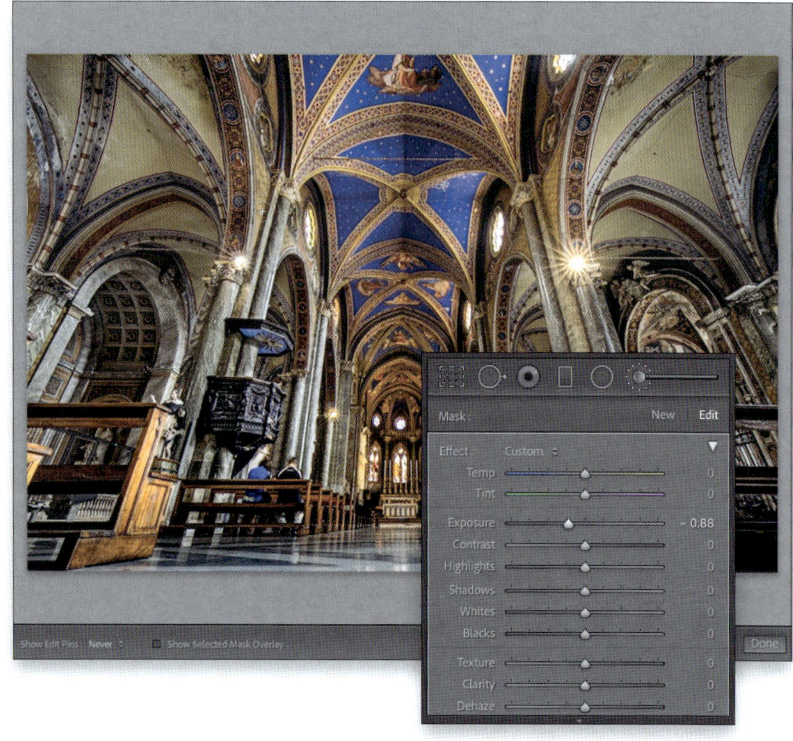

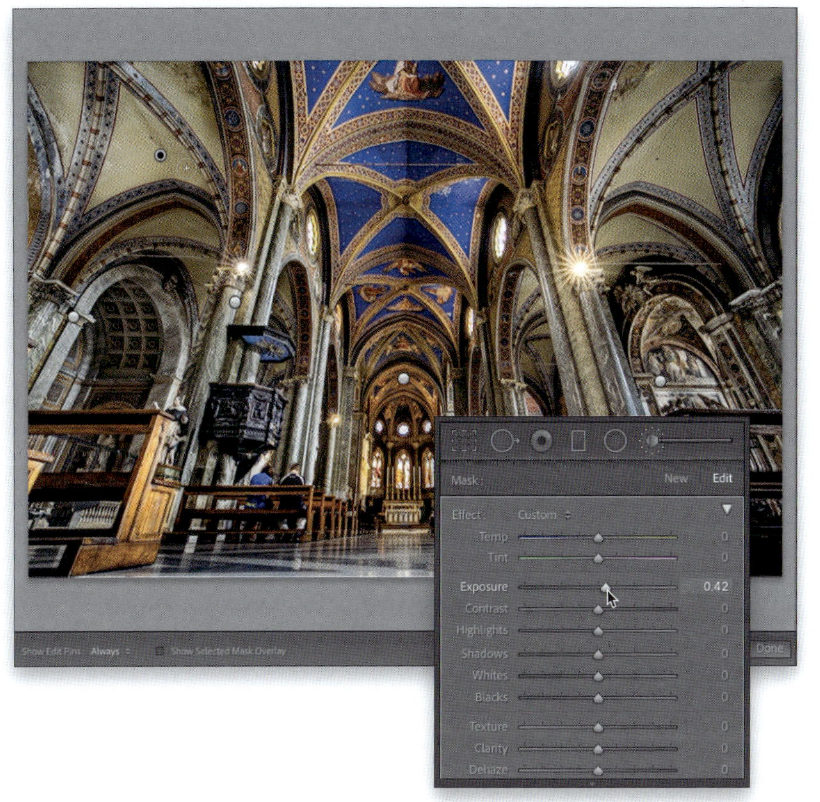

Step 22:

Now, let's brighten that top-left corner a bit. Hit New (the + in Lightroom cloud), increase your Exposure amount to around a half a stop, and then paint over that area to brighten it up so it's balanced with the other side (I started at 0.50, but after I painted over it, it looked a bit too bright, so I backed it off to 0.42). Lastly, as I look at the image, I think the colors are too vivid, and I know why. When we applied that Auto Settings thing back when we first made our HDR, part of Lightroom's auto fix was to increase the Vibrance slider to +15. Ah ha! That's the culprit. So, go to the bottom of the Basic panel (the Color panel in Lightroom cloud) and drag the Vibrance slider to −10 to desaturate the colors a bit. I could have just returned it to zero, but I took it a little farther and I think that looks pretty good (but, of course, set the Vibrance where you want it, or just leave it as is. Again, totally your call).

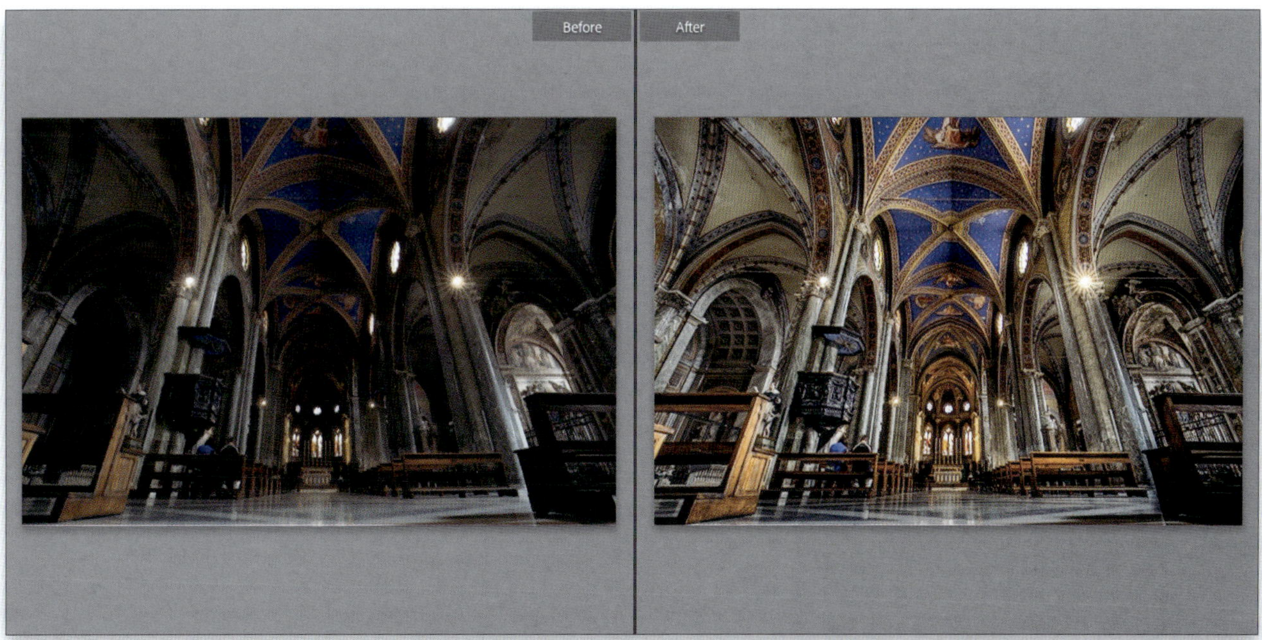

Here's a before and after of our image, with the color Vibrance lowered to −10 (as I mentioned in Step 22).

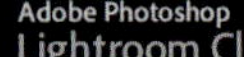

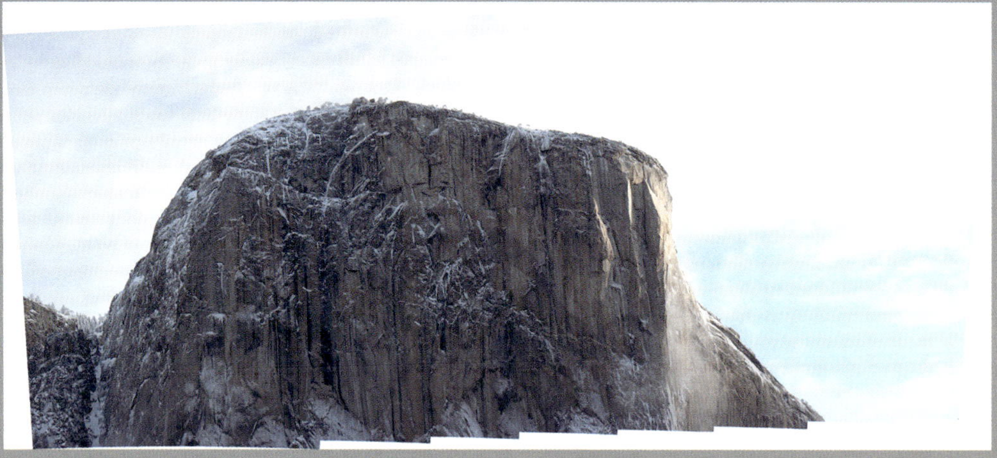

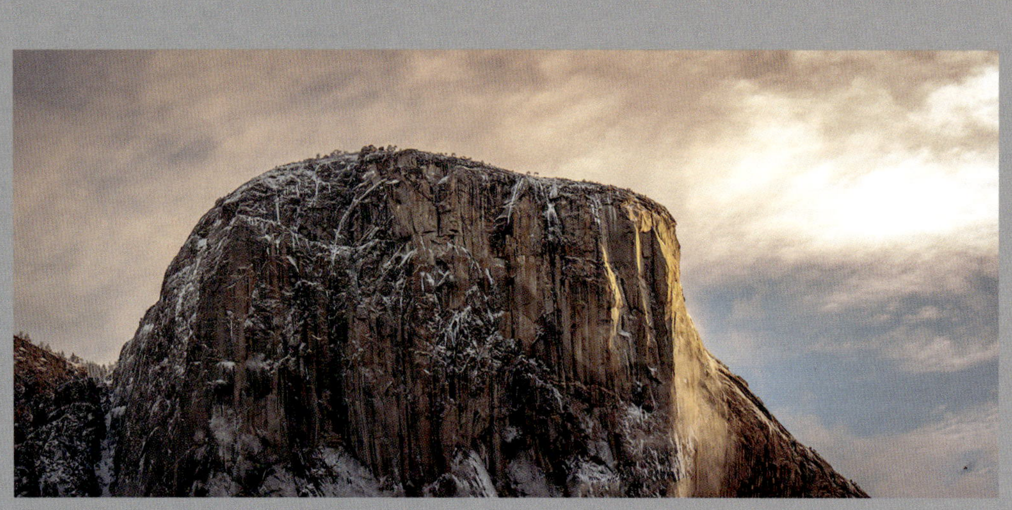

  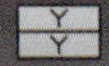 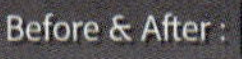  Before & After : 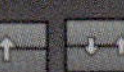  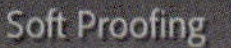 Soft Proofing

YOSEMITE PANORAMA

1. Assigning a RAW Profile
2. Getting the Color Right
3. Expanding the Tonal Range
4. Dealing with Sensor Limitations
5. Painting with Light and Retouching
6. Fixing Lens Issues
7. Finishing Moves

Let's evaluate the image (it's not just one image, though—it's eight images combined into one panoramic image): it looks very flat (it's lacking detail and contrast), there's a pretty strong blue color cast over the whole image, even though the sun is hitting the front of the mountain, the clouds are just kind of "meh," and it lacks sharpness. Ouch!

THE STORY BEHIND THE SHOT:

This shot was taken on my first and only trip to Yosemite National Park in California, where I was a guest instructor (teaching Lightroom) at Moose Peterson's Digital Landscape Workshop Series (DLWS, for short). We got up before dawn one morning (you always get up really early at landscape workshops to catch the dawn light) and headed out to photograph El Capitan. My first thought was to shoot it with a wide-angle lens, but when you do that, you push the mountain farther away and it gets smaller in the frame. So, to keep a sense of scale (and because I love panos), instead, I decided to shoot eight frames and let Lightroom combine them into a single panoramic image. The only thing you need to do in-camera to set things up, so Lightroom can successfully stitch the images together, is overlap each frame by about 30%. If you do that, Lightroom can easily do the rest.

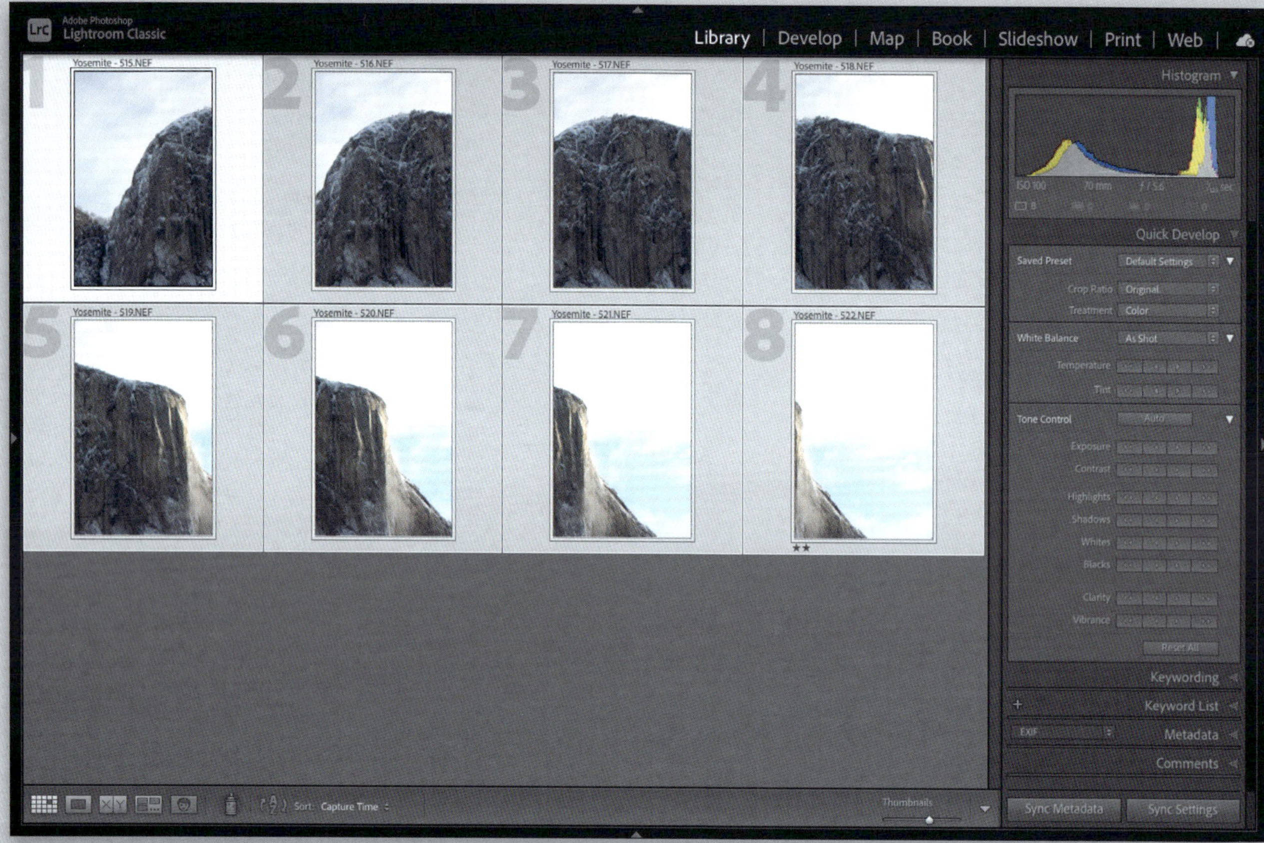

Camera: Nikon D2Xs
Aperture Value: *f*/5.6
Shutter Speed: 1/125 sec
ISO: 100
Focal Length: 70mm

Step 01:

Here are the original eight images in Lightroom Classic's Library module, shot in a vertical format (it's a trick to help reduce the distortion on the edges when you shoot panoramas). Lightroom will stitch a pano together, no problem, as long as you do one key thing: when you're shooting the pano, make sure each frame overlaps the next frame by around 30%. That's it. You can hand-hold it, and you usually don't have to even mess with your settings. (However, you might come across situations where it's better to set your camera to manual mode, so your exposure doesn't change as you move through the scene. If you're doing that, you might as well set your focus on the first frame, then turn off your camera's auto focus, so it doesn't refocus as you move through the scene. And heck, if you're going through all that, you might as well use a tripod. You can make this as easy or as complicated as you'd like, though I usually go with the easy route and it usually works out pretty well.) Anyway, here are our eight frames and we start out by selecting them all, so click on the first frame, then press-and-hold the Shift key and click on the last frame to select it and all the frames in-between (as shown here).

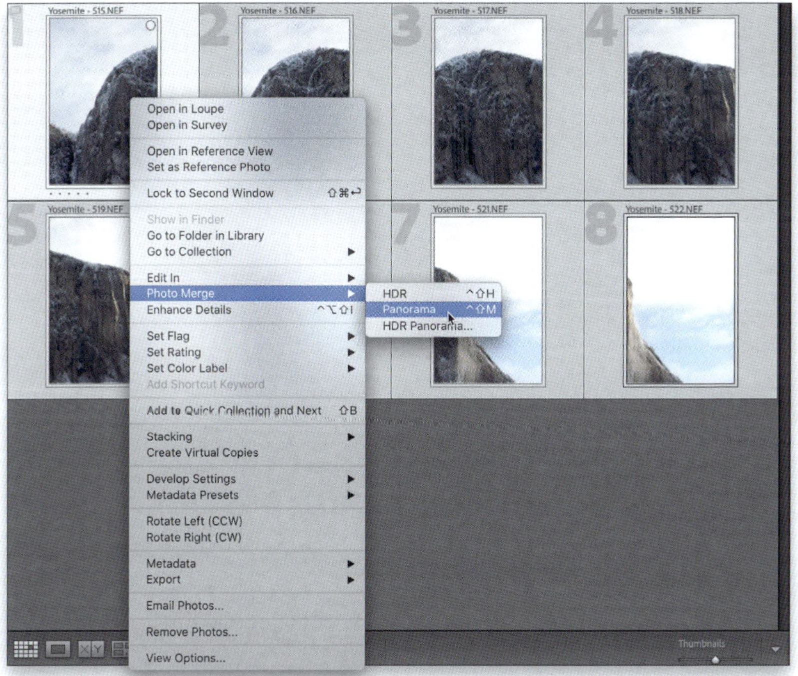

Step 02:

Now that your images are selected, Right-click on any image, and from the pop-up menu that appears, under Photo Merge, choose **Panorama** (**Panorama Merge** in Lightroom cloud), as shown here.

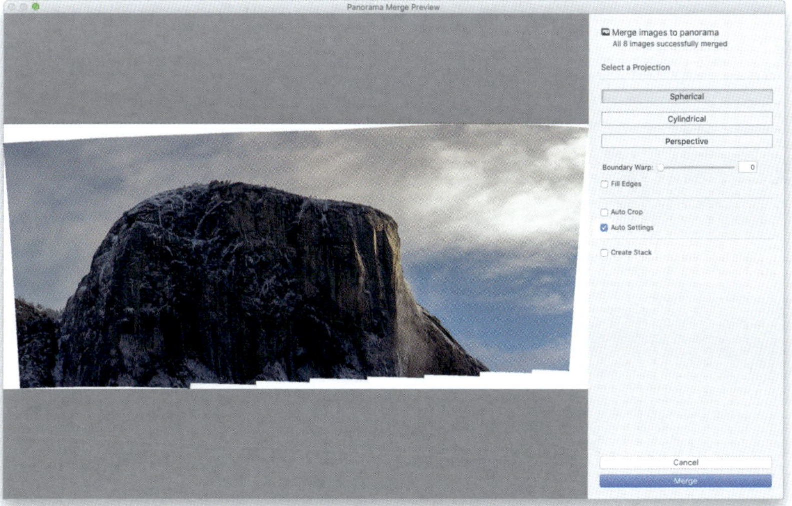

Step 03:

This brings up the Panorama Merge Preview dialog, showing you what, at this point, your pano is going to look like if you click the Merge button. The Select a Projection buttons are normally set to Spherical, which is nice because that's usually the one that looks best. One out of 50 times, I wind up picking another one, but again, it's one out of 50. (I really only click on Cylindrical or Perspective if the Spherical projection doesn't look good, which happens like [say it with me] one out of 50 times. Probably less.) Most likely, your issue won't be the projection—it'll be those white gaps around your image. You could just turn on the Auto Crop checkbox and it will crop all that stuff away, but then your image will be a lot smaller, which isn't awesome when you want to keep as much of your pano as possible (after all, you shot a pano because you wanted a larger view of the scene).

Step 04:

Instead, my go-to choice is to use Fill Edges (just turn on its checkbox). It uses a feature that came from Photoshop, called "Content-Aware Fill," to intelligently fill in those white areas, which is what it did here. Pretty amazing, right? No cropping, no smaller image size, it's like magic. It's not perfect 100% of the time (more like 85%–90%), so if for some reason it doesn't look right, turn off that checkbox and, instead, drag the Boundary Warp slider all the way to the right, which will almost always do the trick if Fill Edges doesn't. The other thing I usually leave turned on here (it's on by default) is the Auto Settings (Apply Auto Settings in Lightroom cloud) checkbox. It applies Lightroom's smart auto adjustment to your image, so you have a decent starting place once the stitched-together pano is done. I also leave the Create Stack checkbox turned on, so when the pano is done, the eight images used to create it are stacked together under a single thumbnail (this option's not in Lightroom cloud. It will stack them automatically). It helps to keep things tidy. Now, click the Merge button.

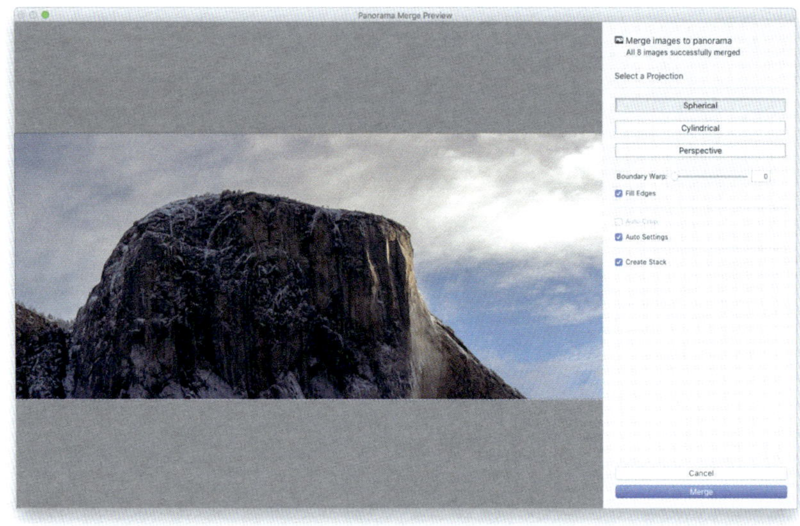

Step 05:

Here's that thumbnail stack—the eight images that make up the pano and the pano itself, all under just a single thumbnail. The number 9 in the top left lets you know it's a stack (and how many images total are under that thumbnail. If you click directly on that 9, it will expand the stack, so you can see all nine images). By the way, you can stack similar images (or any images for that matter) by selecting them and pressing **Command-G (PC: Ctrl-G)** to group them into a stack. If you charge by the hour, you can go under the Photo (Edit in Lightroom cloud) menu, under Stacking (Stack), and choose **Group into Stack**. Okay, we've made our pano, now let's apply the system.

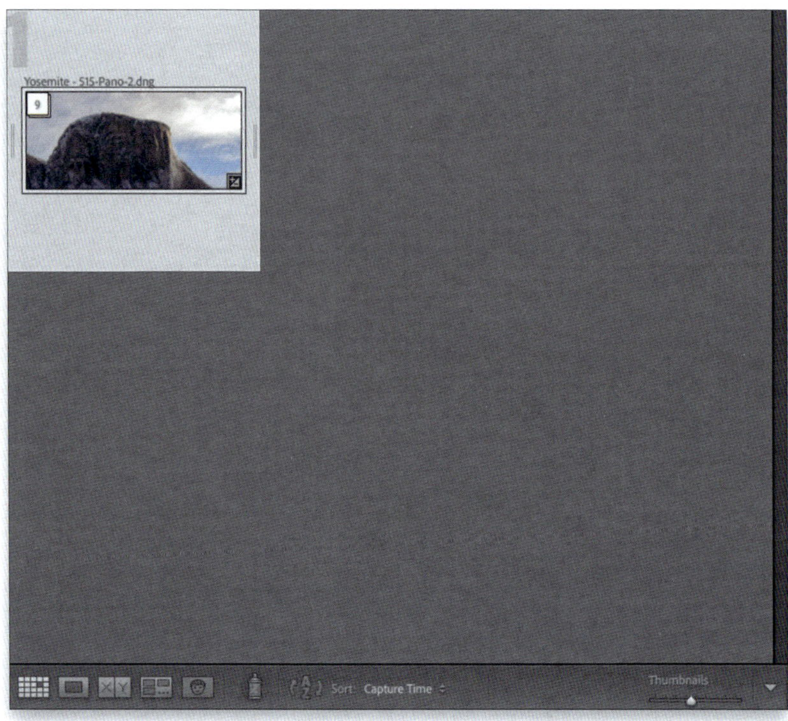

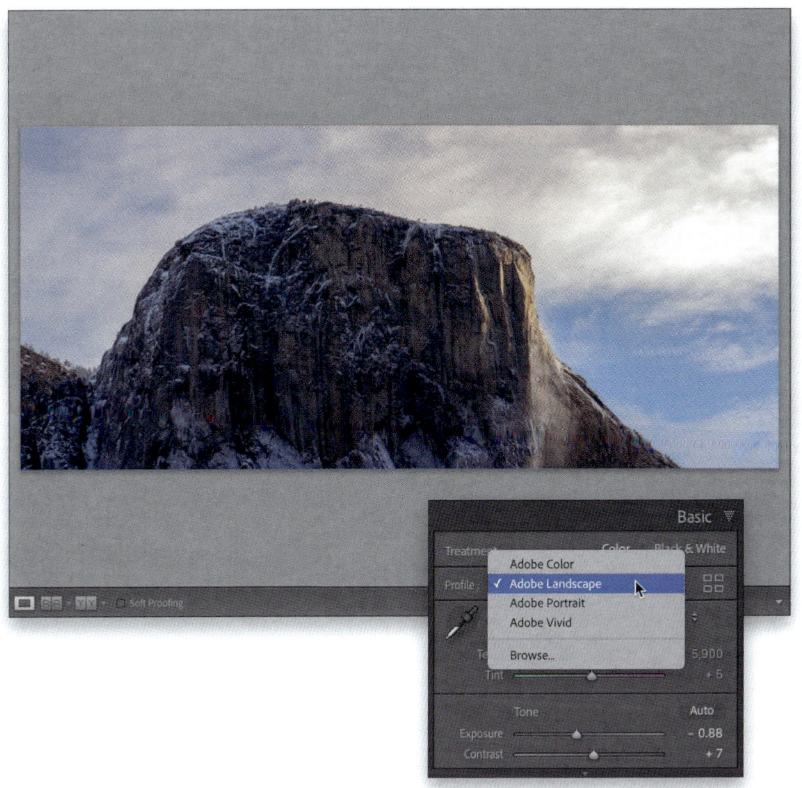

Step 06:

Let's start, as usual, with **Point 1** of the system: head over to the Develop module's Basic panel (the Edit panel in Lightroom cloud) and choose **Adobe Landscape** from the Profile pop-up menu. This is a pretty easy choice, especially with a landscape photo, right? It did a pretty decent job on this image. It's more contrasty and colorful.

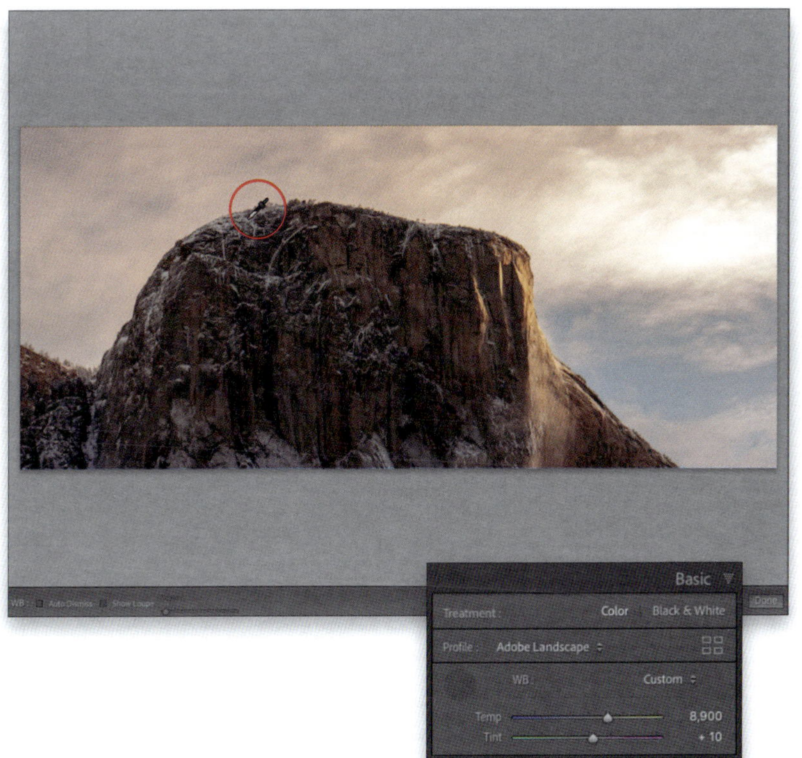

Step 07:

Okay, let's do a quick evaluation of the image (what do we wish were different)? In this case, the first thing that pops out at me is the blue color on the mountain. I used Auto White Balance in my camera, which usually means areas in the shadows will look blue, so let's apply **Point 2** of the system and fix that white balance issue. Get the White Balance Selector tool (**W**; the eyedropper) from the top of the Basic panel (the Color panel in Lightroom cloud) and click it on something that's supposed to be a neutral color. Here, I clicked on some of the snow on the shadow side of the mountain and that looks pretty good. I clicked on a couple of different places on the side of the mountain just to make sure I found a spot that looked good, but I came back to that snowy spot, and look at how much warmer the image looks. The blue is gone and it looks more realistic for a dawn shot.

Step 08:

Now, let's work on the overall exposure (**Point 3** of the system). I know that when we merged the pano, it already applied an auto fix, but that's just a starting point (your Auto Settings may be slightly different than mine). So, let's set the white and black points. Press-and-hold the Shift key and double-click on the word "Whites," and then on the word "Blacks" to expand the tonal range (these sliders are in the Light panel in Lightroom cloud). Doing that sets the Whites and the Blacks to +37 and –37, respectively, so it was worth doing even though it wasn't a night and day change. After we set the white and black points, we head to the Exposure slider and decide if the image looks either too dark or too bright. In this case, I thought it might look better if the sky was darker, so I dragged the Exposure slider to the left to –1.25 to darken the entire image a bit, which makes the sky look better. Again, not a major change in the overall look, but if you compare it to the image in the previous step, it does look a bit better, so we're going in the right direction.

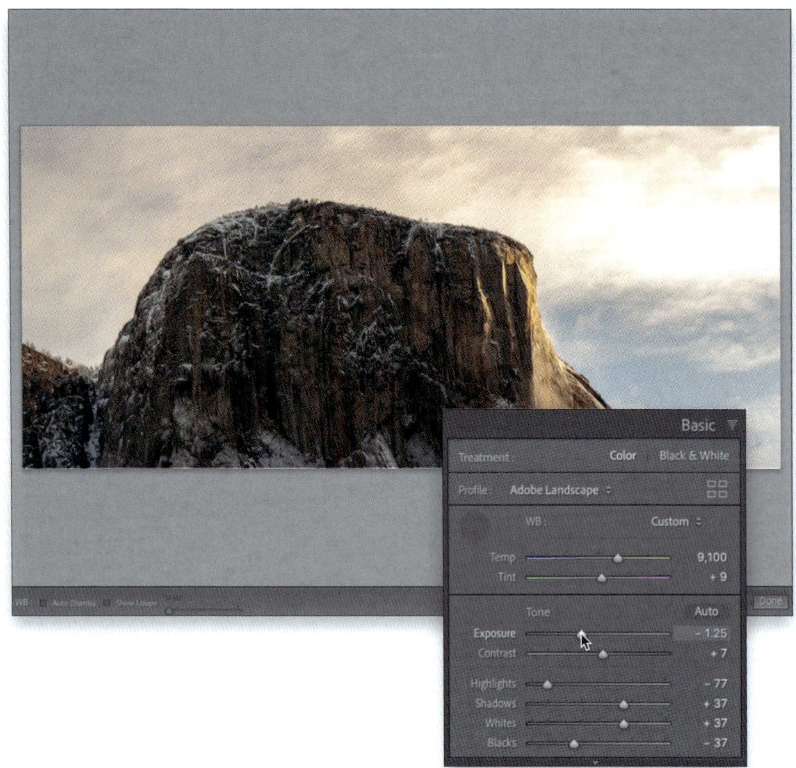

Step 09:

The mountain itself is kind of backlit, so we need to open up those shadow areas (this is **Point 4**), and we're going to use one of my favorite tricks to bring detail back into the sky: lowering the Highlights to –100. So, let's do that. Lower the Highlights to –100, and then open up the shadows until the mountain looks pretty good (here, I dragged the Shadows slider over to +88). When you open up the shadows a lot like this, sometimes that area can look kind of washed out, so you might have to increase the contrast a bit to counteract that, which is what I did here (I dragged the Contrast slider to the right to +18).

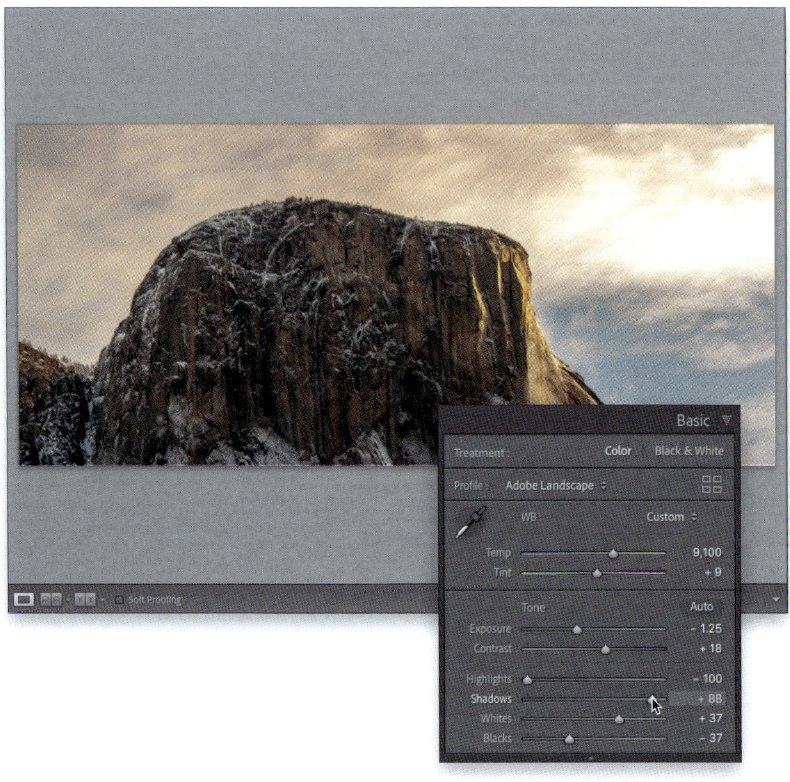

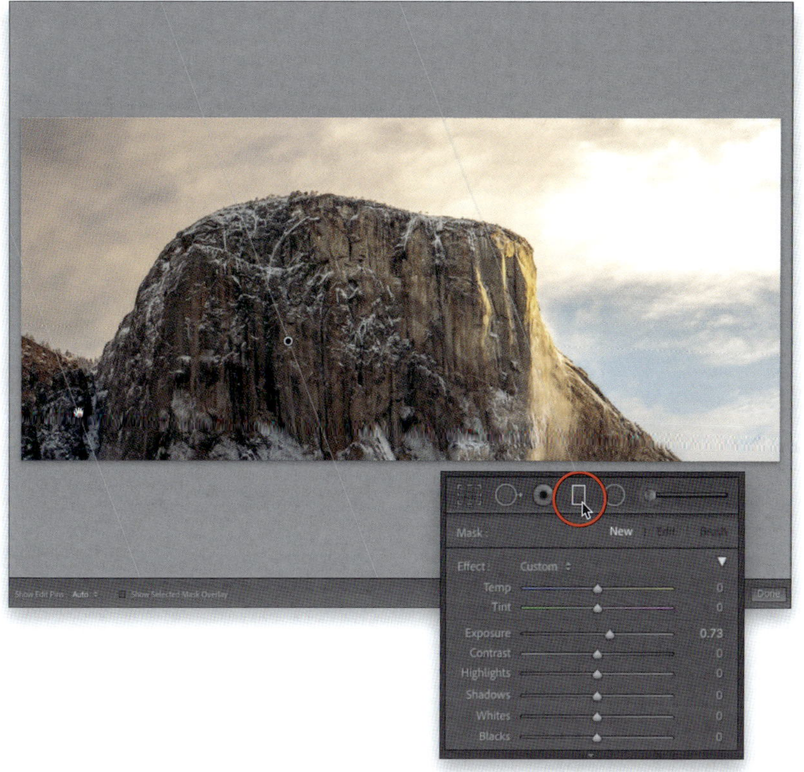

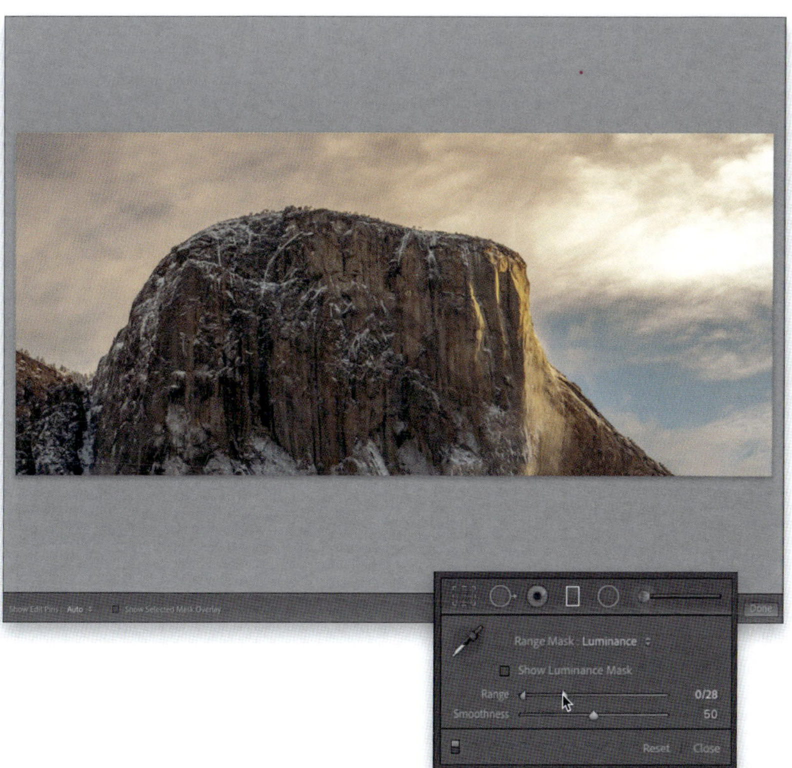

Step 10:

I'm still not crazy about how dark the right side of the mountain is, so we're going to do a little "painting with light"(this is **Point 5**) to brighten that side. But, to save time (rather than painting over the whole mountain with the Adjustment Brush), we're going to use the Graduated Filter (**M**; it's called the Linear Gradient **[L]** in Lightroom cloud) to brighten that whole area, and then we'll use a cool masking trick to select just the mountain. So, get the Graduated Filter tool from the toolbox beneath the histogram (from the toolbox on the right in Lightroom cloud), increase your Exposure around 3/4 of a stop (to around 0.75), and then click-and-drag the tool from where the sun is in the image (in the top-right corner) down through the mountain (as shown here). It brightens everything up, but we're going to fix that in the next step because we want to adjust only the mountain and pretty much leave the sky alone.

Step 11:

So, we're going to remove the effect from the sky and everywhere else we don't want it using a feature called "Range Mask." We literally just move a slider and we can mask away all the highlight areas, leaving us with only the mountain affected by the gradient we just dragged out. You do this by scrolling down to the bottom of the Graduated Filter panel and you'll see the word "Off" next to Range Mask (this feature is not available in Lightroom cloud). Click-and-hold directly on Off and a pop-up menu appears. Choose **Luminance** from this menu and a Range slider appears, which lets us mask our area by its brightness (so you can, for example, apply the gradient to this dark mountain, while ignoring the brighter sky). To remove the highlight areas (the sky) from our gradient, drag the far-right Range slider to the left (as shown here). The farther you drag it to the left, the more of the highlight areas it drops out from that gradient.

Step 12:

So, how far do you drag that slider? Well, this will help: It's a preview of the mask that Lightroom creates behind the scenes to show you what's being affected. Just press-and-hold the Option (PC: Alt) key as you drag. The parts of your photo that turn black are no longer being affected and the parts that are white are the shadow areas still being affected. So, I dragged the far-right Range slider to the left until the sky turned just about black, and now I know that any tweaks I make to the regular Graduated Filter sliders will only affect the areas you see here in white (the mountain), and not the black areas (the sky). There's another Range Mask option called Color, where instead of choosing the area by brightness (like we did here), you create the mask by clicking an eyedropper on the color of what you want to keep.

Step 13:

Let's recap where we are: we dragged a gradient out that made everything bright. Then, we used the Range Mask so only the mountain is now affected by our sliders, so we can do any adjustments we want to the mountain now without worrying about messing up the rest of the image. So, let's do it! We want to make the mountain a little brighter, we want to bring out its texture and detail, and we want it a bit more contrasty. So, drag the Exposure slider a little to the right (to brighten the overall mountain). You can try opening up the Shadows a bit more (dragging to the right), but it was starting to look a bit washed out, so you should probably increase the Contrast, and maybe drag the Blacks to the left a bit, making them a bit darker, which adds even more contrast. Let's also increase the Highlights and Whites just a bit. To bring out the detail, increase the Texture and Clarity amounts. That's all it needs. Click the Done button in the toolbar beneath the Preview area (in Lightroom Classic).

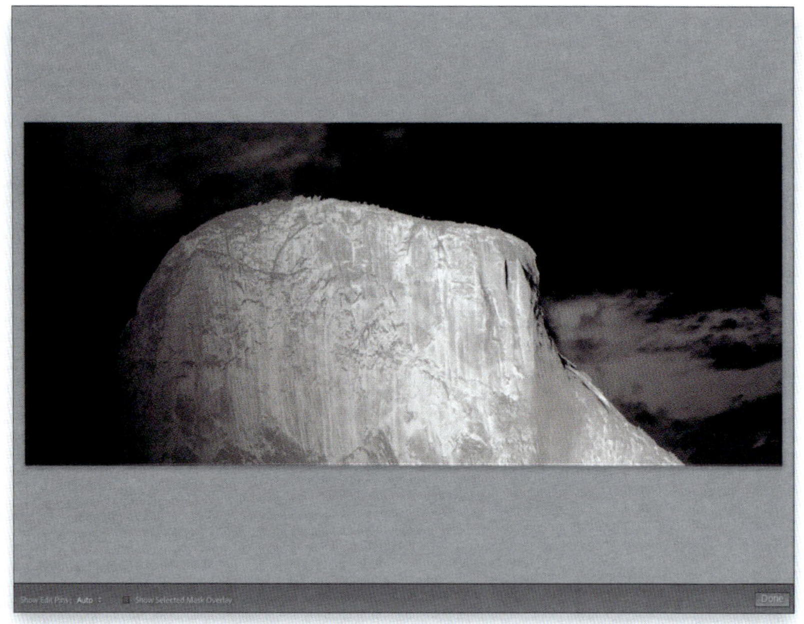

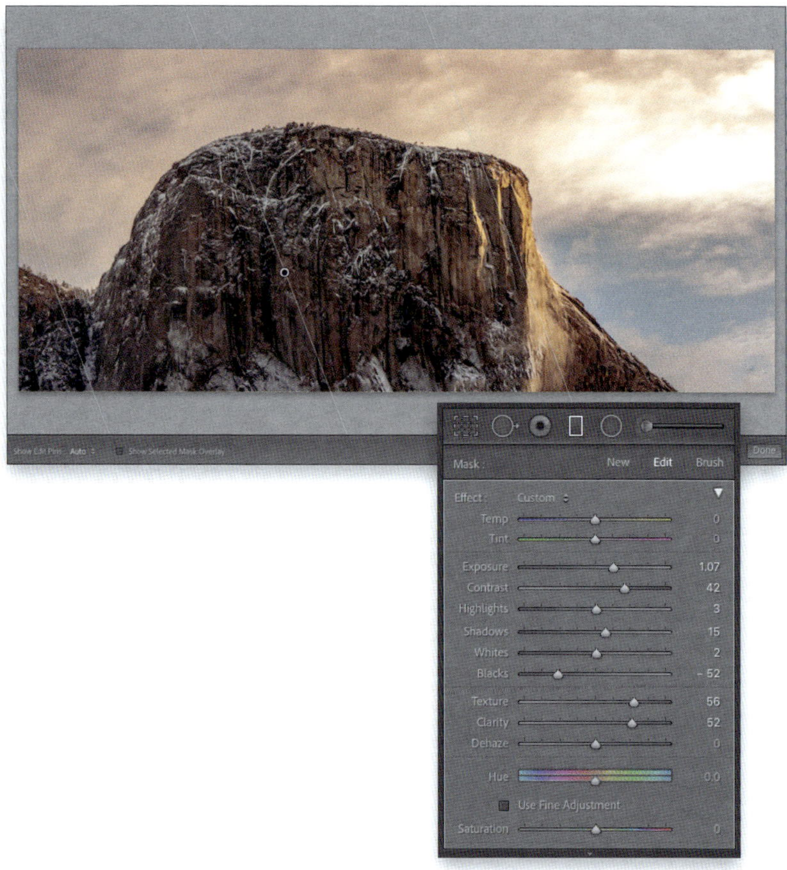

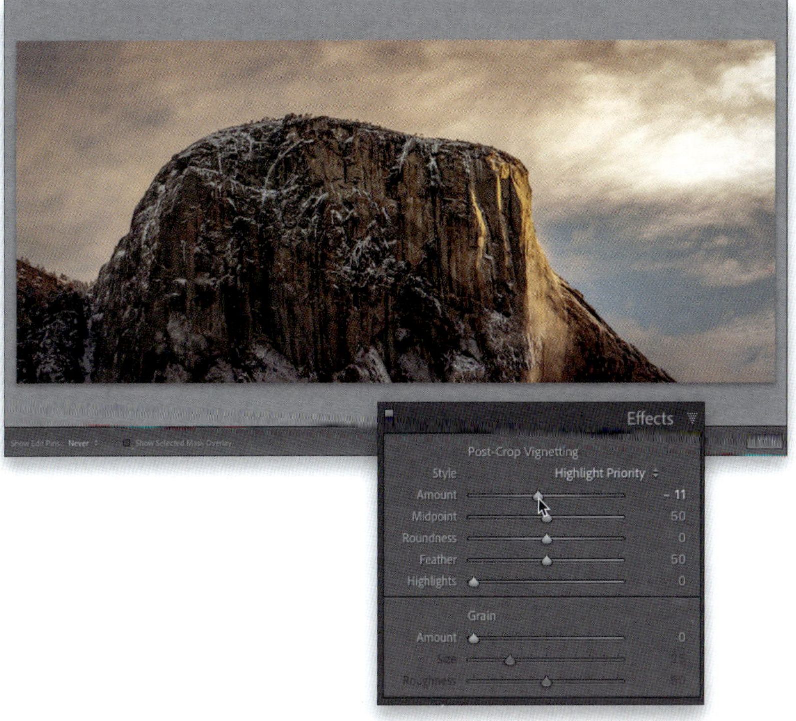

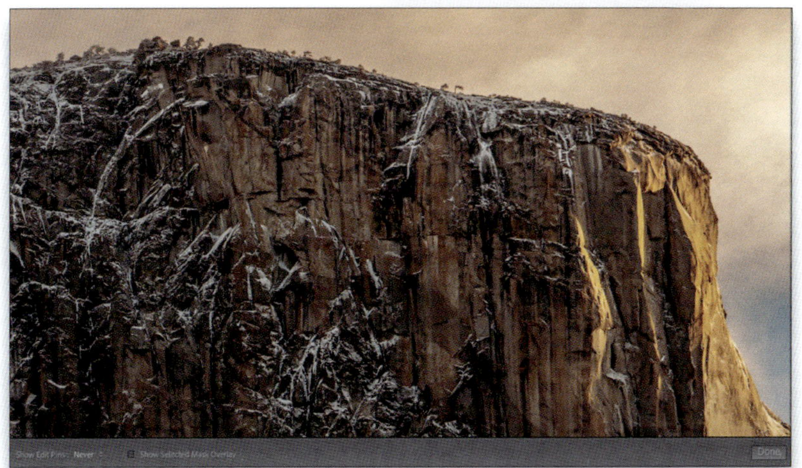

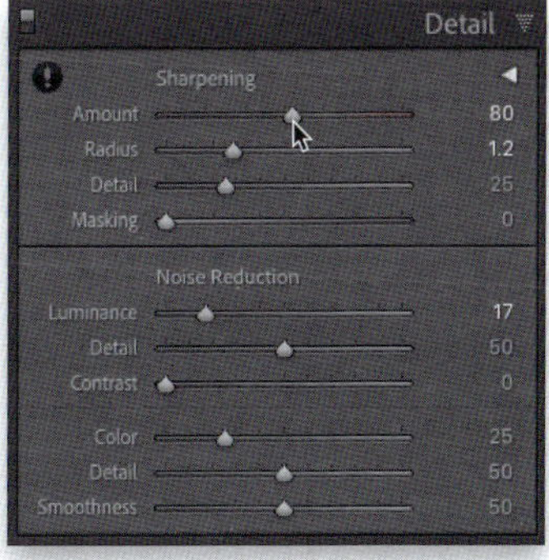

Step 14:

There weren't really any visible lens issues we needed to correct in this image, so we're going to skip over Point 6 in the system, and head straight to the finishing moves (**Point 7**) by darkening the edges just a tad, and then sharpening. So, go to the Effects panel, and under Post-Crop Vignetting, drag the Amount slider (the Vignette slider in Lightroom cloud) to the left to –11 (that magic number that subtly darkens the outside edges of the image all the way around without it looking like you added a vignette). It is pretty subtle, but if you toggle the visibility of the panel on/off a few times (click the button in the left side of the panel header in Lightroom Classic; click-and-hold on the eye icon in the right side of the panel header in Lightroom cloud), you'll see what a nice finishing move it adds.

Step 15:

To wrap this pano up, we're going to apply some sharpening, so head up to the Detail panel, and increase the Amount slider (the Sharpening slider in Lightroom cloud) to 80 (things like land-scapes, city scapes, automobiles, archi-tecture, and things with lots of detail can really look awesome with a lot of sharp-ening, so you can crank the Amount up to 80, or even higher, with shots like these). Also, this image is a pano (a bunch of high-resolution photos stitched together into one big mega photo), so you can usually increase the Radius a bit, as well (here, I took it to 1.2), but depend-ing on the photo, you might go even higher. Don't change the Detail amount (I leave it set at its default of 25, where it actually does a nice job of reducing any bad edge effects that can happen with higher numbers of detail). Adobe rec-ommends viewing your sharpening at 100% size, but unless you're going to be displaying this giant pano printed at full size, I generally don't push in that large (especially with a large pano like this).

Here's the final image. To see this before and after view of your image edits, press the **Y key** on your keyboard (this view is not available in Lightroom cloud, but you can press the \ **[backslash] key** to see a before/after), and there you have it. Remember, we started with eight individual images and stitched them into a single panoramic image before we applied the system, so what you're seeing here on the left isn't the real "before" image because we used the Apply Settings checkbox in the Panorama Merge Preview dialog—when the stitched pano first appeared on your screen, it already had auto settings applied to it. So, I went back and merged the original pano, turning off the check-box, so you could see the real, actual, untouched pano (below left) before any editing was applied. Hope that helps you see how far we came in a very short time. Now, below, let's look at some different white balance settings, so we can have optional versions of this image to choose from (remember, we can also "undo" any we don't like).

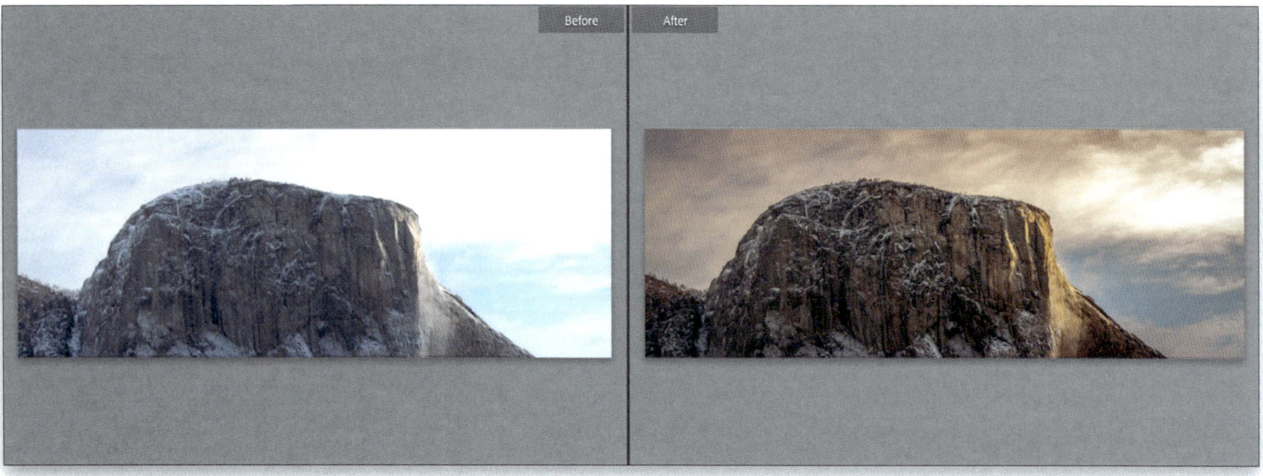

Step 16:

If you want a cooler tone to your image, go back to the Basic panel (the Color panel in Lightroom cloud), and from the WB (White Balance) presets pop-up menu at the top, choose **As Shot** to return the image to the white balance setting I had set in my camera (in this case, I had it set to Daylight, which obviously was not the most accurate choice, but you might actually like this better, so why not at least give it a look, right?). If you don't like how it looks, press **Command-Z (PC: Ctrl-Z)** to undo your white balance change. Okay, let's try another preset.

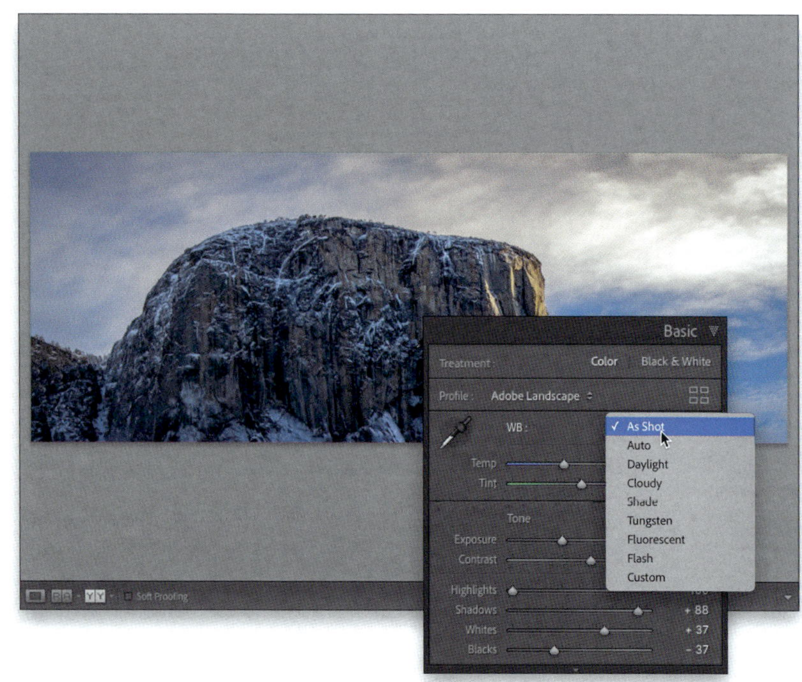

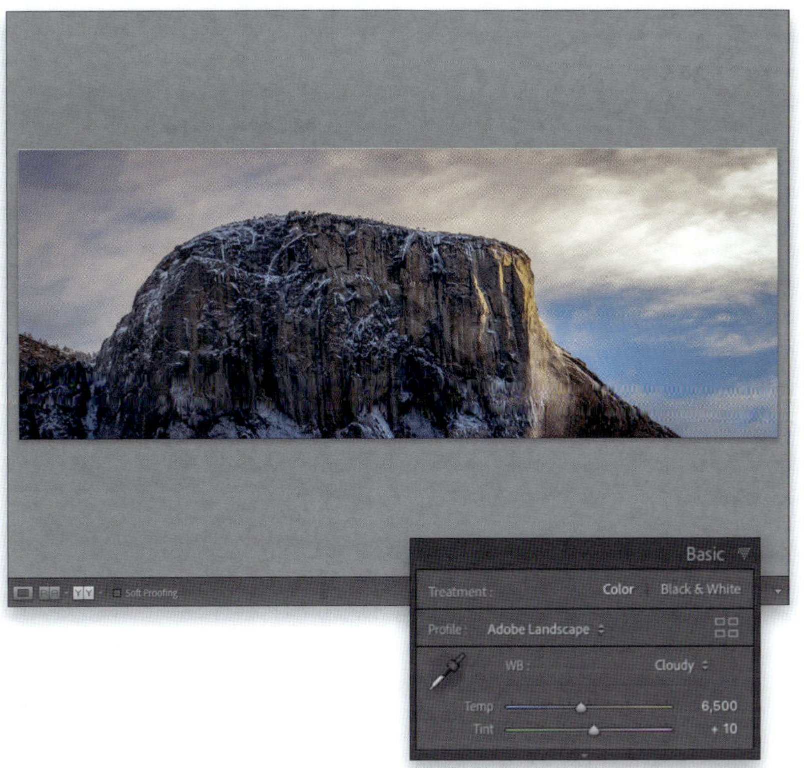

Step 17:
Here's what it looks like if we choose the **Cloudy** white balance preset. Not nearly as blue, and you can see some more magenta in the sky on the left. Overall, it's a more colorful look.

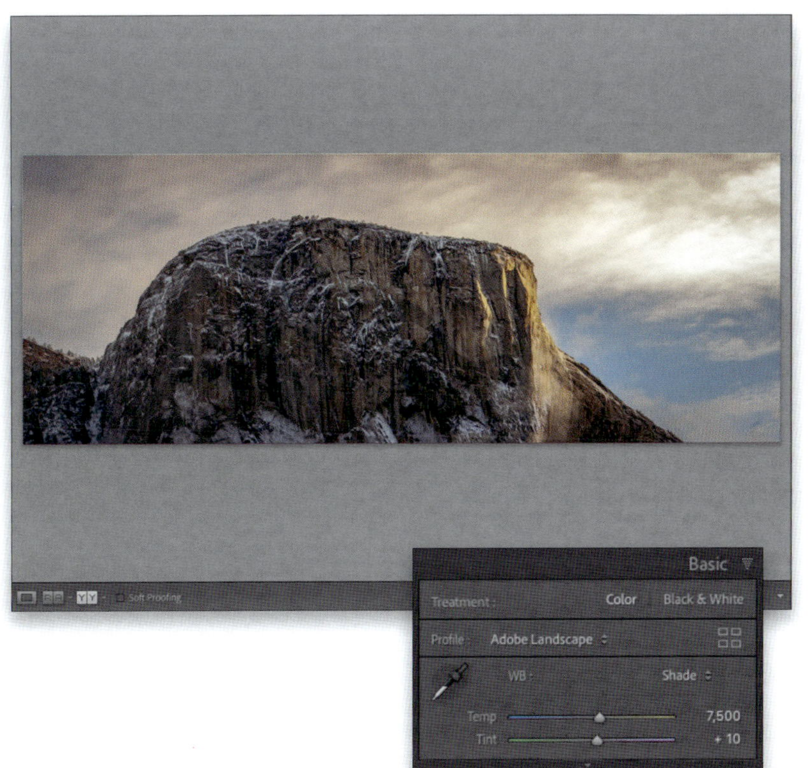

Step 18:
And, here's what it looks like if we choose the **Shade** white balance preset (which is probably what I should have chosen in-camera, right?). Again, less blue and probably a pretty accurate representation of what the color should have been, but these are creative decisions we get to make as the photographer, so whichever one you choose is the right one for you (luckily, there is no international committee ruling on what is the exact proper white balance). In fact, I think out of the four white balances we've looked at, this might be my favorite. A hint of blue in the mountain, and the image isn't too warm or too cold (kind of like porridge), so I personally would probably stick with this white balance and make that my final answer, Regis.

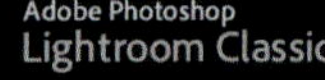
Adobe Photoshop
Lightroom Classic

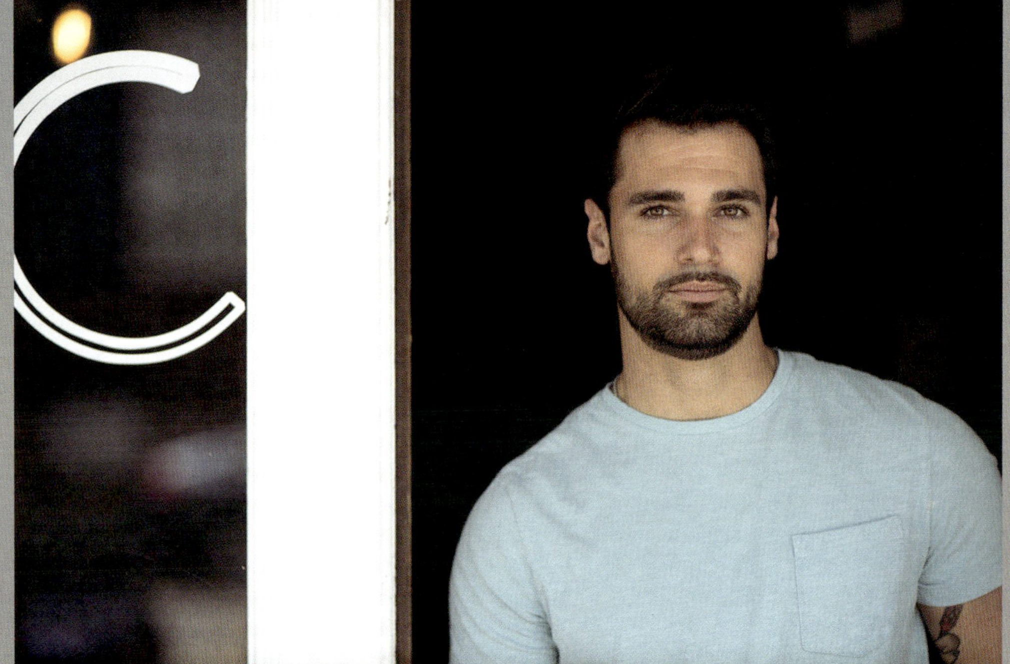
Before

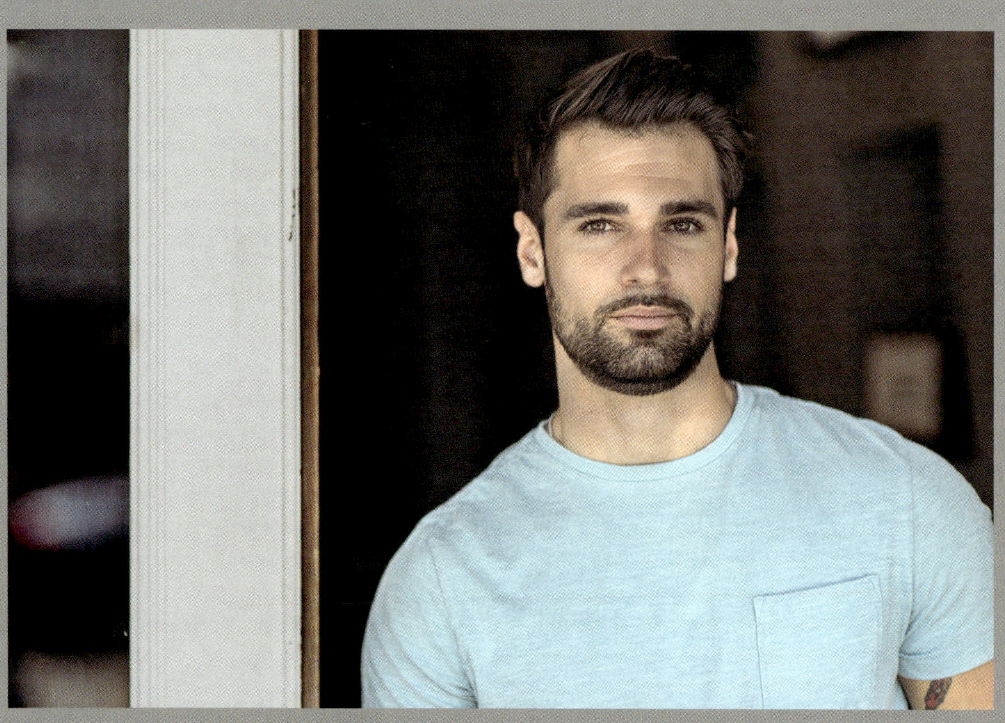
After

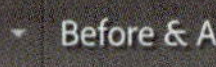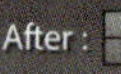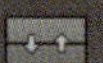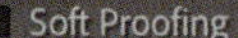
Before & After :   Soft Proofing

LESSON 06

DOORWAY PORTRAIT

1. Assigning a RAW Profile
2. Getting the Color Right
3. Expanding the Tonal Range
4. Dealing with Sensor Limitations
5. Painting with Light and Retouching
6. Fixing Lens Issues
7. Finishing Moves

Here, we're going to do a simple edit on a portrait. No real fancy stuff in this one, but it's important to see how we apply the 7-Point System to all different types of images. Even though our subject is different (in this case, a person), we still use the same sliders for the same things in pretty much the same way. Of course, since our subject is a person, we get to do a few portrait-specific moves, as well.

THE STORY BEHIND THE SHOT:

This portrait was taken in downtown Ybor City, which is just outside downtown Tampa, Florida. Ybor City is the heart of the Cuban community in Tampa, with lots of restaurants and nightclubs, and lots of really cool-looking old buildings and cobblestone streets, so it's a go-to area for Tampa Bay area photographers looking to shoot location portraits. I didn't have a flash or strobe with me, so I wanted to get my subject under some shade so he wouldn't be harshly lit out in the direct, searing, soul-sucking, massive ball of blinding light that is the Florida sun. We had rented a space for this shoot in the back of one of those cool old buildings, and we asked the shop up front if it was okay to do a quick portrait in their doorway (this is asking a lot because it means releasing a few cubic feet of precious air conditioning that is the lifeline of every Floridian), but they were pretty cool about it (see what I did there?).

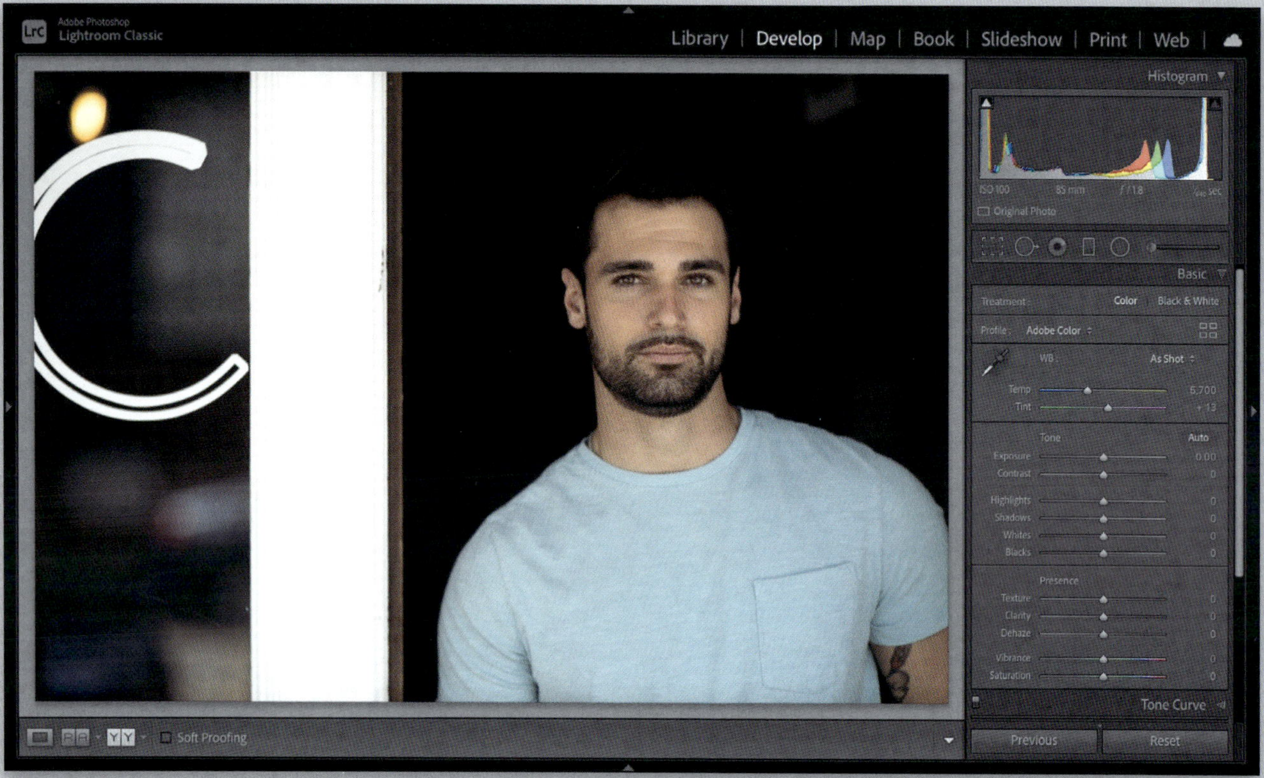

Camera: Canon EOS R 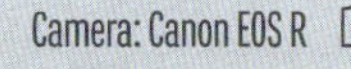
Aperture Value: ƒ/1.8 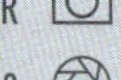
Shutter Speed: 1/640 sec 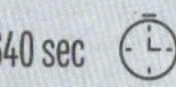
ISO: 100 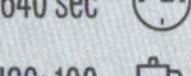
Focal Length: 85mm 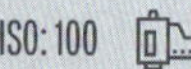

Step 01:

Here's our original RAW image out of the camera, taken in the doorway of a shop downtown. In evaluating the image (that "What do I wish were different" phase), I would say the things that stand out to me are: the white door frame is really pulling the eye, so it needs to be darkened a lot; the big letter "C" with a round, yellow light above it is also very distracting; and the background behind him is way too dark, making his dark hair get lost on it. Also, the lighting, while soft and flattering, isn't all that dimensional, so we could address that, and his shirt is a bit bright compared to his face, so it's drawing the viewer's eye away from the face (not great for a portrait where the person's face is supposed to be the focus). Not too bad overall; nuthin' a little Lightroom won't fix.

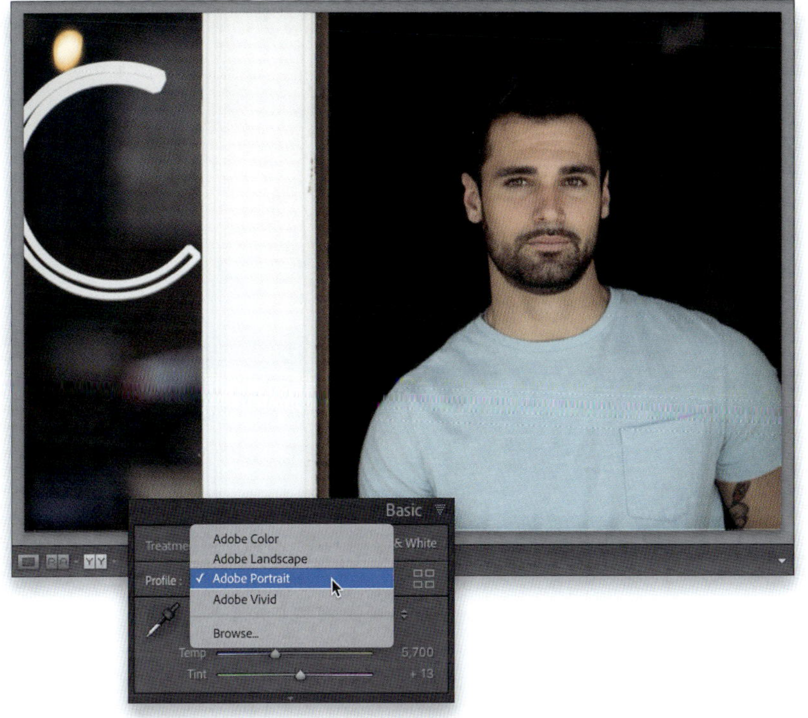

Step 02:

Generally, **Point 1** of the 7-Point System is to change the RAW profile to Adobe Landscape (or maybe even Adobe Vivid, depending on the image), but when it comes to portraits, this is an easy choice—just choose **Adobe Portrait** from the Profile pop-up menu at the top of the Develop module's Basic panel (the Edit panel in Lightroom cloud). It didn't do much at all to this particular image, but it did open up the shadows in the back a little bit, and it's a nice, flat portrait look to start us off, so we'll go with it. Again, just a very minor improvement, but it was just one click, so no biggie (plus, it would double the effort to undo it).

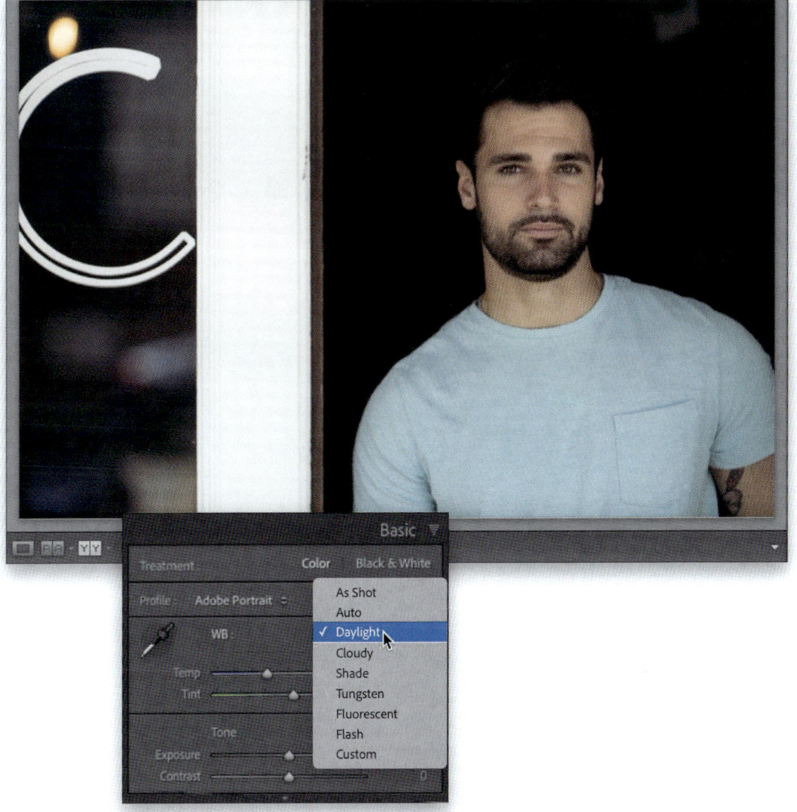

Step 03:

Now, let's check our color (**Point 2** of the system) by choosing a white balance that looks good to us. The white balance in the original really doesn't look too bad, but that can fool your eye, so it's a good idea to try a couple of the white balance presets just to see if one of them looks better. This portrait was shot in the shade of a doorway and just choosing Shade seems like it would be the obvious choice, so go ahead and choose that from the WB (White Balance) pop-up menu at the top of the Basic panel (the Color panel in Lightroom cloud). It looks a bit too warm don'tchathink? Okay, let's try a few more from the menu. How about Auto? Nah, still too warm. Let's try **Daylight**. Okay, now that looks pretty good. Not that much different from the As Shot setting I had in the camera, but just like the previous step, it looks a little better, so let's just stick with Daylight. At this point, things don't look all too different from the original RAW image, but I feel like that's about to change.

Step 04:

Let's move on to getting our exposure where we want it (this is **Point 3**), and we start by expanding our tonal range, right? Right! In the Basic panel (the Light panel in Lightroom cloud), Shift-double-click on the word "Whites," then do the same for "Blacks," and look—it made quite a difference, bumping up the Whites to +58 and the Blacks to –4 (just a reminder: when you drag the Blacks slider to the left, it makes the darkest areas darker, so it's adding more blacks, even though it's a negative number. Kinda weird. I know). Now is when we'd drag the Exposure slider to the right (if we think the overall image needs to be brighter) or left if we think it needs to be darker. I think brightening the midtones (that's what the Exposure slider controls) would help, so let's open it up about 1/2 a stop by dragging it to the right to +0.50. Okay, that did help, and we're moving in the right direction.

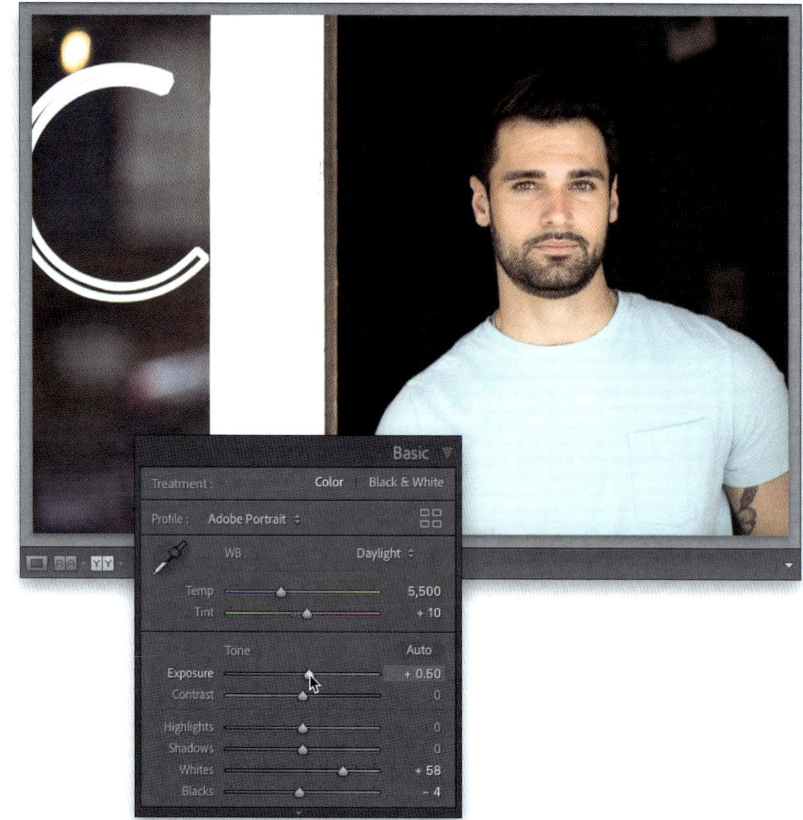

Step 05:

Our overall exposure is now pretty solid, so let's work on our two problem areas: pulling back the very bright highlights (on the door frame and his shirt), and opening up the shadows behind him to help give the image some depth (this is **Point 4**). Let's start by opening up the shadows by dragging the Shadows slider over to around +41, so we can start to see some detail back there. You're even getting some separation in his hair from the background now, and the highlights in his hair are coming out. Drag the Highlights slider to the left to around –61 to pull some of those highlights back. Look at how you can now actually see detail in the wooden door frame. Also, his shirt is darker with more detail as well, and it's not as bright and distracting. Those made a big difference by just balancing out the tones in the image.

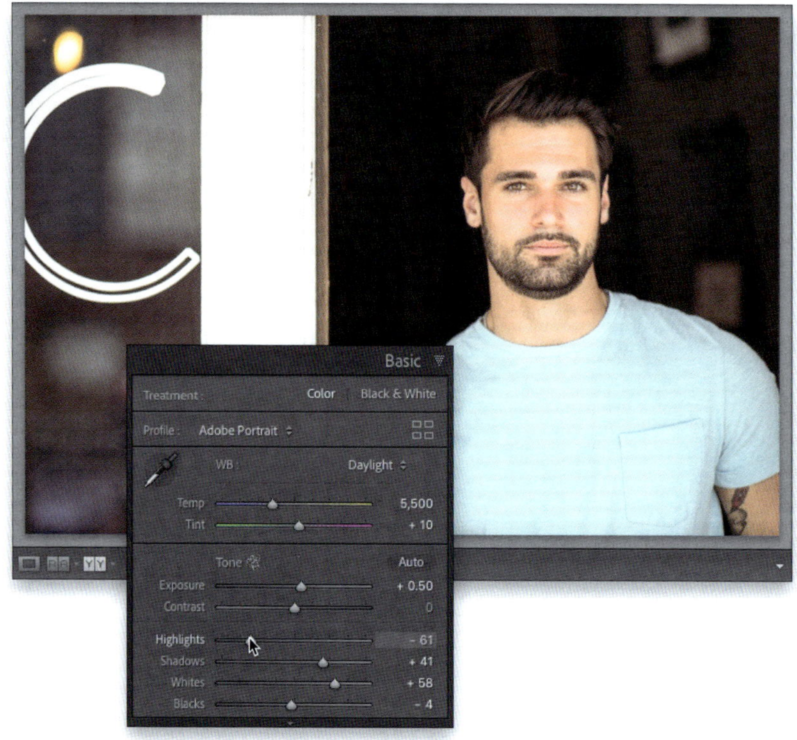

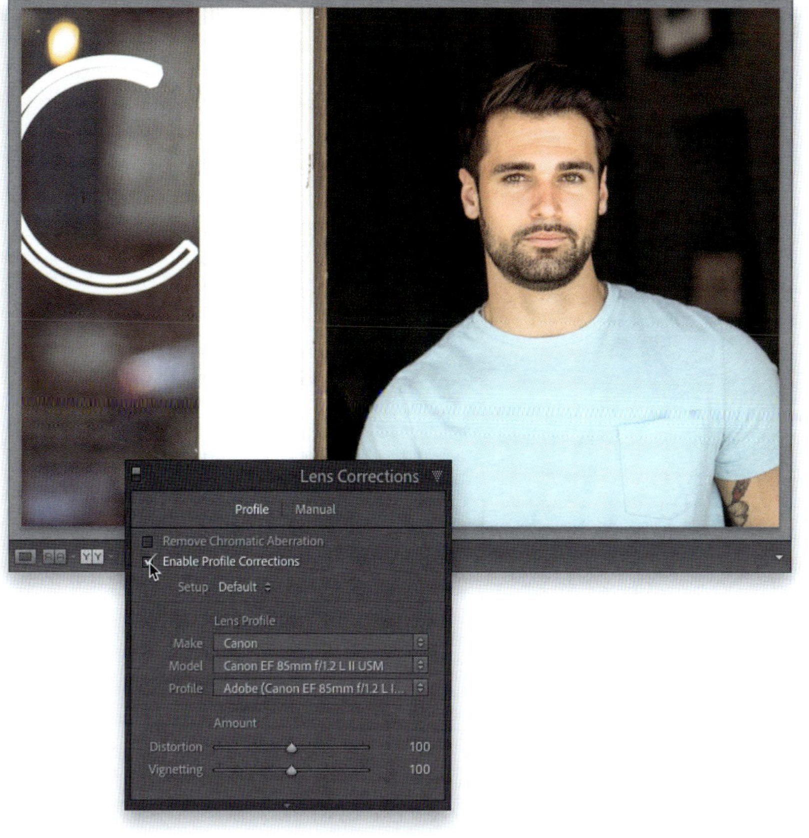

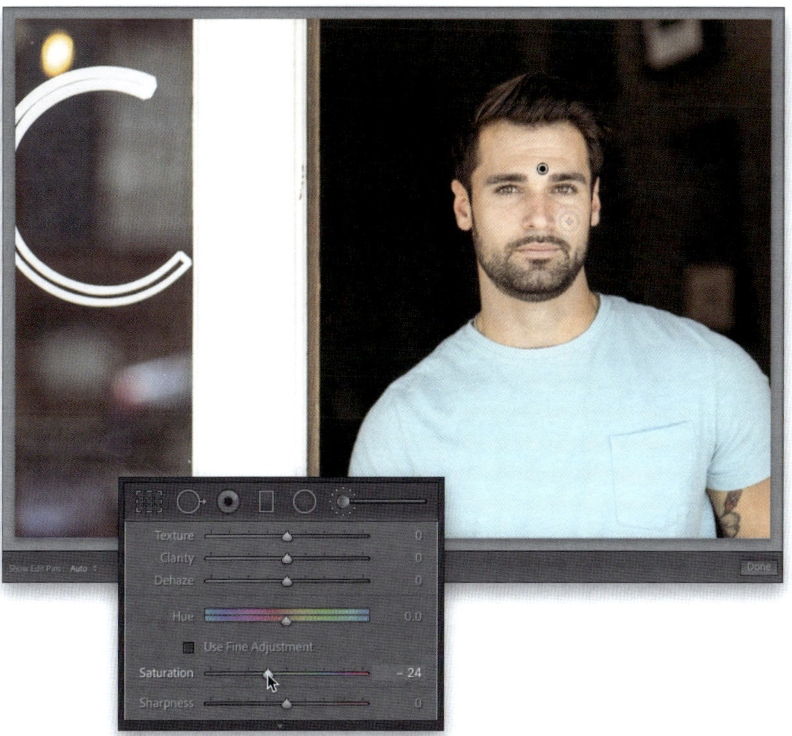

Step 06:

If you look in the corners of the image, you can see some lens vignetting (darkening of the corners caused by the lens itself) and a little bit of lens distortion on both sides of the image. We can deal with all that pretty easily by jumping over to **Point 6**. Go to the Lens Corrections panel (the Optics panel in Lightroom cloud) and turn on the Enable Profile (Lens) Corrections checkbox. Just doing this will fix most, if not all, of the darkening in the corners. Compare the corners in this image, after we've applied the profile correction, to those in the image in Step 05, and you can see they no longer have that darkening. If you see a little left over when you're working on one of your own images, you can drag the Vignetting fine-tuning slider at the bottom of the panel (the Lens Vignetting slider in Lightroom cloud) over toward the right to further brighten the corners—I do have to do this on occasion. Again, it just depends on the photo and the lens you were using (some vignettes are worse than others).

Step 07:

Now we can work on his overall skin tone (this is **Point 5**). I almost always desaturate the skin tone at least a bit, because it gives a more modern look to the image (desaturating the skin a bit is very popular these days). Desaturating skin tone a bunch is a very Hollywood look, but we're not trying to go that far. We just want it looking like portraits are processed today—not like a Hollywood movie poster. Get the Adjustment Brush **(K)** from the toolbox beneath the histogram (the Brush tool **[B]** from the toolbox on the right in Lightroom cloud), double-click on the word "Effect" to reset the sliders to zero, and then drag the Saturation slider to the left a bit (here, I dragged it over to –24). Now, start painting over his face (eyes, lips, and all). Don't forget to do his neck and arm, as well, of course. Any visible skin will need to be painted over, so it all matches.

Step 08:

If you want to open up those shadows in the shop behind him a little more, while you've already got the Adjustment Brush, it's really easy to do. At the top of the panel, click on New (the + [plus sign] in Lightroom cloud), and then double-click on the word "Effect" to reset all the sliders to zero (this happens by default in Lightroom cloud). Now, drag the Exposure slider (which controls overall brightness) to the right a bit (here, I dragged it to 0.60, so a little more than 1/2 a stop), and then paint over the whole area behind him. When you start painting close to his shirt or his head, make sure you turn on the Auto Mask checkbox (**A**) near the bottom of the panel, so the brush won't accidentally paint over those areas even if the edge of your brush crosses over, for example, onto his shirt. Only turn this checkbox on when you're right near an edge—it slows your brush down a bit because it's doing lots of math as you paint when it's turned on. This brightens up that background nicely.

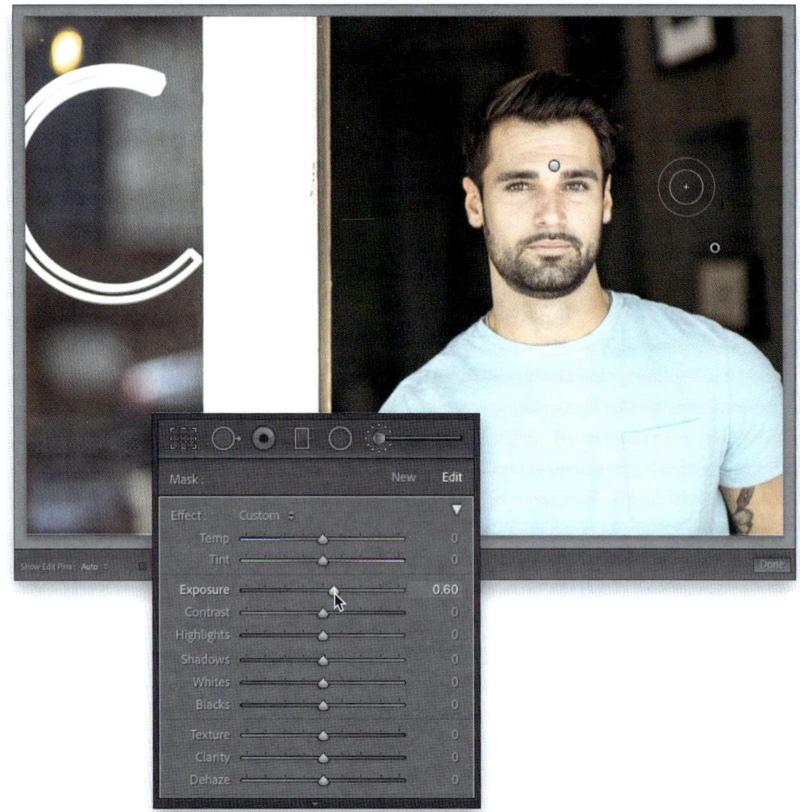

Step 09:

Let's zoom in a bit (press **Command-+** [plus sign; **PC: Ctrl-+**]), so we can add a little more dimension to the light on his face (the light is pretty flat) by adding some subtle shadows. Click on New again, and then double-click on Effect to reset all the sliders to zero. Now, drag the Exposure slider to the left to darken the exposure by around 1/2 of a stop, so we can paint in some shadows (here, I dragged it over to –0.57). Shrink the size of your brush quite a bit (press **Command-[** [left bracket key; **PC: Ctrl-[**]), and then paint over the right side of his face (as shown here)—just his face, not his neck. When you do this, it darkens that side of his face a bit and adds more depth and dimension to the lighting. Remember to keep this subtle or it will look obvious that it was added in post.

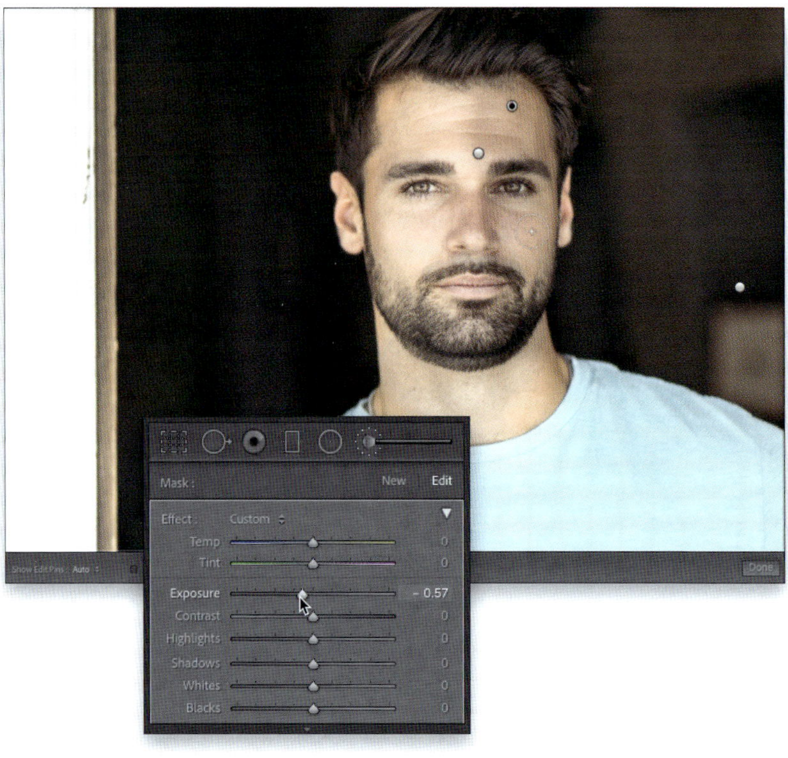

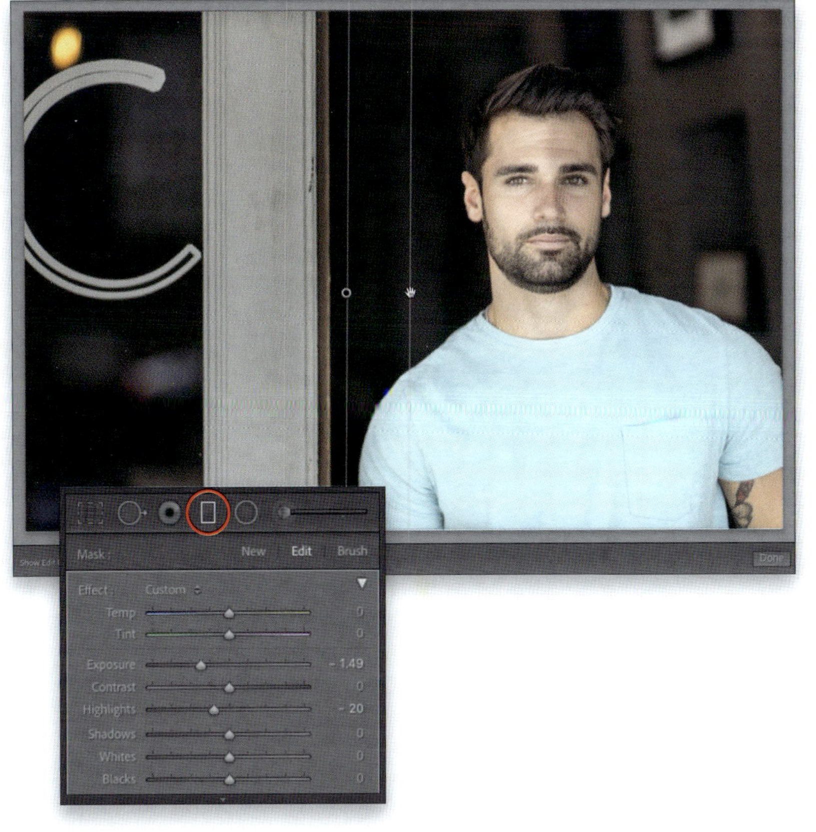

Step 10:

To deal with that overly bright left side of the image (in particular, that door frame), you could just take the Adjustment Brush and paint over it with a dark exposure, but a faster way would be to use its cousin—the Graduated Filter tool (**M**; the Linear Gradient tool **[L]** in Lightroom cloud). Click on it up in the toolbox (its icon looks like a gradient) beneath the histogram (in the toolbox on the right in Lightroom cloud), lower the Exposure amount by around 1-1/2 stops (here, I dragged it to –1.49), then lower the Highlights, too (just to help out with darkening those bright whites of the frame. Here, I lowered them to –20), and then drag the tool from left to right, starting right at the door frame and stopping right around his shoulder (as shown here). Everything to the left of the left vertical line is darkened by 1-1/2 stops, and then it slowly graduates to transparent at the vertical line on the far right (where his shoulder is, so his shoulder doesn't get darkened).

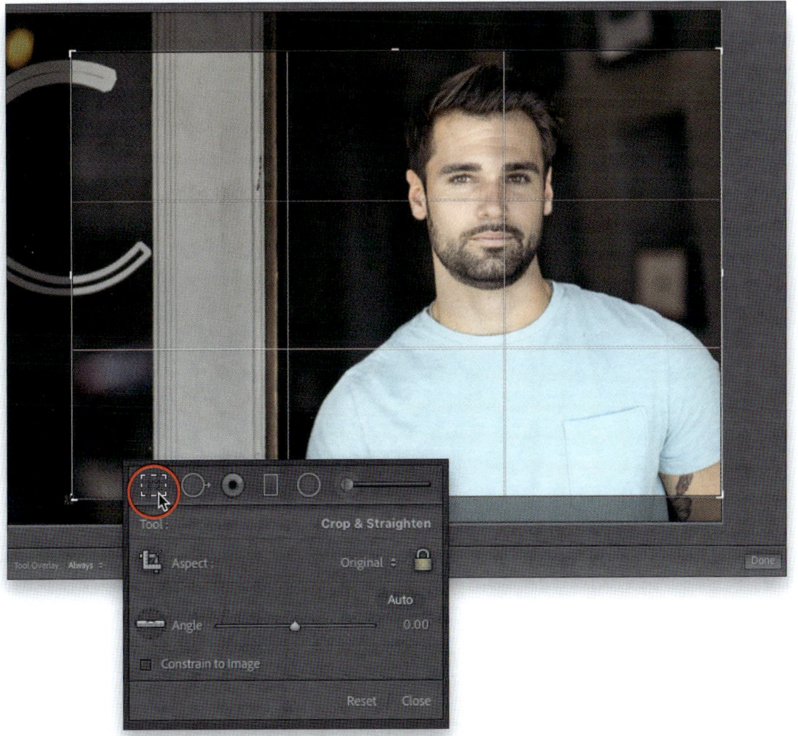

Step 11:

Now, if I were to evaluate the image at this point, I think that big letter "C" on the left is distracting, and so is that round yellow light in the top left (after all, as Henri Matisse would say, if they're not helping the image, they're hurting it). So, I think some cropping would, overall, help this image a lot. Get the Crop Overlay tool **(R)** from the toolbox beneath the histogram (the Crop & Rotate tool **[C]** from the toolbox on the right in Lightroom cloud) and let's crop away a lot of that left side and some of the top, as well. We can even help make this image look stronger and more balanced by pulling in that bottom a bit, too. When you've got it looking like this, hit the **Return (PC: Enter) key** to lock in your changes.

Step 12:

This cropping looks a lot better, and it made the whole portrait more intimate and stronger. However, those lingering parts of the "C" on the left side are still distracting, so let's get rid of them. Get the Spot Removal tool from the toolbox below the histogram (**Q**; the Healing Brush tool **[H]** from the toolbox on the right in Lightroom cloud) and paint right over the bottom part of the "C" (as shown here. When you paint, it paints in solid white). Lightroom will automatically pick a spot to "sample" from (an area nearby to use as a calculation to remove that area). I hate to admit it, but as I mentioned in an earlier lesson, it usually does a pretty bad job of it, so be prepared (in the next step) to override its decision and pick a spot yourself that actually makes sense. Unless what you're removing actually is just a spot (which it does fairly well), you'll almost always have to choose that spot manually. Just so you know.

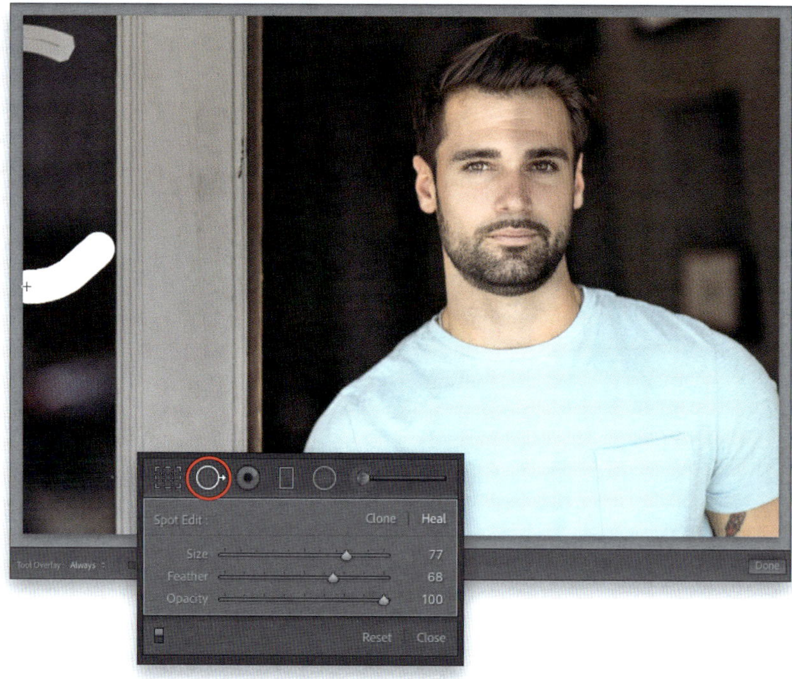

Step 13:

Here's what I mean. You see that second outline of the brush stroke? The one on the wooden door frame here, with a line and a white arrow pointing back toward the area we painted over? That's what it chose as its sample area. Yup, instead of choosing any of the background area (the obvious choice), it decided to choose the door frame (ugh!), so the removal looks pretty bad. In the next step, we're going to move the sample area to a more reasonable spot.

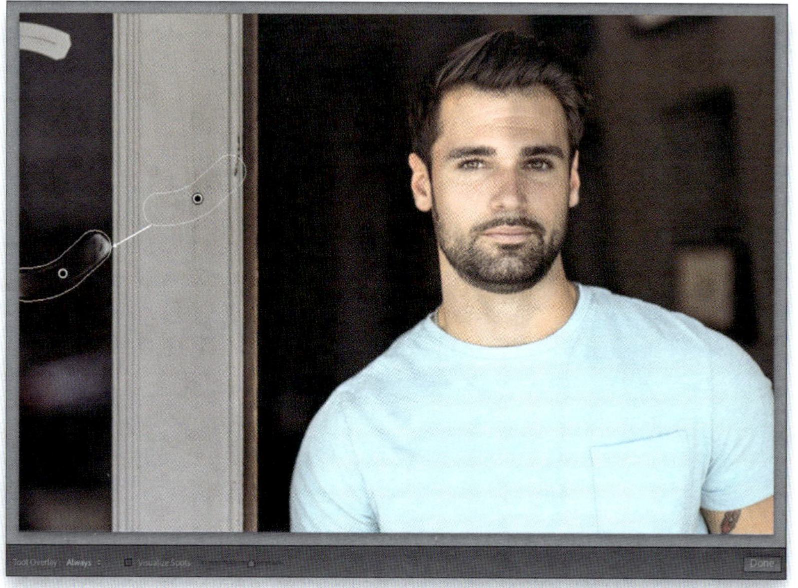

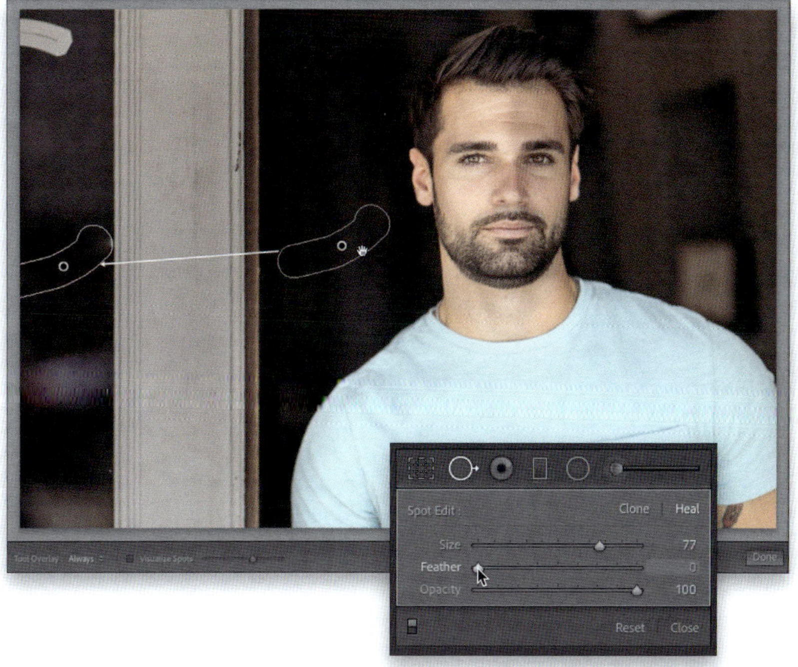

Step 14:

Click inside that second stroke outline (the one on the right) and drag it over to the right until it's on an area of background (as shown here). That helped a lot. If I see smudged edges around the ends (like you'll see when you try this yourself), it's because the amount of Feather (the softness setting for the edges of your painted area) is set pretty high. It should be set at around 50 or even 75, but in this case, it's hurting not helping, so we're going to lower it. Go to the Spot Healing tool's panel and lower the amount of Feather down to 0, and most of the smudging goes away. There's still a little smudge left, but we'll fix that in a minute. For now, just drag the second stroke outline over to the right, lower that Feather amount down to 0, and for the most part, the bottom part of the "C" is gone.

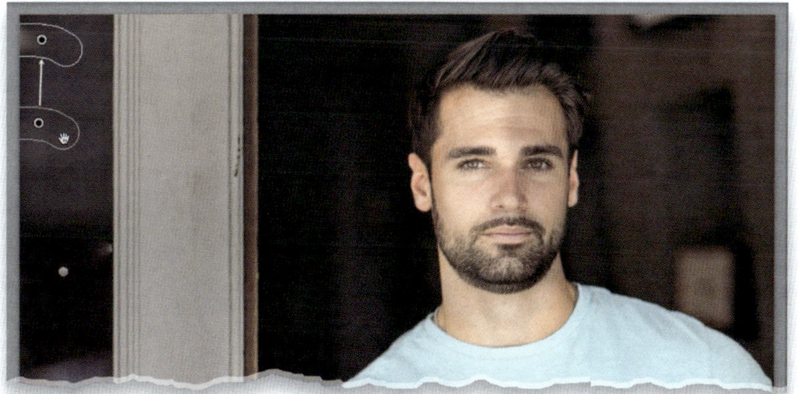

Step 15:

Now, let's paint over the top part of the "C" to get rid of it, and be prepared to drag the second stroke outline to a better spot, like I did here—dragging it right below the first stroke outline—because as expected, it chose a really bad spot on its own.

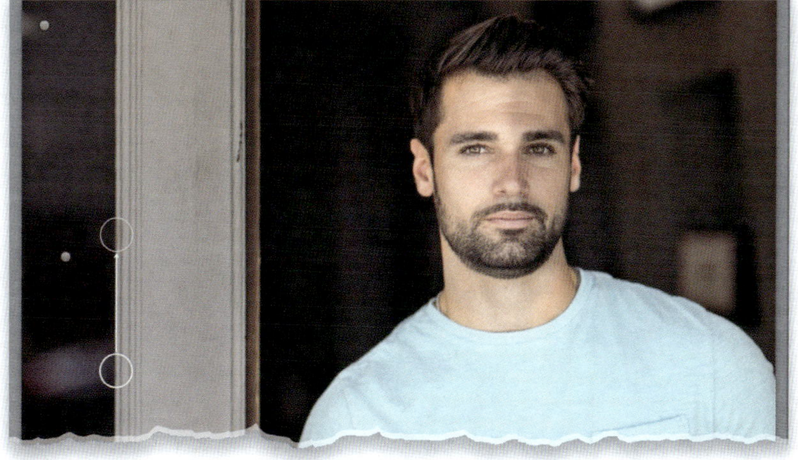

Step 16:

To fix that leftover smudge, click the Spot Removal tool once right over it, and then drag the second stroke outline straight down along that frame to get rid of it. When you're finished, click the Done button in the toolbar beneath the Preview area (only in Lightroom Classic). Okay, you can see what a difference it made getting rid of those two distracting "C" parts.

Step 17:

Now, for our finishing moves (**Point 7**). Let's darken the outside edges of the image all the way around (which will help draw attention away from them and toward our subject) by going to the Effects panel and dragging the Post-Crop Vignetting Amount slider (the Vignette slider in Lightroom cloud) to –11 (as shown here). Compare this image with one on the previous page and you can see what a nice, yet subtle change this made. Okay, just one more step.

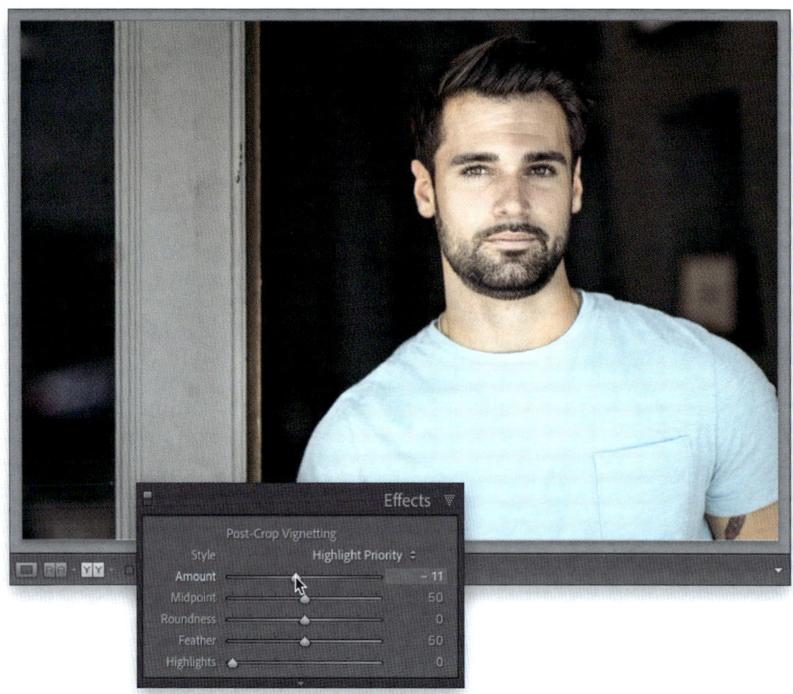

Step 18:

Next, let's sharpen the heck out of the image, so head over to the Detail panel. Shots of men look good with a lot of sharpening, so don't be afraid to crank that Amount slider (the Sharpening slider in Lightroom cloud). Here, I dragged it to 90, and I also dragged the Radius slider to 1.1 (this was taken with a 30-megapixel camera, so it can take a bit of a higher Radius). Also, I zoomed in to 100% to really see the effect of the sharpening (it's the only magnification in Lightroom where you can actually see how the sharpening affects the image. That's why you see a little warning sign—the exclamation point icon—in the top left of the Detail panel when you're applying sharpening at less than a 100% zoomed-in view [in Lightroom Classic]. If you click directly on that exclamation point, it actually zooms your image to 100% for you [in Lightroom cloud, choose **100%** from the Fit pop-up menu in the toolbar beneath the Preview area]). Once you're done sharpening, you can zoom back out to normal view by pressing **Command-–** (minus sign; **PC: Ctrl-–**).

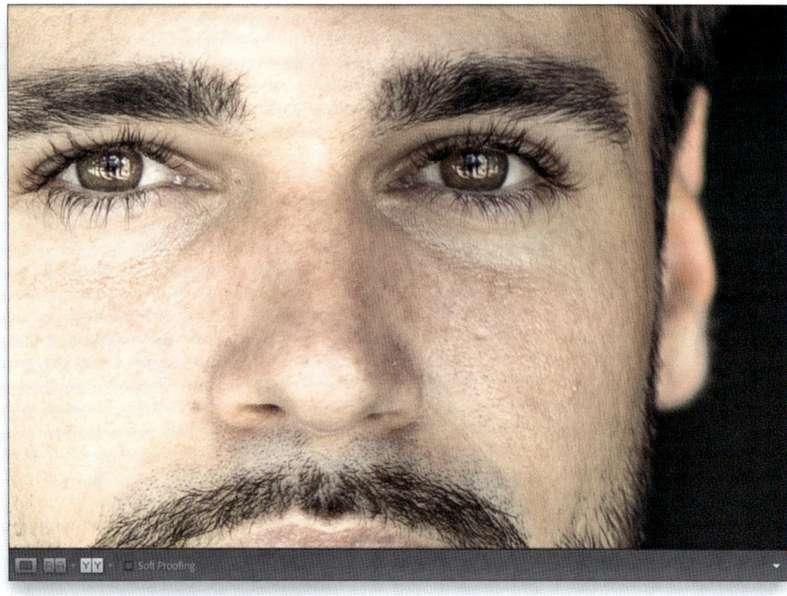

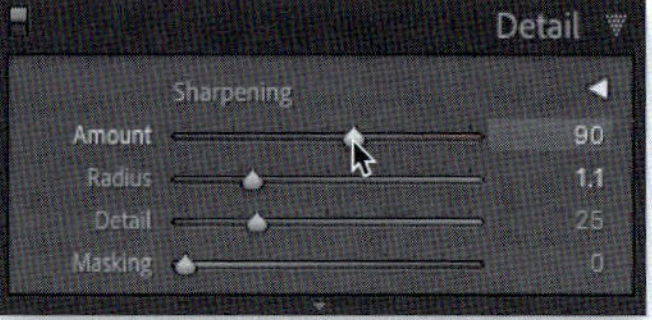

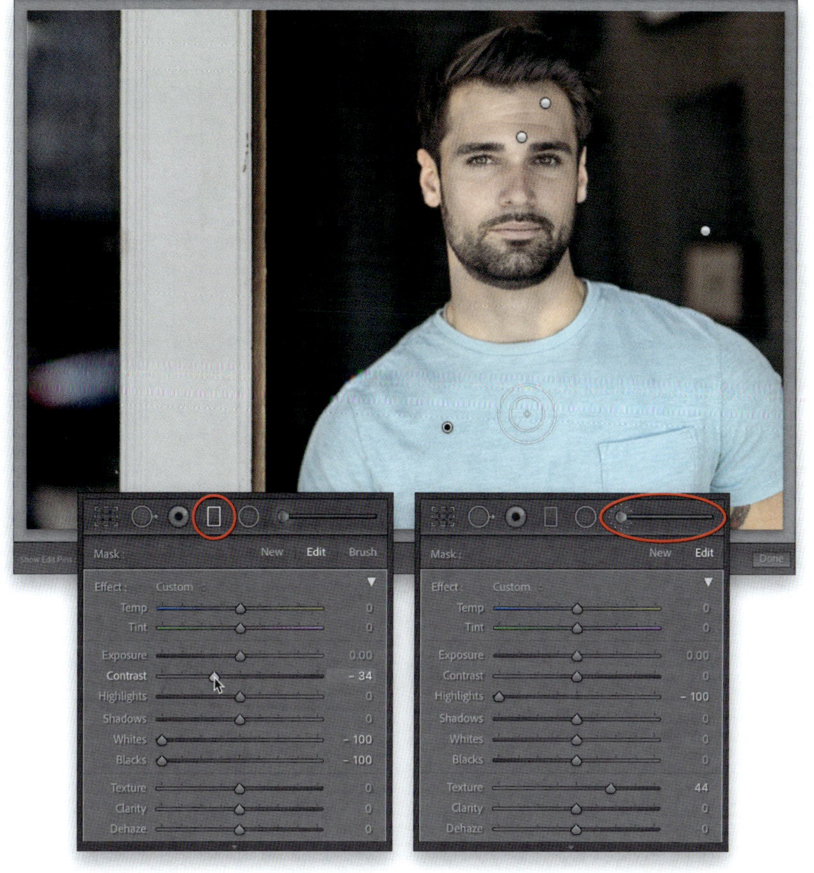

Step 19:

Giving this a last look, there are some things that don't look quite right (which is why we do a final look). First, the white door frame looks too gray (I think I used the wrong sliders for the job). So, get the Graduated Filter tool, again, and click on its Edit Pin to activate the gradient we drew. Double-click on Effect to reset all the sliders to zero, and then drag the Whites and Blacks sliders all the way to the left to –100, then lower the Contrast a bit (I played around with the sliders to find out which ones would work without making the frame look too gray and flat). Also, his shirt still looks too bright, so switch to the Adjustment Brush, zero out all the sliders, and then lower the Highlights to around –100 and paint over his shirt. While you're at it, raise the Texture to +44 to add more detail. Also, his skin needs a little more desaturating, so click on the Edit Pin right above his nose, and then lower the Saturation to –35. Next, click on the Edit Pin for the right side shadow on his face and increase the Exposure to –50, so it's more subtle. Ahhh, that's better.

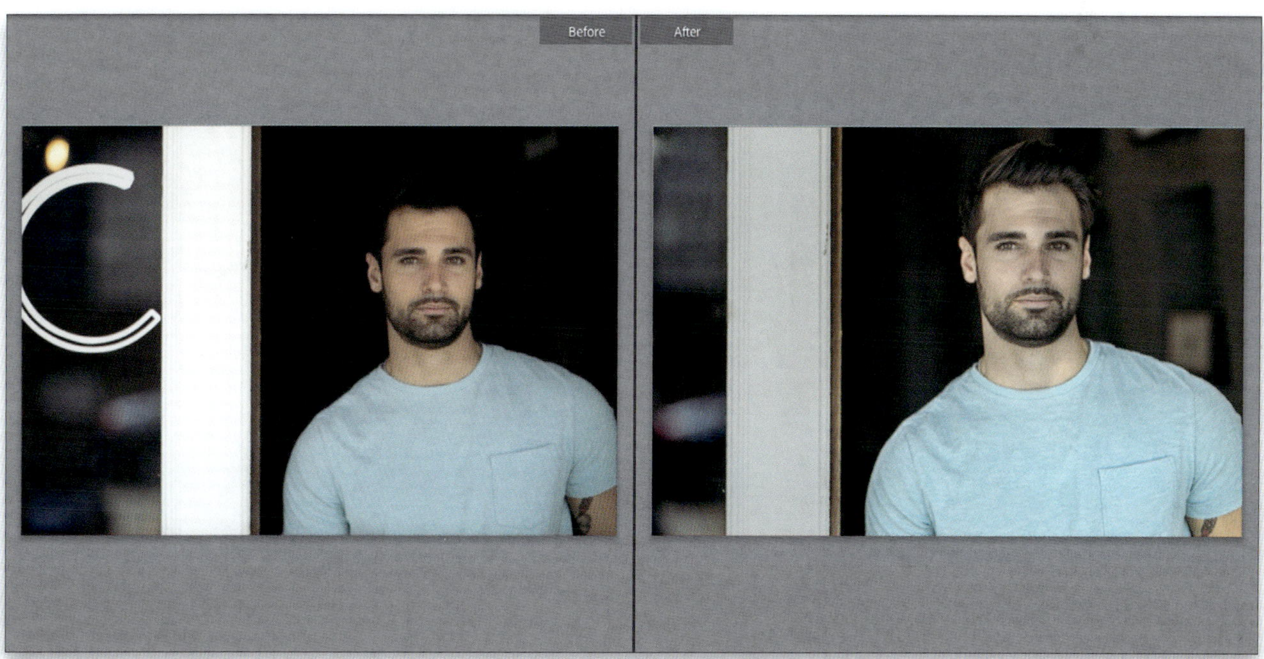

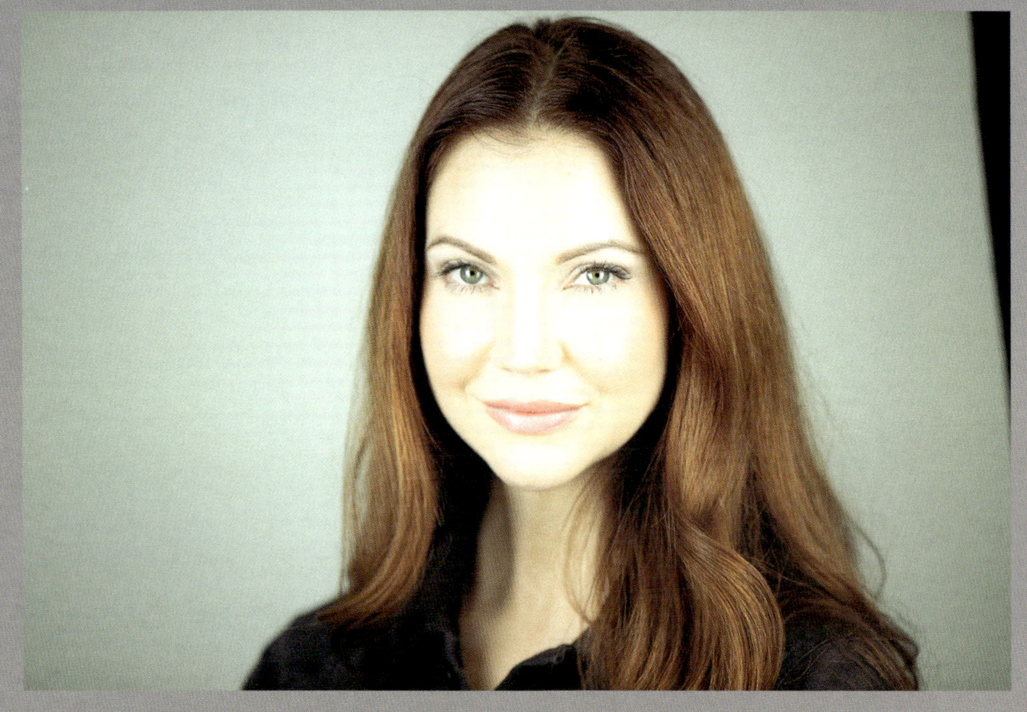
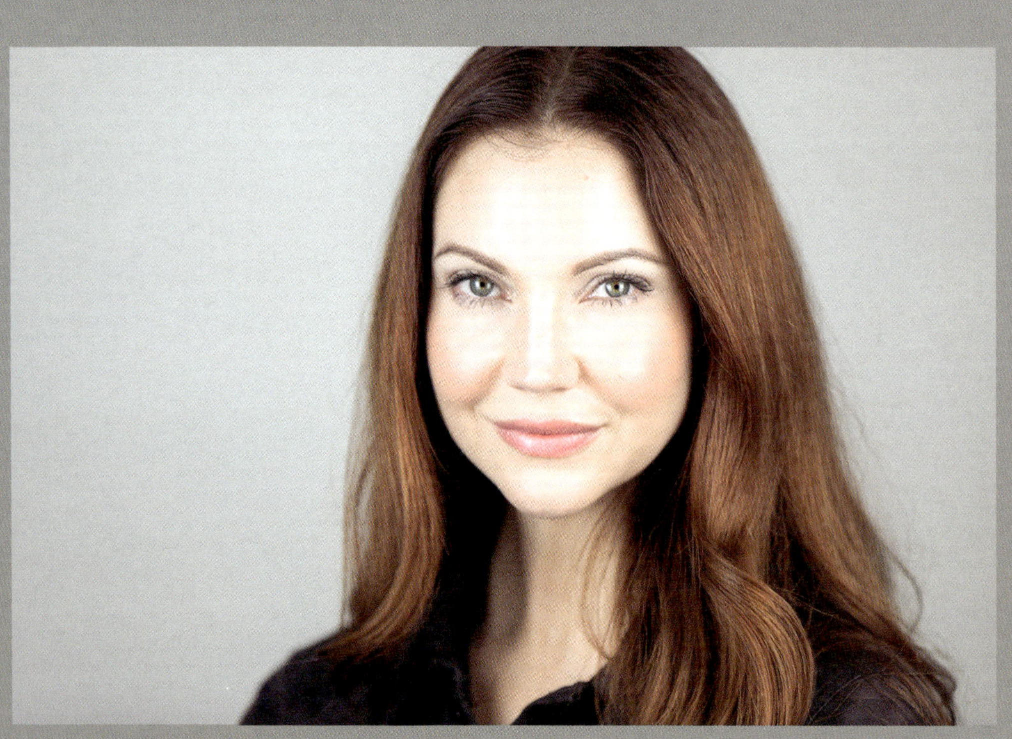
Adobe Photoshop
Lightroom Classic
Before
After
Before & After :
Soft Proofing

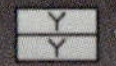
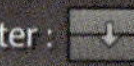
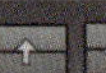
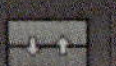
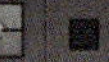

STUDIO PORTRAIT

1. Assigning a RAW Profile
2. Getting the Color Right
3. Expanding the Tonal Range
4. Dealing with Sensor Limitations
5. Painting with Light and Retouching
6. Fixing Lens Issues
7. Finishing Moves

In this lesson, we're going to make our main edits to one photo, and then we'll use the option to apply those exact same changes to other shots taken in the same location and lighting. We'll get to learn a few new things along the way, and still apply the system as we go.

THE STORY BEHIND THE SHOT:

This shot was taken in the studio on a 107"-wide roll of Savage Fashion Gray Seamless background paper. Although I actually shot this on gray paper, most of the time, I photograph people on a white seamless background because it's four colors in one. To make white seamless paper actually look white, you have to light the heck out of it. You can sometimes do it with just one flash, but often, you'll need two to get it solid white evenly, all the way across. If you don't light it, and your subject is 6 to 8 feet from the background, that white paper looks light gray (like the Fashion Gray you see here). If you move your subject 10 feet from the background, your main light won't hit that background too strongly, so you'll wind up with a dark gray. If you move your subject even farther away from that background, your main light won't make it back there at all, so that white background winds up looking black in the photo. So, that's four backgrounds for the price of one, but beyond just the price, you've got a lot of flexibility without having to interrupt the flow of your session to stop and change the paper, which is why I love shooting on white (even though I didn't in this case).

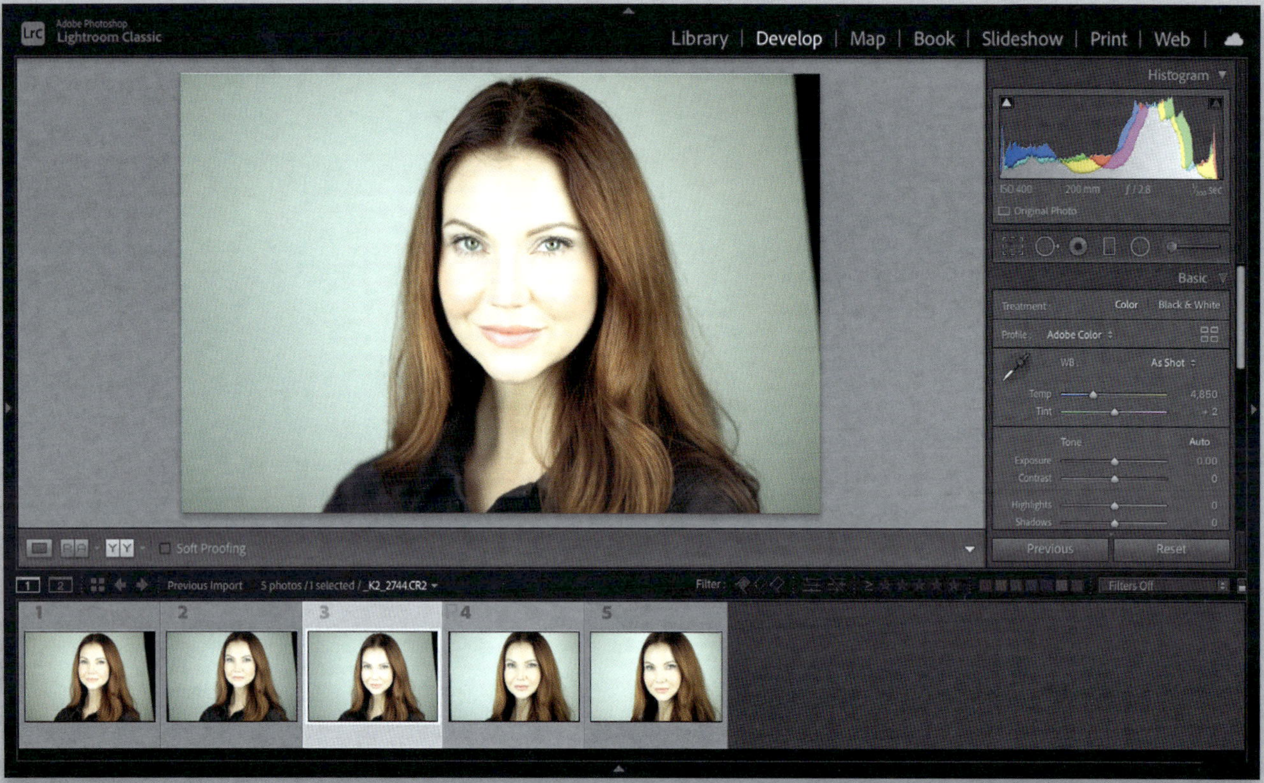

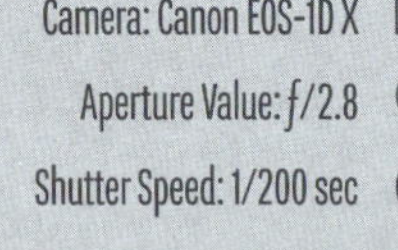

Camera: Canon EOS-1D X
Aperture Value: $f/2.8$
Shutter Speed: 1/200 sec
ISO: 400
Focal Length: 200mm

Step 01:

Here are our original RAW images—taken in the studio on a roll of gray seamless paper. Since all these photos were taken in the same lighting, we can fix one of them, and then apply the same fixes we did to that one photo to all the other photos from the same shoot (here, we're working with only five images, but it's just as easy to fix 50 or 500). There are two ways to do this: (1) You can fix one photo, copy its settings, and then select all the other photos and paste those settings onto them. It's literally just a few clicks. Or, (2) you can select all the images from the start, click on the one photo you want to edit (Adobe refers to this photo as the "most selected photo"), and any edits you make to that "most selected photo" are automatically applied to all the other selected images immediately. They both accomplish the same thing, but when you choose to copy-and-paste, it brings up a dialog where you can choose which things you want to apply. With the other method, it automatically applies anything you do to the one image to all the selected images—no pop-up dialog. So, again, they both accomplish the same thing, but the copy-and-paste version gives you more options (like, which edits to ignore if you want), so we're going to go with option #1 here.

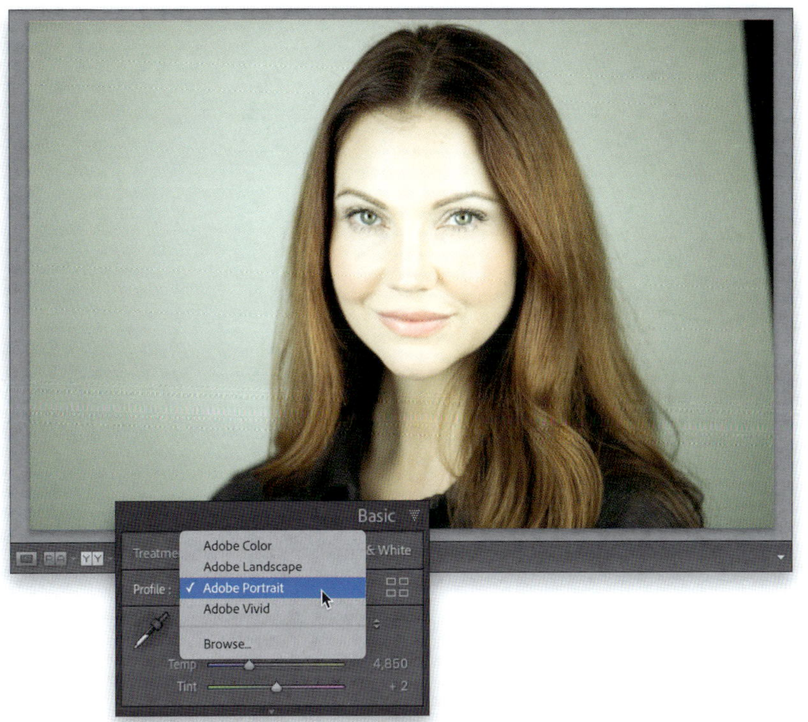

Step 02:

Generally, **Point 1** in the 7-Point System is to go to the Develop module's Basic panel (the Edit panel in Lightroom cloud) and choose a better RAW profile as our starting point. So, this is pretty straight-forward since we're working on a por-trait—just choose **Adobe Portrait** from the Profile pop-up menu (as shown here). This actually gave us a bit of a better starting point than it did in the portrait in Lesson 06, so we're off and running.

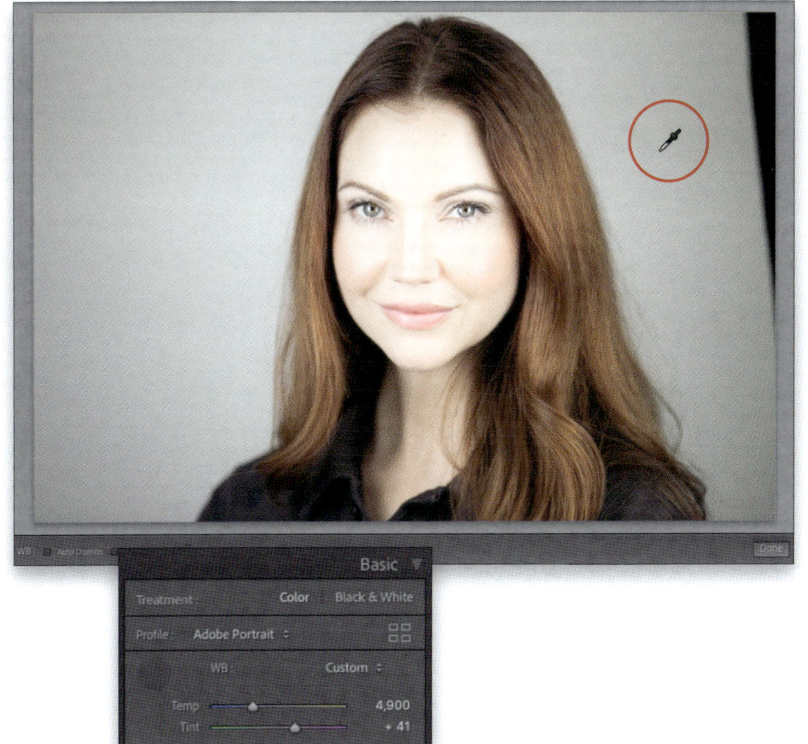

Step 03:

The overall color is way off on this shot, so let's fix that now (**Point 2** of the system). Since there is a neutral color background, this should be easy. Get the White Balance Selector tool (**W**; the eyedropper) from the top of the Basic panel (the Color panel in Lightroom cloud) and simply click it once on the gray background (as shown here), and your white balance is set. You can click in a few different areas on that gray background (they'll probably look a bit different based on how light or dark the area is), so just keep clicking until you find an area you like. In person, our subject is very fair-skinned, but if you want her skin tone to be a bit warmer, you can drag the Temp slider to the right (I didn't do that here, but that's an option you might consider, depending on your subject).

Step 04:

Time to get our Exposure set (**Point 3**), so let's start by expanding our tonal range. In the Basic panel (the Light panel in Lightroom cloud), Shift-double-click on the word "Whites," and then Shift-double-click on the word "Blacks." That will bump up the Whites to +30 and set the Blacks to –4. Our last part of this triangle is to adjust the Exposure amount if we now feel the image is either a bit too bright or too dark. This looks a bit too bright, so let's pull back the Exposure a little—drag the slider to –0.35 (about 1/3 of a stop).

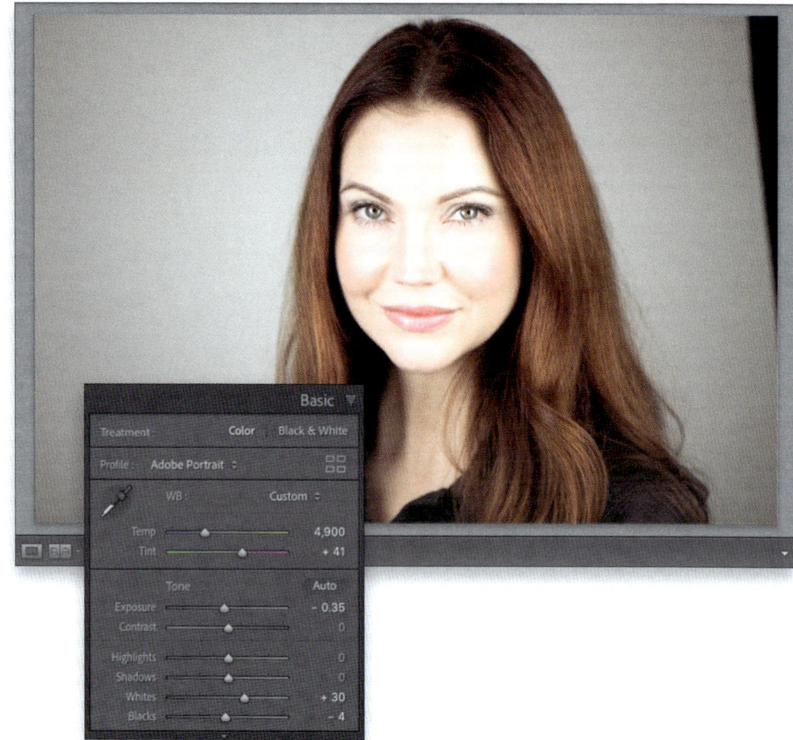

Step 05:

The overall exposure looks pretty good (her hair, her blouse, the background), but I think her face still looks a bit too bright, so let's back the Highlights off a bit, so they match the tonal balance of the rest of image (**Point 4**). Drag the Highlights slider over to the left until they don't look so bright (here, I dragged it over to –31). Ahhhh, that's better. Okay, I think we have a good base exposure and we fixed our problem (our highlights were too bright).

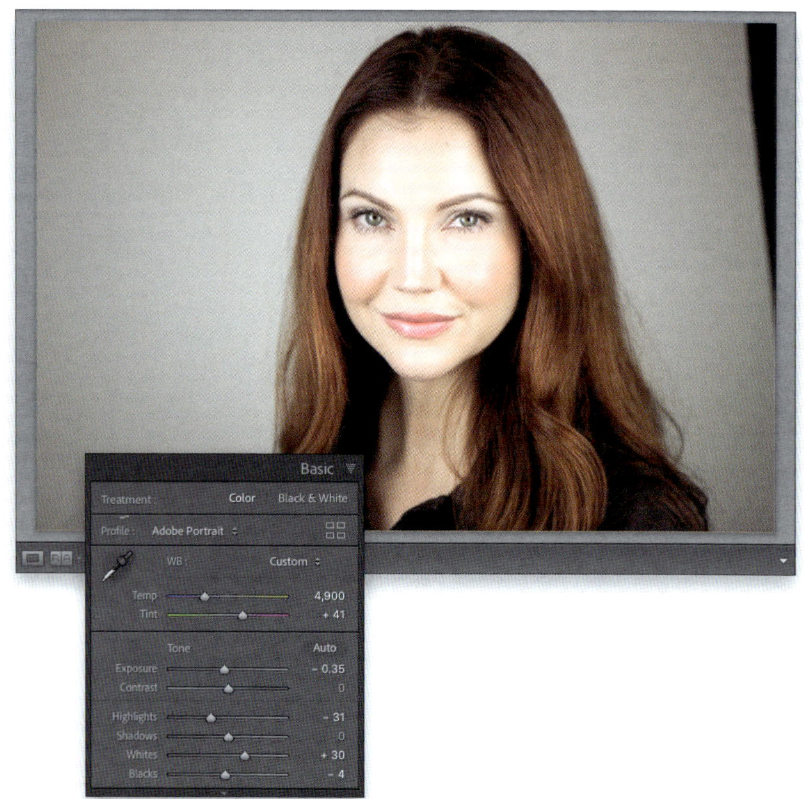

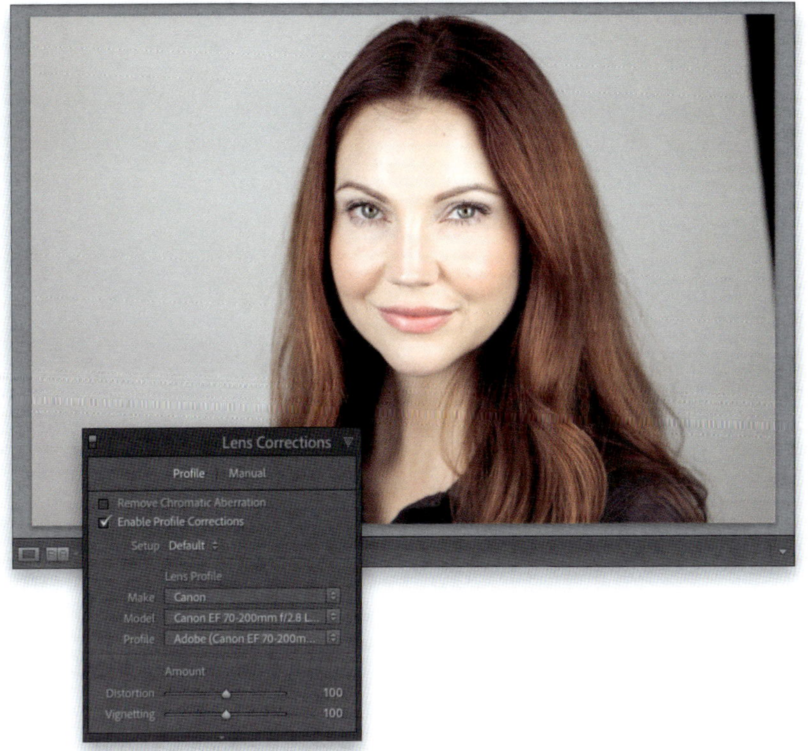

Step 06:

You can see some darkening in the corners (caused by the lens, a 70–200mm f/2.8, one of my go-to lenses for portraits), and a little lens distortion as well, so let's deal with those (and jump over to **Point 6** in the system). Go to the Lens Corrections panel (the Optics panel in Lightroom cloud) and turn on the Enable Profile (Lens) Corrections checkbox. That did a really good job of fixing the distortion and the corner darkening. In fact, the whole background looks brighter now (there was some serious vignetting going on in those corners). Toggle the Enable Profile (Lens) Corrections checkbox on/off a few times and you'll see what I mean on both.

Step 07:

The rest of the edits we need to make are local, like working on her eyes, skin softening, cropping away that black gap in the top-right corner, or adding highlights to her hair. Unless she didn't move her head at all (not even a little) during the entire shoot, we need to stop at this point, copy all the changes we've made so far, and paste them onto all the other similar photos, and then we can come back and pick up our editing on this particular image. This is what Lightroom calls Synchronize, but we get to choose which of the things we've done that we want to copy to the other photos. First, go down to the Filmstrip and select the other images from this shoot that we want to have the same edits we applied to that initial photo. Just press-and-hold the Command (PC: Ctrl) key, and click on all the other photos from the shoot. Now, press **Command-Shift-S (PC: Ctrl-Shift-S)** to bring up the Synchronize Settings dialog. We can turn off any settings we don't want copied over, or click the Check None button to turn them all off, and then turn on the checkboxes for the things we did edit (as seen here. Be sure to turn on the Process Version checkbox to get the best results), so it copies those changes to our other images. When you're done, hit the Synchronize button.

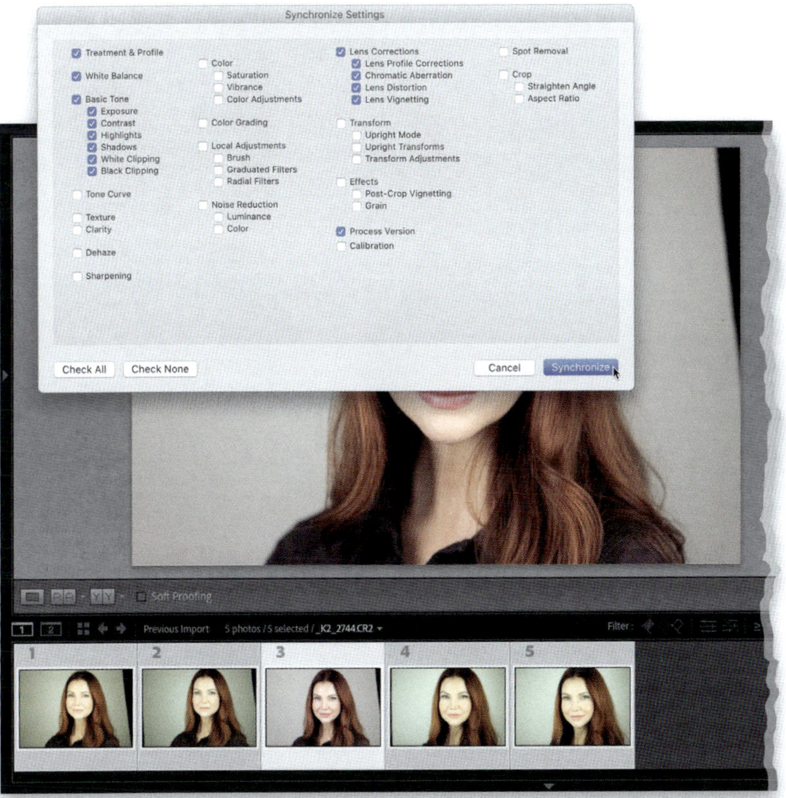

Step 08:

Take a look at those selected images down in the Filmstrip—the fixes we applied to that initial image are all now visible in the rest of the images. Once you're done, press **Command-D (PC: Ctrl-D)** to deselect all the images, and then click on the one you want to edit. Let's choose a different image to work on from this point. *Note:* The Synchronize feature isn't available in Lightroom cloud. Instead, you'll press **Command-Shift-C (PC: Ctrl-Shift-C)** to open the Copy Settings dialog, choose the settings you want to copy, select the other photos, and then press **Command-Shift-V (PC: Ctrl-Shift-V)** to paste those settings onto the selected photos.

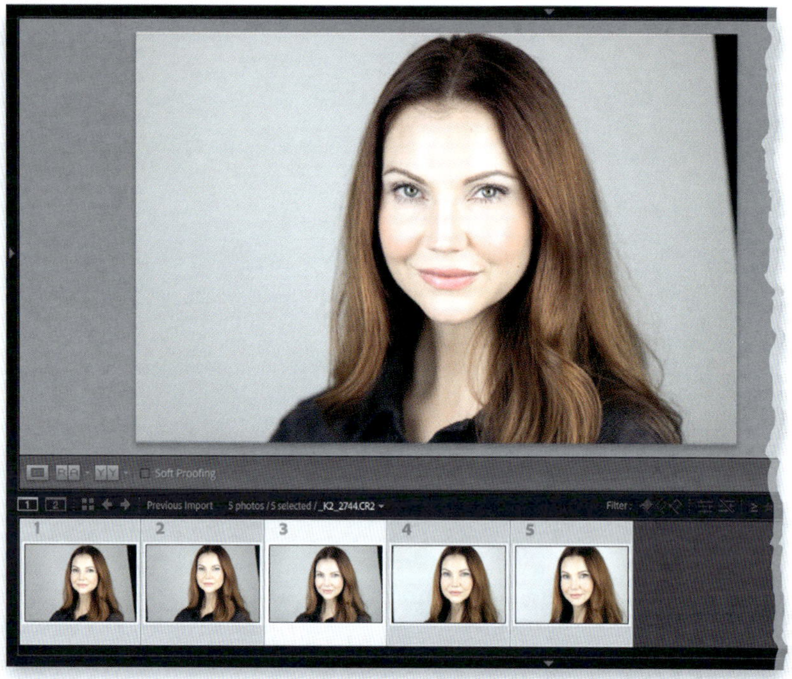

Step 09:

Let's select the second image and deal with those black areas up in the top-right and lower-left corners where the seamless paper ends. We could pop over to Photoshop and fix them easily (you would just select those areas, use Content-Aware Fill, and it would seamlessly fill them with the gray paper background), but to fix it here in Lightroom, we'll have to crop away those areas. So, get the Crop Overlay tool **(R)** from the toolbox beneath the histogram (the Crop & Rotate tool **[C]** from the toolbox on the right in Lightroom cloud), then drag the top-right and lower-left corners diagonally inward until those black areas fall outside the crop, and then hit the **Return (PC: Enter) key** to lock in your crop. You might be thinking "Why didn't we do this before we applied all those edits to the other images?" It's because when I shot these, sometimes I zoomed in or out (using my 70–200mm) or I moved forward or backward during the session. So, if we applied the exact same crop to all the images, in some frames, way too much of her head would be cropped off or the black areas would still be visible.

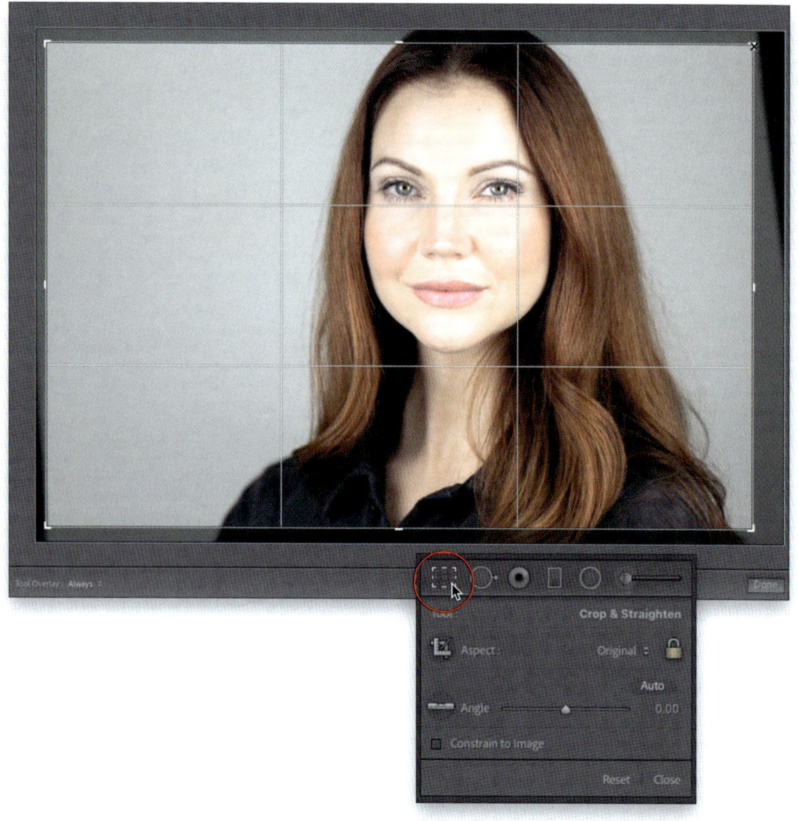

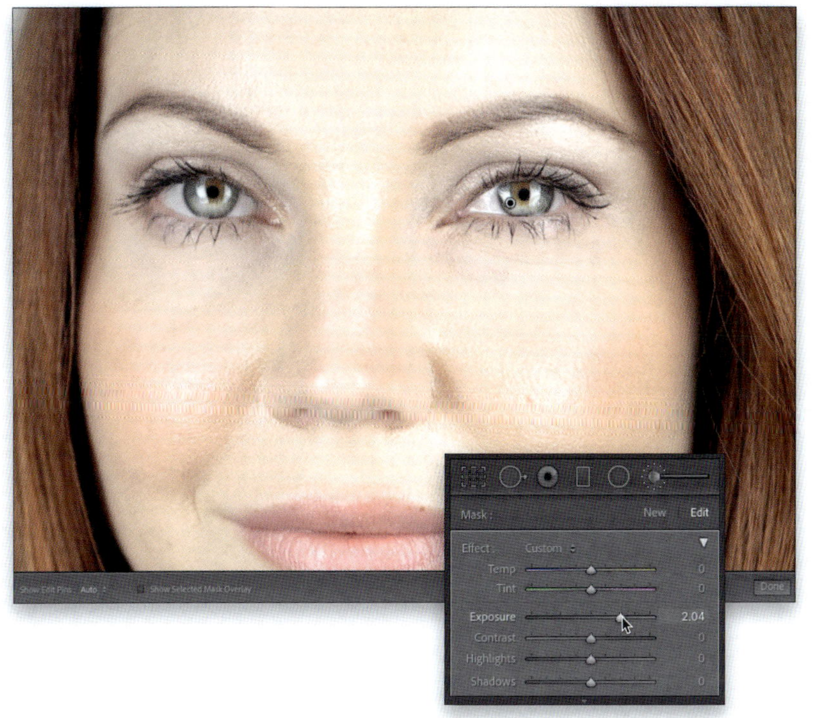

Step 10:

Next, let's jump back to **Point 5** by zooming in tighter on her eyes (press **Command-+** [plus sign; **PC: Ctrl-+**]). Get the Adjustment Brush **(K)** from the toolbox beneath the histogram (the Brush tool **[B]** from the toolbox on the right in Lightroom cloud) and shrink your brush size a bunch by pressing the **[(left bracket) key** on your keyboard. Double-click on Effect to reset your sliders to zero (this happens by default in Lightroom cloud), then increase your Exposure by around 2 stops. Now, paint over the bottom half of both of her irises (just the bottom halves). This "eye kicker" helps brighten the eyes and helps make them look like they sparkle. *Note:* If it looks a little too harsh, adjust your Feather setting to 100 and Flow setting to 75 in the brush settings section of the panel.

Step 11:

Now that we've brightened the bottom halves of her irises, we can add other things to her eyes, as well. Click on New at the top of the panel (click on the + [plus sign] in Lightroom cloud), then double-click on Effect to reset all the sliders to zero. Crank up the Contrast amount (here, I cranked it up big time, to 76), and let's also add just a bit of texture and detail by increasing the Texture slider (to 33) and Clarity slider (to 9). Lastly, go down a little further in the panel and sharpen the eyes by increasing the Sharpness amount (here, I increased it to 32), and then paint over her entire irises. How am I coming up with these numbers? This is going to sound really simplistic, but I keep dragging a slider for as long as it looks good. If it starts to look bad, I stop and backtrack a bit. Don't overthink it.

Step 12:

Next, let's scroll up to her forehead and remove the blemish up there and that stray hair. Get the Spot Removal tool (**Q**; the Healing Brush **[H]** in Lightroom cloud) from the toolbox, make your brush size just a little larger than the blemish itself (as shown here), and then just click it once on the blemish. There's so much skin in this area to choose from that it will probably do a good job of choosing a reasonable area of clean skin to use to fix this blemish.

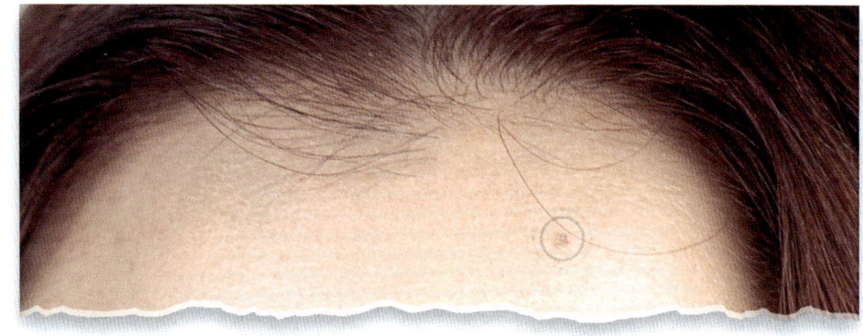

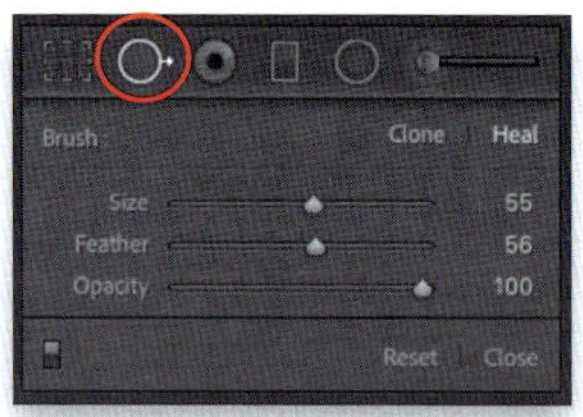

Step 13:

Yup, it worked well this time, nicely removing that blemish altogether. Now, shrink your brush size down to where it's just a bit larger than that stray hair and paint right over the hair (as shown here—it paints the stroke in solid white so you can clearly see where you're painting). When you release your mouse button, it will do a pretty good job of getting rid of that stray hair, as well.

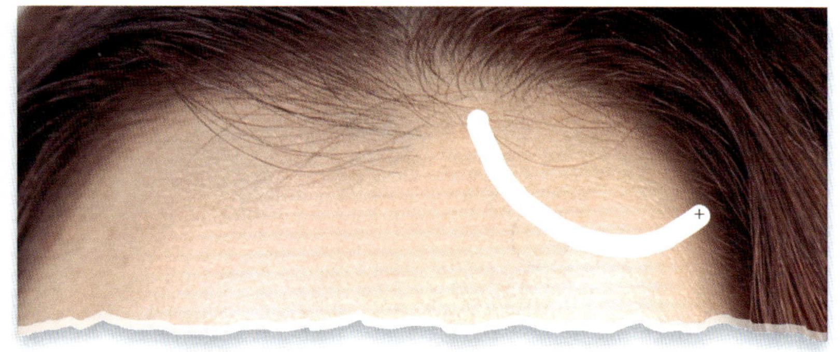

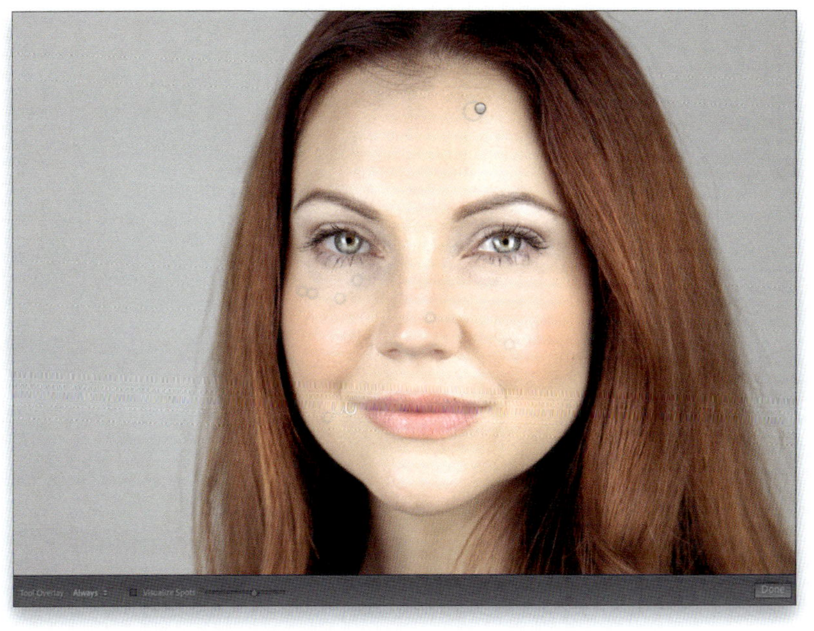

Step 14:

Move around the image and use the same one-click technique to get rid of any other blemishes that need to be dealt with. *TIP*: If there's something on your subject that shouldn't be removed during retouching (like a mole or a scar that is a characteristic of their face, or maybe just wrinkles), that they just wouldn't look like themselves without (or, at the very least, it would be obvious to people who know them that they've been retouched), you can reduce instead of remove. Just take the Spot Removal tool and remove the entire mole (scar, etc.), then in the tool's panel, lower the Opacity. The Opacity slider kinda works like "undo on a slider," and as you drag it to the left, part of the mole starts to come back. So, this way, that facial feature is still there, but not as intense (these things stand out more in a still photo than in real life, so we try to make them look as much like they did in person and this helps a lot).

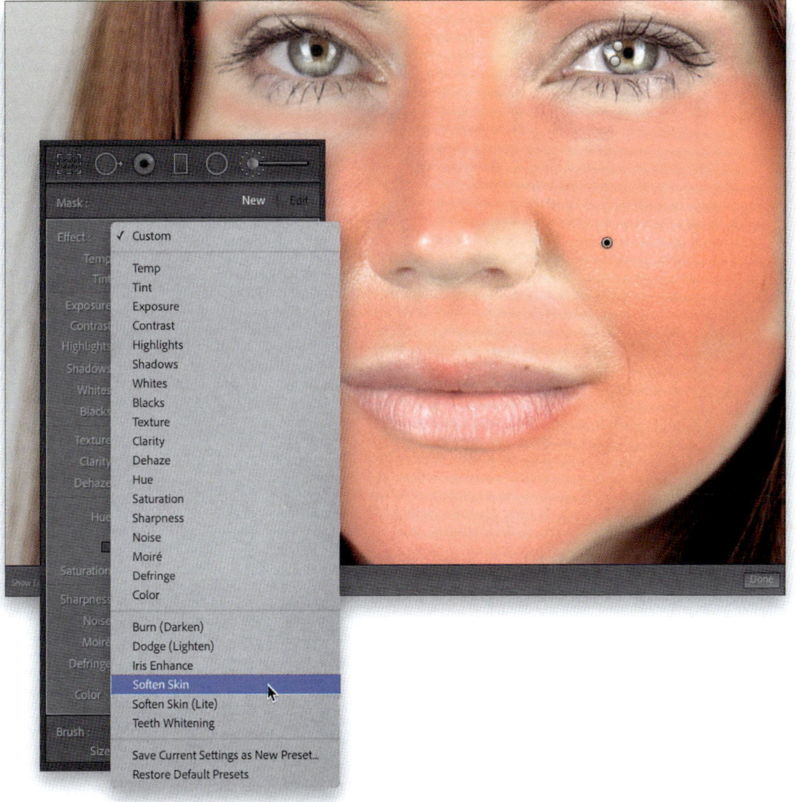

Step 15:

Now, get the Adjustment Brush again, and from the Effect pop-up menu at the top of the panel, choose **Soften Skin** (we're not using this to soften her skin as it's really good already, but it often helps keep your subject's face from looking patchy. *Note:* Lightroom cloud doesn't have brush Effect presets, but you can use the same settings by simply dragging the Clarity slider to –100, then increasing the Sharpness slider to 25, and leaving all the other sliders set to 0). Now, start painting over her skin, being careful not to paint over detail areas that shouldn't be softened, like her eyes, eyebrows, lips, the edges of her nostrils, her hair, etc. To make this easier to see (and so you don't miss any areas), press the letter **O** on your keyboard (press it twice in Lightroom cloud) and the areas you're painting over will appear in a red tint (as seen here). Make sure the Auto Mask checkbox is turned off, the Flow is set to 100, and shrink the brush size when painting in tight areas, like her eyelids and right above her lips.

Step 16:

When you're done, press the O key again to hide the mask and now you can see how your skin softening looks. If it looks like it's too much, you can actually reduce the effect. Go to the top of the tool's panel, click on the down-facing triangle to the right of Soften Skin, and all the sliders will tuck out of sight and you'll just see a single Amount slider. This is (you guessed it) undo on a slider, so let's back the amount of softening off enough so the tones on her face look smooth, but without her face looking blurry (too much softening is probably the most common retouching mistake). Since this Amount slider doesn't exist in Lightroom cloud, you'll have to manually drag the Clarity slider back to the right, and the Sharpness slider back to the left.

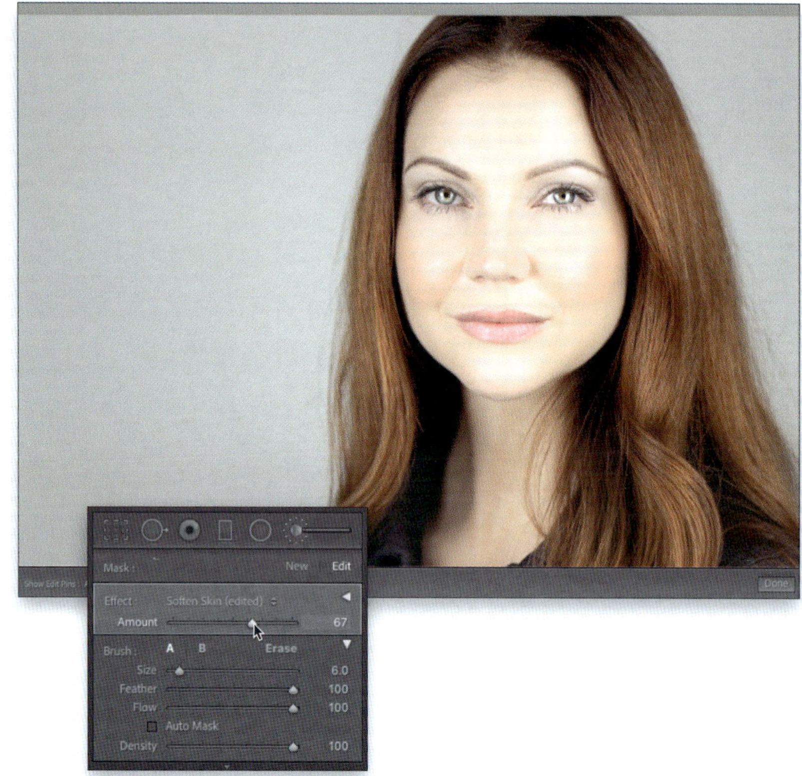

Step 17:

Next, let's accentuate the highlights in her hair. Click on New at the top of the panel (click on the + [plus sign] in Lightroom cloud), then double-click on Effect to reset all the sliders to zero. Increase the Exposure amount by around a half a stop (to 0.50), make your brush size pretty large (like the one seen here), and paint over highlight areas in her hair (and add some where you think they're missing). It's okay to paint brighter than you think it should be because it makes it easier to see where you're painting. After you're done, drag the Exposure slider back to the left to dial in just the right amount (here, I dragged it back to just 0.35).

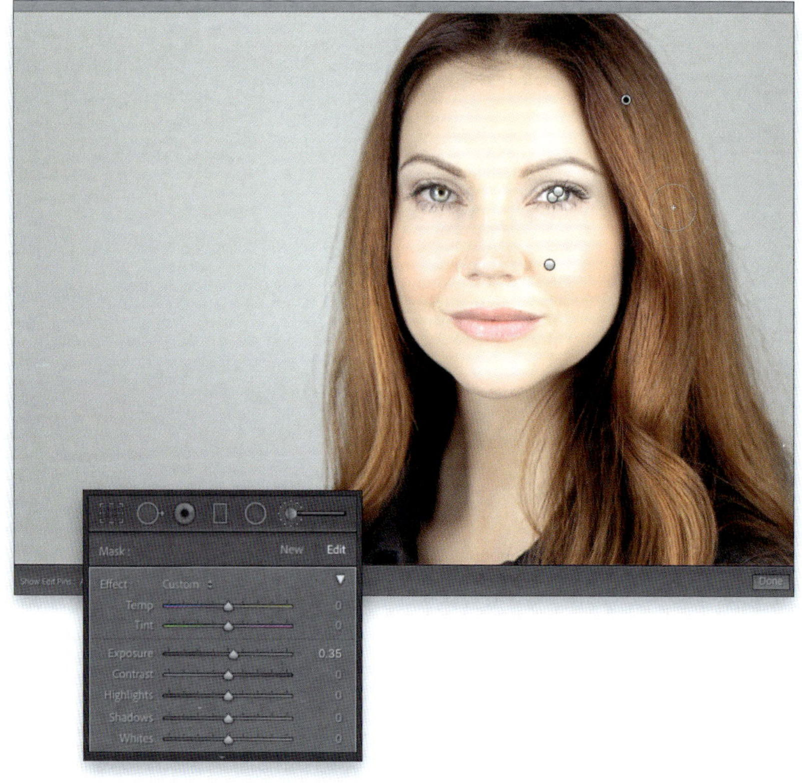

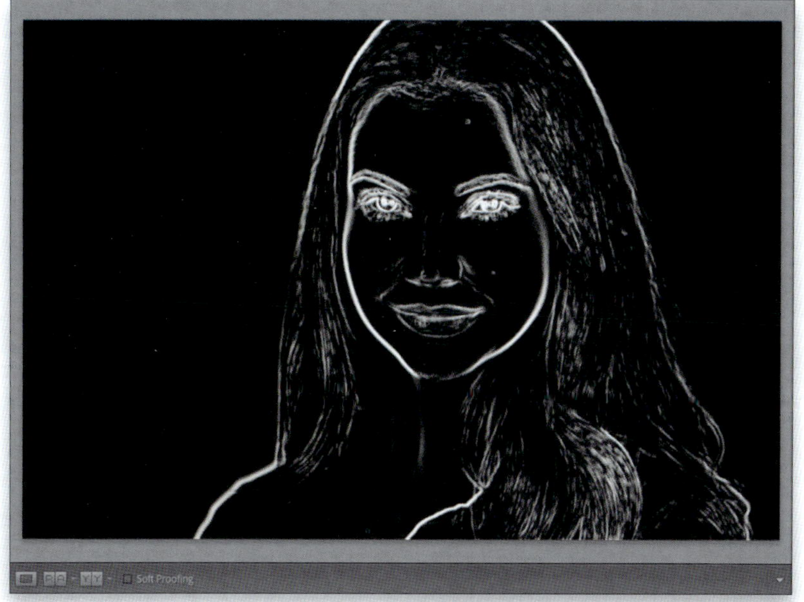

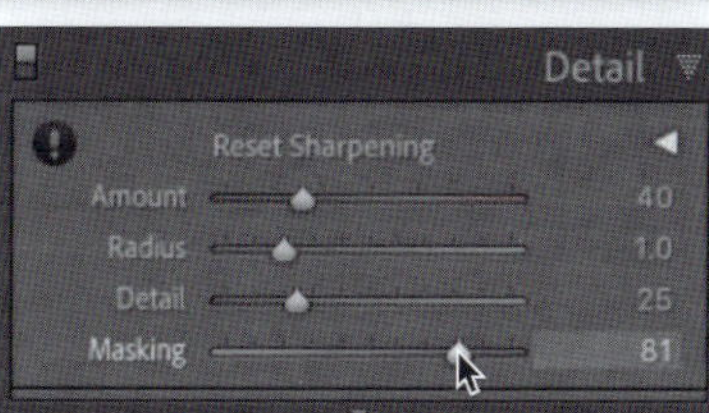

Step 18:

Let's wrap up with **Point 7** and some sharpening. Go to the Detail panel and crank up the Amount to around 40. With men, we sharpen the heck out of them, but with women and children, we're careful not to sharpen their skin (after all, we don't want their pores too sharp and their skin looking craggy). Instead, we want to sharpen their detail areas (eyes, eyebrows, hair, lips, nostril area, edges of the face, etc.), while avoiding sharpening their skin, and the Masking slider will do this for us. Press-and-hold the Option (PC: Alt) key, then click-and-hold on the Masking slider knob. The screen turns solid white, letting you know that everything in the photo is being sharpened. With that key still held down, drag the slider to the right and parts of the image start to turn black. Anything in black is no longer being sharpened, and the farther you drag to the right, the more of those areas are protected (only areas in white are now being sharpened, and look, it's just those areas we want sharpened—her skin is left untouched).

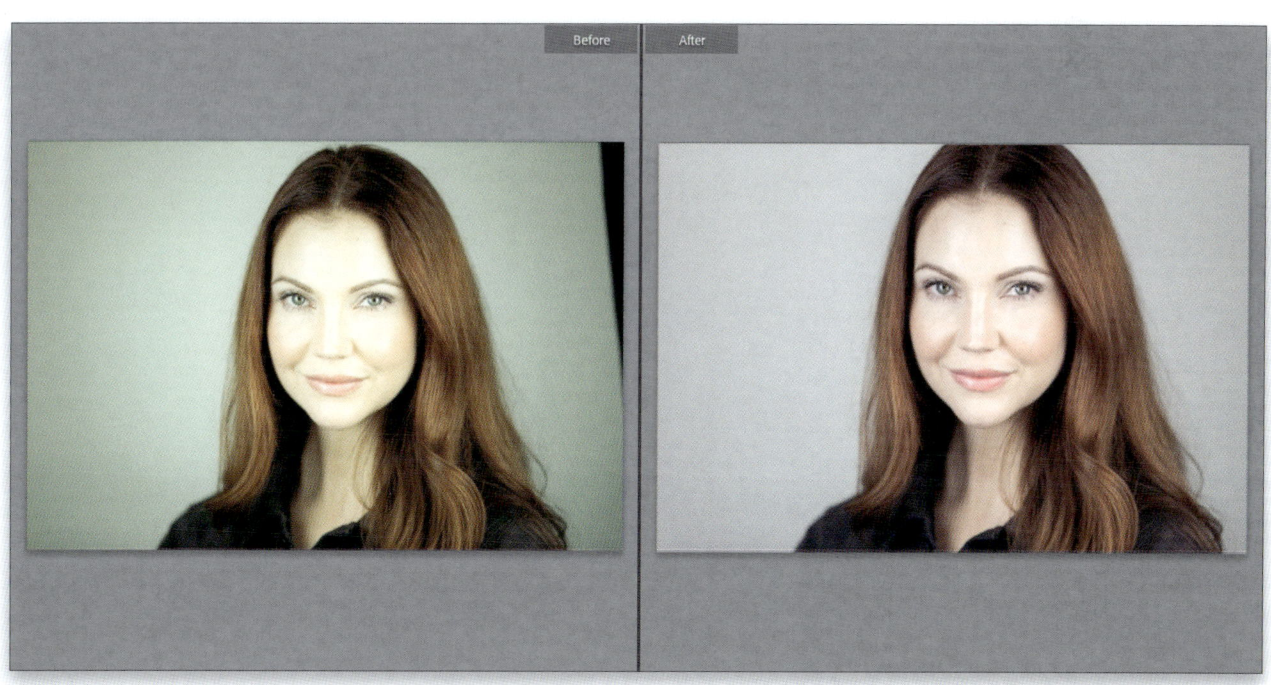

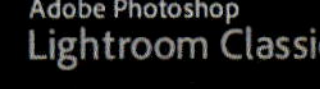

Adobe Photoshop
Lightroom Classic

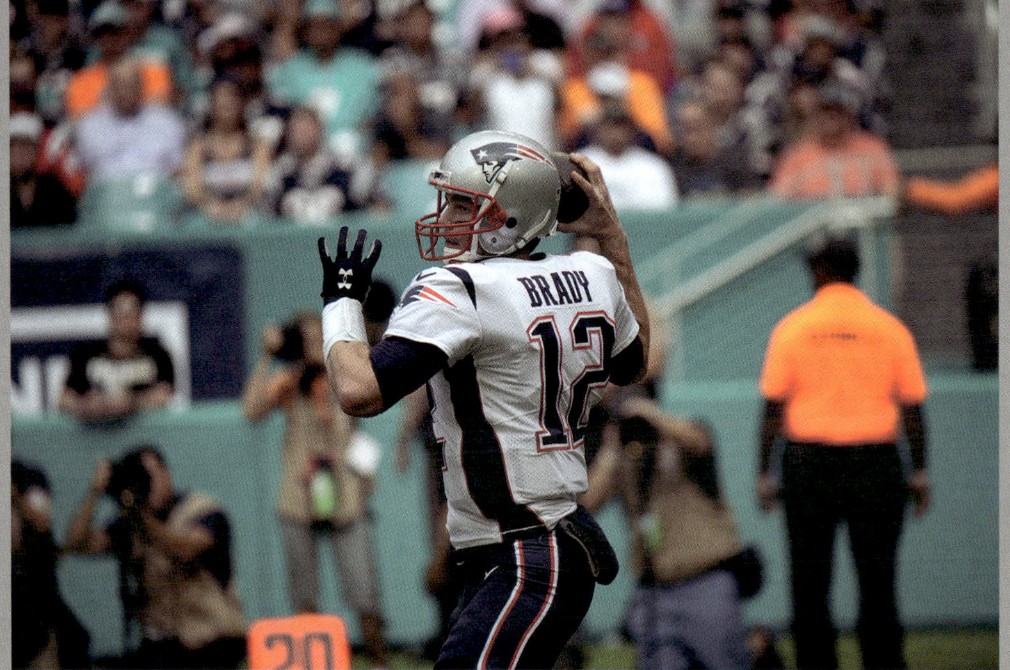

BRADY
12

Before
After

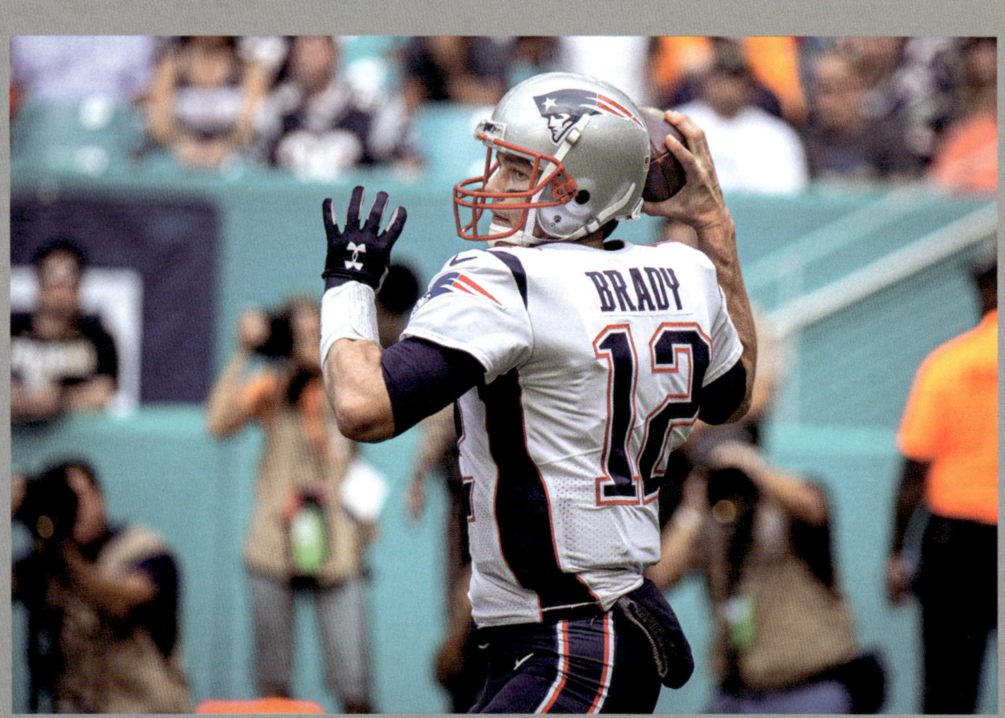

BRADY
12

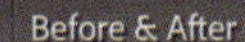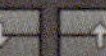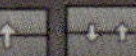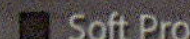

Adobe Photoshop
Before & After :
Soft Proofing

LESSON 08

SPORTS ACTION

1. Assigning a RAW Profile
2. Getting the Color Right
3. Expanding the Tonal Range
4. Dealing with Sensor Limitations
5. Painting with Light and Retouching
6. Fixing Lens Issues
7. Finishing Moves

This time we're working on a sports photo. I had to do a little digging to find a shot in RAW format, as I shoot most of my sports images in JPEG format rather than RAW (for reasons just related to shooting sports, and shooting for a newswire or team). *Note:* We're moving through this edit as if you're shooting to hang a sports print in your home or office. This is not for journalists covering sports because we do things for personal images that we would not do when covering sports for a news outlet.

THE STORY BEHIND THE SHOT:

I spent about six years shooting for a sports news wire service, but I would sometimes get a chance to shoot for the teams themselves. This shot was taken from the sidelines of an NFL Miami Dolphins/New England Patriots game I covered for the Dolphins down in Miami (at Hard Rock Stadium). This was taken the season before Tom Brady left the Patriots and came to my home town of Tampa to take our hapless Bucs from a team incapable of

winning even a Wild Card playoff game in the last 20-something years to immediate Super Bowl champions, all in one year, for which Tom Brady will always be a beloved hero in the hearts and minds of Tampa Bay residents (even though we hated him with the passion of a thousand burning suns when he was with the Patriots, but that's only because they always won everything, all the time. Whew. There. I said it).

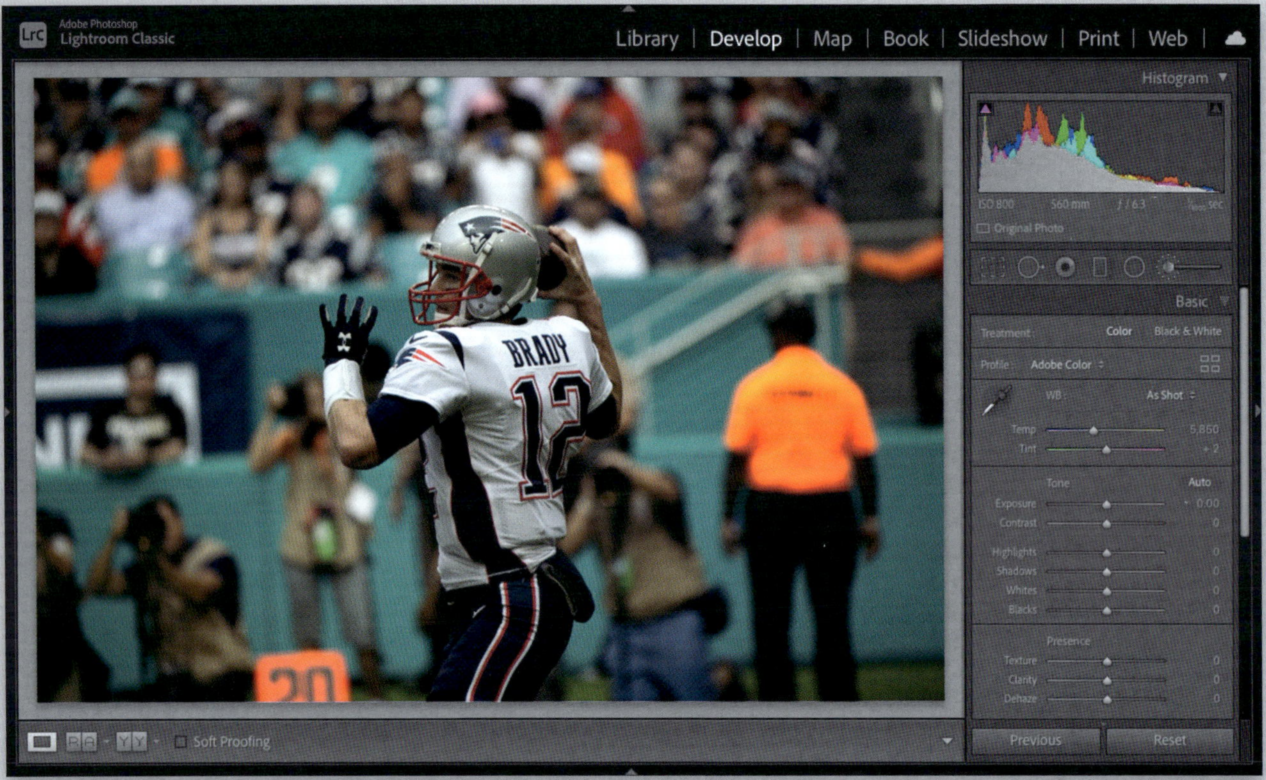

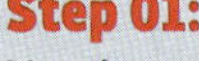

Step 01:

Here's our original RAW image right out of the camera. Let's give it a quick evaluation and ask the question, "What do we wish were different?" Well, the color is off quite a bit (it has a greenish tint), the image is crooked (ack!), it's underexposed and flat, it needs to be cropped in much tighter, and it's just pretty lame all the way around. Okay, let's go to work.

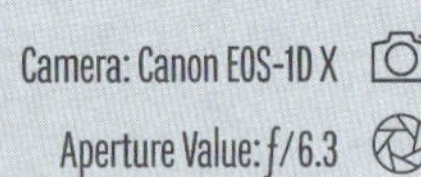

Camera: Canon EOS-1D X
Aperture Value: *f*/6.3
Shutter Speed: 1/1000 sec
ISO: 800
Focal Length: 560mm

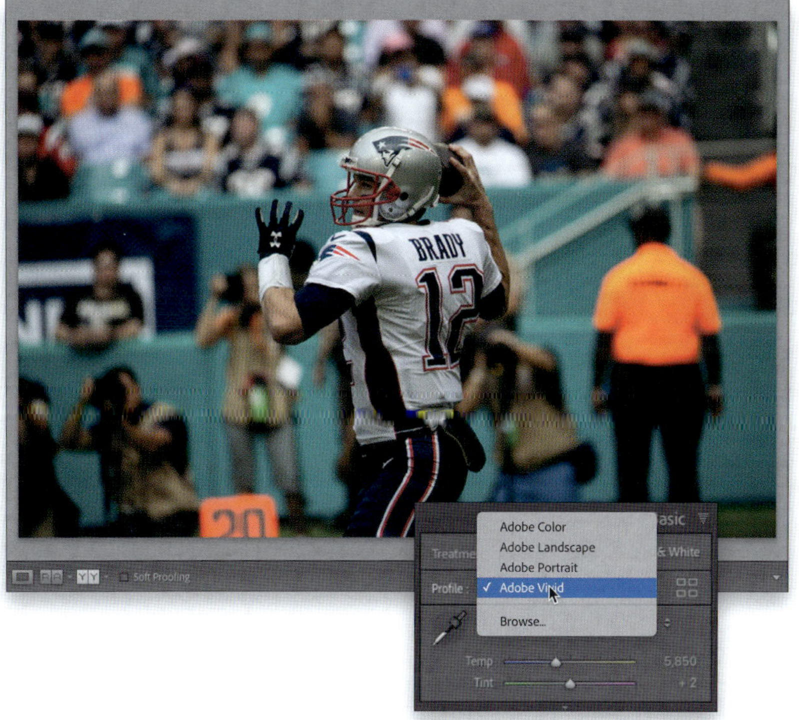

Step 02:

Generally, **Point 1** is going to the Develop module's Basic panel (the Edit panel in Lightroom cloud) and choosing a better RAW profile as our starting point. In this case, I tried Adobe Color, Adobe Landscape, and Adobe Vivid, and Adobe Vivid looked the best (Adobe Color is rarely the best looking choice—it's kind of a "meh" look, which Adobe engineers would probably argue is because it's the most accurate to what your camera's sensor captured without adding any "juice" to the look to make it look better. Frankly, I'd like it to look better). So, choose **Adobe Vivid** from the Profile pop-up menu and you'll see what a difference it makes in the contrast and color (especially in the teal in the background).

Step 03:

Cropping is a big part of sports photography because we can't always get in as tight as we'd like (this was shot with a 200–400mm f/4 lens with a tele-extender—still not nearly tight enough). In a team sport like football, cropping can help focus attention on the player you want the focus on, while cropping away the myriad distractions on the field (refs, other photographers, ads, and players that aren't a part of the action). Luckily, we can crop and straighten at the same time. Get the Crop Overlay tool **(R)** from the toolbox beneath the histogram (the Crop & Rotate tool **[C]** from the toolbox on the right in Lightroom cloud), and click-and-drag in the corners so you're getting as tight on Mr. Brady (Sir Brady? Lord Brady? King Brady?) as you can without cutting off anything important, while leaving room in front of him (a composition trick for things that are moving or can move). Once your crop is about right, move your cursor just outside the cropping border and click-and-drag up/down to rotate the crop until the image looks straight. Press **Return (PC: Enter)** to lock in your crop.

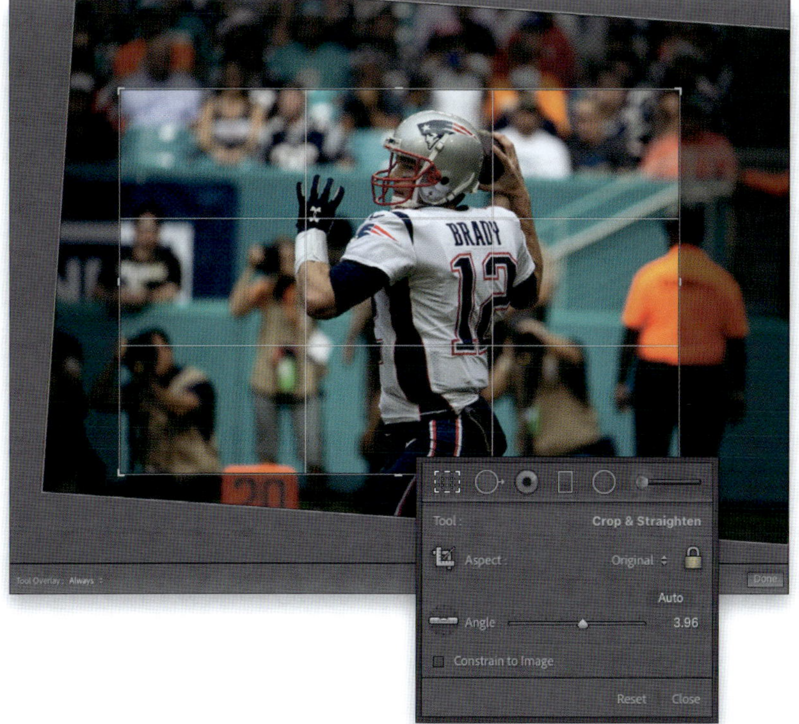

Step 04:

Next up is getting our color right **(Point 2)**, and in this image, the color is pretty wrong, with a green tint over the entire image (you can't see that here because this is where we correct it, so look at the image in the previous step and you'll see the green). In this case, knowing where to start is easy because he's wearing a helmet that's a neutral gray. So, just get the White Balance Selector tool (**W**; the eyedropper) from the top of the Basic panel (the Color panel in Lightroom cloud), click it somewhere on his helmet (as shown here), and it sets the white balance. If you're thinking, "Scott, why don't you just click on his white jersey to set the white balance?" It's because we don't white balance to white in photography (if you were shooting video, then white works).

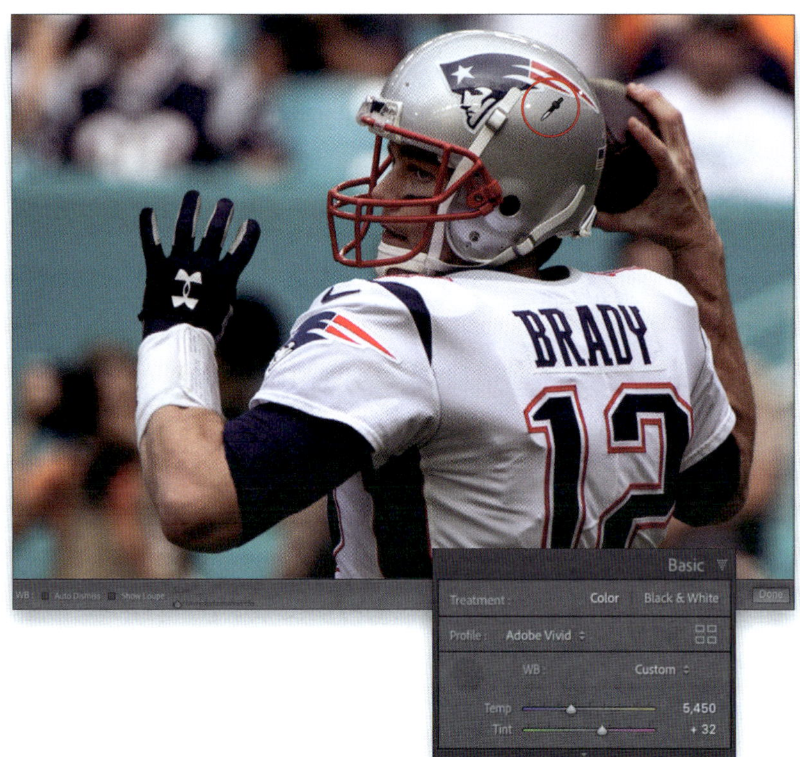

Step 05:

This is a side note about white balance, but an important one: Don't just click once on his helmet and figure, "Well, that's gray, so it must be right." There are all different levels of gray (and highlights and shadows) on his helmet, so don't just click once—click on different areas on the helmet and each time you do, you'll get a different result. That's exactly what I did here—all four images had their white balance set by me clicking on different parts of his helmet and they all look different, which is why you need to do this.

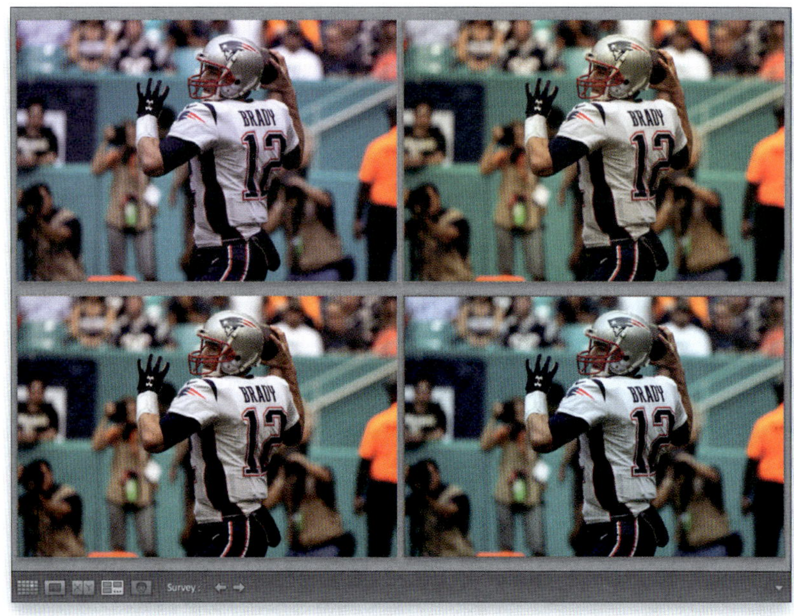

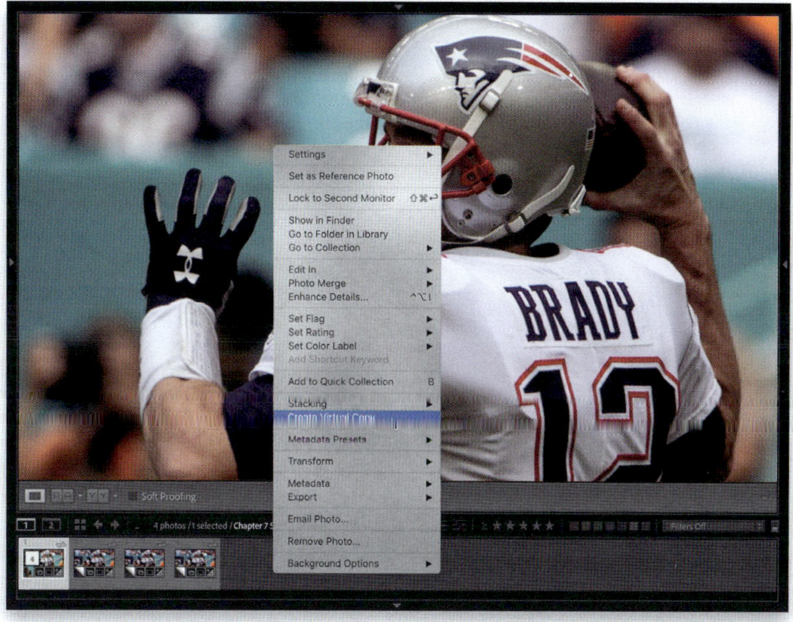

Step 06:

If you were wondering how I showed four versions of the same image onscreen like that, first you need to create three virtual copies of the original by Right-clicking on the image and choosing **Create Virtual Copy** from the pop-up menu a few times. (*Note:* The Virtual Copy feature is currently not in Lightroom cloud.) Then, after clicking the White Balance Selector tool on a different spot on the helmet in each image, I selected all four images down in the Filmstrip and pressed the **N key** on my keyboard to enter that 4-up Survey view (also not in available in Lightroom cloud). Okay, back to our edit already in progress. After clicking around his helmet a few times, I decided I like this white balance better: Temp at 5,750 and Tint at +18.

Step 07:

Now, let's work on the overall exposure and highlight clipping **(Points 3 and 4)**. We start by setting our white and black points by pressing-and-holding the Shift key and double-clicking on Whites, and then on Blacks to get those set. While definitely improved, it still looks a little underexposed, so drag the Exposure slider to the right until it looks nice and bright (after all, it's a day game in the Florida sun. Did I mention Tom Brady lives here in Florida now? About 25 minutes from my house, so we're practically neighbors, right?). Here, I dragged it over to +0.65, so it was still about 2/3 of a stop underexposed even after setting the white and black points. His white jersey is starting to "bloom" a bit (looking too bright while everything else looks good), so let's pull the highlights back, which will help bring some detail back into it, as well. Drag the Highlights slider to the left to around –36 and that should do the trick.

Step 08:

There are no real lens issues here, so we can skip Point 6, but I think we definitely should brighten his face up a bit, so you can see the glory and the majesty that is Tom Brady (did I mention the whole Tampa winning the Super Bowl thing? Oh. I did? Sorry. But, well…we did, thanks to him. But, I digress). Anyway, for **Point 5**, get the Adjustment Brush **(K)** from the toolbox beneath the histogram (the Brush tool **[B]** from the toolbox on the right in Lightroom cloud), drag the Exposure slider over to the right a bit (here, I dragged it to 0.40), and paint over his face (as shown here) with a small brush to brighten that area. Okay, looking good.

Step 09:

While we've got the Adjustment Brush, let's go ahead and make the ball more visible. For some reason, it's really dark (really dark, but you'll have to look at the previous image to see that because we're going to fix it here). Click on New (the + [plus sign] in Lightroom cloud) at the top of the panel, shrink the size of the brush, and then paint over the football. Then, increase the Exposure, Contrast, and Shadows amounts to help make the ball lighter and brighter in his throwing hand, and maybe even pump up the Saturation amount, so we get more brown color in it (as seen here). I bumped the Exposure to 0.61, Contrast to 19, Shadows way up to 49, and Saturation up to 43. How did I know to move these sliders this much? I didn't. Exposure controls overall brightness, so that was easy, and obviously opening up the Shadows would make the shadow areas brighter. Once those didn't work as well as I had hoped, then I tried increasing the Saturation amount, so we'd see more brown, and when things started to look washed out, I went for the Contrast slider (sometimes opening up the shadows a lot can give the image a washed-out look, and adding contrast is usually the fix).

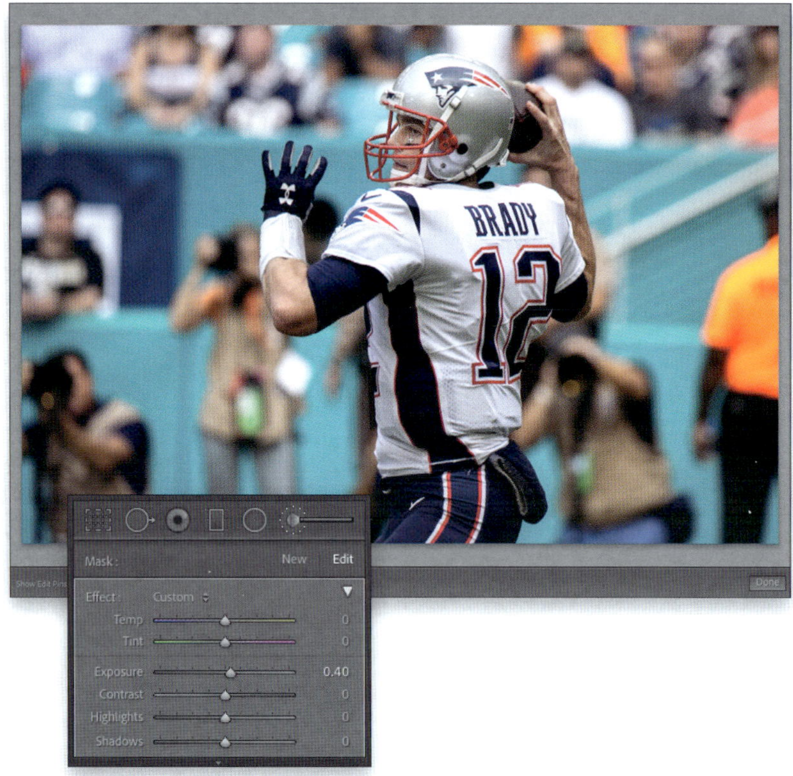

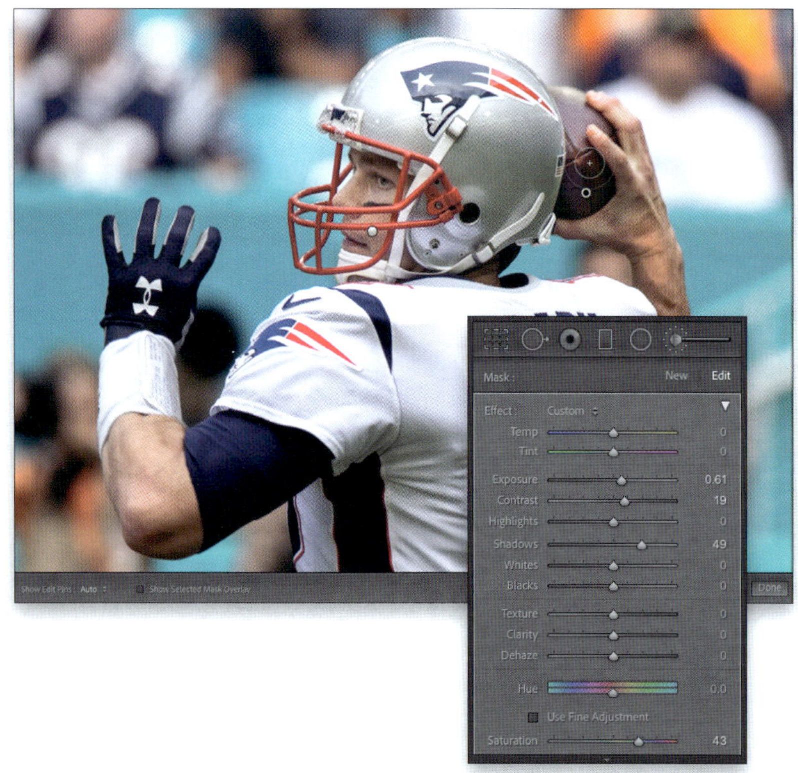

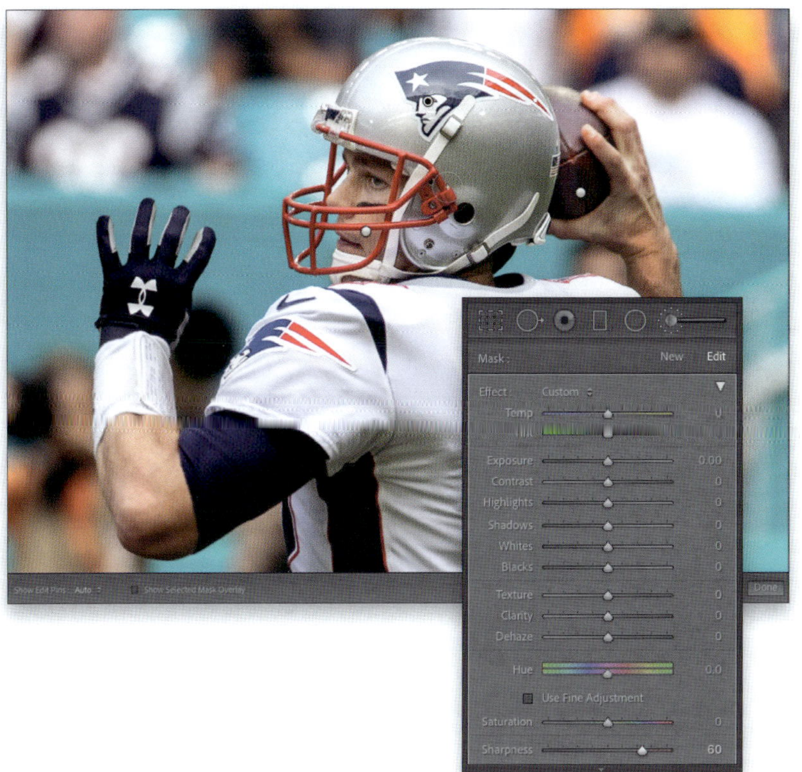

Step 10:

We're going to do a little trick now that has a surprisingly powerful effect on how sharp your photo looks. It's called "creative sharpening" and rather than just sharpening the entire image (which we will do in a minute), we're going to "spot sharpen" certain areas that will make the whole image look much sharper. Click on New again, then double-click on Effect to reset all the sliders to zero, and then increase the Sharpness amount to 60. I start by painting over any text or logos, and anything metal, so paint sharpness over the Patriots logo on his helmet, the front of his helmet, the Under Armour logo on his glove, and the snaps on his helmet. Sharpening those little areas makes the whole image look so much sharper and crisper.

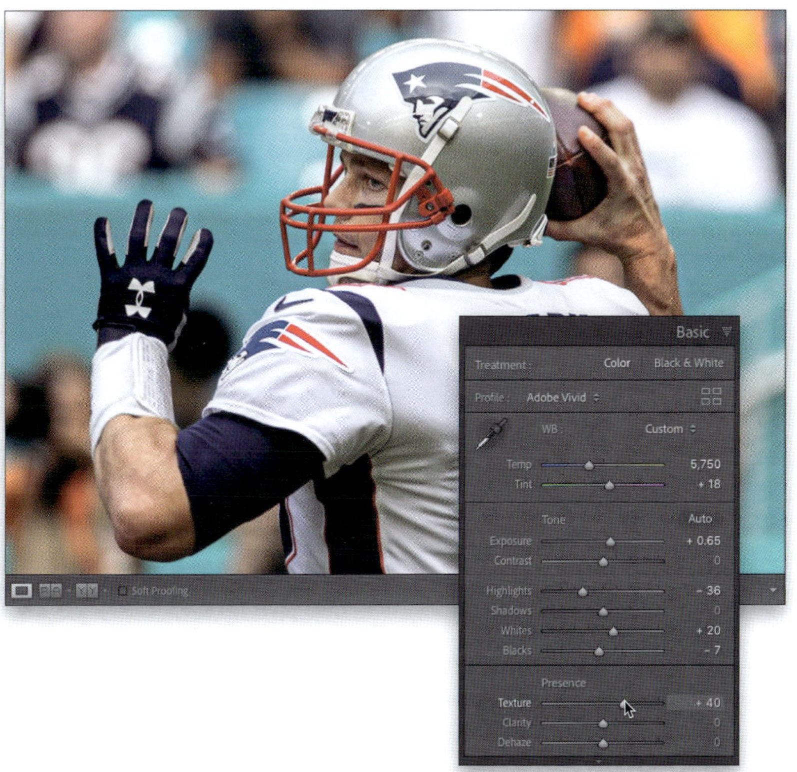

Step 11:

Now let's get to some finishing moves with **Point 7**. Go back to the Basic panel (the Effects panel in Lightroom cloud) and enhance the detail in the photo by dragging the Texture slider to the right, over to +40. Then, if you want, you can add a little Clarity, but you have to be very careful when adding Clarity to sports shots because if you add too much, the images start looking cartoonish, especially if your background is out of focus behind the player, where adding Clarity really looks funky. So, just be really careful (I skipped adding any Clarity to this image). Also, when any player is wearing white (like his jersey here), adding Clarity enhances the wrinkles (by adding midtone contrast), which can look okay, but it also starts to make the jersey look dirty. Use Clarity sparingly and rely, instead, on Texture, which doesn't change the tone of your image very much, but still does a great job of enhancing detail.

Step 12:

Since we're editing this shot for our own purposes (and not for journalistic purposes), we can do what we want to it, and what I'd add is a very subtle darkening around the outside edges. So, go to the Effects panel, and in the Post-Crop Vignetting section, drag the Amount slider (the Vignette slider in Lightroom cloud) over to the left to (you guessed it) –11 (as shown here). Toggle the visibility of this panel on/off a couple of times (click on the little button in the left side of the panel header; click-and-hold on the eye icon in the right side of the panel header in Lightroom cloud), and you'll see what a nice difference this makes.

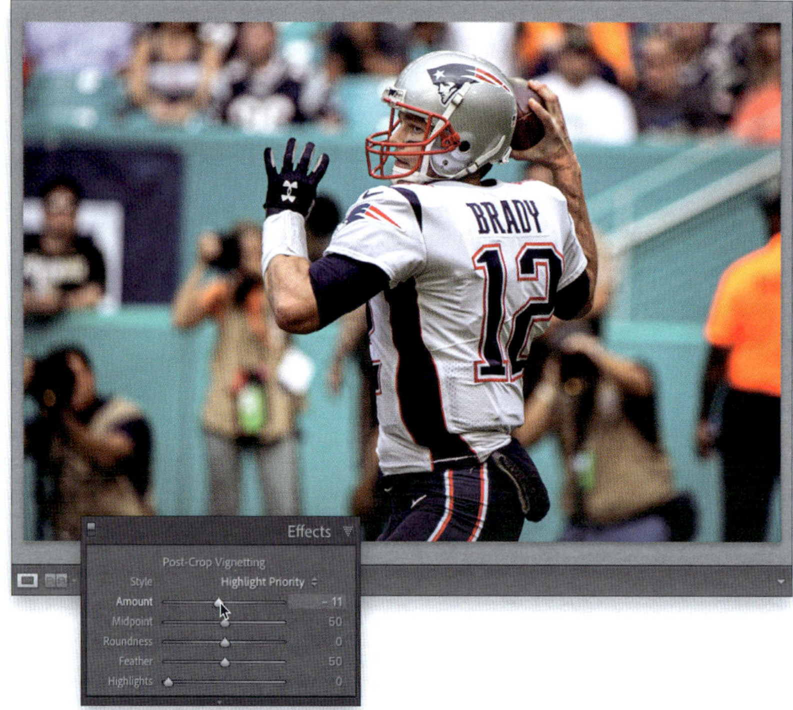

Step 13:

Let's wrap this one up with some really nice, crisp sharpening. Go to the Detail panel, and in the Sharpening section up top, drag the Amount slider (the Sharpening slider in Lightroom cloud) over to 80 (as shown here), leave the rest of the sliders right where they are, and you're done.

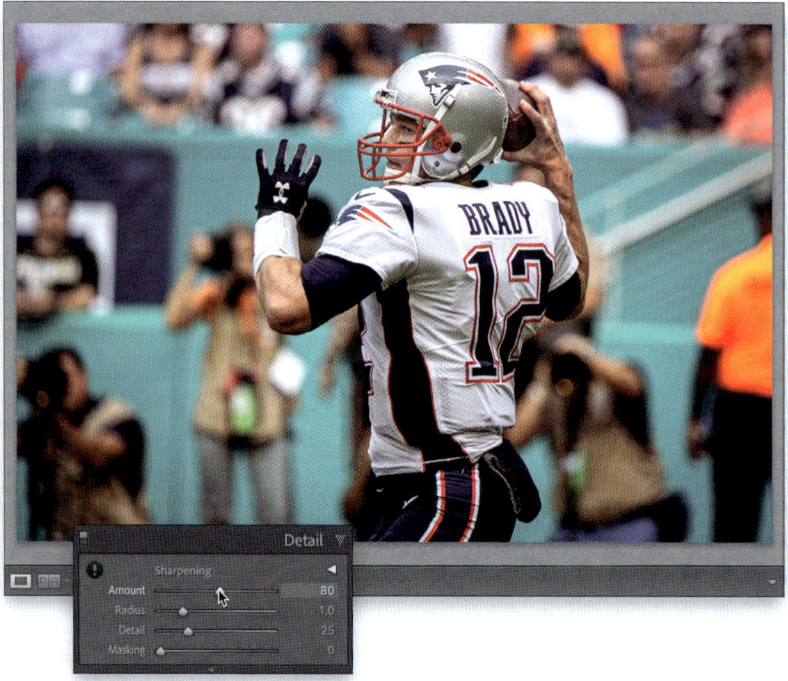

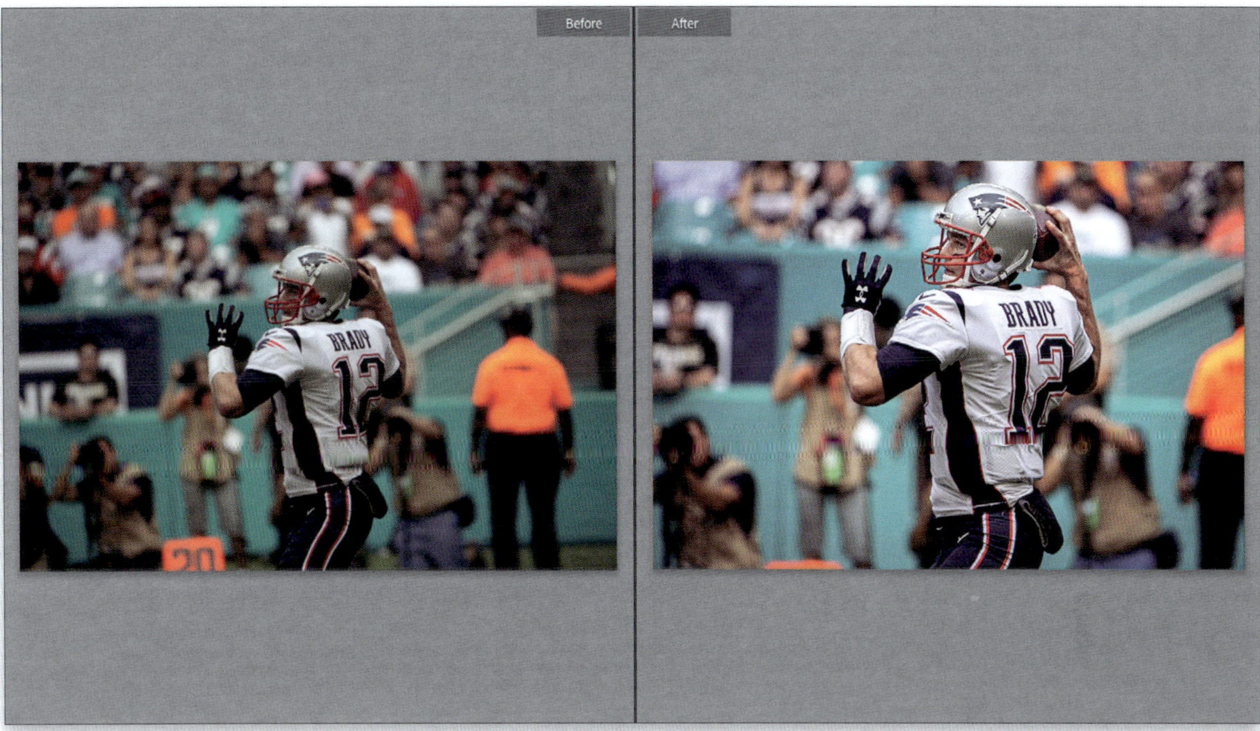

Here's our before and after.

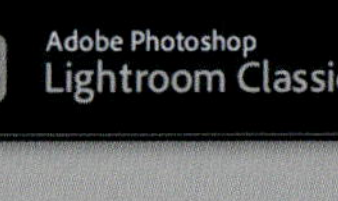

Adobe Photoshop
Lightroom Classic

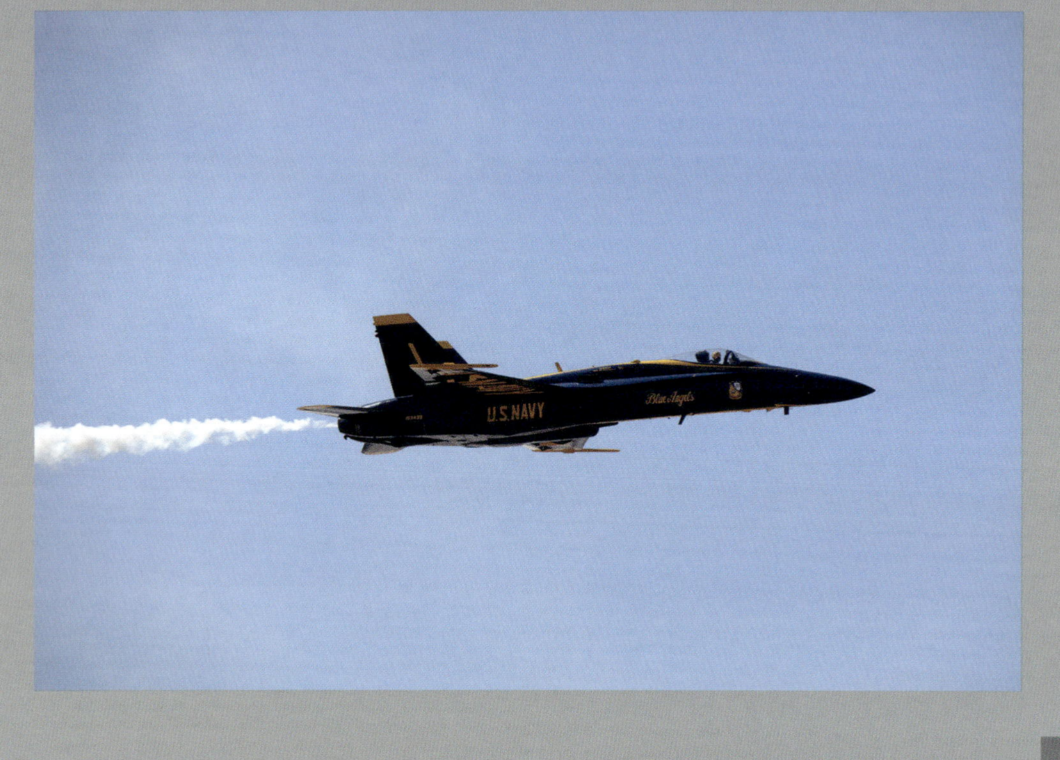

U.S.NAVY
Blue Angels

Before
After

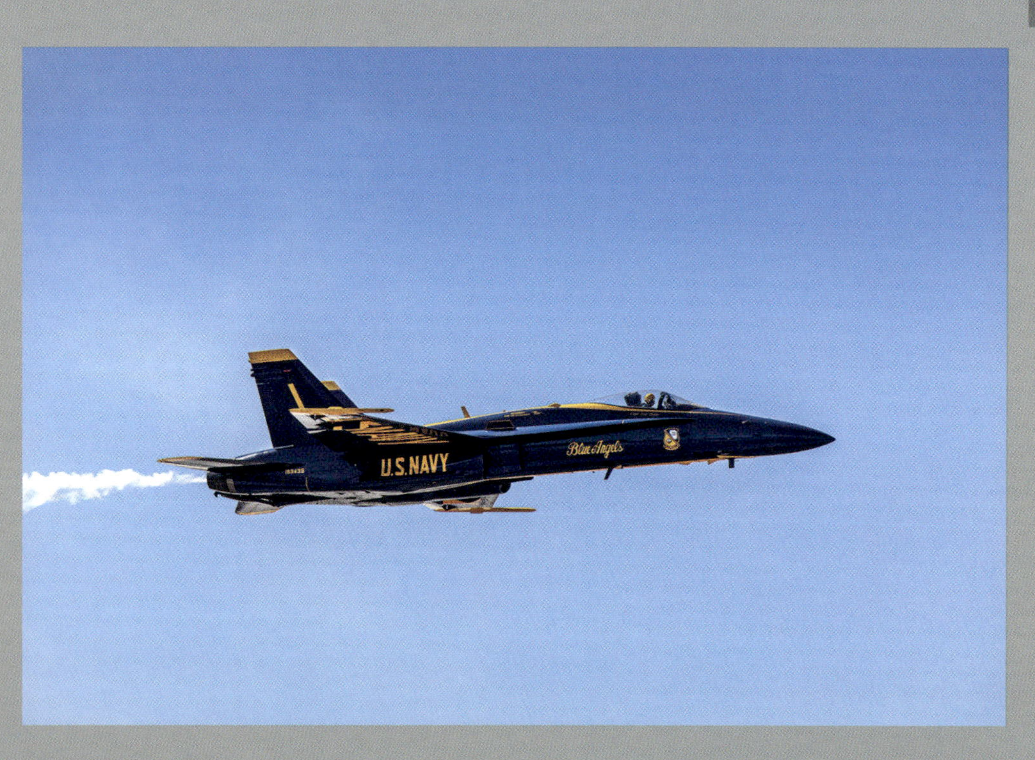

U.S.NAVY
Blue Angels

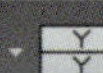
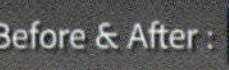
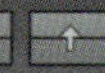

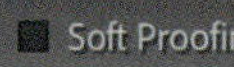
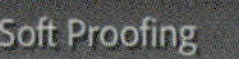

Before & After :
Soft Proofing

AVIATION

1. Assigning a RAW Profile
2. Getting the Color Right
3. Expanding the Tonal Range
4. Dealing with Sensor Limitations
5. Painting with Light and Retouching
6. Fixing Lens Issues
7. Finishing Moves

In this shot, we've got a backlit jet, so the colors are muted, and we've got a composition issue, and our sky needs a bit of work, and we've even got some lens issues to fix. But, even with all of that, the 7-Point System will easily deal with all of it.

THE STORY BEHIND THE SHOT:

This shot, of one of the US Navy's famous Blue Angels Flight Demonstration Squadron, was taken during the Alliance Air Show in Ft. Worth, Texas. I was there with a group of aviation photographers from ISAP (the International Society for Aviation Photography), who have special access to these events, and a group of us were right out next to the runway for most of the day. I was shooting a Canon 200–400mm f/4 lens with a 1.4 tele-extender, which is a beast of a lens in every sense of the word, and is why I now have a 150–600mm lens that's about 2/3 the size, about half the weight, and 1/10 of the price. I could barely lift my arms for two days after this shoot, but it was my first time shooting "The Blues" when there wasn't a gray, lifeless sky behind them, and with the access we had, well…I was really tickled. To learn more about ISAP, visit aviationphoto.org.

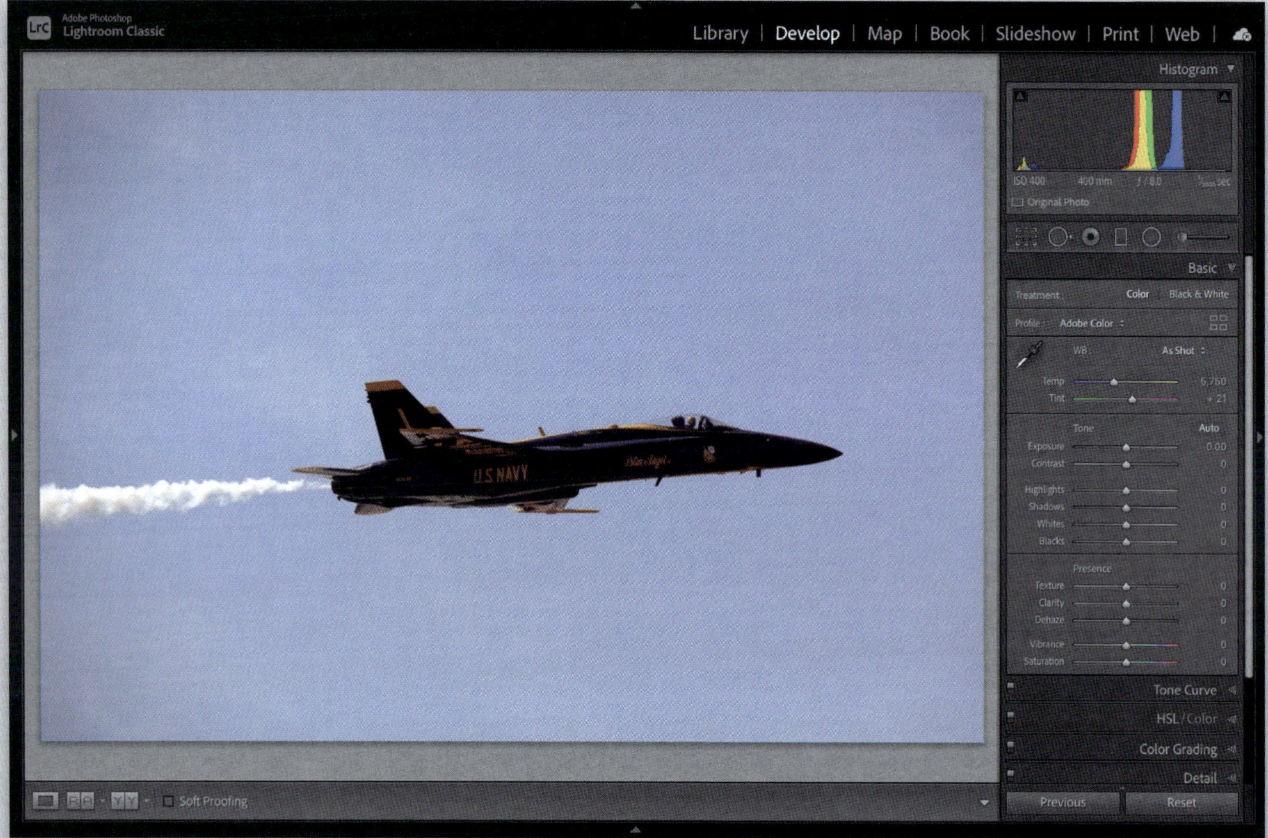

Camera: Canon EOS 5D Mark IV
Aperture Value: *f*/8.0
Shutter Speed: 1/2000 sec
ISO: 400
Focal Length: 400mm

Step 01:

Here's our original RAW image of one of the Blue Angels, taken at an air show, and the whole shot is just pretty "meh." The sky is meh, the jet looks meh, the composition is meh (actually, maybe less than meh), and just…well…meh. Before we get to applying the system, let's fix something compositionally that needs fixing first, and that is we need a little more breathing room in front of the jet versus behind it. It's a psychological thing (isn't everything?) in photos where your moving subject (in this case, a jet) is close to the edge of the frame. That makes the viewer subconsciously uncomfortable because the moving object (be it a jet, or an animal, or an athlete) has a feeling of being "caged in." So, let's start by dealing with that.

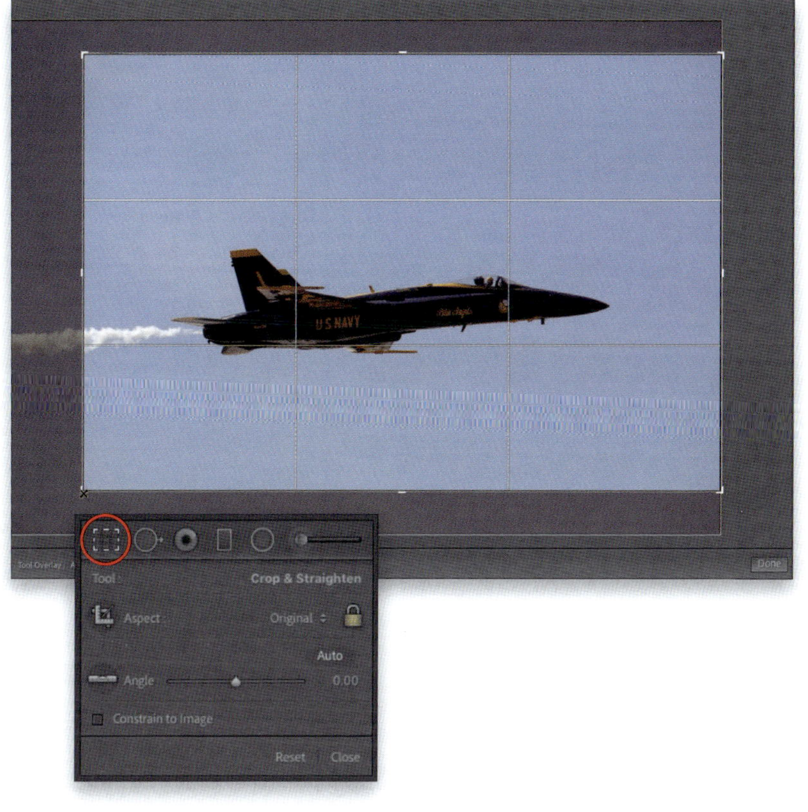

Step 02:

One way to do this would be to jump over to Photoshop, expand the right side of the image area by an inch or so, and then use Content-Aware Fill to fill in that new area in front of the jet with more sky (and it would do a pretty brilliant job of it, too). But, we can actually do a quick fix right here in Lightroom and balance out the composition by cropping. This way, at least it won't appear to have more room behind the jet than in front of it, and that balance will help. So, in the Develop module, get the Crop Overlay tool **(R)** from the toolbox beneath the histogram (or the Crop & Rotate tool **[C]** from the toolbox on the right in Lightroom cloud), and then click on the bottom-left corner and drag up diagonally to crop off some of the left side and bottom (as shown here). You can reposition the jet in the shot by moving your cursor inside the cropping border, where your cursor will change into a grabber hand, and dragging the jet around inside that border to position it where you want. This isn't quite as effective as the Photoshop way, but again, it's a quick fix and gives us a better looking, more balanced composition, and the image now feels less caged in. Press **Return (PC: Enter)** to lock in your crop when you're done.

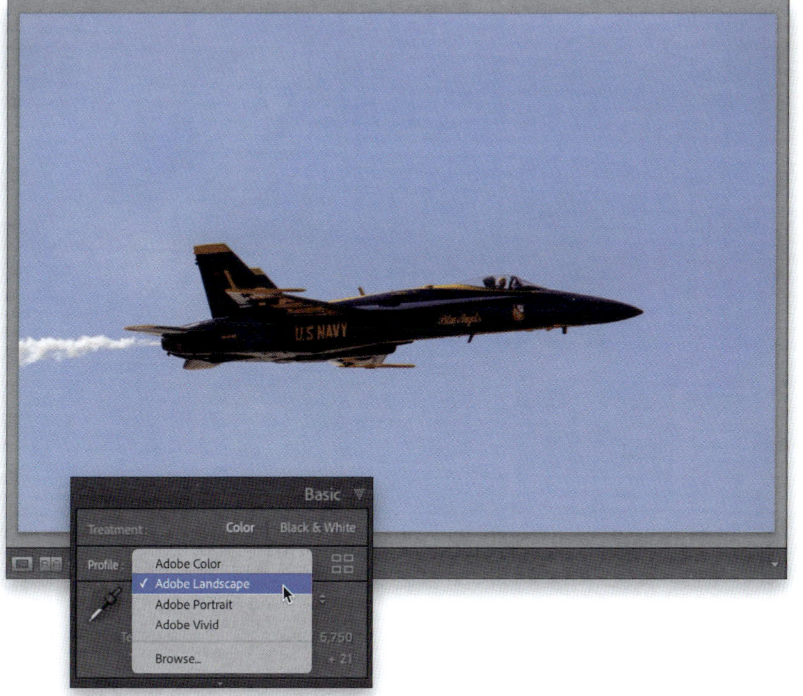

Step 03:

Let's start here with **Point 1** and apply a RAW profile to see if that gets us a better starting place for our editing. At the top of the Basic panel (the Edit panel in Lightroom cloud), from the Profile pop-up menu, choose **Adobe Landscape** (as shown here), and you'll see that the sky looks bluer, the image is more contrasty, and we're on our way.

Step 04:

The color looks okay, so we'll skip Point 2 and get our exposure in the ballpark **(Point 3)**. In the Basic panel (the Light panel in Lightroom cloud), press-and-hold the Shift key, then double-click on Whites, and then on Blacks to set your white and black points (this cranked up the Whites a bunch, to +40, and set the Blacks to –37). Now, look at the image to see if you think the image needs to be a little brighter or darker. It could be just a tad brighter, but you don't want that sky to get much brighter, so let's just increase the overall brightness a smidgen by dragging the Exposure slider to the right to +0.15 (as shown here).

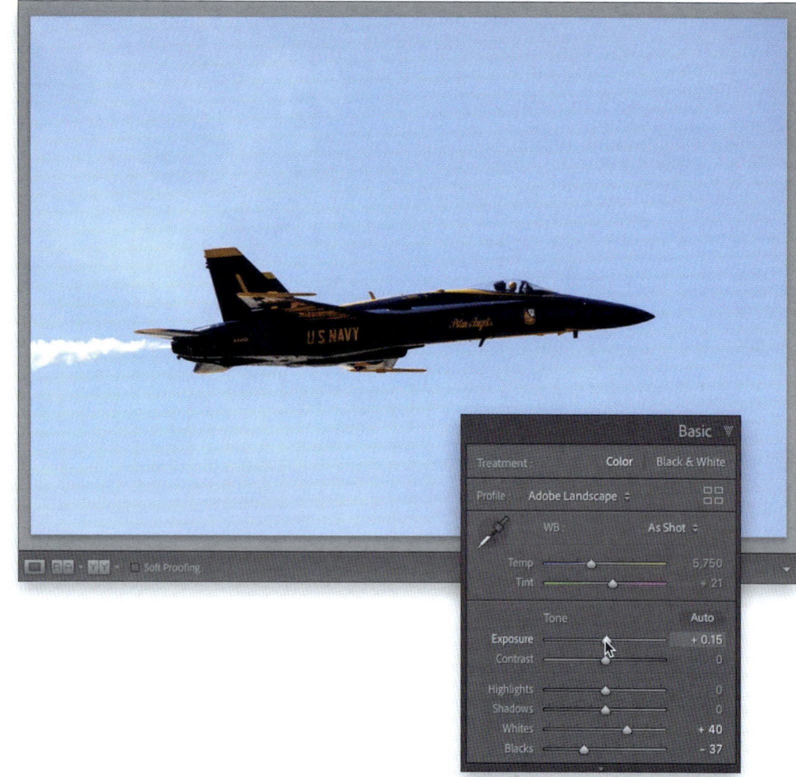

Step 05:

Okay, let's fix our next problem, but the problem here really isn't standard exposure—it's that the jet is backlit for the most part, so we'll deal with that **(Point 4)**. Go to the Shadows slider, crank the amount way up (here, I dragged it over to +47), and look at the difference. Pretty dramatic improvement that one slider made (that sentence kind of sounds the way Yoda might structure it). Anyway, that was a move in the right direction.

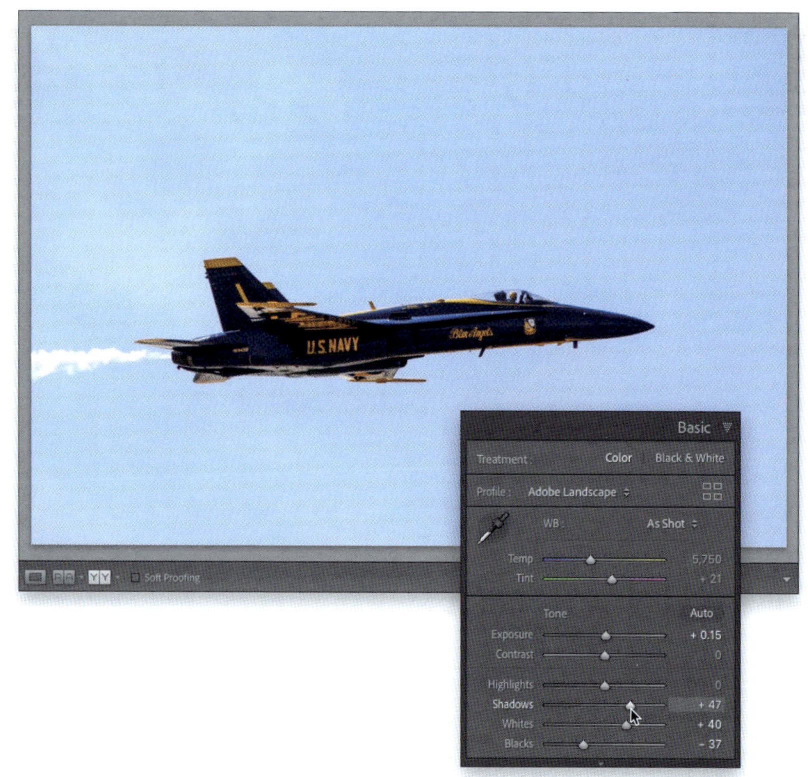

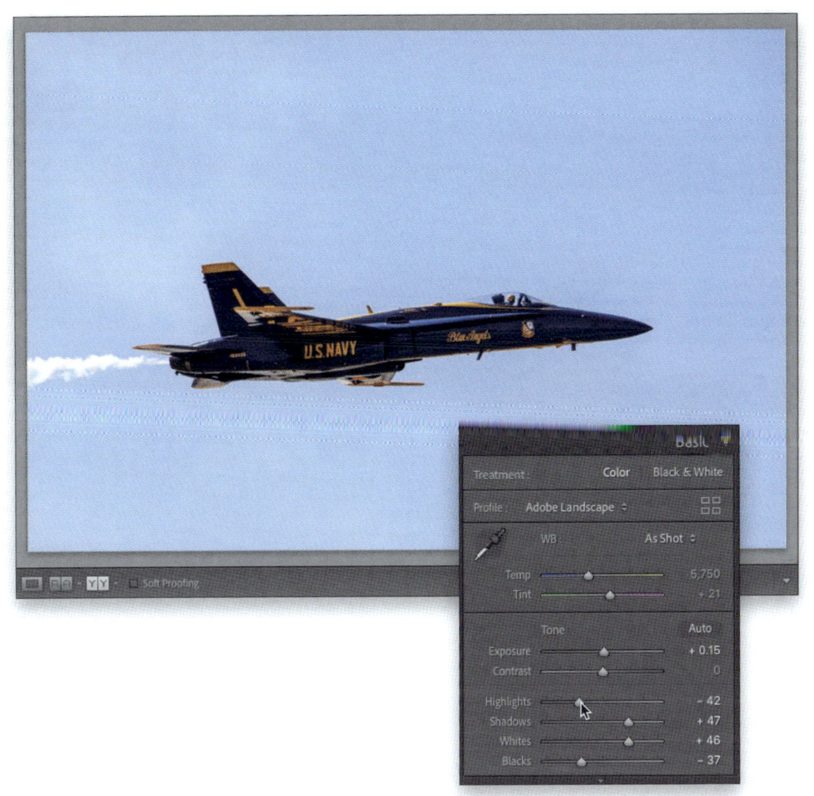

Step 06:

Now, let's help our sky out a little by dragging the Highlights slider quite a bit over to the left (we've used this trick before to make our sky look better and our clouds have more detail). Here, I dragged the Highlights over to –42, and then bumped the Whites up just a little to +46, and you can see the difference it made. It's not enough to get our sky where we want it, but it's a start.

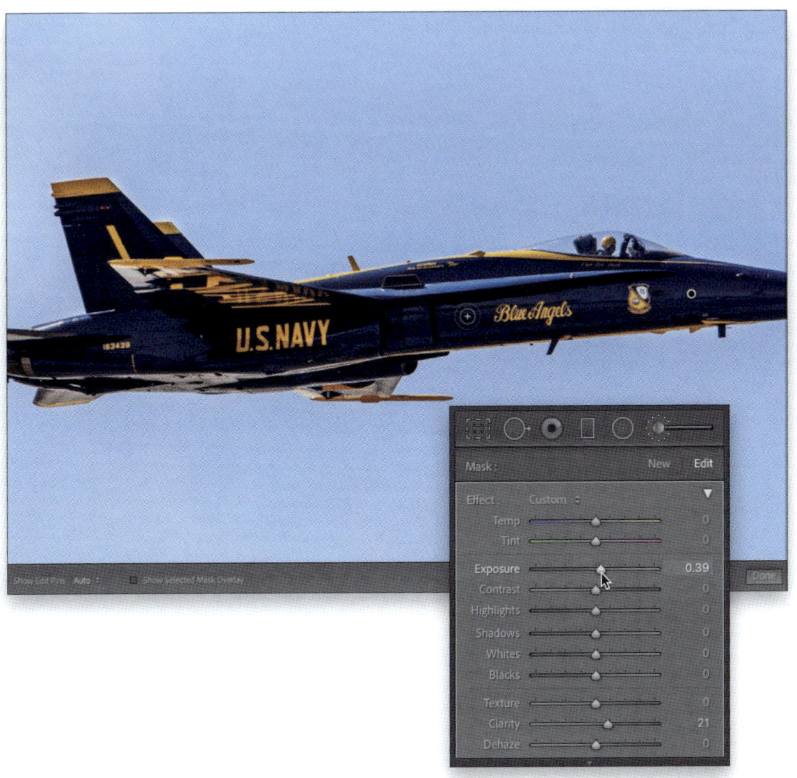

Step 07:

Let's work on making that metal on the jet a little more shiny (this is **Point 5**), so zoom your view in a little tighter by pressing **Command-+** (plus sign; **PC: Ctrl-+**). Get the Adjustment Brush **(K)** from the toolbox beneath the histogram (the Brush tool **[B]** from the toolbox on the right in Lightroom cloud), double-click on the word "Effect" near the top of the panel to reset all the sliders to zero (this happens by default in Lightroom cloud), then drag the Clarity slider over to 21, and then paint over the jet (as shown here). Adding Clarity adds midtone contrast to your image, which will tend to make the area you paint over with Clarity a little darker, so to offset that, drag the Exposure slider to the right a little to around 0.40. Remember, when you get near the edges of the jet, turn on the Auto Mask checkbox (press the **A key** on your keyboard), so you don't "paint outside the lines."

Step 08:

You can't see it in the image shown in this step (because this step corrected the problem), but as the case often is, there's some darkening in the corners caused by the lens (a 200–400mm f/4), but that's an easy fix for **Point 6**. Go to the Lens Corrections panel (the Optics panel in Lightroom cloud), turn on the Enable Profile (Lens) Corrections checkbox, and Lightroom will apply a fix from its built-in collection of lens profiles. A weird thing happened this time, and it's very rare, but when it applied the brightening to the corners to offset the darkened corners, it appears it overcompensated and now the corners actually look too bright. Like I said, this is very rare, but it did happen, so we need to fix it.

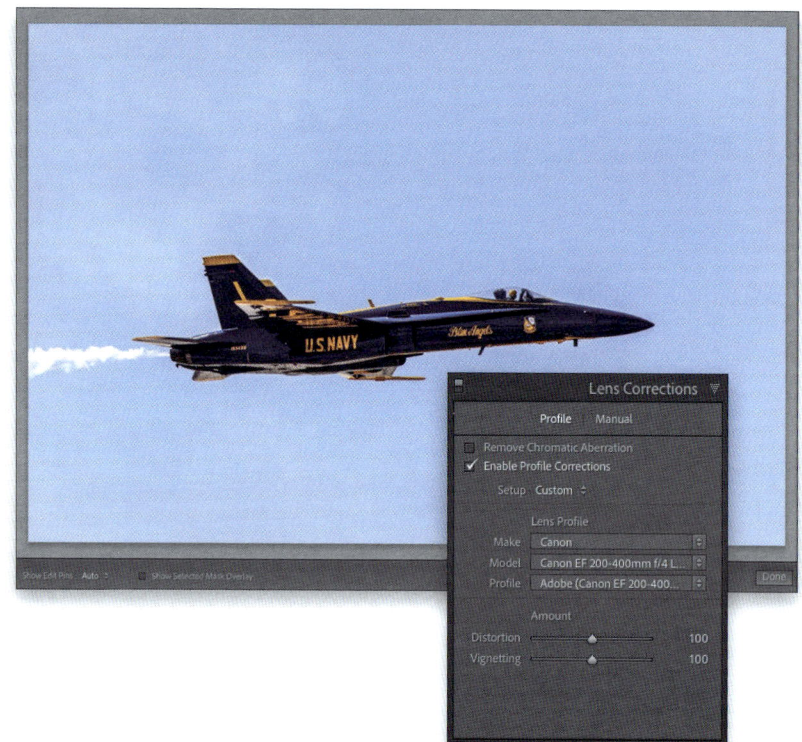

Step 09:

At the bottom of that same panel are two sliders for fine-tuning the adjustment. To tweak the amount of brightening in the corners, drag the (Lens) Vignetting slider to the left until the corners look balanced (not too dark, not too light, like porridge. Did anybody get that joke? Anybody? No? Okay, let's move on then). Here, I dragged the Vignetting slider to the left to 42. That's quite a bit of an adjustment, but that pretty much did the trick.

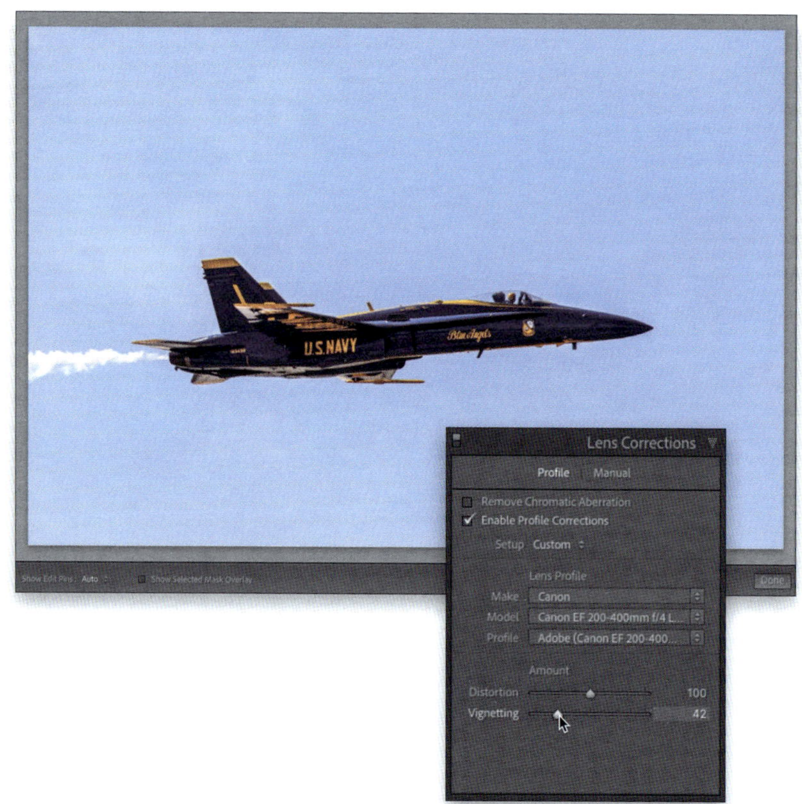

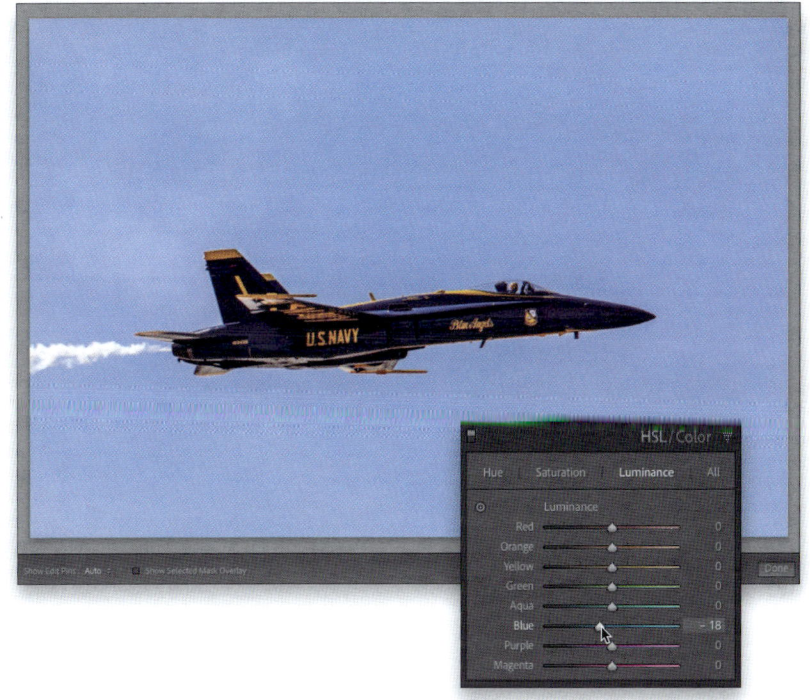

Step 10:

Next, let's make that sky a little bluer by going to the HSL/Color panel (in Lightroom cloud, go to the Color panel, then click on Color Mixer). Click on Luminance up top and drag the Blue slider to the left a bit (like I did here, where I dragged it to –18. In Lightroom cloud, choose Luminance from the Adjust pop-up menu at the top of the panel, and then drag the Blue slider). Okay, the sky is looking better, but you might consider one more tweak—adding a gradient to the sky (like you'd get using an ND filter over the end of your lens. Few people actually try to shoot aviation with an ND filter because getting it in the right position in the sky, and in relation to your jet, would be really tricky, but here in Lightroom, you can put the gradient exactly where you'd like it).

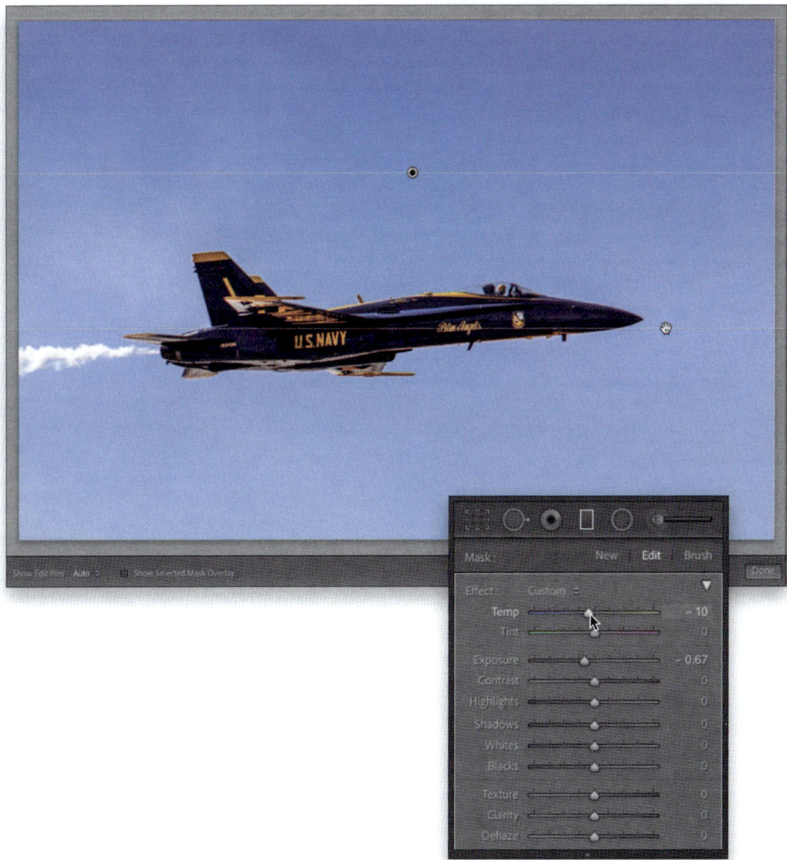

Step 11:

Get the Graduated Filter tool **(M)** from the toolbox beneath the histogram (the Linear Gradient tool **[L]** from the toolbox on the right in Lightroom cloud). Double-click on Effect to reset all the sliders to zero, and then lower the Exposure amount to –0.67 to darken the top of the sky (and then it will gradually move to transparent). Take the tool, click it right at the top of the image, and drag downward until you're right about at the jet (as shown here), so it will be darkest at the top of the image, and then it will stop darkening before it reaches the jet. That does make the sky up there darker, but we can also make that part of the sky a bit bluer by dragging the Temp slider a little toward the left (here, I dragged to –10), which adds some blue white balance to that darker exposure we created up there with the Graduated filter tool. So, we're getting the benefits of a darker sky up top, and a richer sky, as well. Click the Done button in the toolbar beneath the Preview area (in Lightroom Classic) when you're finished.

Step 12:

Let's do some finishing moves now **(Point 7)**, starting off with sharpening. Go to the Detail panel, and in the Sharpening section up top, drag the Amount slider (the Sharpening slider in Lightroom cloud) over to 80 (as shown here), and just leave the rest of the sliders alone.

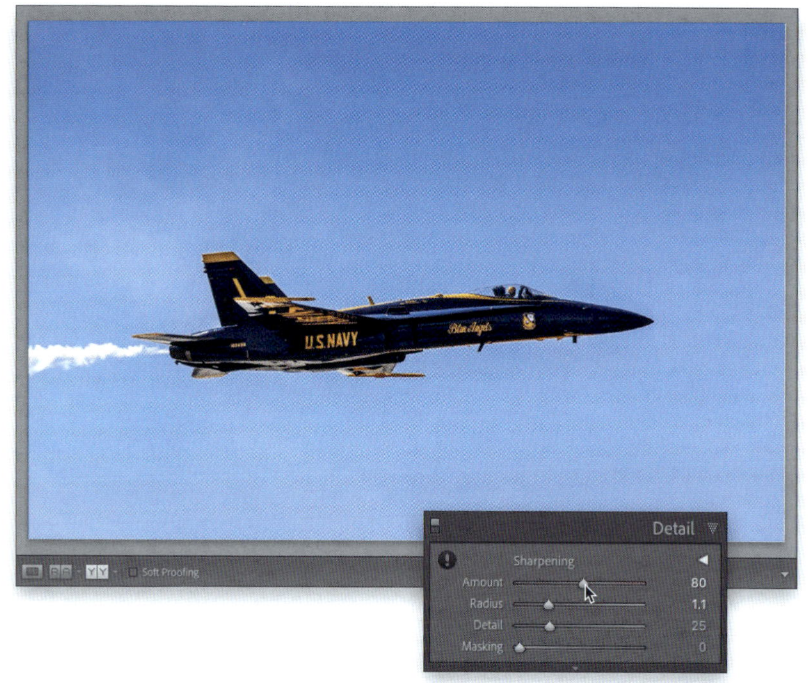

Step 13:

We used a trick earlier in the book that makes our image look even sharper, and that is to "spot sharpen" (also referred to as "creative sharpening") certain areas, and one of my go-to areas to sharpen is any text in the image. It'll help to zoom in tighter on the jet while you're doing this, so you can see the sharpening better as you apply it. Get the Adjustment Brush again, double-click on Effect to reset all the sliders to zero, then increase the Sharpness amount to 23 (as seen here). Now, let's paint over the areas we want to appear really sharp, like the text on the jet. I also painted over the pilot's helmet and the immediate cockpit area, but I didn't paint over the glass. Ahhhh, now that looks a lot better. Click the Done button.

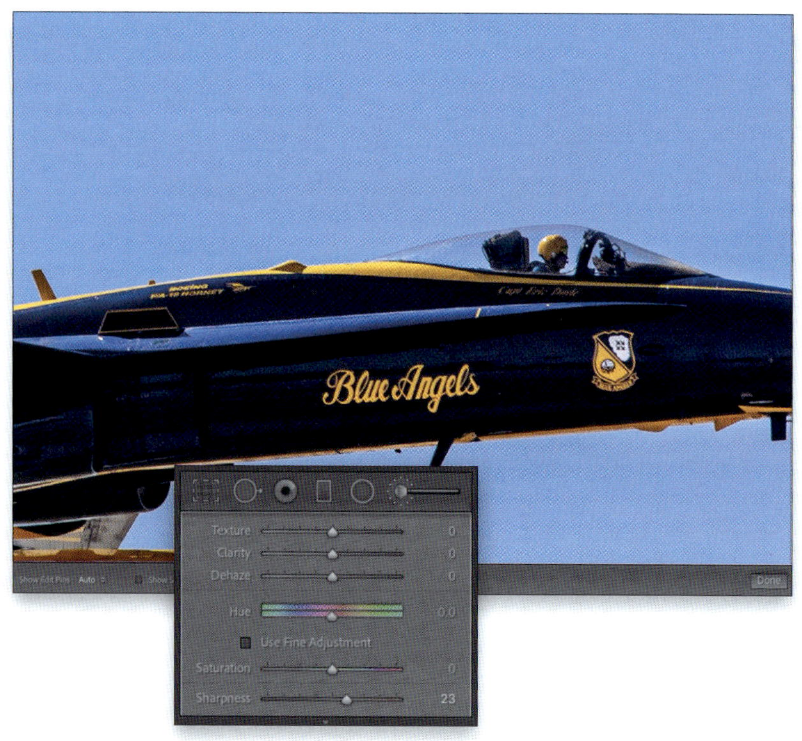

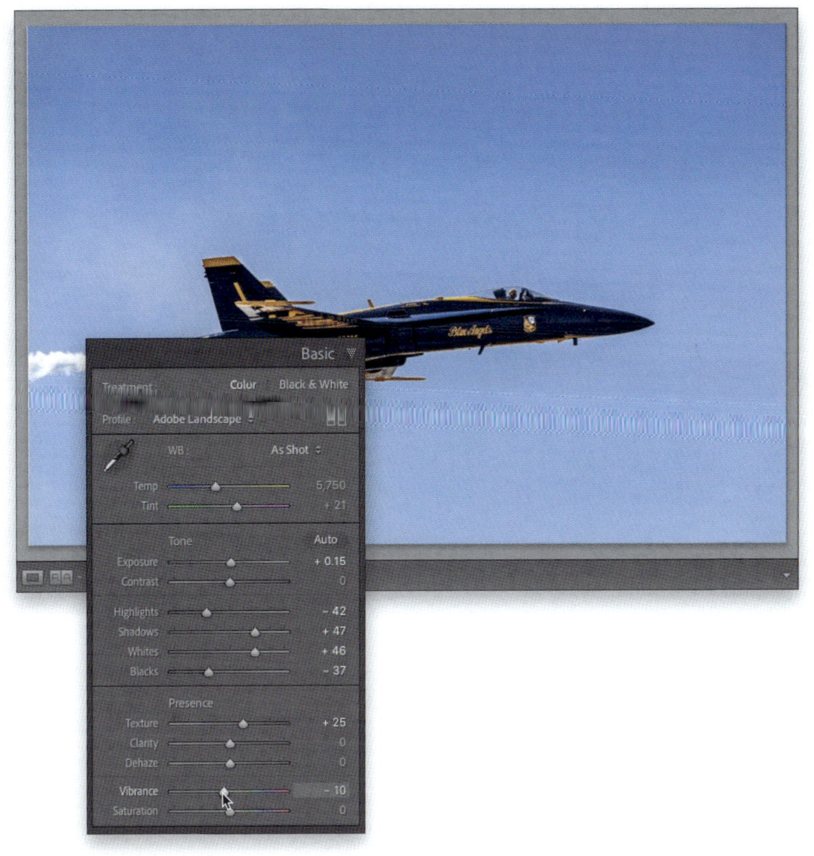

Step 14:

Okay, before we wrap this puppy up, let's step back and evaluate our image to see if we think everything is order. Well, rats, we probably shouldn't have done that (LOL!) because it looks like the overall color in the image is a little too vibrant (well, I guess I should say, "I'm really glad we did that"). This "over-vibrant" syndrome often happens without us really realizing it, as we're focused on fixing and adjusting different parts of the image and lots of little tweaks can really boost the color, especially if some of those steps are just that—boosting the color. Luckily, this is an easy fix. Head back to the Basic panel (the Color panel in Lightroom cloud) and drag the Vibrance slider to the left until the colors look about right to you (here, I dragged to the left to –10). Whew! I'm glad we fixed that. I also ended up increasing the Texture to +25 (that slider is in the Effects panel in Lightroom cloud). Now we're done. You can see our before/after below.

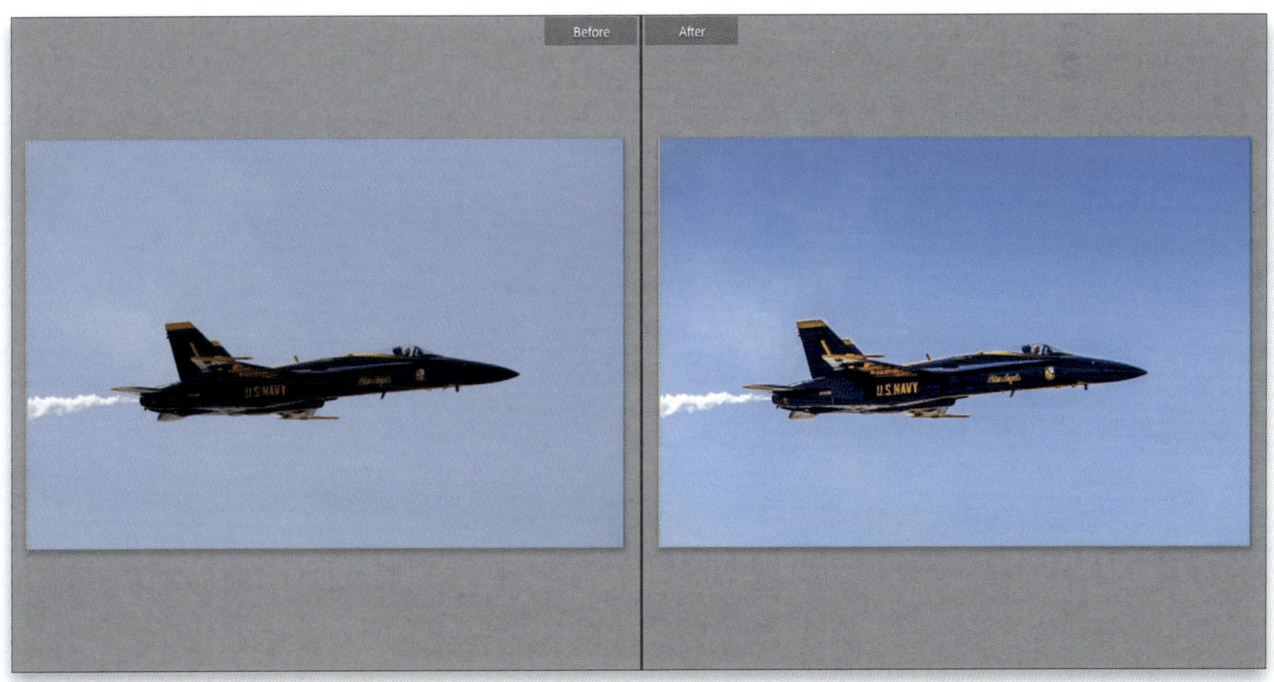

Adobe Photoshop
Lightroom Classic

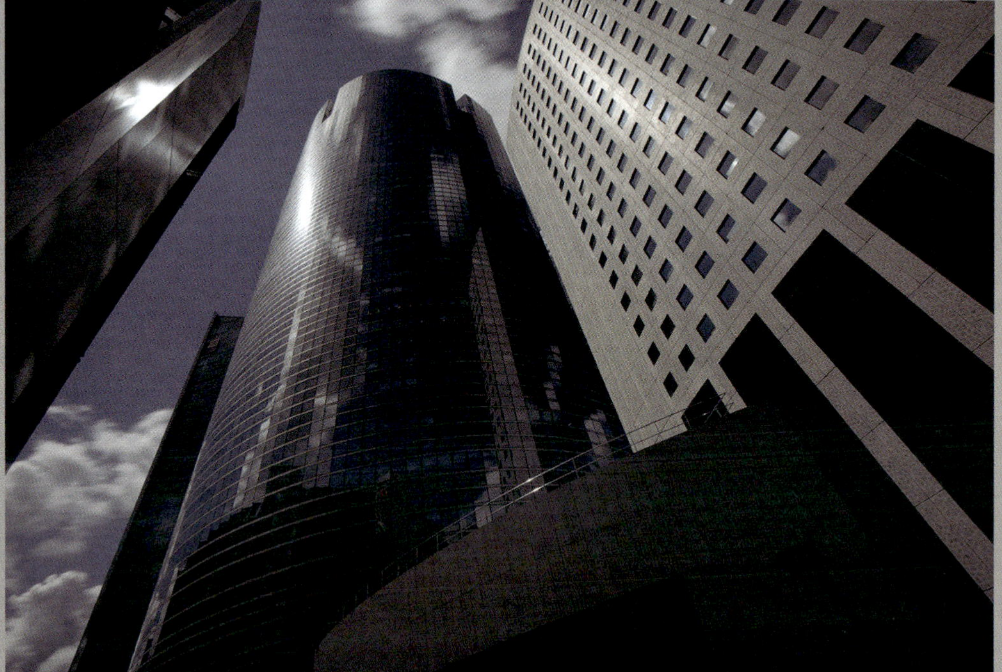
Before

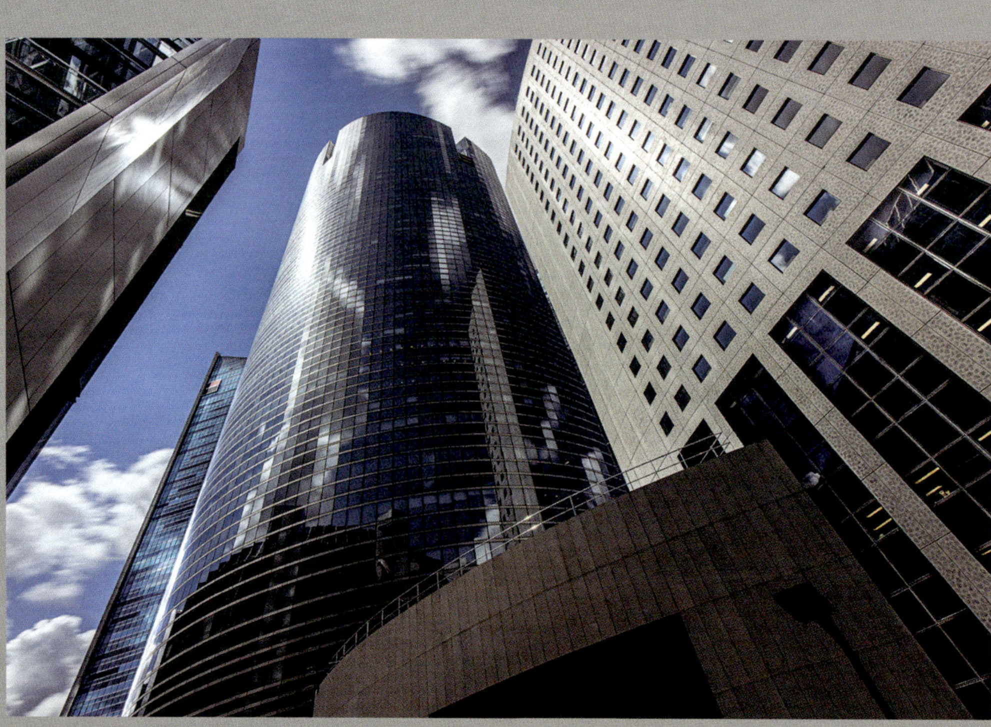
After

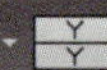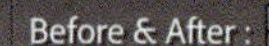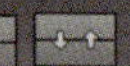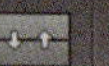
Before & After :
Soft Proofing

ARCHITECTURAL

1. Assigning a RAW Profile
2. Getting the Color Right
3. Expanding the Tonal Range
4. Dealing with Sensor Limitations
5. Painting with Light and Retouching
6. Fixing Lens Issues
7. Finishing Moves

What do I wish were different? Well, the buildings aren't lit very well, the whole image looks a bit underexposed, and the colors don't pop at all. The contrast is kind of flat and the lighting is kind of flat, too, and the buildings need to be much sharper and more detailed. Plus, parts of the buildings are lost in the shadows, so there's a lot to be done here.

THE STORY BEHIND THE SHOT:

This was taken a few days before my most recent travel photography workshop in Paris. I had always seen the modern buildings of La Défense (the large business district just a few kilometers outside the Paris city limits) from afar (like from on top of the Arc de Triomphe, or the Eiffel Tower, or the Tour Montparnasse building), but I'd never actually made it over there. This time, I made it a point to finally take a trip out there to spend a few hours shooting the architecture. I wanted to get some movement in the clouds, so I took a 10-stop ND (neutral density) filter to let me keep my shutter open way longer, even during a bright summer day (keeping my shutter open this long would mean I'd be taking my travel tripod out there with me). I used a 16–35mm wide-angle lens, and I really came to fall in love with the fully articulating LCD screen on the back of the camera for shooting architecture because it made taking these shots, where my camera is aiming nearly straight up, so much easier.

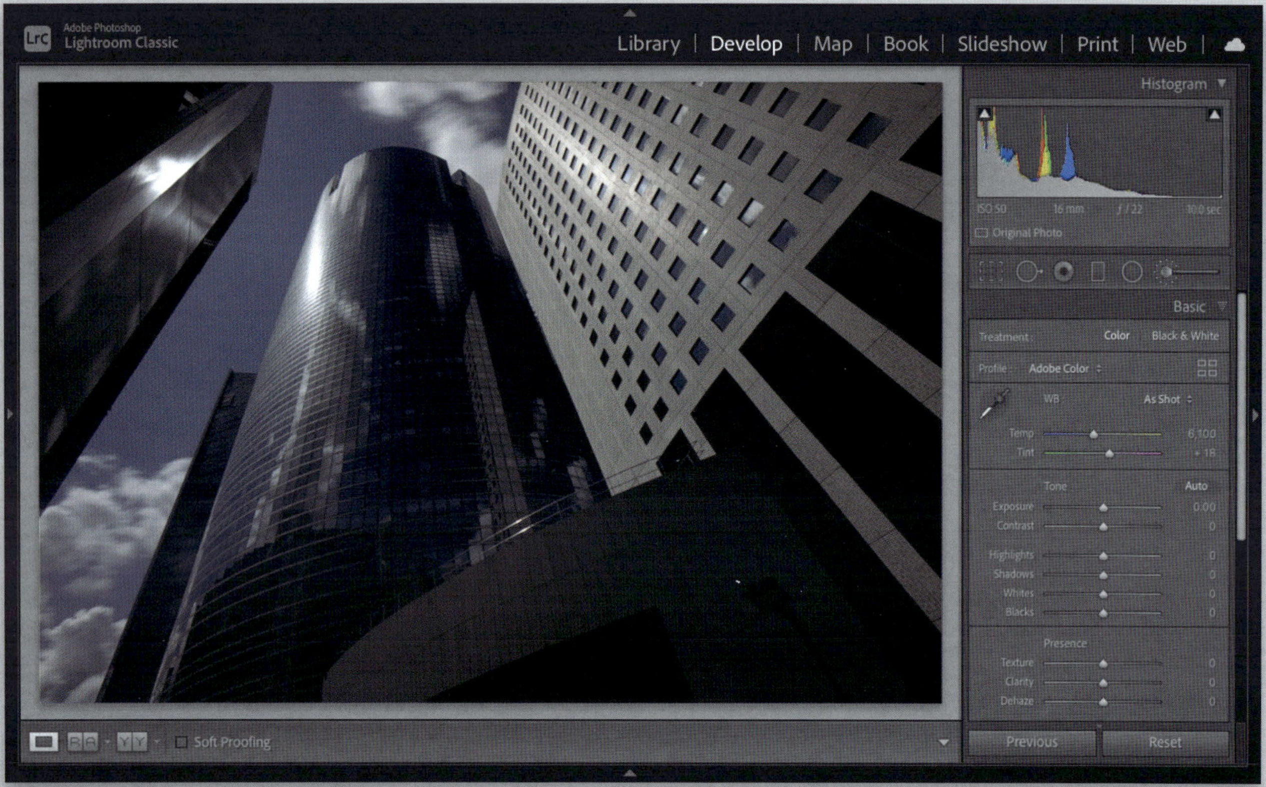

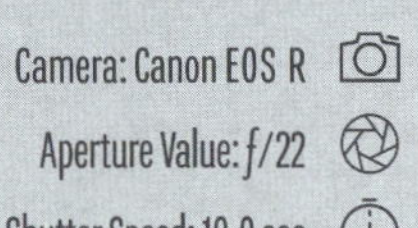

Camera: Canon EOS R

Aperture Value: ƒ/22

Shutter Speed: 10.0 sec

ISO: 50

Focal Length: 16mm

Step 01:

Here's our original RAW image of the buildings in La Défense. The first things that jump out are the fact that the shot is very underexposed, partially backlit, and it looks very flat overall. This is a pretty straightforward fix and shouldn't take long. A nice break now that we're just about halfway through the book.

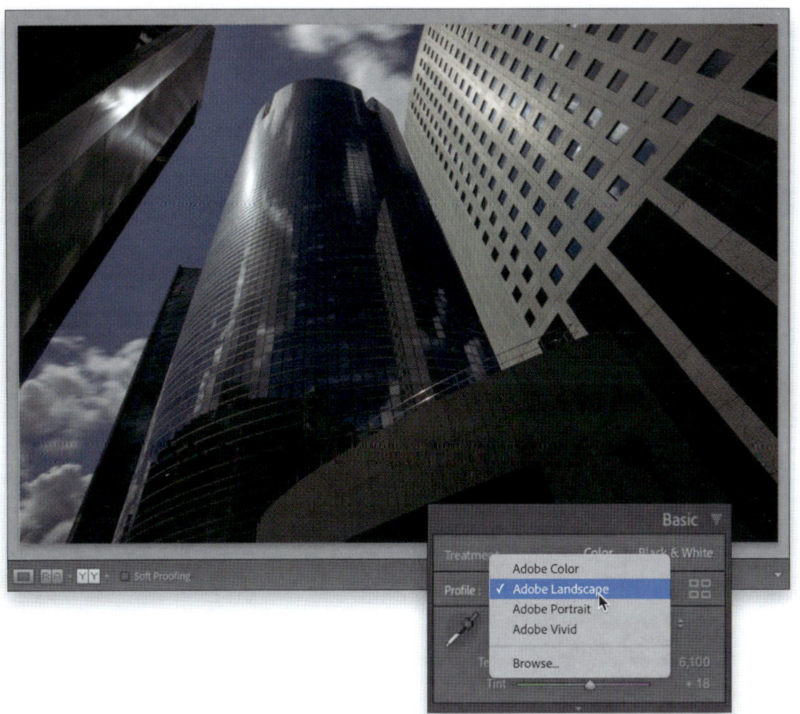

Step 02:

As always, for **Point 1**, let's see if there's a RAW profile that gives us a better starting place for our editing. At the top of the Develop module's Basic panel (the Edit panel in Lightroom cloud), from the Profile pop-up menu, try the three different profiles (spoiler alert—you're going to choose **Adobe Landscape**, as shown here). The sky looks better, and the buildings look a bit better and opened up, as well. Not earth shattering, but still, it's just one click and things are already looking a little better. Let's roll on.

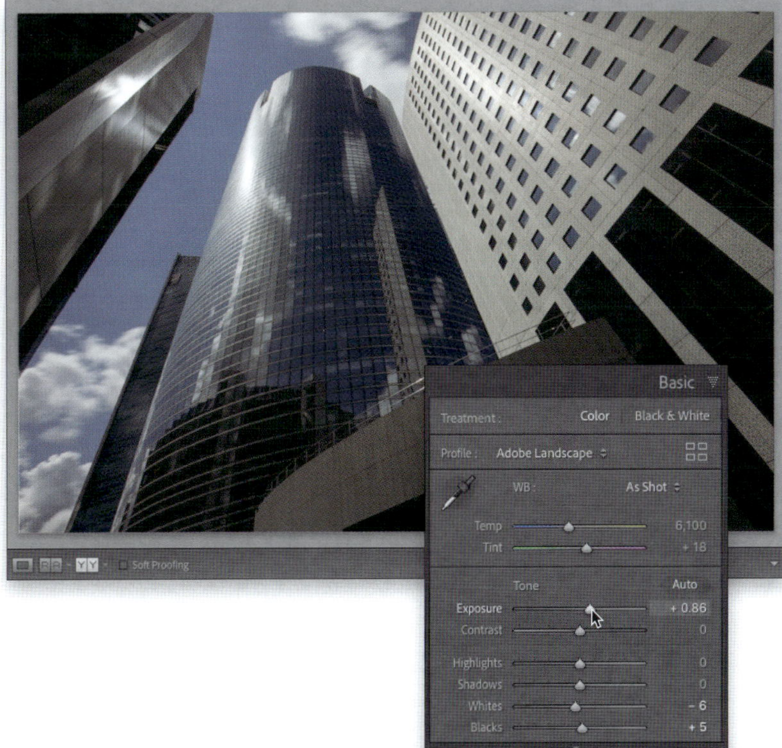

Step 03:

Let's set our white and black points next for **Point 3** (the color looks okay, so we're skipping Point 2 here). In the Basic panel (the Light panel in Lightroom cloud), press-and-hold the Shift key, and then double-click on Whites, and then on Blacks to set your white and black points. This didn't have a big effect, only moving the Whites down to –6, and opening up the Blacks by +5. So, the good news is our tonal range is pretty good. The bad news is it was so good that setting the white and black points really didn't help. Now is when we look to see if we think the image needs to be a little brighter or darker. This image could go quite a bit brighter, so drag the Exposure slider to the right to around +0.86 (as shown here). Okay, things are heading in the right direction.

Step 04:

Now, let's make that sky look a bit better, by pulling the Highlights way back (this will help darken the sky a bit while also helping the clouds stand out better. This is **Point 4**). Drag the Highlights slider to the left to around –61 (as seen here), and then let's open up the shadow areas a bunch, as some of the detail is getting lost in the shadows. So, go to the Shadows slider and crank the amount up to +58.

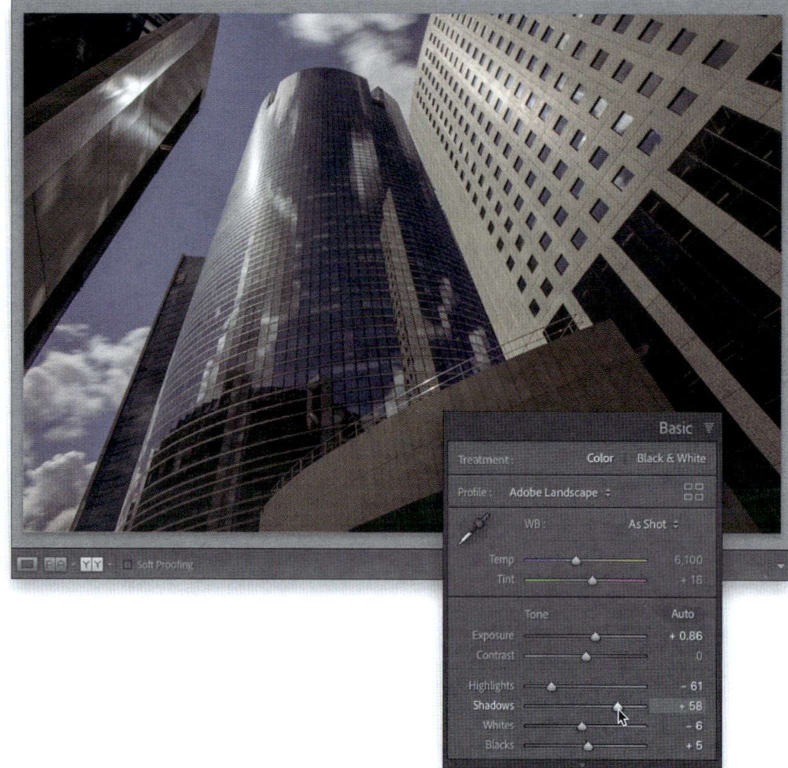

Step 05:

The balance of the tones in the image looks pretty good, but the overall image still looks kinda flat, so let's crank the contrast a bunch by dragging the Contrast slider to +68. Okay, this is starting to get there. Now, let's open up some of the areas those sliders didn't reach.

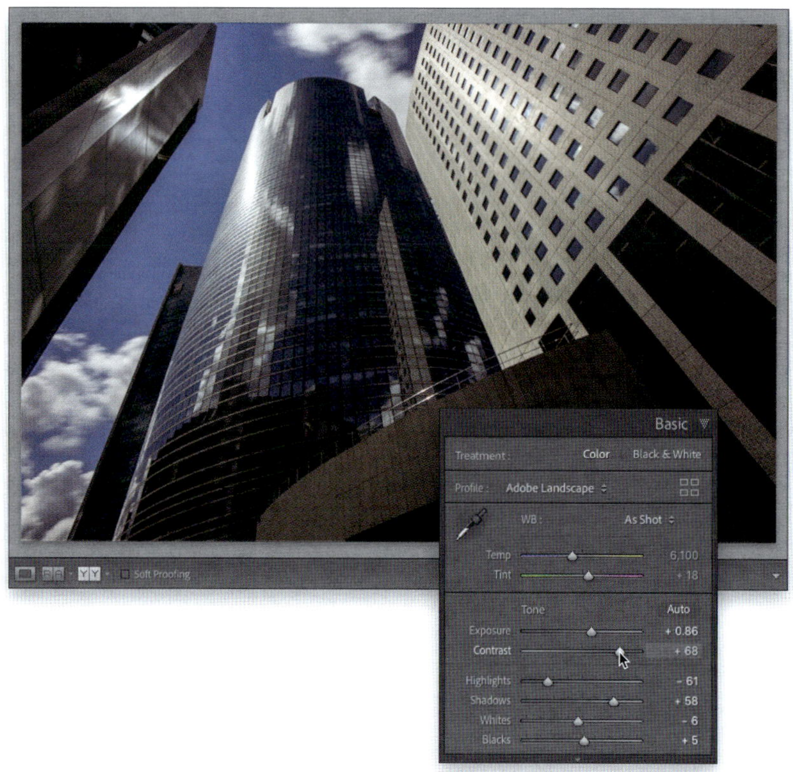

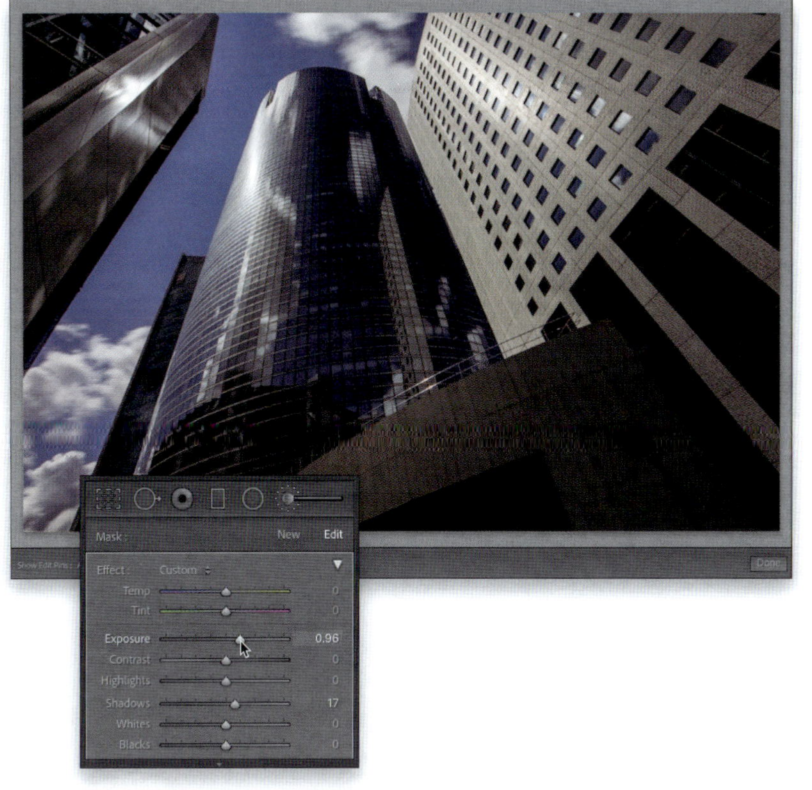

Step 06:

We're going to work on the glass area of the building up in the top-left corner. So, for **Point 5**, get the Adjustment Brush **(K)** from the toolbox beneath the histogram (the Brush tool **[B]** from the toolbox on the right in Lightroom cloud), and double-click on the word "Effect" near the top of the panel to reset all the sliders to zero (this happens by default in Lightroom cloud). Drag the Exposure slider over until you're around 1 stop (here, I dragged over to 0.96, so almost a full stop), and then drag the Shadows slider over a little to the right to around 17 (as seen here). Now, paint over that top-left corner of the building and you'll see all that detail inside the glass, and you get the added bonus of seeing the color of the glass, as well.

Step 07:

Next, let's work on the windows on the bottom right, and then the green glass building on the left behind the round building in the center. Click on New (the + [plus sign] button in Lightroom cloud) at the top of the panel, so our other adjustment will be left as is. We want to make those areas brighter, and more contrasty, so let's crank up the Exposure, the Contrast, the Whites, and the Blacks sliders (remember, making the blacks darker has us dragging the Blacks slider to the left, not to the right like the other sliders). You might want to pull those Highlights back, too, and increase the Shadows just a bit, and then paint over those windows on the bottom right, and that building on the left (that's where I'm painting here, but you can see the Edit Pin on the windows on the right, as well). *TIP:* When painting a straight line, like we're doing here, you can click once at the top of the building or window, then Shift-click at the bottom to paint a straight line between the two points. Click the Done button beneath the Preview area (in Lightroom Classic) when you're finished.

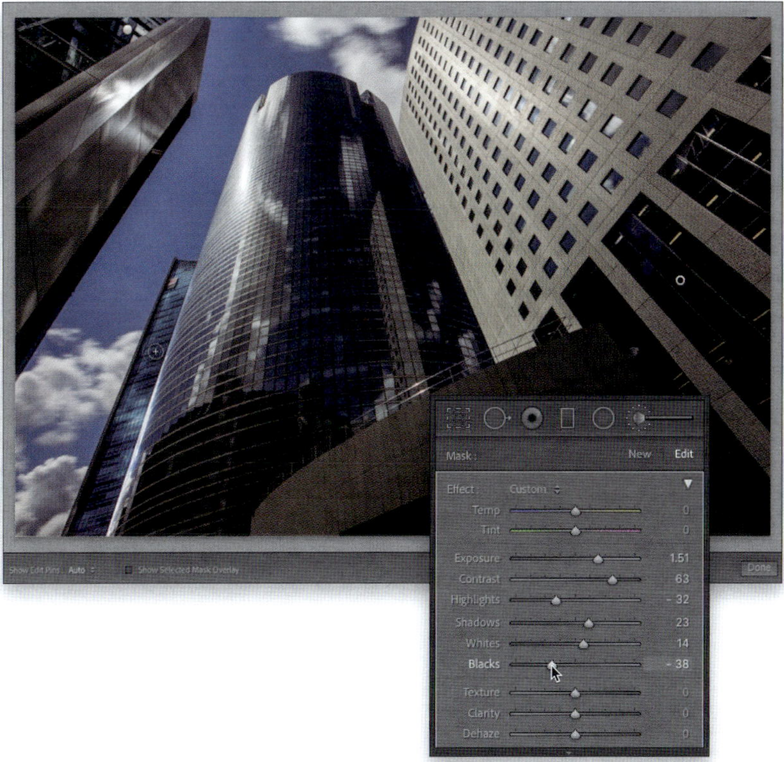

Step 08:

Now, let's bring out the detail and shine in the buildings. Go back to the Basic panel (go to the Effects panel in Lightroom cloud) and drag the Texture slider to the right to around +39 to enhance the detail, and the Clarity slider to +19 (it increases midtone contrast, as you know by now, but a side effect is that is makes metal and glass shiny, which is why we added it here).

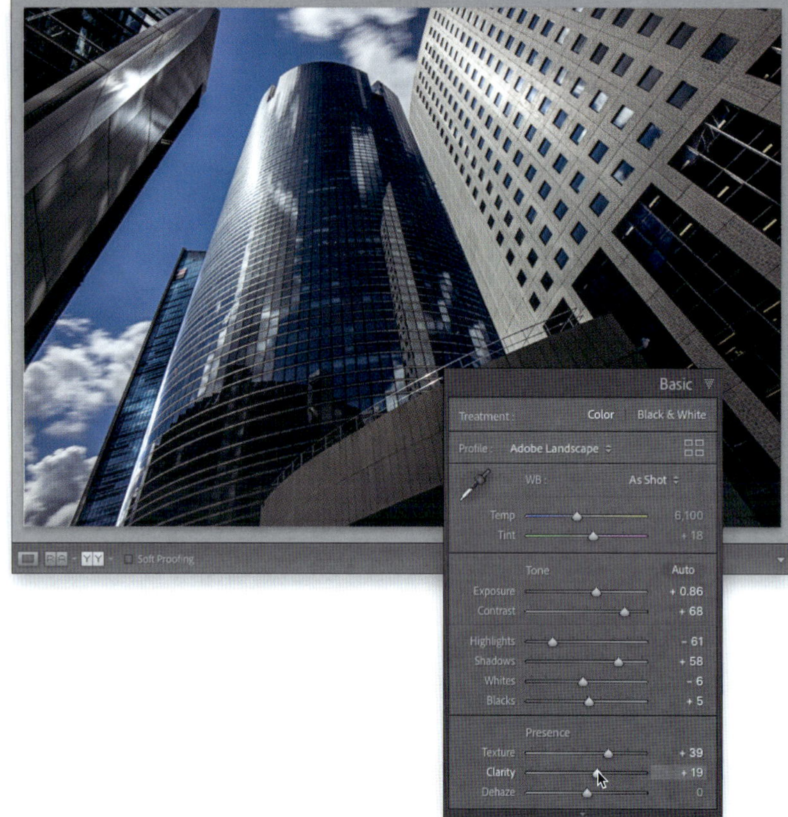

Step 09:

There are some pretty big lens distortion issues due to that wide-angle lens, and some darkening in the corners, as well, so we're going to fix both with just one click for **Point 6**. Head to the Lens Corrections panel (the Optics panel in Lightroom cloud), and turn on the Enable Profile (Lens) Corrections checkbox (as shown here). Lightroom will choose a profile from its built-in database of lens fixes, and just like that— the edges of the image flatten out, the distortion is gone, and the darkening in the corners is gone, as well.

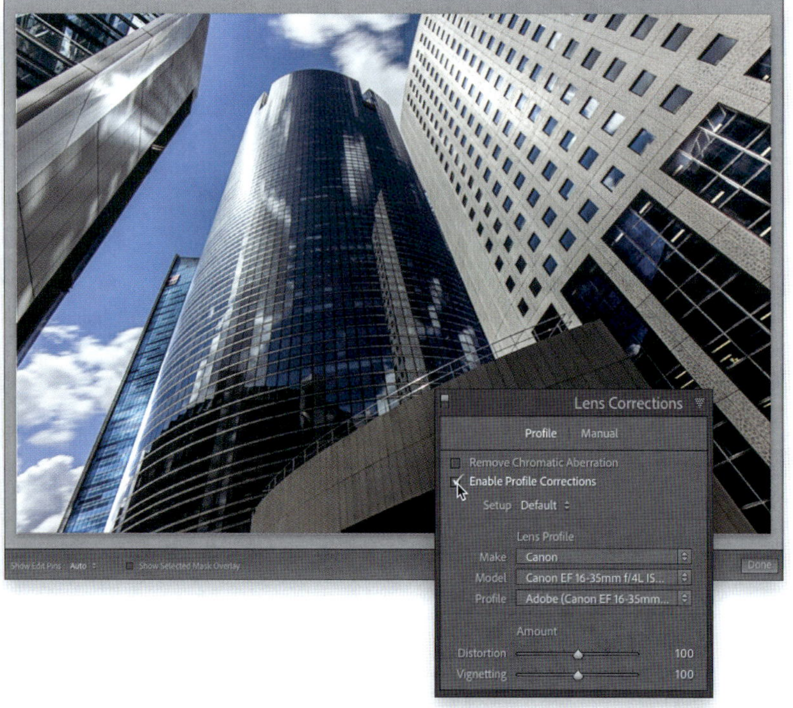

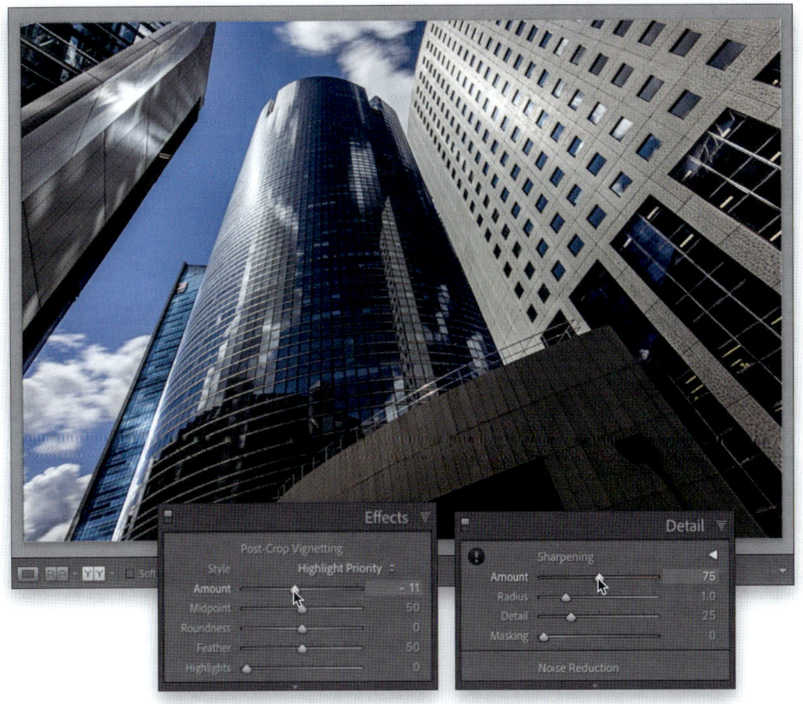

Step 10:

Let's put some finishing moves on this image **(Point 7)**. Head to the Effects panel, and at the top, in the Post-Crop Vignetting section, drag the Amount slider (the Vignette slider in Lightroom cloud) over to –11 (yup, I pretty much use the same setting every time) to subtly darken the edges of the entire image all the way around. Let's finish up by applying a decent amount of sharpening (after all, it has lots of edges and detail), but we're not going to go crazy because we added lots of Texture and Clarity, so the image already looks pretty crisp. Go to the Detail panel and drag the Amount (Sharpening) slider over to 75, leave the other sliders as is, and you're done. This is more of that repetition that I talked about in the book's introduction, so if you're thinking, "This is a lot of the same thing applied again and again"…well…that's the whole idea.

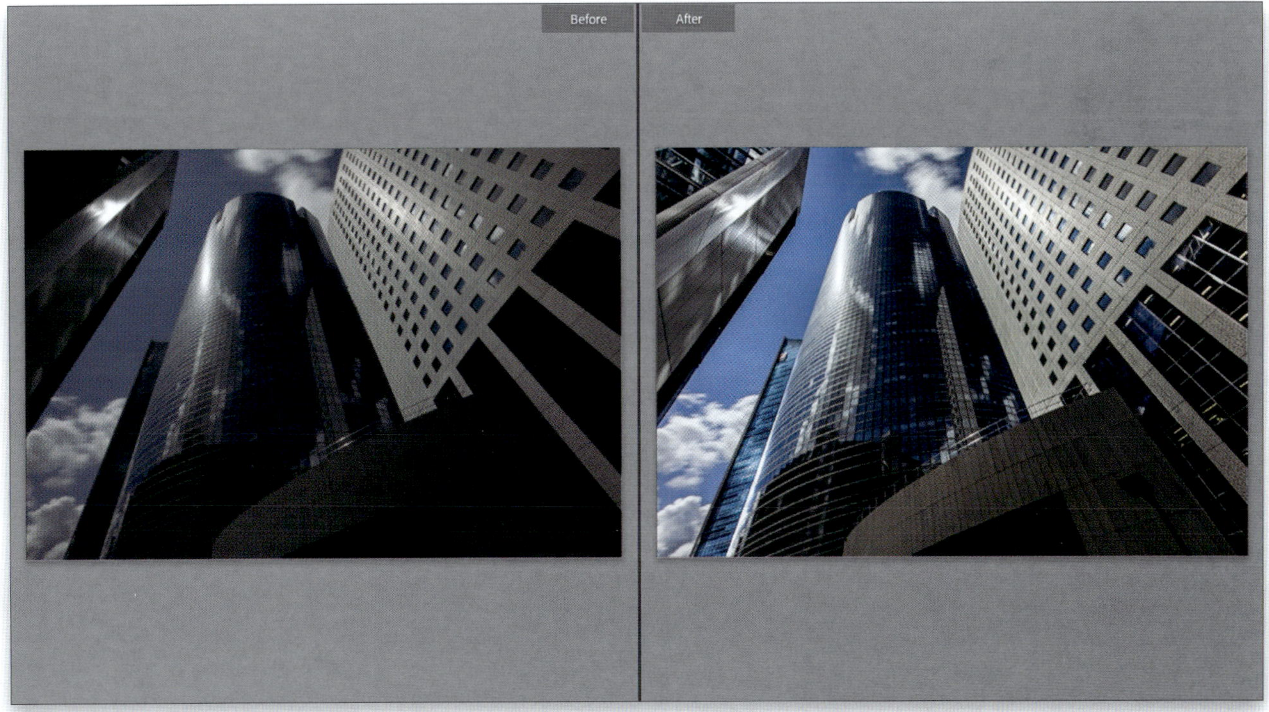

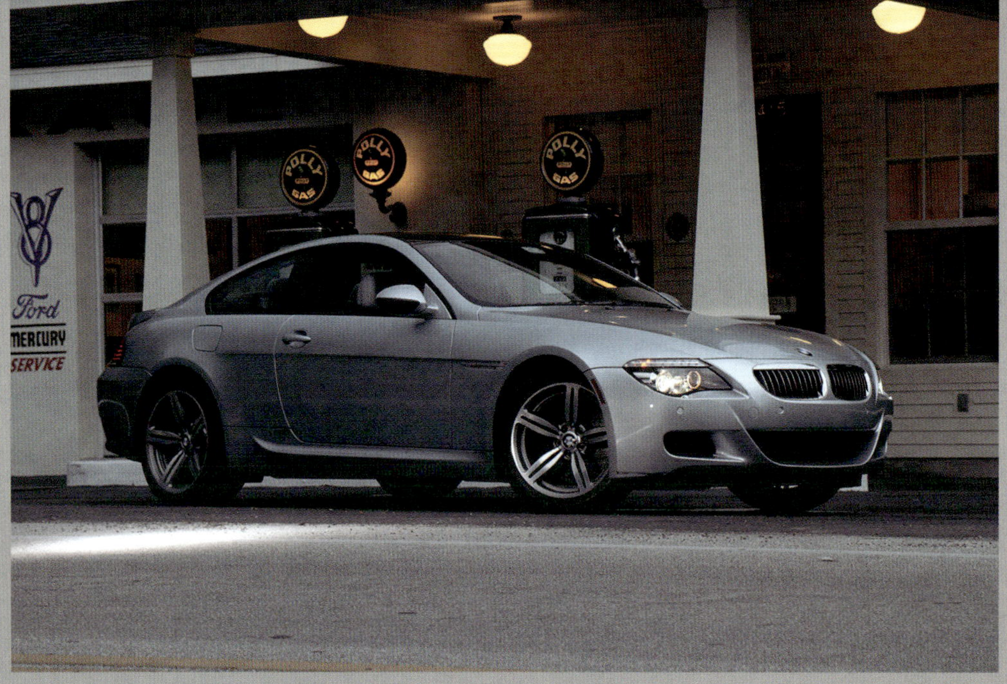

Before

After

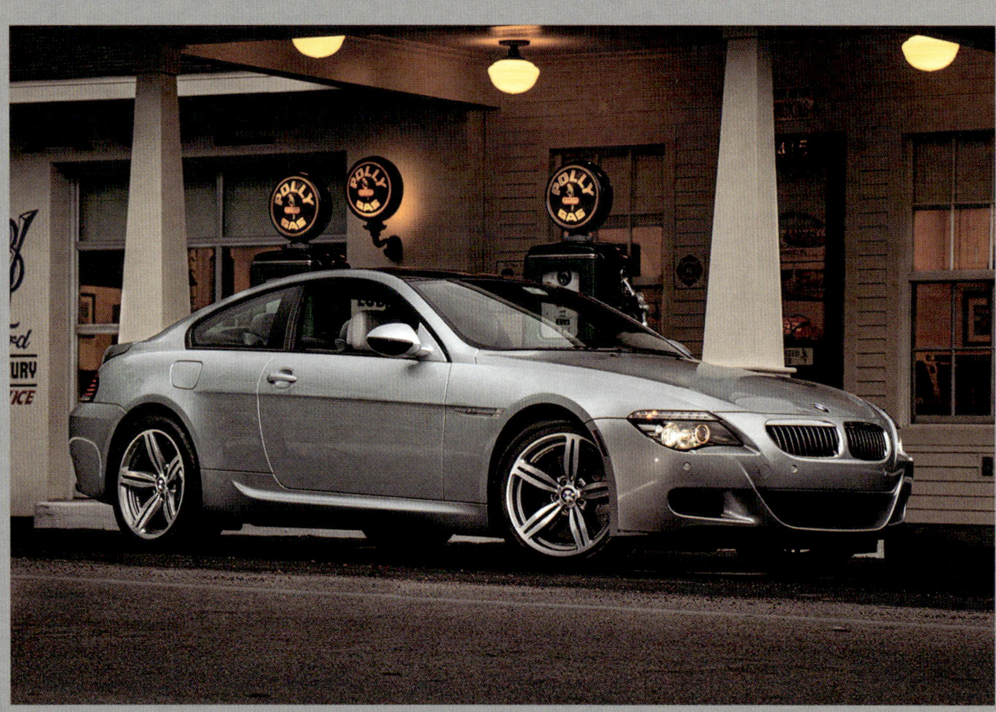

AUTOMOTIVE

This one has a little bit of everything wrong, from the fact that the gas station is crooked (the station sits on a small hill, but in making the car look straight in the shot, the gas station itself looks crooked), and the color is way off (it's a silver car), and there's light spill on the ground from the lights, and the lighting is really uneven on the car (look at the wheels in the back), and it just needs a lot of work.

THE STORY BEHIND THE SHOT:

I live in the Tampa Bay area of Florida and when I want to do a location shoot, I call my dear friend, photographer Kathy Porupski. She always knows of a lot of cool locations for shoots (she helps run the large, local Strobist group), and when I told her "I found a car—now I just need a location," she told me about this fully restored old gas station not far from us that was now the offices of an ad agency, and they were cool with letting photographers take shots out front (they were super-nice and very accommodating). I thought this would make an interesting juxtaposition with the modern car and the antique background, so off we went. We hauled out a couple of strobes, a large octa softbox to light the side and rear, and a 4' strip bank to light the front. The goal was to blend the existing light with the light from the strobes. Well, it was my first time lighting a car on location like this, and I did not do an awesome job (to say the least), so Lightroom is going to have to come to the rescue to fix the many lighting mistakes I made (I learned a lot that day).

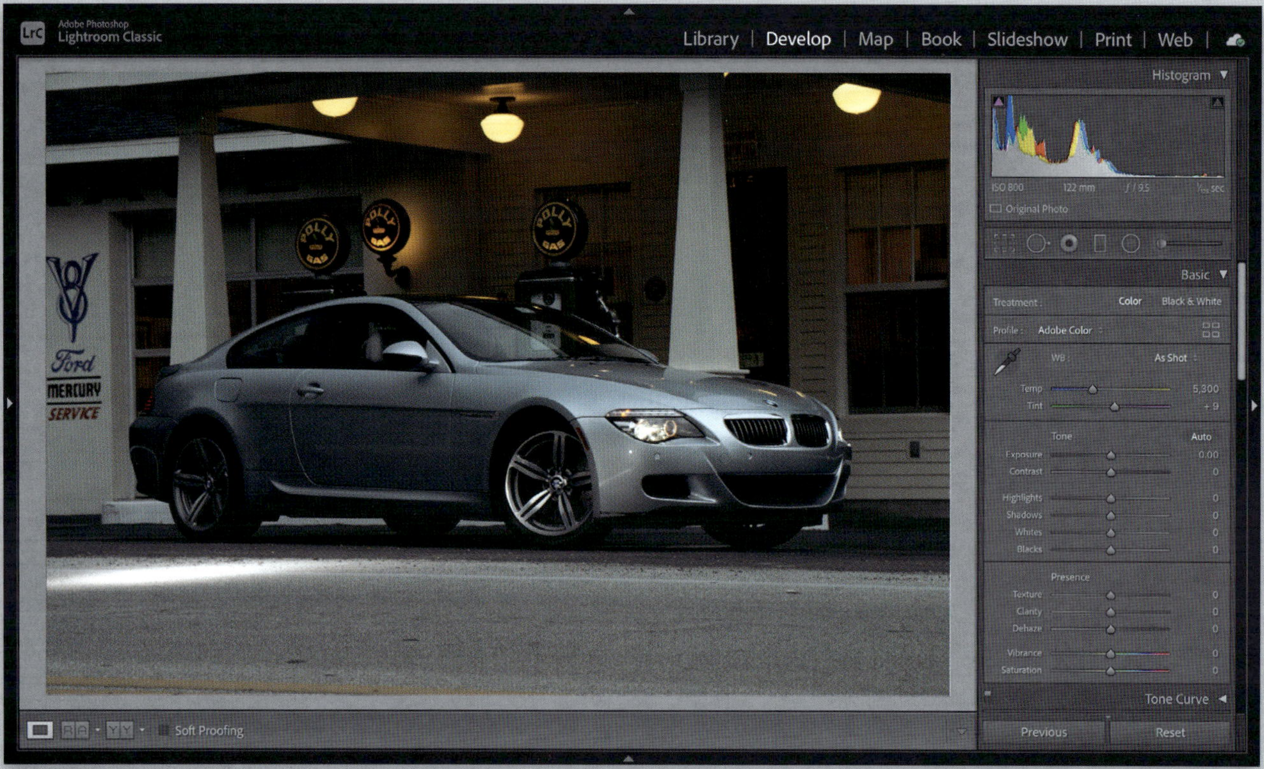

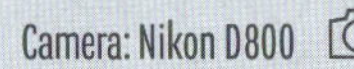

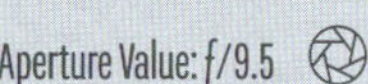

Camera: Nikon D800
Aperture Value: ƒ/9.5
Shutter Speed: 1/125 sec
ISO: 800
Focal Length: 122mm

Step 01:

Here's our original RAW image of the car, and you can see all the issues we're going to have to deal with, plus a few bonus things we're going to do (like lighting the signs above the gas pumps themselves) that aren't a part of the system, but are easy (and fun), and it makes a big difference in the final image. To fix the light spill on the ground and the reflections on the car, you might think we'd need to jump over to Photoshop (and, of course, we could), but I think you'll be surprised at how much we can address right here in little ol' Lightroom.

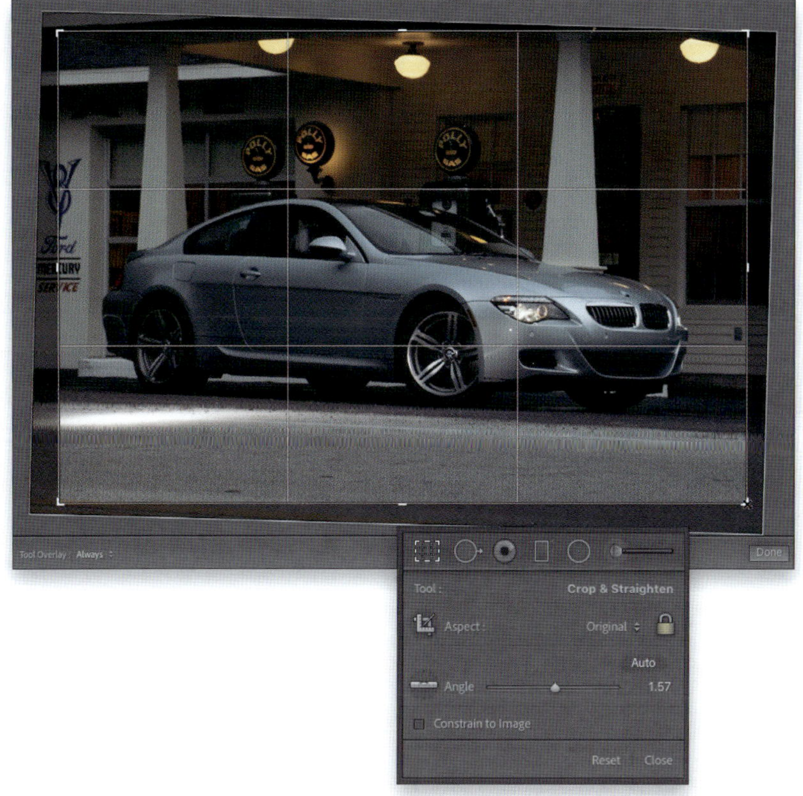

Step 02:

We always check to see if there's a RAW profile that can get us a better starting place for our editing **(Point 1)**, so go to the top of the Develop module's Basic panel (the Edit panel in Lightroom cloud), and from the Profile pop-up menu, try the different profiles. I tried Adobe Landscape and Adobe Vivid, but neither really looked better than **Adobe Color** (which is rare), so I just left it at that. We do have an issue with the image being straight, so let's deal with that really quickly. The car looks fairly straight (see the image in Step 01), but the gas station looks weirdly tilted, and that's because it kind of sits on a little hill. So, let's straighten the gas station and if the car aims slightly downhill, it's okay because that's how it really looks. Get the Crop Overlay tool **(R)** from the toolbox beneath the histogram (the Crop & Rotate Tool **[C]** from the toolbox on the right in Lightroom cloud) and click-and-drag the bottom-right corner inward a little, then move your cursor just outside the cropping border, where it changes into a two-headed arrow. Click-and-drag in a clockwise motion to rotate the crop until the gas station looks fairly straight (as seen here). Press the **Return (PC: Enter) key** to lock in your crop.

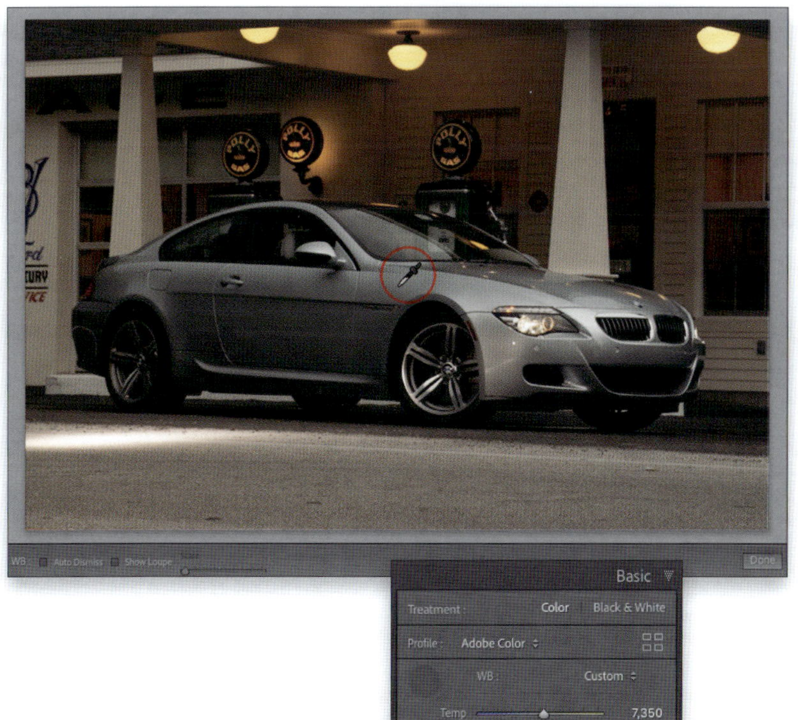

Step 03:

Now, let's get our color where it needs to be (and not so blue. **Point 2**). Near the top of the Basic panel (the Color panel in Lightroom cloud), get the White Balance Selector tool (**W**; the eyedropper) and click it on a nice, light gray part of the car, like I did here just behind the front wheel well. Again, it's always worth clicking in a few different places, as each will give you a slightly different color, so click around until you find a white balance that looks good to you. Ahhh, that's better—the blue tint is gone and now the car looks like it was shot near sunset, instead of at dawn.

Step 04:

Let's set our white and black points now, and get our overall exposure where we need it to be **(Point 3)**. Press-and-hold the Shift key and double-click on the word "Whites," and then on "Blacks" (in the Light panel in Lightroom cloud) to set your white and black points. This dropped the Whites down to –32, and opened up the Blacks by +21. Now look and see if you think the image needs to be a little brighter or darker. This could go a little brighter, but not too bright because it's a "near sunset" shot, so drag the Exposure slider to the right to around +0.20 (as seen here). I also bumped the Tint slider toward green just a bit (to +23). So far, so good.

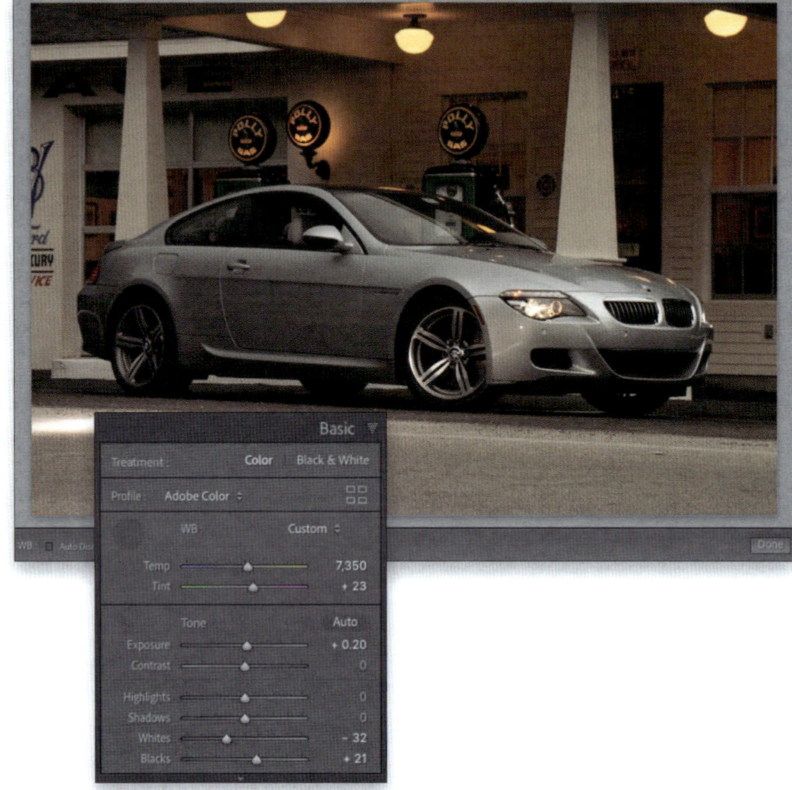

Step 05:

The image looks a bit flat, so let's crank up the contrast by dragging that slider to the right to +39. This adds some nice contrast and vibrance to the shot, but when you add contrast (which makes the brightest parts of your image brighter, and the darkest parts darker), it often makes the image look darker overall, which it did here (especially in the dark areas of the car), but we're going to address that later. For now, let's make sure we have enough contrast, so the image doesn't look flat.

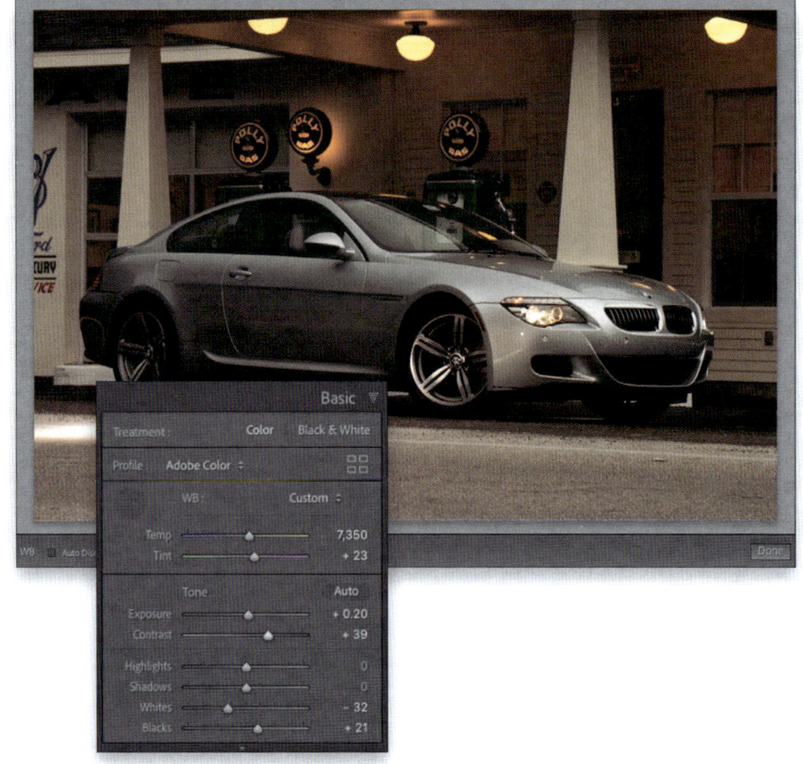

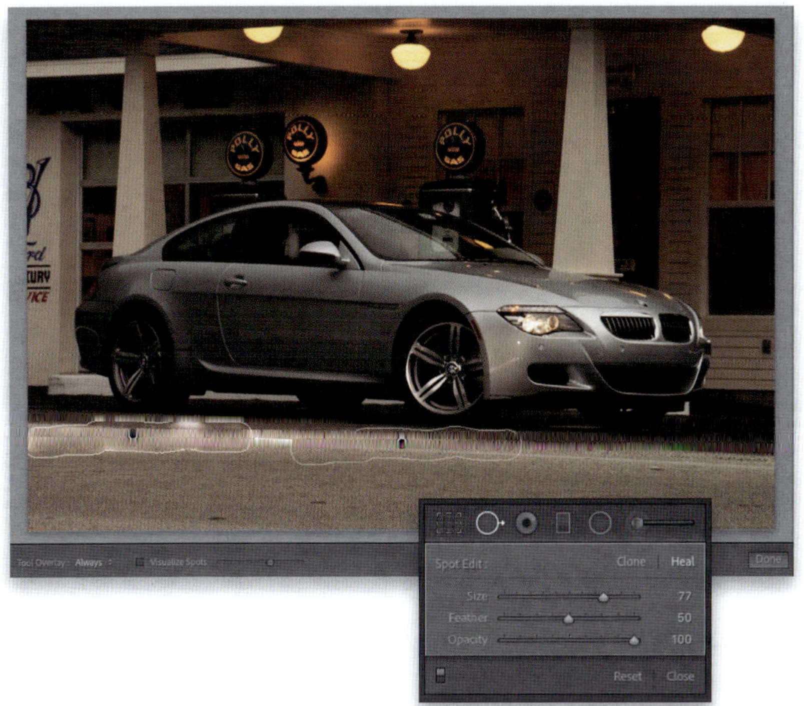

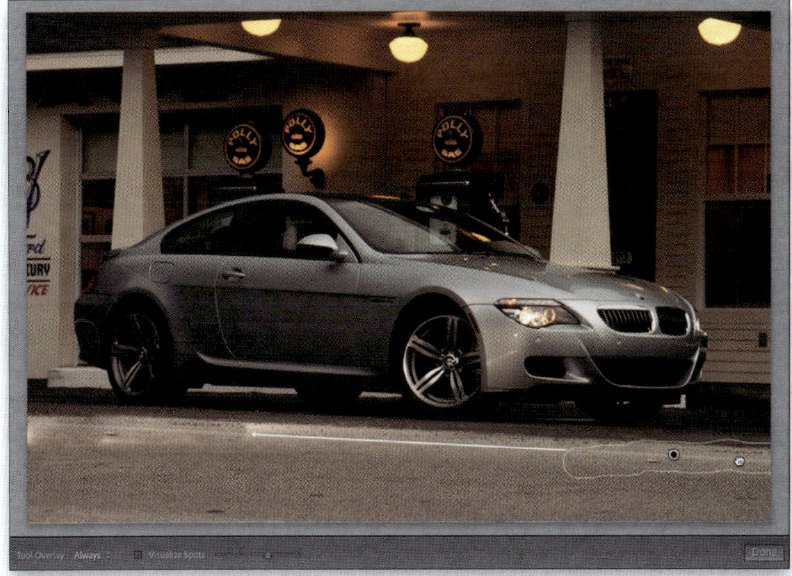

Step 06:

Before we go any further, let's jump to **Point 5** and deal with that light spill on the ground over on the bottom left (we don't have any highlight clipping or shadow issues, so we can skip Point 4). As I've mentioned before, the Spot Removal tool **(Q)** in Lightroom Classic (the Healing Brush **[H]** in Lightroom cloud) is good at removing spots and fairly lame at everything else, but it's the only tool we have, so let's give it a shot. Get this tool from the toolbox beneath the histogram (in the toolbox on the right in Lightroom cloud), make your brush Size a little larger than the light spill itself, and then starting on the far left, paint over the spill. It will choose an area to sample from, and you'll see an outline of that area with an arrow pointing back to an outline of the area where you painted (as seen here). You can also see it didn't do a very good job, which is pretty much how it works.

Step 07:

We can try to manually pick a better sample spot by just clicking inside that second outline (the one with the arrow pointing outward) and dragging it farther over to the right. While this sample area over on the far right here isn't great, it's better than what we had, so at least that's a start. *Note:* Yours may look a bit different depending on how you painted over the light spill.

Step 08:

Now, let's try to fix those areas where it left gaps and such. Once you've painted a brush stroke like we did, it doesn't really like you to try to paint another stroke inside it (which is kind of what we need to do). So, our workaround is to shrink our brush Size and try clicking once right over a gap (if it lets you), or just try painting over those areas by starting your stroke in an area outside the original painted stroke, coming in from a different angle, and see if that works. That's what I did here (and it's why you see that grouping of little gray Edit Pins on the left). Then, I tried to fix another gap by painting a short stroke, and then manually moving the second outline over—right down that white line on the pavement (as shown here). By the way: one quick trip over to Photoshop would fix this seamlessly, but hopefully, our next step will help hide some of those brighter gaps.

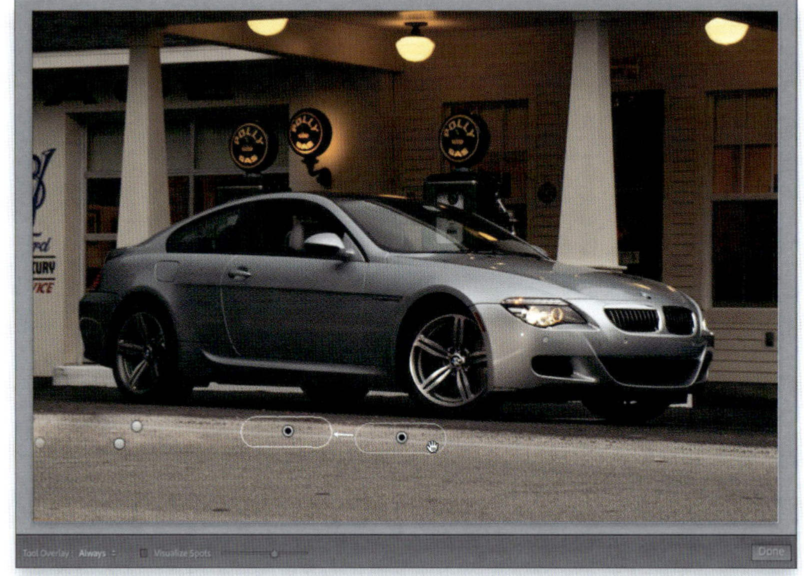

Step 09:

Let's darken the road (after all, it's not about the road, it's about the car and the gas station), which might help hide some of those light gaps. Get the Graduated Filter tool **(M)** from the toolbox beneath the histogram (the Linear Gradient tool [L] from the toolbox on the right in Lightroom cloud), double-click on Effect to set all the sliders to zero (this happens by default in Lightroom cloud), then drag the Exposure amount to about 3/4 of a stop darker (I dragged to –0.74) and the Highlights to around –47. Click at the bottom center of the image and drag upward at the same angle as the road to darken that area. Where you see the grabber hand here is totally transparent, so I stopped dragging when it reached the bottom of the car. That helped, but we'll need to do a little more work with the Spot Removal tool to see if we can get that area looking better. I'm not going to show another image here with more Edit Pins (boring), but I'm going to try clicking a few more times to see if I can clean it up a bit more.

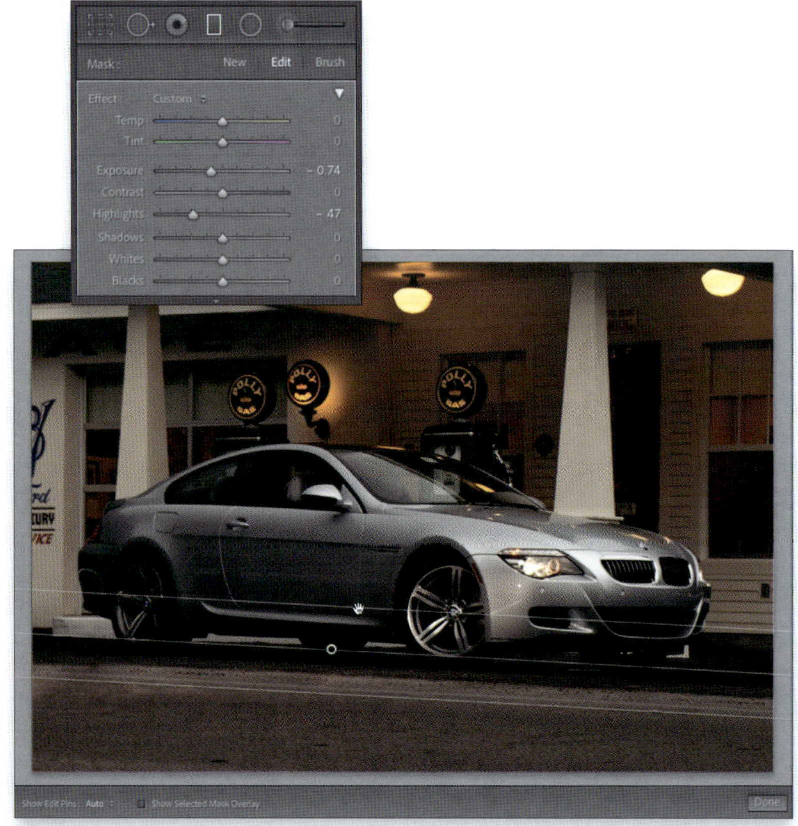

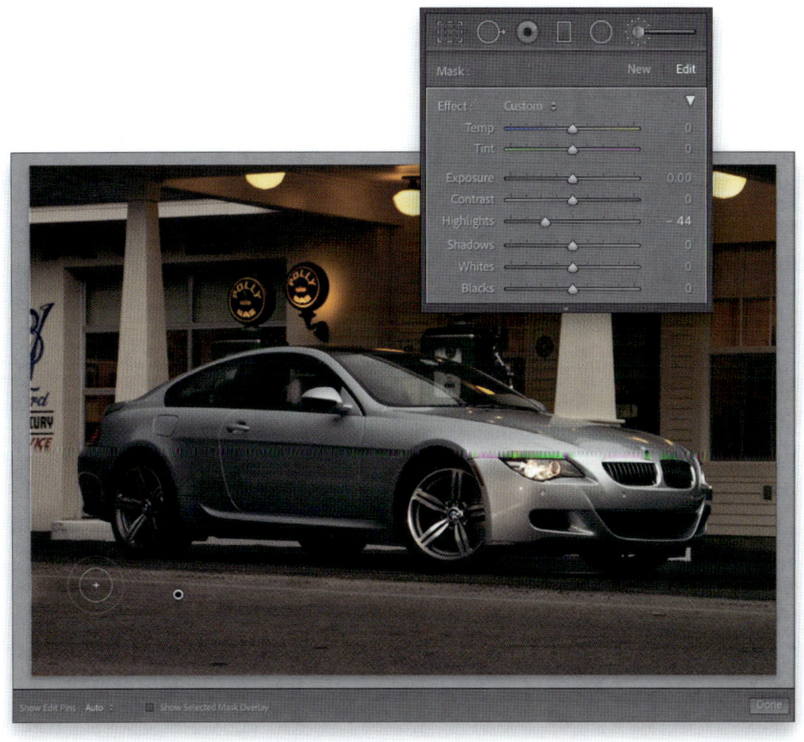

Step 10:

Okay, here's what I did to get here: (1) I did click on two more areas with the Spot Removal tool and it got a little better, but the thing that actually made a big difference was (2) getting the Adjustment Brush (**K**; the Brush tool **[B]** in Lightroom cloud) from the toolbox, resetting the sliders to zero, lowering the Highlights to –44, and then painting right over those brighter light gaps, and son of a gun it did a decent job. Not perfect. Not pristine, but certainly better. How did I know that –44 would be the perfect amount? I'm awesome that way. I wish that were the case, but in reality, I started with –20 and it didn't darken it enough, so I kept dragging the slider to the left until it pretty much matched the darkness of the rest of the road. Basically, trial and error. It could use a tiny bit more tweaking, but if we spend another page on removing spots, I imagine you'll bail on this lesson altogether, so let's roll on.

Step 11:

Now for some fun stuff—balancing out the tones on the side of the car. The front is okay (in fact, it might be a tad bright), but the side is really dark, so let's tackle that. Zoom in a bit, then with the Adjustment Brush still active, click on New at the top of the panel (the + [plus sign] in Lightroom cloud), and then double-click on Effect to reset all the sliders to zero. Drag the Exposure slider to the right to brighten the area we're going to paint by 1 stop (so, to 1.00), then start painting over the body of the car (as shown here). Remember, if 1.00 isn't right (too bright or too dark), we can adjust that after the fact. For now, just paint from the front wheel well on back. Also, when you get to the outside edges, turn on Auto Mask **(A)**, so you don't spill over and make the background a stop brighter. Go ahead and paint over the visible interior, but don't paint over the wheels yet (we want to control that separately), and don't paint over the front windshield because it will just make the reflection more obvious.

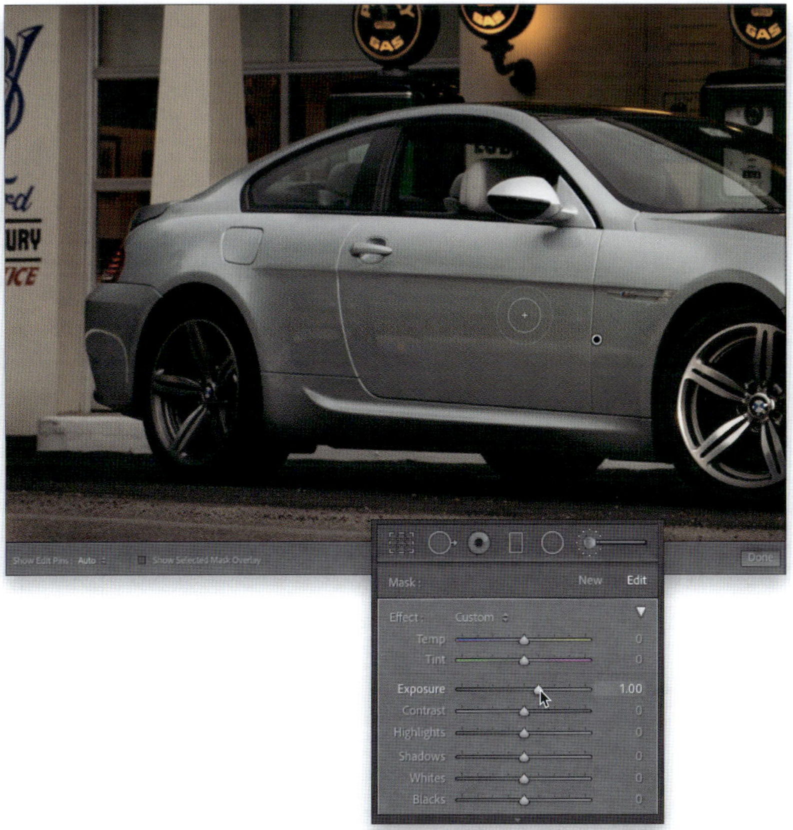

Step 12:

We now have a "transition of tones" problem. You see on the body, right above the front tire where we started painting the side brighter? Well, there's kind of a dark patch there where the area we brightened meets the existing tone that was there (you can see it back in the Step 11 image, since I've already started fixing it here). We want that to be a smoother transition (we don't want that area to stand out, right?). Well, our plan is to paint a lighter amount of exposure over that area to help smooth the transition. Click on New, shrink the size of your brush, set the Exposure to around 1/4 of a stop (here, I chose 0.25), and then paint right over that area above the front tire. Be careful not to paint over the side of the car where you brightened earlier, but go ahead and paint up to the front headlight. Once we've done that, there's still a little dark patch right above the front tire, so click on New, make your brush a bit larger, lower the Exposure to 0.12, and simply click once to add just a hint of soft-edged brightness right there (you'll see how that looks in the next step).

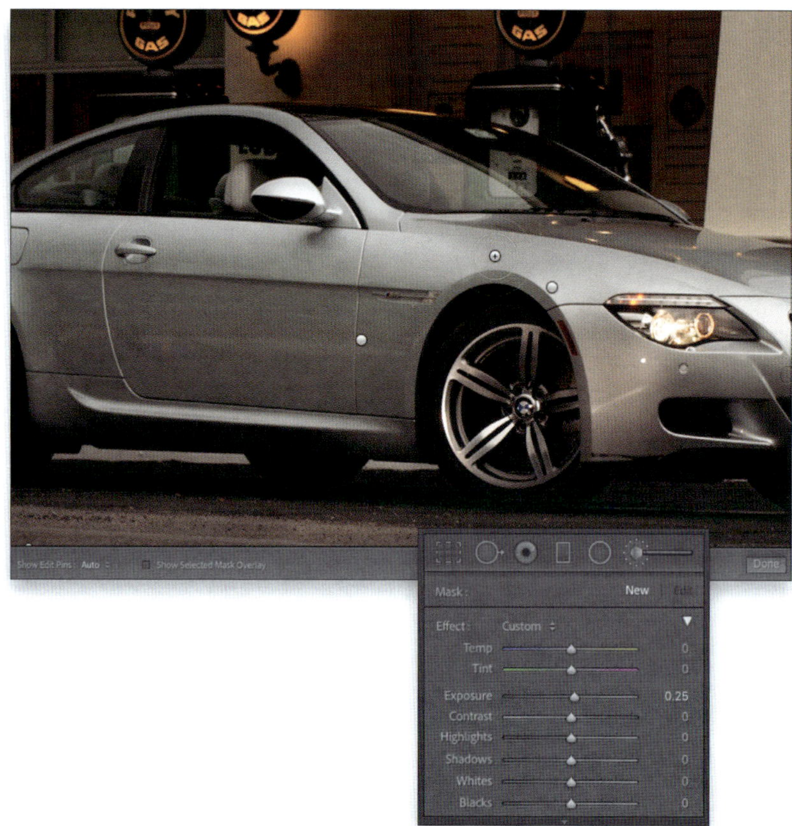

Step 13:

Now, let's balance out the bright tones on the front of the car. Start by clicking New again, then decrease the Exposure by around a half a stop (here, I went to –0.53), and then pull back the Highlights a little, too (here, I dragged just a little over to the left to –8). Now, paint over the front of the car, so it's not as bright and balances out better with the tones on the side of the car. You can paint over the hood and the front grill area, as well (as shown here).

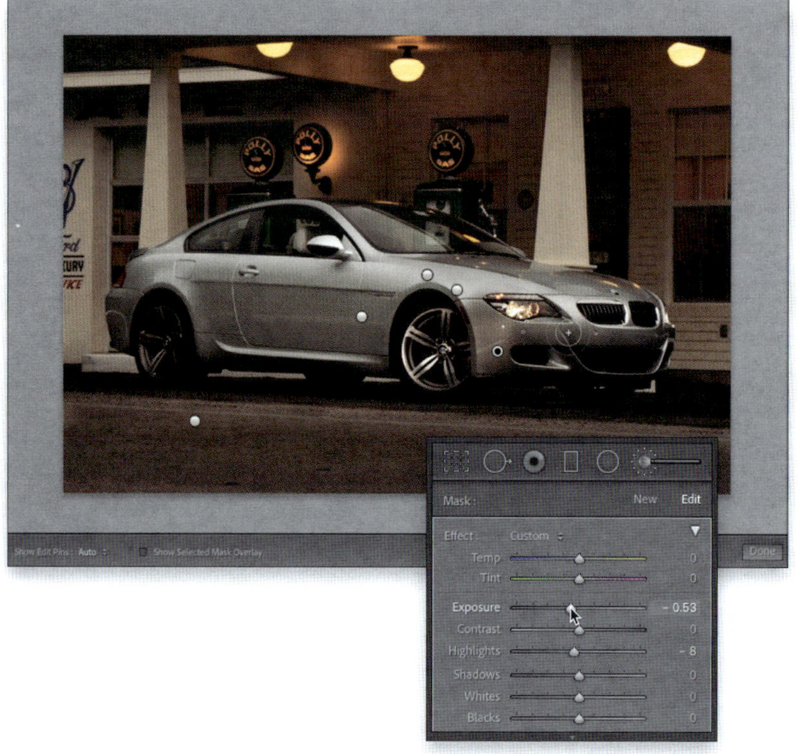

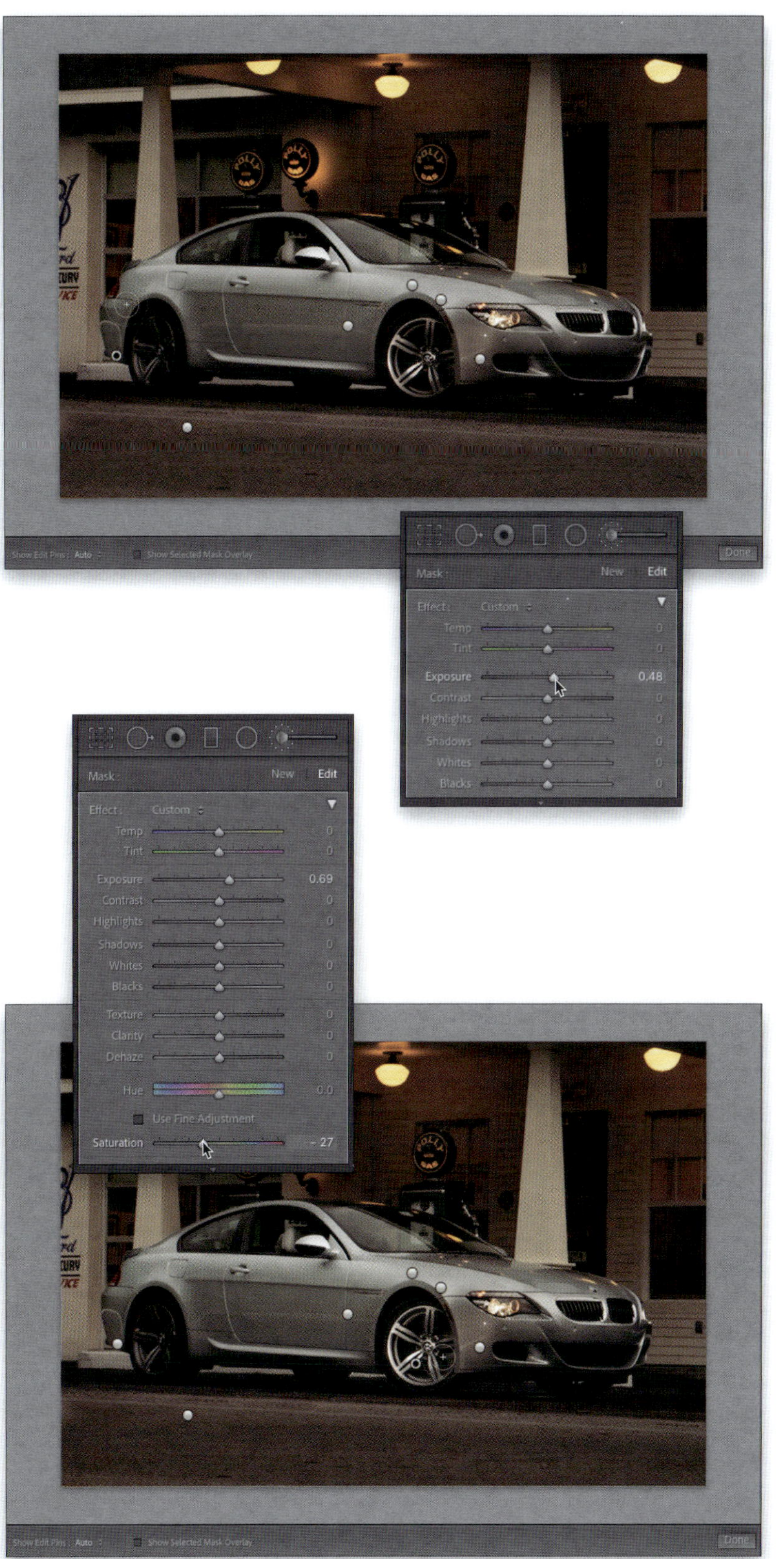

Step 14:

Okay, we're getting pretty close on the car—just a few more tweaks. Next up is the rear side of it (the area behind the rear wheel), which needs just a little brightening to match the rest of the car. Click New again, reset all the sliders to zero (double-click on Effect; this happens by default in Lightroom cloud), then increase the Exposure amount by around a half a stop (here, I went to 0.48), and then paint over just that rear side section (as shown here) to even everything out brightness-wise.

Step 15:

Let's move on to brightening the tires and wheels. Click on New, reset all the sliders (you know how—you just did it), and then increase the Exposure amount by 3/4 of a stop (here, I went to 0.69). Now, paint over that front tire and wheel (as shown here) to brighten it up. If you look at that wheel back in the image in Step 14, you can see it's a little yellowish, but that's easy enough to get rid of—just drag the Saturation slider to the left a bit (here, I dragged it to –27), and any yellowing in the wheel or tire will pretty much go away. If you drag that slider farther to the left, it will remove all the color and the wheel will turn black and white. That's actually a great trick, and I probably would have done just that were it not for the BMW logo in the center of the wheel, which has a lot of blue in it, so I didn't drag as far as I might have.

Step 16:

Next, let's do the rear wheel, but we want to be able to edit it separately from the settings we used for the front, so…you know the drill, right? Click New, reset the sliders, then add some Exposure (here, I dragged it over to 1.69 because that wheel is a lot darker than the front one). Once you paint over it, you'll find it's not nearly as shiny as the front one, but luckily you know a feature that makes thing look shinier (you remember it, right? It's Clarity). So, drag the Clarity slider over to around 46 (as shown here), and let's also increase the Contrast a bit (to 15), and now that wheel's looking pretty good.

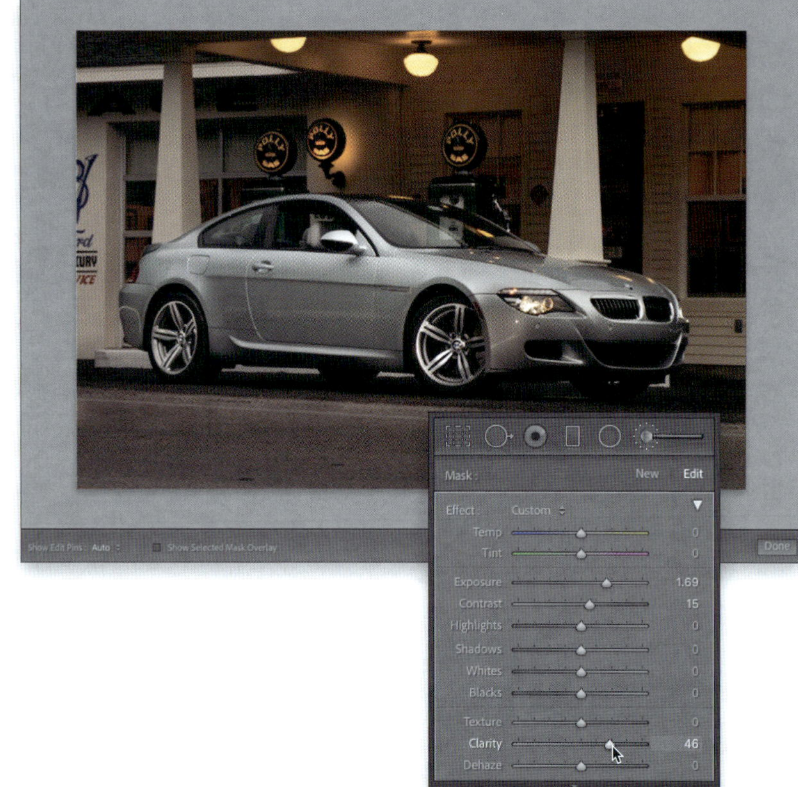

Step 17:

Take a look at the hood and the windshield, and even the roof of the car and you'll see lots of distracting reflections from the yellow overhead lights. We can get rid of a lot of these (even most of them) by getting the Spot Removal tool again (but, wait, didn't I say this tool was trash? It pretty much is, but as I mentioned earlier, it does a decent job on "spots" and these are mostly spots). So, zoom in tight on the hood, shrink your brush way down in size, and just click once over a spot, or if it's a streak of light, make sure the brush is just a little larger than the streak and paint over it. You'll end up with quite a few Edit Pins as you remove all the little reflections (well, as many as you can), but that's okay—you won't see them in the final image. Just remember, the key here is to use a very small brush.

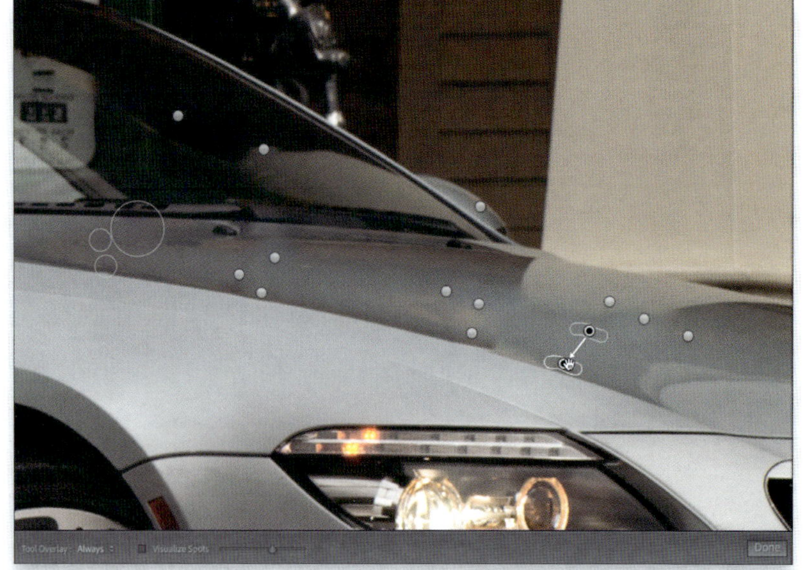

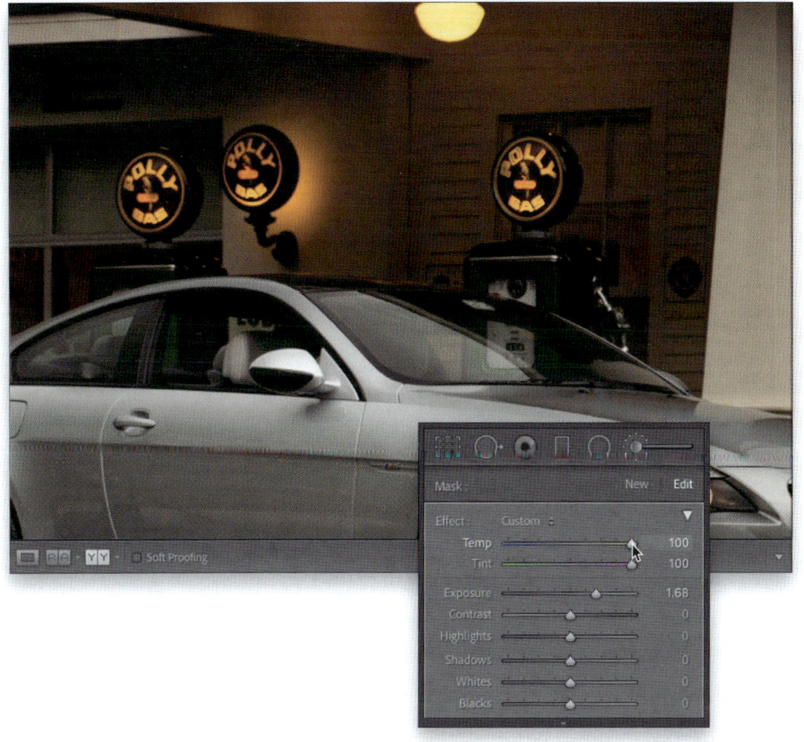

Step 18:

The car is looking pretty good, so let's take care of the few minor things we have left to finish this image off. Next up is to "light" the two signs above the gas pumps. Look back at the image in Step 16, and you can see that one of the Polly Gas signs is clearly lit, while the other two are kind of dark, so we're going to light them. Zoom in a bit (so they're easier to see), switch back to the Adjustment Brush, reset all the sliders to zero, and then increase the Exposure amount by more than a stop and a half (here, I went to +1.68). To match the color of the lit sign, drag the Temp and Tint sliders over to 100 (as shown here). Now, paint over the two signs above the pumps, and the center of the sign mounted on the wall, as you can't really see the parrot logo in that one. I know this is a little thing, but it makes a difference. Click the Done button beneath the Preview area (in Lightroom Classic) when you're finished.

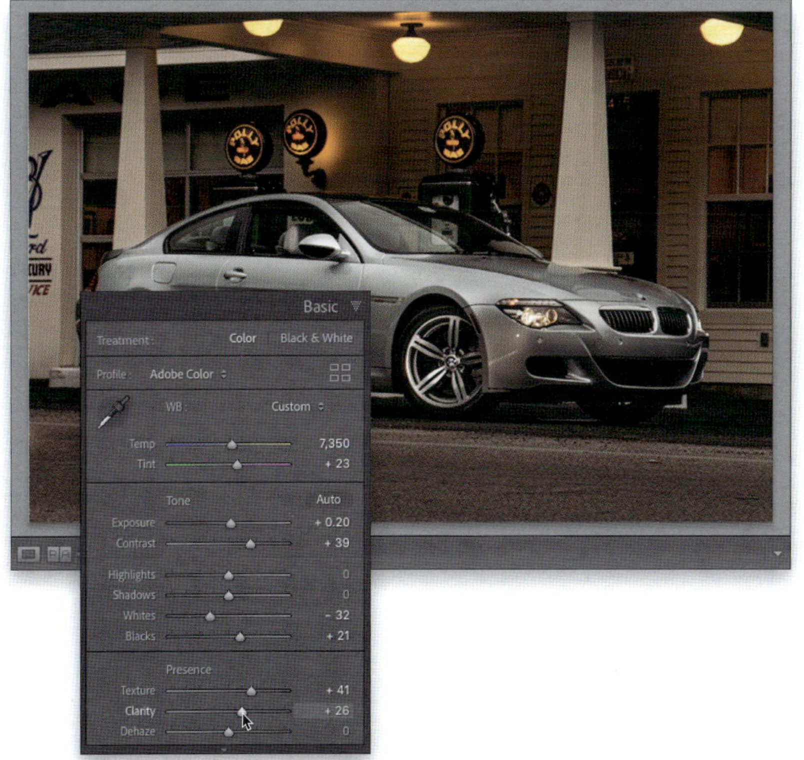

Step 19:

We don't have any lens issues to fix (Point 6), so let's add our finishing moves **(Point 7)**, starting with bringing out the detail and shine in the car. Go back to the Basic panel (the Effects panel in Lightroom cloud) and drag the Texture slider to the right to around +41 to enhance the detail, and then the Clarity slider to +26 to give the car more shine and midtone contrast. In short, some Clarity makes cars look great.

Step 20:

Next up, go to the Effects panel. At the top, in the Post-Crop Vignetting section (in Lightroom Classic), drag the Amount slider (the Vignette slider in Lightroom cloud) over to –11 (there it is again) to subtly darken the edges of the entire image all the way around.

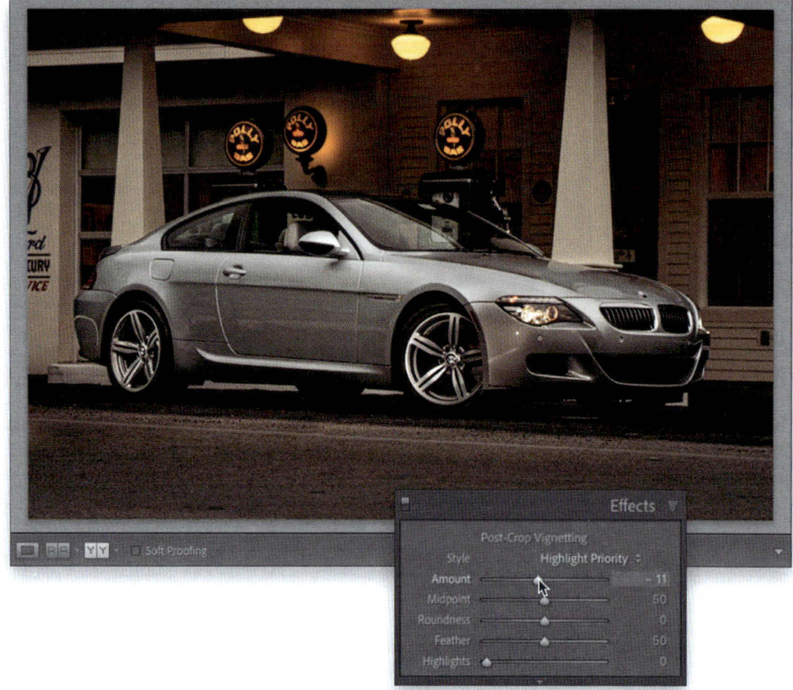

Step 21:

Let's wrap this one up with some sharpening. It has lots of detail and edges, so let's hit it hard. Go to the Detail panel and drag the Amount slider (the Sharpening slider in Lightroom cloud) over to the right to around 80, and we're done.

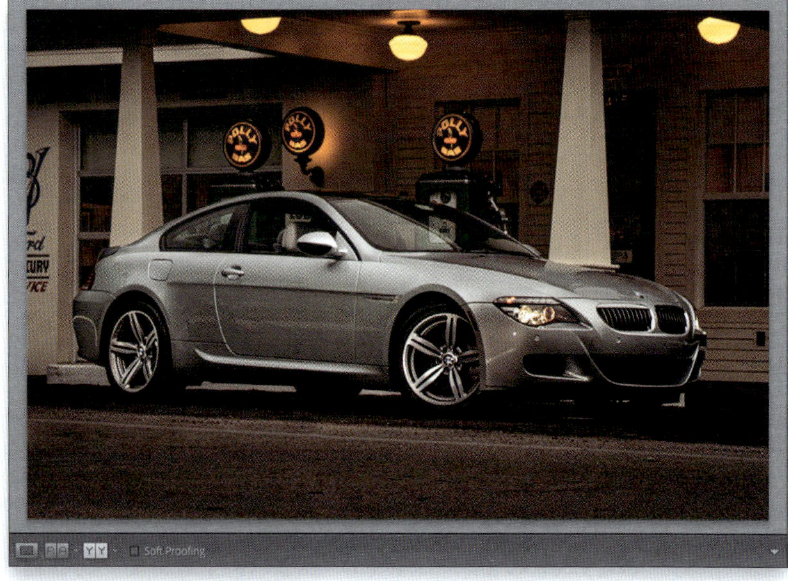

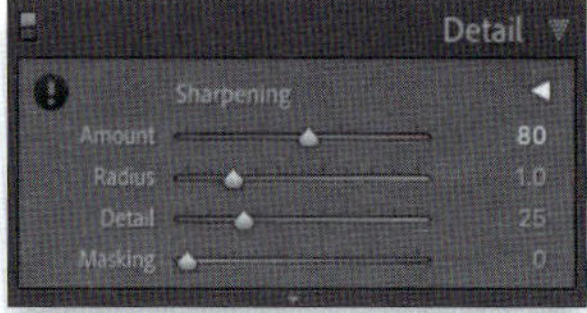

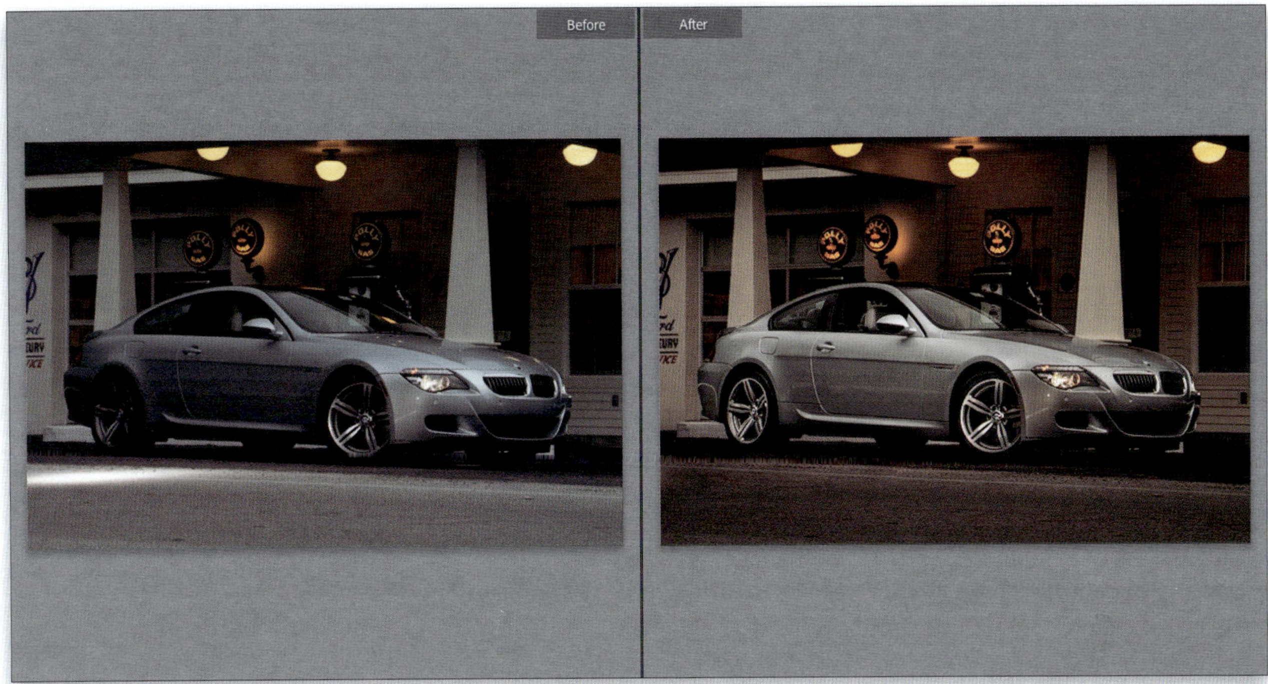

Here's our before/after.

Adobe Photoshop
Lightroom Classic

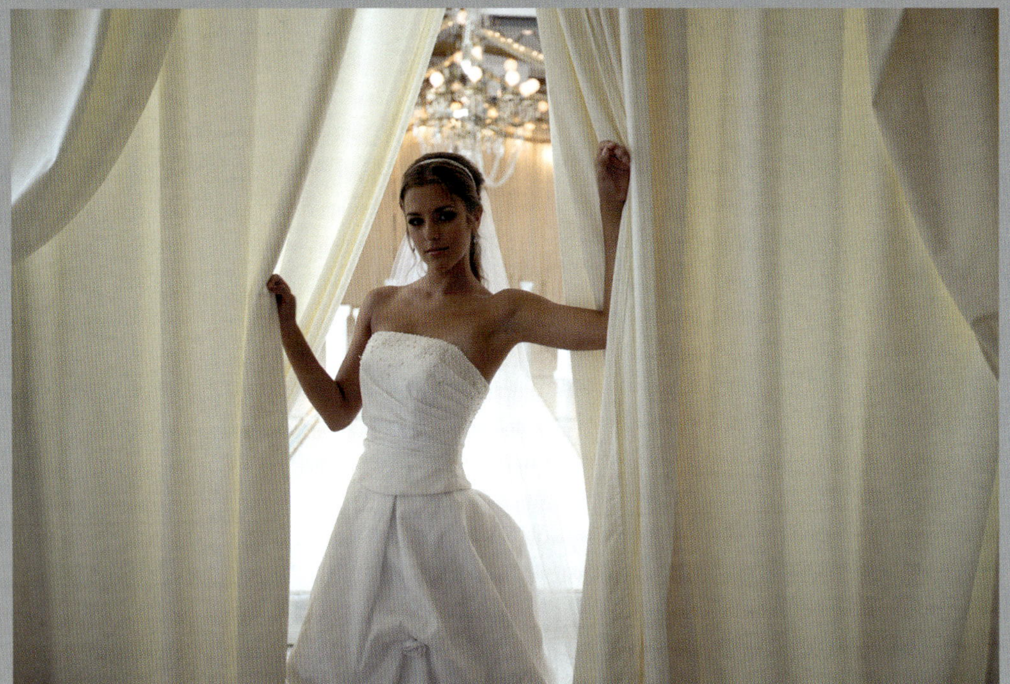

Before

After

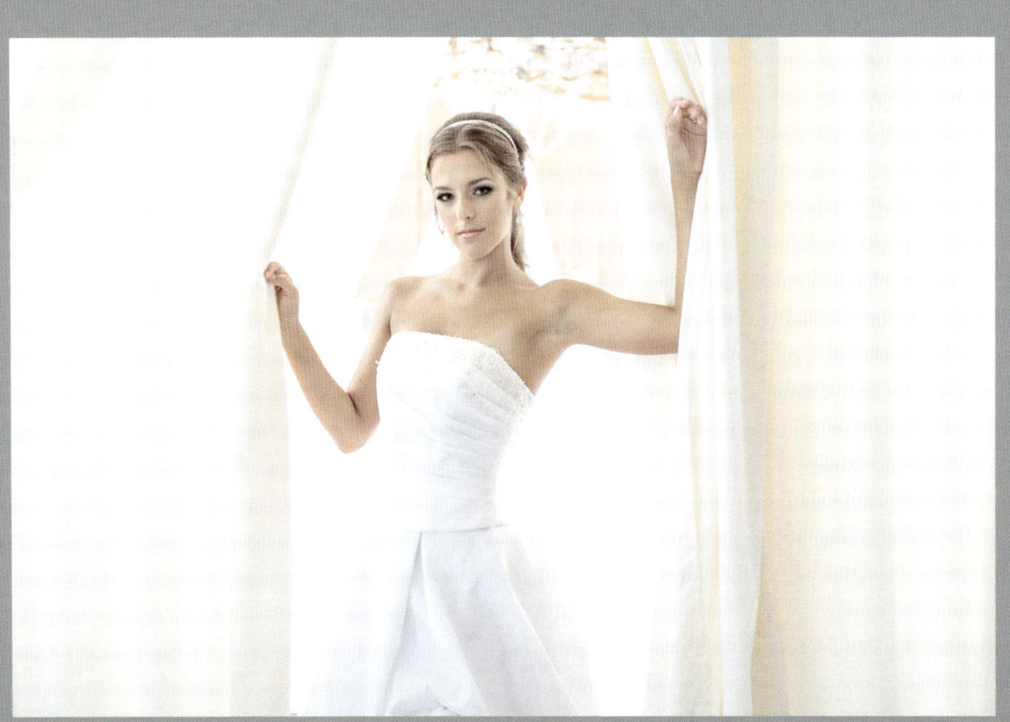

Before & After :   Soft Proofing

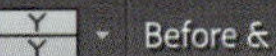
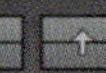
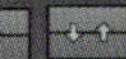
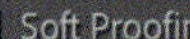

WEDDING PORTRAIT

1 Assigning a RAW Profile

2 Getting the Color Right

3 Expanding the Tonal Range

4 Dealing with Sensor Limitations

5 Painting with Light and Retouching

6 Fixing Lens Issues

7 Finishing Moves

We've got a lot to deal with on this one, starting with the fact that our subject is backlit, and the whole shot is way underexposed. There's an ugly fold in the top-right corner, and the color needs some work, as well. A little crop here, a little exposure adjustment there, a color tweak or two, and I think we can make a very happy bride.

THE STORY BEHIND THE SHOT:

This was taken at the sprawling Kapok Special Events Center in Clearwater, Florida, which is a very popular location for high-end weddings and receptions. It has lots of beautiful areas throughout, and an epic main ballroom with a stunning spiral staircase. Photographically, there are many great places there to make stunning shots, including a wonderful Greek garden area outside. All this might make you wonder why I chose to make this portrait at the back of one of the reception/ceremony areas where they store the set pieces and extra chairs. It was because of those drapes and the chandelier behind the bride. I thought it might make an interesting shot, like she was pulling back the curtain to see the reception hall or the crowd gathered inside, but the reality of this shot is that she's looking into that messy storage area—with boxes and stacked chairs—and I'm standing in the middle off all that junk. There's great natural light, but it's behind her, streaming into the hall, so she's backlit and the drapes look dingy from this back view, but I knew Lightroom could save the day!

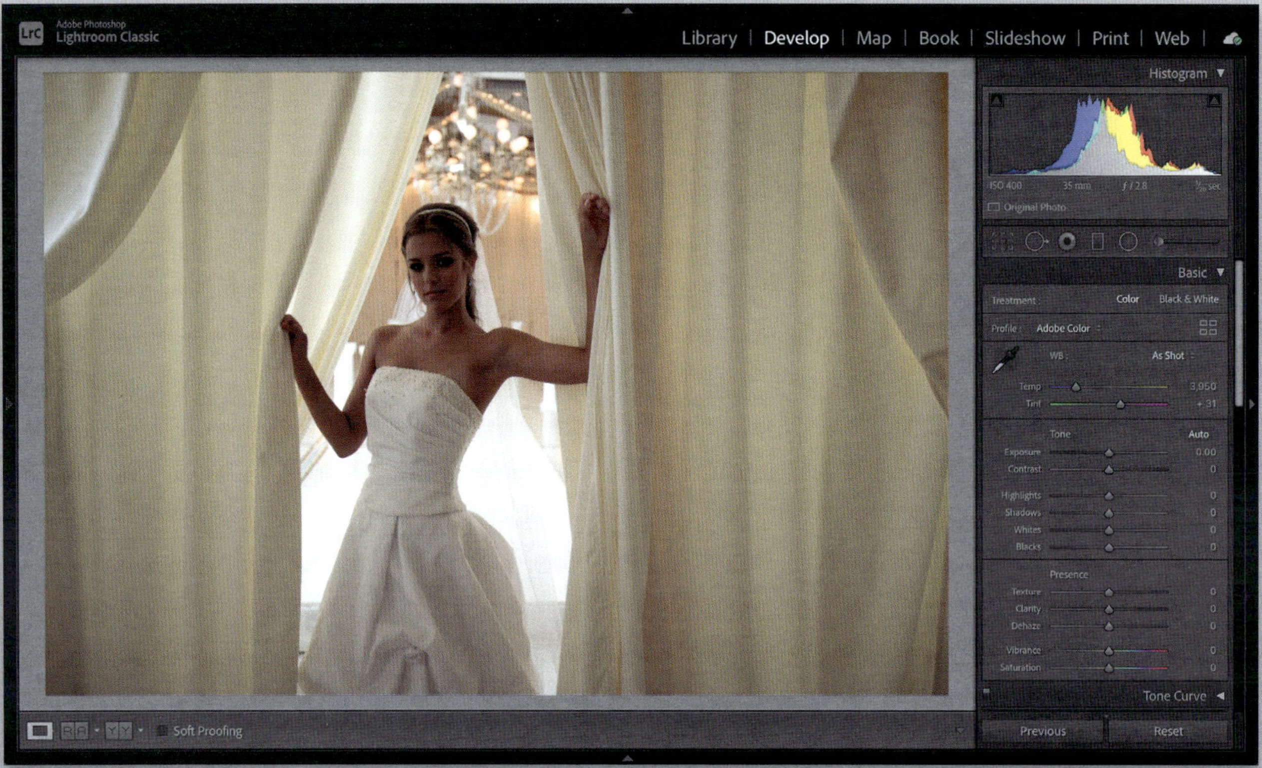

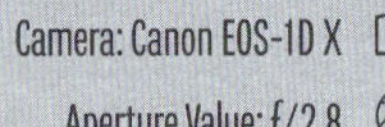

Camera: Canon EOS-1D X

Aperture Value: ƒ/2.8

Shutter Speed: 1/20 sec

ISO: 400

Focal Length: 35mm

Step 01:

Here's our original RAW image of our bride. The biggest issue we're going to have to deal with is the exposure and overall light in the scene (I envisioned it as a high-key, very bright scene, which it clearly is not), and the color being off isn't helping (her white bridal gown is yellowish), and her skin tone is off, and there's darkening in the corners, and this is just kind of a mess. We can fix every bit of it, though.

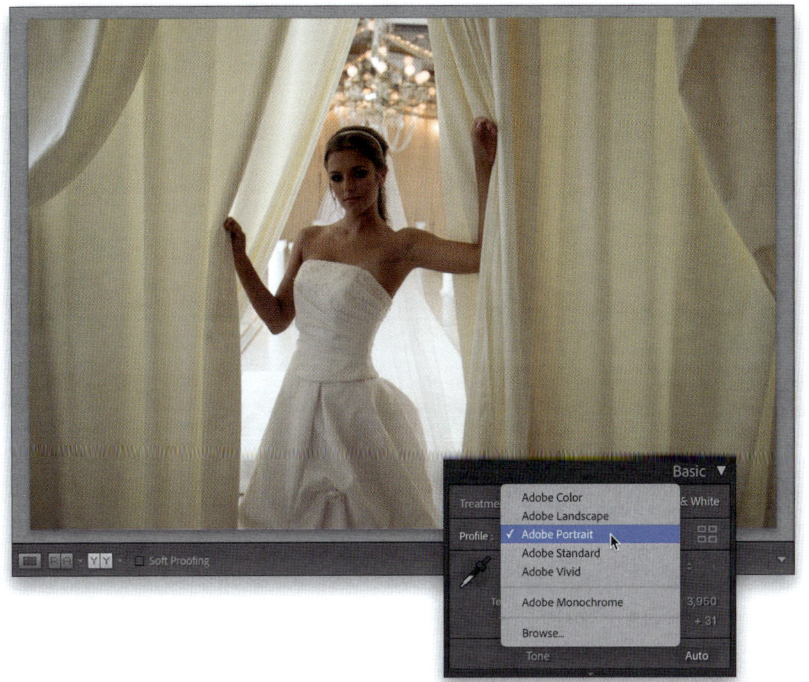

Step 02:

Let's start by checking the RAW profiles **(Point 1)** in the Profile pop-up menu at the top of the Develop module's Basic panel (the Edit panel in Lightroom cloud). I can pretty much tell you that we're probably going to choose Adobe Portrait as our starting place, but give all the other options a try. See what I mean? Yup, **Adobe Portrait** it is (not a big improvement, but it's a little better starting place for editing a portrait).

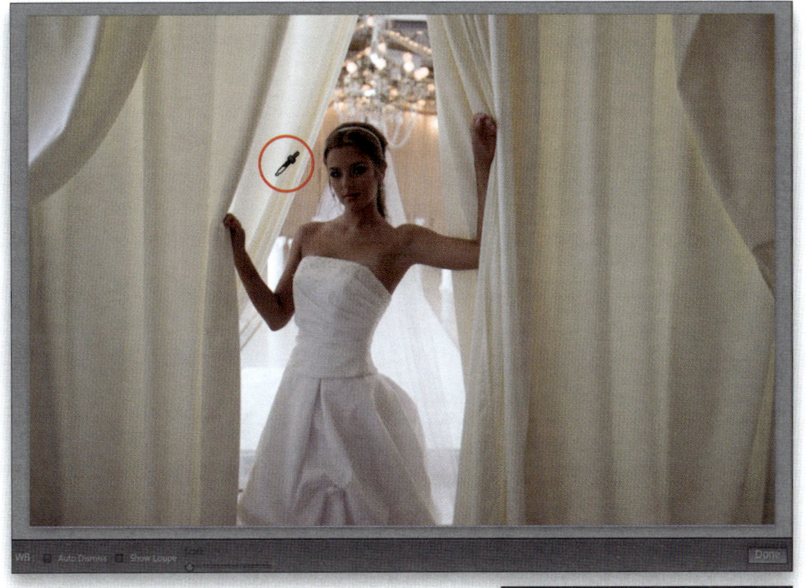

Step 03:

Next, let's get that color looking better **(Point 2)**. In the Basic panel (the Color panel in Lightroom cloud), get the White Balance Selector tool (**W**; the eyedropper) and click on something that's supposed to be a neutral color. You'll probably have to click in a few different places to find a white balance that makes her dress look white again (well, it took me a few clicks, anyway). Here, I clicked on the drapes to the left of her head (as shown here). Okay, that at least gives us a good starting place color-wise, but the image is still really underexposed, so it's kind of hard to judge the color.

Step 04:

Now, let's get that Exposure looking right. (*Note:* This is supposed to be a "high-key" shot, meaning a really bright, airy-looking shot.) We'll start (like usual with **Point 3**) by setting our white and black points. So, press-and-hold the Shift key, and then double-click on Whites, then on Blacks to set them automatically. This didn't have a big effect on the Whites, only moving them up to +3, but it did darken the Blacks to –34. That didn't do enough to brighten our image where we want it to be, so let's really crank up the Exposure amount (here, I dragged it up to +1.45). It's getting in the ballpark now, but she's still a bit backlit (we'll fix that next).

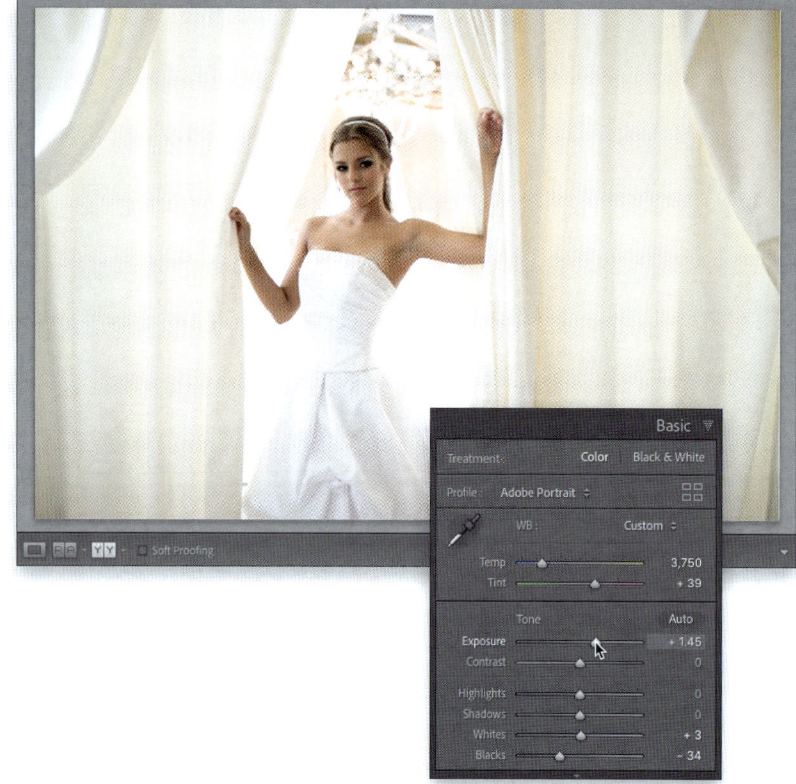

Step 05:

Let's head over to the Shadows slider **(Point 4)** and drag it over to the right quite a bit (as shown here, where I dragged it over to +61, and that helped a lot). Her skin tone is a bit funky, and we'll get to that, but we're going in the right direction.

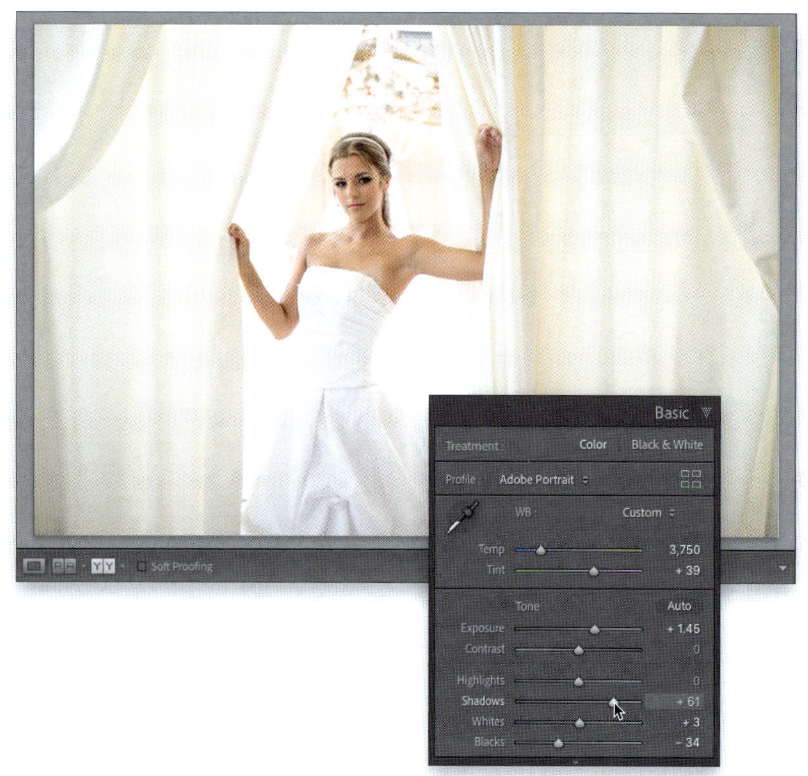

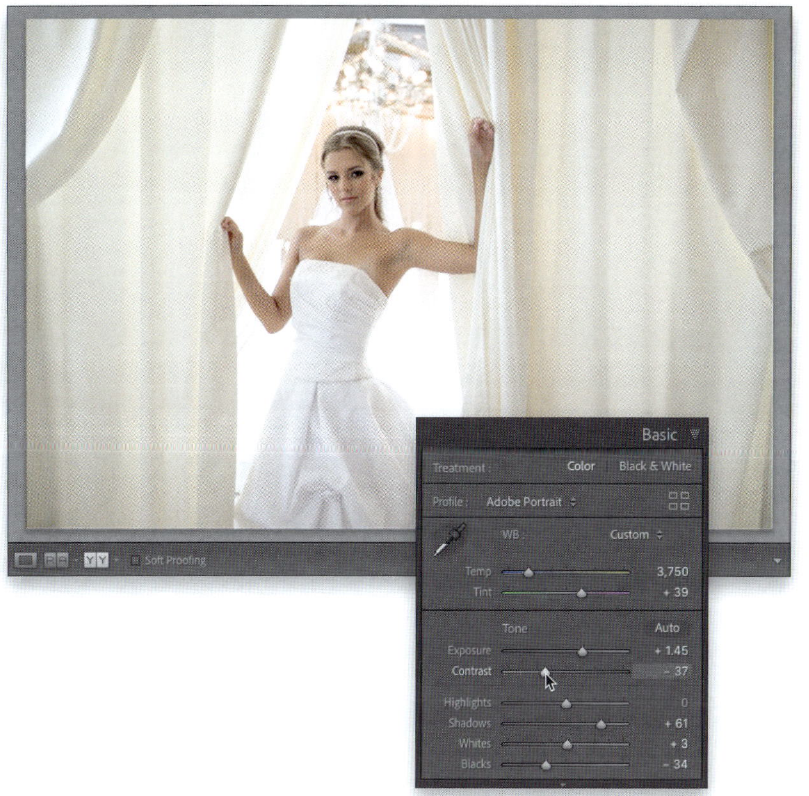

Step 06:

With landscapes, architecture, travel, cars, and so on, we're usually bumping up the contrast a lot, but this image is actually looking pretty contrasty already (perhaps too contrasty). Well, not the image here—you can see it in Step 05—because here, I dropped the Contrast by –37, which helped flatten out the image, making it smoother and softer, and you'll also see it even helped her skin tone.

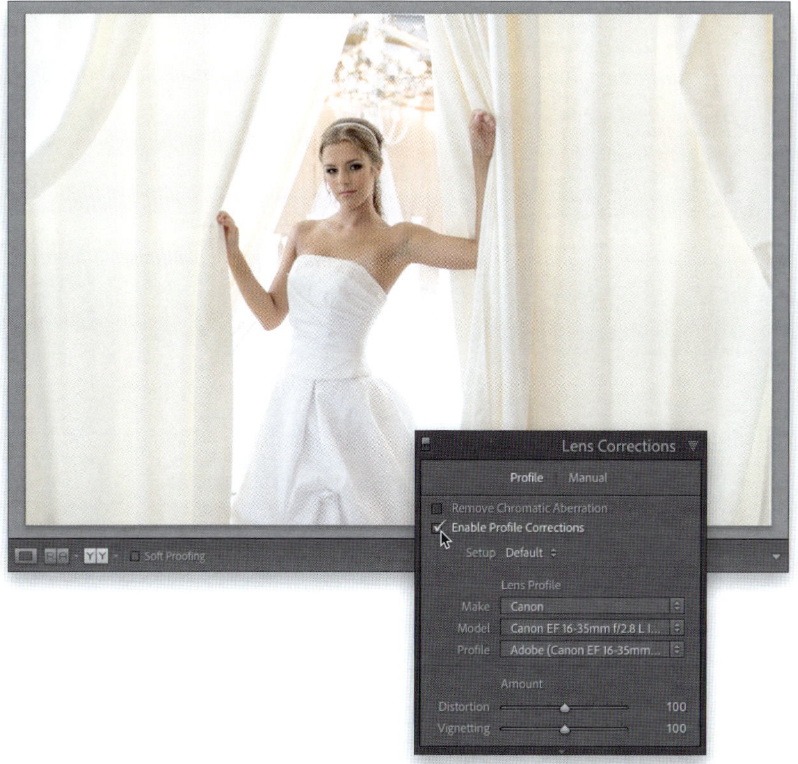

Step 07:

A lens issue is causing the corners to be really dark, so let's fix that next (by jumping over to **Point 6**), and it should make the whole image look brighter. Go to the Lens Corrections panel (the Optics panel in Lightroom cloud) and turn on the Enable Profile (Lens) Corrections checkbox. That should do the trick. Look at how much brighter that made the entire image look, just by fixing those darkened corners.

Step 08:

Her flesh tones are still a little funky, so let's deal with that next **(Point 5)**. Get the Adjustment Brush **(K)** from the toolbox beneath the histogram (the Brush tool **[B]** from the toolbox on the right in Lightroom cloud), double-click on Effect to reset the sliders to zero (this happens by default in Lightroom cloud), and then let's do this (don't paint yet): we're going to add a little yellow back into her skin by dragging the Temp slider to 7, and then add a little green by dragging the Tint slider to –12 (I gotta tell ya, it has been a minute since I had to add green to a flesh tone, but her skin was a bit magenta). Now that we've balanced the colors, let's back off the saturation a little bit, so they're not so intense, by dragging the Saturation slider to the left (here, I dragged it over to –28). Then, increase the Exposure a bit (to 0.22), and now (finally!) paint over her face, arms, shoulders, etc.—anywhere you see flesh tone.

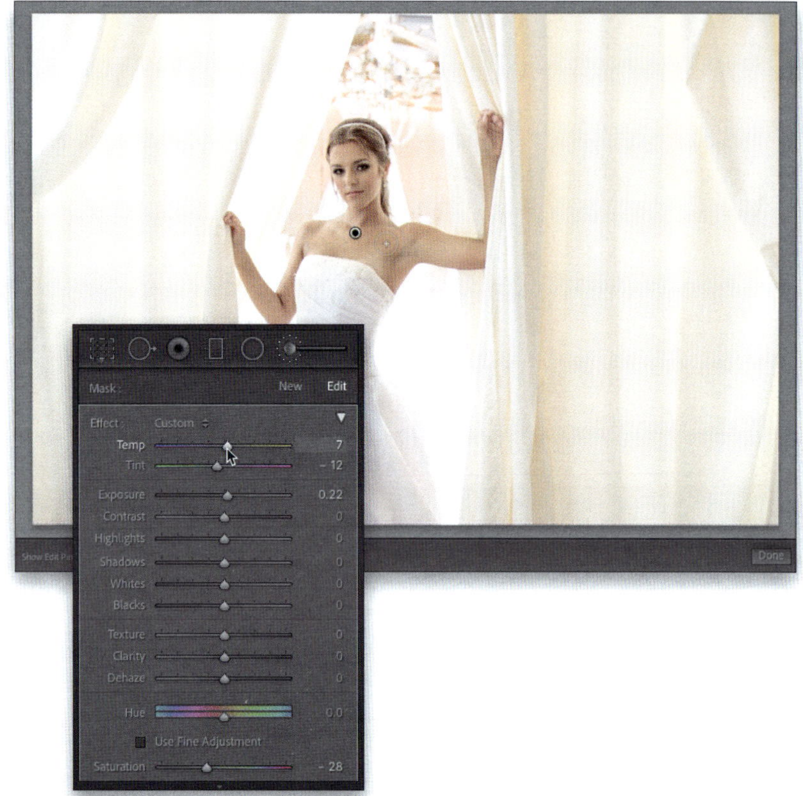

Step 09:

Okay, see that distracting, ugly, "it needs to go away" folded area of curtain up in the top-right corner? Yeah, that one. It's probably too large to remove with the Spot Removal tool (if it's bigger than a spot, it's probably not going to work too well), so let's crop it out of the frame, which will also give us a closer, more intimate portrait of our bride. Get the Crop Overlay tool **(R)** from the toolbox beneath the histogram (the Crop & Rotate tool **[C]** from the toolbox on the right in Lightroom cloud), then grab the bottom corners and drag inward until that piece of cloth Is out of the frame (as seen here). Don't commit to your crop quite yet.

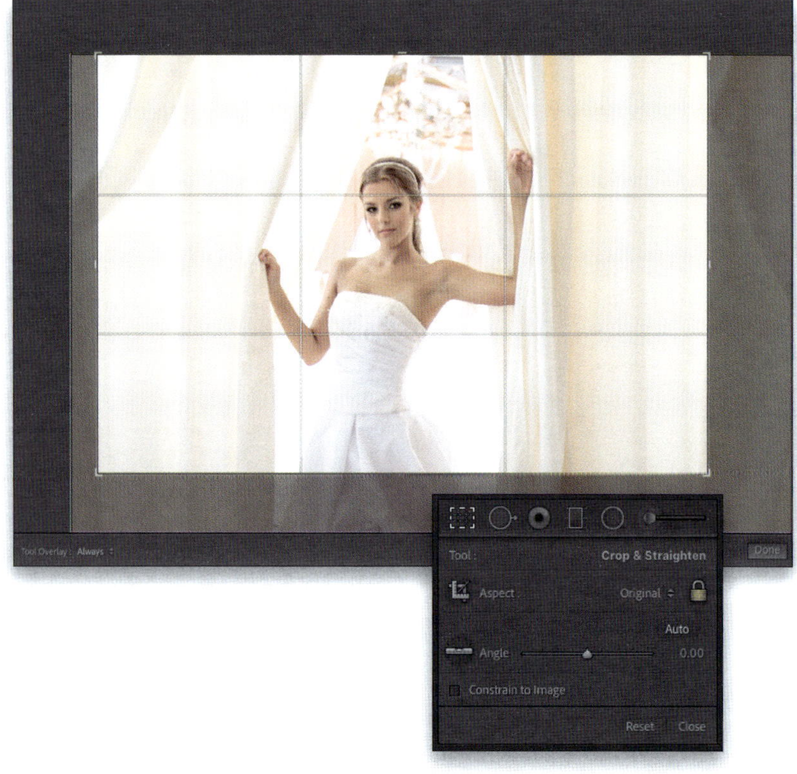

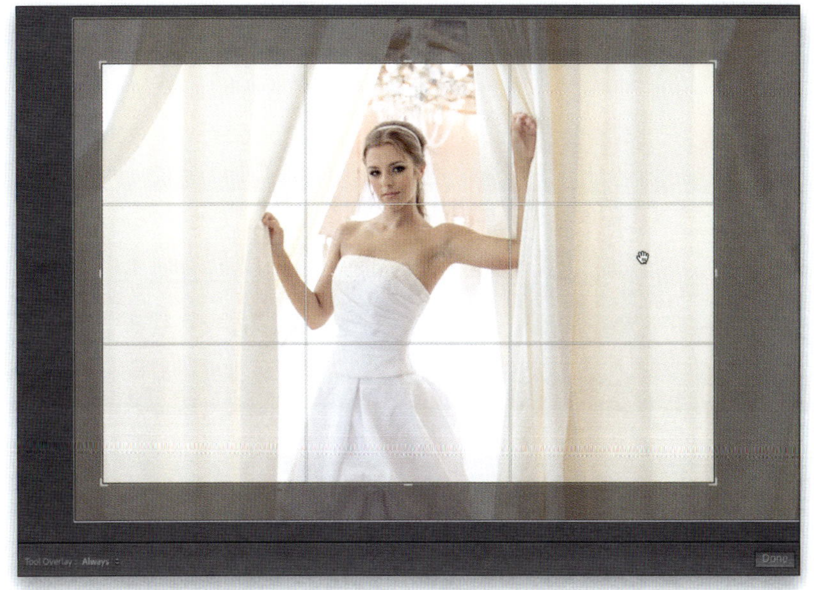

Step 10:

So, we got rid of the bad curtain part, but now our composition is…well…let's just say it's lacking. Click your cursor inside the crop border and drag the image, so your composition looks better. I actually would like to drag it a little to the right, but then we'd pretty much completely lose the chandelier in the back, so at least this is a lot better. Hit **Return (PC: Enter)** to lock in your crop.

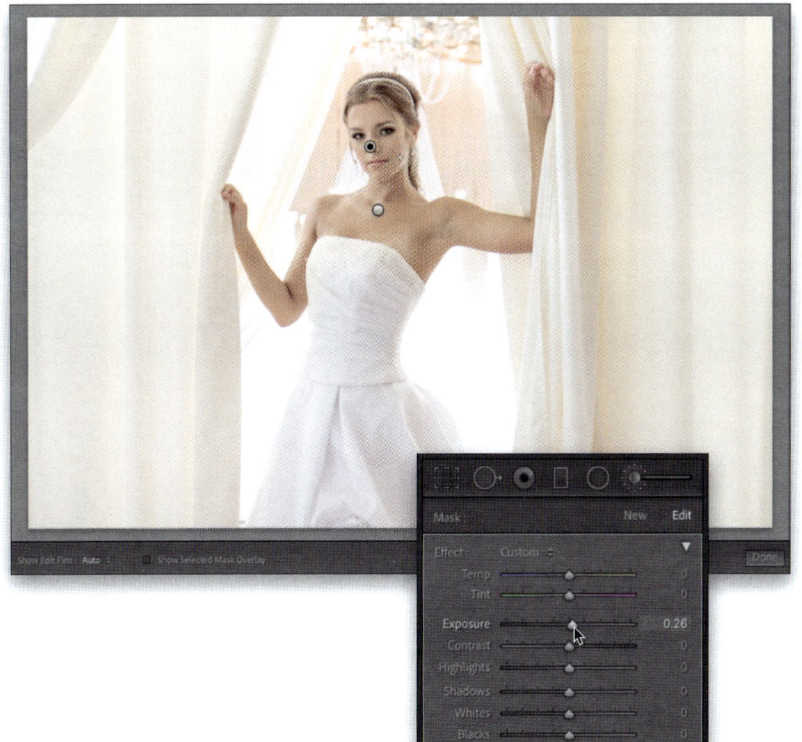

Step 11:

A finishing move **(Point 7)** I nearly always do to portraits, right near the very end of the editing process, is to subtly brighten the face, so let's do that here. Get the Adjustment Brush again, double-click on Effect to reset the sliders to zero, and then increase the Exposure amount—usually anywhere from 0.25 to 0.50 (it depends on the image). It's supposed to be subtle, so for this image, just drag the Exposure slider over to the right to 0.26 (around 1/4 stop brighter), and then paint over her face (as shown here).

Step 12:

All that's left is to do now is sharpen our image. I'm going to use the technique you learned back in Lesson 7, on page 83, where you mask away the skin areas, so just things like her eyes, eyebrows, lips, hair, dress, and so on will have sharpening applied and her skin will remain unsharpened. We do this in the Detail panel, under Sharpening. Drag the Amount slider (the Sharpening slider in Lightroom cloud) over to around 60 (as shown here), then press-and-hold the Option (PC: Alt) key, and drag the Masking slider to the right (here, I dragged it to 82). If you remember from back on page 83, the screen will turn solid white, telling you the entire image is being sharpened equally. As you drag the slider to the right, anything that turns black is no longer being sharpened (as seen here at the bottom); only the white areas are being sharpened (which is exactly what you want in a portrait of a bride). That wraps this one up.

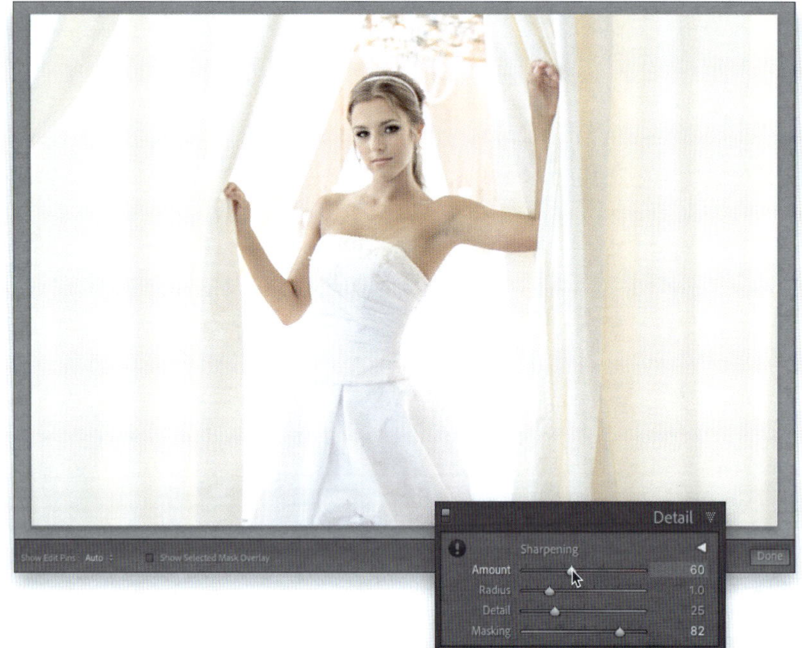

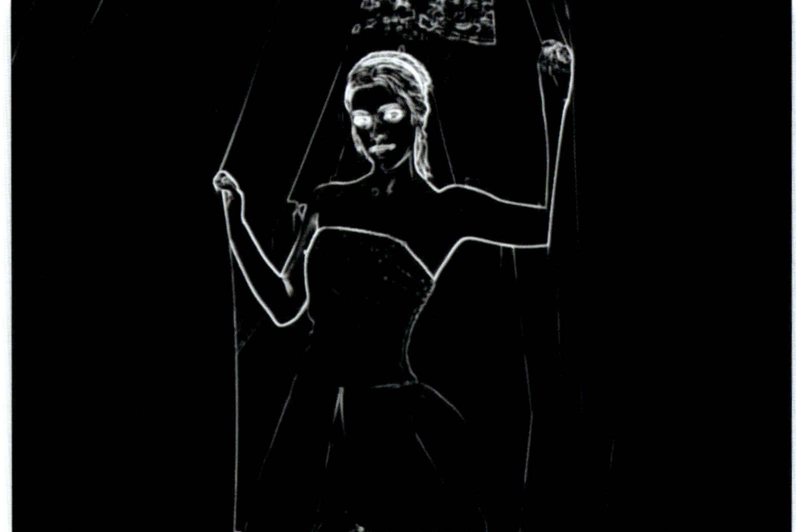

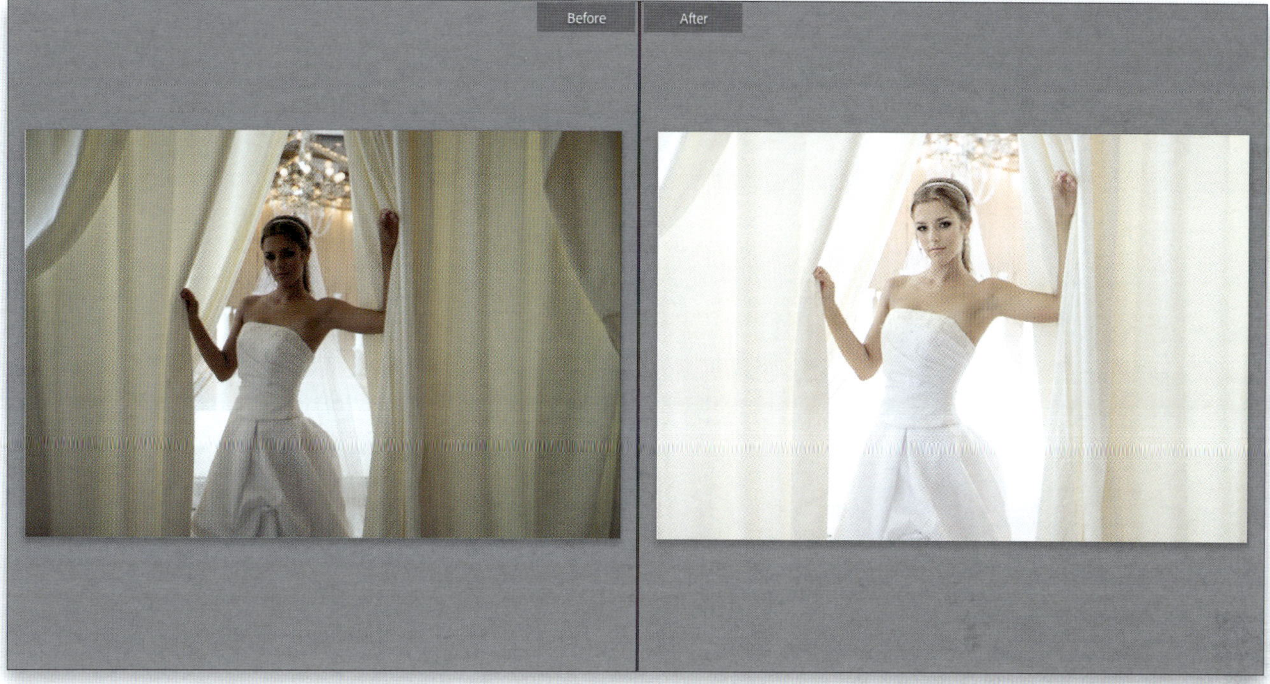

Here's our before/after.

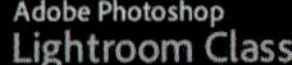
Adobe Photoshop
Lightroom Classic

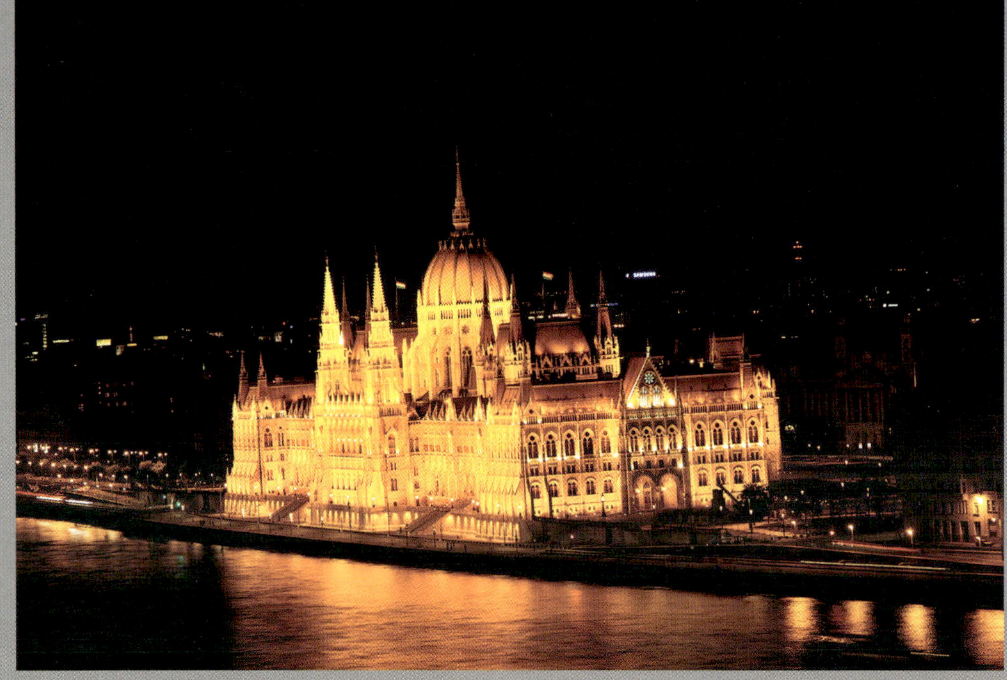
Before

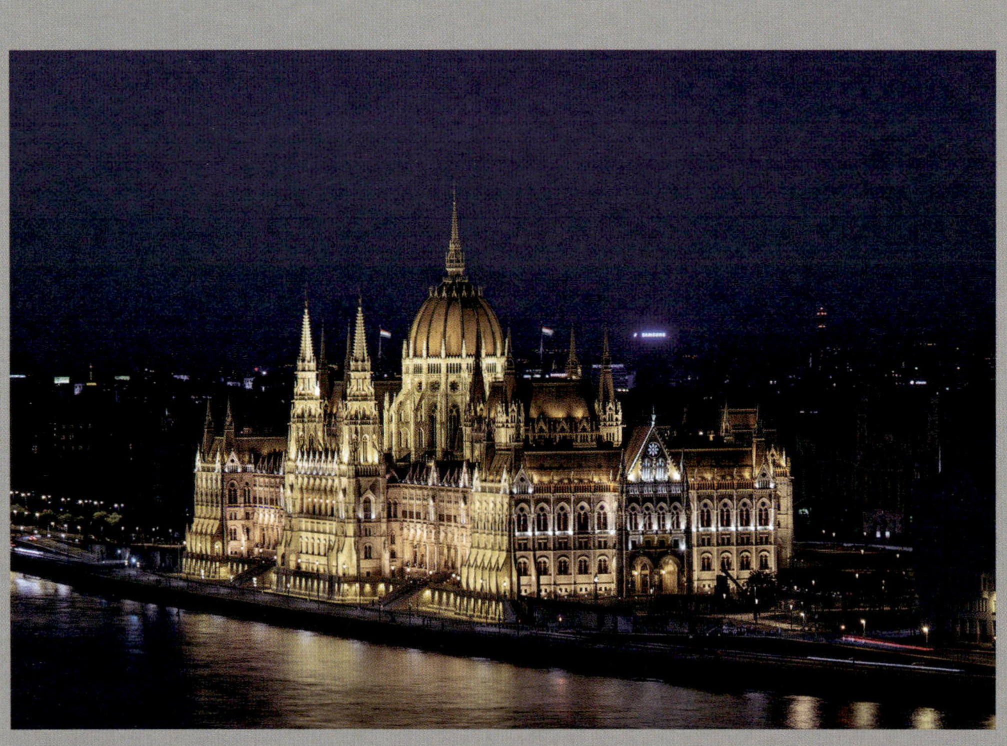
After

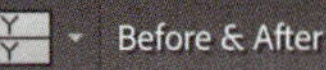
Before & After :

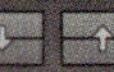
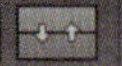

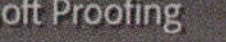
Soft Proofing

LESSON 13

NIGHTTIME SHOT

1. Assigning a RAW Profile
2. Getting the Color Right
3. Expanding the Tonal Range
4. Dealing with Sensor Limitations
5. Painting with Light and Retouching
6. Fixing Lens Issues
7. Finishing Moves

This time, we're working on a travel shot taken at night. It has a number of issues, starting with the fact that I obviously wasn't paying enough attention to keeping the image straight. Beyond that, the color is way too warm, the sky is just solid black, and the lights are too bright, which is a common issue for night photography shots like this.

THE STORY BEHIND THE SHOT:

My wife and I took a 10-day cruise down the Danube River on one of those flat, river barge–style boats (it was way better than I was expecting—so relaxing, with great shooting opportunities and incredible food!). One of the stops along the river was in Budapest, Hungary (where I got to spend the day shooting with my buddy, high-end portrait retoucher and generally cool guy Viktor Fejes). Just like the classic Paris shot is one of the Eiffel Tower, the classic Budapest shot is one of the Hungarian Parliament building (seen here). This isn't the most popular view of it (that's more the head-on shot from across the river, or one from the closest bridge), but we wound up having dinner up high on a hill across the river from it. As we were leaving the restaurant, this was the view I saw, so I had to set up my tripod and get a quick shot (and you'd think since I had a tripod, I would have a straighter shot, but…well…it is what it is. I blame it on the amazing Hungarian stew I had for dinner).

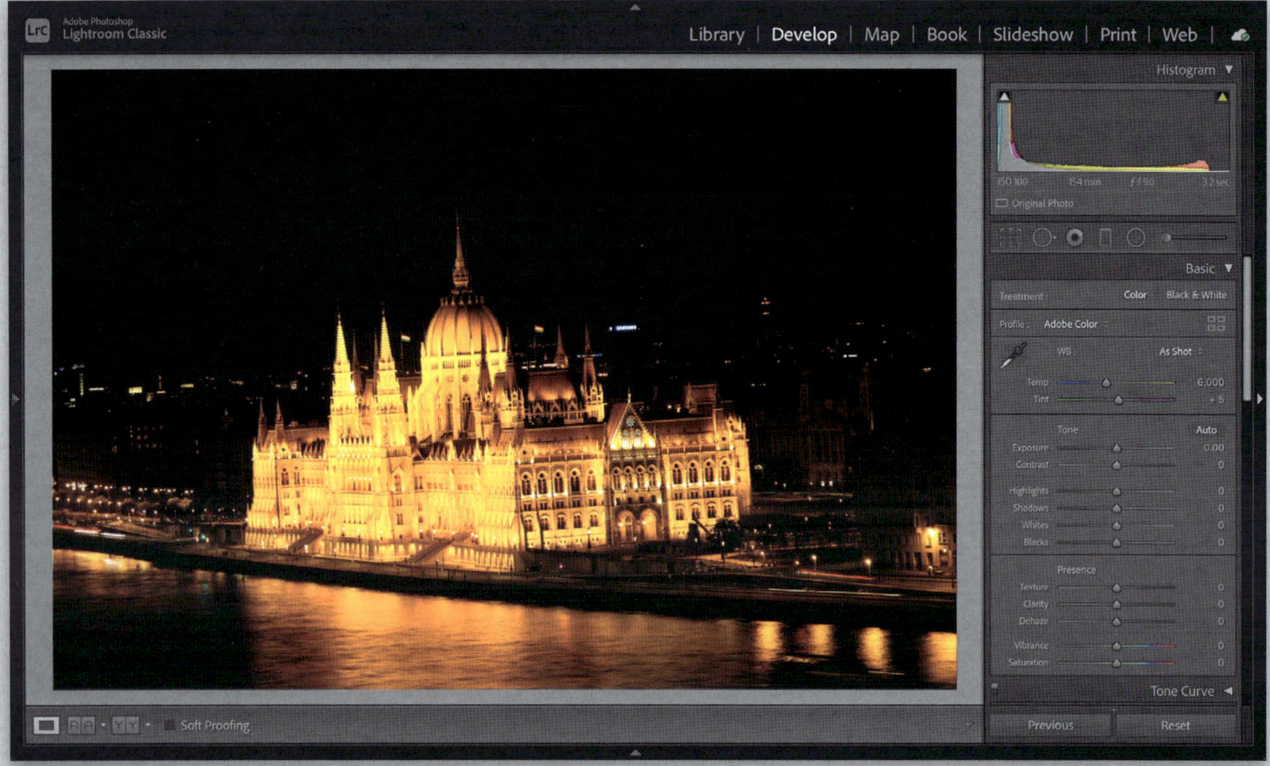

Step 01:

Camera: Canon EOS 5D Mark III
Aperture Value: f/9.0
Shutter Speed: 3.2 sec
ISO: 100
Focal Length: 154mm

Here's our original RAW image of the Hungarian Parliament building at night. Let's give the image a quick evaluation: Well, there's the whole crooked thing, and the overly yellow color. Not to mention the boring, solid black sky, or the fact that the building is so bright it's nearly all highlights, and well…it's just not awesome (and that's being kind, but I can say something mean like that because I took the shot, so I'm basically giving myself a harsh critique and from looking at this image, I had that coming). Okay, let's fix this mess!

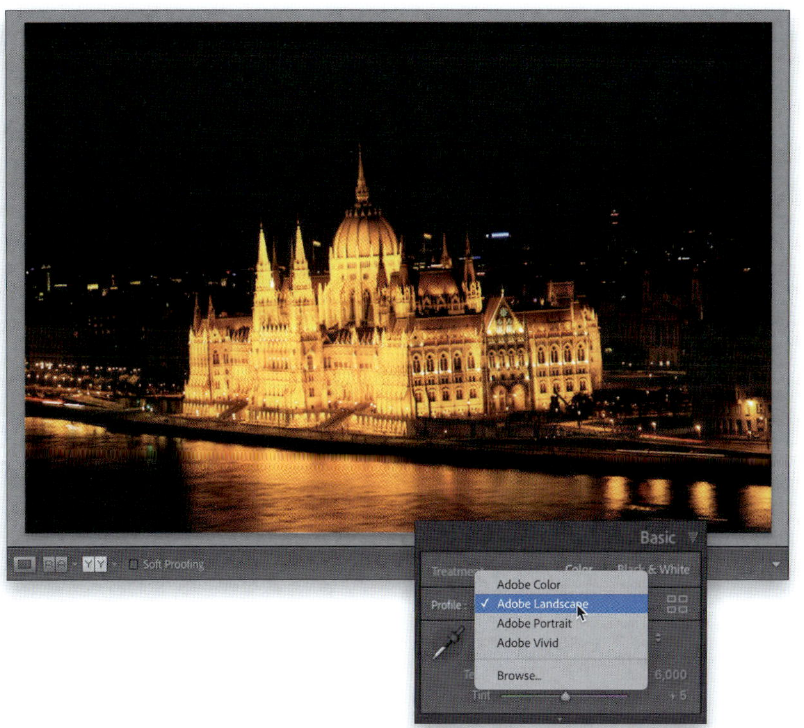

Step 02:

Let's see if there's a RAW profile to get us a better starting place for our editing **(Point 1)**. At the top of the Develop module's Basic panel (the Edit panel in Lightroom cloud), from the Profile pop-up menu, try the different profiles. The only one that looks to be an improvement (no big surprise) is Adobe Landscape. It actually helped pull back some of the brightness in the building, but outside of that, color-wise, it didn't do a whole lot. But, it's the best of what the choices are, so go ahead and choose **Adobe Landscape**.

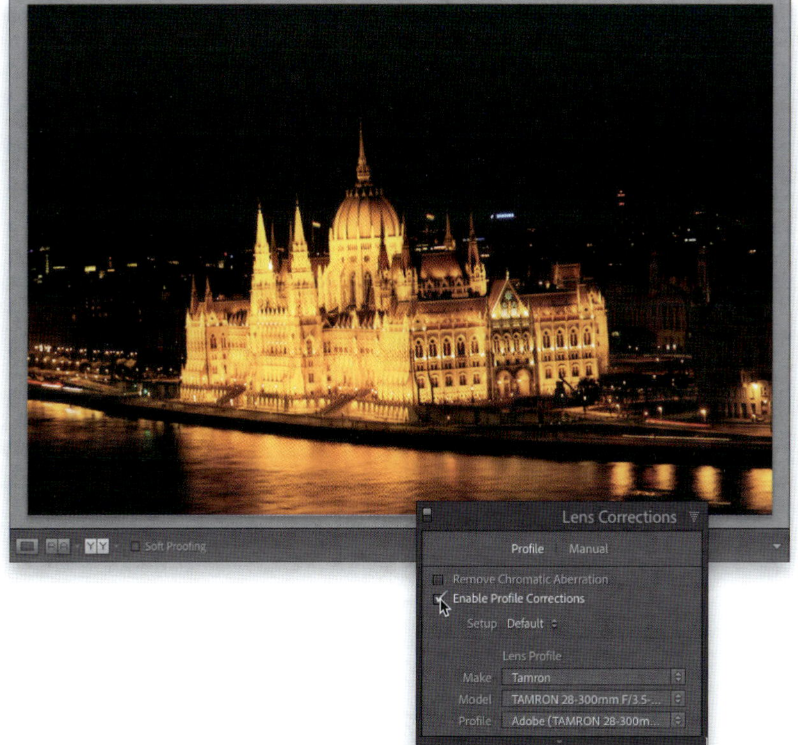

Step 03:

I usually save lens correction issues for a bit later in the system **(Point 6)**, but we're going to use the Lens Corrections panel's cousin, the Transform panel, to fix the crookedness of this image, so while we're right there in that neighborhood (lens stuff), we'll go ahead and fix the lens distortion now. Head to the Lens Corrections panel (the Optics panel in Lightroom cloud) and turn on the Enable Profile (Lens) Corrections checkbox (as shown here), and that should take care of the lens distortion (you'll see the change as soon as you turn on that checkbox).

Step 04:

Now, let's go to the Transform panel (the next panel down; the Geometry panel in Lightroom cloud) and drag the Rotate slider to the right to +2.8 (as shown here; be sure the Constrain Crop checkbox is turned on, below the sliders). Okay, now you might be wondering why we did the rotation here, rather than using the Crop Overlay tool (the Crop & Rotate tool in Lightroom cloud), cropping in, and then dragging in a circular motion to free-rotate the image until it's straight. Well, this is just another way to straighten your image, and doesn't it sound like a lot less trouble than using the whole Crop Overlay tool method? I use this method of straightening a lot.

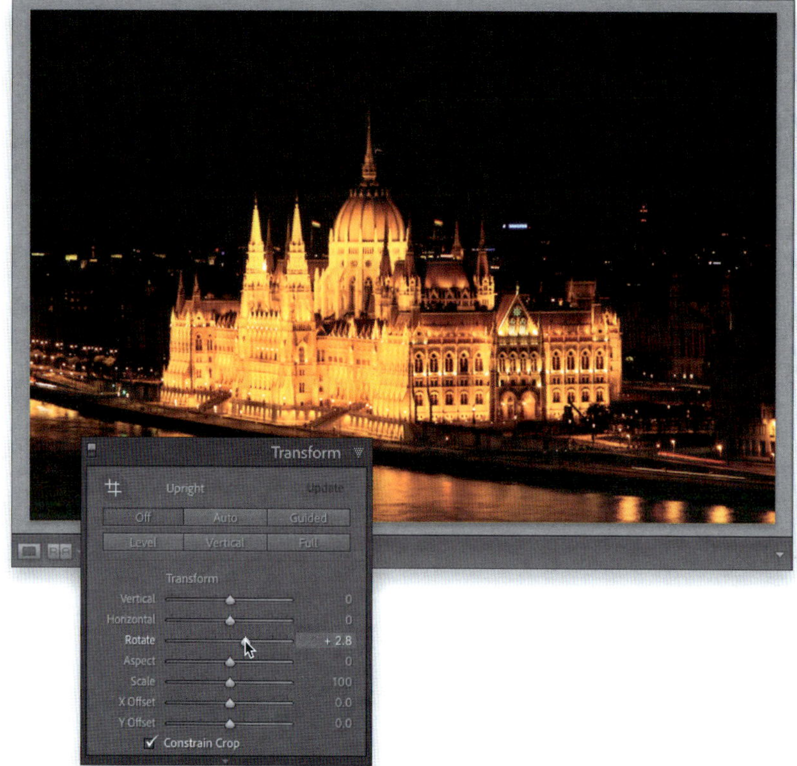

Step 05:

I wish I could remember the name of the photographer who I learned this trick from (I think it was on a blog) for turning a black night sky to a blue color, because I would certainly give him credit here—it works like a charm, and I've used it many times since I learned it. Go back to the Basic panel (go to the Color panel in Lightroom cloud) and drag the Temp slider way over to the left to around 2,450-ish to get that blue hour–looking sky **(Point 2)**, but just a heads up: you don't always have to go that far to get a nice, blue night sky. If you want to make that night sky even bluer, just increase the Shadows amount (drag the slider to the right to around +41; back in the Light panel in Lightroom cloud) to get the nice, even bluer sky you see here. Also, look at what that white balance adjustment did for the Parliament building itself. I ended up increasing the Tint amount to +21, as well. Okay, we're on the right rack.

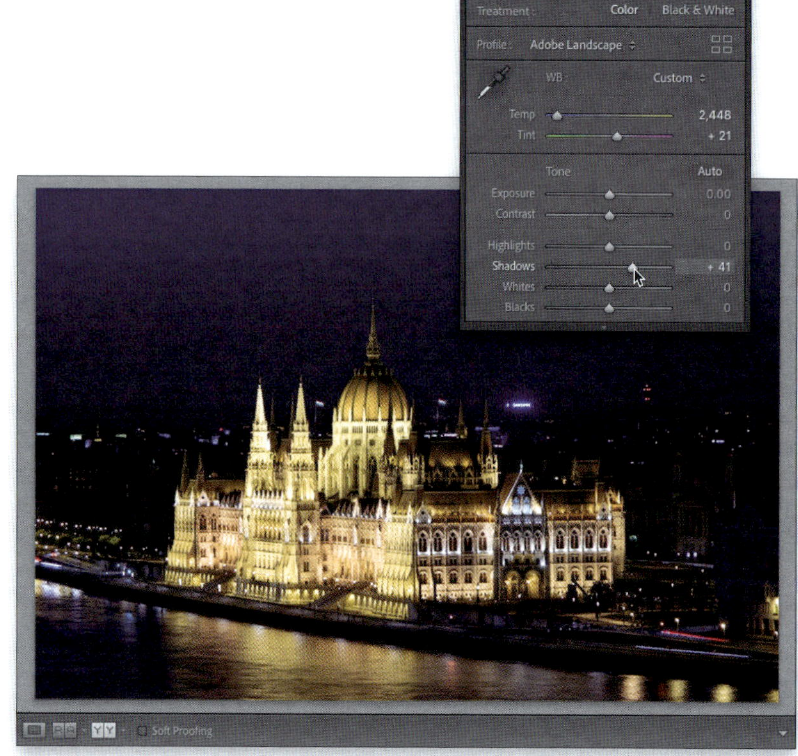

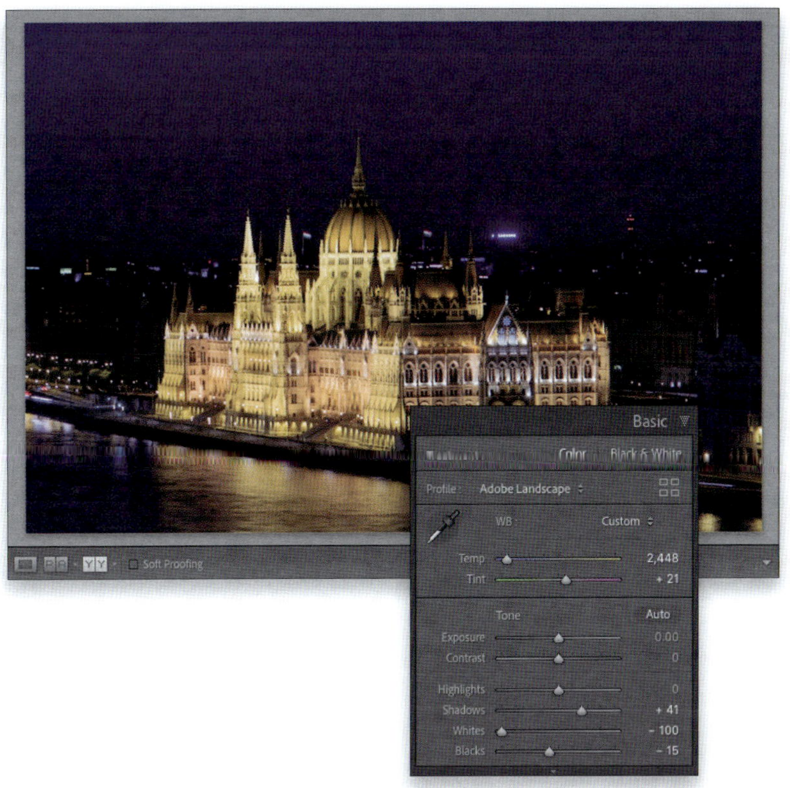

Step 06:

Let's set our white and black points next **(Point 3)**. Press-and-hold the Shift key and then double-click on the word "Whites," and then on "Blacks" to set them automatically. Look at how it kicked down those Whites to –100. That gives you some idea of how bright that building had gotten. No big change on the Blacks, just moving them to –15, and now the overall exposure is pretty good. I don't think we even have to touch the Exposure slider, so let's just roll on.

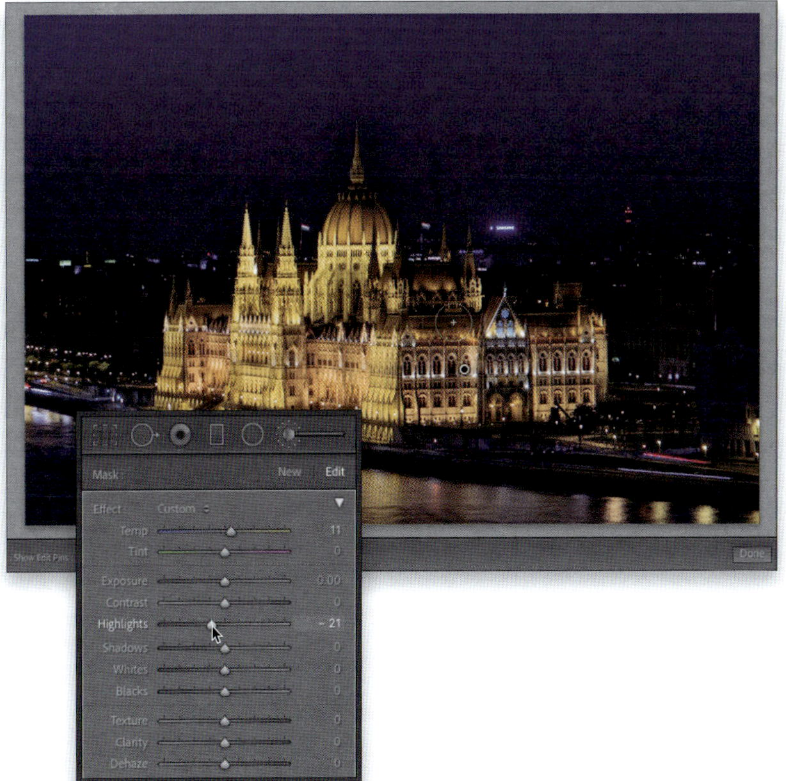

Step 07:

Next, let's work on the building itself. We can warm up the color a bit and maybe pull back some more of those highlights by painting over it with the Adjustment Brush (so, we'll skip Point 4 and jump to **Point 5**). Get the Adjustment Brush **(K)** from the toolbox beneath the histogram (the Brush tool **[B]** from the toolbox on the right in Lightroom cloud), double-click on Effect to reset the sliders to zero (this happens by default in Lightroom cloud), and then we're going to add a little yellow back into to the building. So, drag the Temp slider to 11, and then drag the Highlights slider to the left to –21. Now paint over the entire building with the brush (as shown here).

Step 08:

If you want to make sure you completely covered the building with your painting, press the **O key** on your keyboard and the area you painted over will appear in a red tint (like you see here). You can see that I missed a few areas, but that's okay. That's why we have this feature—so we can find any areas we missed, and we can erase any areas where we spilled over.

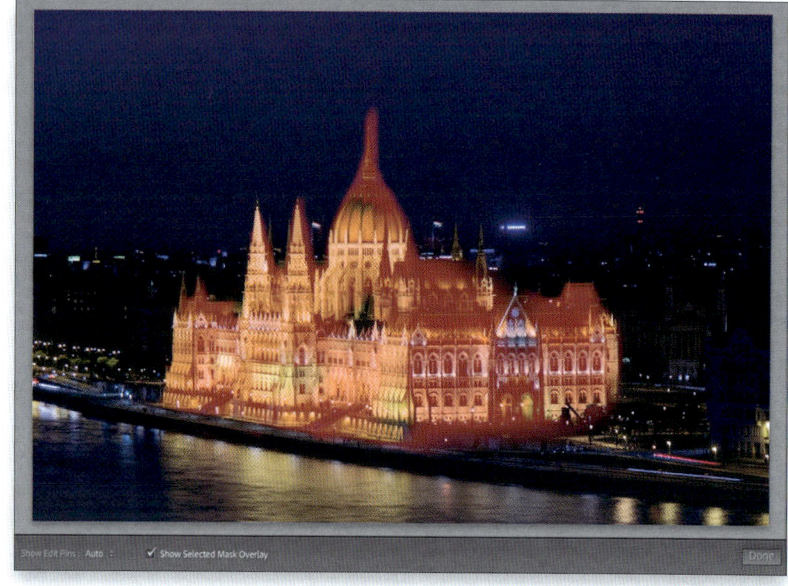

Step 09:

Shrink the size of your brush and paint over any areas you missed. While you're at it, if you see any areas where you spilled over onto the background (like I did in a bunch of areas), press-and-hold the **Option (PC: Alt) key** to temporarily switch to the Erase brush and paint those areas away (those areas you erase won't appear in that red tint anymore). Okay, now that we've refined our mask, you can press the O key again to turn the mask off and return to normal view (in Lightroom cloud, you'll need to press it three times to return to just seeing the Edit Pin).

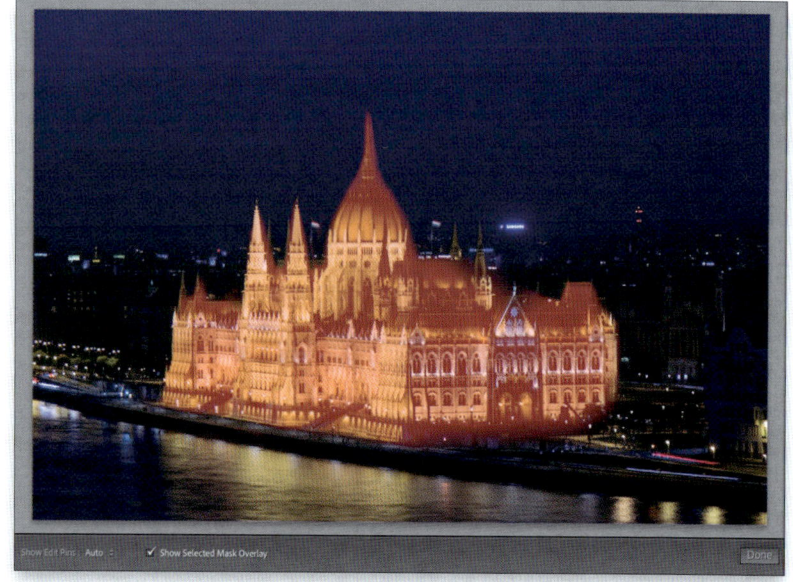

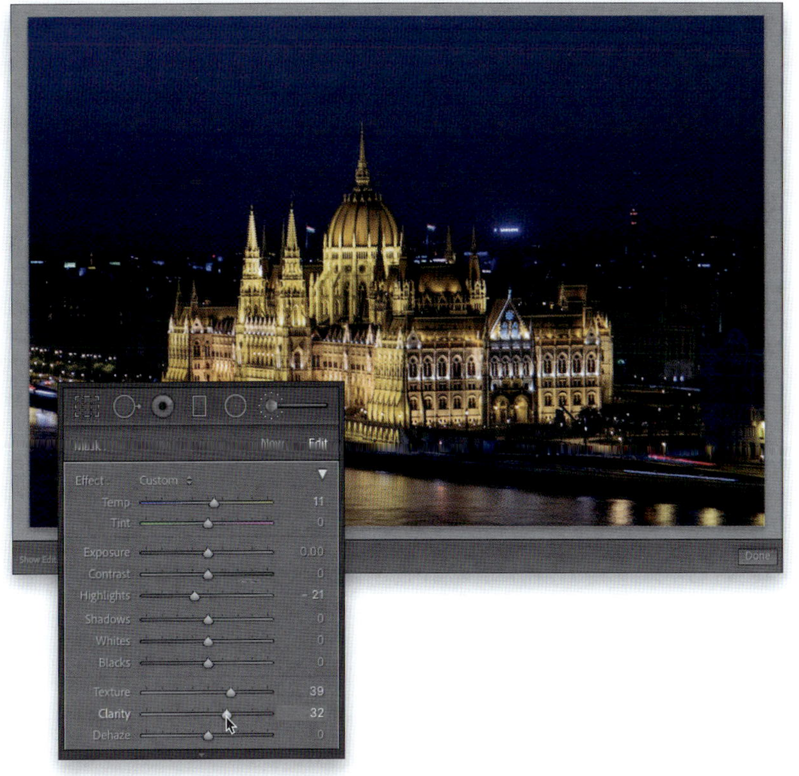

Step 10:

While we have the building still masked by the brush, let's add in some Clarity and Texture to bring out more detail. Drag the Texture slider to around 39 and the Clarity slider to 32. Okay, it's looking better. By applying the Clarity and Texture to just the building, it keeps from accentuating any noise in the sky. Click the Done button beneath the Preview area when you're finished (there isn't a Done button in Lightroom cloud).

Step 11:

If you feel the image is a little too color-ful or punchy, you can back it off a bit by going back to the Basic panel (the Color panel in Lightroom cloud) and dragging the Vibrance slider to the left (here, I dragged it over to −26). I think the color overall looks a bit more realistic now (but most non-photographers would probably prefer the color from the image in Step 10. The public loves punchy color, so if you're thinking of selling your images, you should probably skip this step).

Step 12:

Time for some finishing moves **(Point 7)**. Go to the Effects panel, and in the Post-Crop Vignetting section, drag the Amount slider (the Vignette slider in Lightroom cloud) over to –11 (sound familiar?) to subtly darken the edges of the image all the way around (as shown here). It's a little harder to see with night shots like this, but toggle it on/off (by clicking on the little switch in the left side of the panel header, or by clicking-and-holding on the eye icon in the right side of the panel header in Lightroom cloud) and you'll see it still has an effect.

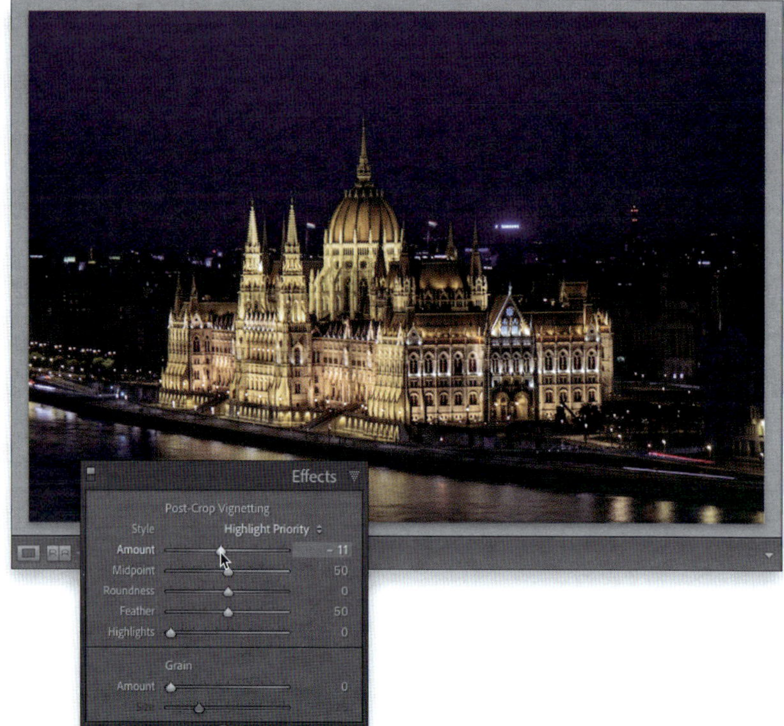

Step 13:

Let's finish up by adding some sharpening. Go to the Detail panel, drag the Amount slider (the Sharpening slider in Lightroom cloud) over to 80, and we're done.

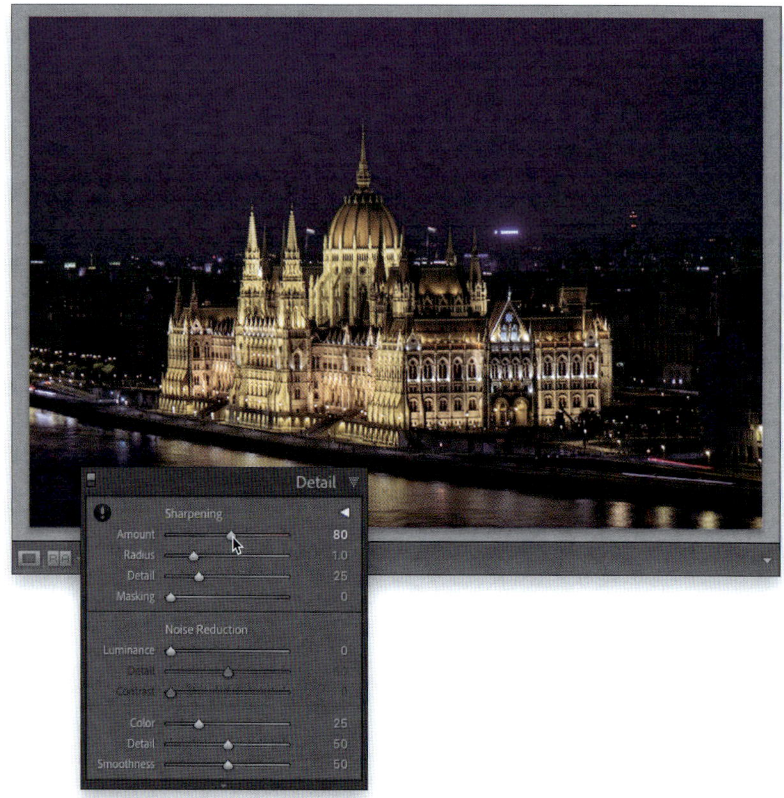

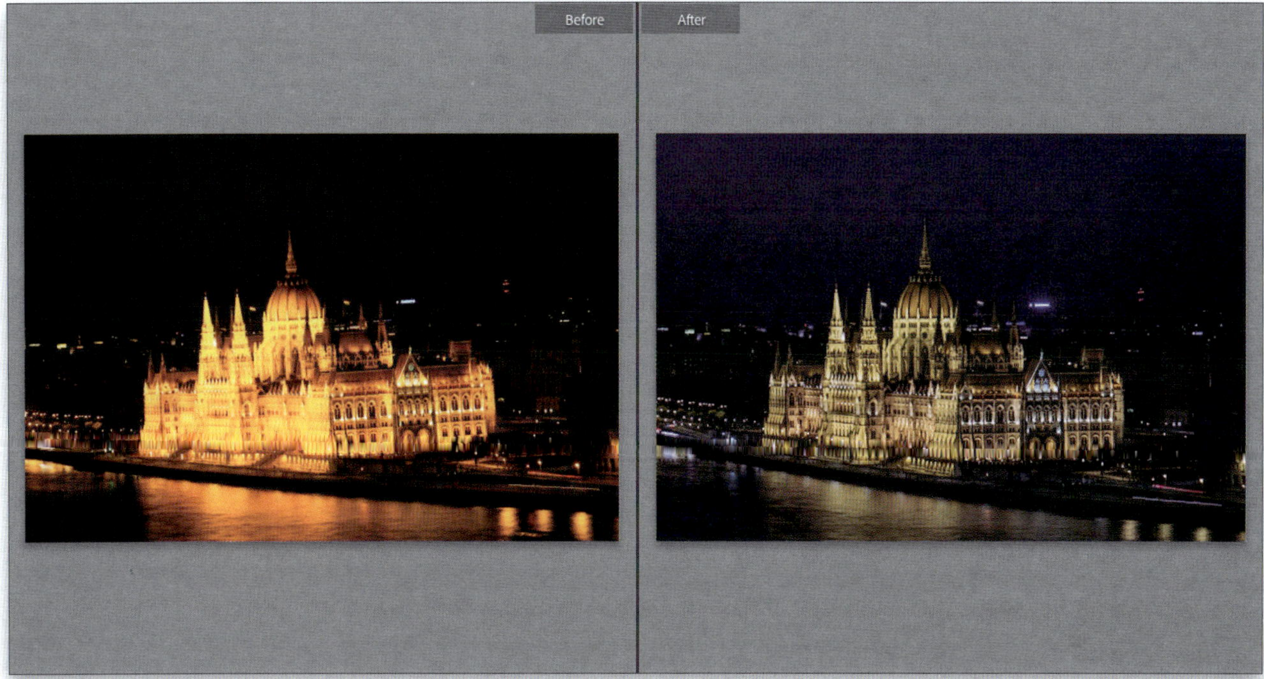

Here's our before/after.

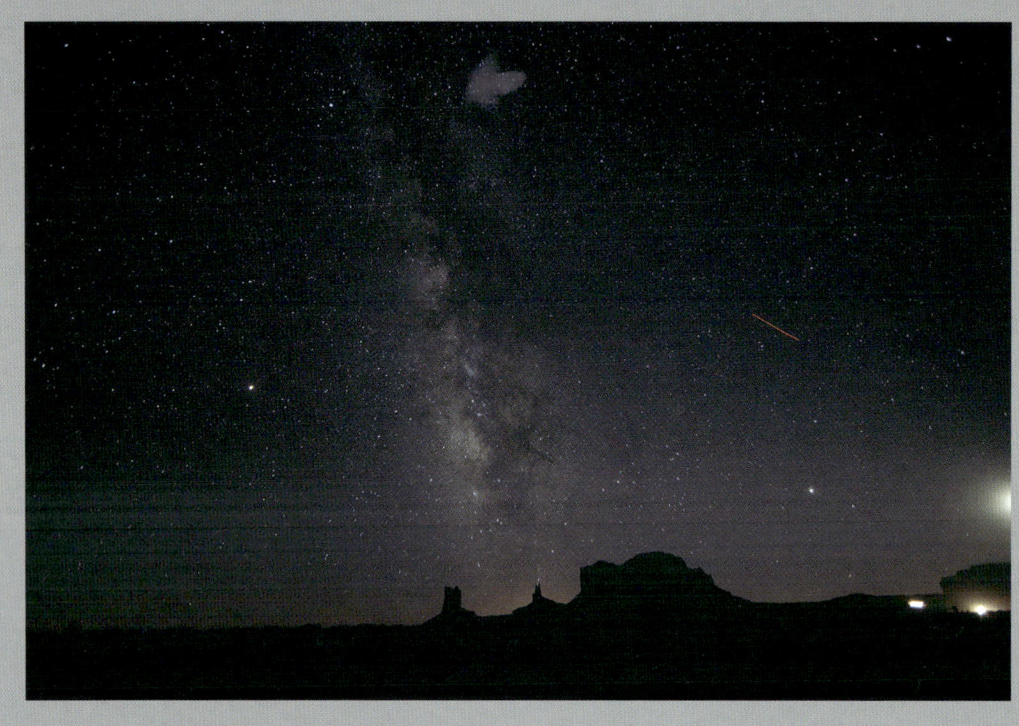

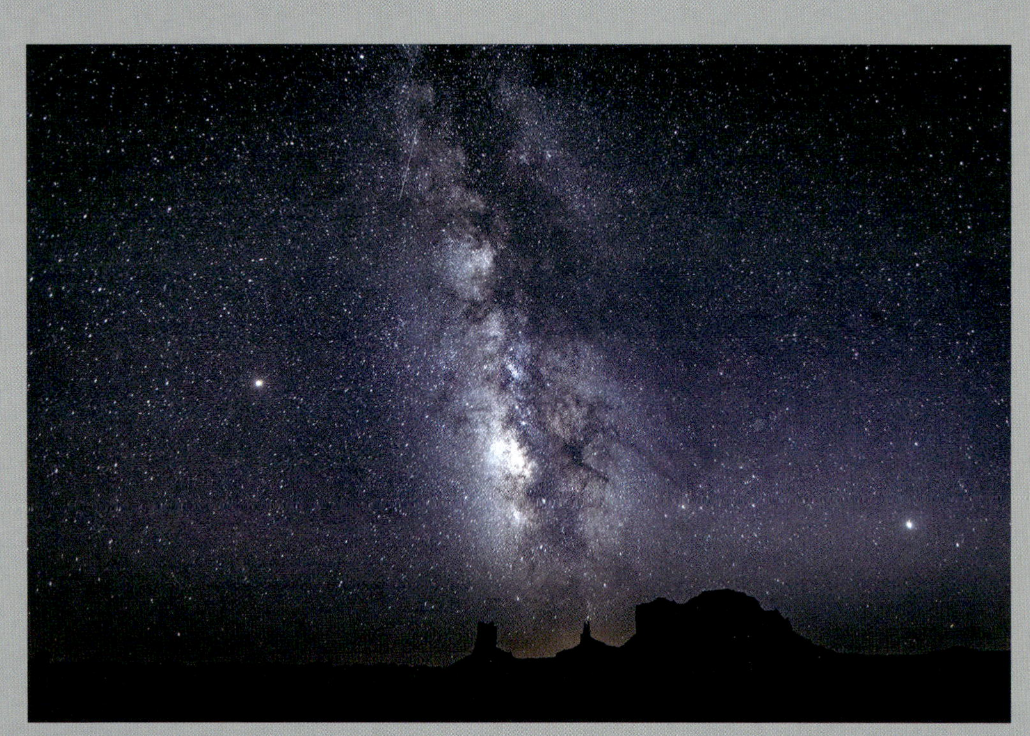

Before

After

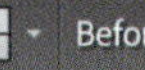

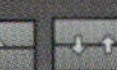
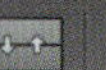
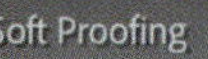

LESSON 14

MILKY WAY SKY

We've all seen shots of the Milky Way before, and I think you'd agree that our Before shot doesn't look like any of them. That's because the stars and the Milky Way aren't nearly as bright you'd think they'd be (they're pretty far away as it turns out), so we have to do a lot in-camera, and a lot in post, to bring out the brightness and color to keep our shot from looking dark and boring.

THE STORY BEHIND THE SHOT:

This shot was taken on a trip out west with my buddy and fellow photographer Erik Kuna. We had been shooting sunset in Monument Valley, Utah, and then we drove in the opposite direction of the visitor's center to get far away from any light pollution (a big thing when you're trying to shoot the Milky Way—you need a clear, cloudless sky with as little external light as possible). Unfortunately, light found us as a car drove by on the road behind us (as you can see in the bottom-right corner of the Before image). Also, there's some light pollution coming from that visitor's center, but we can deal with that. Of course, since shooting the Milky Way is a long exposure, I'm shooting on a tripod and using a wireless trigger to fire the camera, so I don't touch it and create any vibration (it's hard enough to get the stars reasonably sharp because there's that whole "earth is rotating on its axis" thing that's just so annoying. Well, it's great for gravity, but bad for photographing stars).

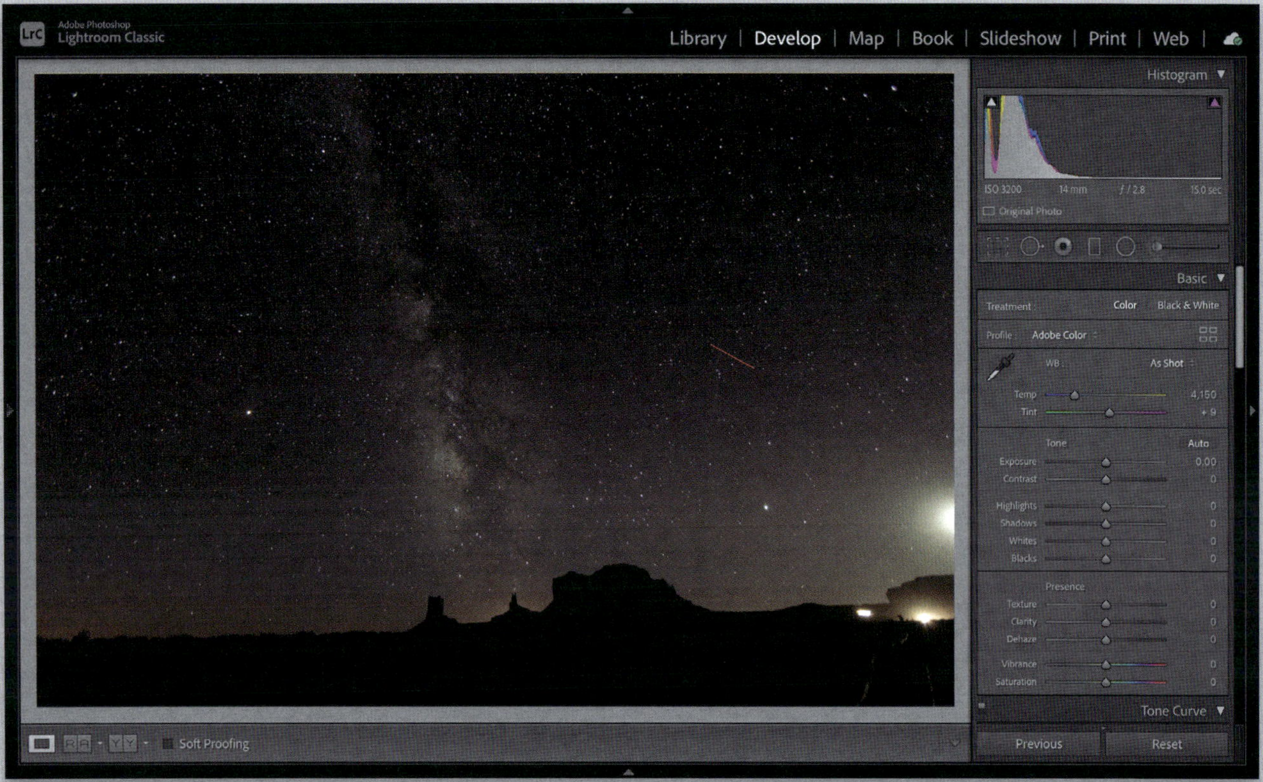

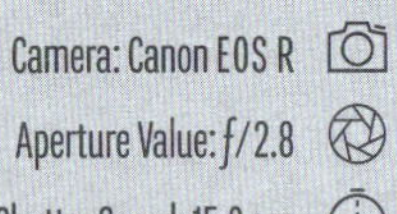

Camera: Canon EOS R
Aperture Value: *f*/2.8
Shutter Speed: 15.0 sec
ISO: 3200
Focal Length: 14mm

Step 01:

Here's the original RAW image of our Milky Way photo from Monument Valley. Let's do a quick evaluation of the photo: Well, it's a lifeless, soulless, nothing of a photo (but, somehow, it has potential). The color is pretty awful, there are car headlights on the right (generally a shot killer when it comes to Milky Way photos), there's a streak from a falling star, and there's a hazy sky, and well…it's another photo that needs a bit of work.

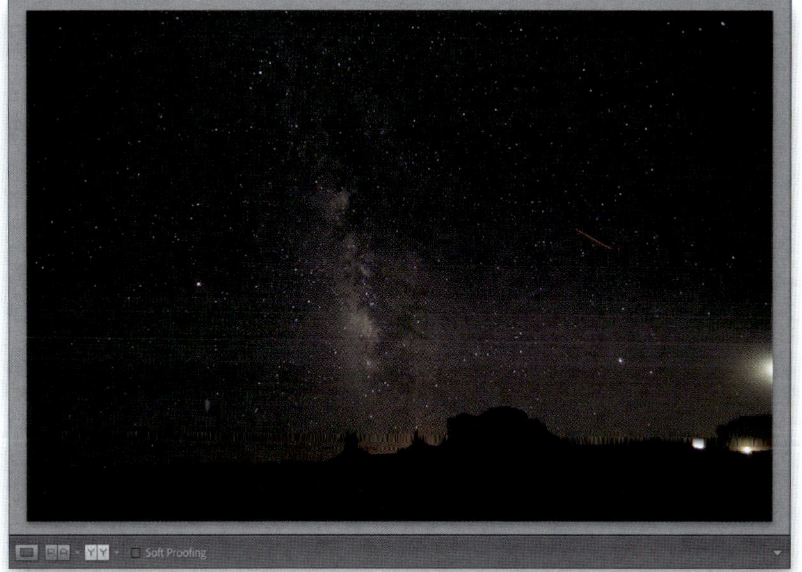

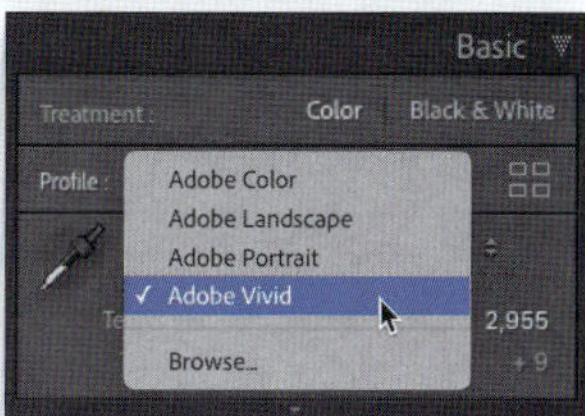

Step 02:

Let's start by running through the different RAW profiles **(Point 1)** to see if we can find one that will give us a better starting place. Try all of them from the Profile pop-up menu, but while your first thought, and mine, would be to choose Adobe Landscape, in this case, **Adobe Vivid** looks best (adding a nice pop of color and contrast). I'm actually surprised Adobe Vivid doesn't wind up as our starting place more often than it does, but I imagine it only looks better in 5% to 10% of the cases (at best).

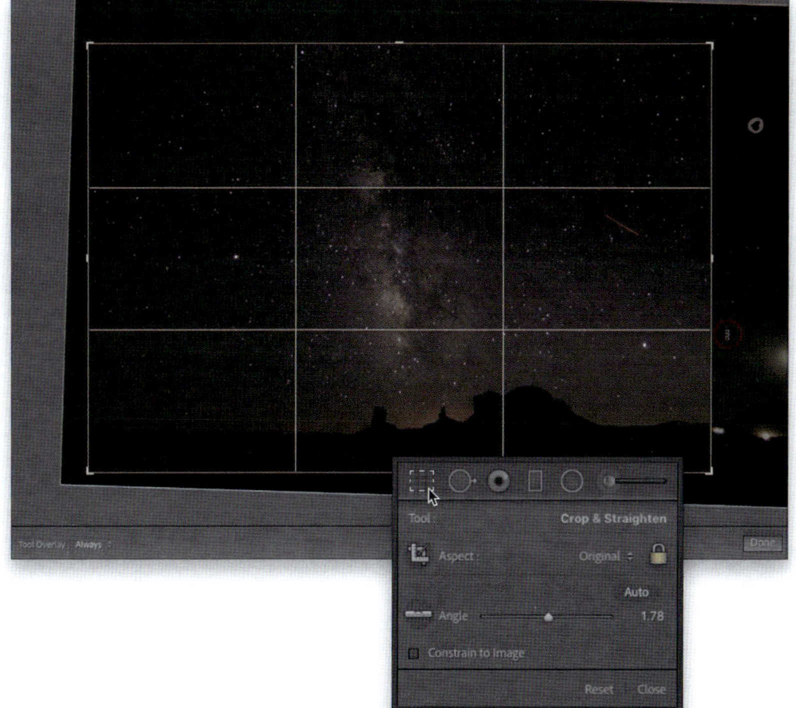

Step 03:

Before we get to tweaking the exposure, let's fix two problems at once: (1) the photo is a bit crooked, and (2) those car headlights are killing the right corner of the shot, which in turn, pretty much kills the whole shot. So, get the Crop Overlay tool **(R)** from the toolbox beneath the histogram (the Crop & Rotate tool **[C]** from the toolbox on the right in Lightroom cloud), click-and-drag the corners inward enough to where those headlights fall outside the frame (as seen here), and then move your cursor outside the cropping border, where it turns into a two-headed arrow (circled here in red). Click-and-drag to rotate the cropping border until our landscape looks fairly straight. Once it does, press **Return (PC: Enter)** to lock in your crop.

Step 04:

Two more things before we head into adjusting the exposure—the first one is getting rid of any lens distortion and darkening in the corners by going to the Lens Corrections panel (the Optics panel in Lightroom cloud) and turning on the Enable Profile (Lens) Corrections checkbox (as shown here. We're jumping over to **Point 6**). This fixes the distortion and the darkening of the edges (you'll see this clearly if you toggle the little switch in the left side of the panel header on/off a few times. In Lightroom cloud, click-and-hold on the eye icon in the right side of the panel header). Because doing this brightens the corners, which, as a result, brightens the image, it also brightens the light pollution glow behind the mountains, which somehow doesn't look bad (a happy accident?).

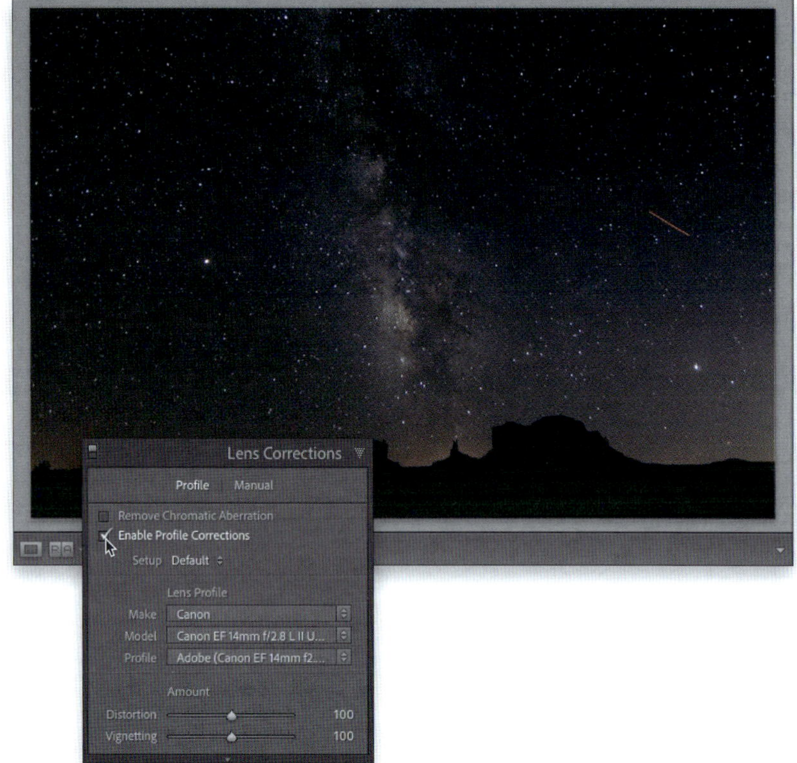

Step 05:

The other thing we should deal with is that streak from the shooting star (which you only have to deal with if you think it looks funky. I think it's distracting, so I'm going to remove it, but it's your call. We're jumping over to **Point 5** for this). Get the Spot Removal tool (**Q**; the Healing Brush tool **[H]** in Lightroom cloud) from the toolbox and paint right over the streak (as shown here, where the painted area appears in white).

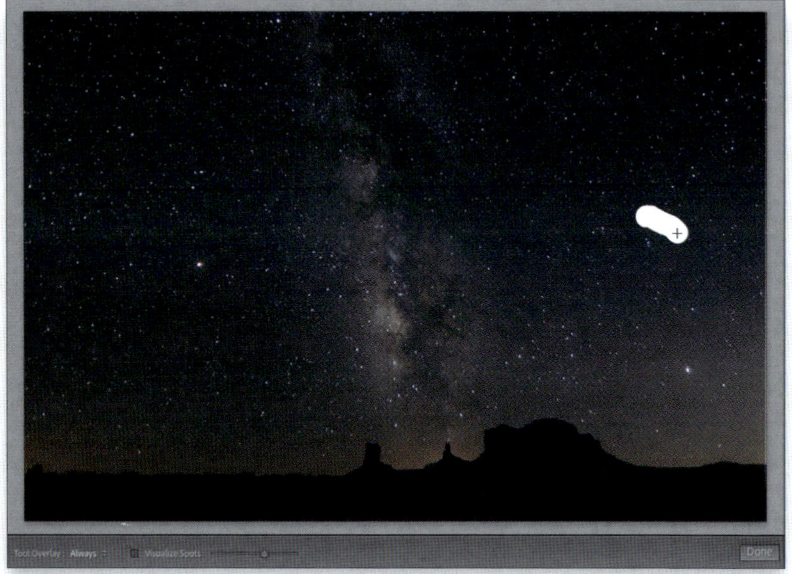

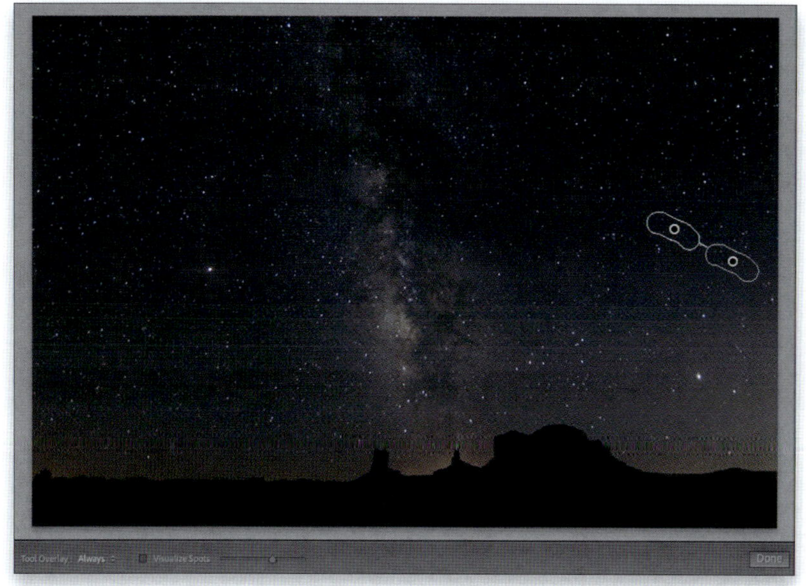

Step 06:

That did a pretty decent job because (a) the thing we wanted to remove wasn't touching anything else, so it didn't smear (which is the case when the thing you want to remove is touching another object), (b) this tool is actually pretty good at removing spots, specks, and small little lines all alone and by themselves, like this one, and (c) we got lucky. Click the Done button beneath the Preview area when you're finished (Lightroom cloud doesn't have this button).

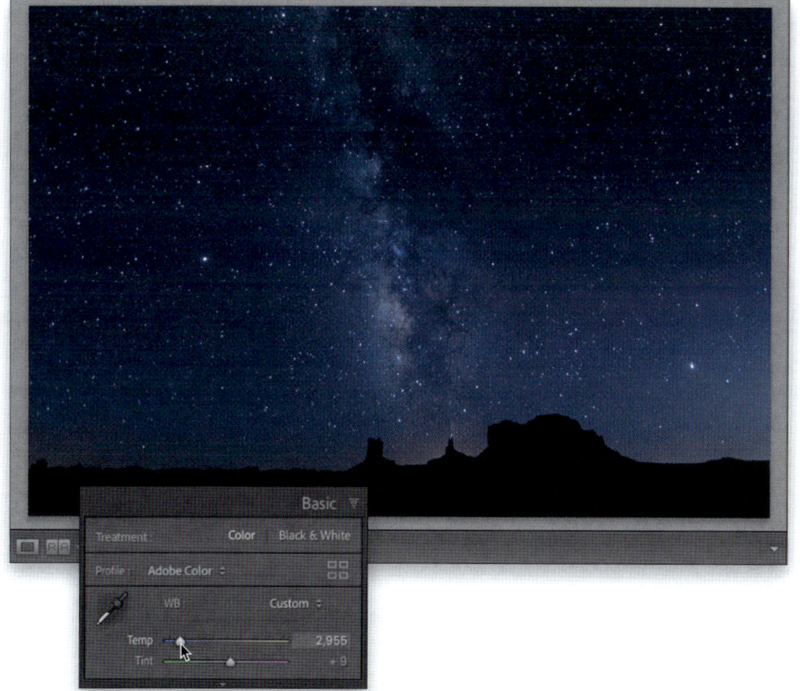

Step 07:

Now, let's bring some color and life into the image by adjusting the white balance **(Point 2)**. My go-to white balance for night skies is to go blue, so go to the Basic panel (the Color panel in Lightroom cloud) and drag the Temp slider way over to the left to make that night sky blue. Go ahead and drag it to around 3,000.

Step 08:

Okay, now we can finally work on our exposure **(Point 3)**. Let's start by expanding our tonal range: press-and-hold the Shift key, then double-click on Whites, and then on Blacks to automatically set your white and black points. This didn't do much at all (it set the Whites to +3 and the Blacks to –6), so our tonal range is pretty good.

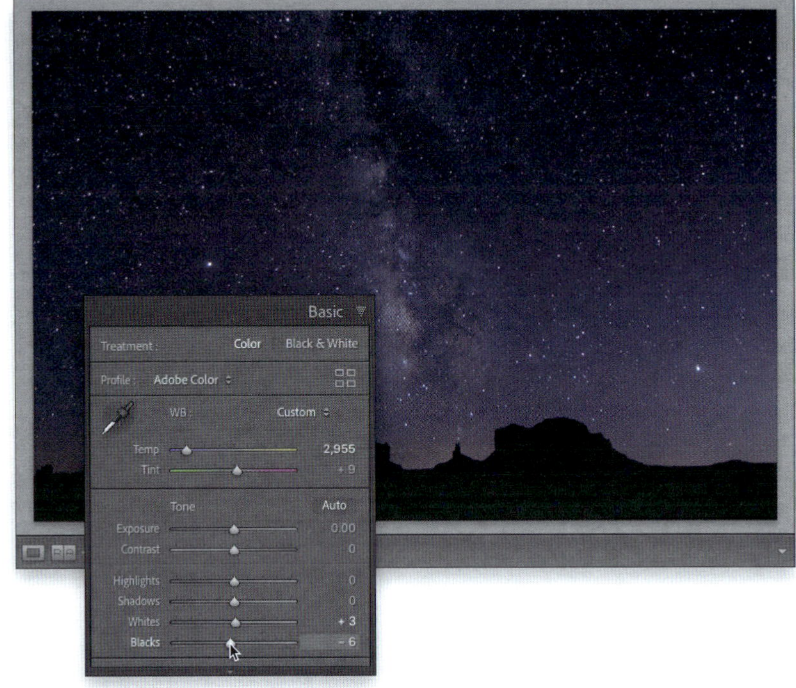

Step 09:

We're going to add some things later (Contrast and Dehaze) that are going to darken the image, so drag the Exposure slider to the right to +0.55 (as shown here).

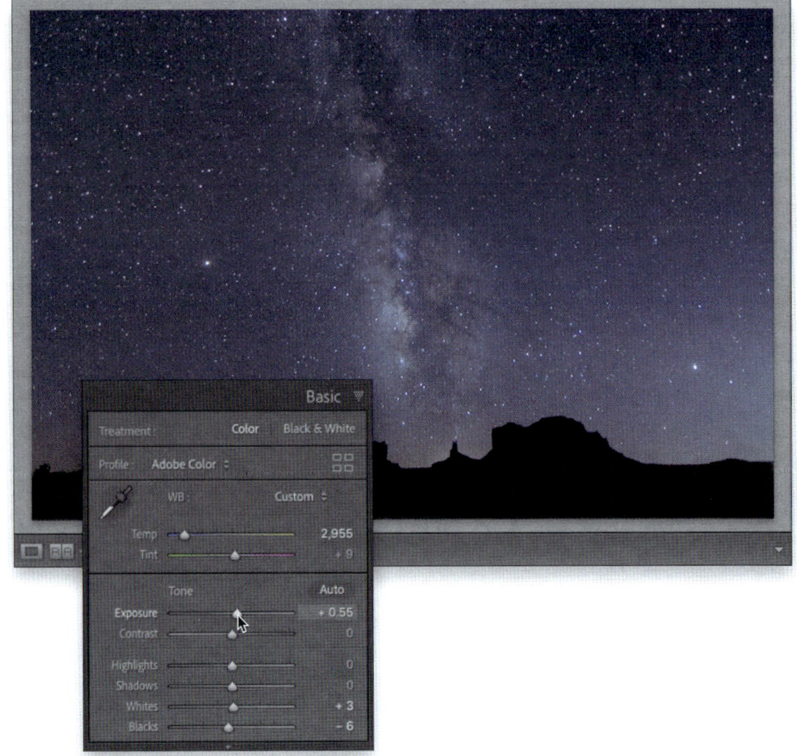

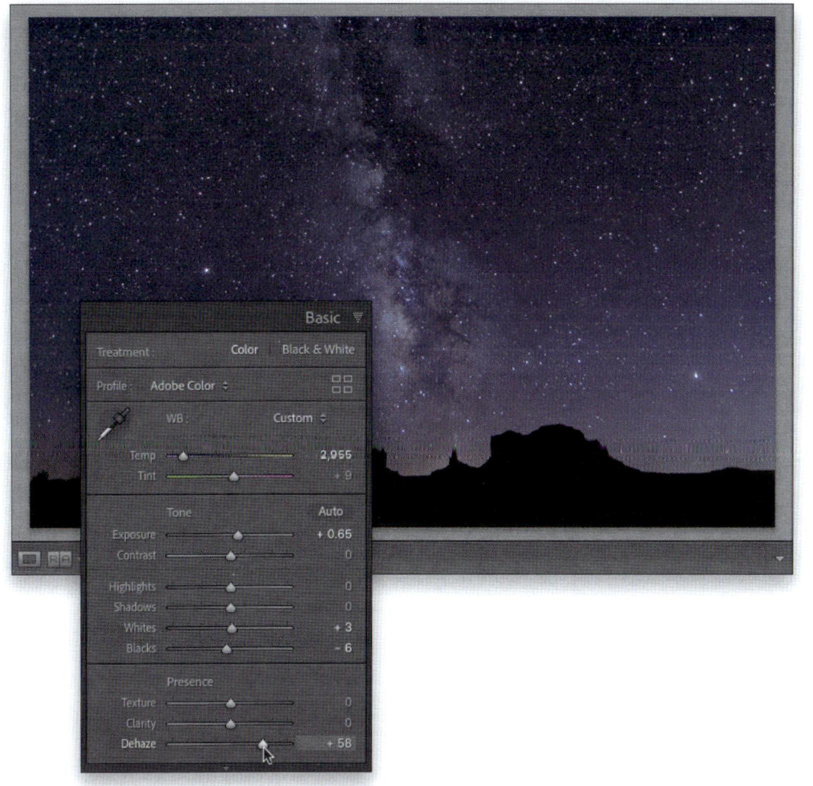

Step 10:

Now, let's cut some of that haze in the sky, and nothing does the job like Dehaze. It's light magic, and its only real side effect is that it adds blue to the image, but since our image is already quite blueish, that extra blue won't stand out. In fact, it will blend in, so we're good to go (and that brightening of the Exposure we did in the previous step worked out pretty well for us here, where I dragged Dehaze to +58, although I did end up bumping up the Exposure just a bit to +0.65).

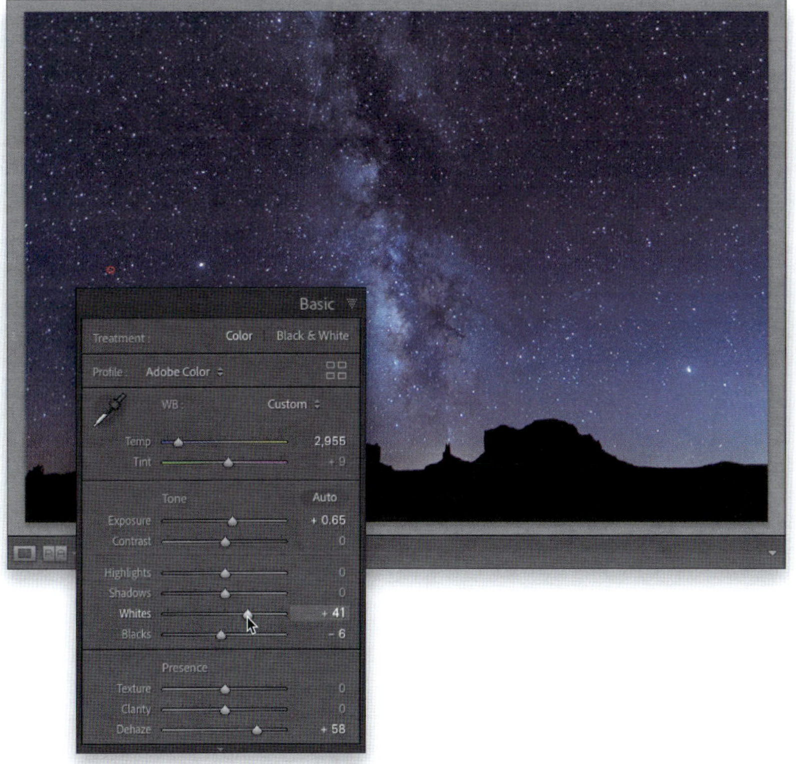

Step 11:

Okay, now let's make those stars brighter **(Point 4)**. Think about it: we want something that's already bright to be even brighter. Which sliders could we use? Highlights? (That's one.) Whites? (Yes.) So, go ahead and increase the Highlights (dragging the slider to the right) to see how that looks. Then, double-click directly on the word "Highlights" to reset it to zero and try the Whites slider. Which one looks better? Whites, because it mostly brightened the stars and didn't affect the rest of the image as much. Highlights worked too, but it brightened more of the sky. Between the two, Whites seems to look best, so drag the Whites slider over to +41.

Step 12:

Let's add a little more contrast to the image to make the dark parts of the sky darker and the bright parts even brighter. Drag the Contrast slider to the right until it looks good to you (here, I dragged it over to +36).

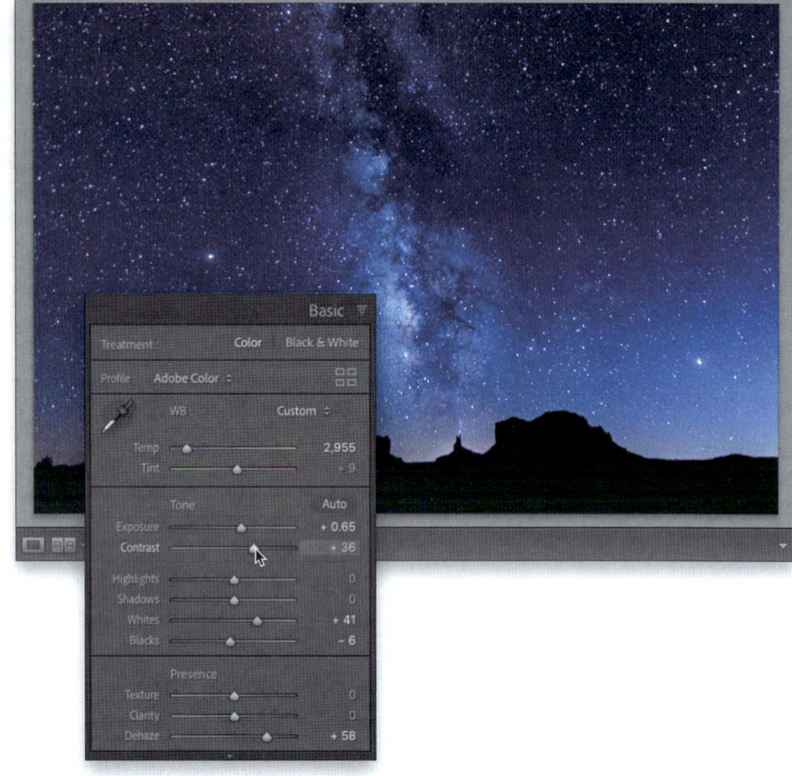

Step 13:

Now, let's bring out some detail in the Milky Way itself by adding a bunch of Clarity (way more than you would for most other images). Go ahead and drag the Clarity slider over to around +42 (as shown here).

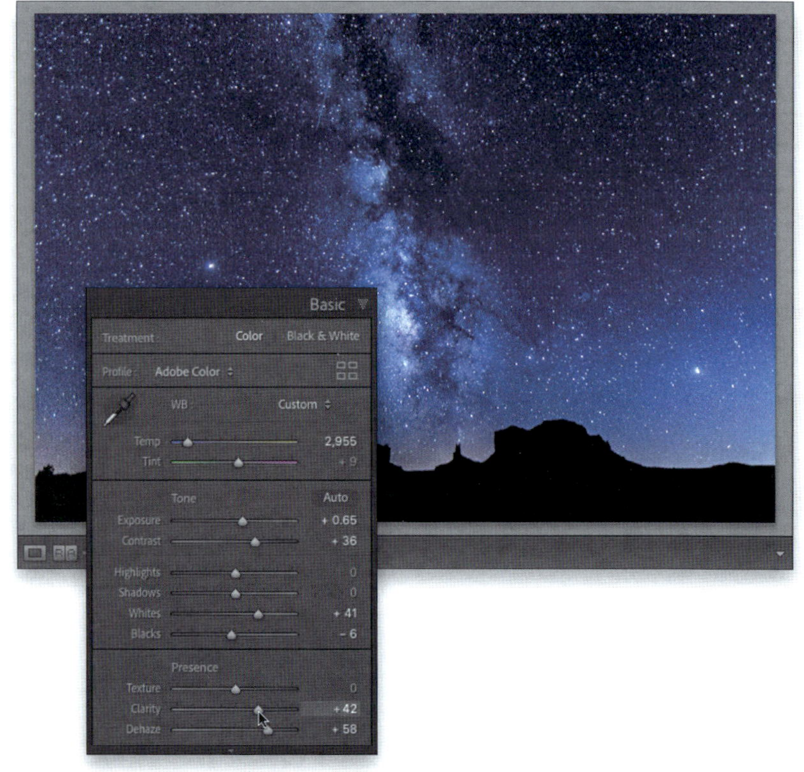

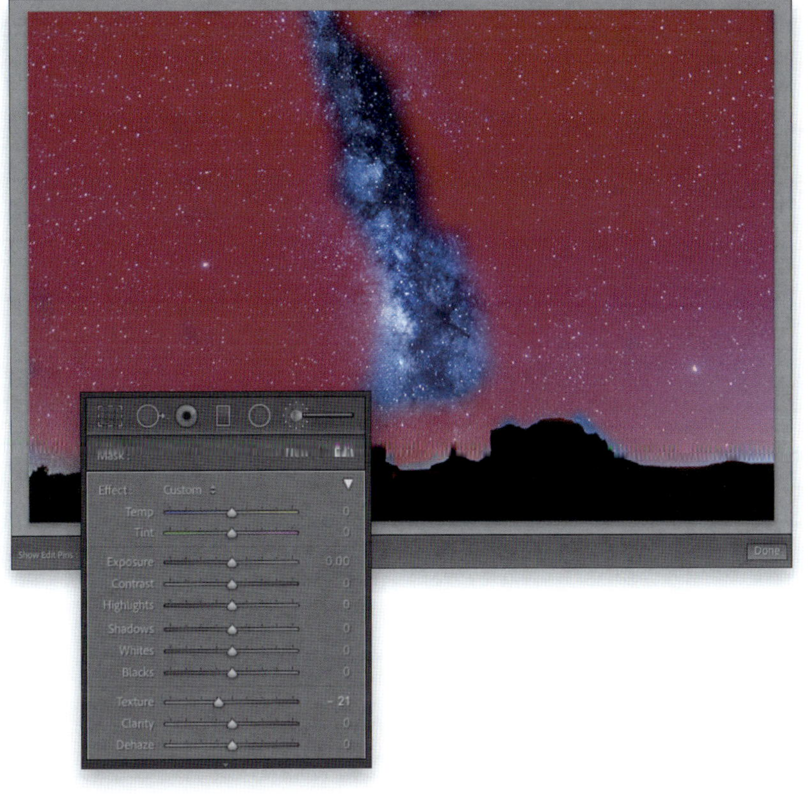

Step 14:

This next move is going to sound counter-intuitive, but it works wonders because we're going to paint with negative Texture on all the areas outside the Milky Way core (back to **Point 5**). This softens the outside edges of the core and helps draw your eye to the Milky Way as we're going to keep it really sharp. (I picked this tip up from my buddy and co-host of our weekly photography talk show, *The Grid*, astro and rocket photographer Erik Kuna). So, get the Adjustment Brush (**K**; the Brush tool [**B**] in Lightroom cloud), double-click on the word "Effect" to reset all the sliders to zero (this happens by default in Lightroom cloud), then set your Texture amount to –21 and paint over everything outside the Milky Way. Press the **O key** to see the mask, so you can clearly see if you missed painting over any areas of the sky (remember, the red tint shows you where you painted). When you're done painting, press the O key again (press it three times in Lightroom cloud to get back to showing just the Edit Pin).

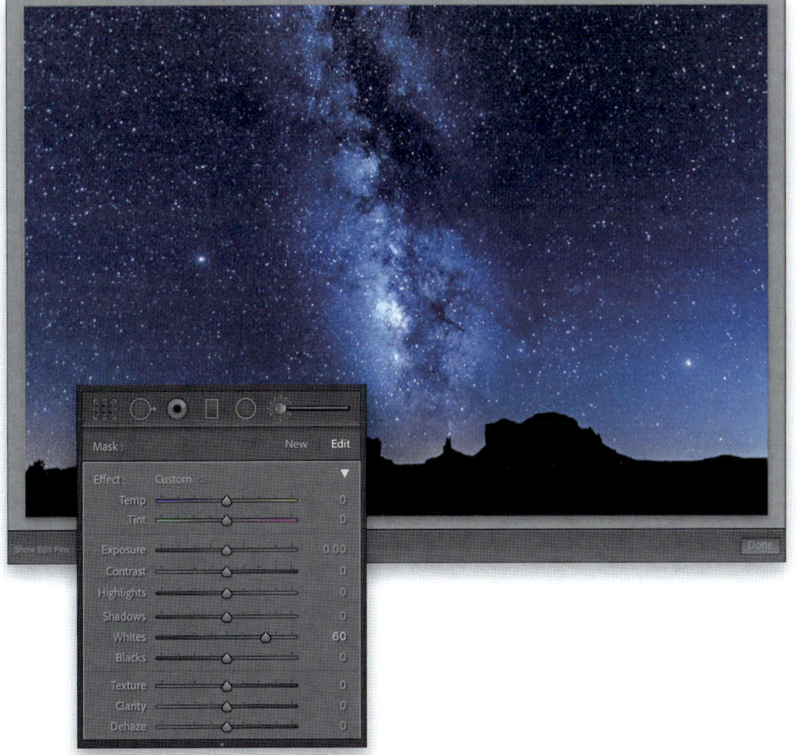

Step 15:

Now that the stars outside the core are softened, click on New (the + [plus sign] in Lightroom cloud), and then reset your sliders to zero because we're going to create a glow just in the core area by painting over it with the Whites cranked way up. So, drag the Whites slider over to around 60, and paint right over the core, and that's what creates that glow (compare this image to the one in Step 13). Click the Done button when you're finished.

Step 16:

We're not getting a whole lot of variation in the color of the Milky Way because earlier we made the white balance way too blue. So, let's go back to the Basic panel (the Color panel in Lightroom cloud) and drag the Temp slider back to around 3,820 and the Tint to around +10. Ahhhh, that's better—now we're seeing more color in the core, which is what was missing.

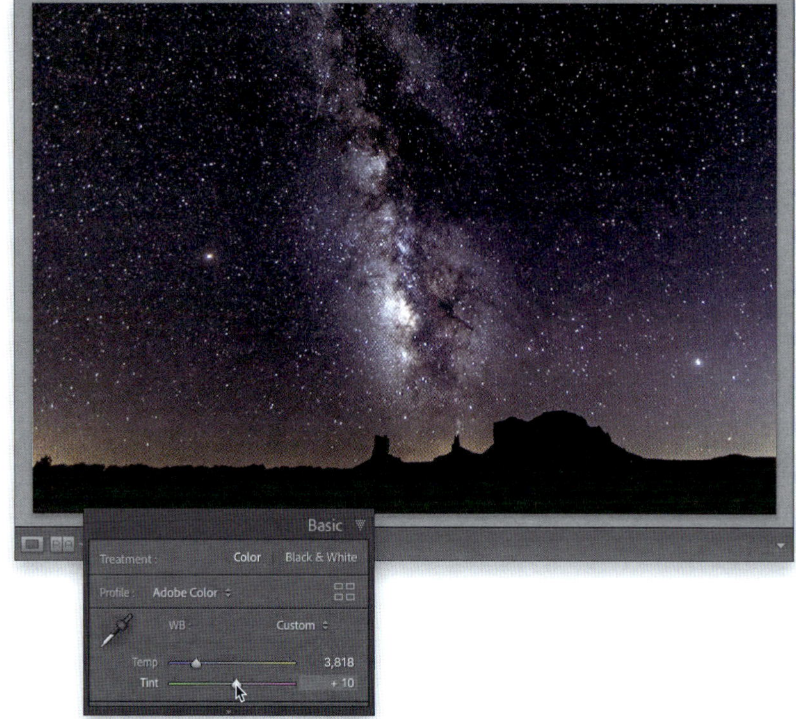

Step 17:

Now, we're going to finish this off **(Point 7)** by killing two birds with one stone: we're going to darken the edges all the way around big time, which will give us a black sky in those outside areas (focusing the viewer's attention on the Milky Way), and doing so will reduce that glow (light pollution) behind the mountains. Go to the Effects panel, and in the Post-Crop Vignetting section, lower the Amount (Vignette in Lightroom cloud) to –27 (yes, I know this is a *lot* more than our standard –11, but this is a special case, right?). Look at how that helps the sky and the glow. Normally, at this stage, we would add some sharpening, but with high-ISO Milky Way shots like this, you're better off skipping the sharpening, which will mostly just accentuate any noise already in the photo. So, in this one instance, we skip the sharpening. That's it—we're done!

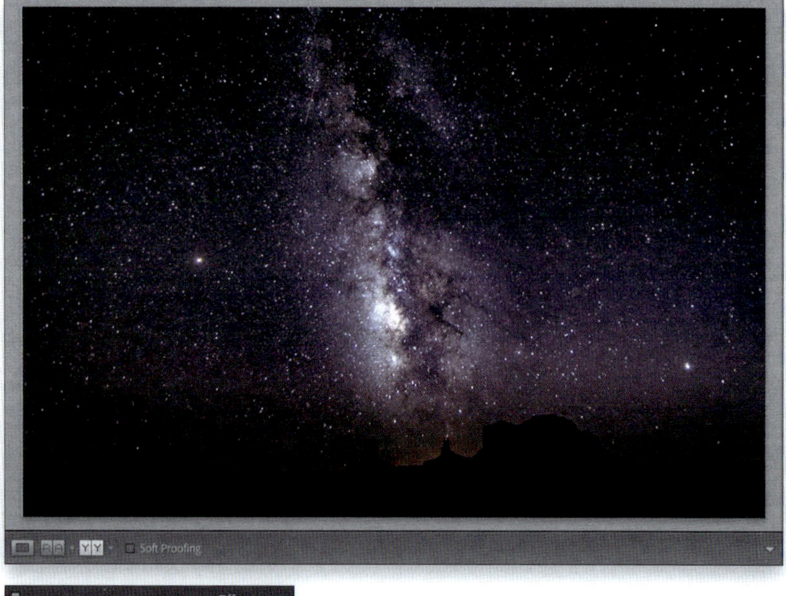

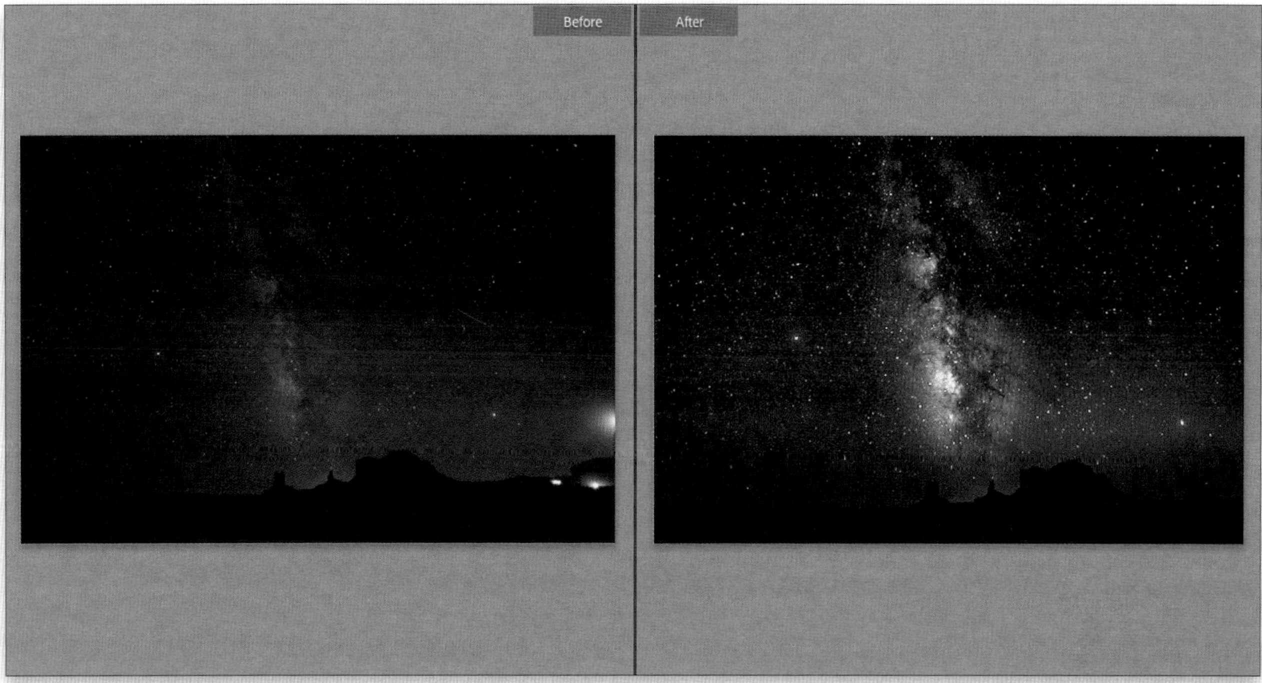

Here's our before/after.

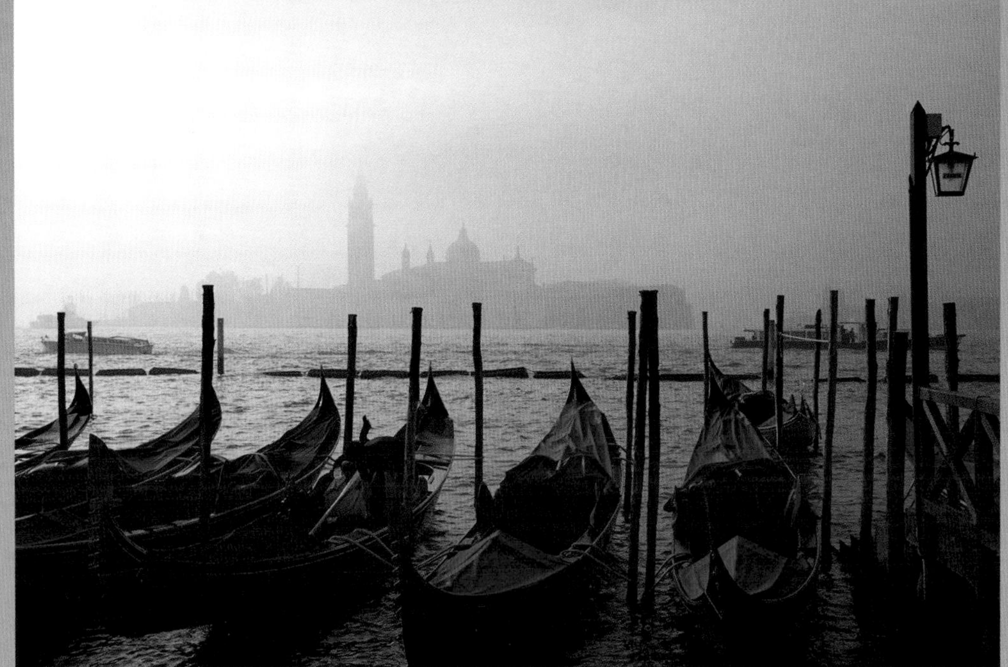

Adobe Photoshop
Lightroom Classic
Before

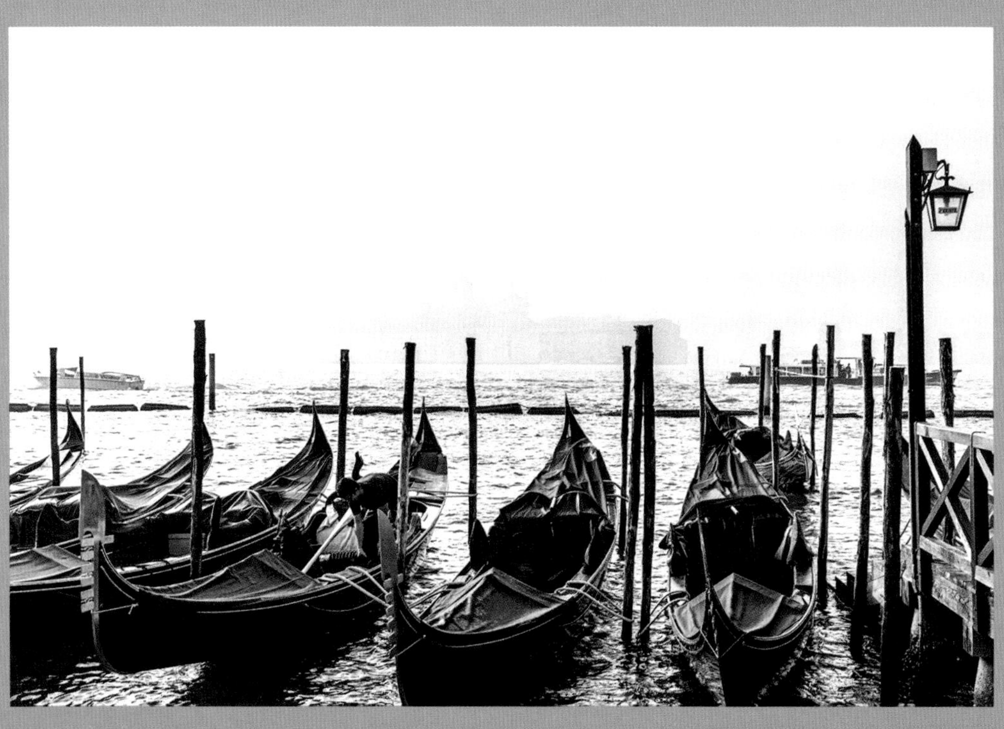

After

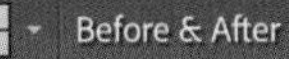
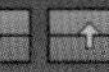
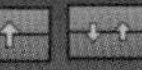
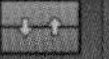

Before & After :
Soft Proofing

BLACK & WHITE CONVERSION

1. Assigning a RAW Profile
2. Getting the Color Right
3. Expanding the Tonal Range
4. Dealing with Sensor Limitations
5. Painting with Light and Retouching
6. Fixing Lens Issues
7. Finishing Moves

Let's evaluate the shot. (What do we wish were different?) First, the colors are very flat throughout (which, right there, is a trigger for me to consider converting it to a B&W image). The sky looks like just a foggy mess, the contrast is really low, and it's just kind of a "meh" shot all the way around. Converting to B&W will surely help, and I've always felt the key to a great B&W is a ton of contrast. It just gives black-and-white images that snap.

THE STORY BEHIND THE SHOT:

This shot was taken in Venice (I know, duh) at the edge of St. Mark's Square with the tiny island of San Giorgio Maggiore in the background (you just hop a water bus to get over there. It takes less than 5 minutes). The previous time I was in Venice (many years earlier), I wanted to get a similar shot, but my son and I both caught a terrible flu during that family vacation and spent our whole time there flat on our backs, sick as dogs, in our hotel room, so we never even got to see the city. During this trip, I was feeling perfect, got up at dawn, and got my tripod set up to get the shot. It's not obvious at first glance, but I love that there's a gondolier there prepping his boat for the day (he's on the third boat from the left). He gets lost in the tones, but I still see him every time I look at the image. I came back later on this trip with a 10-stop and a 3-stop ND (neutral density) filter to darken the scene, so I could do a long exposure and get the water looking nice and silky, and I have that one hanging as a print.

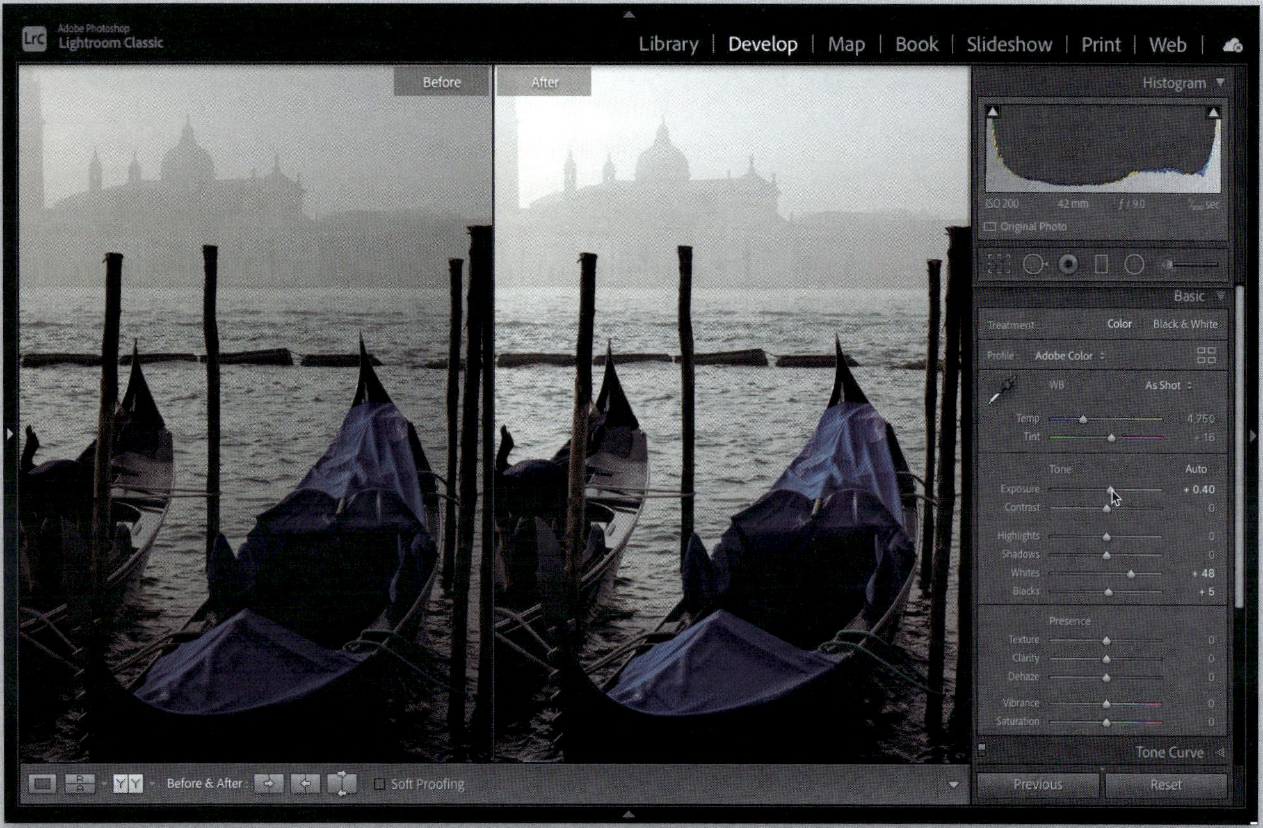

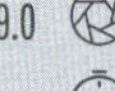

Camera: Canon EOS 5D Mark IV
Aperture Value: *f*/9.0
Shutter Speed: 1/800 sec
ISO: 200
Focal Length: 42mm

Step 01:

Normally, our first step would be to choose a RAW profile, but as you saw in the before/after in this Lesson's introduction, this image is going to wind up being a black-and-white photo anyway, so getting the color right isn't going to help our cause. So, in this case, we're going to skip choosing a RAW profile (Point 1), and skip fixing the white balance (Point 2) because we're going to apply a B&W creative profile instead. But, before we get to that, I find it's harder to choose a great black-and-white conversion when your tones are this flat in the initial color image. So, let's kind of get our exposure in the ballpark first **(Point 3)**, and then we'll look at converting it to black and white once the tones in the image look better. Press-and-hold the Shift key and double-click on the word "Whites," and then on "Blacks" to expand the tonal range. Okay, that didn't do a whole lot (but it did bump up the Whites by quite a bit). Let's also increase the Exposure amount to +0.40. Above is a before/after of just those exposure adjustments (white point, black point, and moving the Exposure slider). *Note:* You can get this view by pressing the **Y key** on your keyboard (this view is not available in Lightroom cloud, but you can press the **\ [backslash] key** to see your original image).

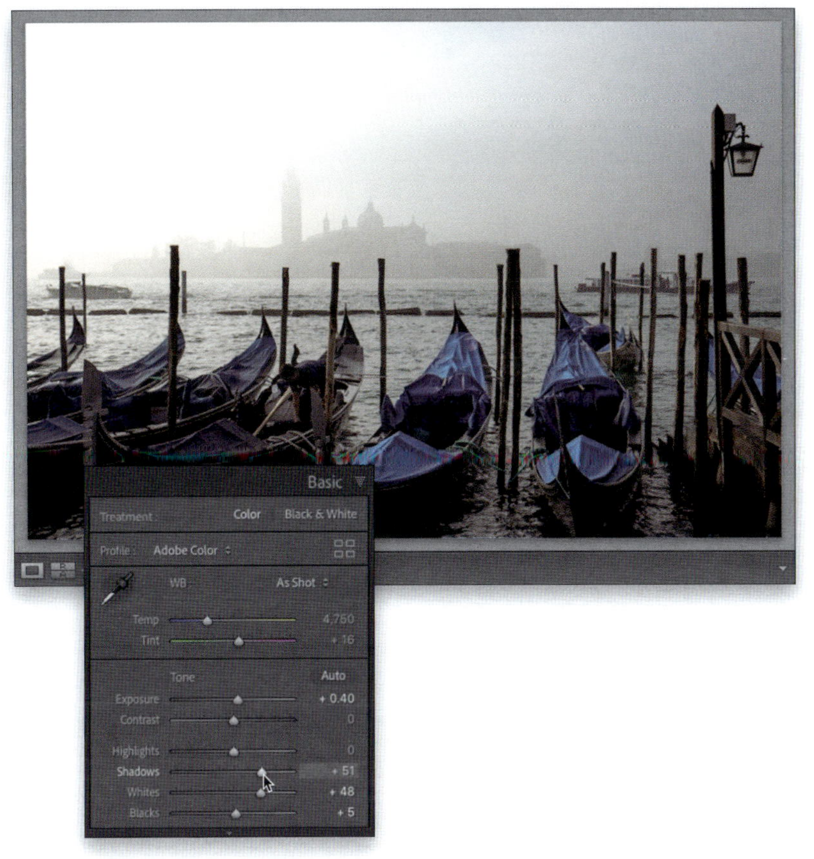

Step 02:

Now, let's open up the shadow areas a bit (since these boats are kind of backlit; **Point 4**) by dragging the Shadows slider to the right quite a bit (here, I dragged it over to +51).

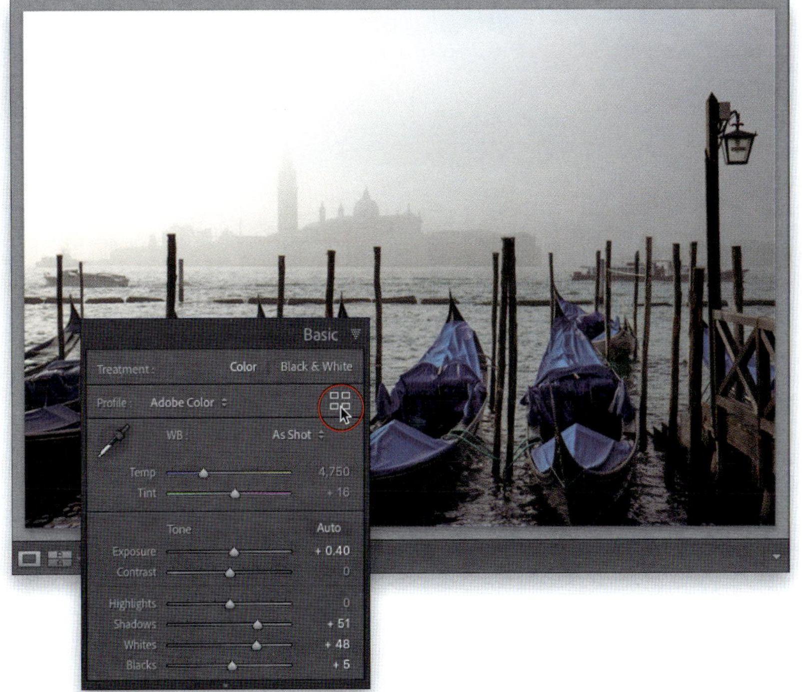

Step 03:

Okay, I think we did enough with those few moves to set us up for success when we choose our black-and-white creative profile. At the top of the Basic panel (the Edit panel in Lightroom cloud), to the right of the Profile pop-up menu, you'll see an icon with four little squares (shown circled here in red). Go ahead and click on that to bring up the Profile Browser (seen in the next step).

Step 04:

Once the Profile Browser appears (seen here), in the list of creative profiles, open the B&W set. There are 17 different black-and-white conversions here to choose from, and the thumbnails show your image with each of them already applied. To see an onscreen preview of any of them, just hover your cursor over one of the thumbnails and it updates your onscreen image (as shown here, where I'm hovering over B&W 07, and the image has updated to show how it would look if we decided to go with that one. Spoiler alert—we're not going with B&W 07. This conversion makes the gondolas too dark).

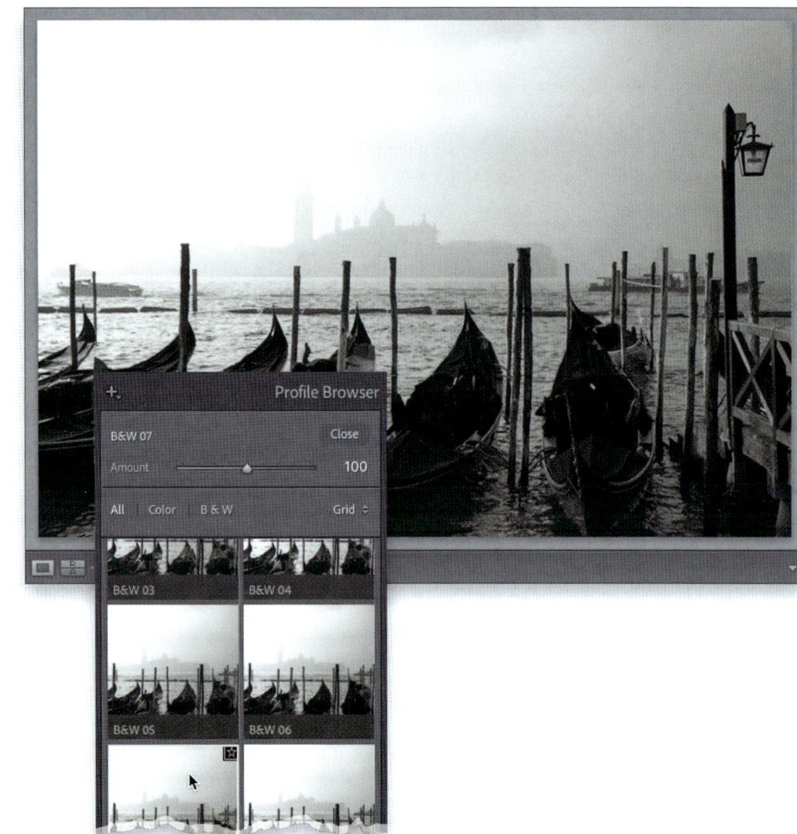

Step 05:

Go ahead and hover your cursor over each of the 17 B&W creative profiles to see which one looks best for this particular image. There is no official "right answer" for this, but I try to look for a conversion that has nice contrast overall. Of course, we can (and will) add lots of contrast after we make this initial conversion (this is just our starting point), but I want to look at the image, even at this stage, and think, "Hey, this looks okay." For me, I thought out of all of them, B&W 09 actually looked best (the gondolas look so much better), so click on B&W 09, then hit the Close button in the top right of the panel to apply this profile (click on Back in the left of the panel header in Lightroom cloud).

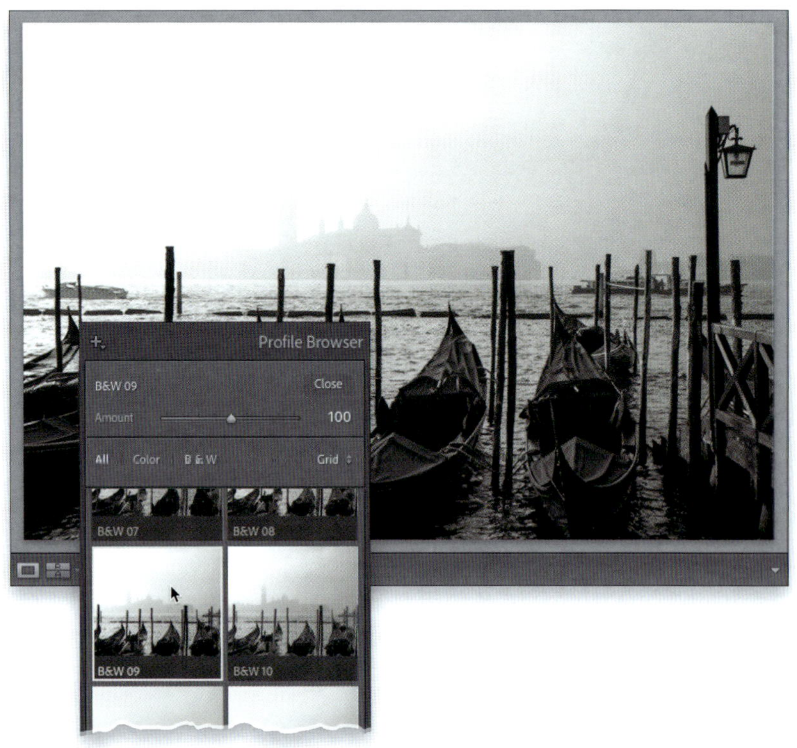

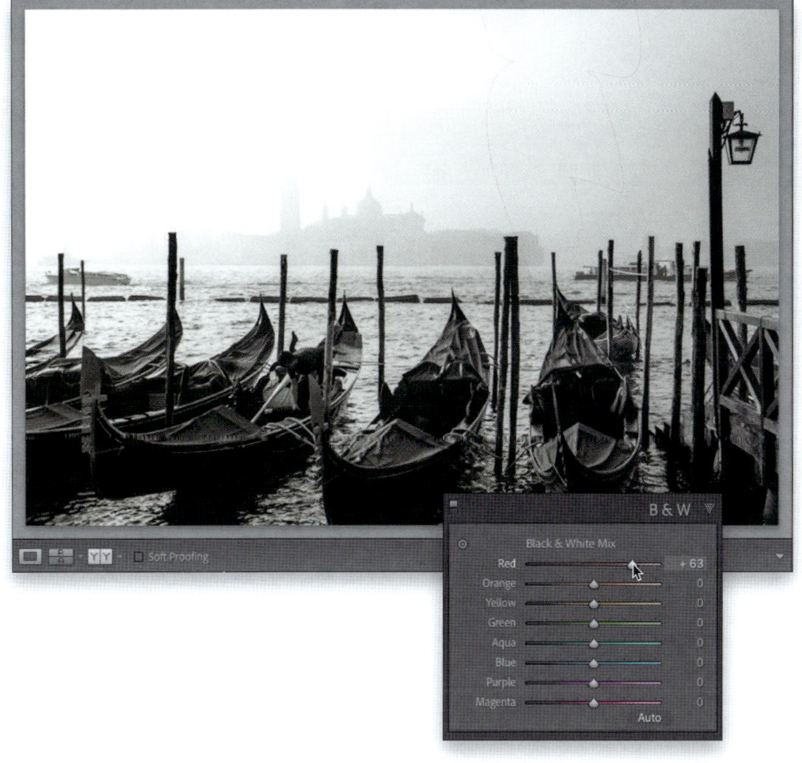

Step 06:

Next, let's go to the B&W panel (the B&W Mixer panel in Lightroom cloud). Wait. What? Why didn't we see this panel before? Where has it been hiding? It only appears when you convert your image to B&W (it replaces the HSL/Color panel [the Color Mixer panel in Lightroom cloud] while you're working on a B&W image). The thing that throws a lot of people is that what it brings you is a set of color sliders (Red, Orange, Yellow, Green, and so on), and yet you're working on a black-and-white image. There are a few that are obvious, right? Like, the Blue slider would control the tones of the sky (well, if there was a blue sky in the image at least), and Green would control the grass (of course, there's no grass in this photo). So, what I've found that's quick and easy is to simply drag each slider back and forth once or twice, and you'll immediately see which tones in your black-and-white image each slider controls. For example, here, I dragged the Red slider all the way to the left, then back to the right (to +63), and learned that it controls the tones for the gondola covers on the left side, and that dragging it to the right opened them up nicely.

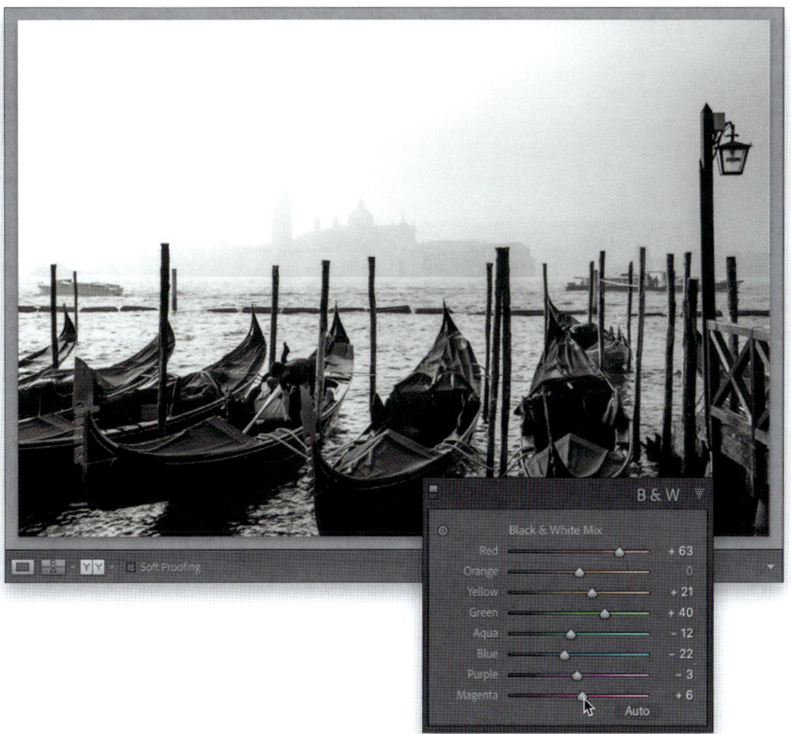

Step 07:

Go ahead and do this process of dragging the sliders back and forth and you'll be surprised at which sliders control which parts of the image (for example, the Green slider only adjusted the brightness in the water between the two gondolas on the far right). The main thing we're doing with these sliders is taking control over different parts of the image—dragging a particular slider to the right lightens that tone in that color area, and dragging it to the left darkens that area—so it gives you a nice level of control over the different areas of your image (you can see all my slider settings here). After making those adjustments I ended up going back to the Profile Browser and switching to B&W 02, instead, because I thought it looked better.

Step 08:

Let's start adding in a bunch of contrast now (different types of contrast). We'll start with the standard ol' Contrast slider. Go back to the Basic panel (the Light panel in Lightroom cloud), and drag the Contrast slider to the right to make the brightest parts of the image brighter and the darkest parts even darker (here, I dragged it over to +48). Okay, that's a start.

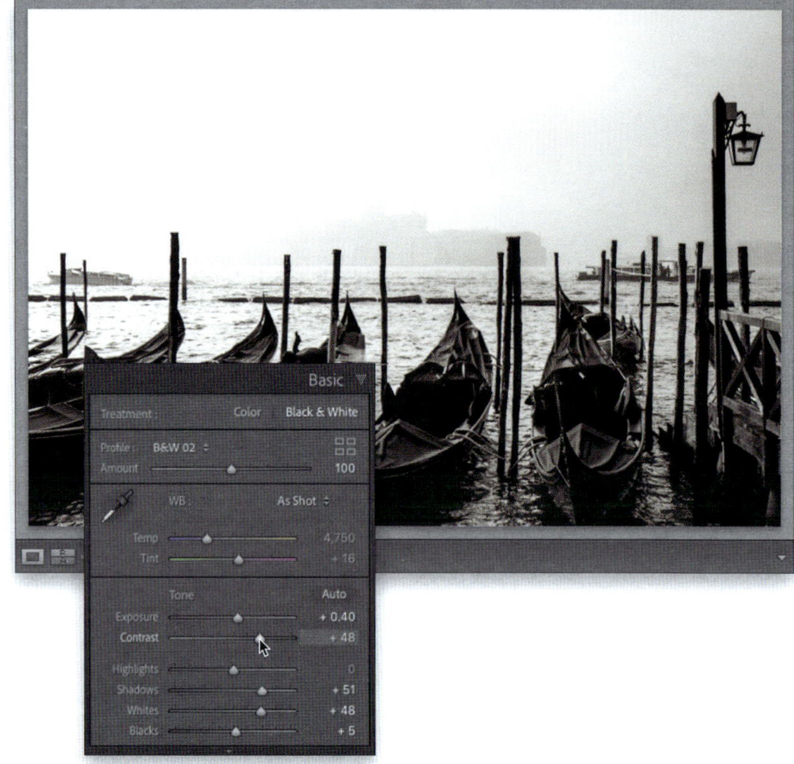

Step 09:

Now, let's add lots of midtone contrast, and we do that using the Clarity slider. On black-and-white images like this, I often add a lot more Clarity than usual, as this tends to give the image its shine and grit. So, drag the Clarity slider (in the Effects panel in Lightroom cloud) over to the right (here, I dragged it all the way over to +46. That's a lot of Clarity, folks, but it's also bringing that nice midtone contrast and shine to the image). Compare this image with the one in Step 08—in particular, look at the highlights on the tops of the boats. Much punchier.

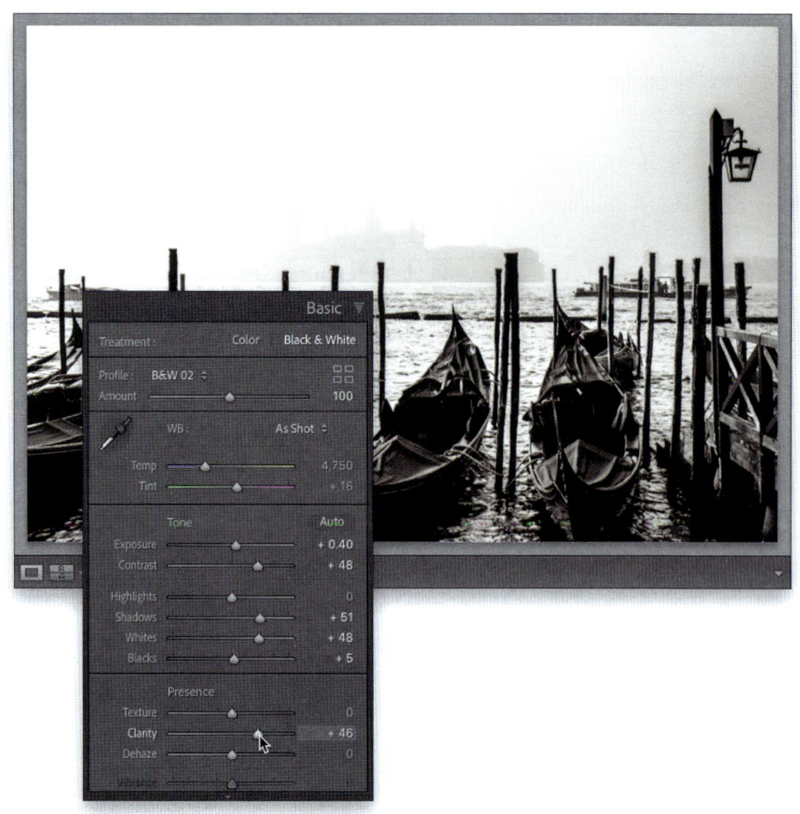

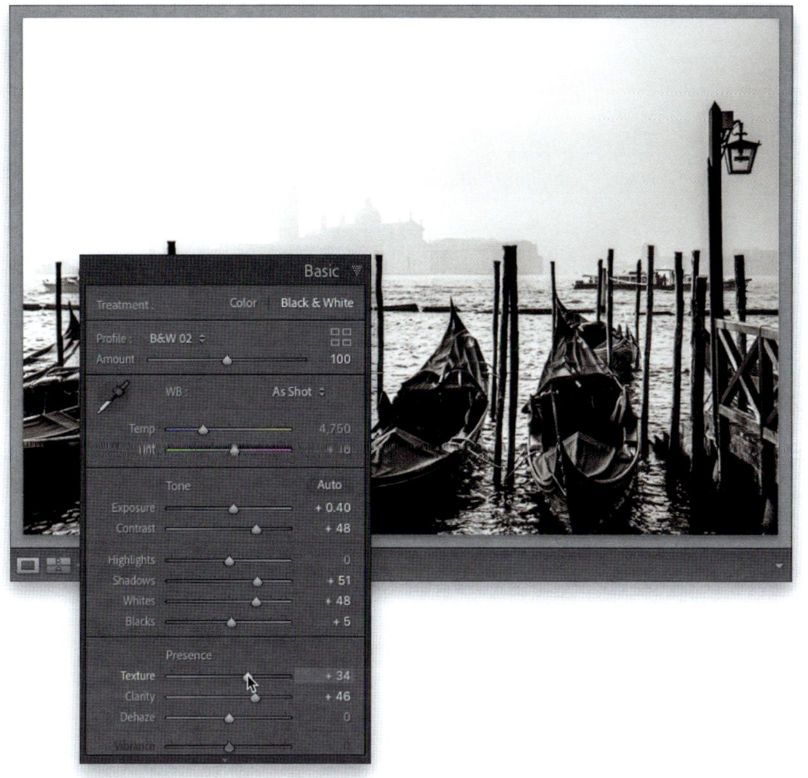

Step 10:

Next, let's bring out some extra detail using the Texture slider. Here, I dragged it out to +34. *Note:* This is the opposite balance of Clarity and Texture than what I usually do, where the Texture amount is higher, and the Clarity amount is often half as much or even less. Black and white is different, and here contrast is king!

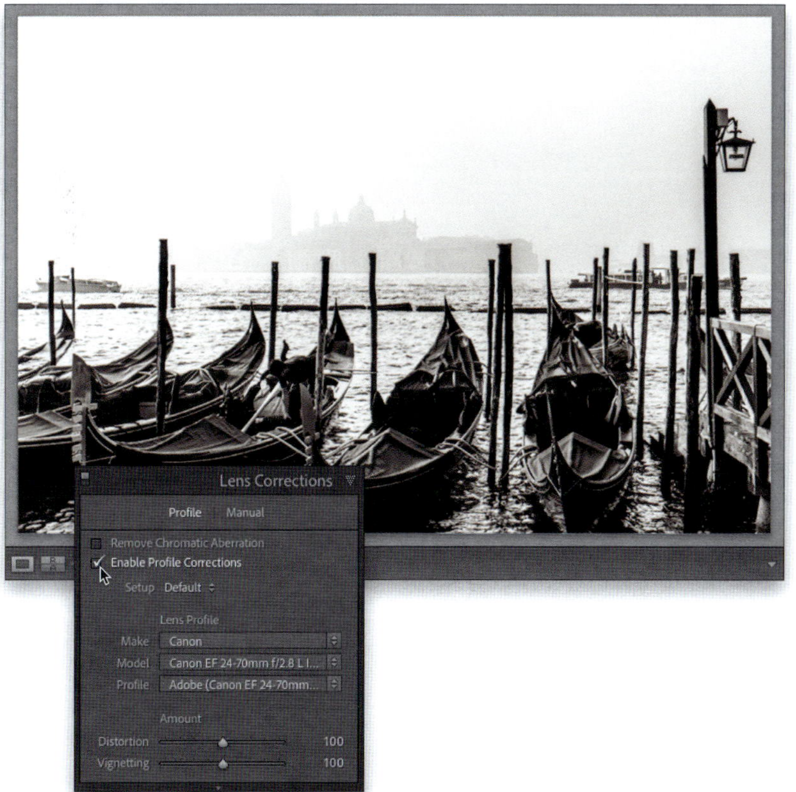

Step 11:

There is (as usual) a little lens distortion—not enough that it's distracting, but the darkening in the corners is pretty severe, so let's deal with it **(Point 6)**. Go to the Lens Corrections panel (the Optics panel in Lightroom cloud), and turn on the Enable Profile (Lens) Corrections checkbox. That alone—just turning on that one checkbox—not only fixed the lens distortion (granted, it wasn't too bad in this shot), but it also did a great job cleaning up those dark corners. Compare the corners here (especially, the top-right corner around the light pole) to those in Step 10. Night and day! It's just one checkbox, but it can make a big difference.

Step 12:

While falling under the finishing moves point **(Point 7)** of the 7-Point System, this is a move I only do on black-and-white images, and that is to add some film grain to the image. Grain (not the noise we think of from today's digital cameras) was a trademark of traditional film—it's a signature feature, if you will—and adding some grain gives your black-and-white image a "legit" feeling and a bit of romance (if that makes sense). You can consider this an optional step if you like, but anybody serious about black and white is going to tell you to add grain so…go ahead and add some (I did a before and after here, so you can see the difference grain makes, and it absolutely helps to zoom in to see how it affects your image). In the Effects panel, drag the Grain Amount slider to 60 (this is totally a "salt to taste" thing), set the Size to 30, and the Roughness (of the paper) will be already set to its default setting of 50.

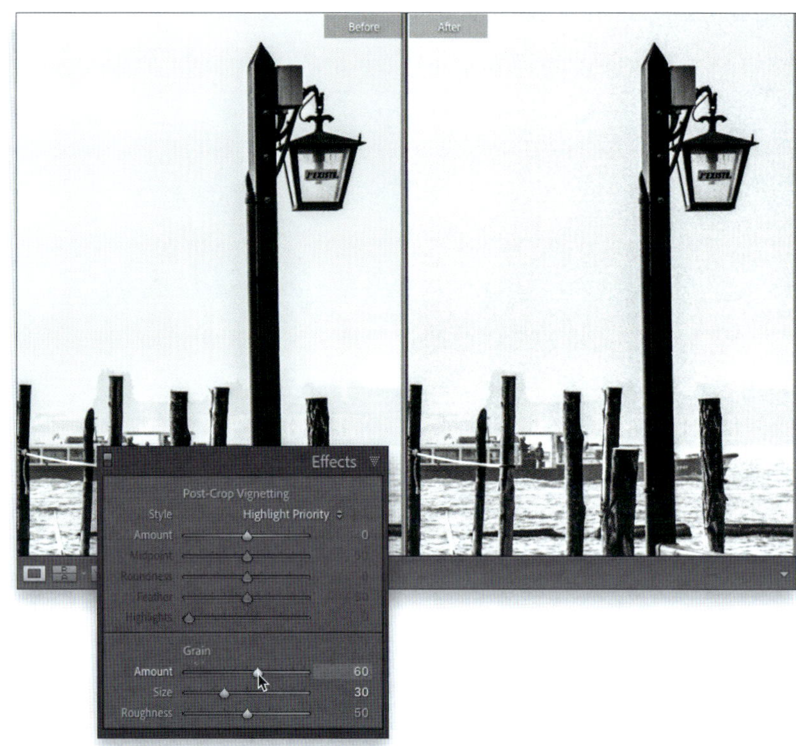

Step 13:

Let's wrap up with some sharpening, but since we added a bunch of grain to the image, we'll want to keep the noise in the sky from being sharpened (it will be most apparent in the sky, where there's not much detail and it's just a smooth, flat surface). To do that, go to the Detail panel, and in the Sharpening section up top, increase the Amount slider (the Sharpening slider in Lightroom cloud) to 70. At this point, we're sharpening the entire image (sky and all), but we can limit our sharpening to just the boats, the water, and the island in the background by pressing-and-holding the Option (PC: Alt) key while dragging the Masking slider. The screen will turn solid white (letting you know that everything is being sharpened), but as you drag to the right, any parts of the image that turn black are no longer being sharpened (like the sky, as seen here, when we drag over to 52). Now, the noise in the sky is no longer being sharpened, but the rest of the image is.

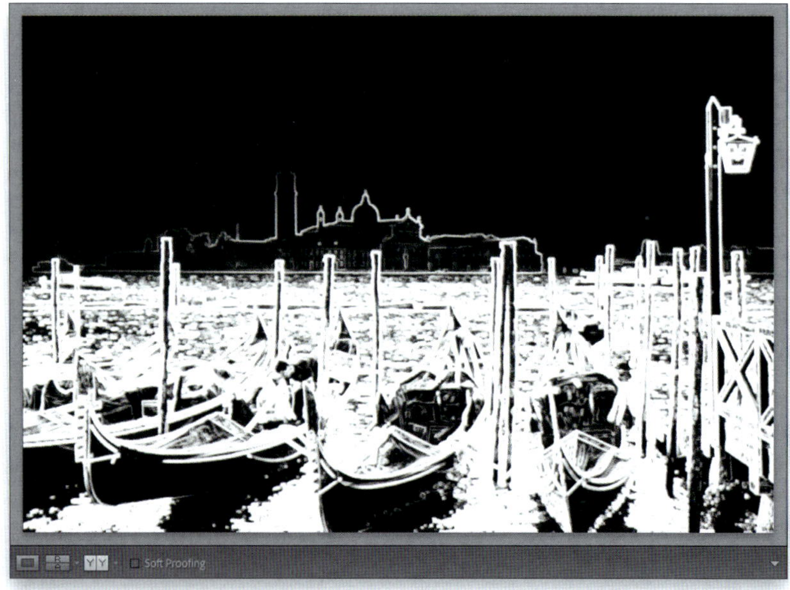

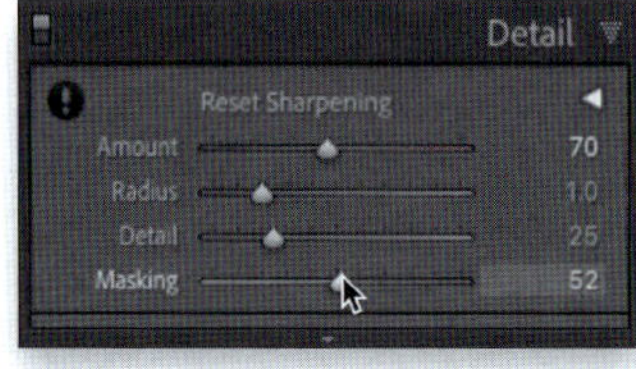

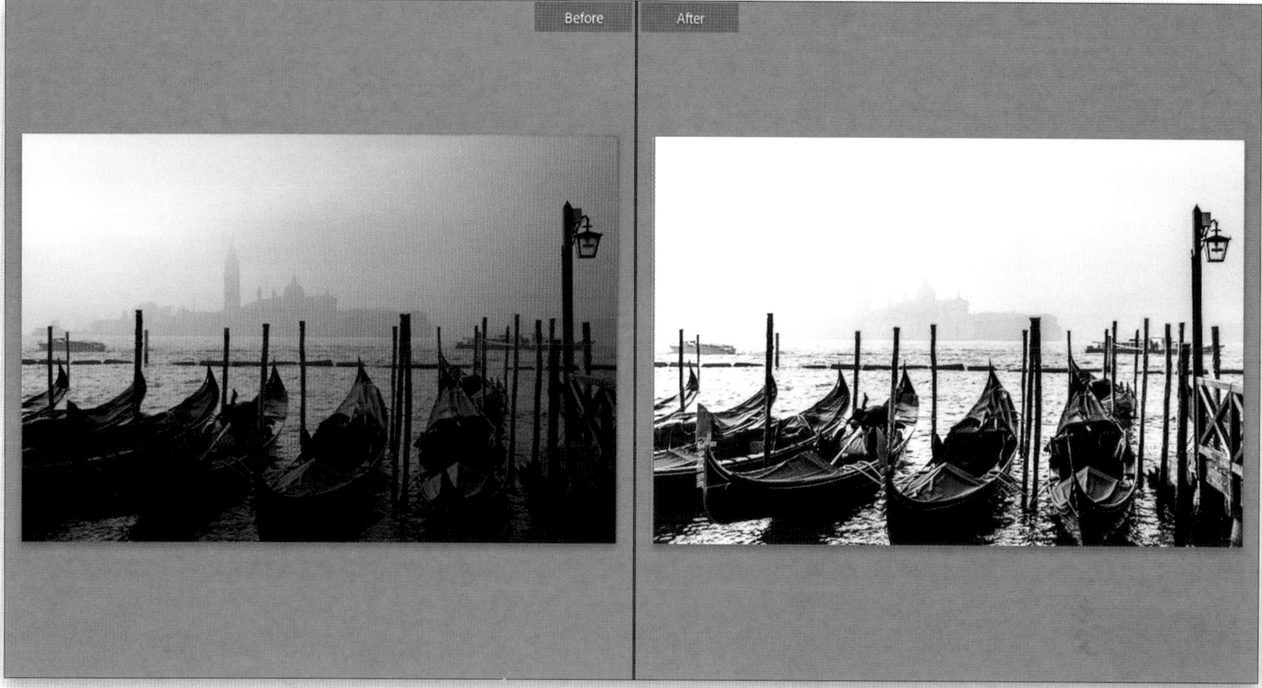

Here's our before/after.

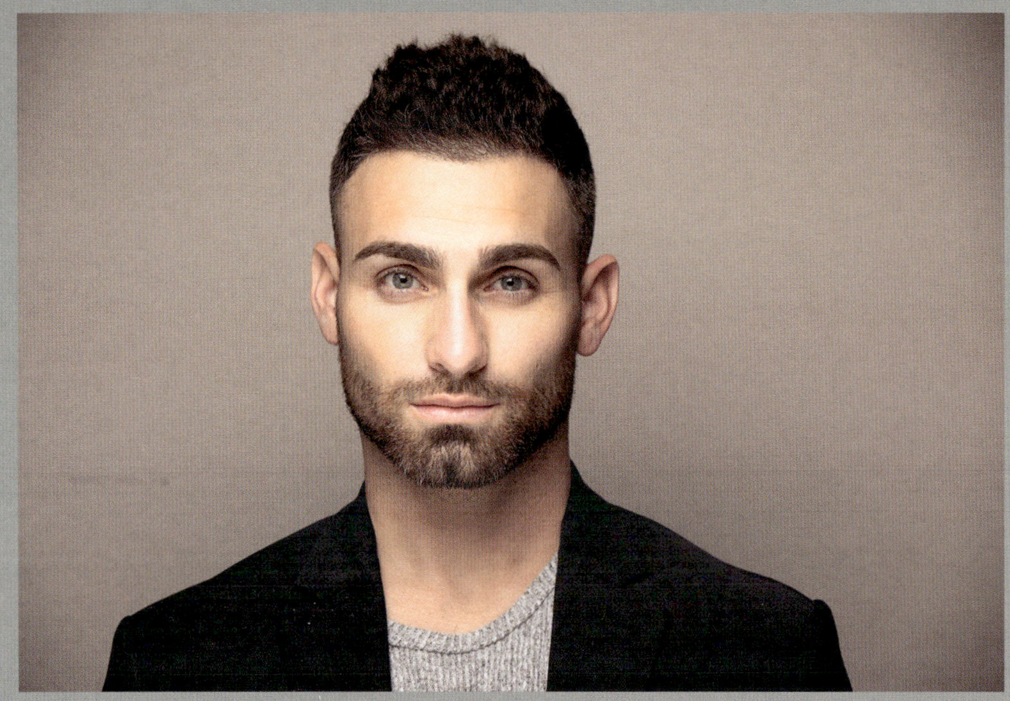

Before

After

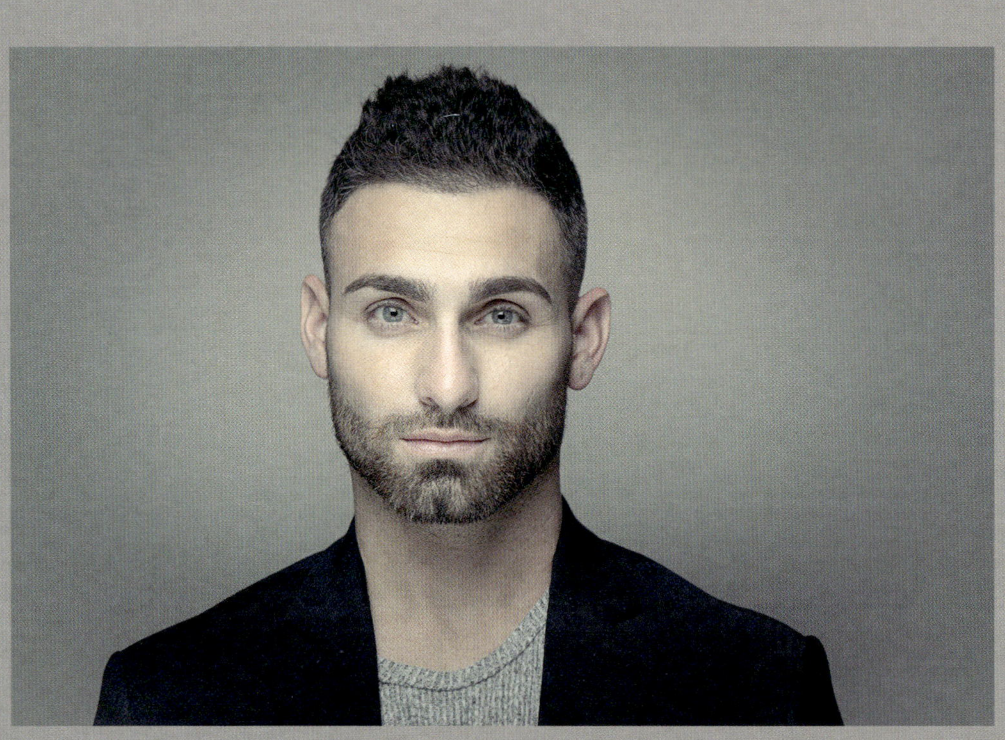

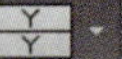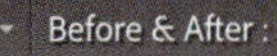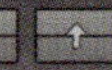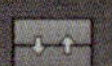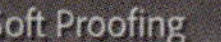

LESSON 16

COLOR GRADED PORTRAIT

1. Assigning a RAW Profile
2. Getting the Color Right
3. Expanding the Tonal Range
4. Dealing with Sensor Limitations
5. Painting with Light and Retouching
6. Fixing Lens Issues
7. Finishing Moves

Let's evaluate the shot. Two big things jump out: the color is all off, which makes his skin tone look overly warm, and the vignetting in the corners (caused by the lens) is really severe (it stands out so clearly because he's on a flat, neutral background, which gives you a great idea of why we try to fix this corner-darkening issue in our shots). We also have some sensor smudge on the center left. Once we're done with the fixes, we'll add some color grading (a very popular look today).

THE STORY BEHIND THE SHOT:

This portrait was taken indoors in Ybor City (just outside of downtown Tampa, Florida). It looks like a studio shot because he's on such a neutral background, but that's just a plain wall inside the building we rented for the shoot. Most of the building had brick walls, and I had so many shots of our subject on those that I just wanted a different look for a few of the shots. It's lit with a single light (a Profoto B1X 500-watt battery-powered strobe with a medium-sized Profoto softbox mounted on a light stand). I have no idea why my white balance was this far off, but if I had to guess, it would be that I had been shooting outdoors with my white balance set for a totally different lighting situation, and when we came indoors to take this shot, I never changed it to match. If you're wondering why I didn't see the color issue while looking at the image on the back of my camera, it's because I was focused on the lighting and didn't really notice the issue at the time.

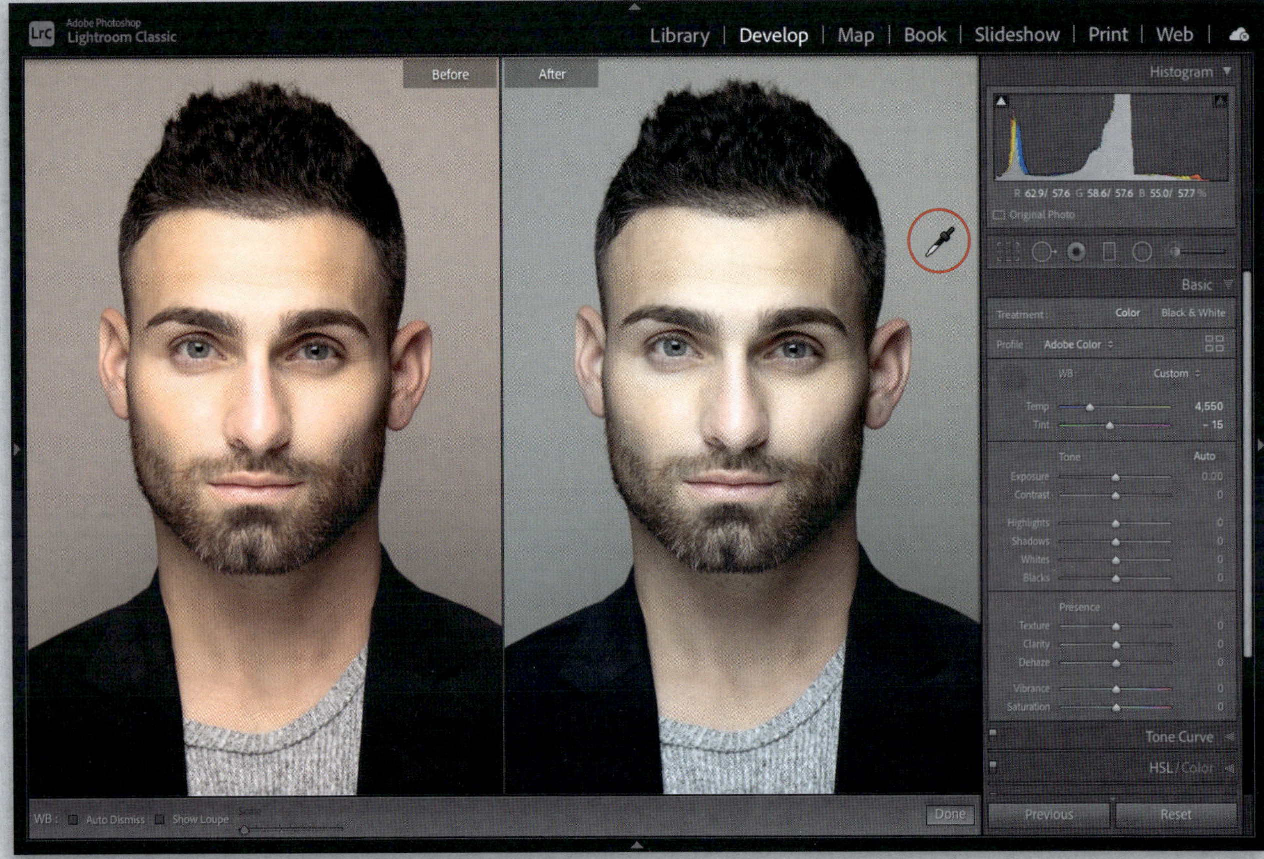

Camera: Canon EOS 5D Mark IV
Aperture Value: f / 6.3
Shutter Speed: 1/125 sec
ISO: 100
Focal Length: 110mm

Step 01:

Normally, we don't start by fixing the color, but in this case, because it's so far off (the colors are so strong it actually looks like the Before image has already been color graded), it's harder to make decisions about things like exposure, so let's fix that now **(Point 2)**. In the Basic panel (the Color panel in Lightroom cloud), get the White Balance Selector tool (**W**; the eyedropper) and click it on something in the photo that should be a neutral gray, like his gray shirt. His skin tone looks okay now, but try clicking on the neutral wall behind him where it looks a lot better. The reason we generally fix the white balance so early in the 7-Point System is that it can really affect the overall exposure. Look at the histogram (at the top of the right side Panels area) as you click on different areas, and you'll see how the color is changing the exposure of your image. By the way, if you've ever watched my weekly photography talk show *The Grid* (it airs live every Wednesday at 1:00 p.m. ET), when I'm asked, "What do you fix first in an image," my answer is, "I fix the thing that's distracting me the most." It's hard to focus on things like exposure and composition and well, just about anything if something is really bugging you about the shot. So, that's why we're fixing this now, which is a little bit out of order with how we do things using the system, but no harm done whatsoever by doing this a step or so early. Click the Done button when you're finished.

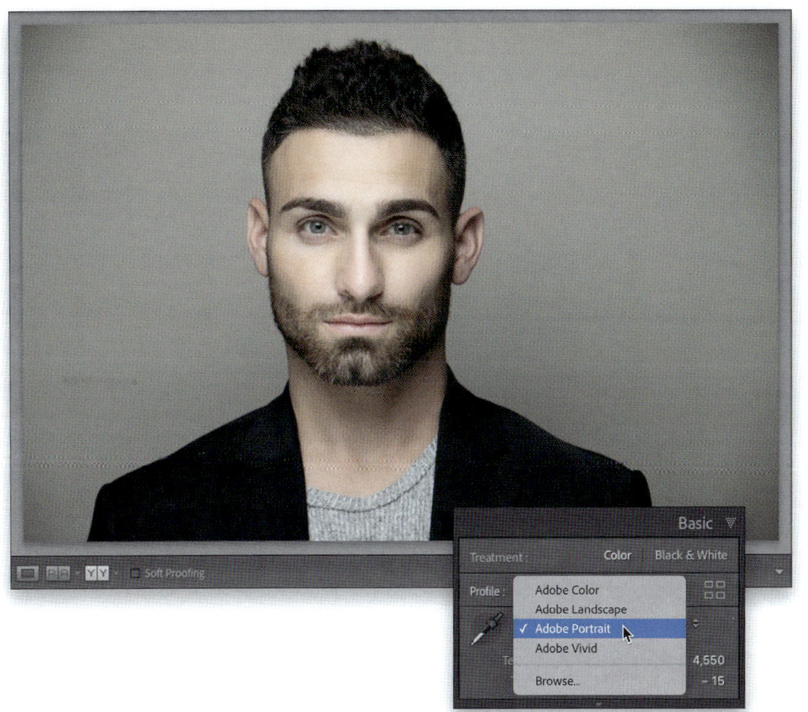

Step 02:

Next, let's pick our RAW profile from the Profile pop-up menu **(Point 1)**. Our go-to profile for portraits is (no big surprise) **Adobe Portrait**, so go ahead and choose that. It didn't do a ton to this photo (it made the tones a little bit flatter and opened the shadows a tiny bit). The effect of these profiles really just depends on the image. Sometimes you're surprised at what a big difference it makes, and sometimes you're surprised at how little it does. But, since it's literally just one or two clicks, it's certainly worth doing for those times when it does give us a nice head start on our editing.

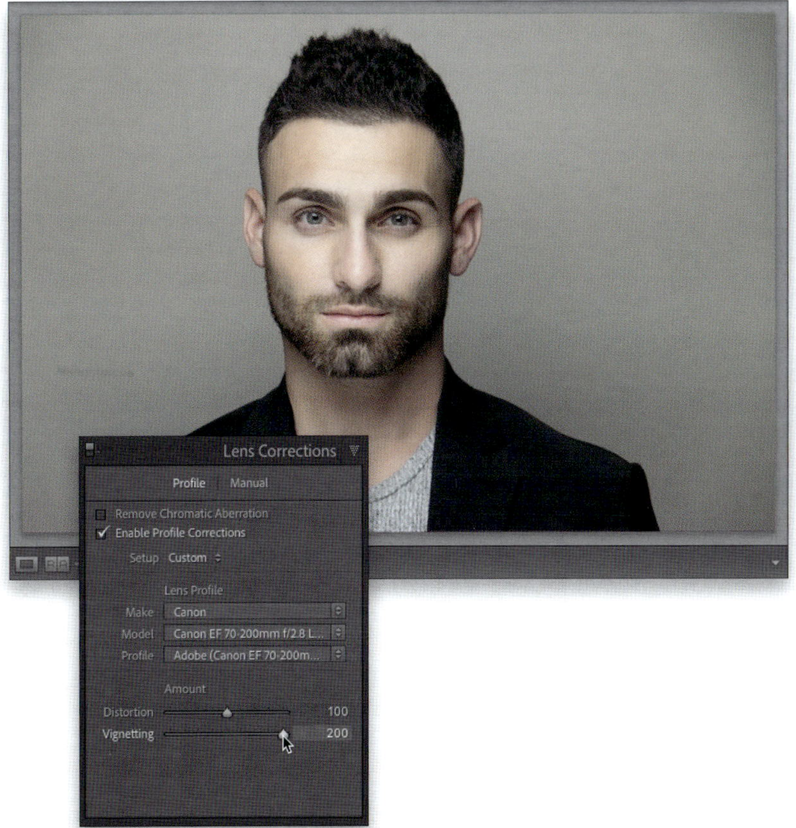

Step 03:

Seeing as we're already a little out of order with the system, let's go ahead and deal with that heavy corner darkening **(Point 6)**. Go down to the Lens Corrections panel (the Optics panel in Lightroom cloud), and turn on the Enable Profile (Lens) Corrections checkbox (as seen here) to see how that does. Well, not great. I mean, it is better, but it didn't really fix enough of it. Let's go to the Vignetting slider (the Lens Vignetting slider in Lightroom cloud) at the bottom of the panel (used to fine-tune the profile correction) and drag it all the way over to the right to see if that helps. Well, it did. A little. I mean, if you look at the image back in Step 02, it certainly is better, but it's not great. Okay, let's dig a little deeper.

Step 04:

We rarely have to go as far as we're about to, but now we have to pull out "the big guns" to try to manually fix those dark corners. Go to the Effects panel, to the Post-Crop Vignetting section, and drag the Amount slider (the Vignette slider in Lightroom cloud) to the right to +17 to help brighten those corners. The other sliders here (you'll need to click the little left-facing arrow to the right of Vignette to reveal all these sliders in Lightroom cloud) affect the position, shape, and softness of your brightening, and I had to drag them around, while trying not to have this brightening extend too far into the image (you want it just in the corners). The Mid-point slider helps with that and dragging it to the right moves the correction closer to the corners, which helps. The problem here now is that the corners on the left side look a little too brightened, and the top-right corner still looks too dark. So, at this point, we can either (a) crop in, so those corners are out of the image altogether; (b) hope that when we darken the edges later, it hides what's left; or (c) jump over to Photoshop where its Content-Aware Fill feature would fix this in 15 seconds flat. Let's go with "b" and roll on.

Step 05:

Let's work on our overall exposure now, and we'll start by setting our white and black points **(Point 3)**. Back in the Basic panel (the Light panel in Lightroom cloud), press-and-hold the Shift key, and then double-click on Whites and then on Blacks. Yikes! Okay, setting the white and black points did not do us any favors this time around. The Blacks at –6 look fine, but those Whites are way too hot at +61. This may be, somehow, technically correct (according to how Lightroom does its math to calculate this, as his face is not clipping or blown out), but it doesn't look good. He looks like he has "hot spots" on his face, so we'll need to fix that in the next step.

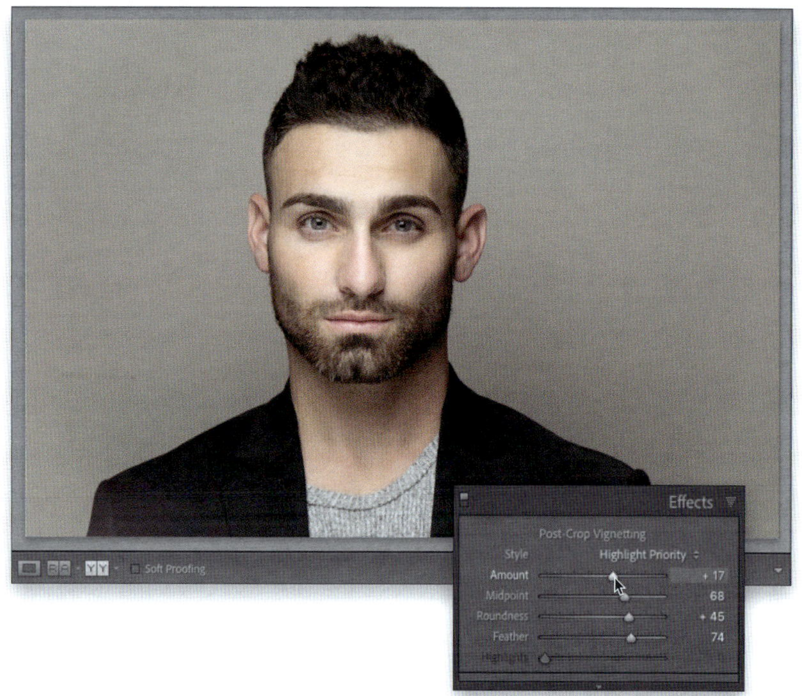

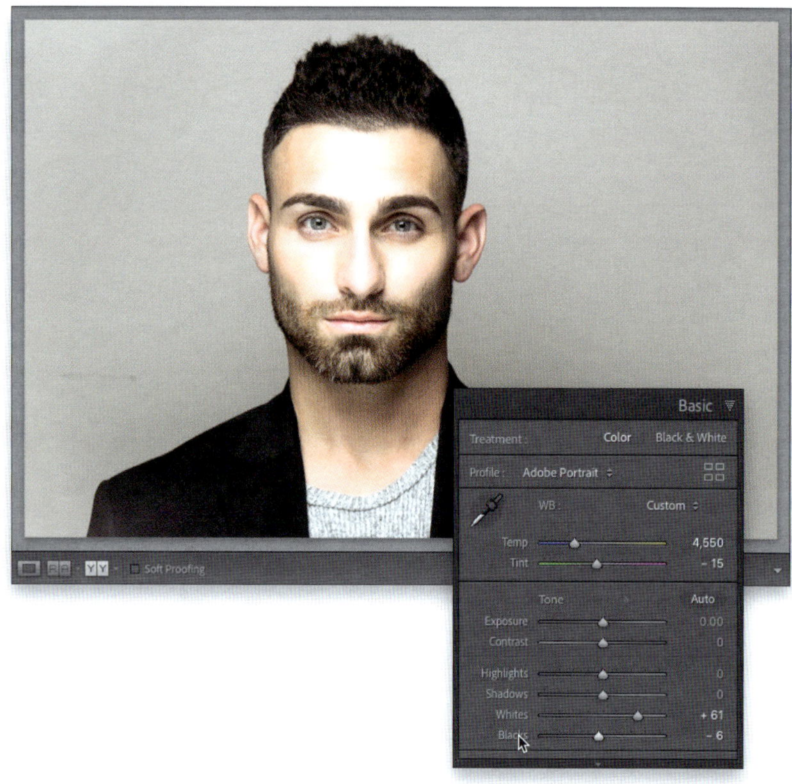

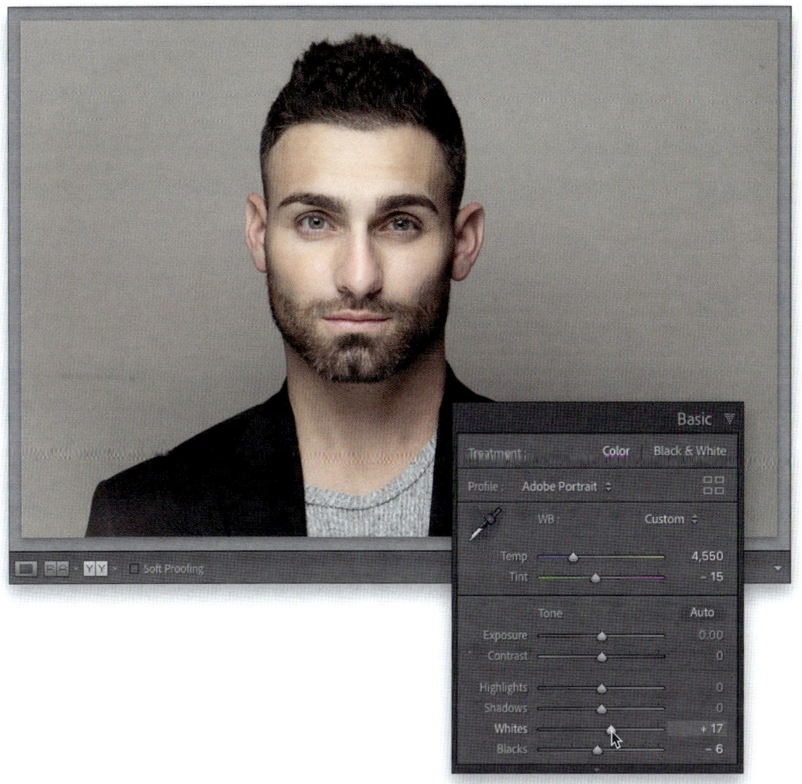

Step 06:

Grab the Whites slider and drag it back over to the left a bit until it looks a lot more balanced. Here, I lowered it from +61 down to +17, so it did need a boost in the whites, but just not so darn high. It's looking pretty good overall at this point (we can see detail in his hair and coat), and I don't think we need to adjust the Exposure slider at all—I think our overall exposure looks pretty good. So, while setting the white and black points didn't give a great result, fixing it took us all of just dragging the Whites back down a bit. Easy fix.

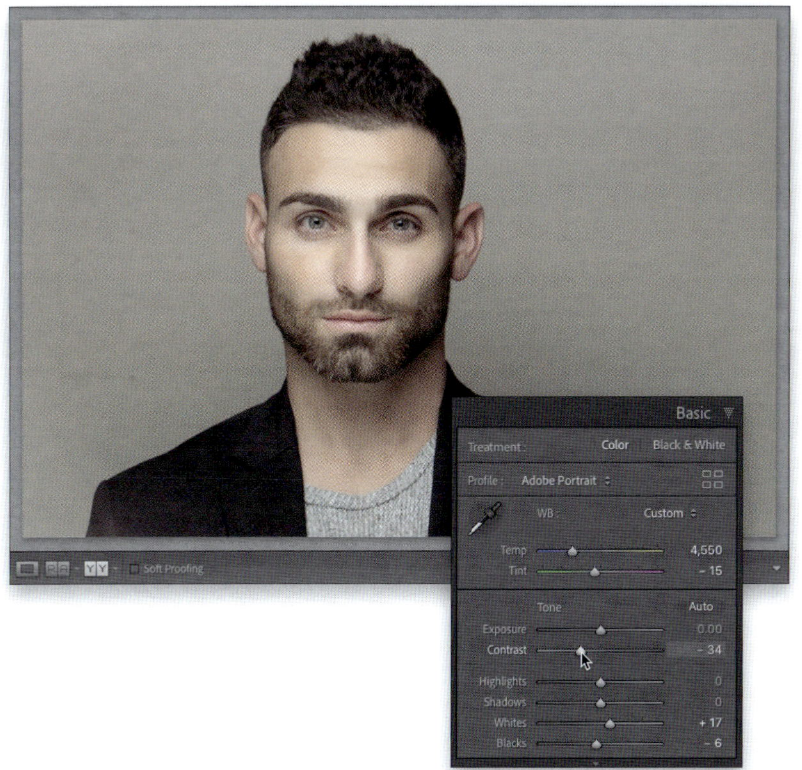

Step 07:

In this particular portrait, we're going to go for a very different look than we normally do—one that's intentionally flatter than usual (this is also a popular look today, made so by the filters people use a lot in Instagram, which themselves, are based on old traditional film looks). So, we're going to reduce the contrast in this image to get that flat look by dragging the Contrast slider to the left. Here, I dragged it to –34. Now compare how his face looks here with how it looked in the previous step. You can really see the difference in flatness between the two.

Step 08:

Normally, with portraits of men, I add Clarity to enhance the midtone contrast and add some "grit" to the image, but in this case, we're trying to take away contrast, so adding Clarity will work against our flat look. Instead, we're only going to add Texture, so drag the Texture slider to the right quite a bit (here, I dragged it to +50. This slider is in the Effects panel in Lightroom cloud). The Texture slider enhances detail without affecting the tone of the image to any major extent. The Clarity slider also enhances detail, but it definitely messes with the tone a bunch because it adds midtone contrast, so that's why we skipped it here and just went with Texture.

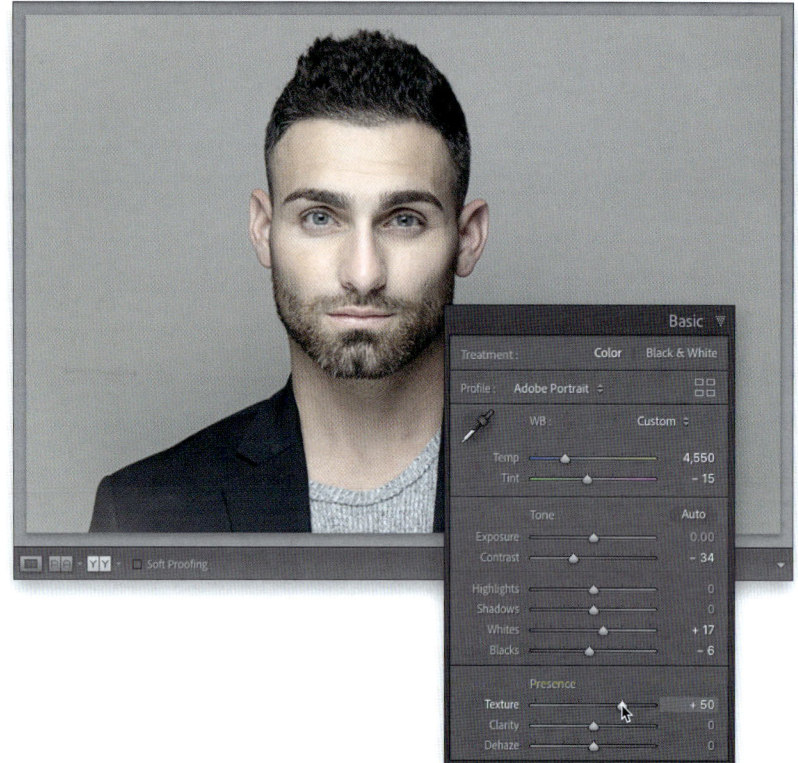

Step 09:

Okay, that sensor dust, or crud on the wall, or whatever it is on the left is starting to get on my nerves, so can we please remove it before we go any farther? (Thank you! We're going to skip Point 4 here and move on to **Point 5**.) Get the Spot Removal tool (**Q**; the Healing Brush [**H**] in Lightroom cloud), make the size of the tool a little larger than the stuff on the wall itself, and paint a stroke right over it. As you paint, the area you painted over turns white (as shown here).

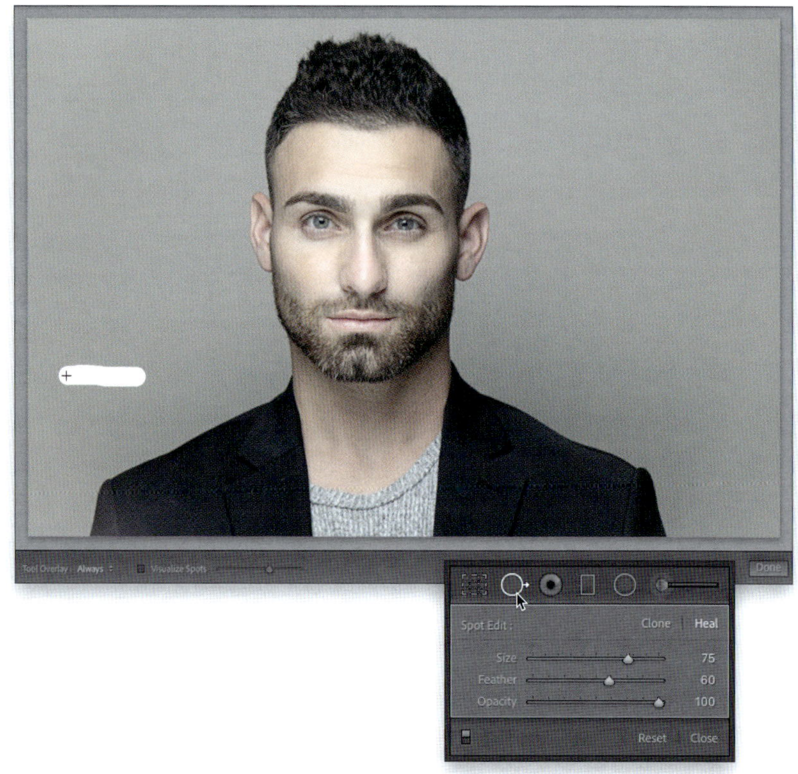

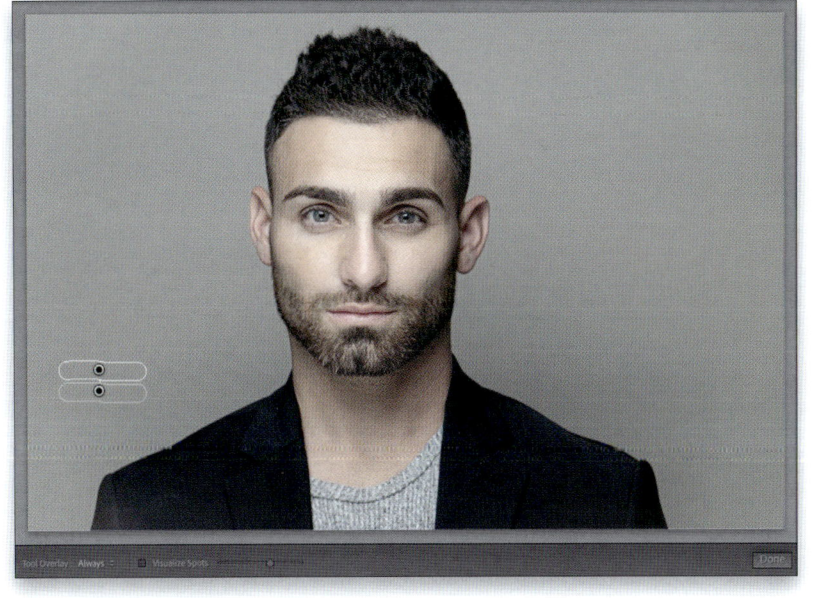

Step 10:

When you let go of your mouse button, you'll see a second stroke outline of the area you painted over showing you which part of the image Lightroom used as a source to remove your smudge/crud/whatever. In this case, it made a good choice, choosing an area right nearby, and it got rid of that mess without any fuss. This is the stuff the Spot Removal tool (Healing Brush) does best—removing stuff like a speck or a line that is off by itself like this. Thanks for getting rid of that—it was kind of driving me crazy.

Step 11:

To darken the edges all the way around (which will hopefully help hide our corner vignetting issue some more), we usually go to the Effects panel and lower the Post-Crop Vignetting Amount. But, we already used that panel to get rid of the bad corner vignetting, and if we move those sliders, it will undo the fix we did earlier. So, we'll have to go another route. Instead, get the Radial Filter tool **(Shift-M)** from the toolbox beneath the histogram (the Radial Gradient tool **[R]** from the toolbox on the right in Lightroom cloud), and we'll use this to create a subtle spotlight effect around our subject, which will darken the area outside our spotlight area. With this tool, starting in the center of his face, click-and-drag outward to create an oval. To resize the oval, just click-and-drag one of the four control points on it (as shown here). Now, go to the Exposure slider (reset the sliders, if needed) and drag it to the left (here, I dragged to –0.56) to darken the area outside the oval (if, instead, it darkens the area inside the oval, just turn off the Invert checkbox near the bottom of the panel [it's near the top in Lightroom cloud]). This not only did a good job of hiding our dark corner problem, but we got the bonus that it gives the effect of having a background light behind him, as well. Now, hit the Done button.

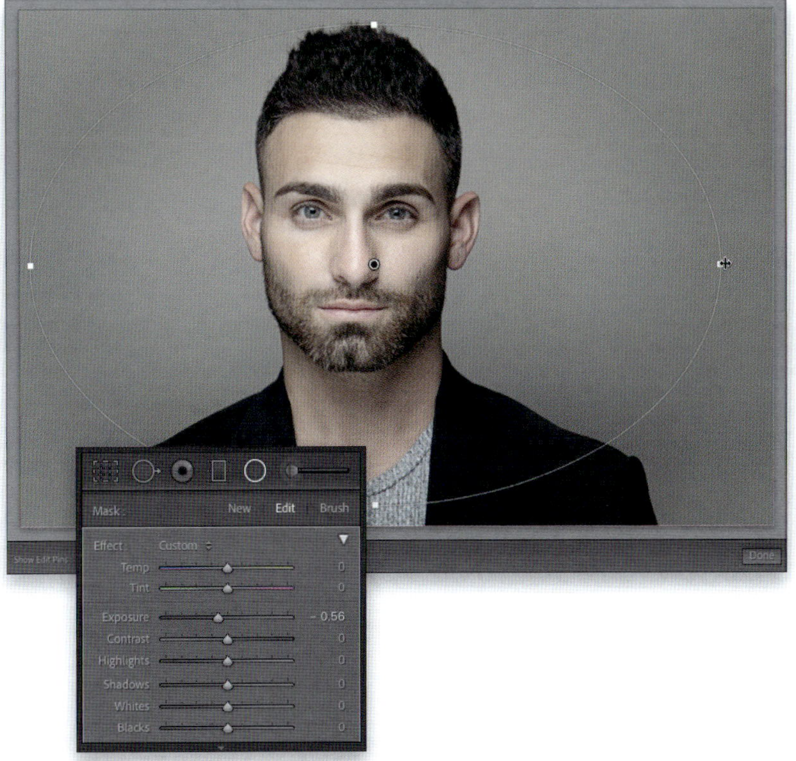

Step 12:

If we were going for a more traditional portrait, we'd stop here, add some sharpening, and we'd be done. But, for this lesson, we're giving it more of a modern feel by adding a color tint to the shadow areas, another color tint to the midtones, and a third color tint to the highlights. We do this in the Color Grading panel, using the three color wheels (seen here). We'll start by adding a blue tint to just the shadow areas, using the color wheel on the bottom left. Click on the circle in the center of the wheel and drag it diagonally downward toward blue (as shown here). The blue circle that appears on the outside of the wheel shows you the hue (the color) you've chosen. The hollow circle within the color wheel (the one you dragged) determines how vivid (saturated) the color will be. For example, as you drag that circle toward the outside edge, the color gets deeper and more vivid. As you drag back toward the center, the color gets less saturated and more pastel looking.

Step 13:

You might find it easier (and more precise) to just see the one color wheel you're currently working on (rather than all three). To do that, click on the Shadows icon (the black circle) at the top of the panel to just see the Shadows color wheel (as seen here). Doing this also gives you access to more features. For example, there's a little color swatch at the bottom left of the color wheel and if you click on it, out pops a set of commonly used colors (seen here) to choose from. But, in our case, just choose a nice medium blue from the color wheel. *Note:* Click on the little, left-facing arrow at the bottom right of the wheel, and two additional control sliders appear (Hue and Saturation). *Tip:* If you mess up and want to start over, double-click on the word "Shadows," directly above the color wheel and it resets. If you just want to temporarily hide the color you applied, click-and-hold on the eye icon at the bottom right (top right in Lightroom cloud) of the color wheel.

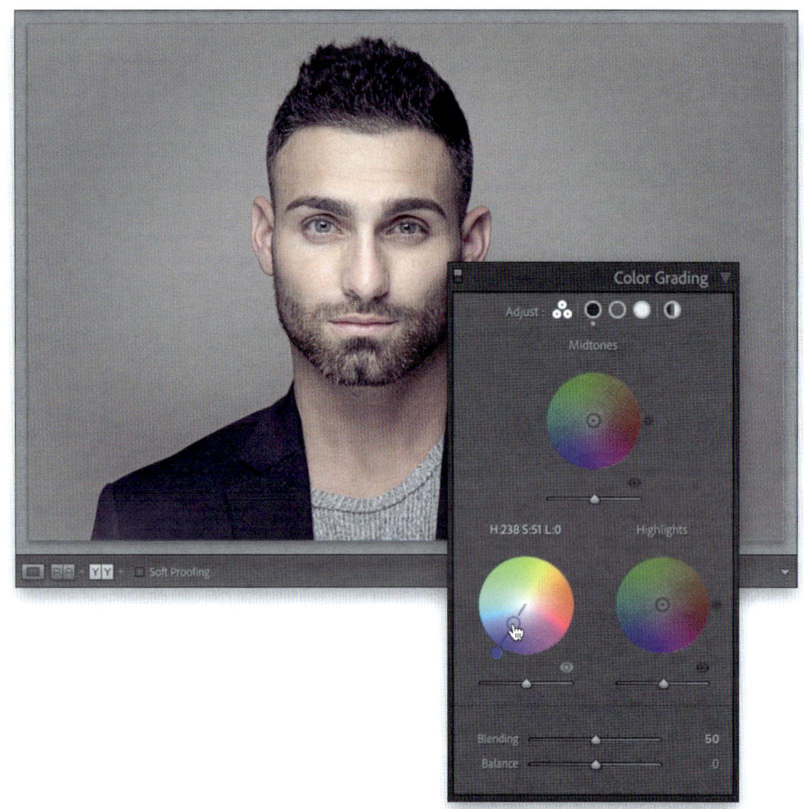

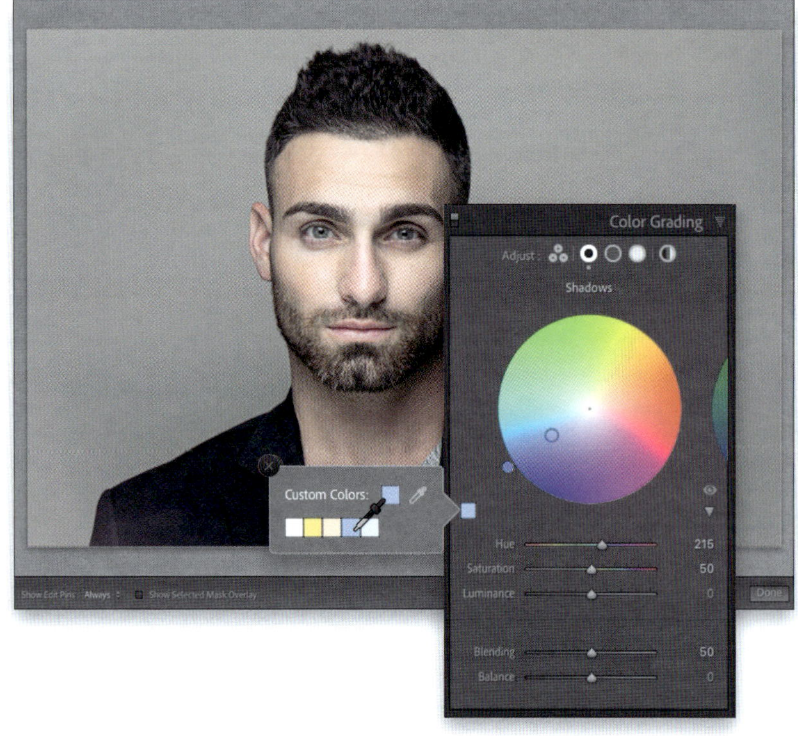

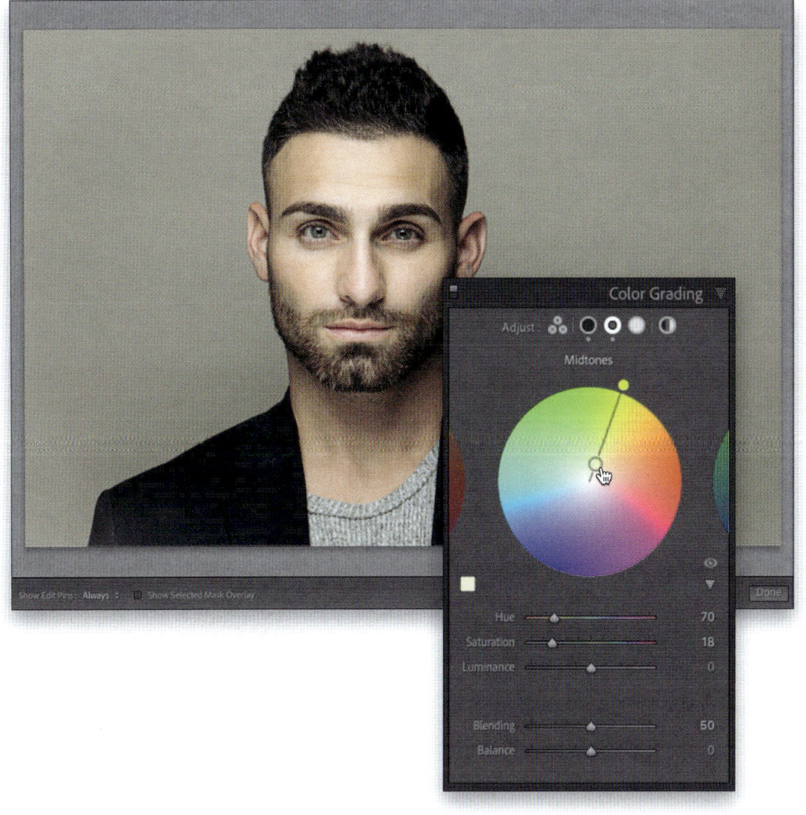

Step 14:

Now, let's add a tint to the midtones. Click on the gray circle at the top of the panel to switch over to the Midtones color wheel (seen here). We want to put a very light, greenish/yellow color in the midtones, so click on the center and start dragging it in the direction of green/yellow, but as you see here, don't drag very far from the center, so it doesn't become a really vivid greenish/yellow. Look at how much this little bit of color affected the midtones. Much like how the Exposure slider (which mostly controls the midtone areas of our photo) has such an effect on the brightness of the whole image, this Midtones color wheel, even when you just apply a little bit of color, has a big influence over the whole image. Adding blue in the shadows did a little, but adding this green/yellow color added a ton! By the way, another advantage of working with these individual color wheels is the Hue, Saturation, and Luminance (controls the brightness of the color) sliders. If you'd prefer, use them instead of the wheel.

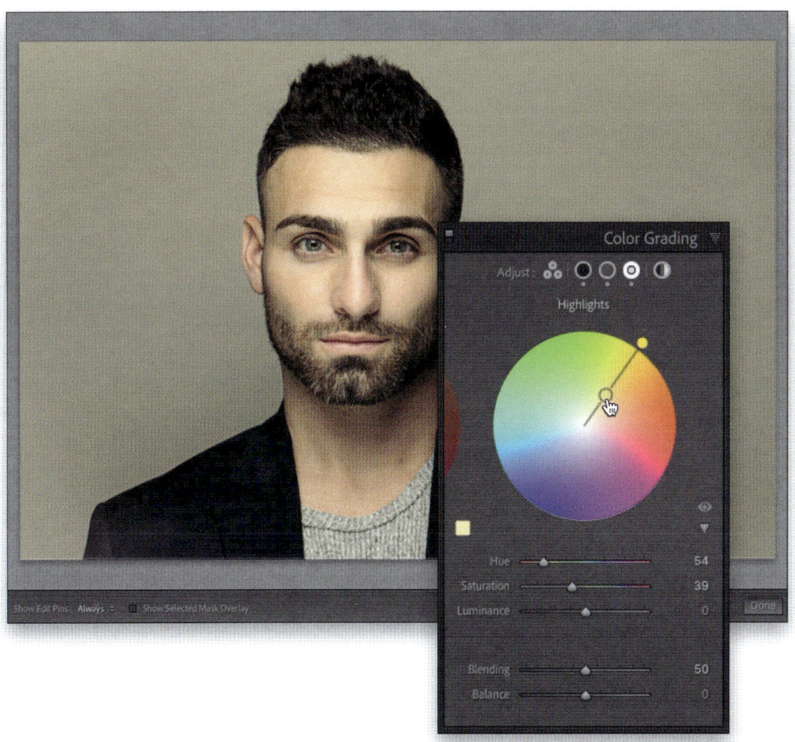

Step 15:

To add a tint to the highlight areas, click on the white circle up top to bring up the Highlights color wheel (seen here). Click on the circle in the center and drag it a little less than halfway to the edge to add a light yellow to the highlights. You could also choose a yellow color from the color swatch's pop-up menu. You can see it added that yellow to his face and some to the highlight areas of the background, as well. Here's another tip: Let's say you like the Saturation amount of the color you've chosen (you like where the hollow circle is saturation-wise), but you want to try some different colors with that same amount of saturation. You can do that by pressing-and-holding the Command (PC: Ctrl) key and a second circle will appear inside the wheel, and now when you drag the outside Hue circle, the center circle starts in the same relative position (try this out and you'll see what I mean).

Step 16:

Before we get to this next thing, here's yet another handy little tip: if you want to try out different Saturation amounts without changing the color (Hue), press-and-hold the Shift key and it locks your Hue circle in place, so you can now slide along a straight path from the center outward to the edge, seeing all the levels of saturation for that particular hue. Okay, back to our project. At the bottom of the panel are two sliders, and the one I think you'll really find helpful is the Balance slider. It allows you to bias your color grading more toward the Shadows color (and reduce the Highlights color) or more toward the Highlights color (and reduce the Shadows color). In this case, for example, let's tilt our color more toward the blues we added in the shadows, so drag the Balance slider to the left, and you'll see some more of those blues appear (and less of the highlights. Here, I dragged it over to –52 to bring some of those blues back into the image since it looked so warm/yellow). Drag it to the right instead, and you'll see the yellows from the highlights appear more prominently in the image. One last thing: this is a global change, so whether you move this slider when you're in a single color wheel view or viewing all three at once, it affects the balance of everything the same way.

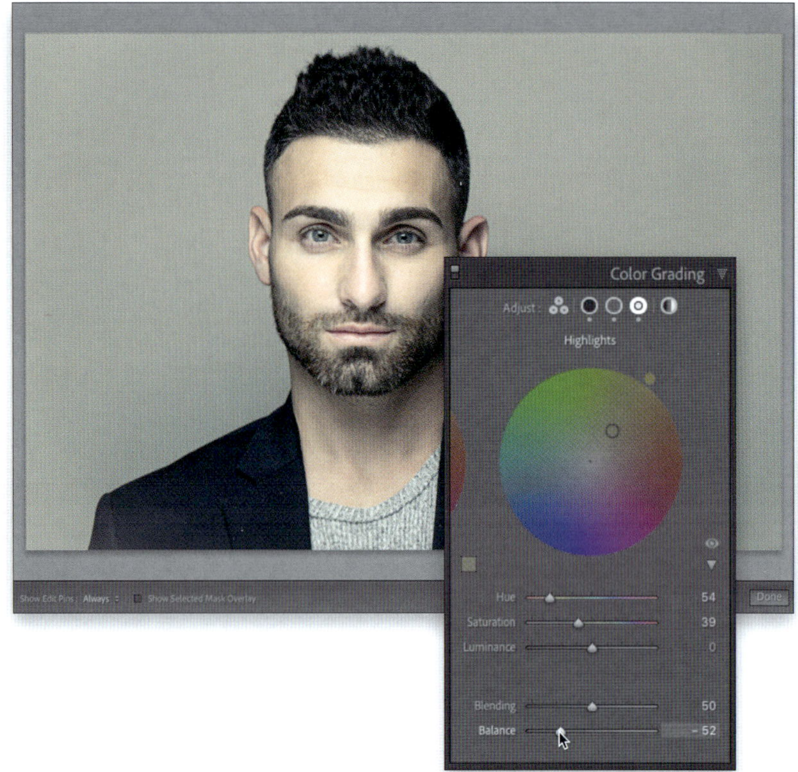

Step 17:

The other slider down at the bottom of the panel is the Blending slider, and it controls the transition between the highlights and shadows (how fast that transition happens). Go ahead and drag this slider back and forth a few times to see how it affects your image and seeing that will help you better understand what it does. Then, go ahead and set the Blending amount to 25 (as shown here).

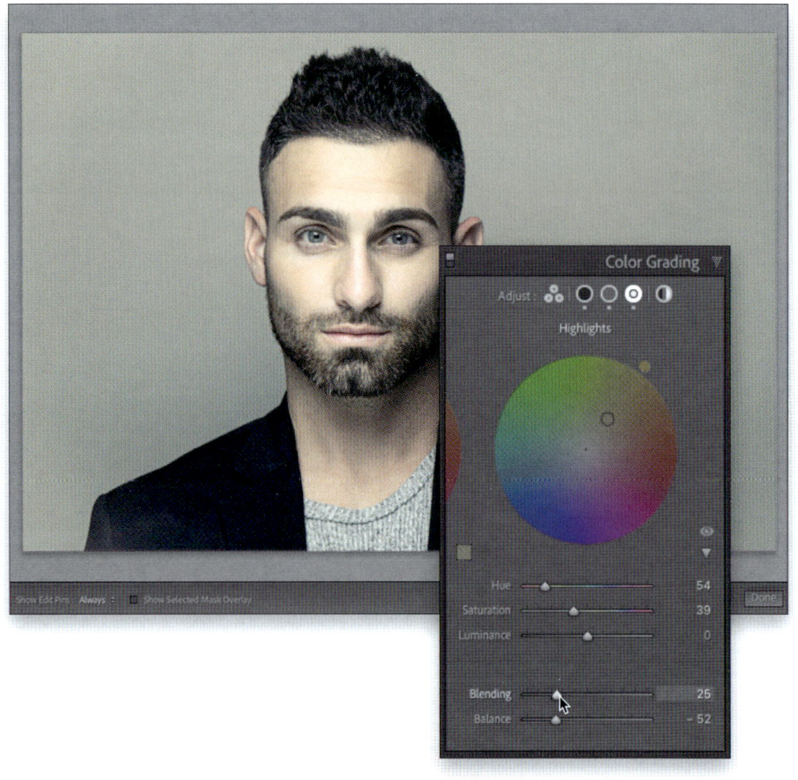

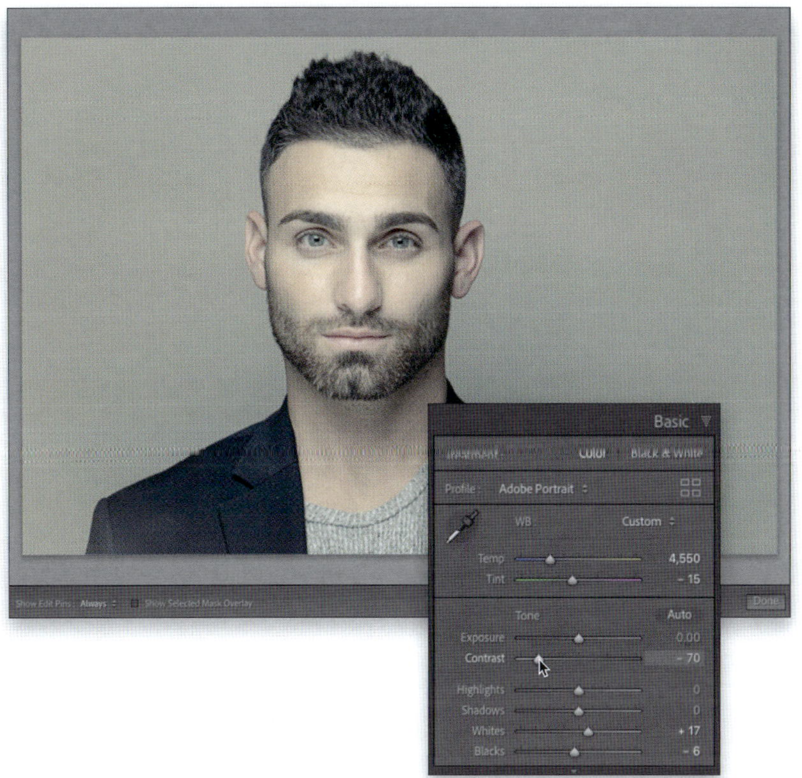

Step 18:

Let's kind of step back now that we've added our color grading to see how things are shaping up. I feel during this process that we've lost some of that flat look we were looking for, so head back to the Basic panel (the Light panel in Lightroom cloud) and drag the Contrast slider farther over to the left to around –70 (as shown here). Okay, the flatness is back!

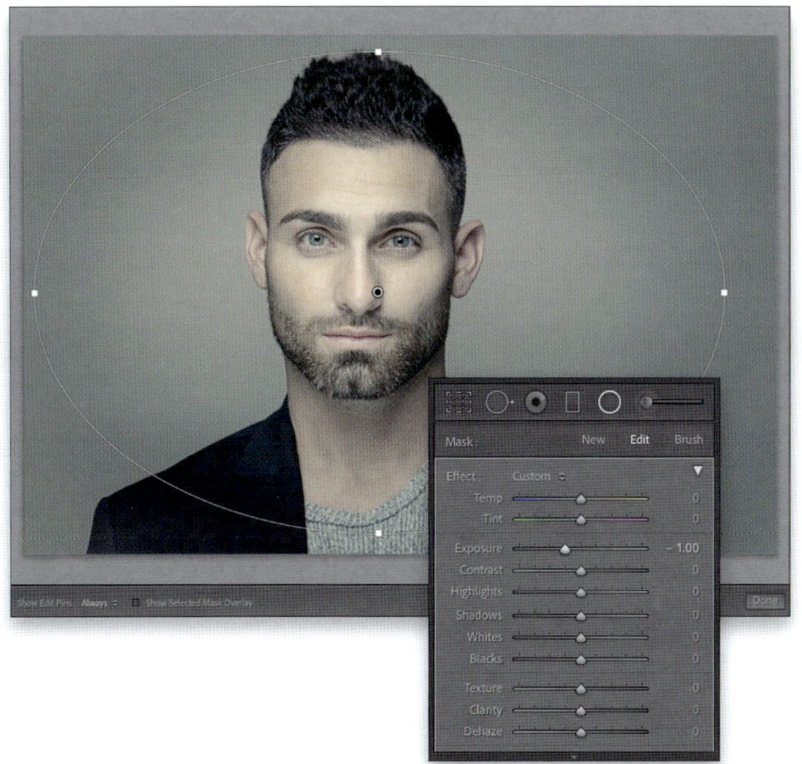

Step 19:

That dark corner repair still isn't looking that good, so let's get the Radial Filter tool (the Radial Gradient tool in Lightroom cloud) again and click on the Edit Pin for the adjustment we created earlier. Once it's active, let's drop the Exposure amount down to around –1.00 (as seen here), which darkens the outside edges and enhances the spotlight effect behind him, and since we're adding more shadows to the image, it brings out our color grading in the shadow areas nicely. That's a lot for just dragging the Exposure slider to the left a bit more, eh?

Step 20:

Let's wrap this one up by going to the Detail panel to add some sharpening **(Point 7)**. With photos of men, we usually apply a good amount of sharpening because it accentuates their pores and brings out detail, which is a good thing. So, we crank up the Amount slider (the Sharpening slider in Lightroom cloud) quite a bit on portraits of men. Let's drag it over to around 85 (as shown here), but you might even go a little farther, if you like, depending on the photo and the age of the subject. The older they are, the more detail and character you can bring out with sharpening, so don't be shy. I also increased the Radius to 1.1 here, again, to increase the sharpening effect on this type of shot.

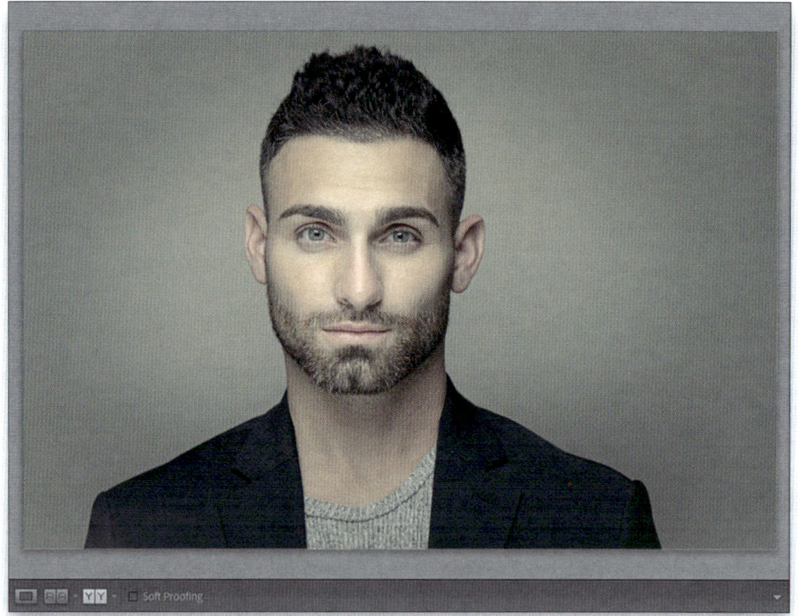

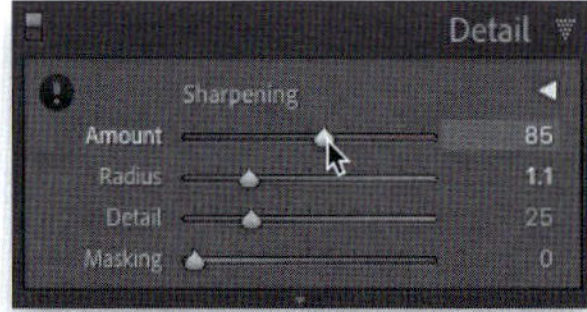

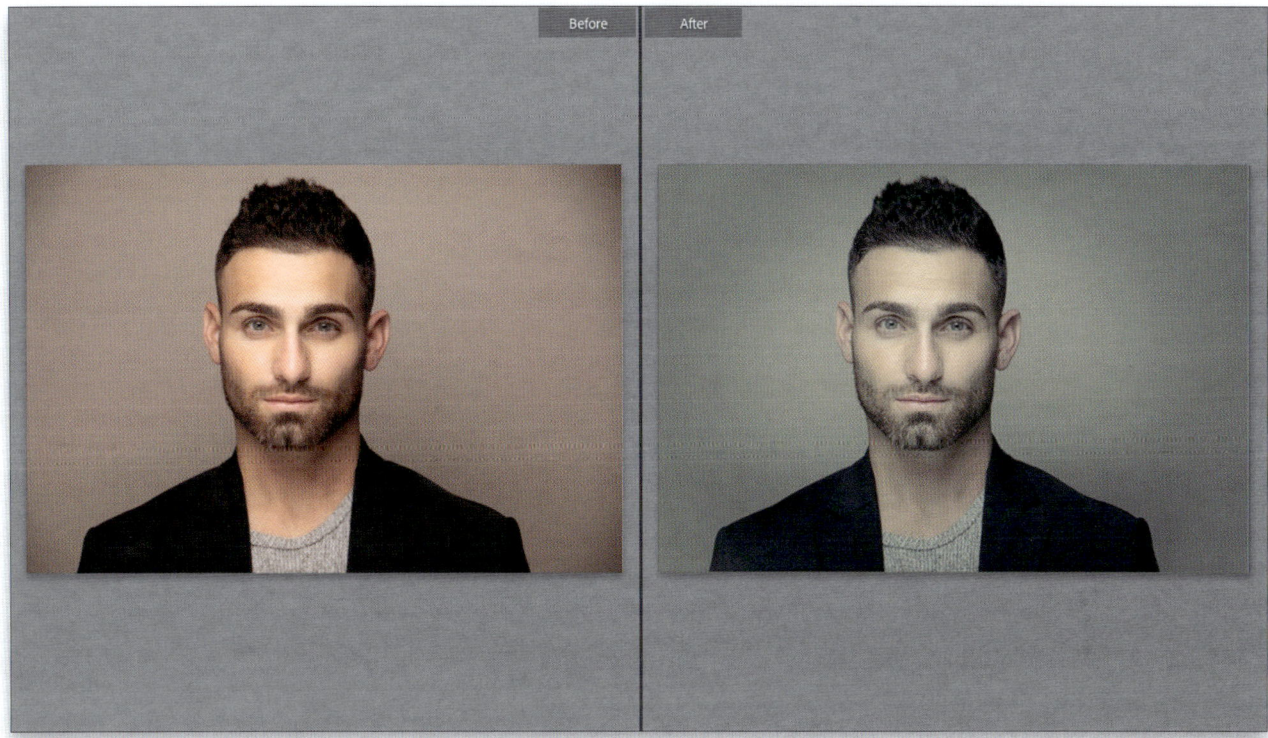

Here is our Before/After.

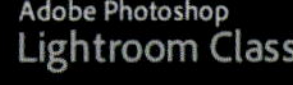

Adobe Photoshop
Lightroom Classic

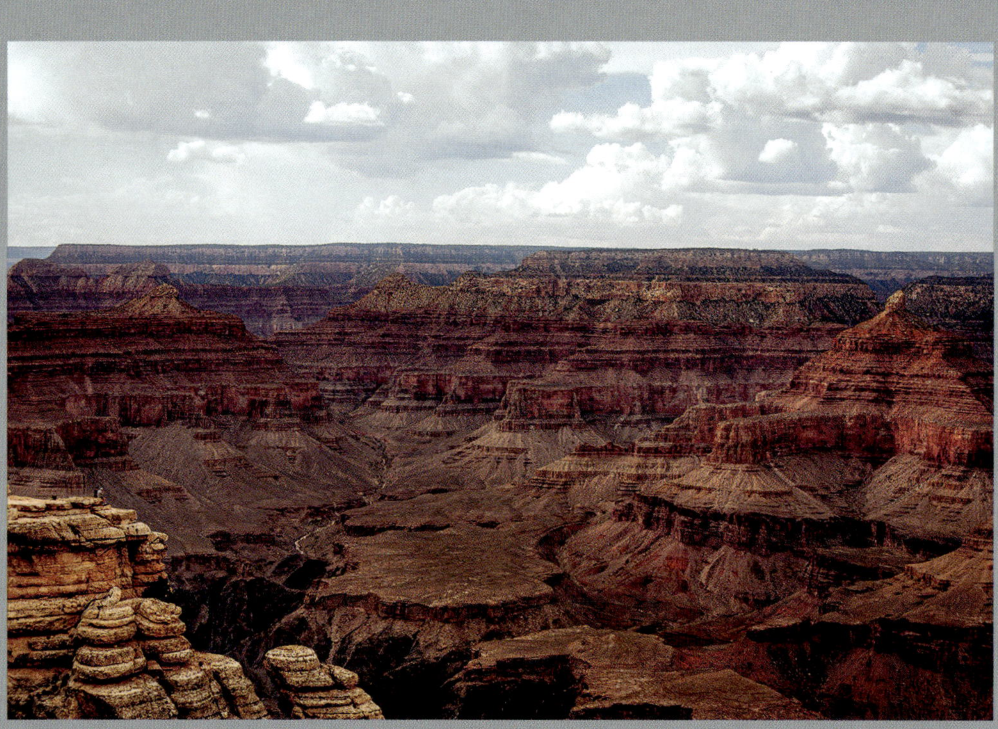

Before
After

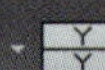
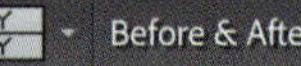
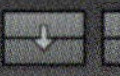
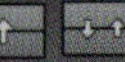
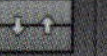

Before & After :
Soft Proofing

GRAND CANYON OVERLOOK

Let's evaluate the shot: It's super-over-exposed, so it's lacking everything—color, contrast, detail, etc. The sky looks like it has some areas that are clipping (blown-out pixels), and the image has a lot of haze. This shot doesn't have a lot going for it exposure-wise, and it has some pretty significant lens distortion (just look at the horizon line—it's bent), so we'll be pretty busy getting this one back in the box.

THE STORY BEHIND THE SHOT:

This shot of the Grand Canyon was taken on a trip out west with some buddies a few years back (might be more than just a few). It was my first trip to the Grand Canyon (I've only been twice), and it's pretty overwhelming to see in person. I found it really challenging to get a great shot there because you're looking at this awesome, epic scene in front of you, but when you put the camera up to your eye, you're only capturing a small portion of its epicness, which is really frustrating. This was taken from the visitor's center, which is not by any means a hot spot to shoot from (every tourist there will be getting pretty much the same shot, and it's not a good one). The most interesting shots I've seen of the canyon have come from down inside it, rather than up top, looking down into it. What drew me to take this shot was the people out on the ledge, on the far left. I'm super-scared of heights, so I was freaked out just shooting it, even though I was safely away from the ledge.

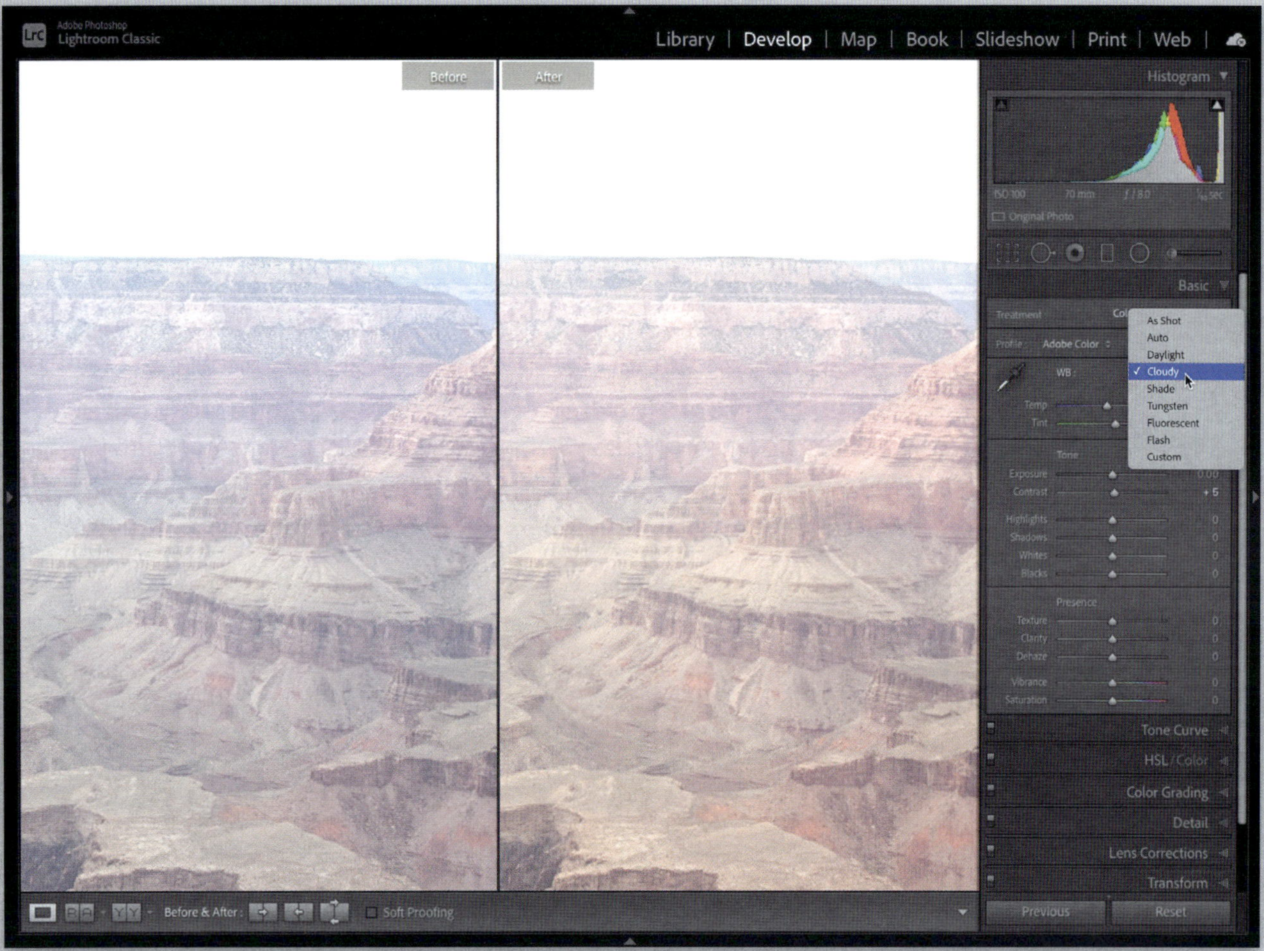

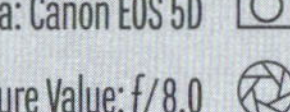

Camera: Canon EOS 5D

Aperture Value: ƒ/8.0

Shutter Speed: 1/80 sec

ISO: 100

Focal Length: 70mm

Step 01:

We'd normally start out by picking our RAW profile (Point 1), but this image is so overexposed that I'm not sure we'd even see anything at this stage. So, let's skip making that choice for now, and instead, let's get the color in the ballpark **(Point 2)**. Head over to the Basic panel (the Color panel in Lightroom cloud) and from the WB (White Balance) preset pop-up menu, go ahead and try out the different presets (and, yes, you can skip Tungsten and Fluorescent since we're shooting outdoors). In this case, it seems like **Cloudy** looks the best, which makes sense because it was fairly overcast that day (and believe it or not, hidden within all that overexposure and clipping are clouds). That warmed things up nicely (you can see how blue the Before image on the left is, which probably means my camera was set on Auto White Balance at the time). Great on sunny days; not so great on cloudy days.

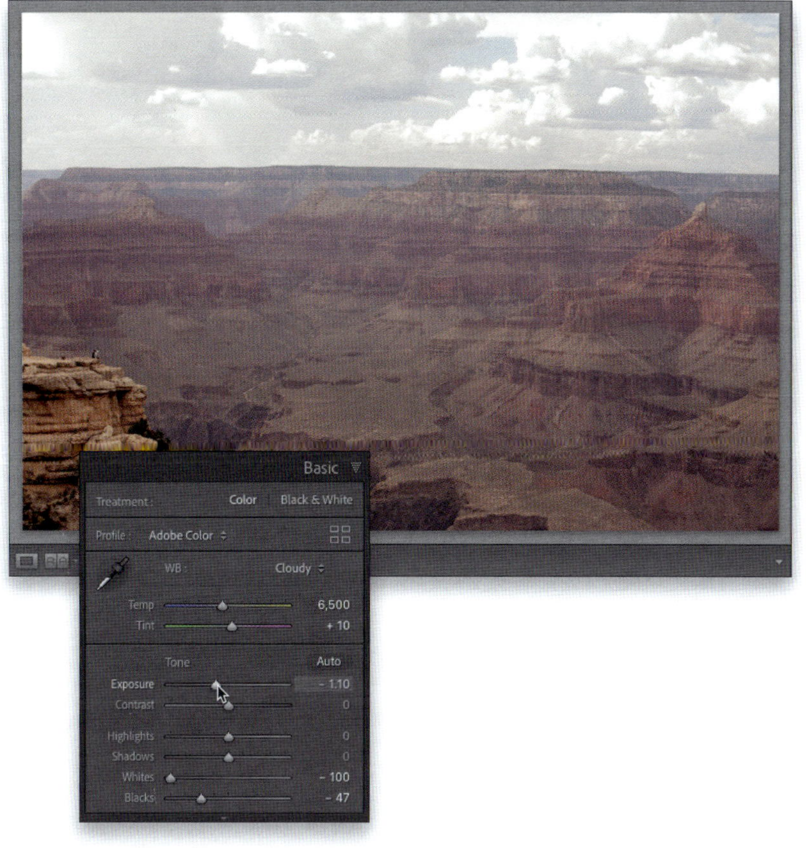

Step 02:

Let's get to fixing our exposure next **(Point 3)** by setting the white and black points first. Press-and-hold the Shift key and double-click on Whites, and then on Blacks. That helped a bunch, bringing back some contrast, and now you can actually see some of the clouds, and that's probably thanks to the fact that it set the Whites to –100. It set the Blacks to –47, making the dark areas much darker, so you can see how out-of-whack this image's exposure was. After setting the white and black points, it's still overexposed, so let's drop the Exposure slider a little more than a stop (here, I dragged it to the left to –1.10).

Step 03:

This image is super-lacking in the contrast department, so let's bring some back by dragging the Contrast slider over to +53 (as shown here). Okay, we're starting to get somewhere.

Step 04:

Let's do a little quick fix on that sky, seeing that part of it is clipping **(Point 4)**. Take a look at the image back in Step 01, up in the top-right corner of the histogram (at the top of the right side Panels area). See that solid white triangle? That's a warning that there are some areas in the image so bright that they have "clipped," and there's no detail in those areas—no pixels, no nuthin'. So, if you printed this, there would be gaps in the sky where it was just the paper—there would be no ink. Luckily, in most cases, if you have some clipping like this, you can fix it by dragging the Highlights slider over to the left until you see that white triangle turn dark gray, which means the clipping is gone. Here, I dragged the Highlights slider to –100, and while I didn't have to go that far to get rid of the clipping, I had to drag it that far to start to get the sky looking at least halfway decent.

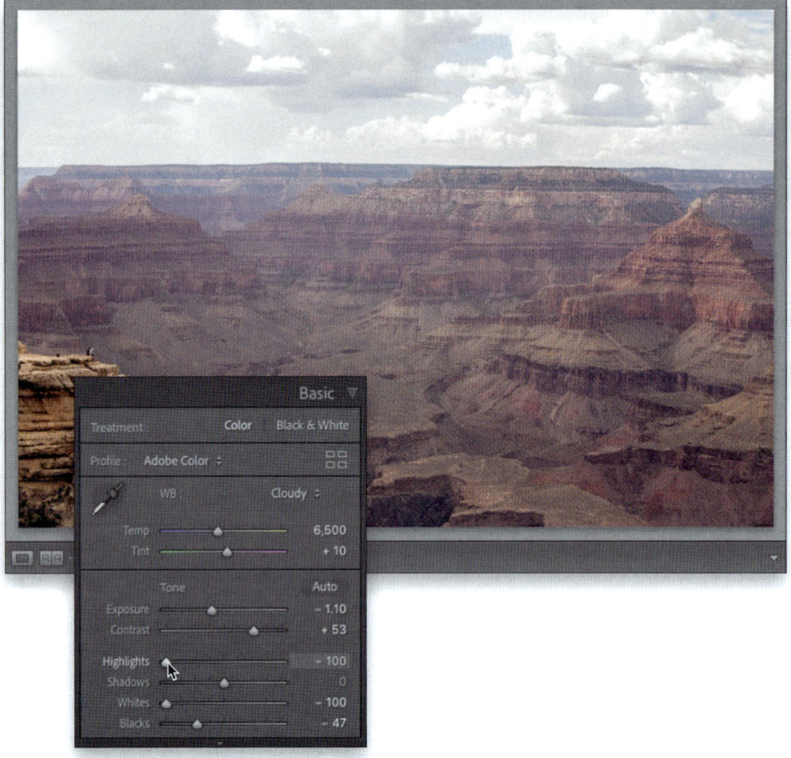

Step 05:

To get those mountains in the middle ground (the focus of the shot) to not look so flat and hazy, we're going to need to crank up the Dehaze a bunch. So, drag the Dehaze slider (in the Effects panel in Lightroom cloud) over to the right until you start to see it cut through the haze and bring some nice contrast to those mountains. Here, I dragged it over to +59, which did a pretty darn nice job cutting that haze, but I'm not sure I like what it did to the clouds (they look a little funky now). But, we have a way (or two really) to keep that Dehaze off the sky. So, now that you've seen how Dehaze looks on those mountains, let's undo it (double-click right on the slider's little knob to reset it to zero), and then let's apply our Dehaze in a different way, so it avoids messing with the sky **(Point 5)**.

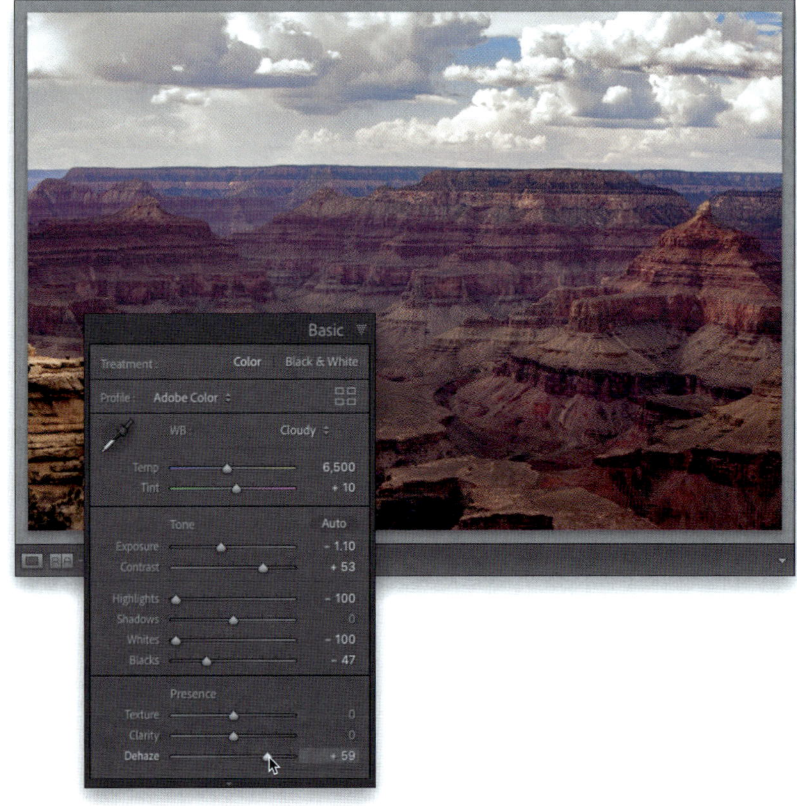

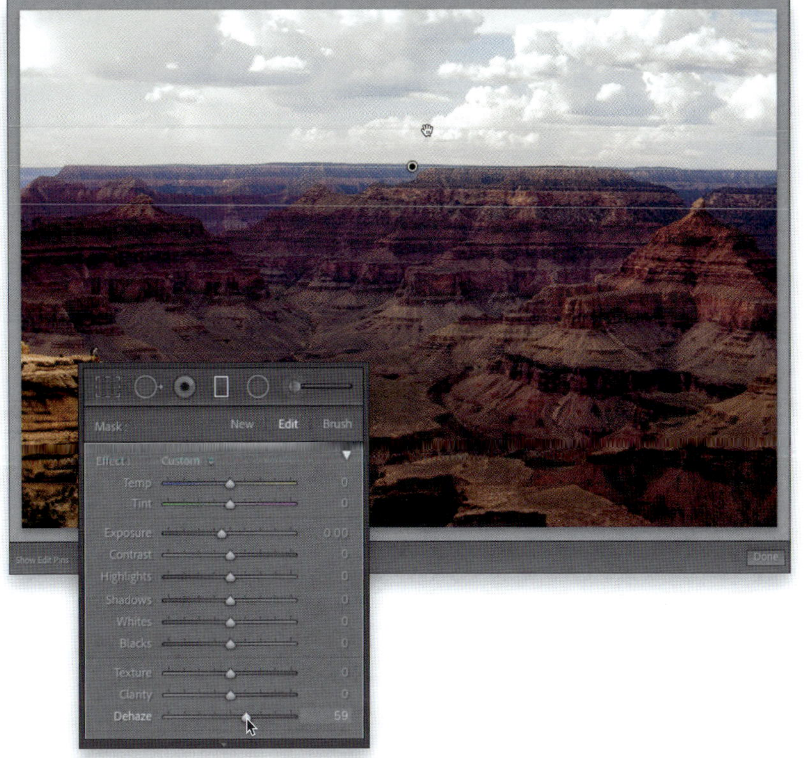

Step 06:

Get the Graduated Filter tool (**M**; the Linear Gradient tool **[L]** in Lightroom cloud) from the toolbox, double-click on Effect to reset all the sliders to zero, then drag the Dehaze amount over to 59. Now, starting at the bottom center of the image, click-and-drag up above the horizon line. Once this is done, we want to compress the height of our gradient, so the mountains get pretty much all the Dehaze, so click-and-drag the top and bottom lines in toward each other, so it's just a thin area where the gradient is (as shown here). That way, all the darkening happens down on the mountains and none of it really hits the sky (that top line where you see my grabber hand here is transparent—no Dehaze is happening up at that end of the gradient).

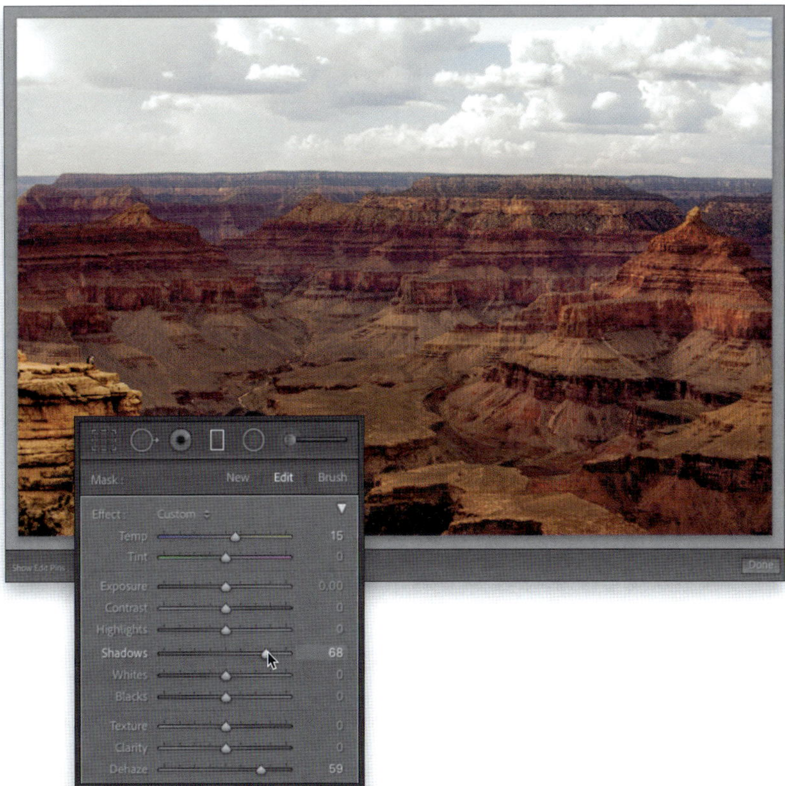

Step 07:

One side effect of using a lot of Dehaze is that it adds a blue tint over those areas (look at the mountains way in the back in Step 06, and you can see they're turning purple). We can counteract this by adding some yellow (warmth) into this gradient while it's still active. To do this, drag the Temp slider to the right toward yellow (here, I dragged it over to 15, and you can see that made a big difference color-wise). Also, areas in the canyon are pretty dark now, so let's open up the shadows a bunch (here, I dragged the Shadows slider to 68). Now that we've got just this part of the image (the canyon) that we can adjust, what else do we need to do to help this along? *Note:* I hid the Gradient Filter tool's overlay here by pressing the **H key** on my keyboard (in Lightroom cloud, press the **O key** to cycle through the tool overlay options).

Step 08:

If you were thinking, "We can enhance the detail in the canyon," then you get five points (and a chance to play in our bonus round). Let's drag the Texture slider over to 37 and the Clarity slider to 14, and just remember—these sliders we're moving are just affecting the area inside our Graduated Filter (we haven't switched off this tool yet), so we're not messing with the sky at all.

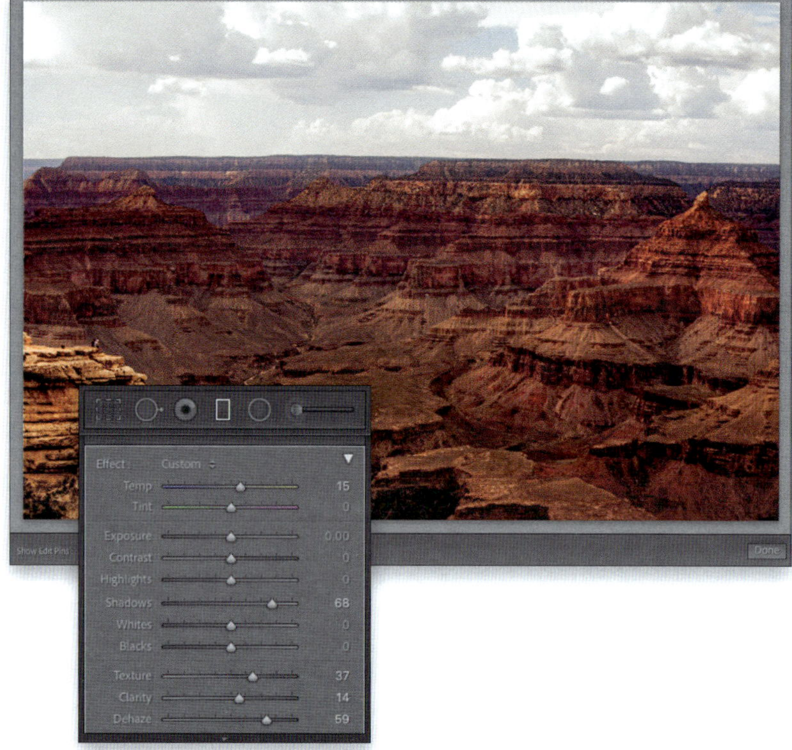

Step 09:

Now that things have balanced out a bunch, we can hit the Done button (beneath the Preview area) and jump back over to the Basic panel (the Edit panel in Lightroom cloud) to pick our RAW profile **(Point 1)**. Of course, I reached for Adobe Landscape as my first choice, but it didn't look that great. I tried Adobe Vivid and—boom—that was the one (well, the one that looked best). So, choose **Adobe Vivid** from the Profile pop-up menu (as shown here). These colors are getting quite vibrant, which means at some point soon, we might have to rein them back again, but from where we started, the fact that we have to actually worry about too much color just shows how far we've come.

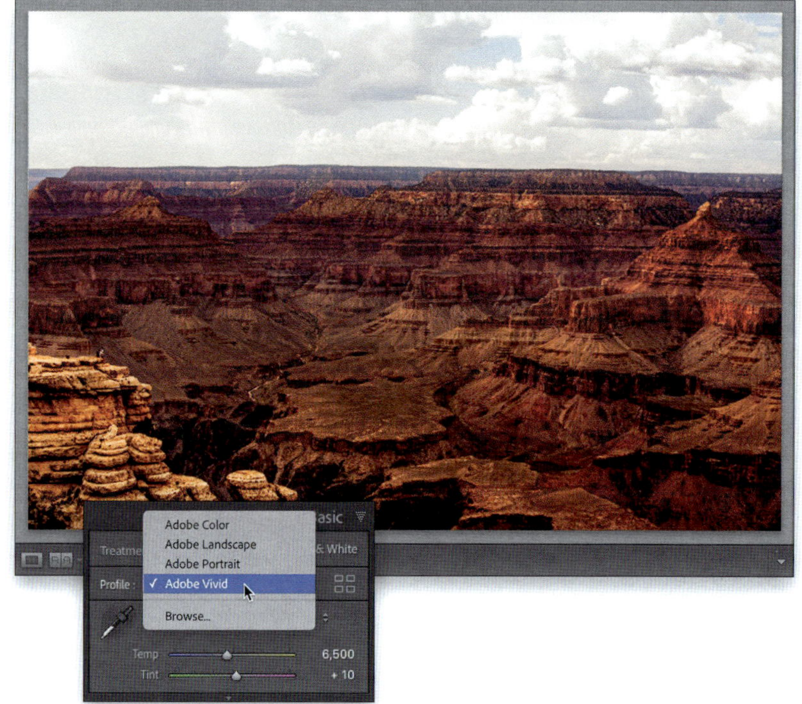

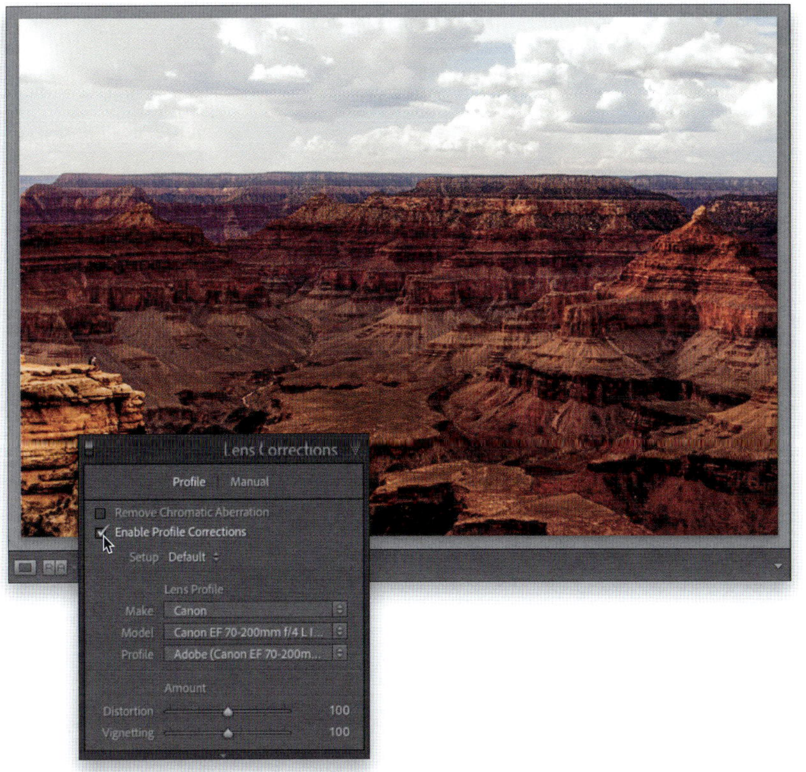

Step 10:
There's a pretty serious lens issue going on (the horizon line is bent—well, it's bowing anyway), so go to the Lens Corrections panel (the Optics panel in Lightroom cloud), and turn on the Enable Profile (Lens) Corrections checkbox (as shown here. **Point 6**). That straightened out the sides of the image and flattened things out pretty nicely. Toggle this checkbox on/off a few times and you'll see why we do this (and why it's so important).

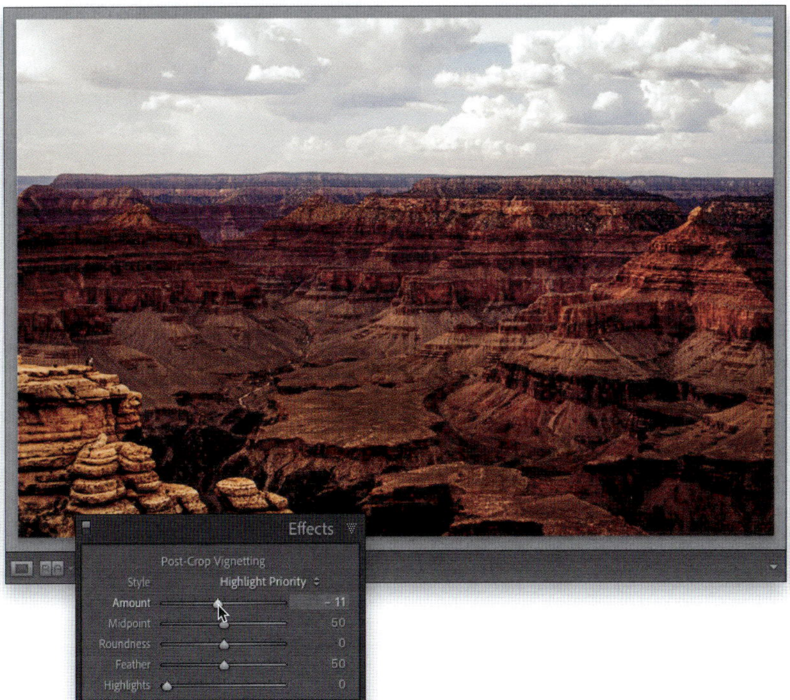

Step 11:
Let's darken those outside edges now (very subtly) all the way around (drawing your attention to the center. **Point 7**). Go to the Effects panel, and under Post-Crop Vignetting, drag the Amount slider (the Vignette slider in Lightroom cloud) over to –11 (as shown here).

Step 12:

As is sometimes the case, when we step back to look at this image, it looks a little too colorful and a little too contrasty (well, not in what you see here, because this is after I fixed it. But, look back at the image in Step 11, and you'll be like, "Yeah, that was gettin' kinda saucy"). So, go back to the Basic panel (the Color panel in Lightroom cloud) and drag the Vibrance slider to the left just a bit (here, I dragged it to –13 to pull back that color a little), and then lower the Contrast amount (drag it back to just +21). That should do it.

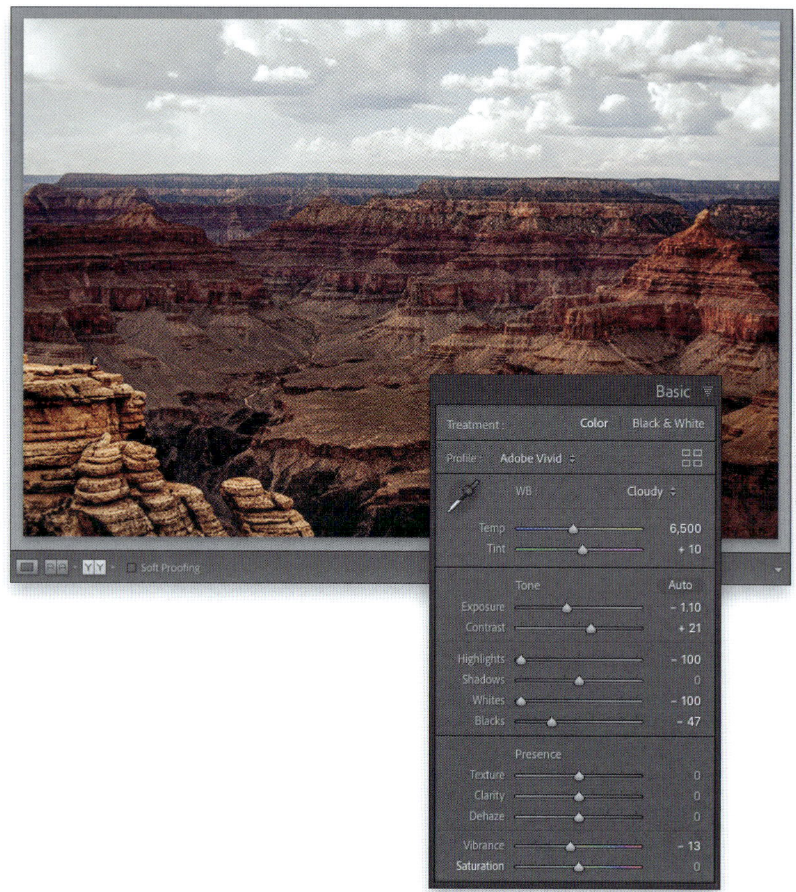

Step 13:

Let's finish things off with some sharpening. Go to the Detail panel and drag the Amount slider (the Sharpening slider in Lightroom cloud) to 60. The image is already pretty sharp due to adding so much contrast and texture and clarity, so we can be kind of conservative with it here. Now, if you want, you can avoid sharpening the sky by using the Masking slider, pressing-and-holding the Option (PC: Alt) key as you drag it to the right, until the sky turns black (indicating that the sky isn't being sharpened any longer). Or, you can skip doing the sharpening here in the Detail panel, and instead, get the Graduated Filter tool again, click on the Edit Pin for the gradient we created earlier (the one that just covered the mountain areas), then drag the Sharpness slider over to the right, and it will just sharpen the mountains and not the sky. Both methods accomplish the same thing, and now we're done.

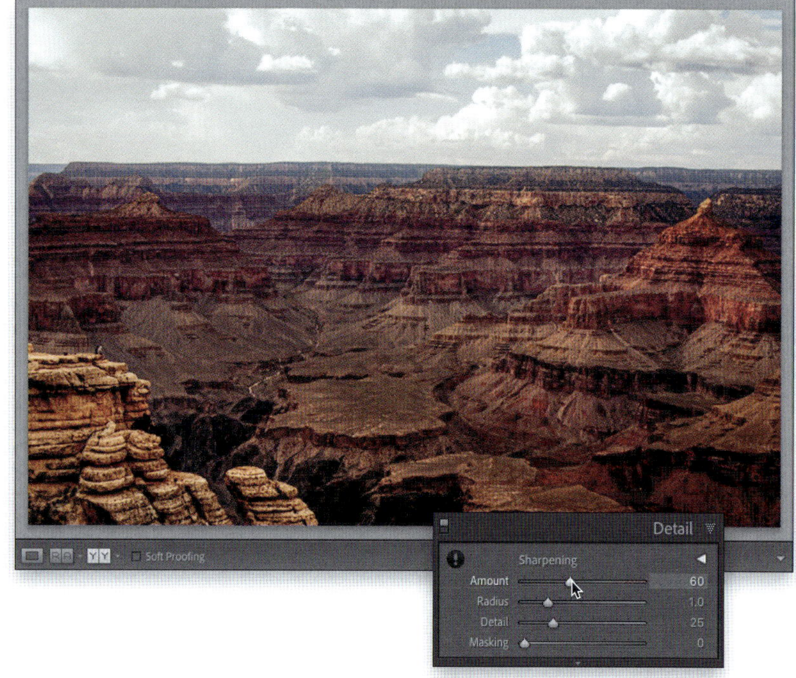

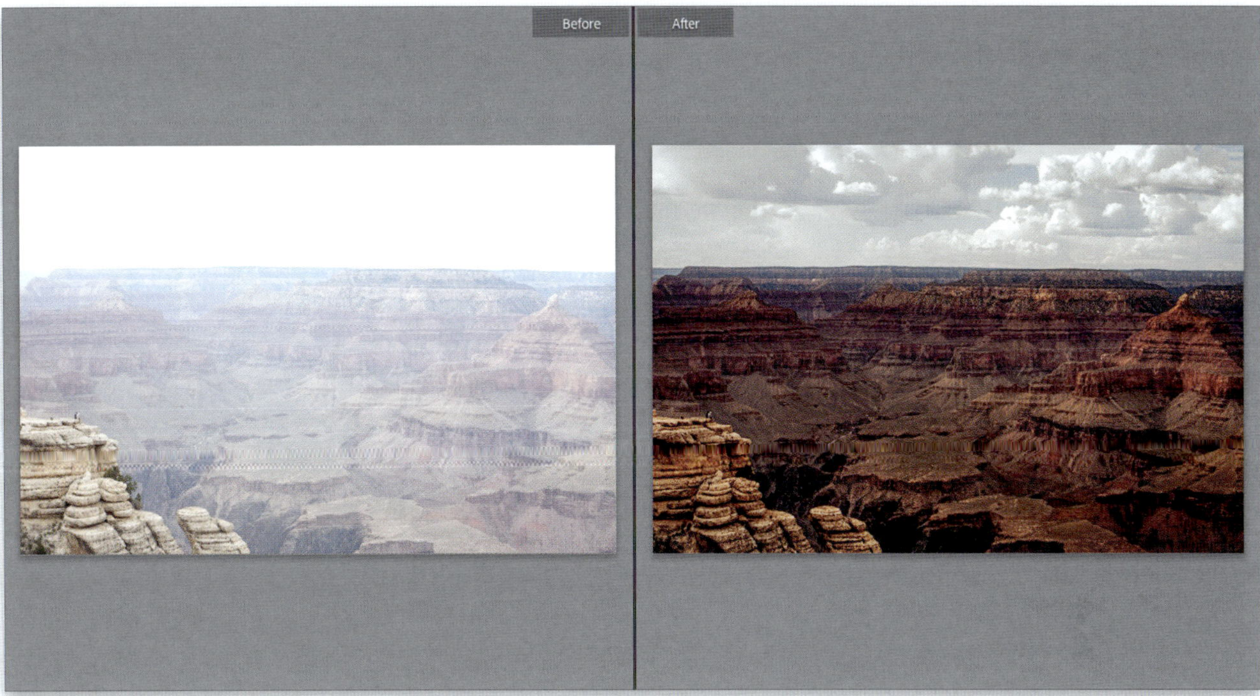

Here's our before/after.

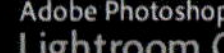

Adobe Photoshop
Lightroom Classic

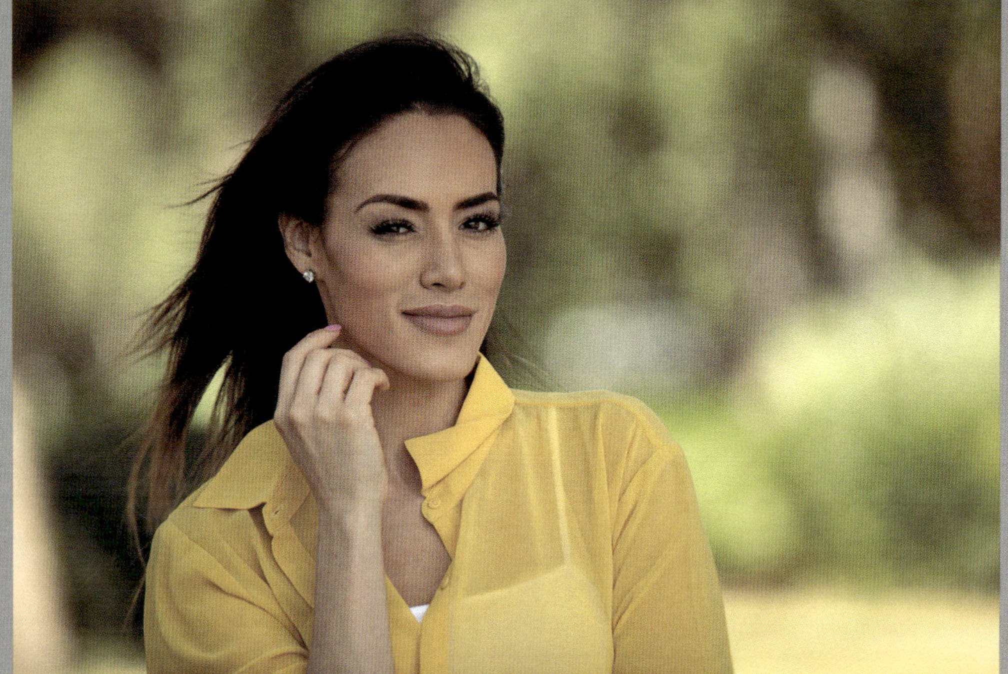

Before

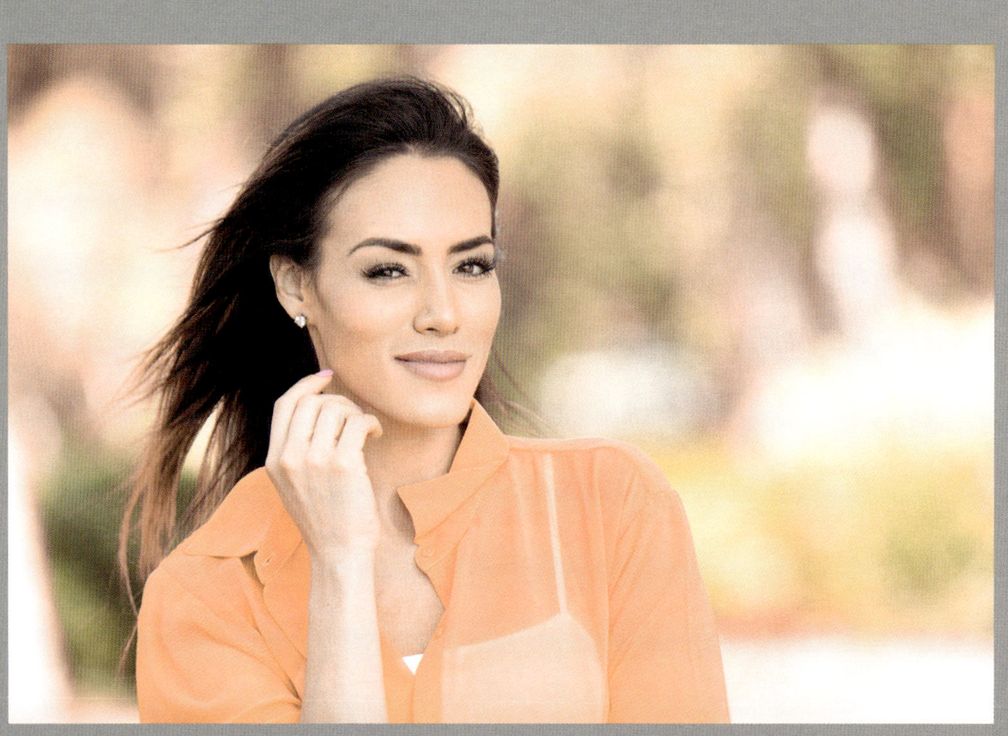

After

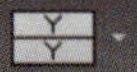

Before & After :

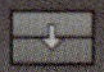
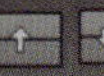

Soft Proofing

LESSON 18

OUTDOOR PORTRAIT RECOLOR

1. Assigning a RAW Profile
2. Cotting tho Color Right
3. Expanding the Tonal Range
4. Dealing with Sensor Limitations
5. Painting with Light and Retouching
6. Fixing Lens Issues
7. Finishing Moves

Let's evaluate the shot: It's not really in too bad a shape overall. It's a little underexposed, but that's an easy fix (and we will fix that). Instead, in this case, we're going to give this image a new look and a strong color treatment that changes the feel of the image, and we get to work with the Tone Curve feature (something born in Photoshop many years ago that made its way into Lightroom) to tweak our tone just the way we want it.

THE STORY BEHIND THE SHOT:

This shot was taken in a park right near our offices for a book project on shooting in natural light, and most of the shots in this series were either taken in the shade of the huge oak trees, or by placing a 1-stop diffuser over our subject's head to soften and spread the light (though, I believe this one was just shot in the shade). When we're booking a model for a shoot and they ask what they should wear to the shoot, we have a simple rule that works great: bring solid colors. Unless it's a fashion shoot, where the clothes are the subject, having your portrait subject wear solid colors helps to keep the focus on them and not on what they're wearing. Since they're not going to be wearing patterns, one thing we recommend is for them to dress in light layers, like the yellow blouse you see here over a white tank top, and to bring lots of accessories (from hats to sunglasses to purses, etc.) to add visual interest without drawing attention away from the subject.

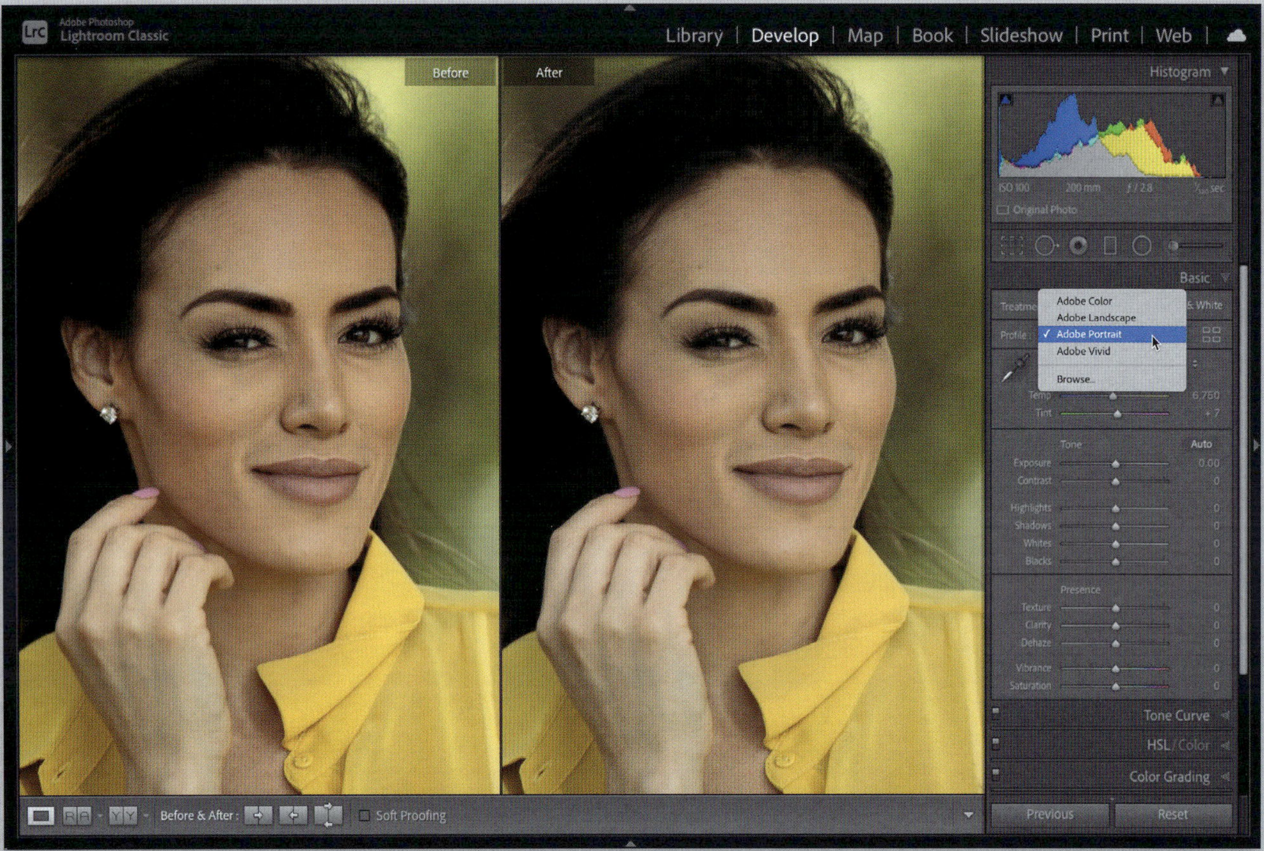

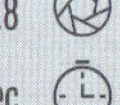

Camera: Canon EOS 5D Mark IV
Aperture Value: *f* / 2.8
Shutter Speed: 1/320 sec
ISO: 100
Focal Length: 200mm

Step 01:

Let's start by choosing a RAW profile **(Point 1)**, and as you've learned by now here in the book, when it comes to portraits, going with Adobe Portrait is usually the best looking scenario. The others (Adobe Landscape and Adobe Vivid) generally boost the colors too much for them to make a good starting place for a portrait, and even if you just stuck with Adobe Color for your portraits, it's a good, simple place to start. So, go ahead and choose **Adobe Portrait** from the Profile pop-up menu. I did a before and after here, and it didn't do a ton to help us, but it didn't hurt us, and it gives us a little better starting place for a portrait, so why not, right?

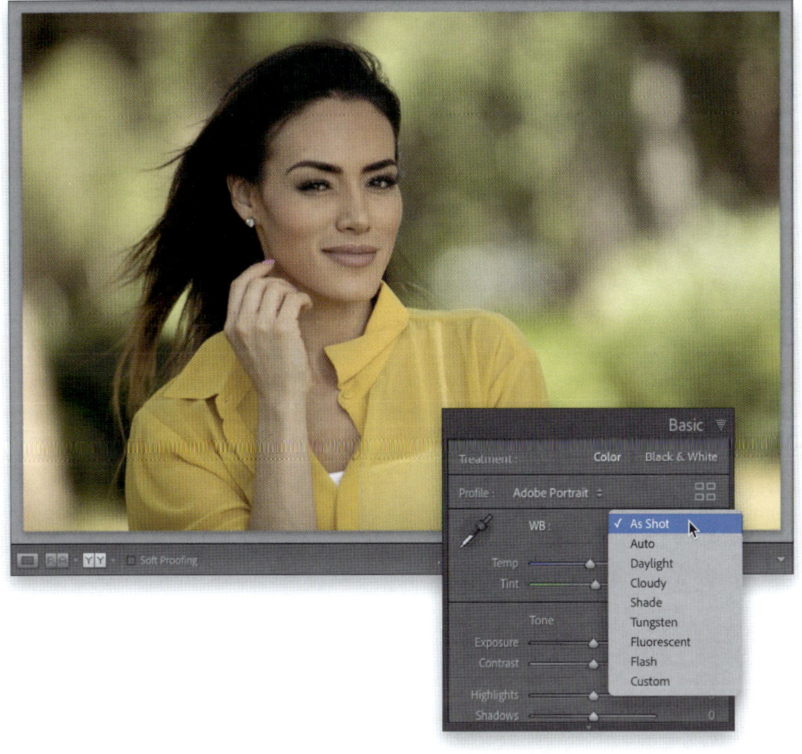

Step 02:

We're not going to mess with the white balance (Point 2) because a big part of this lesson is changing the overall color tone of the image, so just leave the WB (White Balance) set to **As Shot** (as shown here). By the way, I've heard people say many times over the years that they don't worry about setting the proper white balance in their camera because they're shooting in RAW and they can always change it later in Lightroom. First, you don't have to shoot in RAW to change your white balance in Lightroom—you can change it for JPEGs and TIFF images here, as well. But, more importantly, getting it right in-camera (just changing the White Balance setting on your camera to match your lighting situation) not only saves you time later in post, but when you're looking at an image on the back of your camera whose color is way off and you're thinking to yourself, "I know it looks bad, but I'll fix it later" isn't inspiring. It doesn't boost your creativity. It doesn't "get you in the zone." Okay, stepping off my soap box now.

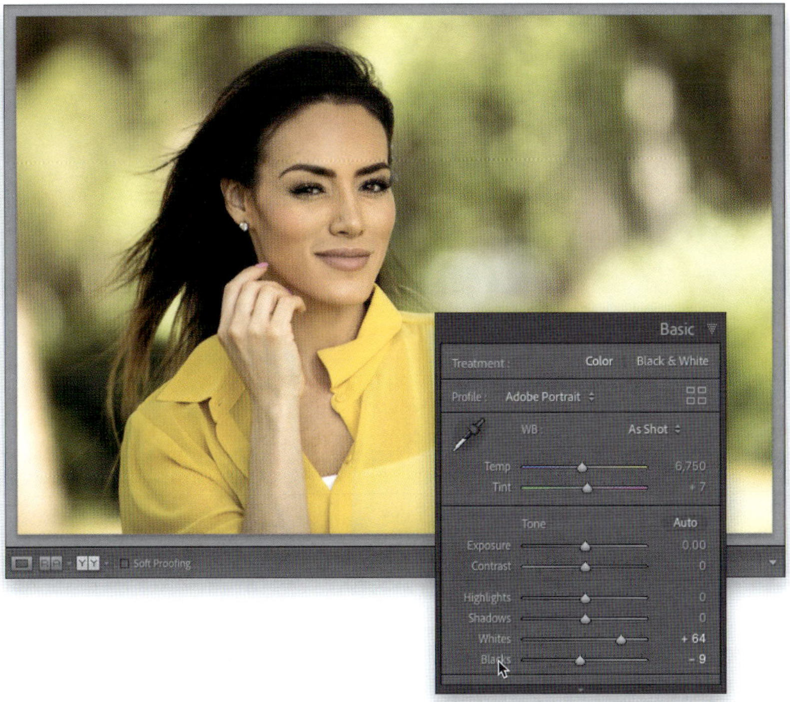

Step 03:

Let's go ahead and set our white and black points now **(Point 3)**. Press-and-hold the Shift key and double-click on Whites, and then on Blacks. This didn't affect the Blacks that much, increasing them by –9 (a negative number for Blacks means making them darker), but it jumped those Whites way up to +64. This would be ideal if we were just doing a standard edit to this photo. But, because we're going for a flatter look, in this instance, we can try something a little different, which is to back off those really bright whites, and instead, boost the exposure. This will boost the midtones and give us a different look, while still keeping the image looking brighter.

Step 04:

So, to get this bright midtone look, drag the Whites slider way back to the left to around +10, and then we'll raise the midtone brightness by dragging the Exposure slider up to +0.60 (as shown here). I'm showing you a side-by-side here, with the Whites at +64 (in the Before photo on the left), and then backing the Whites off to +10 and brightening the Exposure instead (in the After photo on the right). You can see that while they both have similar brightness overall, the one on the right has a different, more muted look (which is nice for a portrait like this). Also note that the Before image has a very punchy yellow in her blouse and in the background, and it's much more muted in the After image. So, just a different look, while still keeping the image bright (and a trick to keep in your back pocket for when you need it).

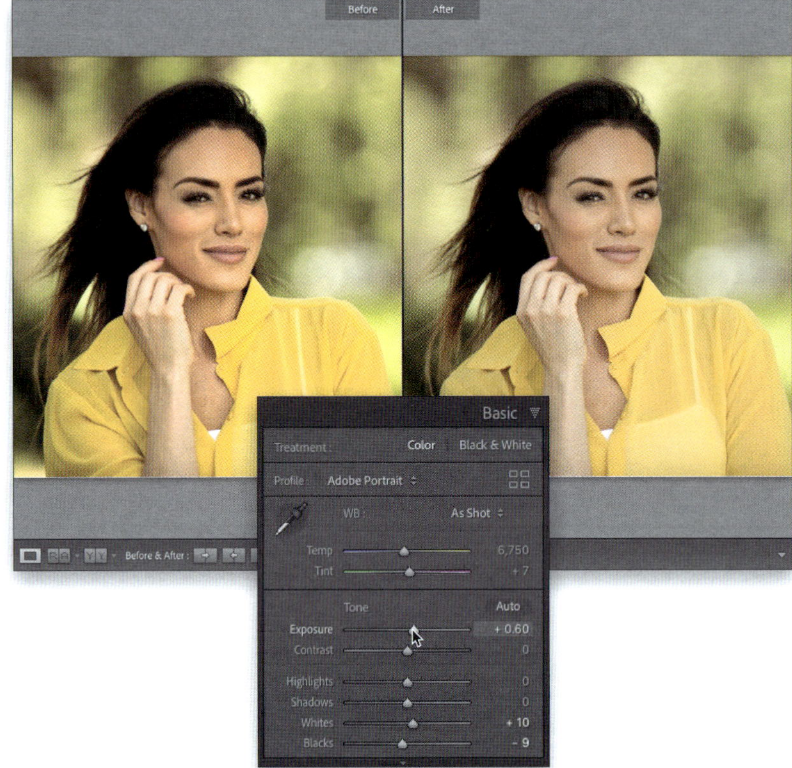

Step 05:

We are now going to take this nice midtone brightness up a notch using the curve in the Tone Curve panel. This curve allows you to get very precise with how you want to adjust an image's tone because it's not just a coarse slider—you can adjust very specific tones within the image using this curve. By the way, it doesn't look like a curve at first—it's just a straight, diagonal white line (like you see below left)—until you adjust it to create a curve. So, click once directly in the center of that diagonal line (the center of that line controls the midtones), which adds a control point to the curve, then gently drag up and to the left (as seen below right) to boost the midtones in that area of the curve. Look at how much brighter that little change made the overall image, especially visible in her face, compared to the After image in the previous step. Okay, now this is starting to look really good, but we're not done with our curve yet.

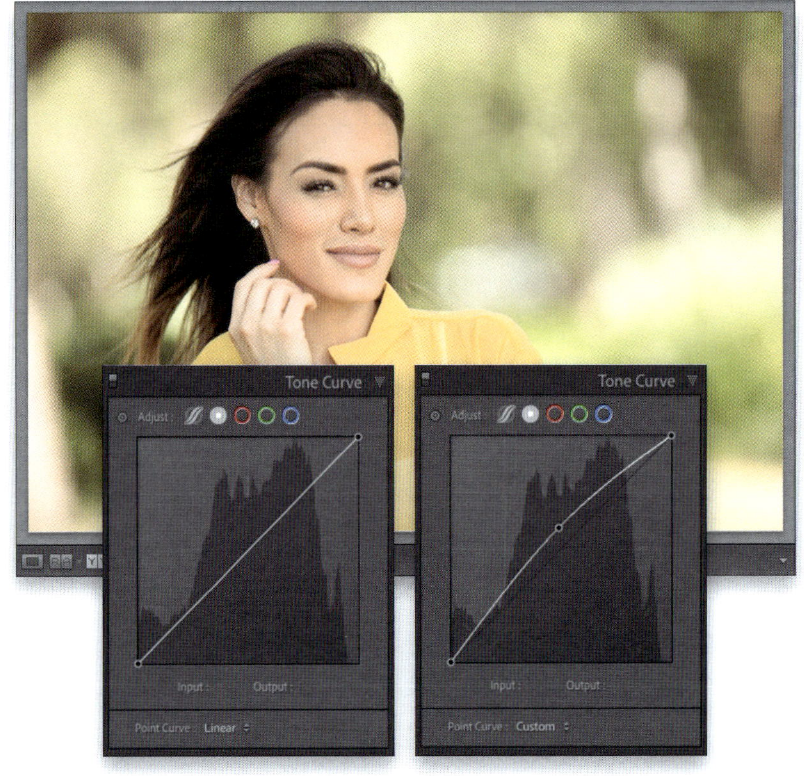

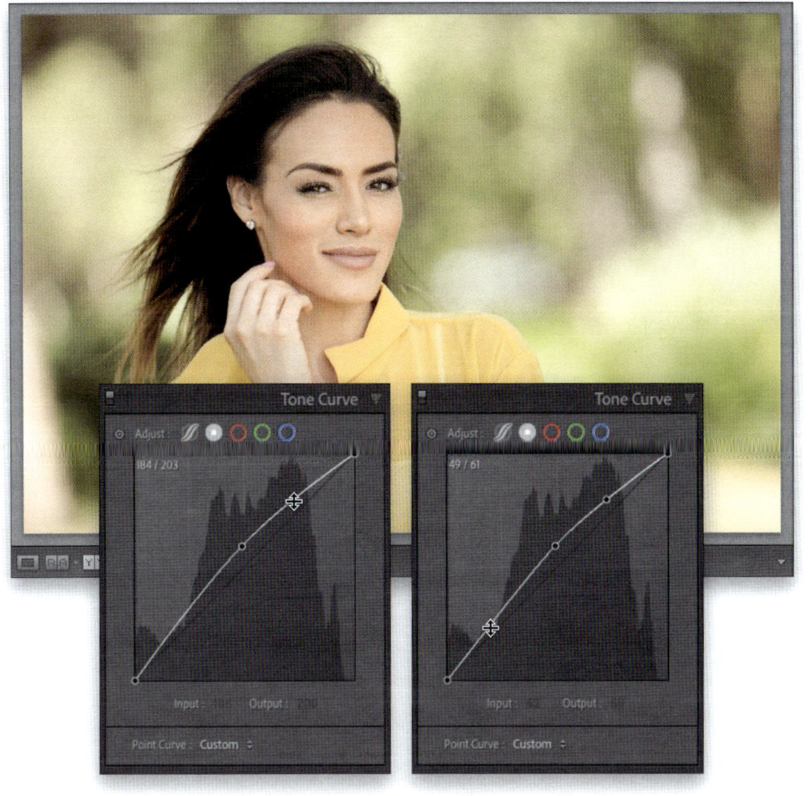

Step 06:

To adjust the upper midtones (called the quarter tones in "curve talk"), click once in between the center point we created in the previous step, and the end point up in the top-right corner—that area controls those bright upper midtones. Let's drag them up a tiny bit diagonally to the left (as seen below left—your cursor will change into a two-headed arrow, letting you know you can move that point up or down). If you drag that point diagonally down, it will darken the brighter midtone areas of your image (so dragging up diagonally to the left brightens those upper midtones; dragging down diagonally to the right darkens them). If you want, you can add a separate control point for the lower midtones (called the three-quarter tones) by clicking once in between the center point and the bottom-left corner point (as seen here, below right), and now you can adjust that a tiny bit upward, as well. Now our image has some really nice bright midtones and we're almost ready to add our color.

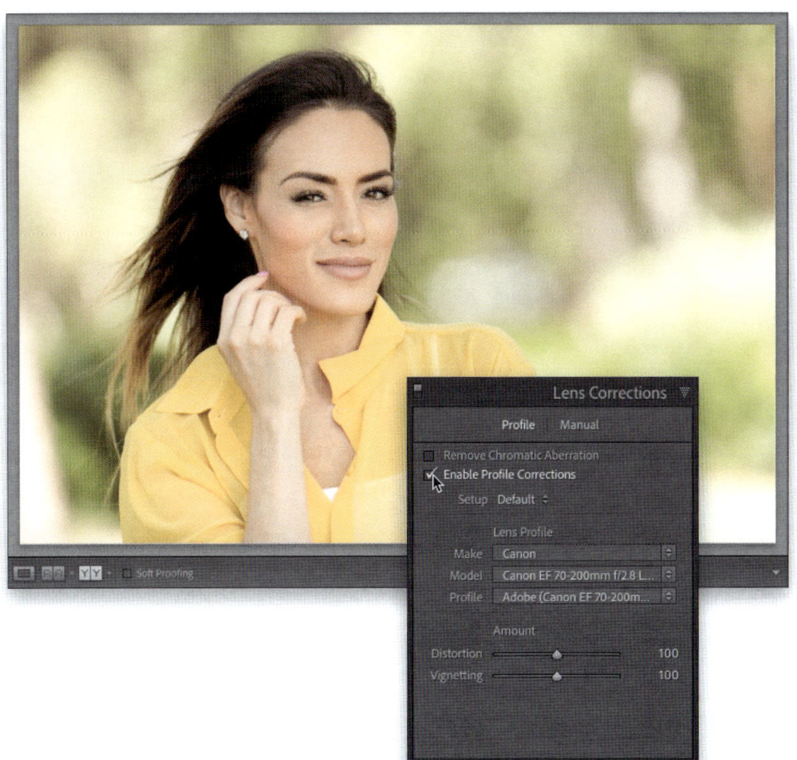

Step 07:

As usual, we have a few lens issues we can fix that will remove any lens distortion and brighten the corners in the image, so let's do it **(Point 6)**. Go to the Lens Corrections panel (the Optics panel in Lightroom cloud), and turn on the Enable Profile (Lens) Corrections checkbox (as shown here). Besides fixing the distortion issue, look at how much brighter the overall image is now that those corners are at the proper brightness. Okay, I think we're in a good place to add our color. *Note:* If you don't want to do the color effect we're about to add, you can just skip the next step, head over to the finishing moves, and you'll be done. But, you might want to stick with me just to try this out for the sheer educational purpose of it. Learnin' is good fer ya.

Step 08:

To add our color (we're skipping our usual Point 4 here and moving to **Point 5**), we're going to go to the HSL/Color panel (in Lightroom cloud, go to the Color panel, and then click on Color Mixer). There are four tabs across the top of the panel (in Lightroom cloud, there's an Adjust pop-up menu up top) where you can choose to adjust the Hue (color), Saturation (how vibrant each color is), and Luminance (how bright each color is). We're just going to adjust the color, so click on the Hue tab (in Lightroom cloud, choose **Hue** from the Adjust pop-up menu). The big move we're going to make here is to drop the yellows big time by dragging the Yellow slider way over to the left (here, I dragged it to −90). Now you can play around with the other sliders to see how they affect the overall color of your image. In this case, I lowered the Red hue to −20, and took a little out of the Purple (−10) and Magenta (−15), but those actually did very little to the look at all—it was dropping the yellows that did all the work.

Step 09:

If it were me (and it is), I'd now subtly darken those outside edges all the way around **(Point 7)**. Go to the Effects panel, and under Post-Crop Vignetting, drag the Amount slider (the Vignette slider in Lightroom cloud) over to −11 (as seen here).

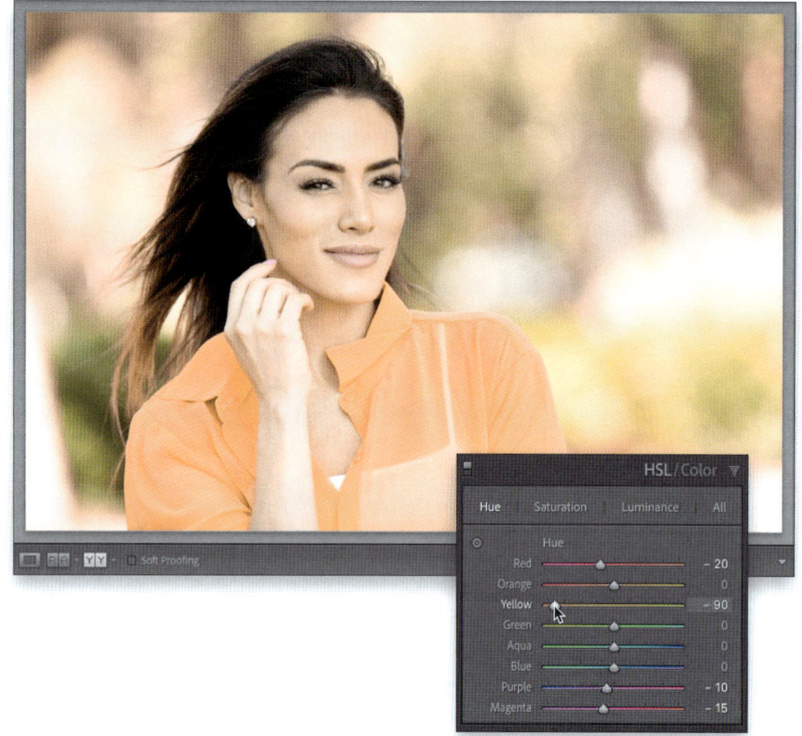

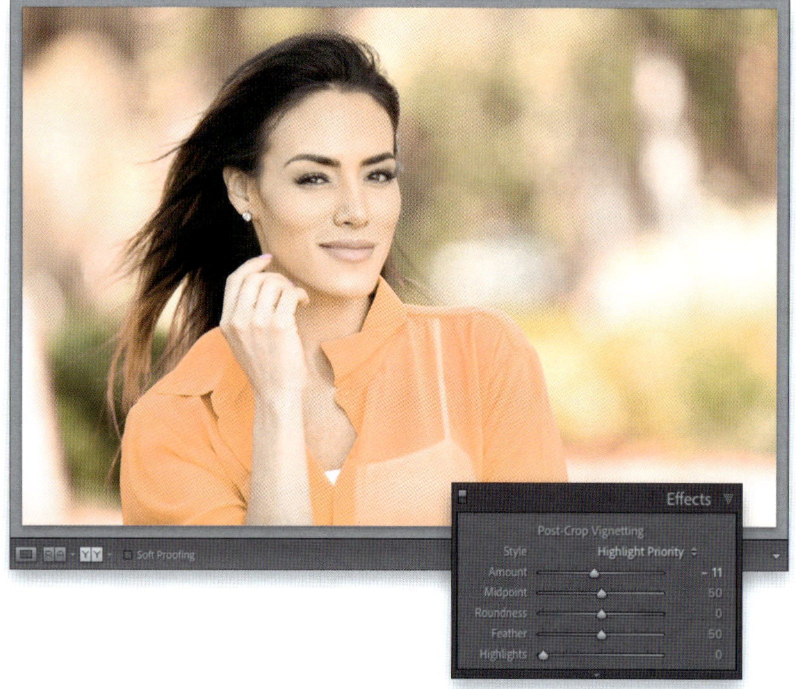

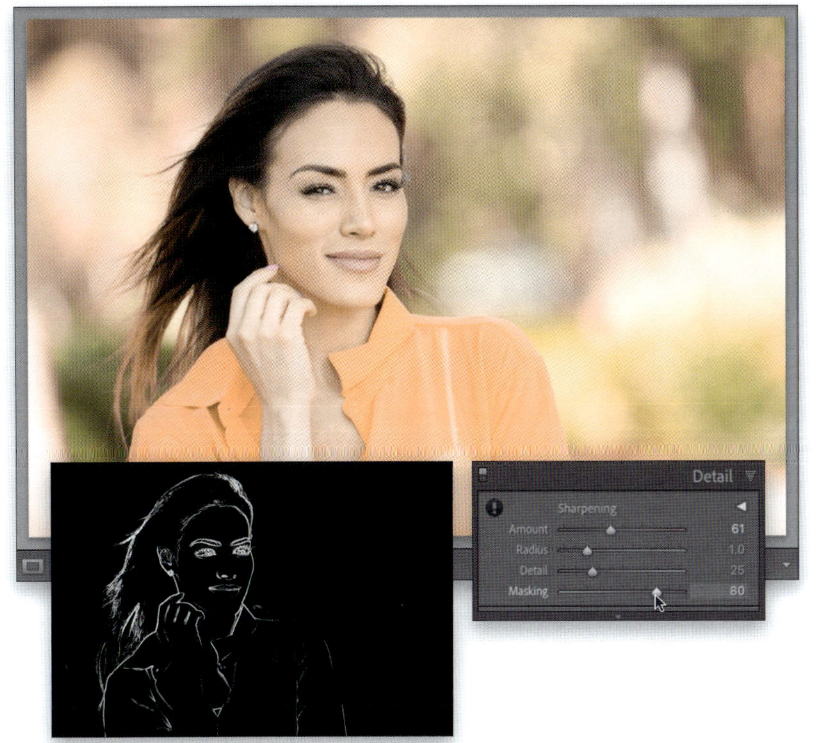

Step 10:

Now, let's sharpen our image. We're going to use that technique you learned back in Lesson 7, on page 83, where we just apply the sharpening to the detail areas (eyes, eyebrows, lips, hair, clothing, and so on), and avoid sharpening her skin altogether, so it stays soft. Go to the Detail panel, and under Sharpening, drag the Amount slider (the Sharpening slider in Lightroom cloud) over to around 61 (as seen here), then press-and-hold the Option (PC: Alt) key, and drag the Masking slider to the right. The screen will turn solid white at first, letting you know that the entire image is being sharpened, but as you continue to drag to the right, parts of the image will turn black (as seen here, in the bottom left). Those parts are no longer being sharpened—you'll notice her skin is fully in the black, so it's not getting sharpened, which is our goal. Congrats for sticking in there 'cause you're done.

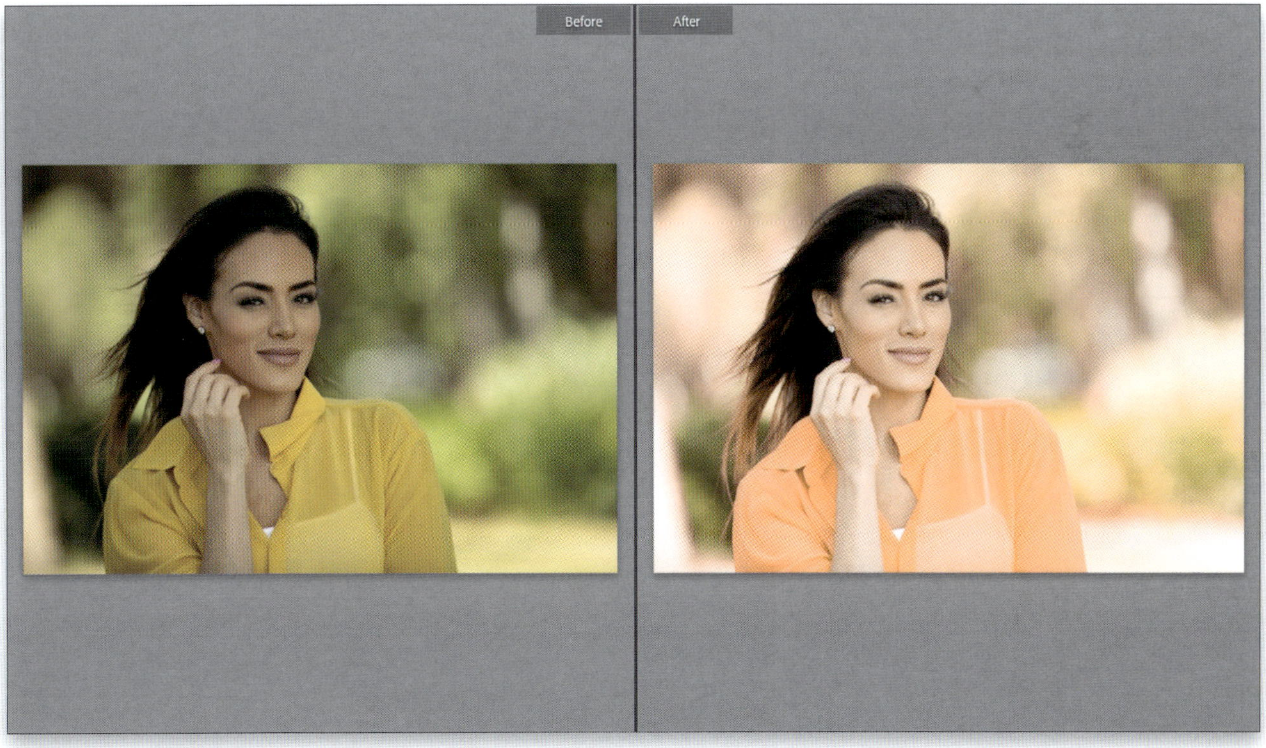

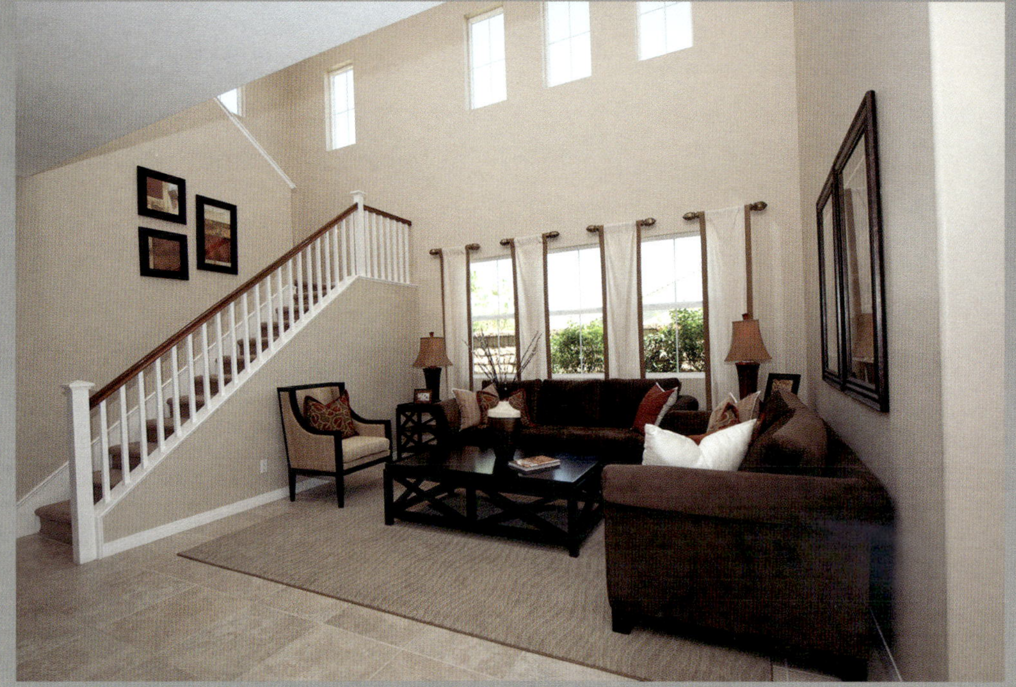

Before

After

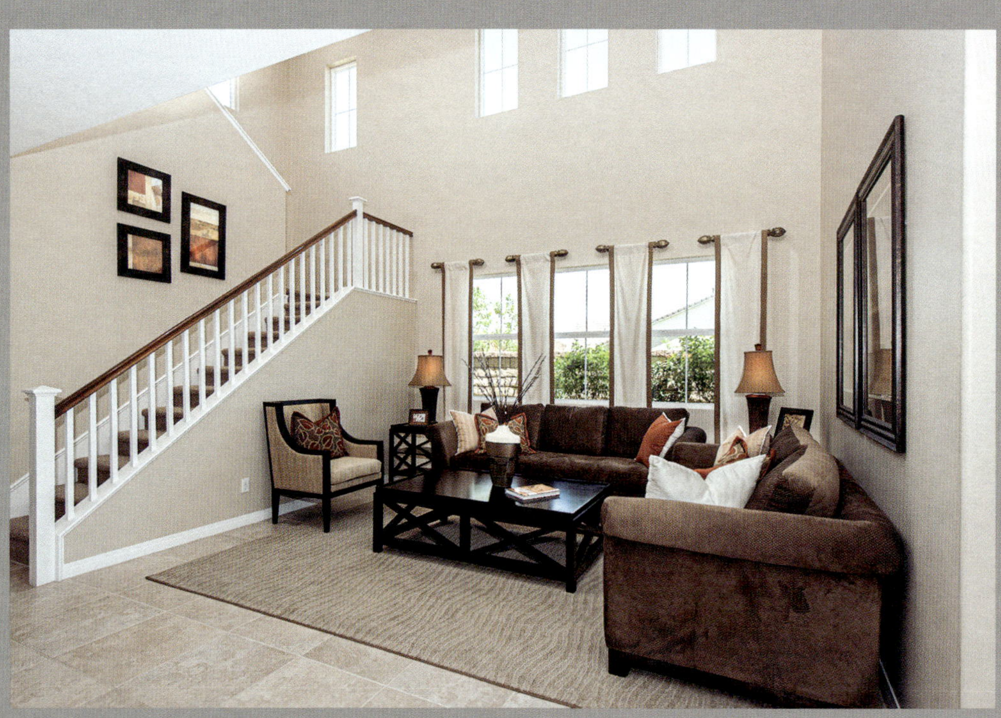

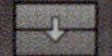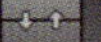

LESSON 19

HOME INTERIOR

1 Assigning a RAW Profile

2 Getting the Color Right

3 Expanding the Tonal Range

4 Dealing with Sensor Limitations

5 Painting with Light and Retouching

6 Fixing Lens Issues

7 Finishing Moves

Let's evaluate the shot: Even though it's lit with multiple flashes, the interior is still dark—buyers want to see nice, bright, sunny homes. There's a distortion issue (look at how the wall on the right is leaning inward. Could be a construction issue with this home, but more likely, it's a lens problem. Okay, it's a lens problem). Mostly, we'll be working on brightening and balancing the light throughout the image (plus, we have to do something about that dingy-looking ceiling in the top-left corner). We got this.

THE STORY BEHIND THE SHOT:

This shot was taken a number of years ago, inside a builder's model home, at a hands-on workshop I was a participant in out in California. At one point, we were set loose with a couple of flashes to light and photograph a few rooms to see how we'd do, and they would evaluate the images afterward. The basic idea (lighting-wise) was to either (a) get your exposure set so the scene looked good outside the house, which would mean it would be dark inside, but then you'd use flashes to brighten the interior (which is what I did here). Or, (b) you could let the windows blow out and go to white (another popular type of shot you'll see in today's real estate images). But, the rule was if it looked good outside, then you'd expose for the outside and light the interior. If the outside view was boring (or, worse yet, unattractive), then you'd expose for the interior and let the windows blow out to white (which they generally will do if you expose the interior enough to the point that it looks nice and bright).

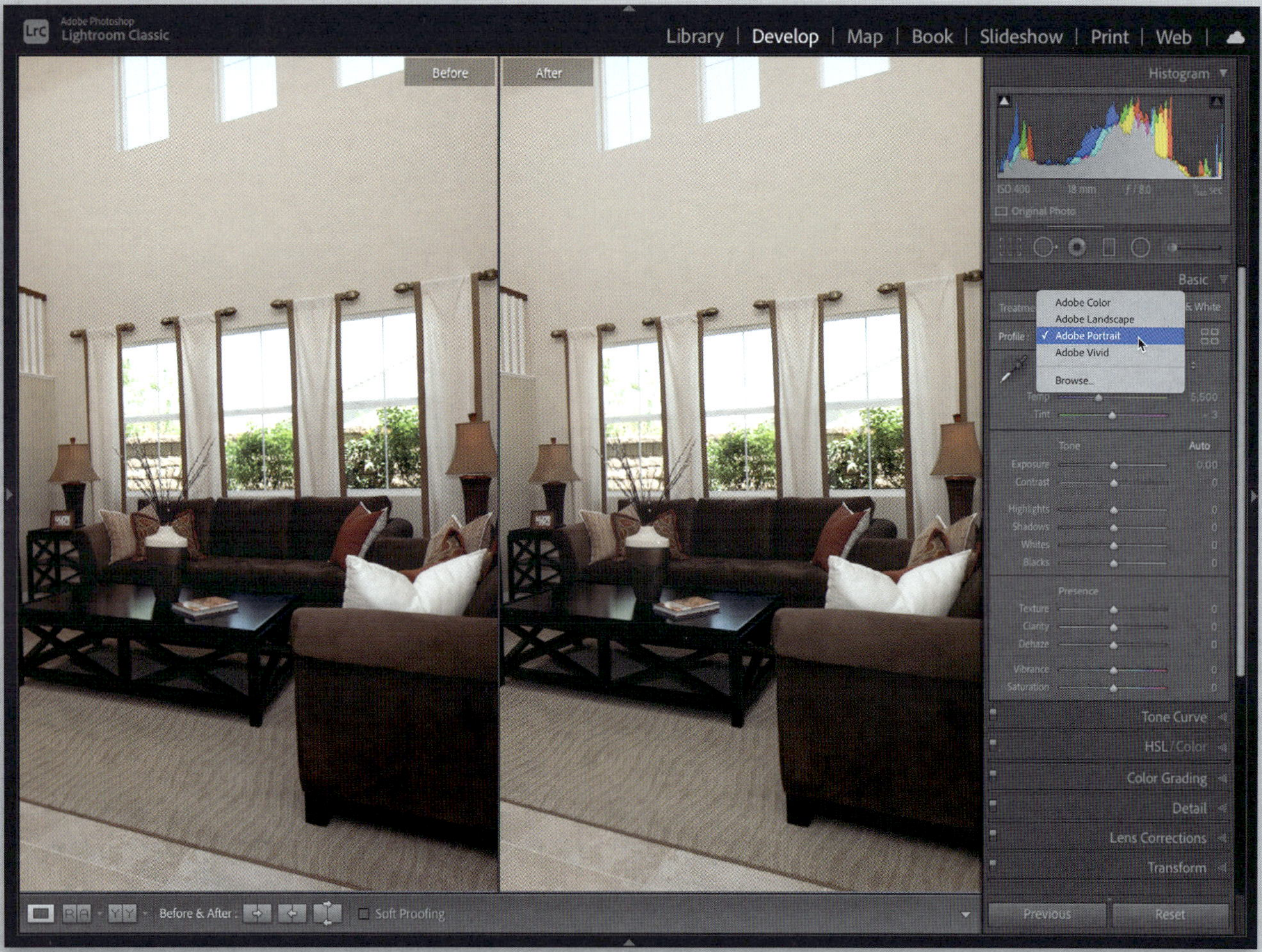

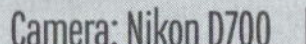

Camera: Nikon D700

Aperture Value: ƒ/8.0

Shutter Speed: 1/160 sec

ISO: 400

Focal Length: 18mm

Step 01:

Let's start by seeing if there's a RAW profile that gives us a better starting place **(Point 1)**. I tried my "go-to" RAW profile, Adobe Landscape, and it didn't look right for this interior shot. Adobe Vivid was even worse, saturating the colors a bit and adding contrast. So, I was a little surprised that **Adobe Portrait** turned out to be the best choice for this.

Go ahead and choose it from the Profile pop-up menu at the top of the Develop module's Basic panel (the Edit panel in Lightroom cloud). You can see the slight difference it made when looking at the couch in the center. If we're looking for brighter and airier, Adobe Portrait is the best choice of the four RAW profiles, so we're starting there.

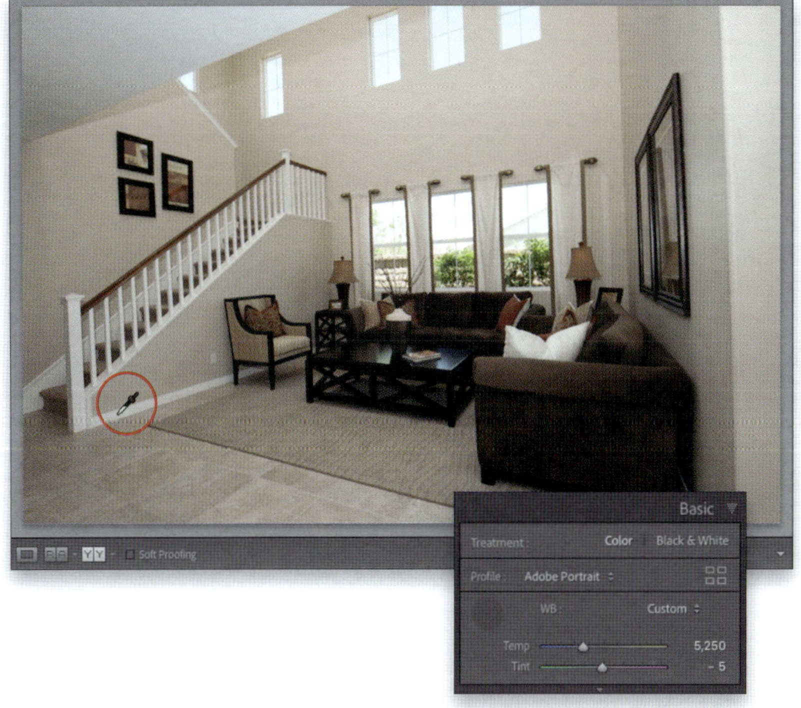

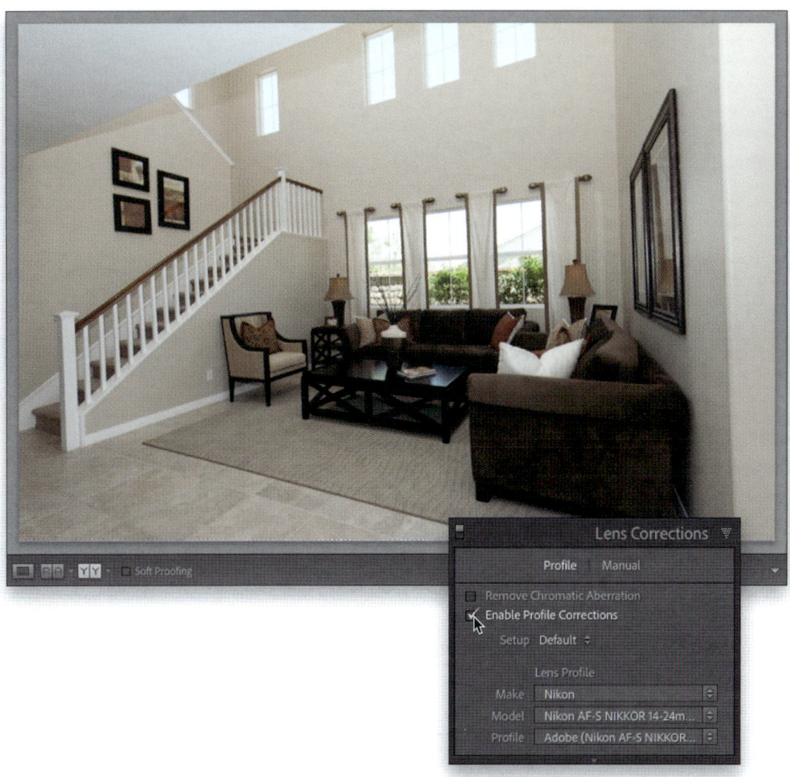

Step 02:

Point 2 of the 7-Point System is to get our color right, but I gotta tell ya, the color doesn't look too bad here, right out of the camera. But, I know that it can sometimes fool the eye, so let's give it a quick white balance correction to see if it actually does need an adjustment. In the Basic panel (the Color panel in Lightroom cloud), get the White Balance Selector tool (**W**; the eyedropper) and click it on something that's light gray (provided, of course, you can find something light gray). In this case, click on the baseboard along the staircase (as shown circled here), though that barely changed the color at all. Try clicking on the neutral color wall along the staircase, and that does a decent white balance fix, but it definitely has a blue bias to it, so that's not ideal. Let's try the WB (White Balance) preset pop-up menu to see how the different presets look. Auto actually looked good, and so did Flash (which makes sense since this was lit with flashes), and Daylight wasn't too bad either, but it made the walls look a little pink. The rest are either too warm (Cloudy, Shade), or too blue. So, let's just go with **Auto**, or use what you got clicking the eyedropper on the baseboard along the stairs. Click the Done button when you're finished.

Step 03:

There are two levels of lens issues and I want us to deal with them now because they're affecting the brightness (and architecture) of this shot, and since it's only a couple of clicks, let's do it **(Point 6)**. Go to the Lens Corrections panel (the Optics panel in Lightroom cloud) and turn on the Enable Profile (Lens) Corrections checkbox (as shown here). That brightened the darkening in the corners and flattened out the distortion on the edges (toggle this checkbox on/off a few times to see how big a difference this makes), but this one has a second level of lens issues—the walls are still leaning inward, so we have to dig a little deeper.

Step 04:

Go to the next panel down, the Transform panel (the Geometry panel in Lightroom cloud), and near the top of it, you'll see the Upright options (well-named since they're for making things like walls straight and upright). There are six buttons here (in Lightroom cloud, it's a pop-up menu instead), so go ahead and click on Auto, which generally gives the most balanced correction, and as you can see here, the wall on the right is now perfectly straight and the horizontal perspective issues are fixed, as well. Click the Off button, and then click Auto, going back and forth a few times, and you'll see that this is a pretty "wow" fix for this room, and an awful lot of improvement for just two clicks (one to turn on Enable Profile [Lens] Corrections and one to click the Auto Upright button).

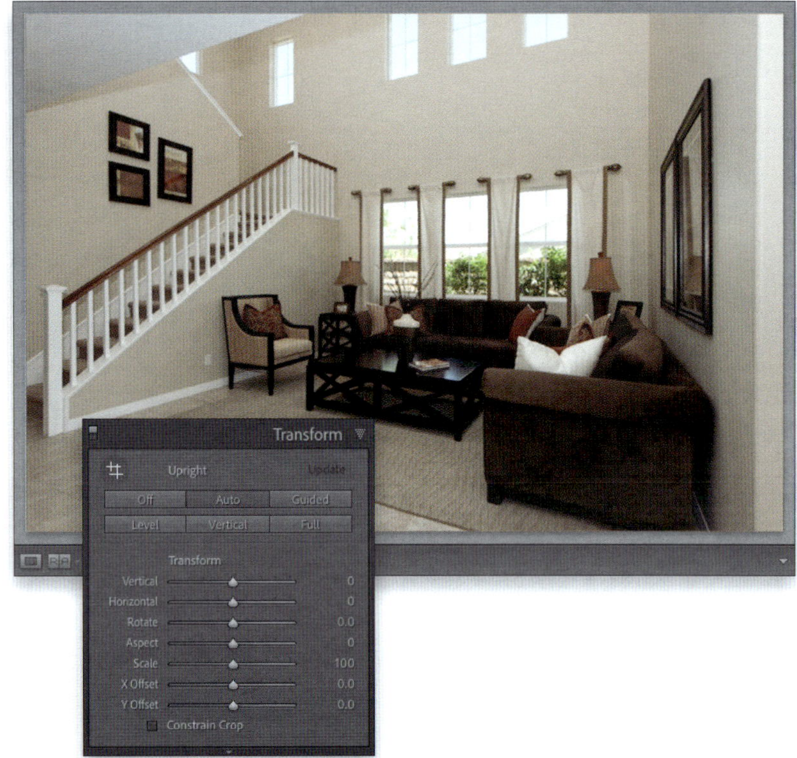

Step 05:

Next, let's get to fixing our exposure **(Point 3)**, and we'll start by setting the white and black points. Head back up to the Basic panel (the Light panel in Lightroom cloud), press-and-hold the Shift key, double-click on Whites, and then on Blacks. Well, because of that bright light coming in from the window, its reaction was to pull the Whites way back to –55, and it opened up the Blacks to +17 to lighten the dark areas. Basically, it didn't do a lot to help our image here, but we're not done. Let's bring some major brightening to the scene by dragging the Exposure slider to the right to open everything up by about 1/2 a stop (here, I dragged it to +0.55). Ahhhh, now it's brighter inside (and, unfortunately, a little bit outside, too, but we can fix that).

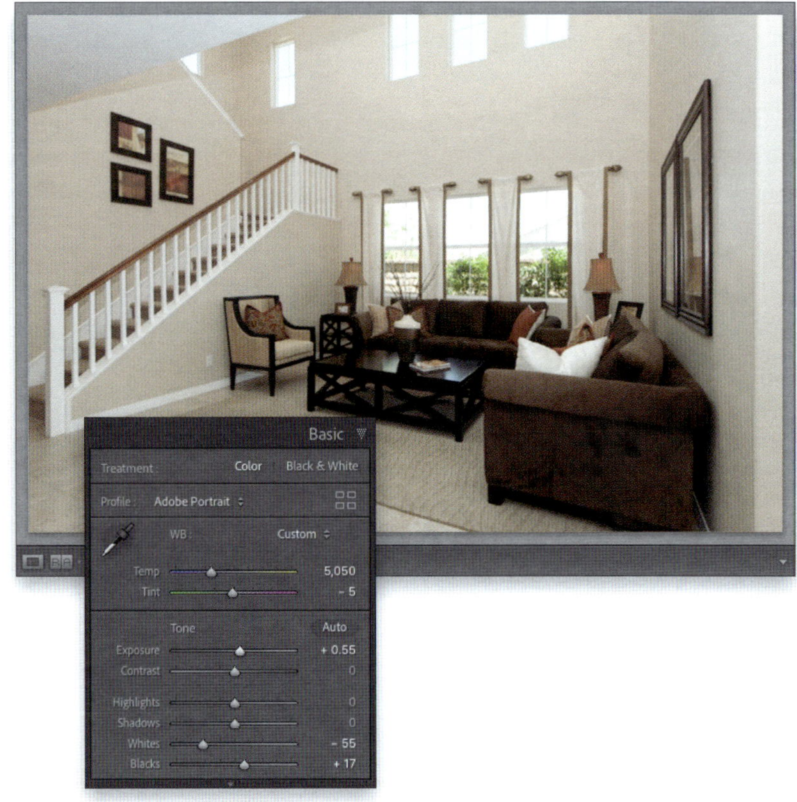

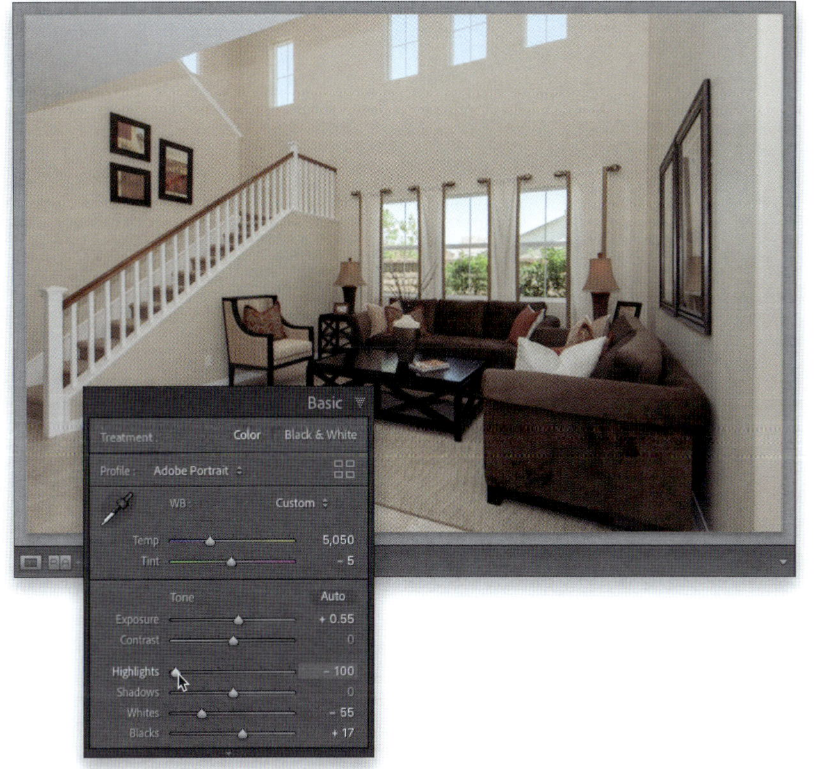

Step 06:

Let's go ahead and pull those highlights back a bunch to see if we can get some detail back in that area outside, and maybe in the windows up top, too **(Point 4)**. Drag the Highlights slider all the way over to –100, and then take a look at that row of windows up top. There's some sky out there! Also, there's more detail outside the windows behind the couch. That's all good, but I think we need a little more overall brightening.

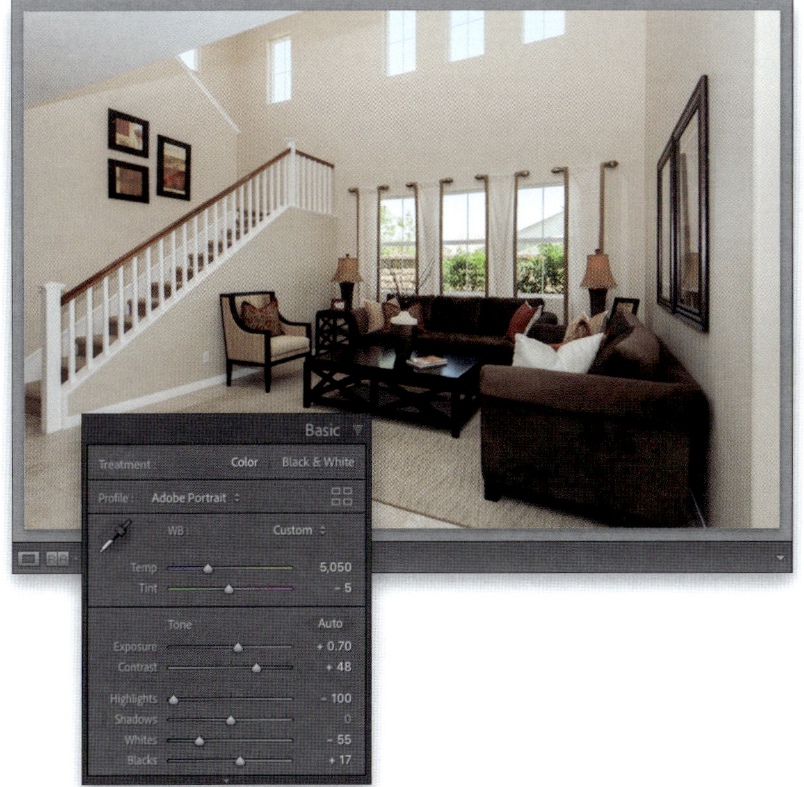

Step 07:

Not only do we need a little tweak to our overall brightness, I think we need to bump up the contrast a bit, so the image doesn't look as flat. When you add contrast (which makes the brightest parts of your image brighter, and the darkest parts darker) it tends to make your overall image look a bit darker. So, let's add the contrast first (dragging the Contrast slider over to the right to around +48), which makes the room more contrasty (which is good), but it also makes it a bit darker (in this case, that's bad). We can counteract that darkening by just increasing the Exposure amount since it controls the midtones, which has the biggest single effect on our brightness. It was set to +0.55, so let's bump it up a little to +0.70. That's better (and brighter).

Step 08:

We'll do our "spot brightening" (**Point 5**) using the Adjustment Brush (**K**; the Brush tool [**B**] in Lightroom cloud), so get it from the toolbox, double-click on the word "Effect" to reset all the sliders to zero, and then increase the Exposure amount about 3/4 of a stop (here, I went to 0.75). Now, paint over the couches (but avoid that white pillow on the couch on the right). While we're at it, let's paint over the end table, coffee table, and those pictures on the wall over the stairs. Hit the **O key** on your keyboard to see the areas you've painted over (you'll see the mask appear in a red tint, as seen here). If you spill over, press-and-hold the **Option (PC: Alt) key** to switch to the Erase brush and paint away any of those spillovers. When you're done, hit the O key again to turn off the red tint overlay (in Lightroom cloud, press it three times to return to just the tool overlay). Now those couches, the end table, the pictures, and most of the coffee table are 3/4 of a stop brighter.

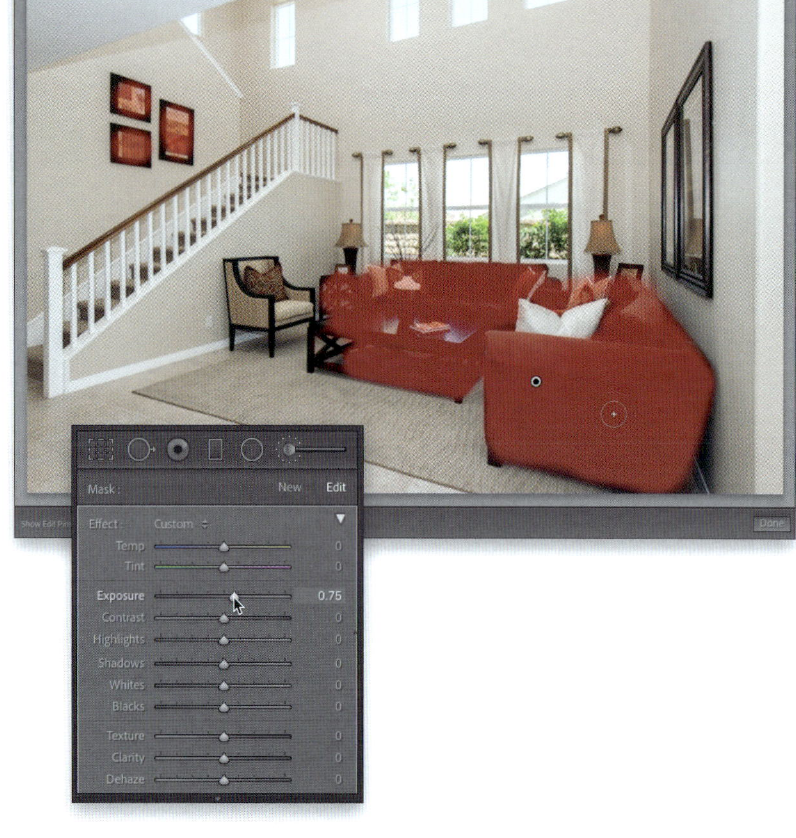

Step 09:

Next, let's "turn on the lights." Click on New at the top right of the panel (the + [plus sign] in Lightroom cloud), so it leaves the brightening we just did alone and allows us to paint somewhere else. We're going to click a single, large brush over both lamps, but we'll need to add a little yellow into our brightening to make it look legit. Drag the Temp slider over to 16 (as shown here), so now when we click, it will make it 3/4 of a stop brighter and a bit yellow. Press **Command-+ (plus sign; PC: Ctrl-+)** to zoom in a bit, so you can clearly see the lamps, make your brush Size a little larger than the lamp shade on the right, and then position it over the center of the lamp shade (as shown here).

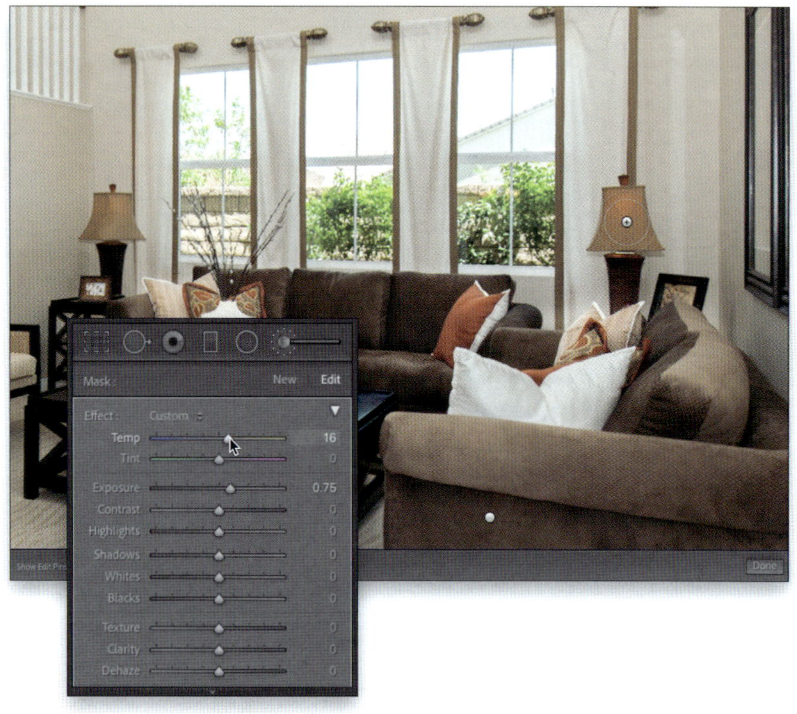

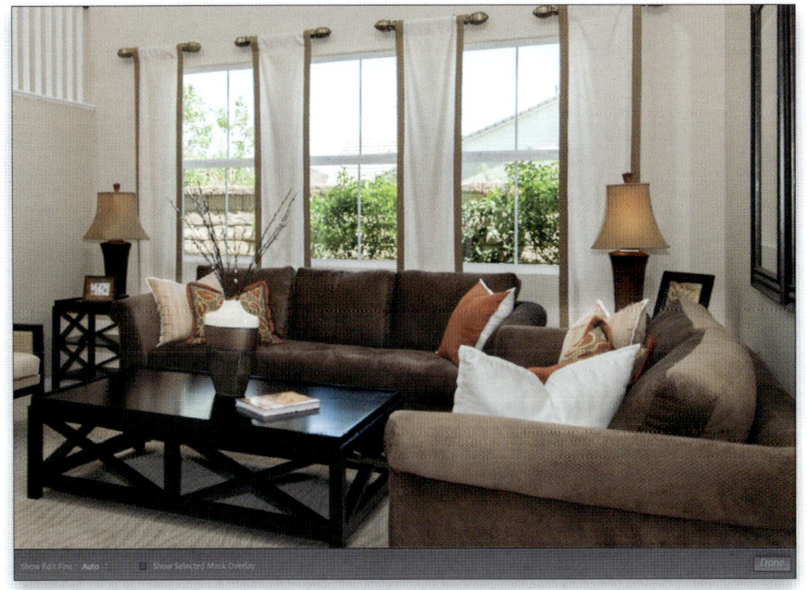

Step 10:

Now, don't paint—just click once. That puts the brightest part of the brush in the center, and then the feathering that's applied to the brush has that brightness fade out as it gets toward the edges. That helps make the light look lit (as seen here).

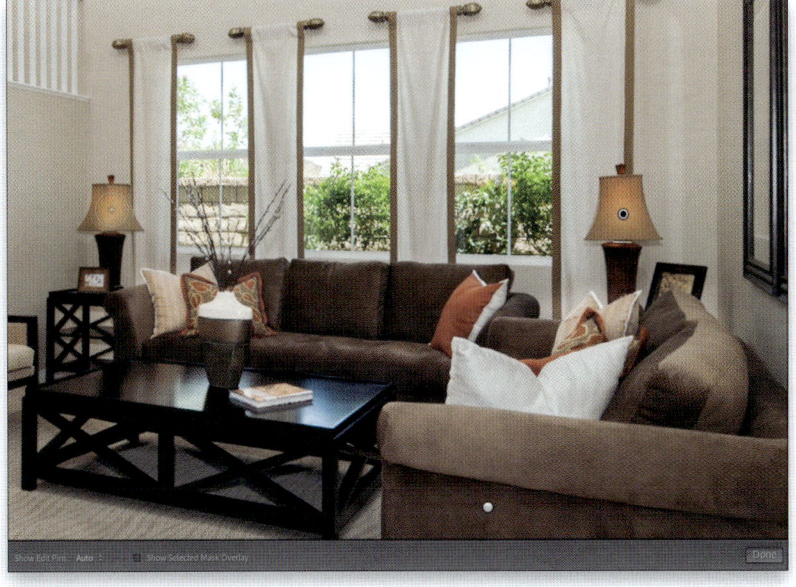

Step 11:

Let's move over to the lamp on the left and do the same thing, but since it's farther away, you'll need to shrink your brush size a little (remember, you can change the brush Size by hitting the **bracket keys** on your keyboard—the left bracket key makes the brush smaller; the right bracket key makes it larger. The bracket keys are to the right of the letter P on a standard US keyboard). Just click once to light that other lamp, but when you do this, you might find (well, at least I did) that it doesn't match the color of the other lamp for some reason. So, go ahead and undo that click on the lamp on the left by pressing **Command-Z (PC: Ctrl-Z)** because we're going to have to create a separate edit—one where we can change the white balance of our lamp brightening to closer match the other lamp.

Step 12:

Hit New at the top of the panel again (the + [plus sign] in Lightroom cloud), to leave the brightening we did on the right lamp alone, and allow us to adjust the left lamp separately. Size your brush down a bit, and then over in the brush options panel, drag the Tint slider over to the right a bit (to 37), and maybe add some contrast (here, I increased the Contrast setting to 43. I had to try a few sliders to find out which ones would get me in the ballpark. This doesn't nail it, but it's close). Now, just click once over the shade of that lamp on the left. If it's not bright enough, either click the brush once again on the same spot, or try increasing the Exposure amount (here, I increased it to 0.83).

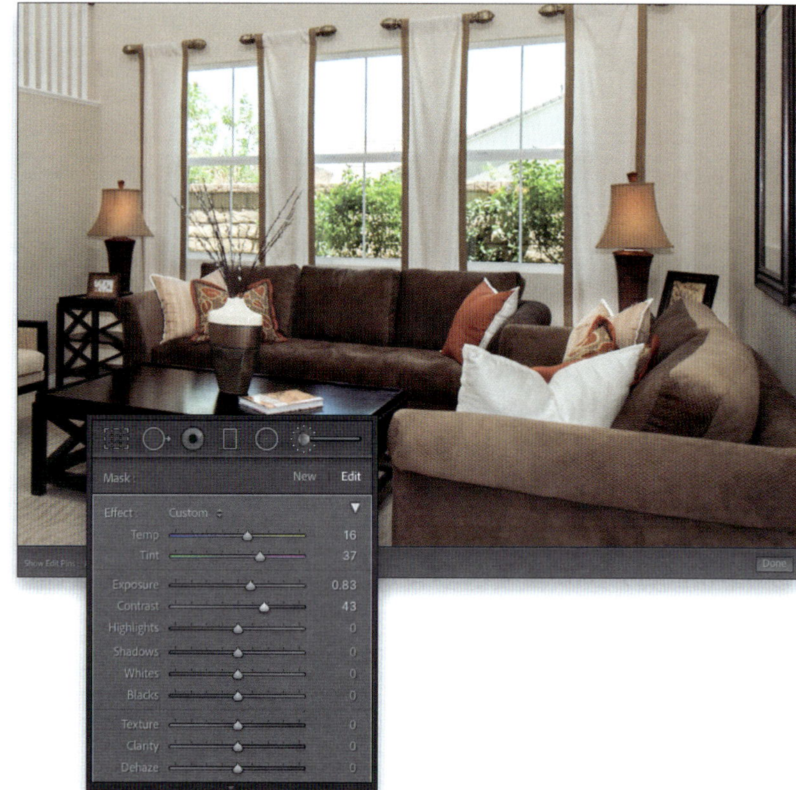

Step 13:

Time to paint somewhere new, so hit New once again, because now we're going to brighten that dingy-looking, top-left corner of the ceiling. Reset your sliders, and then increase the Exposure to 0.36. To keep from painting "outside the lines," turn on the Auto Mask checkbox at the bottom of the panel (at the top of the panel in Lightroom cloud), and then paint over that area (as shown here). As long as that + (plus sign) in the center of the brush doesn't stray over onto that beige wall, it won't spill over and brighten outside that white area of ceiling. Click the Done button beneath the Preview area when you're finished.

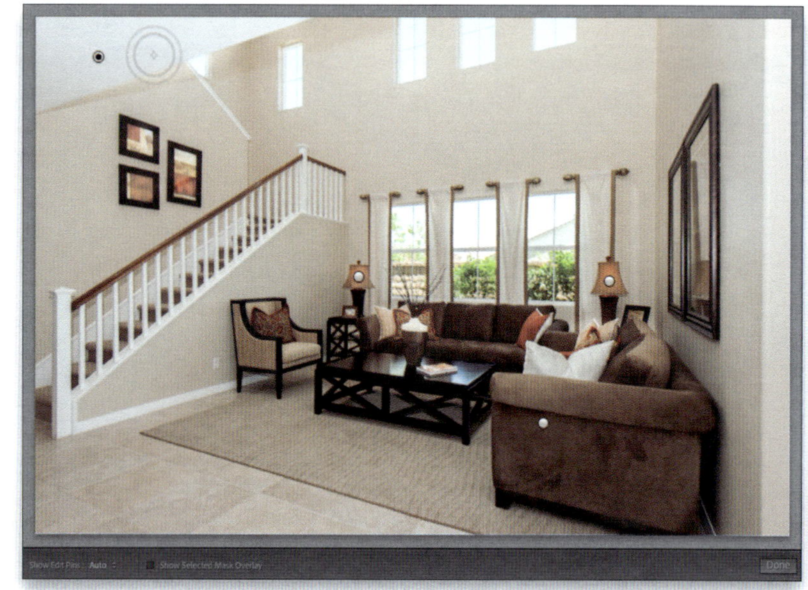

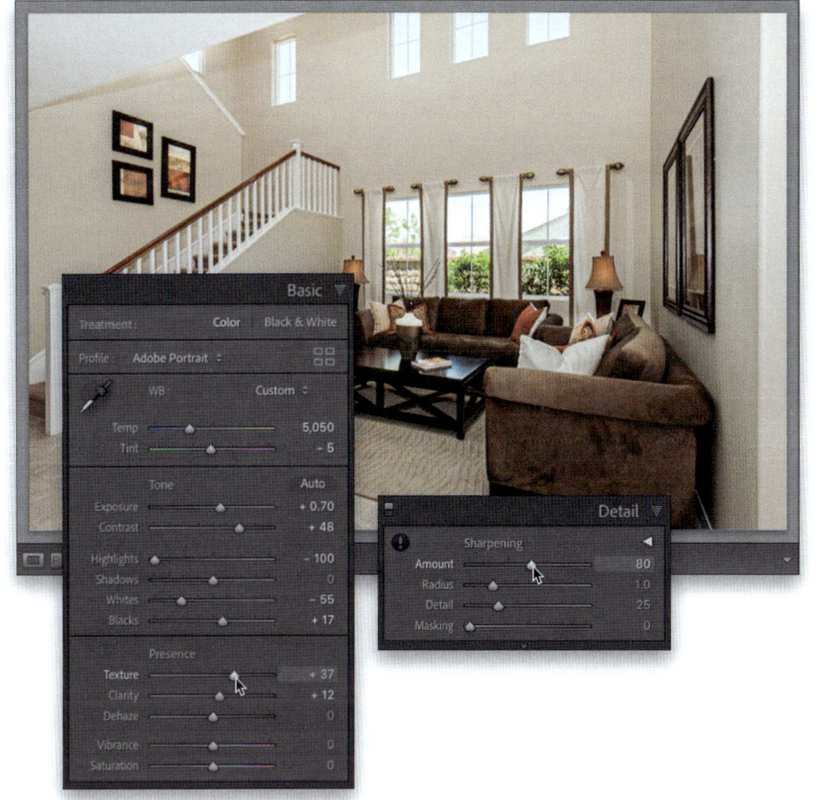

Step 14:

We're going to skip the edge darkening that we would normally do, because we want to keep this image looking nice and bright throughout, but we are going to bring out some detail in the image by increasing the Texture and Clarity. So, go back to the Basic panel (the Effects panel in Lightroom cloud) and drag the Texture slider over to the right to around +37 and the Clarity slider over to around +12 (we don't want to go much further with Clarity because it's increasing the midtone contrast. Too much will make the image a bit darker and can make it look a bit grungy, which is great on the right image, but would mess up this one). Let's finish up by sharpening the interior **(Point 7)**. Go to the Detail panel and drag the Amount slider (the Sharpening slider in Lightroom cloud) to 80 to apply some really nice, snappy sharpening. That's all we need to do to finish this one off.

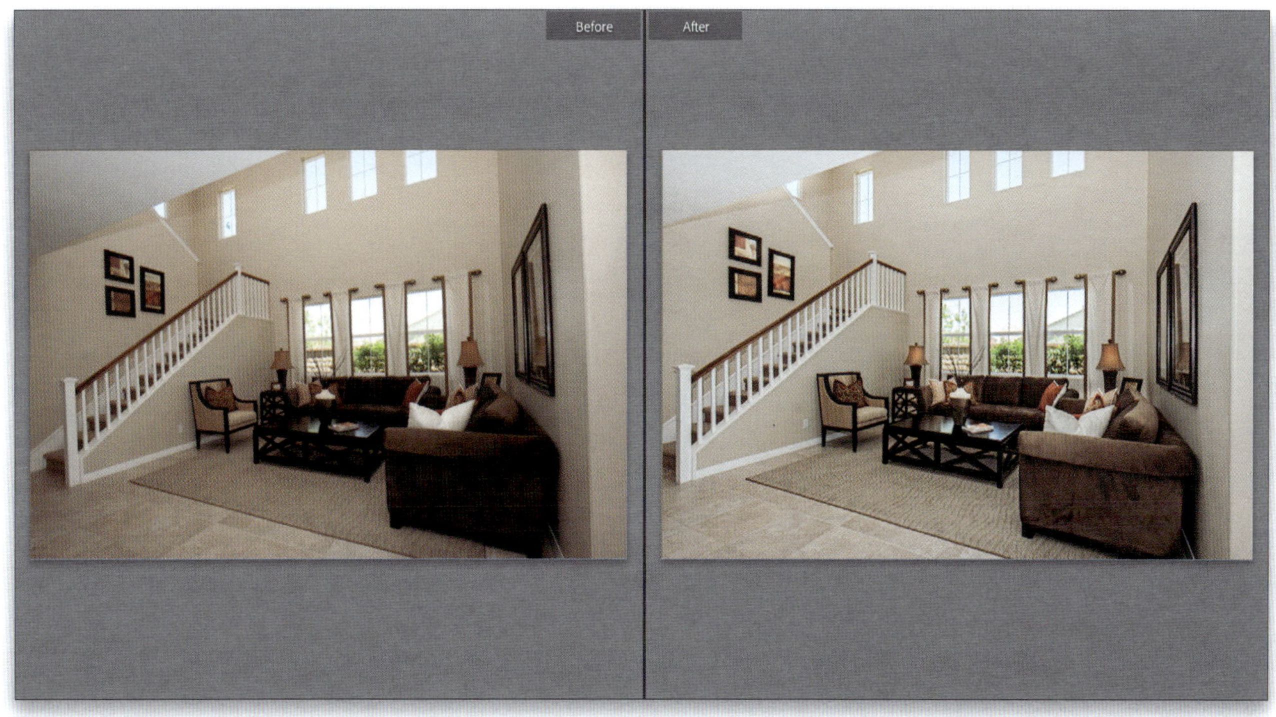

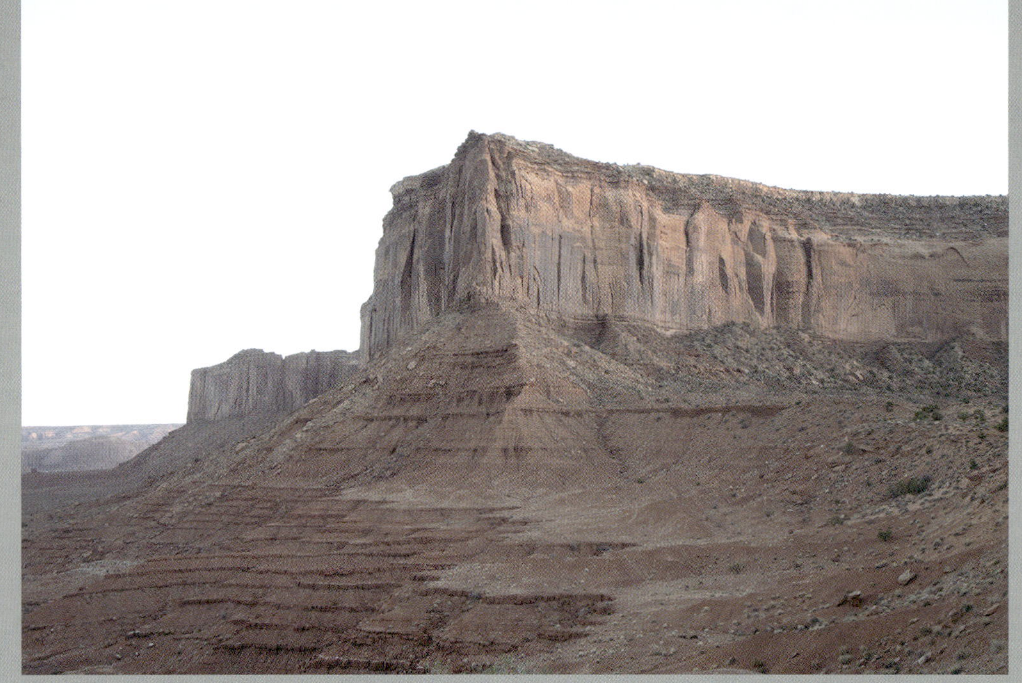

Before

After

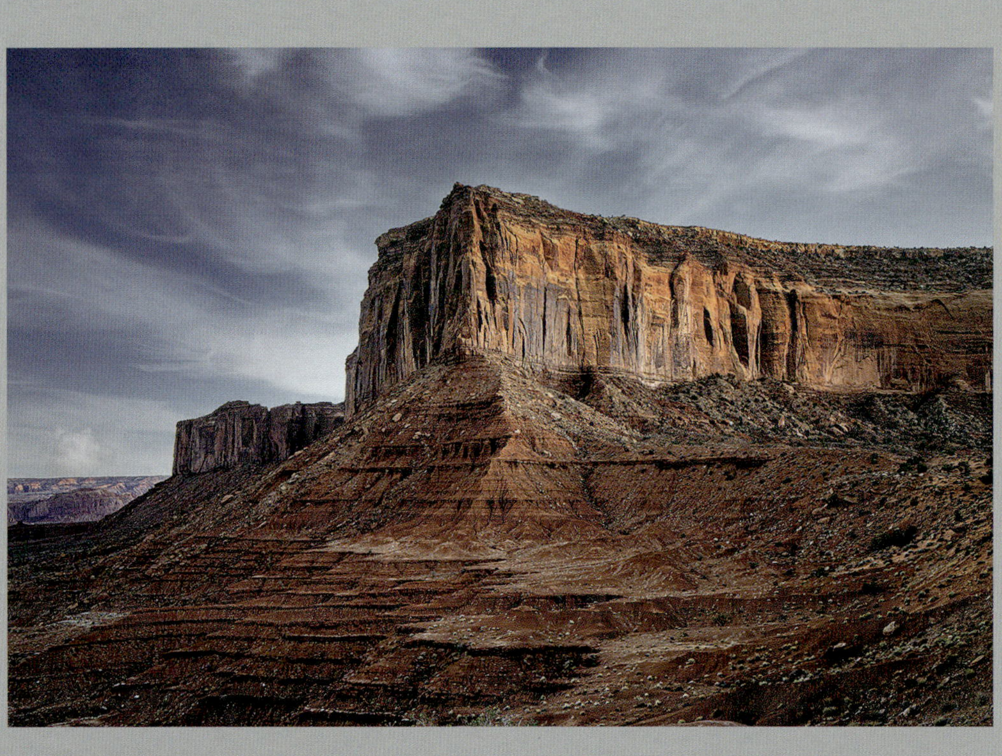

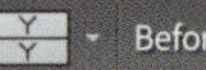
Before & After :
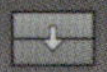

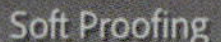
Soft Proofing

LANDSCAPE OUT WEST

1. Assigning a RAW Profile
2. Getting the Color Right
3. Expanding the Tonal Range
4. Dealing with Sensor Problems
5. Painting with Light and Retouching
6. Fixing Lens Issues
7. Finishing Moves

This is the first of our two bonus lessons where we do most of the work in Lightroom (the Before image here is really flat, and needs more detail, better color, more contrast, and sharpening), then jump over to Photoshop to do things we can't do in Lightroom (like sky replacement), and then we jump back to Lightroom to put our finishing moves on the image.

THE STORY BEHIND THE SHOT:

This is another shot from my trip out west with my buddy Erik. This was taken at Utah's Monument Valley from the back side of the Visitor's Center, where we were all set up, tripods in place, well before sunset and waiting for the light to get good on that classic scene (the one you've seen a million times, but you still have to shoot it). We had at least another hour or so before the light got really good on that side, but when I looked behind me, I saw this interesting looking scene and the light was getting kind of interesting, so I rotated my ballhead 180° and took this shot. Erik and I spent three days in that area, and never saw a cloud the entire time we were there. On the way to the airport to head home, we saw half a cloud, but that was as close as we got. Luckily, there's Photoshop, so it wasn't a bald, flat sky for long, and luckily, there's Lightroom, so it wasn't a flat, washed out, hazy, dull-looking image for long.

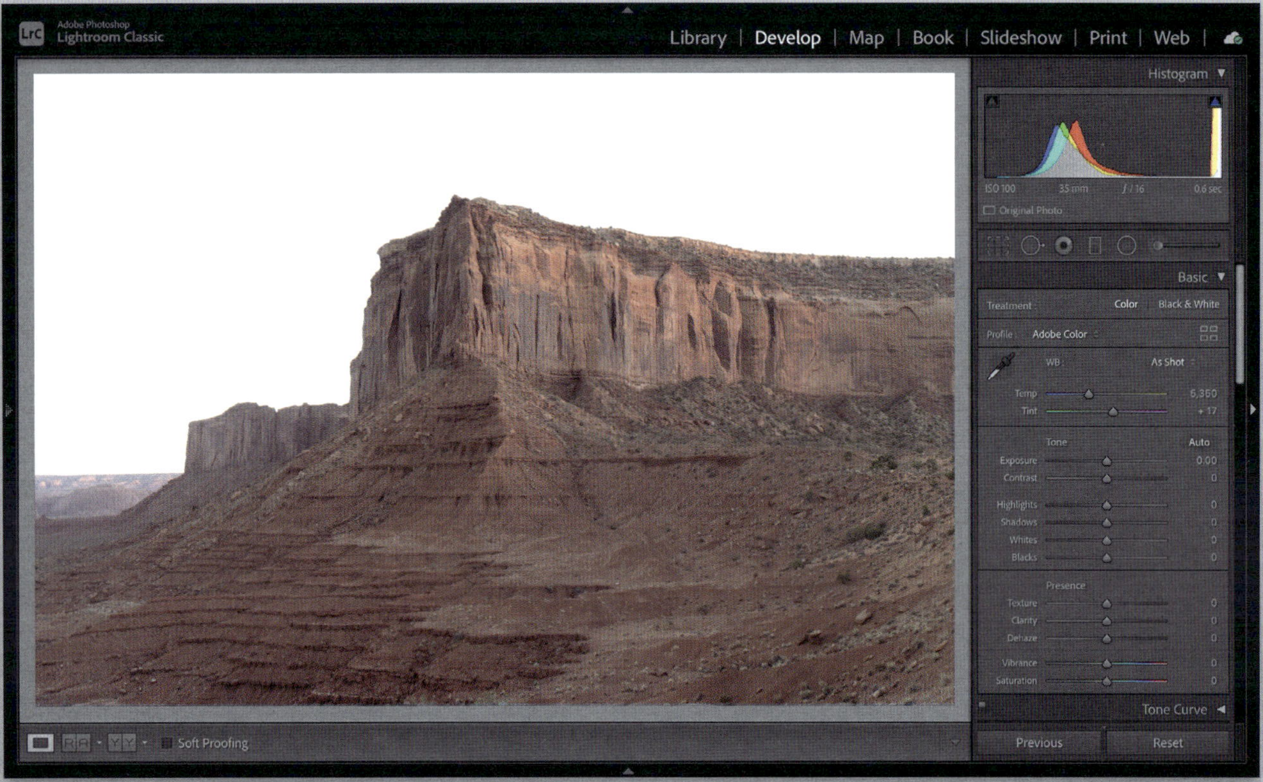

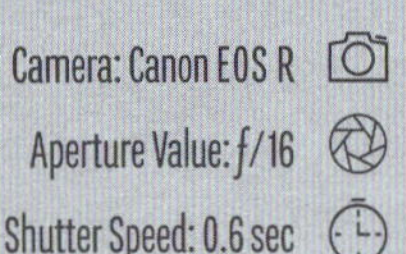

Camera: Canon EOS R
Aperture Value: ƒ/16
Shutter Speed: 0.6 sec
ISO: 100
Focal Length: 35mm

Step 01:

Here's our original RAW image of our landscape photo from Monument Valley. Let's do a quick evaluation of the photo by asking that all-important question: "What do I wish were different?" First, I wish I had turned to my left, so I'd at least actually have the classic Monument Valley shot. Besides that, the image is washed-out, flat, and hazy with a bald sky, and has boring color. In this bonus lesson, we're going to bounce over to Photoshop to do one or two critical things, and then we'll bop back over to Lightroom (and yes, "bop" is a real word).

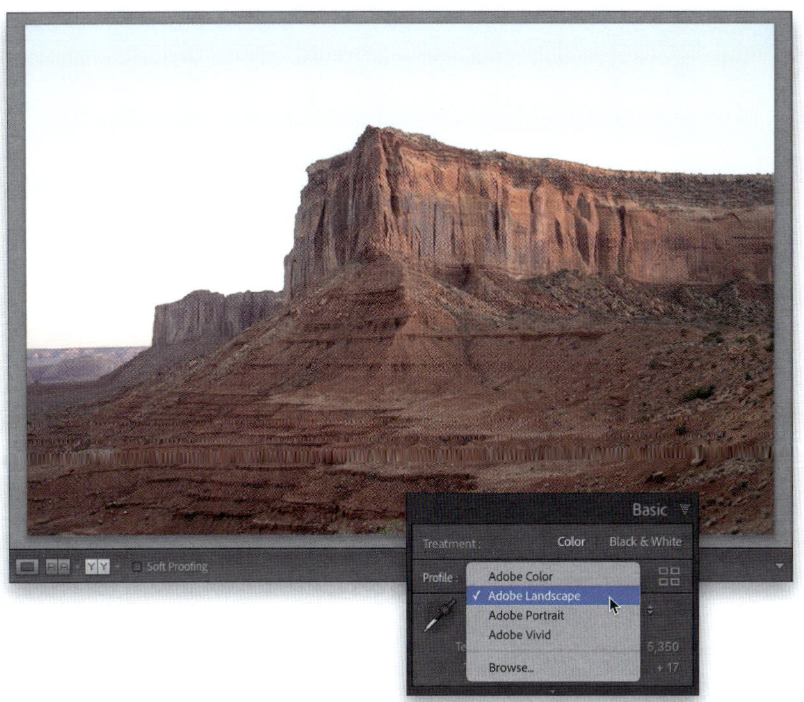

Step 02:

Let's start with the easiest decision we'll have to make with this image: in the Develop module's Basic panel (the Edit panel in Lightroom cloud), choose **Adobe Landscape** from the Profile pop-up menu **(Point 1)**. Well, that was easy. You can really see the difference in the color and contrast by making this one, fairly obvious move.

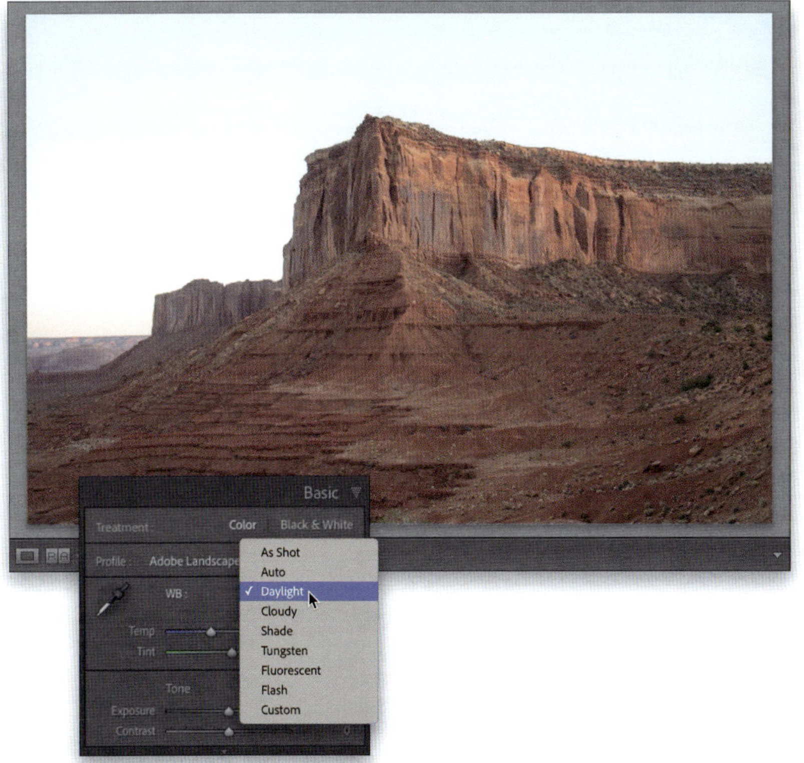

Step 03:

The As Shot white balance is pretty "meh," so let's try the WB (White Balance) preset pop-up menu to see if there's anything in there that looks good (in the Color panel in Lightroom cloud; **Point 2**). Since this was taken later in the day and the mountain is somewhat in the shade, I tried Shade as the white balance and well…give it a try and you'll see why you'll probably choose **Daylight** instead (Shade and Cloudy are both too warm).

Step 04:

Let's get our exposure looking right now **(Point 3)**. Press-and-hold the Shift key and double-click on Whites, and then on Blacks to set your white and black points. This lowered the Whites to –14 (probably because of that washed-out sky), but it deepened the Blacks, moving them to –49, and that made a big difference. Now look at the image to see if you think it needs to be brighter or darker. I think it could be a little brighter, so drag the Exposure slider to the right to +0.20 (as shown here). The exposure on the mountain looks pretty good now (we're not counting the sky in the overall exposure because we're going to address that over in Photoshop).

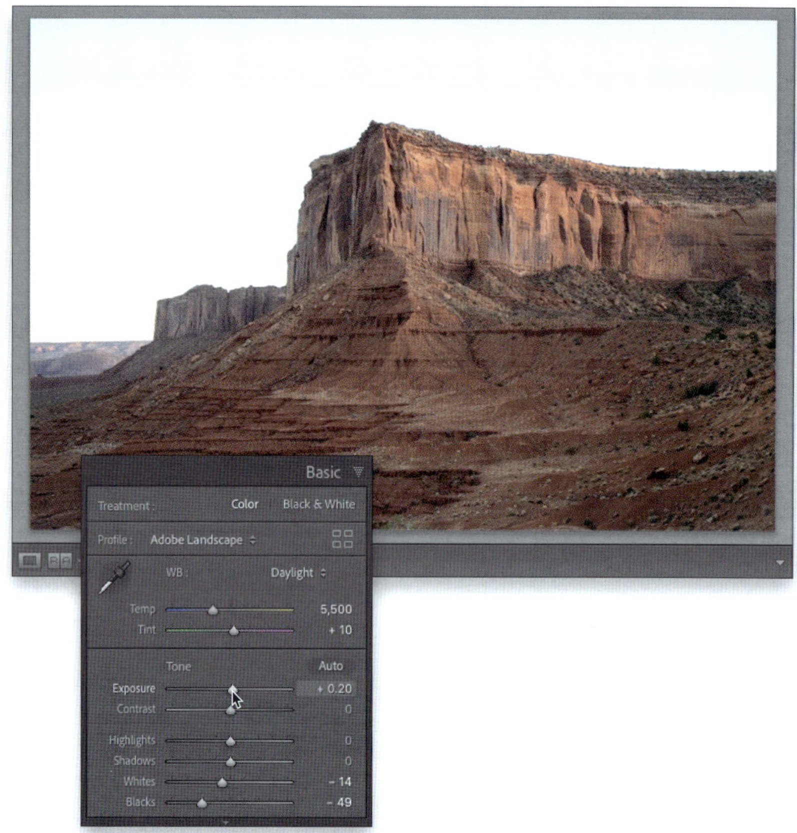

Step 05:

Next, let's get some nice contrast in here. Landscape photos generally look great with lots of contrast, and we'll add some using the Contrast slider (drag it over to +24). But, the thing that will probably have a much bigger impact is the Dehaze slider (in the Effects panel in Lightroom cloud), as you can see visible haze in the image, and this slider does a pretty good job. So, drag the Dehaze slider over to +35 (as shown here) and look at the difference! Even the sky looks better (but that's really no consequence to us right now).

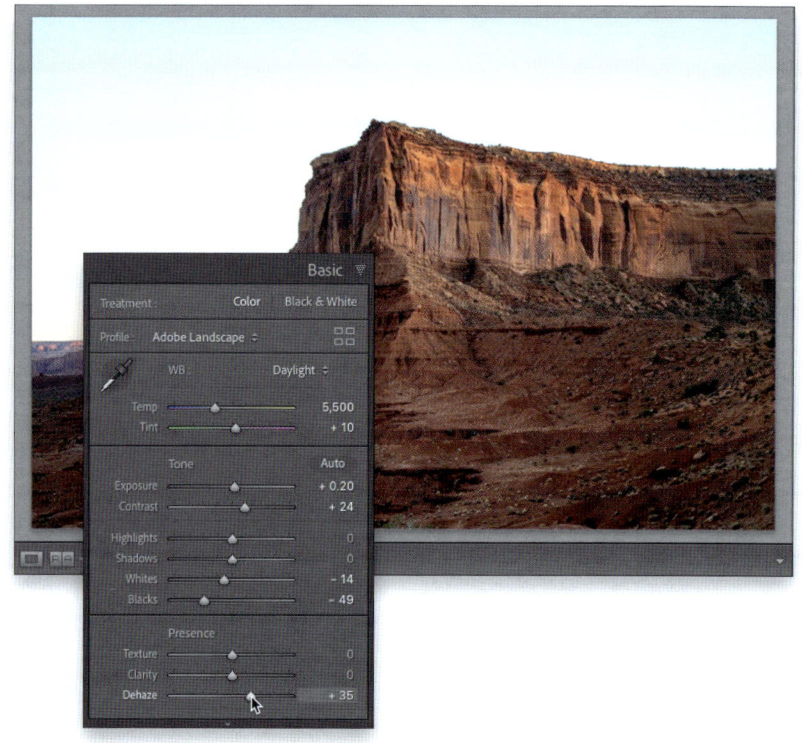

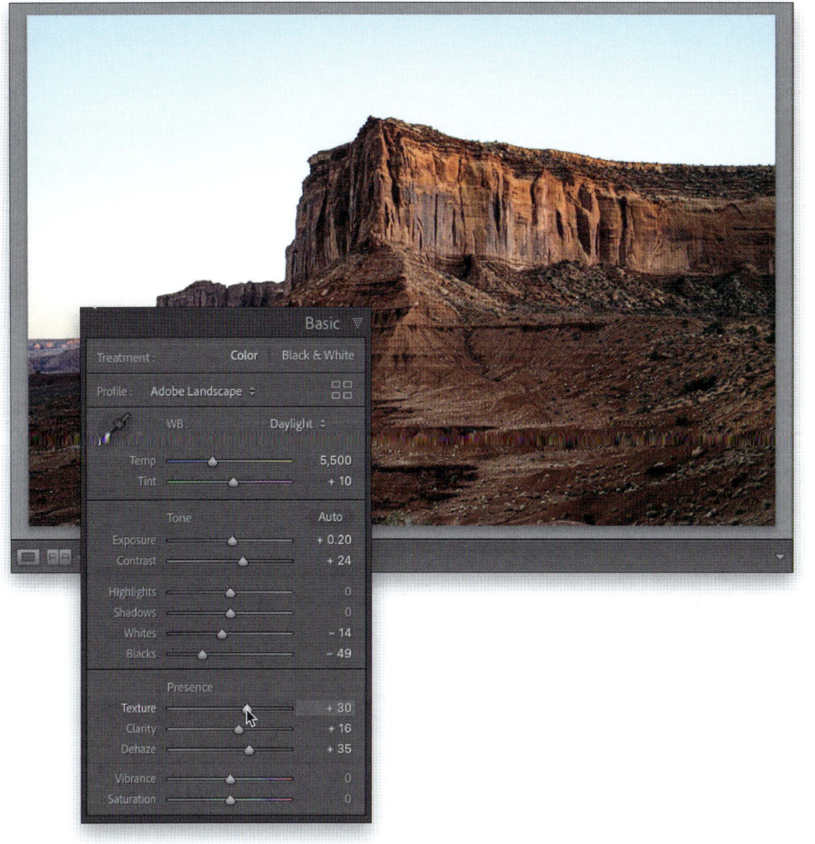

Step 06:

Okay, let's crisp up the image and bring out all that glorious mountainous detail by increasing the Texture and Clarity amounts (drag the Texture slider to +30 and the Clarity slider to +16). You could actually go a litter higher with both if you'd like—landscapes like this can take a lot of detail enhancing, so don't be afraid to push it.

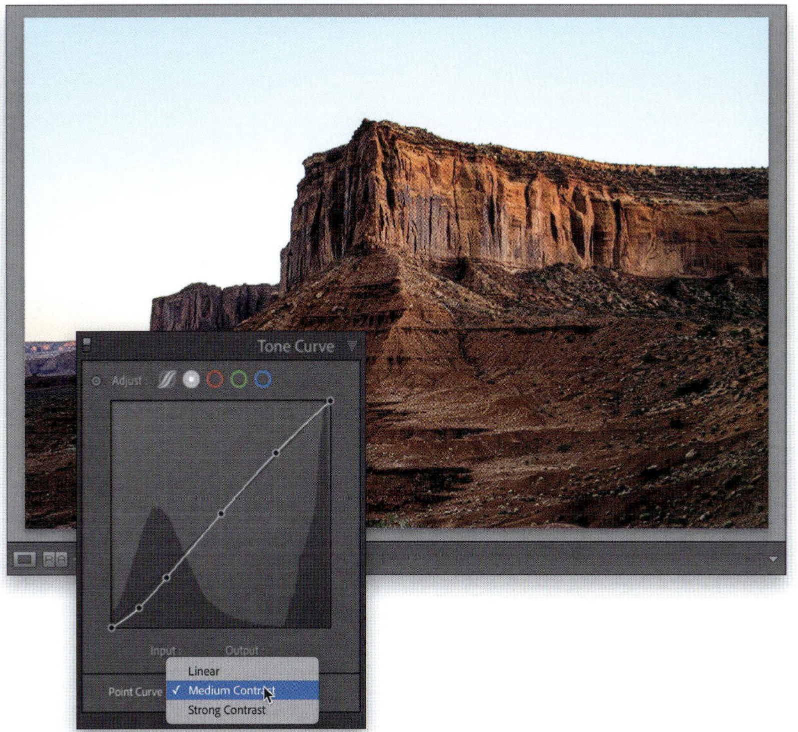

Step 07:

When you have a really detailed image like this that can take a lot of contrast, you might consider (well, I say consider, but we're doing it, right?) heading to the Tone Curve panel (which is in the Light panel in Lightroom cloud) and applying a subtle "S-curve" (it's a preset) that adds a nice kick of contrast. Right at the bottom of the panel, from the Point Curve pop-up menu, choose **Medium Contrast**, and you can see the extra level of contrast that gives us. If you wanted to open up the midtones a little (using the curve), you could click on the center point on the diagonal line (known as the curve) and drag diagonally upward and to the left a bit. Totally optional. Your call. (*Note:* The Point Curve pop-up menu is not in Lightroom cloud, so you'll have to click on the curve and create the S-curve yourself.)

Step 08:

Okay, now let's work on our lack-of-sky situation (we're skipping our usual Point 4 here, and moving on to **Point 5**). Press **Command-E** (**PC: Ctrl-E**; **Command-Shift-E [PC: Ctrl-Shift-E]** in Lightroom cloud) to take your image over to Photoshop. If you're working on a RAW image, it will just appear in Photoshop (if Photoshop isn't open, it will launch for you). If you're working on a JPEG, a dialog will pop up asking how you want it to go over to Photoshop. Choose Edit a Copy with Lightroom Adjustments, and then click Edit. That way, your original stays intact in Lightroom and you're working on a copy. Once your image is open in Photoshop, go under the Edit menu and choose **Sky Replacement** (as shown here). We're going to pop in a new sky, and then save this image. We're not going to go into the ethical aspects of whether replacing skies is the right thing to do or not. Just know that most of the big name photographers we all look up to have been doing it for years. Years. I think I'm the last photographer left on earth that has not been doing it, so… well…I'm finally on board. Even if you're not, go ahead and try this just for fun.

Step 09:

When the Sky Replacement dialog appears, click on the Sky thumbnail up top, and you'll see that it comes with a bunch of built-in Adobe skies for you to practice with, so let's take a look at what they've got. In the Sky pop-up menu is a scrolling list of skies, and all you have to do is click on one (as shown here, where I clicked on the seventh one down), and it automatically masks the image (putting the clouds behind the mountain), and it puts a light tint over the image that has the same basic color tone as the sky you chose (so if you choose one from the Sunsets folder of skies, it makes the mountains warmer). Okay, let's try a different sky.

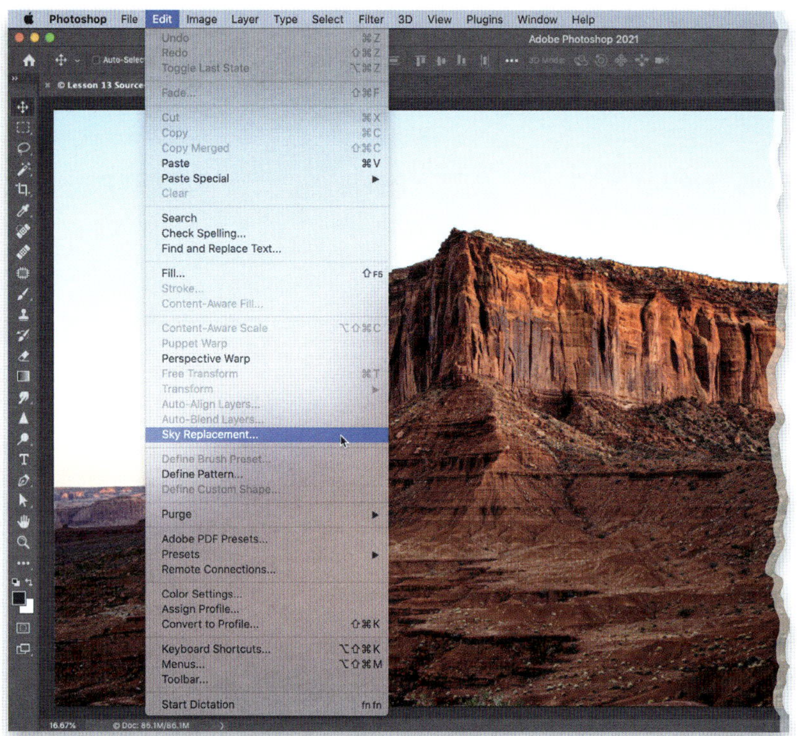

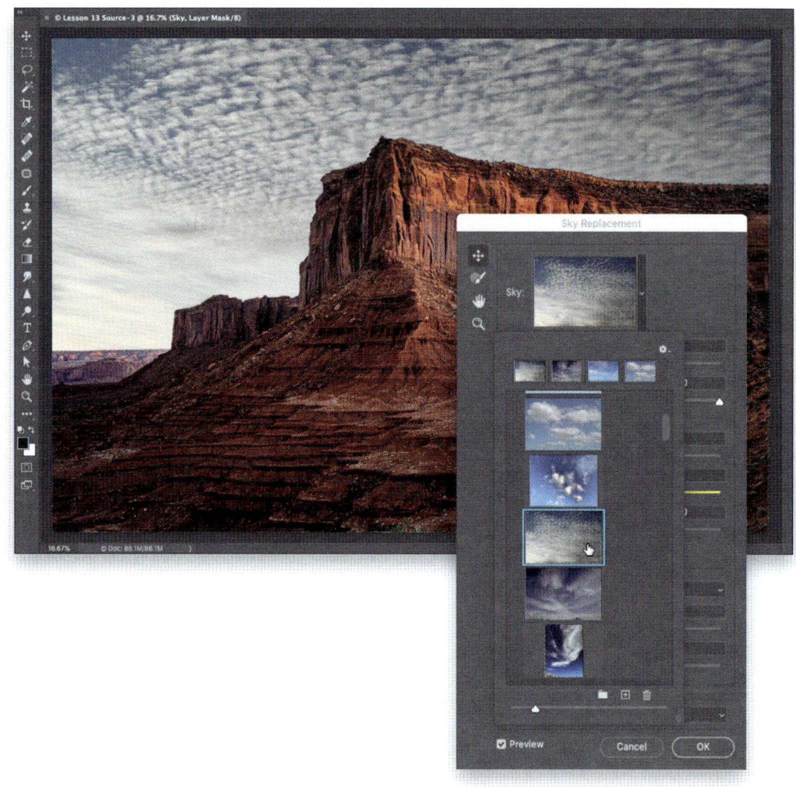

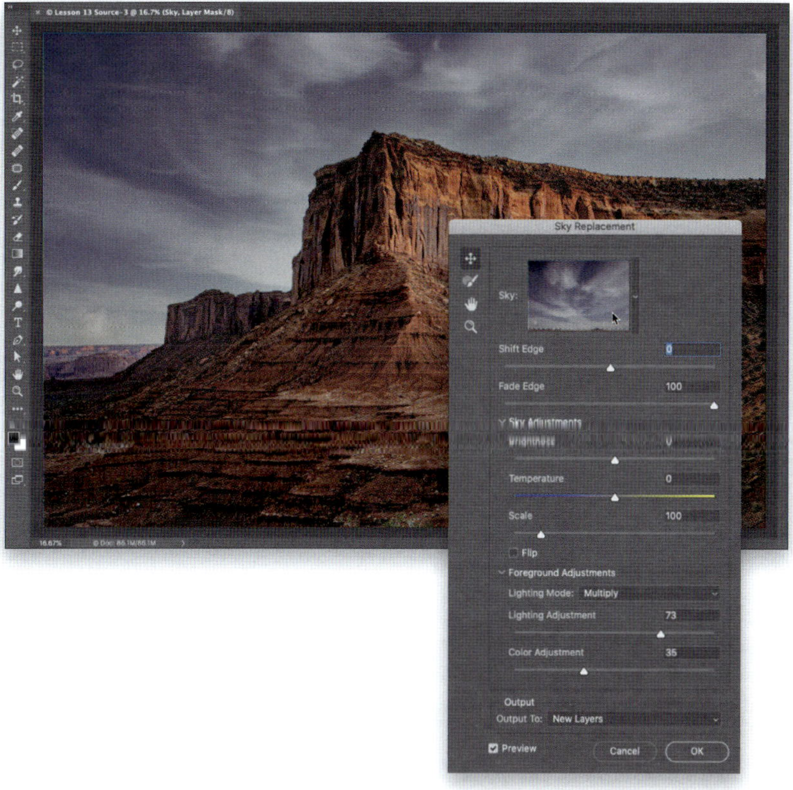

Step 10:

Scroll down and try the next one down (shown here). Okay, that looks a little better. If you want to tweak how this all looks, then click outside the pop-up menu (in some empty, gray area), it tucks away, and you can see the rest of the options. The top two, Shift Edge and Fade Edge, are more useful when you're dealing with a flat landscape and it didn't automatically mask it perfectly (however, most of the time, it does an astonishingly good job). The Sky Adjustments are for tweaking the brightness, white balance, and size of the sky image. The next section down is for tweaking the tint it automatically puts over your foreground. We actually don't have to do much to this. In fact, I rarely have to tweak these settings at all. So, at this point, let's click OK and move on. One last important thing, though: don't actually use Adobe's skies in your work other than for practice. Since millions of other Photoshop users have those same built-in skies, you'll get called out for it on social media if you post a photo with a Photoshop built-in sky. Shooting your own skies is easy. Aim up.

Step 11:

While we're over here in Photoshop, it has a super-sharpening technique we can employ that would look great here. Head over to the Layers panel on the right, and start by pressing **Command-Shift-E (PC: Ctrl-Shift-E)** to merge the four layers you see there into a single Background layer. Now, press **Command-J (PC: Ctrl-J)** to make a duplicate of the Background layer, then go under the Filter menu up top, under Other, and choose **High Pass**. We're going to use this filter to sharpen our image. Your image (on this duplicate layer) will turn nearly solid gray (as seen here). Drag the Radius slider all the way to the left, and then slowly drag it to the right until you see lots of well-defined edges (here, I dragged over to 4.2 pixels), and then click OK. We're now only one minor step away from achieving super-mega-sharpening.

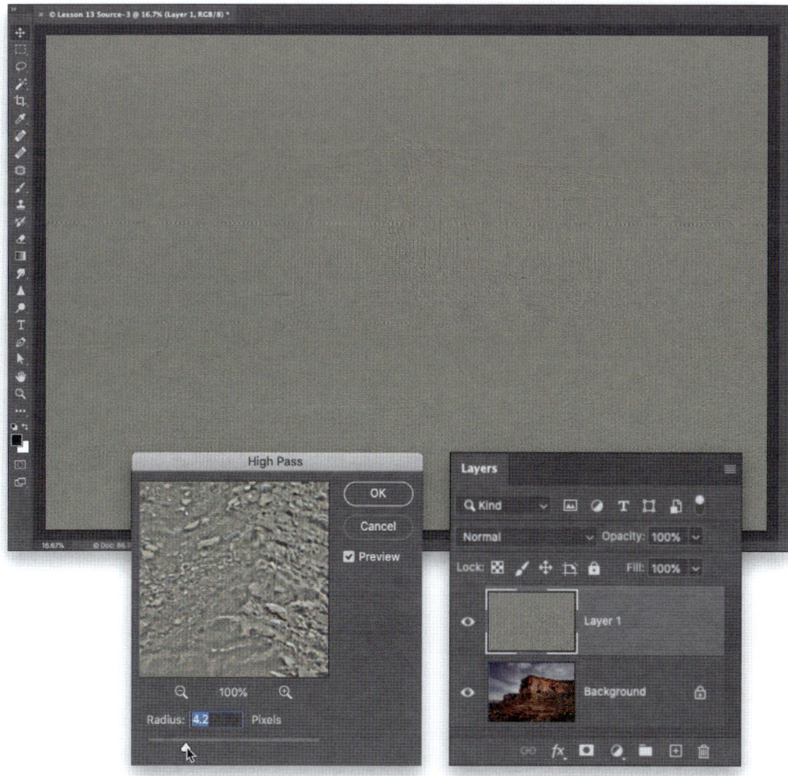

Step 12:

At the top of the Layers panel, you'll see the word "Normal." Click-and-hold on it and a pop-up menu appears with different blend modes (seen here). For super-mega-sharpening, scroll down and choose **Hard Light**. If that seems like too much sharpening, then try Soft Light. If even Soft Light seems like too much (which I doubt, but hey, it could happen), you can lower the amount of sharpening by lowering the Opacity of this layer. Where it says "Opacity: 100%," just click on the downward-facing arrow to the right, and a slider appears, which you can drag to the left to lower the Opacity of this layer. This lowers the strength of the sharpening. In this case, let's leave it set to Hard Light at 100%. Man, that's some mega-sharpening. By the way, if we do our sharpening here in Photoshop, we don't need to resharpen again in Lightroom. Besides, this image is already so sharp we could cut diamonds with it.

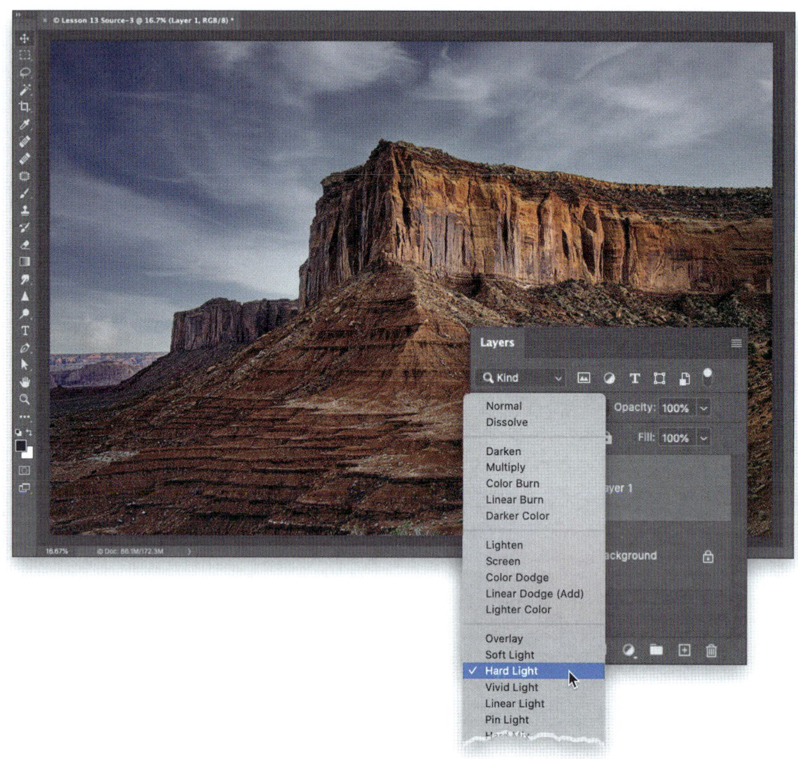

Step 13:

Okay, now that we've added our sky, and sharpened this image to death, how do we get this image back into Lightroom? Simply save and close it. Press **Command-S (PC: Ctrl-S)** to Save the file, and then close it (click on the little close button on the window), and when you go back to Lightroom, you'll see this new Photoshop-edited copy (a PSD file) right there in Lightroom (as seen here), right next to the original. So, that's the "roundtrip" between Lightroom and Photoshop. You hit Command-E (PC: Ctrl-E) to get your image from Lightroom over to Photoshop. Then, you make any changes you want to it in Photoshop, and simply save and close it, and your image bops right back over to Lightroom. These two programs were designed to work like this from the very start. Since we don't have any lens issues to fix (Point 6), let's finish this one off.

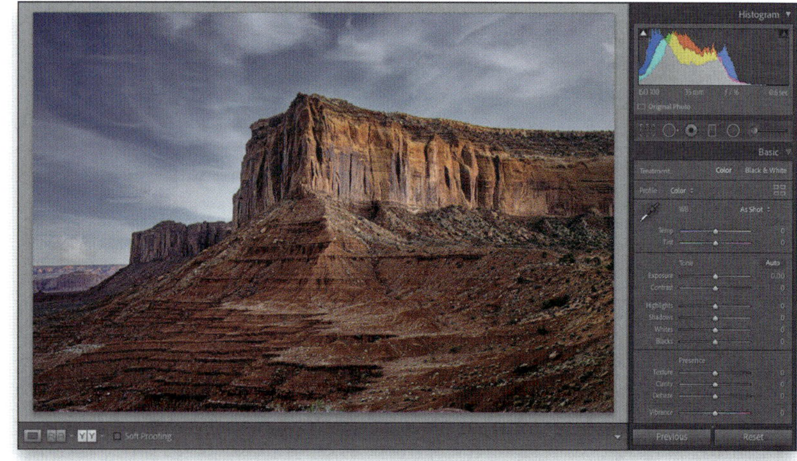

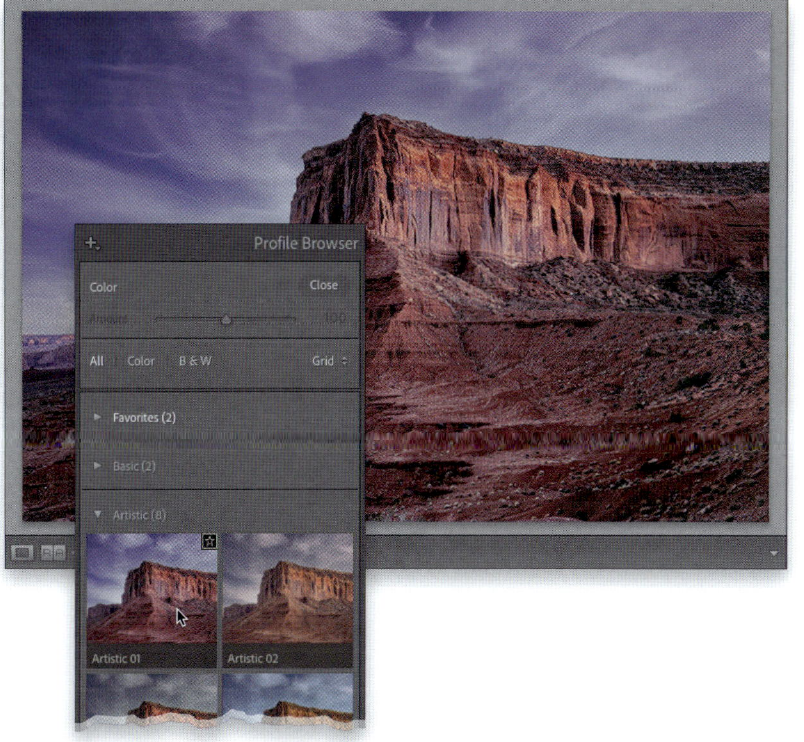

Step 14:

As a finishing move **(Point 7)**, we can apply a creative profile. These are different than the RAW profiles in that they actually add a "look" to our image that changes the tone, contrast, and color, all with just one click. A bunch of them come with Lightroom and they live in the Profile Browser. To get to this browser, go to the top of the Basic panel (the Edit panel in Lightroom cloud), and to the far right of Profile, you'll see an icon with four little squares. Click on that to bring up the Profile Browser (seen here), which has a scrolling list of profiles, with the RAW profiles up at the top. There are four sets of profiles that come with Lightroom: Artistic (some of which are seen here) has eight creative profiles, the B&W (black-and-white) set has 17, the Modern set has 10, and the Vintage set has 10 (and you can add other profiles that you download from the Internet). As you move your cursor over one of the profile thumbnails in the browser, you'll see an instant onscreen preview. Go ahead and hover over that first one in the Artistic set, Artistic 01, and you'll see how your image would look if you went ahead and clicked on it to choose it. Okay, not my first choice, but at least you can see how they work.

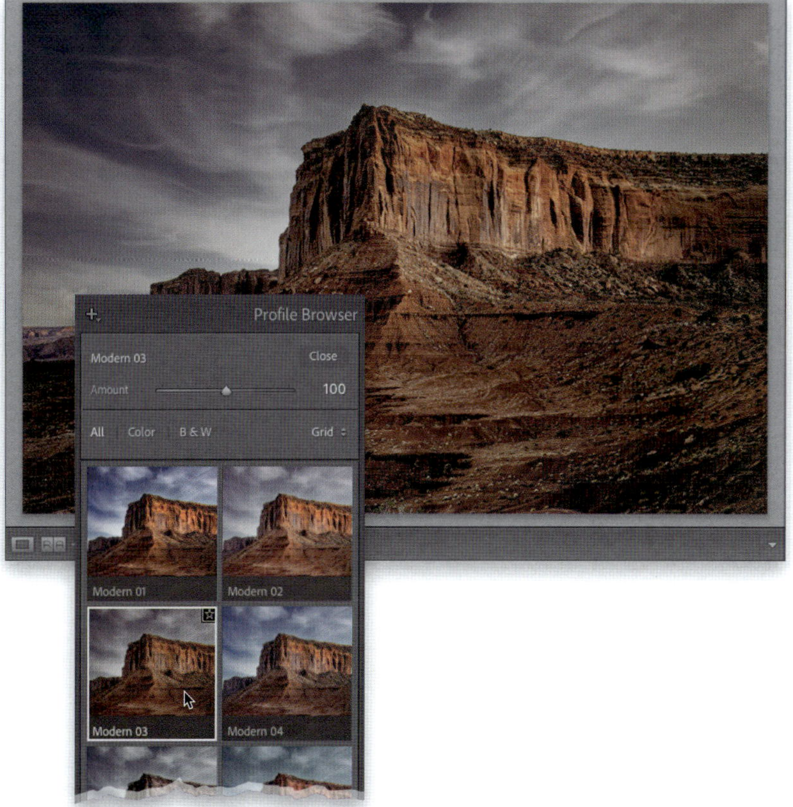

Step 15:

Keep scrolling down in the Profile Browser until you get to the Modern set and try out some of these. Here's what Modern 03 looks like. It reminds me of a Bleached Bypass look with that desaturated sky and overall tone. Again, you just have to hover your cursor over a thumbnail to see a preview. But, it's also nice that the thumbnails displayed are of the image you're working on, so you can already see a mini-preview of how the effect looks on your image without even having to hover over it.

Step 16:

Keep scrolling on down to the Vintage set and try out a few of those. Don't let the name "Vintage" fool you—it's just another collection of looks, so go by what it looks like, not by what it's called. Here, is Vintage 01, which looks pretty good. In fact, let's go with this one, so click on it to select it. Now that you've done that, look at the top of the Profile Browser and you'll see an Amount slider (in Lightroom cloud, you'll see this slider beneath the selected profile's thumbnail). This lets you add more or less of the effect that you see onscreen, so if you like a look but think the effect is too intense, drag the Amount slider to the left, or if you want it more intense, drag it to the right (here, I dragged the Amount slider over to 145, just as an example. I think that's a bit much, so I'll back off to 100, the default, so the image you see in Step 17 is just the default setting, not the bump to 145, which is seen here). When you're done, click the Close button in the top right of the panel (click on Back in the top left of the panel in Lightroom cloud).

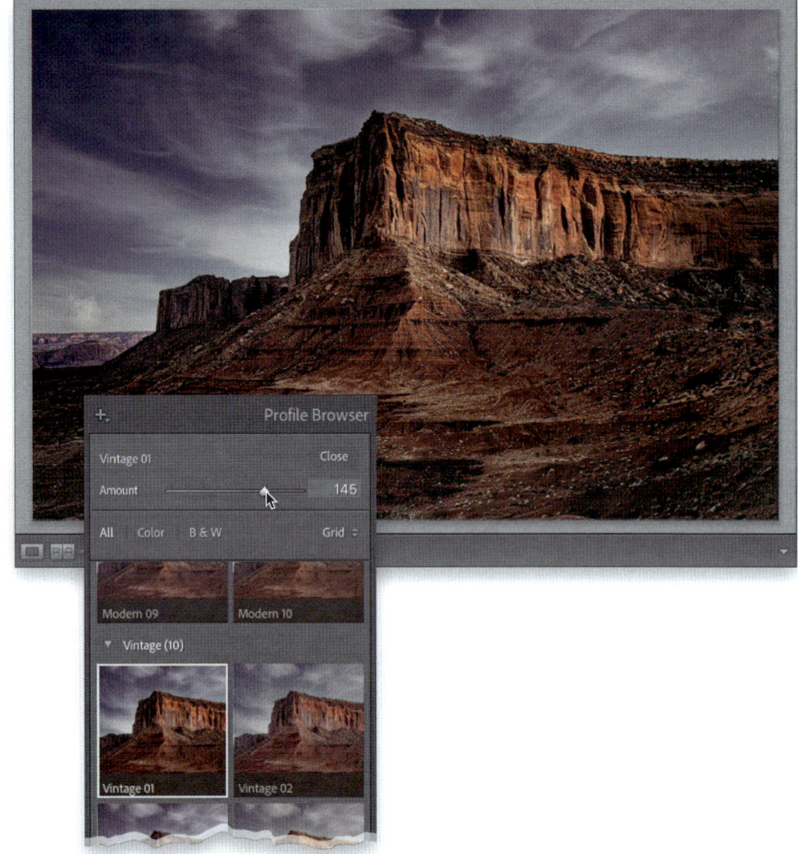

Step 17:

This is the point where we usually add a subtle edge darkening, but I'm not sure this one needs it. Just for the heck of it I went and applied it by going to the Effects panel and dragging the Amount slider over to –11 (as seen here). But, again, I don't think this particular image looks better with it. I'm showing it here just as an example, but in the final image (shown on the next page), I took the Post-Crop Vignetting Amount back down to zero, and that wraps this one up. *TIP:* You've seen me do this throughout the book, but if you look at the image at this ending stage and you think the colors are a bit too punchy, go to the Basic panel (the Color panel in Lightroom cloud) and drag the Vibrance slider to the left a bit until the colors look more natural. This isn't a "must do," but it is an option.

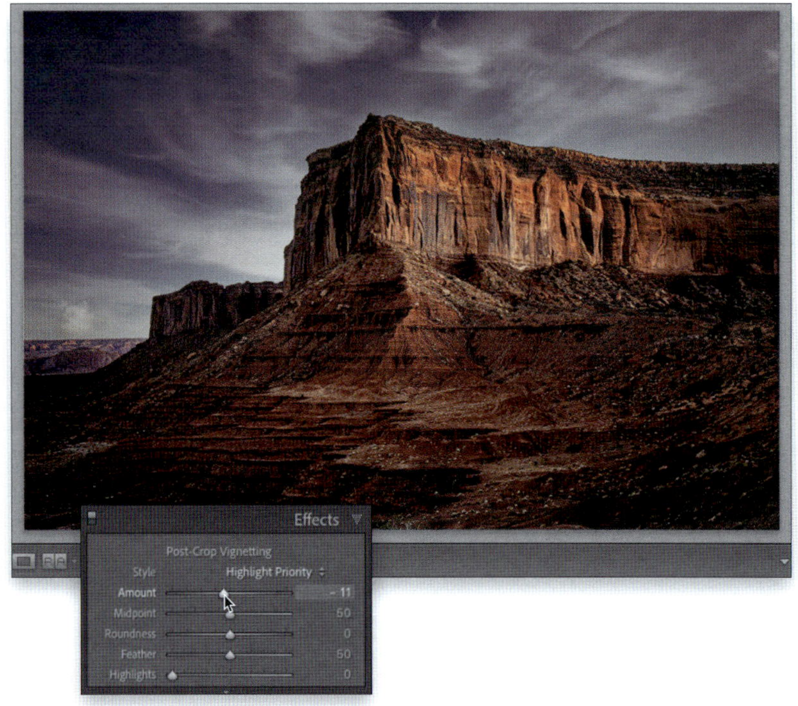

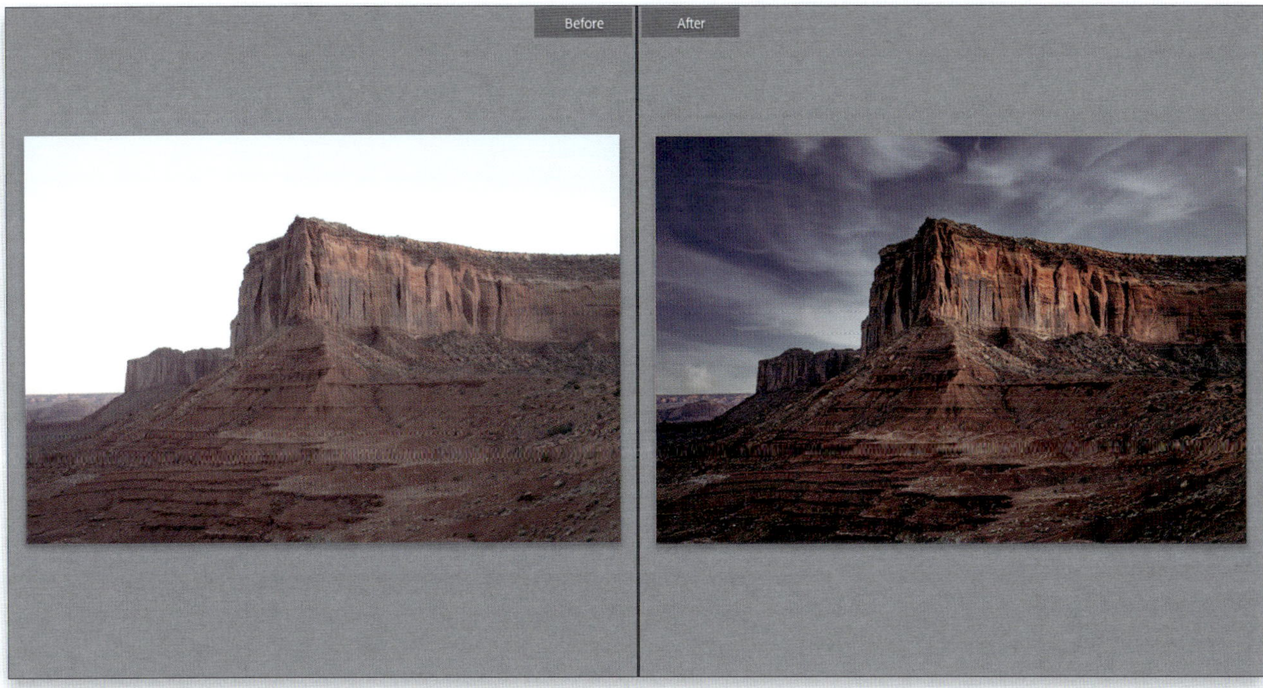

Here's our before/after.

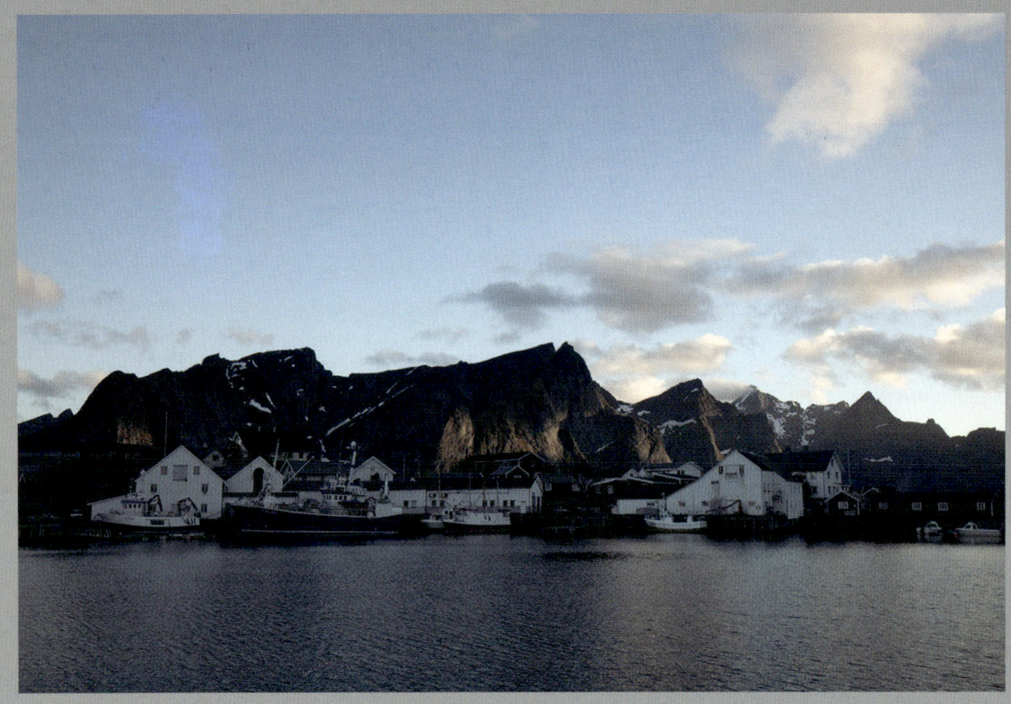

Before

After

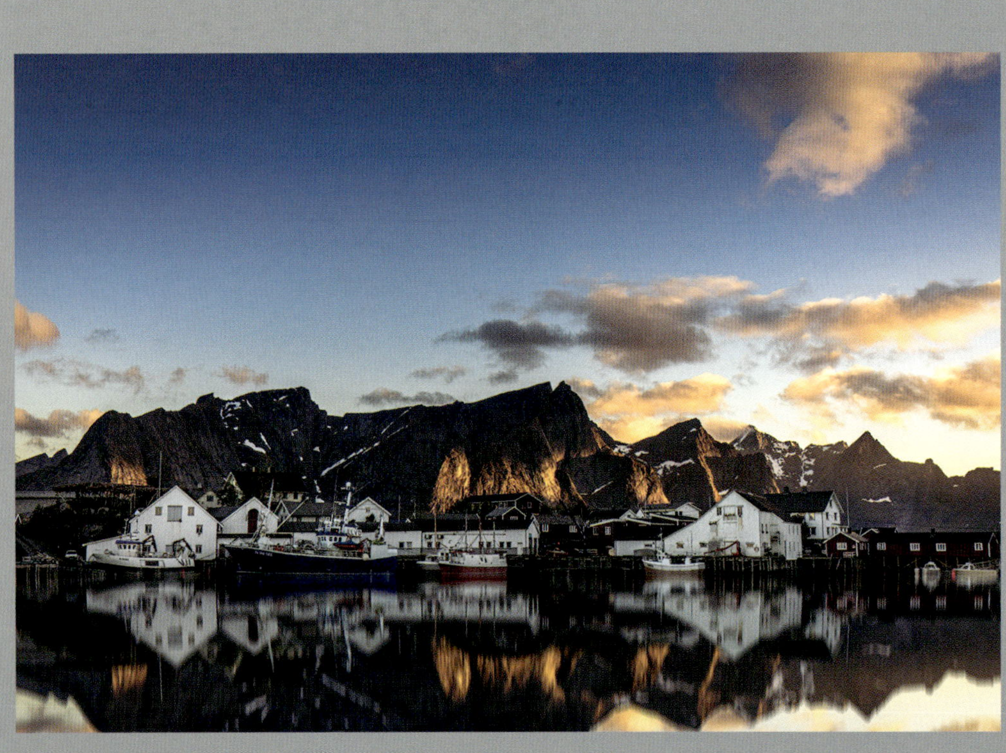

   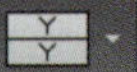 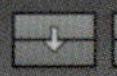 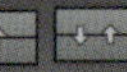  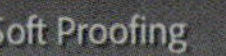

TRAVEL PHOTOSHOP MAGIC

1. Assigning a RAW Profile
2. Getting the Color Right
3. Expanding the Tonal Range
4. Dealing with Sensor Limitations
5. Painting with Light and Retouching
6. Fixing Lens Issues
7. Finishing Moves

Let's evaluate the shot. Well, it has potential, but it has lots of problems, too, starting with the fact that the sun is setting behind the mountains, so they're backlit. The sky could be good, but it's too bright, and the water does not look awesome—kind of choppy and not reflective enough. Since this is a bonus lesson, where you'll jump over to Photoshop, we can make this image look good pretty quickly and easily. We'll do almost all the work in Lightroom, but the thing we'll do in Photoshop has a big effect.

THE STORY BEHIND THE SHOT:

This shot was taken in the Lofoten Islands of Norway, on a summer trip with the family. The awesome thing about being that far up north in Norway during the summer is that the sun never really sets at night. It gets really low in the sky, but then it comes right back up again, so you have a really, really long "magic hour" with great light—it literally lasts for hours! We had gone to one of the most Instagrammed scenes in Norway (so you know I had to shoot that), and as we were leaving, right around the corner from the famous "fishing village on the rocks scene" was this scene, so we pulled over so I could grab a few quick shots.

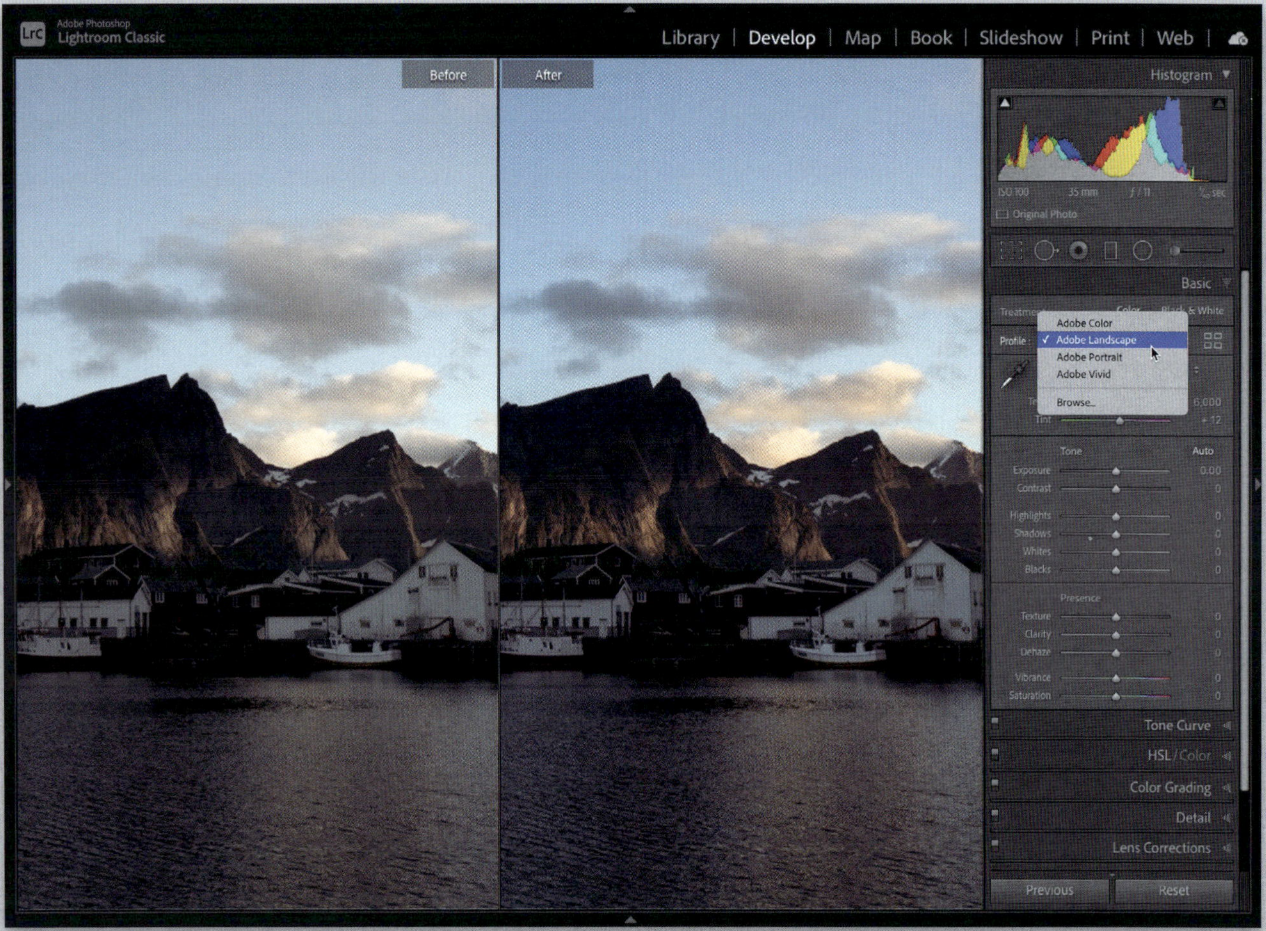

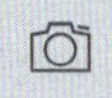

Camera: Canon EOS 5D Mark IV

Aperture Value: ƒ/11

Shutter Speed: 1/40 sec

ISO: 100

Focal Length: 35mm

Step 01:

Let's start off by assigning a RAW profile **(Point 1)**. Go ahead and try out all of them, but my guess is you'll want to go with **Adobe Landscape** (choose it from the Profile pop-up menu)—you can see the difference it makes, especially in the sky and the water (as seen here). By the way, if you open an image and you see Adobe Standard as the profile (instead of Adobe Color, like usual), that just means you probably took the photo a while ago (before Adobe introduced the current default, Adobe Color RAW profile), and at some point, you opened it, so it was assigned that old profile (it was the default profile for 11 or 12 years). But, when you open a new photo, these new photos will automatically be assigned the Adobe Color profile. So, if you see that Adobe Standard profile, just know it's using the old math, with less sharpening and less contrast. I used to joke that Adobe Standard was mis-named. It should have been named the more accurate "Adobe Dull."

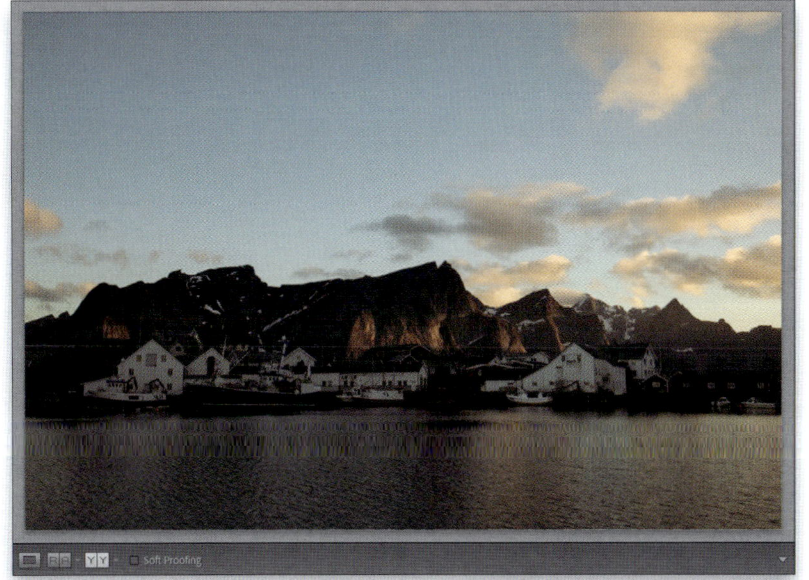

Step 02:

Next, let's get our color where we want it **(Point 2)**. In this case, let's run through the pop-up menu of White Balance presets to see if any of them look good. (*Note:* If you shot in JPEG, you won't have all these choices in the menu—just Auto.) Auto actually doesn't look bad, but if you go down to Shade, you'll probably like what it's doing to the light hitting the sides of the mountains, giving it more of a late-in-the-day-toward-sunset look, like you see here. That's probably the best of the presets, but I'll bet we can do better.

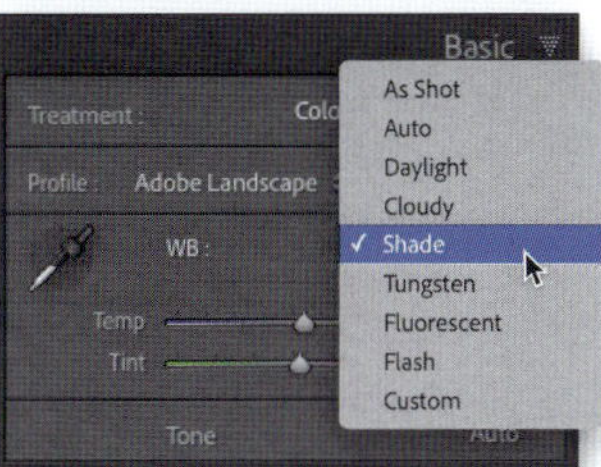

Step 03:

Let's see if we can get something better by using the White Balance Selector tool. Remember, we're looking for something that's a neutral color (like a light gray or a beige or tan). In this image, let's try that house over on the far left. Yes, it's a white house, but in that full shade, it's far from white—it's more of a light gray, so it should work just fine. Get the White Balance Selector tool **(W)** and click it once on the house (as shown here), and now we have a pretty decent white balance, with a nice color on the mountains and in the clouds, and at least a decent color in the sky (but, we'll have an opportunity to make that look better in just a minute). Click the Done button when you're finished (or just click the tool back in its circle in the panel).

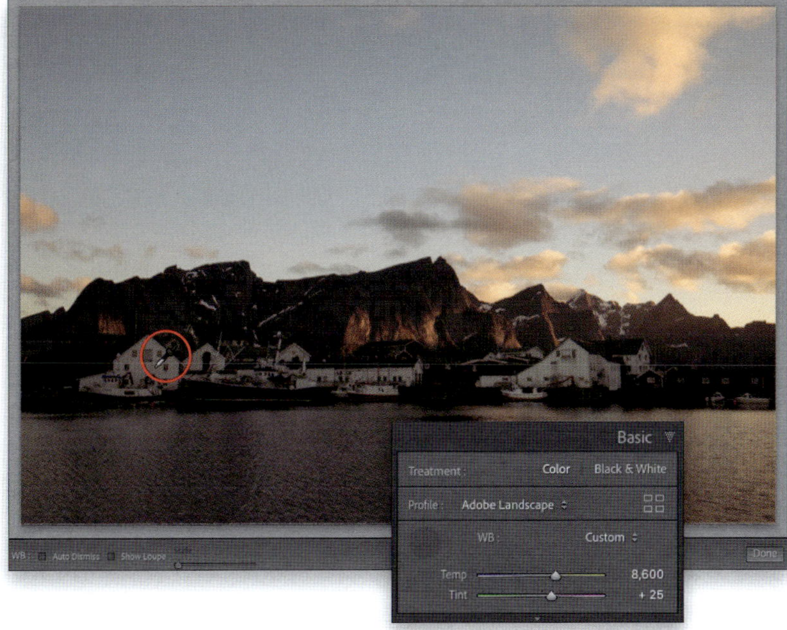

Step 04:

Let's work on our overall exposure next **(Point 3)**, starting with setting our white and black points. Press-and-hold the Shift key and double-click on Whites, and then on Blacks. That bumped up the Whites to +51 and set the Blacks to +16 (making them lighter). That helped make the image a lot brighter, but so things don't get too out of hand, let's darken the overall exposure by dragging the Exposure slider to about –0.35.

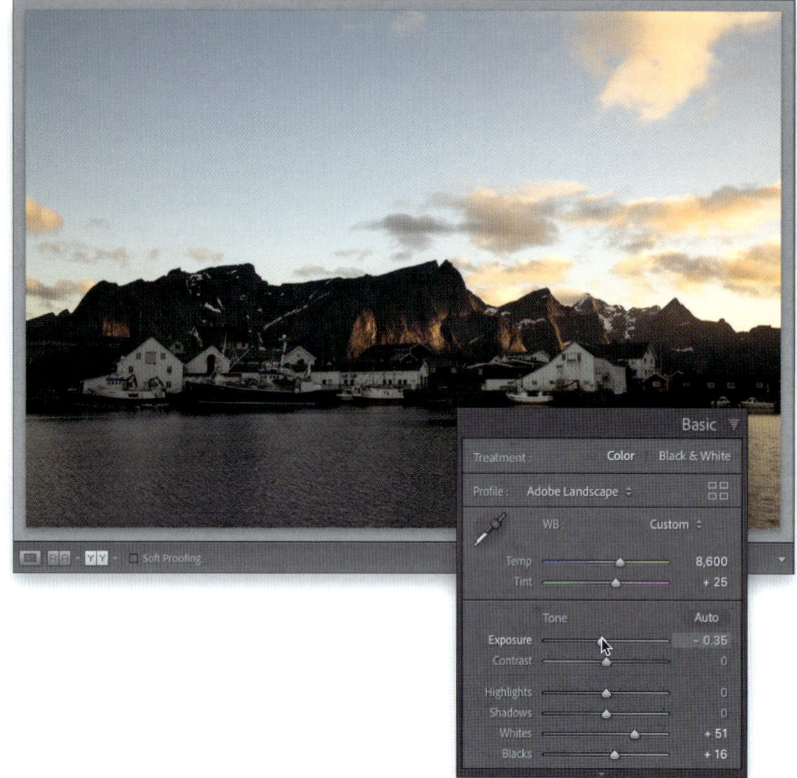

Step 05:

Next, let's fix our backlit problem, and help out our sky a bit **(Point 4)**. Start by dragging the Shadows slider over to the right to bring the mountains, boats, and houses out of the shadows. Drag it over to around +76. That's going to open up those areas nicely, but opening up those shadows this much is probably also going to make it look a bit flat, so we'll have to add some contrast in a minute. Now, let's pull back those highlights (as shown here, where I'm dragging the Highlights slider to –98), and that will help bring some definition back to the clouds and "blue up" that sky a little at the same time.

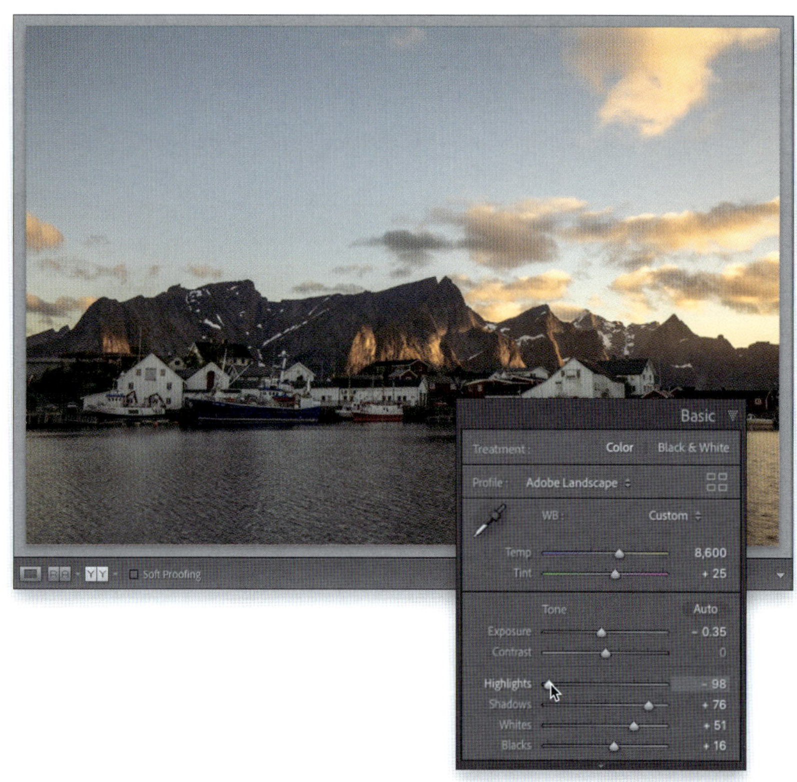

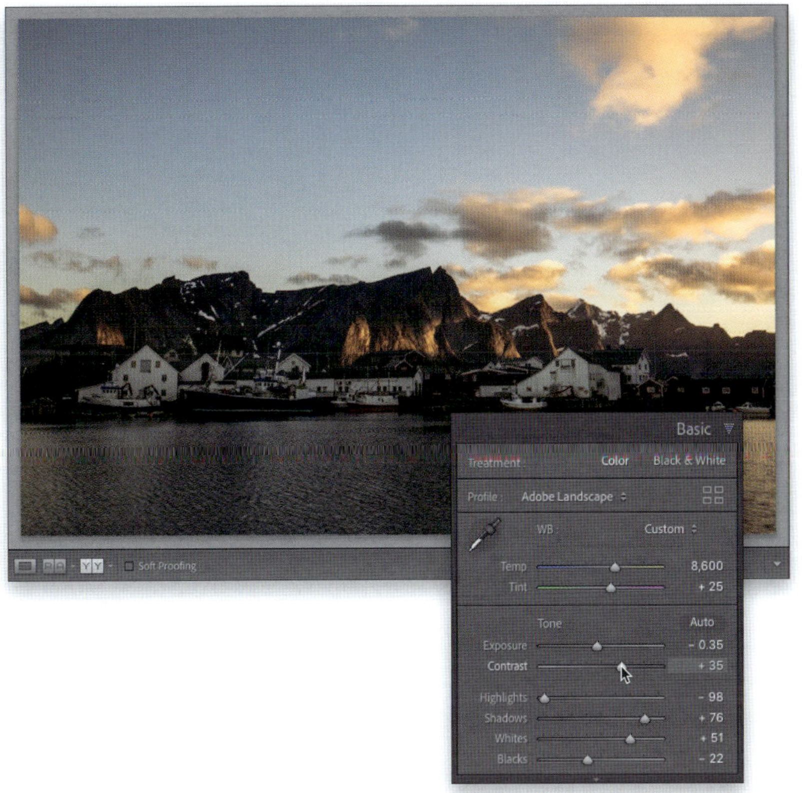

Step 06:

Now, let's bring some of that contrast back and we'll start by fixing those blacks. I know that when we set our white and black points it opened up the blacks, but it's making things look washed out, so let's pull them back the other way (darkening them, which adds contrast) by dragging the Blacks slider to around –22. Not a terribly big move, but when we add what we're going to do with the Contrast slider (cranking it up to +35, as shown here), it helps. Okay, this is looking a lot better, but of course, when you make darker areas darker, you wind up with the mountains and houses and boats being a little darker than we'd like. Of course, we can fix that, so for now, let's get that nice snappy contrast back.

Step 07:

Let's now get that shine, more detail, and more contrast (midtone contrast, in particular) by increasing the Texture and the Clarity amounts. Drag the Texture slider to the right, over to around +27, and the Clarity slider to around +17 to add that snap it needs (these sliders are in the Effects panel in Lightroom cloud).

Step 08:

Next, let's work on that sky **(Point 5)**, adding the Lightroom equivalent of a neutral density gradient filter (an ND filter) by using the Graduated Filter tool (**M**; the Linear Gradient tool **[L]** in Lightroom cloud). Get the tool and double-click on Effect to reset all the sliders to zero. Drag the Exposure slider to the left to darken the sky by 1 full stop (so, drag it to around –1.00), and then start at the top center of the image and drag straight downward, stopping near the tops of the houses (as shown here). This darkens the sky at the top, but it doesn't do much for the color (we'll fix that in the next step).

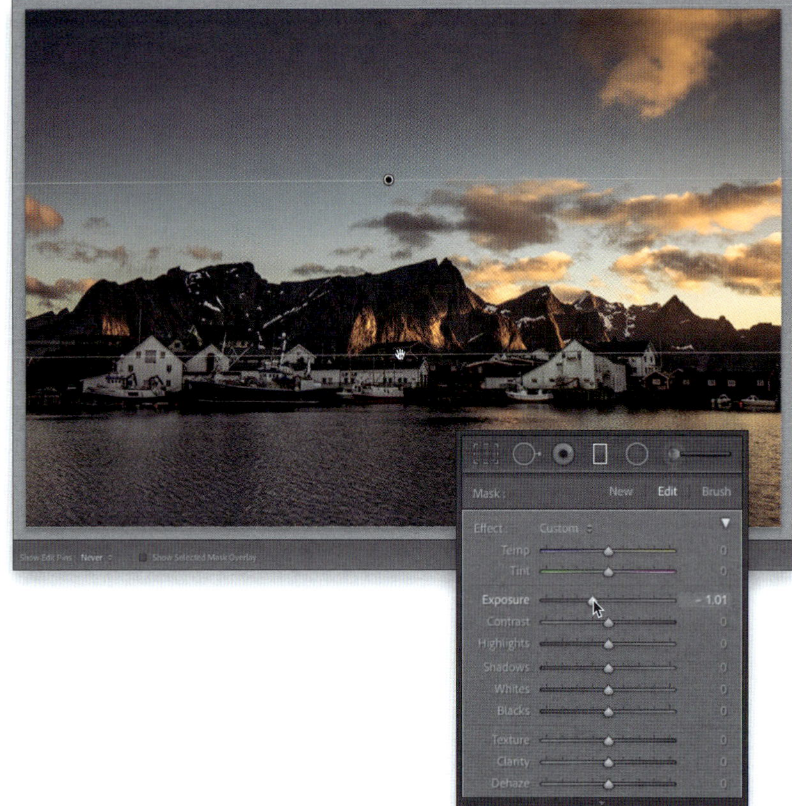

Step 09:

While we still have that gradient active, we can add some blue into the sky by dragging the Temp slider to the left to –30, and look at what the gradient did for the sky—darkening the top of it in Step 08, and then kicking in that nice blue here in this step. Okay, that's looking pretty good, but we still have work to do. Click the Done button when you're finished.

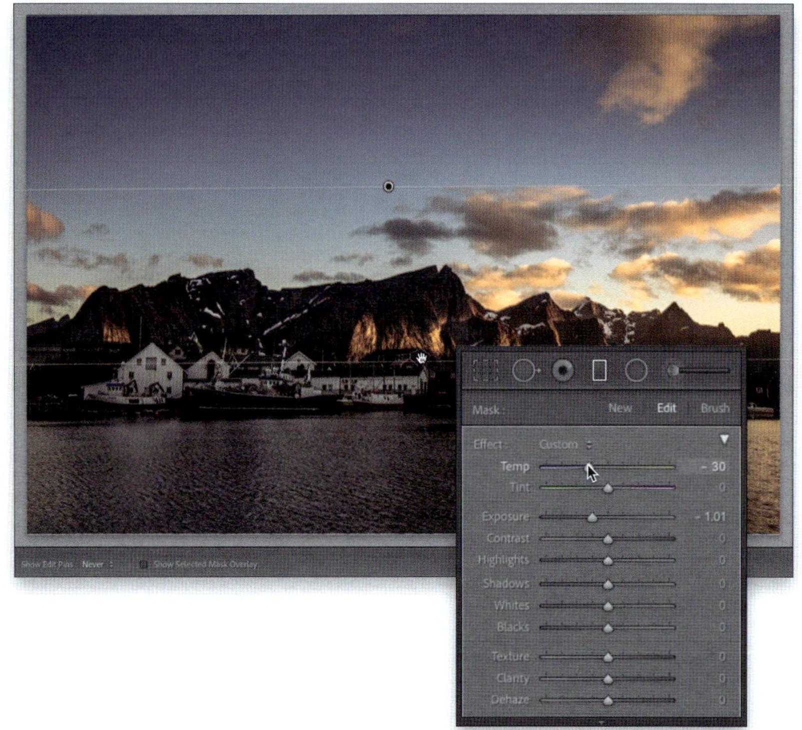

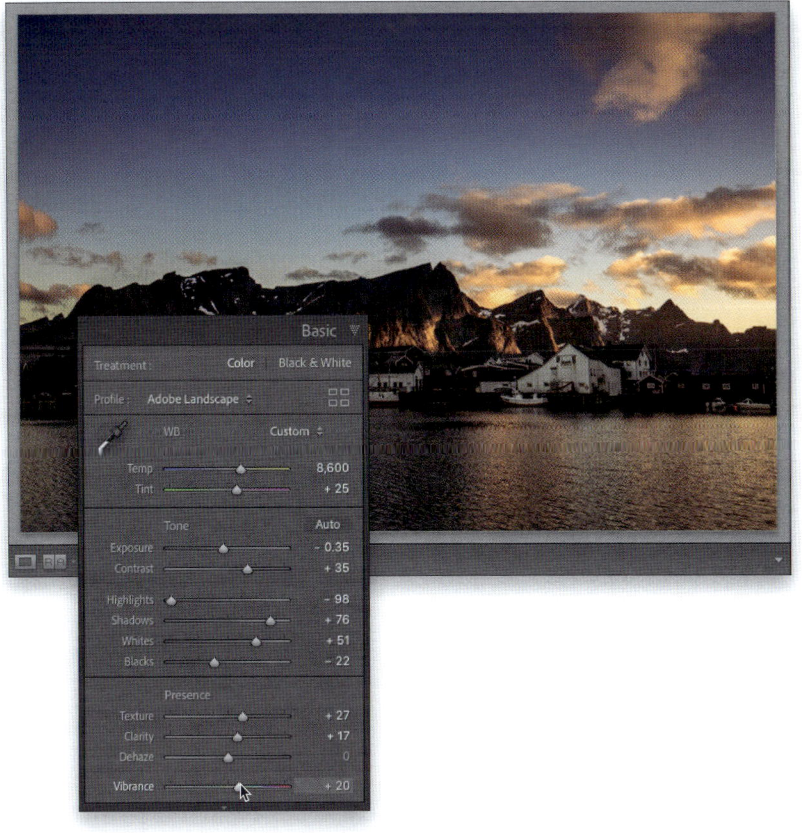

Step 10:

Let's goose the color just a bit. Head back to the Basic panel (the Color panel in Lightroom cloud) and drag the Vibrance slider over to +20 to give that color a little boost. By the way, the reason we use the Vibrance slider in the Basic panel, rather than the Saturation slider, is that Vibrance is kind of like "Smart Saturation"—it has some crazy math going on behind the scenes. When you increase the regular Saturation amount, it makes all the colors in your image more colorful and because of that, it's easy to go too far and make your colors look funky. Vibrance, on the other hand, is smart in that if it sees a dull color, it boosts it a lot; if it sees a color that's already vibrant, it only boosts that color a tiny bit. It also has a special mathematical algorithm that avoids boosting skin tones, which is great if you have people in the shot (they don't wind up looking sunburned). That's why our go-to is Vibrance (however, Vibrance isn't available for the Adjustment Brush. Just Saturation. Boo!).

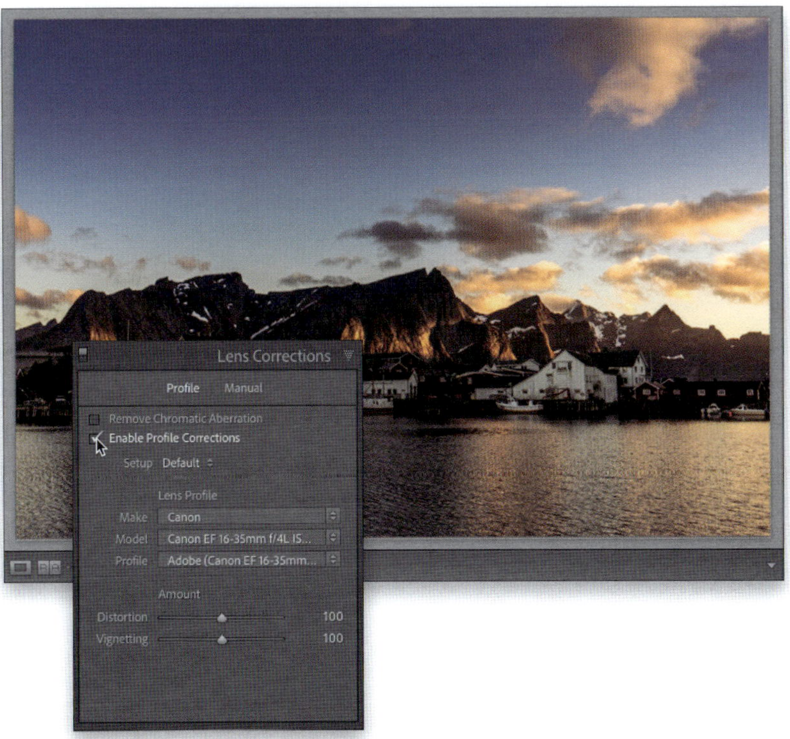

Step 11:

Next, let's do a "2-for-1" and get rid of the lens distortion issue (you'll see it once you go and remove it), and the dark vignetting in the corners of the image **(Point 6)**. Just head to the Lens Corrections panel (the Optics panel in Lightroom cloud) and turn on the Enable Profile (Lens) Corrections checkbox (as shown here). That's all you have to do and Lightroom will take care of both issues for you. Just that one click works wonders.

Step 12:

Now, let's jump over to Photoshop to do a little "Photoshop Magic." We're just going to do one thing there, but it's a good one. Press **Command-E** (**PC: Ctrl-E**; **Command-Shift-E [PC: Ctrl-Shift-E]** in Lightroom cloud) and if you're working on a RAW image, Photoshop will launch (if it's not already open), and your image will just appear there. If you're working on a JPEG or TIFF, then you'll get a dialog (shown here) asking if you want to "Edit a Copy with Lightroom Adjustments." That's the one you want (the top choice), so click that (again, you'll only see this if you're working on a JPEG or TIFF). The other choices—Edit a Copy (without any of the changes you've made in Lightroom) or Edit Original—are (do I even have to say it?) bad choices. Just go with the top choice—Edit a Copy with Lightroom Adjustments.

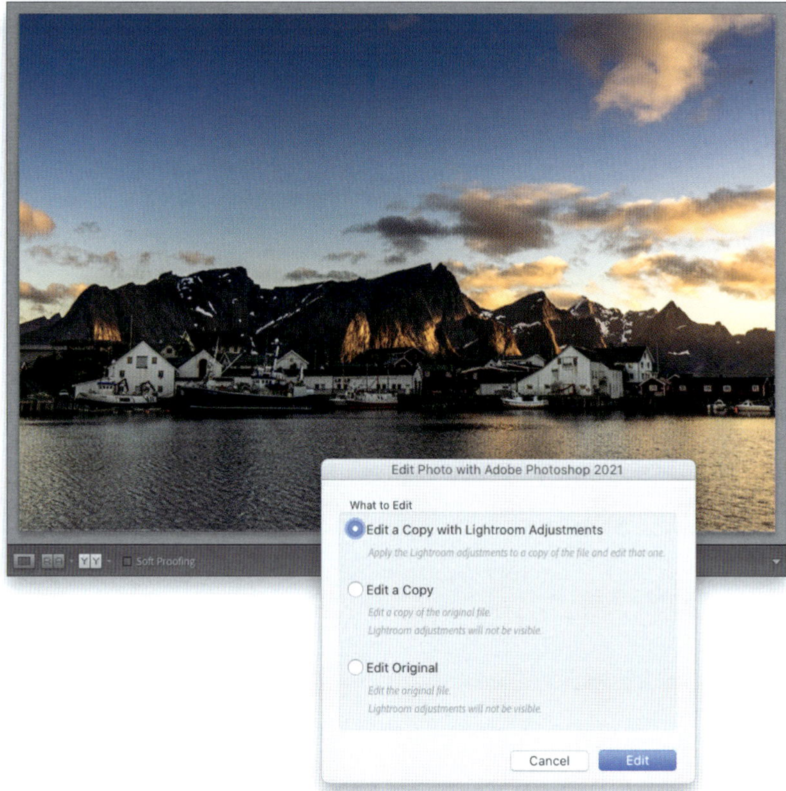

Step 13:

Here we are in Photoshop and here's what we're going to do: We're going to create a reflection in the water, so it no longer looks choppy, but instead, looks smooth like glass. Get the Rectangular Marquee tool from the Toolbar on the left (**M**; as shown here, right near the top-left corner) and drag it out over the top 2/3 of the image, stopping at the bottom right under the boats (as seen here).

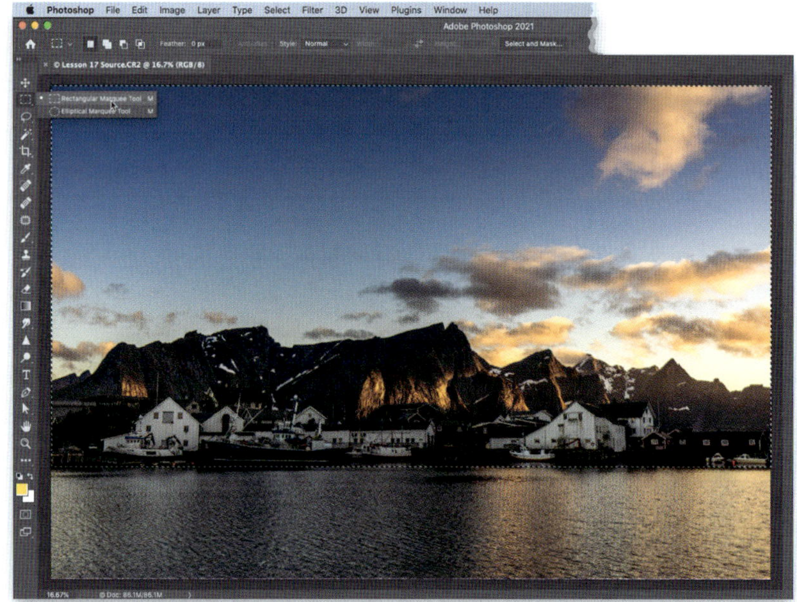

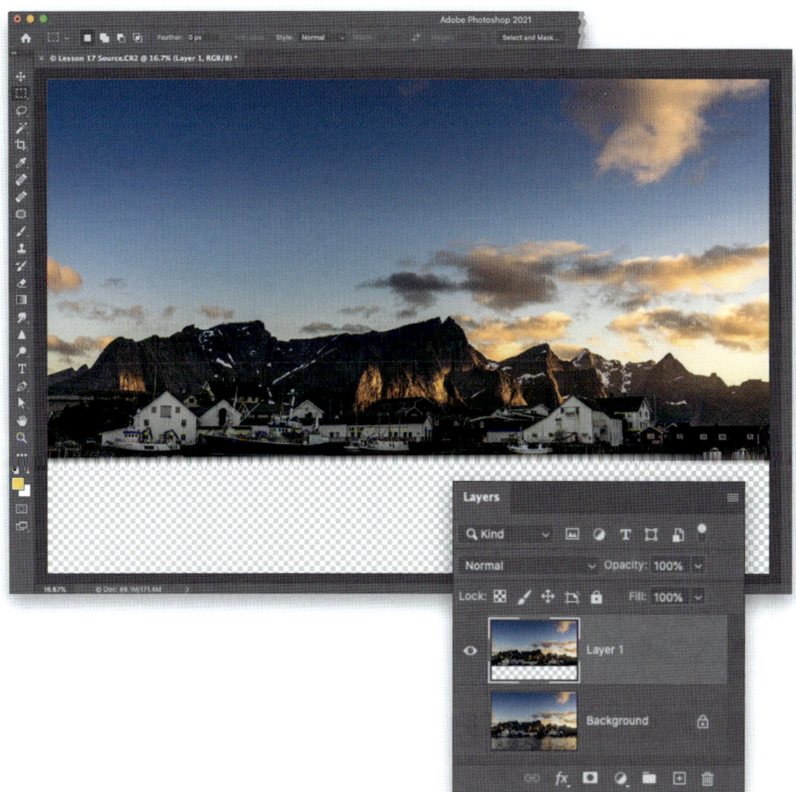

Step 14:

Next, we need to put this selected area (the top 2/3) up on its own separate layer (above the Background layer), and you do this by pressing **Command-J (PC: Ctrl-J)**. I hid the Background layer (the original image we brought over from Lightroom) from view here, by clicking on the eye icon to the left of the layer, so you can see the area we selected up on its own separate layer (now known as Layer 1). The checkerboard pattern you see below it is just showing areas that are transparent (just an FYI—it doesn't really affect you).

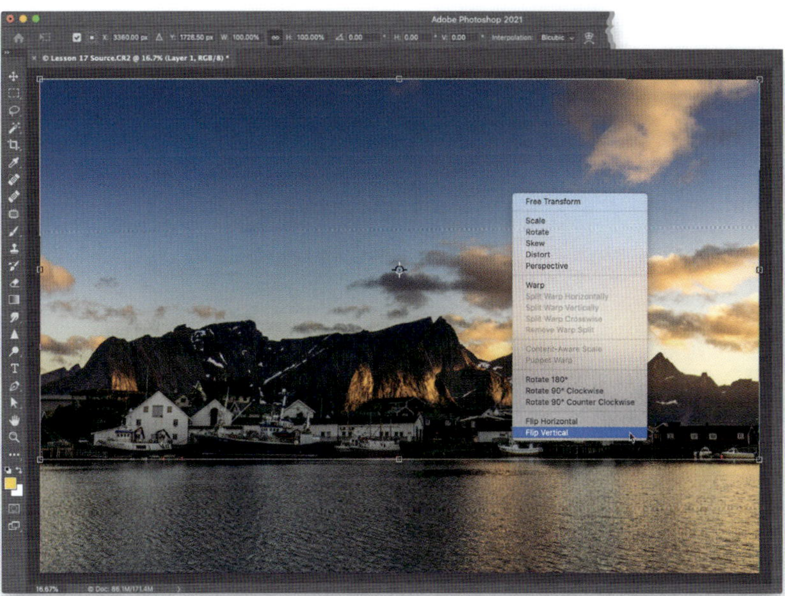

Step 15:

We're gonna flip this sucker upside down now. Press **Command-T (PC: Ctrl-T)**, which is the keyboard shortcut for Free Transform. This is the feature in Photoshop that lets you change the sizes of things, or rotate, warp, distort, etc. It lets you transform things. When you press that keyboard shortcut, it puts a bounding box around your layer (as seen here). Once that's in place, Right-click anywhere inside it, and a pop-up menu appears with all of the transformations you can do to your image on this layer. So, bring up Free Transform, Right-click, and then choose the very last option in the pop-up menu—**Flip Vertical** (as shown here. By the way, I clicked where the eye icon used to be to the left of the Background layer in the Layers panel to turn it back on here).

Step 16:

Once you choose to flip this layer upside down (vertically), you'll need to lock in your transformation by hitting the **Return (PC: Enter) key**. Then, press the **V key** on your keyboard to switch to the Move tool (shown circled here in red). This is the tool that we use to (wait for it…wait for it…) move things.

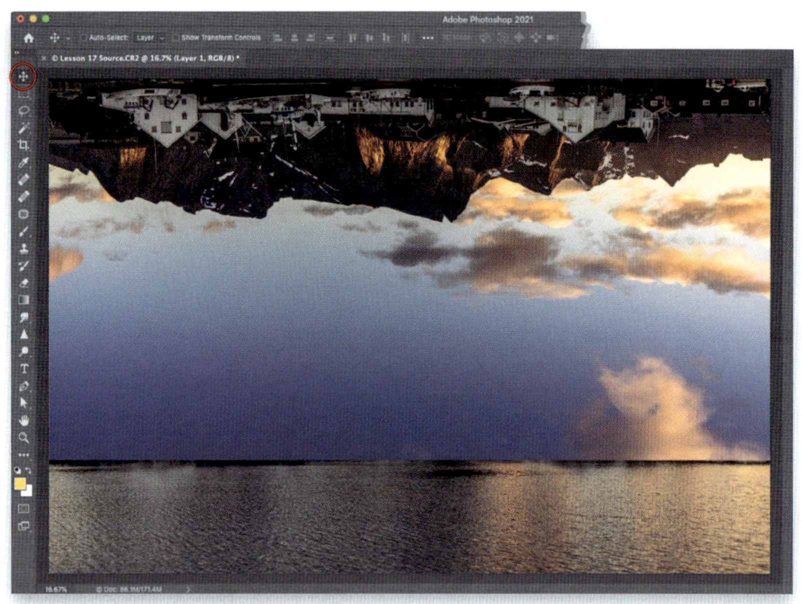

Step 17:

Press-and-hold the Shift key (that makes things move in a straight line), and drag that flipped layer straight down to where the bottom of this layer meets the bottom of the boats (as shown here). That's what creates the reflection. We're not done yet, but that's a big part of it.

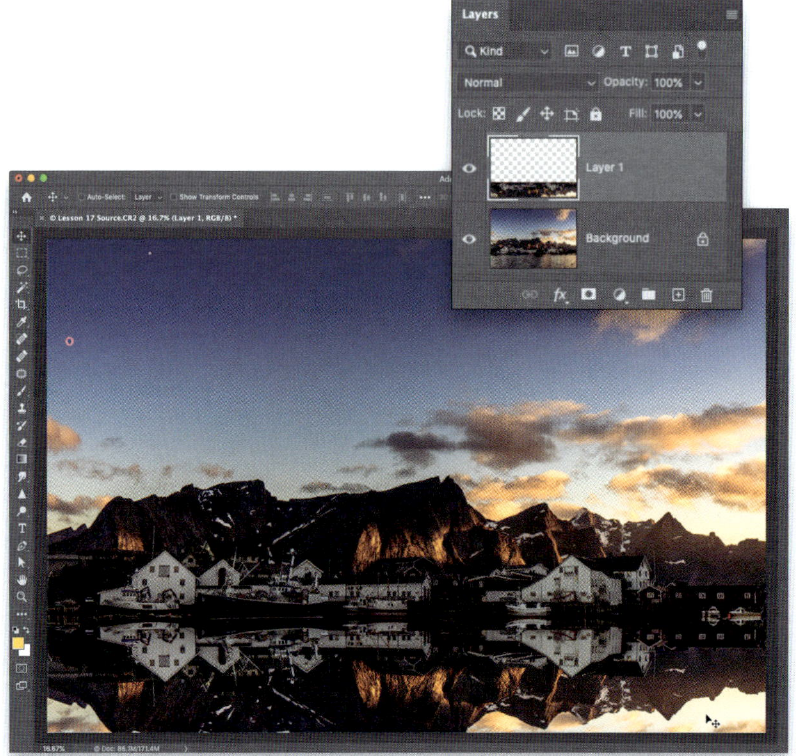

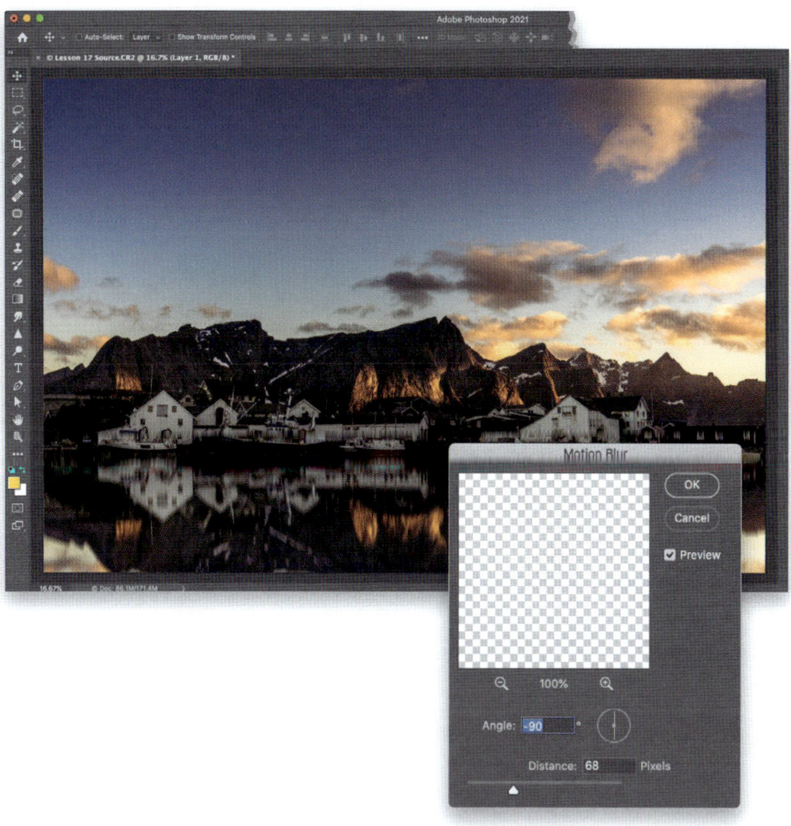

Step 18:

You could leave the image with that perfect glass reflection, but I like to add a bit of motion blur so it looks more realistic. Go under the Filter menu (up at the top of the screen), under Blur, and choose **Motion Blur**. When the filter's dialog appears (seen here), set the Angle to –90° (you can move that little angle indicator circle, but honestly, it's easier to just type in –90), then set the Distance to around 68 pixels or so, and that creates the movement in the water (as seen here). Click OK to apply this motion effect, and we're done with our Photoshop part.

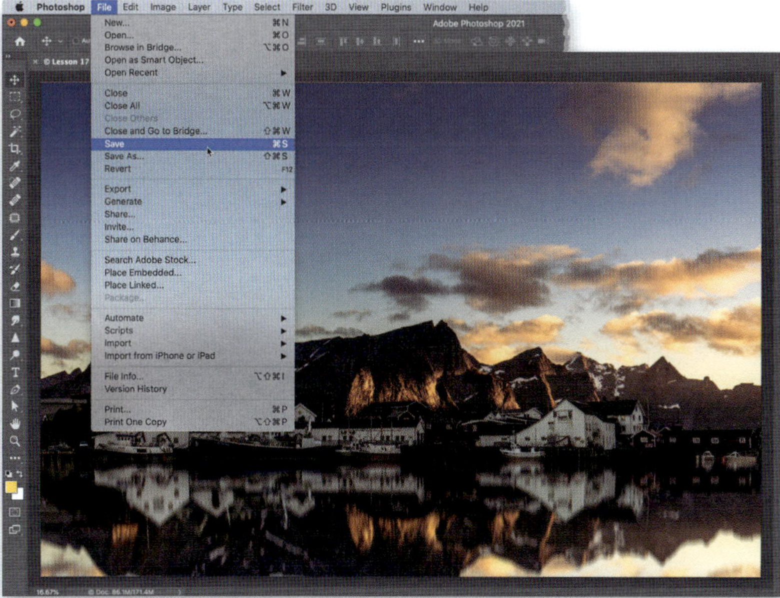

Step 19:

To get this image back to Lightroom is simple: just Save and Close. That's it. Either press **Command-S (Ctrl-S)** or go under the File menu and choose **Save**, and then just close the image window. That sends this copy back to Lightroom.

Step 20:

When you head back to Lightroom, there's your "edited in Photoshop" file waiting for you (here it is, right back in Lightroom). We'll wrap up with a few little tweaks and a finishing move or two (**Point 7**), and then we're done.

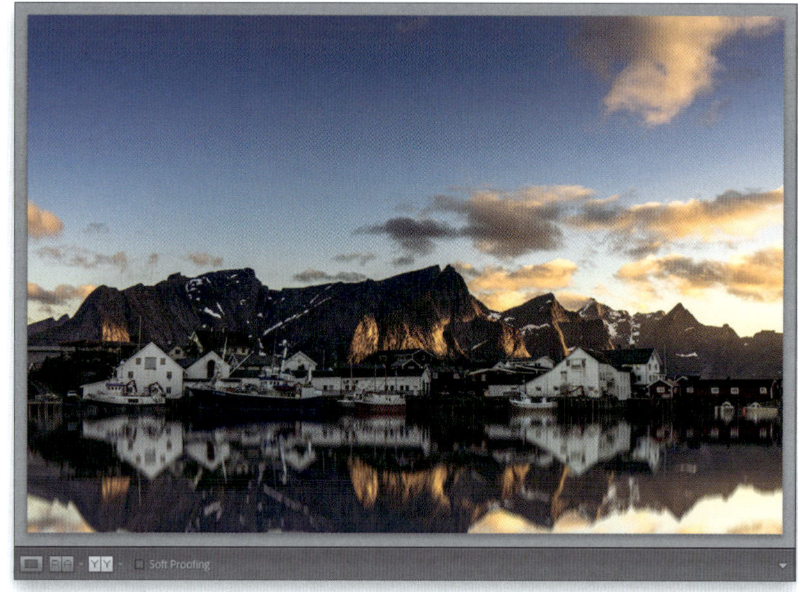

Step 21:

We can do a really simple move here that will help a lot: we're going to quickly brighten all those houses and boats with one brush stroke. So, get the Adjustment Brush (**K**; the Brush tool **[B]** in Lightroom cloud), double-click on Effect to reset all the sliders to zero, then drag the Exposure slider over to 0.71. Now, make your brush big enough to cover the houses and boats, and just paint a stroke right over them, going from the left and ending on the right (as shown here, though, technically, it doesn't really matter which way you paint). *Cool tip:* You can paint a perfectly straight line by clicking once where you want to start your line (so, say, over on the left side), then pressing-and-holding the Shift key (that's the secret), and then moving your cursor over to the far right, and clicking again, and it paints a straight line between the two points. Super-handy and, of course, you could use that here.

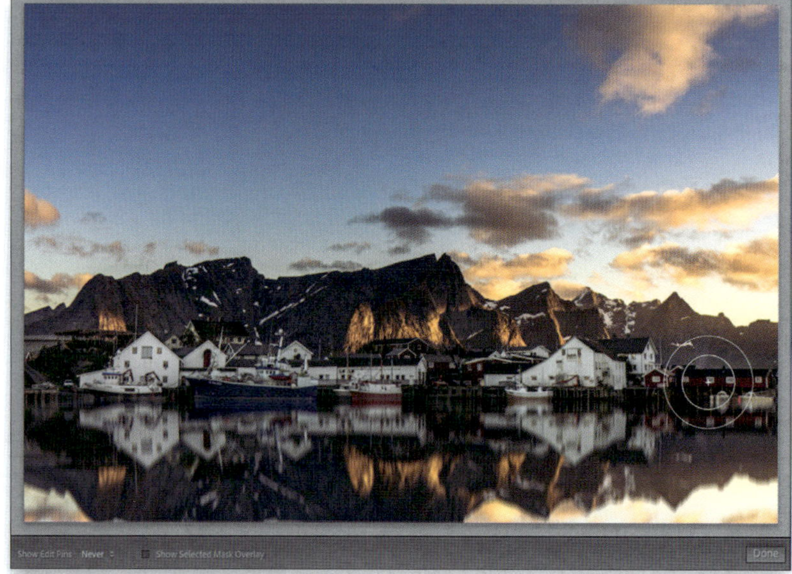

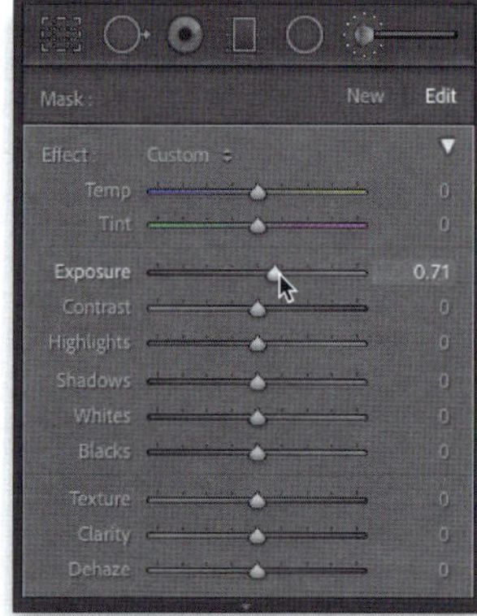

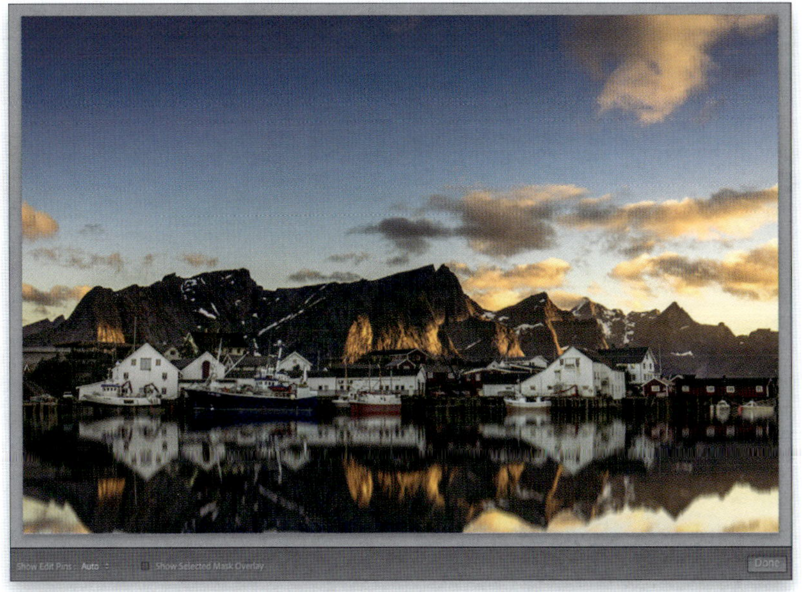

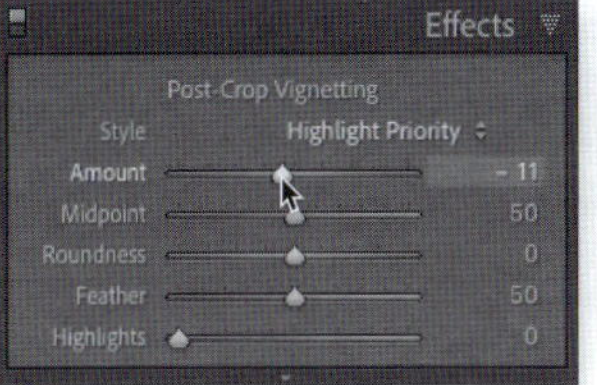

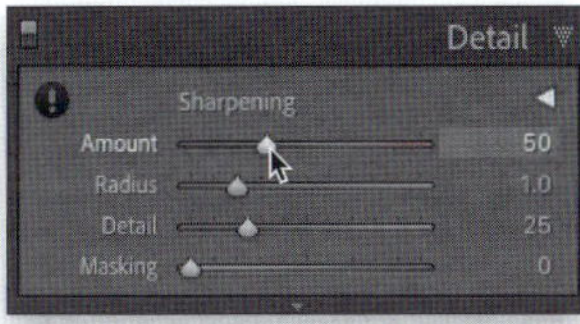

Step 22:

It's time to add a very subtle darkening around the outside edges, all the way around the image. Go to the Effects panel, and under Post-Crop Vignetting, drag the Amount slider (the Vignette slider in Lightroom cloud) over to (that's right) –11. Lastly, let's add some sharpening. Go to the Detail panel and drag the Amount slider (the Sharpening slider in Lightroom cloud) to 50. Why only 50? Because this image has already been sharpened with the Amount set to 40 back before it went over to Photoshop. So, it was pre-sharpened (all RAW photos are, by the way. The default sharpening for RAW photos is 40). But, once you make a copy and go to Photoshop, this is now a different file (it's no longer a RAW file), so when it comes back to Lightroom, the Amount slider isn't set to 40, it's set to zero. Adding 50 here goes on top of the 40 that was already added earlier, so it's really getting sharpened to around 90, and that's a bunch. If things look too crunchy when you zoom into the image at a 100% view, you could back off that Amount to 40. Your call (though I went with 50, as seen here).

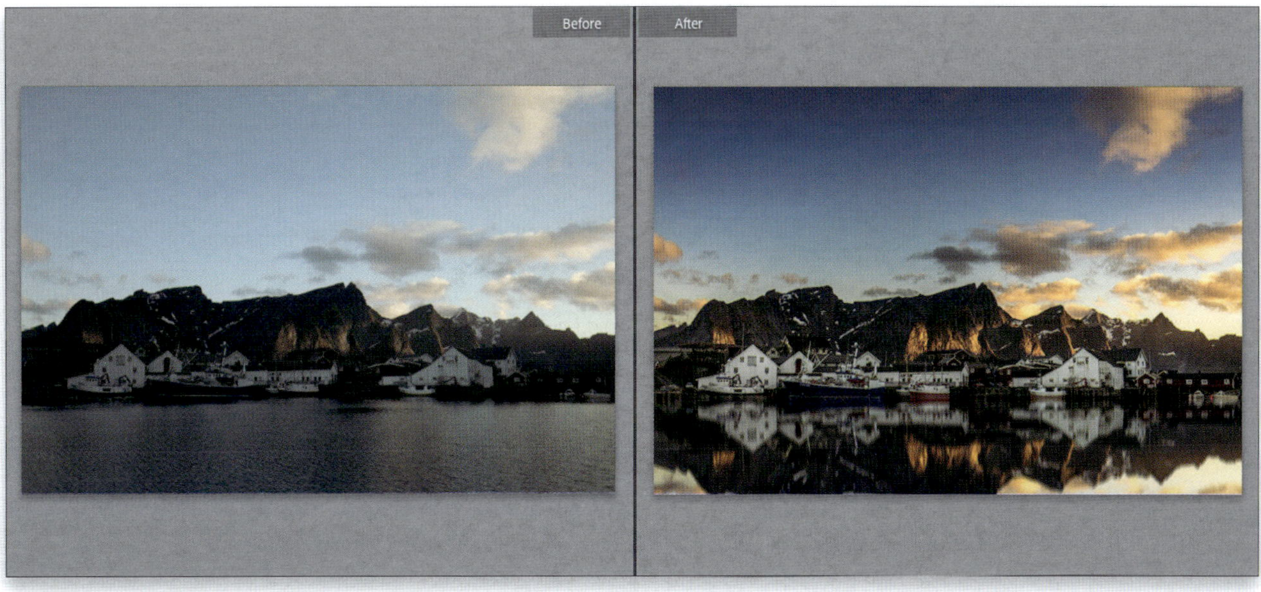

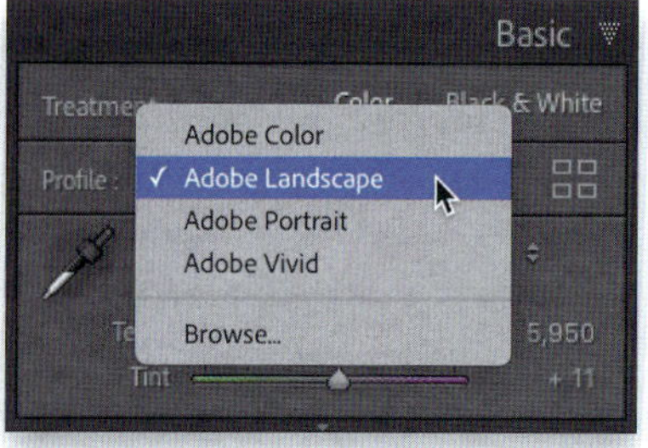

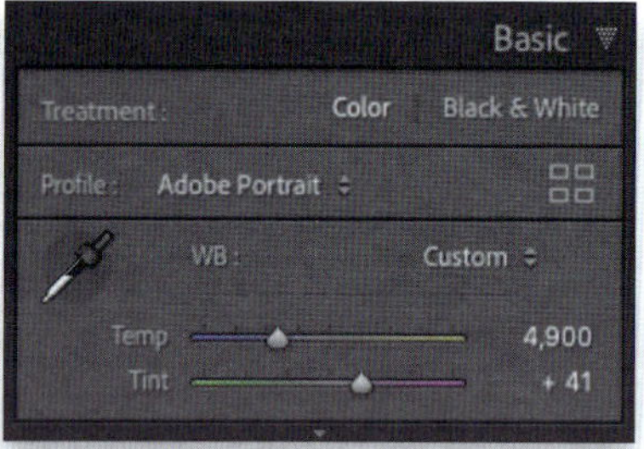

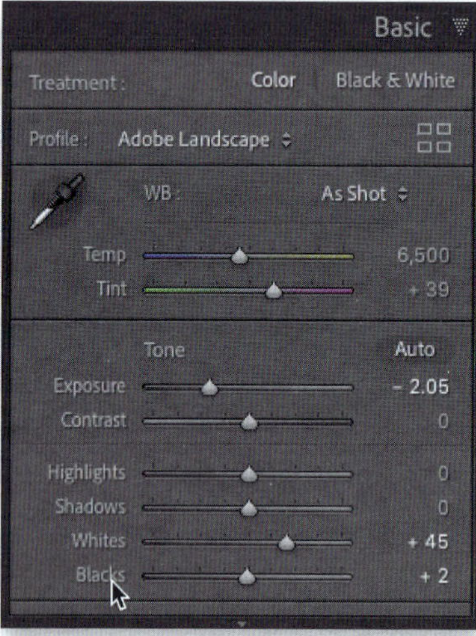

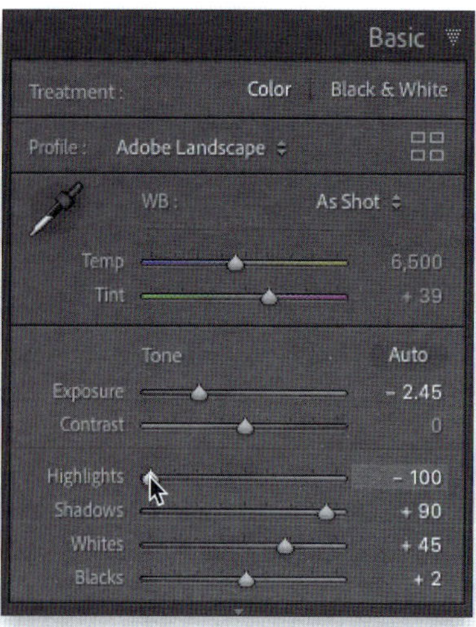

01: Assigning a RAW Profile

You want a better starting place for your RAW photo than Adobe's default Adobe Color setting, so go to the top of the Basic panel (the Edit panel in Lightroom cloud), and from the Profile pop-up menu, try Adobe Landscape or Adobe Vivid as your profile, unless you're editing a portrait, in which case, choose Adobe Portrait. I wind up choosing Adobe Landscape most of the time, but of course, like everything in image editing (say it with me now…), it just depends on the photo. So, try both Adobe Landscape and Adobe Vivid and chances are one of those two will look better than Adobe Color.

02: Getting the Color Right

We need to get our color right early in this process because (a) the color being off will distract us from making the proper exposure choices, and (b) changing our White Balance settings later in the process can change our exposure, and we don't want that. I primarily use the White Balance Selector tool (the eyedropper; in the Color panel in Lightroom cloud) when I'm trying to get an accurate (like, real-life) color for my image, by clicking it on something that's supposed to be a neutral color (ideally, something light gray, but if there's no light gray, a tan or beige color), or one of the WB (White Balance) presets. If you want a creative look (for artistic purposes), then skip the eyedropper and use the Temp and Tint sliders to make your color whatever you want it to be.

03: Expanding the Tonal Range & Getting Your Base Exposure

To make sure our image uses its full tonal range, we have Lightroom set the white and black points for us, making the brightest areas of the image as bright as possible without clipping the highlights, and the dark areas as dark as possible without making them go solid black. We do this by pressing-and-holding the Shift key and double-clicking directly on the word "Whites," and then on the word "Blacks" (in the Light panel in Lightroom cloud). Depending on the image, this could have a huge impact or it could be subtle, in which case, our image range captured in-camera was already well-expanded. We then use the Exposure slider if we feel the image is a little too bright or too dark. This will probably be a small move in either direction.

04: Dealing with Sensor Problems

There are issues caused by the fact that our camera sensors don't have nearly the range that the human eyes does. That's why we wind up with things like backlit subjects where they look like a silhouette (though, they didn't look like that when we were standing in front of them), or shots where your highlights are clipped and damaged. Use the Shadows slider—dragging it to the right—to bring out backlit subjects and reveal hidden details, and drag the Highlights slider to the left if you've clipped the highlights. You'll know you've clipped highlights if you see a white triangle in the upper-right corner of your histogram (at the top of the right side Panels area). Click on that triangle and any clipped areas will appear in a red tint.

05: Painting with Light and Retouching

The sliders in Lightroom affect everything in the photo, so if you drag the Exposure slider to the right, it makes the whole photo brighter. But, if you want to adjust just one area of your photo, you could, for example, switch to the Adjustment Brush (**K**; the Brush tool [**B**] in Lightroom cloud), and just paint over specific areas you want to be brighter or darker (called "painting with light"). It's the same sliders you normally use, that do the same things, but now you're painting those adjustments to apply them. Like, you can paint white balance, by painting over a blue area in yellow to remove the blue, or paint on sharpening in an area, etc.

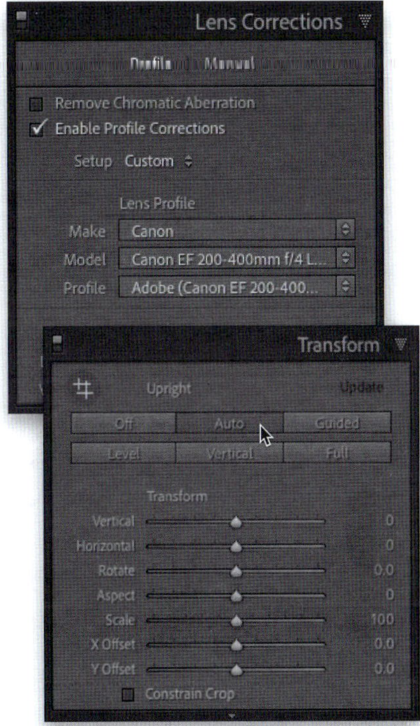

06: Fixing Lens Issues

Lens issues include distortion within the edges of your images, or the corners of your images are all darkened (called lens vignetting, and it's very common), or maybe you have buildings leaning backward in your photos (also very common). We fix these in two steps: (1) By going to the Lens Corrections panel (the Optics panel in Lightroom cloud), and turning on the Enable Profile (Lens) Corrections checkbox. This tells Lightroom to search through its built-in database of lens fixes and apply the one for your particular lens (it has about a ba-gillion profiles built in, so the one for your lens is probably there). That will usually fix the distortion and corner darkening, but if it doesn't, there are two fine-tuning sliders right below that checkbox that can help. Next, (2) go to the Transform panel (the Geometry panel in Lightroom cloud), and if your buildings are leaning backward, or the photo is crooked, or there are other problems along those lines, click the Auto button in the Upright section (choose it from the Upright pop-up menu in Lightroom cloud), and that will usually do the trick.

07: Finishing Moves

At the end of our editing process, we add a few things to finish the image off. I generally darken the outside edges of the image all the way around by a very subtle amount, so it doesn't look like I added a vignette, but it refocuses the light and attention away from the edges. You do this in the Effects panel by dragging the Amount slider (the Vignette slider in Lightroom cloud) to –11. At this point in the system, this is also where you add sharpening to your image (in the Detail panel, using the Amount slider [the Sharpening slider in Lightroom cloud]), or you bring out texture and detail in your subject using mostly the Texture slider and about half as much of the Clarity slider (so, if you apply Texture set to 30, you'd only apply Clarity set to around 15). If the image doesn't feel colorful enough, you can drag the Vibrance slider (never the Saturation slider) to the right to make the colors more vibrant without them looking too horsey.

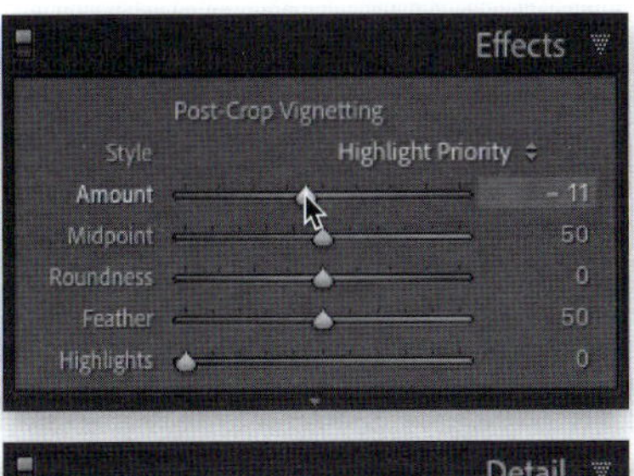

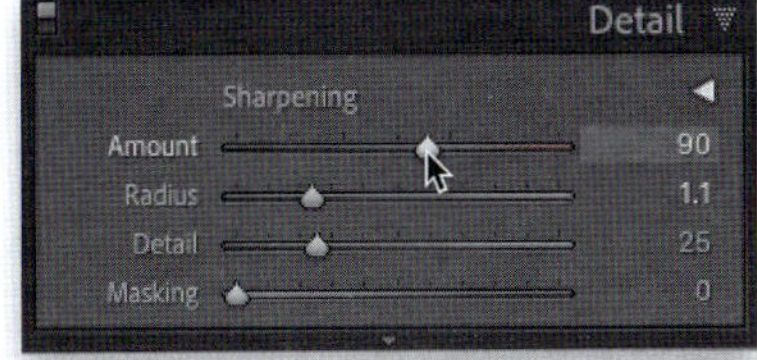

INDEX

H

hair retouching, 80, 82
Hard Light blend mode, 218
haze reduction
    for landscape photos, 186–187, 214
    for Milky Way sky photo, 153
HDR images, 37–38
HDR Merge Preview dialog, 37
Healing Brush tool, 27, 68, 80, 117, 150
    See also Spot Removal tool
High Pass filter, 217
high-key shots, 130
highlight adjustments, 236
    architectural photo and, 108
    aviation photo and, 99
    home interior photo, 205
    landscapes and, 17, 54, 186
    nighttime photo and, 141
    portraits and, 64, 76, 177
    sports action photo and, 89
    travel photos and, 6, 24, 141, 226
highlight clipping, xv, 89, 186
Highlights color wheel, 177
Highlights slider, 6, 17, 24, 54, 64, 99, 236
home interior photo, 201–209
horizon line straightening, 3
HSL/Color panel
    Hue adjustments, 198
    Luminance adjustments, 31, 101
Hue adjustments, 198

I

images
    bracketing, 36
    downloading for lessons, xxi
    editing multiple, 74
    shooting for panoramas, 50
    stacking, 37, 52
interior photos
    classic interior, 35–45
    home interior, 201–209
Invert checkbox, 175

J

JPEGs
    Photoshop editing of, 216, 230
    RAW profiles and, xiii, 15
    white balance setting for, 195, 225

K

kelbyone.com website, xxi
Kuna, Erik, 147, 155

L

lakeside reflection photo, 13–19
landscape photo lessons
    Grand Canyon overlook, 183–191
    lakeside reflection, 13–19
    Monument Valley, 211–221
    western landscape, 211–221
    Yosemite panorama, 49–59
landscape photos
    black and white points, 16, 54, 185, 214
    Clarity adjustments, 18, 188, 215
    contrast adjustments, 17, 54, 185, 190, 214, 215
    darkening edges of, 57, 189, 220
    exposure adjustments, 54, 56, 185, 214
    haze reduction, 186–187, 214
    highlight adjustments, 17, 54, 186
    lens distortion fix, 189
    Photoshop adjustments, 216–218
    RAW image profiles, 15, 188, 213
    shadow adjustments, 16, 54, 56, 187
    sharpening, 19, 57, 190
    texture adjustments, 18, 188, 215
    tonal range, 16, 54, 185, 214
    Vibrance adjustments, 190, 220
    See also travel photos
layers, merging in Photoshop, 217
Layers panel (Photoshop), 217, 218
Lens Corrections panel, xviii, 237
    architectural photo and, 110
    aviation photo and, 100
    black & white conversion and, 165
    home interior photo and, 203
    landscape photo and, 189
    Milky Way sky photo and, 150
    nighttime photos and, 139, 150
    portraits and, 65, 77, 131, 171, 197
    travel photos and, 3, 29, 40, 139, 229
lenses
    distortion issues from, 3, 65, 77, 110, 139, 165, 229
    profiles for, 3, 4, 29, 65, 77, 100, 110
lesson photo downloads, xxi
light
    painting with, xvii, 25, 55, 237
    spill removal, 117
Light panel, 5, 15, 23, 54, 64, 76

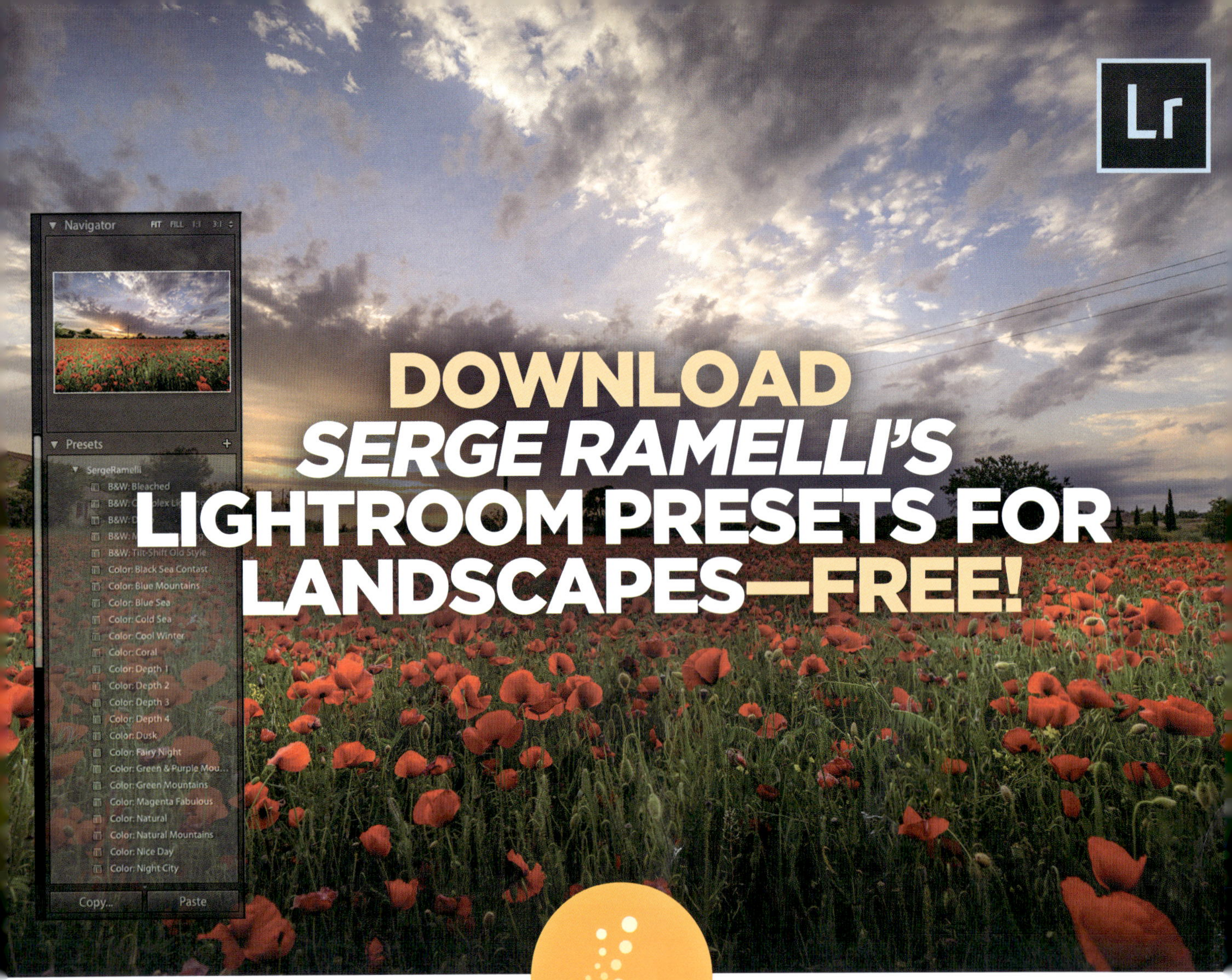